Contributions to Finance and Accounting

The book series 'Contributions to Finance and Accounting' features the latest research from research areas like financial management, investment, capital markets, financial institutions, FinTech and financial innovation, accounting methods and standards, reporting, and corporate governance, among others. Books published in this series are primarily monographs and edited volumes that present new research results, both theoretical and empirical, on a clearly defined topic. All books are published in print and digital formats and disseminated globally. This book series is indexed in Scopus.

Selim Yazıcı
C. Coşkun Küçüközmen • Michael Salmony
Editors

Tokenisation of Money

From Fiat Currencies to Stablecoins

Springer

Editors
Selim Yazıcı
Faculty of Political Sciences
Department of Business Administration
Istanbul University
Istanbul, Türkiye

C. Coşkun Küçüközmen
Faculty of Business
İzmir University of Economics
Izmir, Türkiye

Michael Salmony
CEO
Payments Innovation Consulting
Heidelberg, Germany

ISSN 2730-6038 ISSN 2730-6046 (electronic)
Contributions to Finance and Accounting
ISBN 978-3-032-22945-8 ISBN 978-3-032-22946-5 (eBook)
https://doi.org/10.1007/978-3-032-22946-5

This Springer imprint is published by the registered company Springer Nature Switzerland AG
The registered company address is: Gewerbestrasse 11, 6330 Cham, Switzerland

Contents

Editors and Contributors

About the Editors

Selim Yazıcı is Professor of Management and Strategy at the Department of Business Administration, Faculty of Political Sciences, Istanbul University, and Co-Founder of FinTech Istanbul. He holds a BSc in Mechanical Engineering from Yıldız Technical University and MSc and PhD degrees in Business Administration from Istanbul University. In addition to his full-time academic position, he has served as Adjunct Professor at Marmara University (Banking and Insurance Institute), Özyeğin University (Financial Engineering and Risk Management Program), and Sabancı University (Master in Finance Program), teaching financial technologies at both undergraduate and graduate levels.

His research focuses on digital transformation, disruptive technologies, entrepreneurship, financial technologies (FinTech), insurance technologies (InsurTech), project management, and business continuity. He has published extensively in peer-reviewed national and international journals indexed in Scopus and Web of Science, contributing to the academic literature on digital financial innovation, technology-driven business models, ecosystem development, and strategic transformation in financial services. His work combines qualitative inquiry and strategic frameworks to bridge theory and practice in emerging financial technologies. In addition, he has authored and edited several books in Turkish, including *Electronic Insurance* (2002) and *The Transformation of Finance with FinTech and InsurTech* (2021).

He is a frequent keynote speaker at international conferences, industry summits, and academic forums on FinTech, InsurTech, and digital transformation. He has delivered keynote addresses and executive briefings for financial institutions, regulators, technology firms, and startup ecosystems, focusing on the strategic implications of digital assets, embedded finance, and emerging financial infrastructures. His speeches typically bridge academic insight with real-world industry experience, offering forward-looking perspectives on the future of money and the evolving global financial architecture.

Beyond academia, Prof. Yazıcı plays an active role in the financial technology ecosystem. As Co-Founder of FinTech Istanbul, he has contributed to the development of Türkiye's FinTech landscape and designed the country's first "FinTech 101" training program for entrepreneurs, corporates, and investors. He mentors startups in incubation and acceleration programs and has previously served on the boards of İş Private Equity and İş Leasing.

He brings together academic rigor and industry insight in his role as Editor of *Tokenisation of Money: From Fiat Currencies to Stablecoins*, contributing to scholarly and policy debates on the future of digital assets and monetary transformation.

C. Coşkun Küçüközmen is a faculty member in the Department of International Trade and Finance at İzmir University of Economics. He holds an MSc in European Economics and Finance from Loughborough University (Jean Monnet Scholarship) and a PhD in Finance from the University of Exeter. Prior to academia, he built a 25-year career in public financial institutions, serving 20 years at the Central Bank of the Republic of Türkiye (TCMB) and 5 years at the Banking Regulation and Supervision Agency (BDDK), where he worked on risk measurement and management, research, financial stability, and banking regulation within the framework of Basel Committee regulatory and supervisory standards.

He joined the FSI of BIS/BCBS as a guest speaker, lecturing on market, credit, and operational risks, hedge funds, and risk management in emerging markets. Drawing on this institutional foundation, his research focuses on financial risk measurement, financial econometrics, central bank digital currencies (CBDCs), the tokenisation of financial assets, fintech innovation, sustainable finance, and the transformation of global financial systems and blue finance. His work explores how distributed ledger technologies (DeFi) and artificial intelligence are redefining monetary sovereignty, cross-border payments, and the architecture of global finance.

Professor Küçüközmen is an invited speaker and keynote contributor at international conferences and high-level policy forums. His recent engagements include academic and policy dialogues in Geneva (WTO), London, Cairo, and Singapore, where he delivered talks on artificial intelligence, as well as financial transformation in Shanghai, and leading universities in Uzbekistan, including contributions to international summer schools. He also frequently contributes to public debate through appearances on national media, including BloombergHT and other major television channels, as well as podcasts and expert interviews, where he interprets developments in global finance, monetary policy, geo-economics, geopolitics, and emerging technologies for broader audiences.

These engagements reflect his active role in shaping cross-border conversations on digital finance and global monetary governance. His scholarship argues that the future of money will be determined not only by technological innovation, but also by regulatory foresight, institutional credibility, and the evolving geopolitical balance of financial power in an increasingly digital world. His academic publications include articles indexed in Web of Science (SSCI) journals and other international peer-reviewed outlets, contributing to the scholarly literature on digital finance and financial system transformation.

Michael Salmony is an internationally recognised leader on strategy of business innovations in digital and financial services with a particular focus on Payments, Open Finance, FinTech, Digital Identity, B2B/e-Invoicing/SCF, AI for Financial Services and Electronic Money/CBDC/Stablecoins.

He is board-level advisor to major international banks, industry associations, regulators, global consultancies, service providers, and investors across the world. He regularly helps shape future directions in all key decision-making bodies (e.g. European Commission/ European Parliament/ECB/CEPS Think-Tank in Europe, and central banks from Japan to Uruguay and Kazakhstan). For 10 years he served as Executive Adviser to the Board of Worldline Financial Services, helping to bring them from a local player to become the world's 4th largest financial processor of transactional services, which handles over 17 trillion Euro per year.

He also works with multiple regions where financial innovations are currently emerging—for example, with the World Bank in Central Asia, as Board Member of Fintech Africa, as Advisory Board Member to Mastercard in Latin America, as strategic partner to FinTech Istanbul.

His views are much in demand as keynote speaker at international events and he appears on TV/Radio/all electronic media on advances in finance and is quoted extensively (e.g. Financial Times, Harvard Business Manager, New Scientist, The Economist and governments from Ghana to Malaysia). He teaches at the Oxford Business School on "AI in Fintech and Open Banking" and at further universities such as in Australia, Turkey, and Germany. He has published much own original work which has been translated into many languages including German, Italian, Dutch, Finnish, Polish, Danish, Turkish, Russian, Chinese, and Japanese and is cited in hundreds of publications around the world. He is extensively networked into the new financial services space and has one of the top most viewed profiles on business social media platforms.

He is a Freeman of the Worshipful Company of International Bankers, Freeman of the City of London and a Fellow of the Royal Society for Arts, Manufactures and Commerce FRSA.

Previous positions include Director Business Development of leading national central bank (Bank of the Year, Best Innovator Award).

Before entering the world of finance, he helped transform companies and business models in many industries as IBM's Director of Market Development Media and Communications Technologies.

He studied at the University of Cambridge UK and is married, with two millennial children.

Contributors

Emrah Ahi Özyeğin University, Istanbul, Türkiye

Gabriel R. Bizama Institute for Civil Law, University of Bern, Bern, Switzerland

Paul Desprairies Directorate Digital Euro, European Central Bank, Frankfurt, Germany

Claus George DZ BANK AG, Frankfurt, Germany

Jean-Michel Godeffroy Independent consultant, former Director General at the European Central Bank (1998–2014), Paris, France

Christian Grothoff Bern University of Applied Sciences, Biel, Switzerland

GNU Taler, Biel, Switzerland

Levent Güntay Department of International Finance, Özyeğin University, Istanbul, Türkiye

Mikolai Gütschow GNU Taler, Biel, Switzerland

TUD Dresden University of Technology, Dresden, Germany

Jung Ho StanChart, Singapore, Singapore

Lars Hupel Giesecke+Devrient advance52 GmbH, Munich, Germany

Feride Hilal İmal İstanbul Bar Association, İstanbul, Türkiye

Haluk İnanmış Inted Ltd., İstanbul, Türkiye

Zennon Kapron GL Insight, Cambridge, MA, USA

Mehmet Kerse Regulation and Policy for Digital Innovation, Frankfurt, Germany

John Kiff Kiffmeister LLC, Hillsboro, VA, USA

C. Coşkun Küçüközmen Faculty of Business, Izmir University of Economics, Izmir, Türkiye

Inutu Lukonga Lukonga Global Consulting LLC, Vienna, VA, USA

Paula Martins Giesecke+Devrient Currency Technology GmbH, Munich, Germany

Erin McCune Forte Fintech LLC, San Francisco, CA, USA

Tony McLaughlin Ubyx, Wilmington, DE, USA

London, United Kingdom

Philipp Neubauer Directorate Digital Euro, European Central Bank, Frankfurt, Germany

Kamila Nigmatulina Said Business School, University of Oxford, Oxford, UK

Pinar Ozcan Said Business School, University of Oxford, Oxford, UK

Thibault Pele Worldline Financial Services, Paris, France

Michael Juul Rugaard Independent author and creator of TVAC - Tokenization Value-Add Calculator, Copenhagen, Denmark

Michael Salmony Payments Innovation Consulting, Heidelberg, Germany

Valentin Seehausen Digital Euro Association, Frankfurt, Germany

Wolfram Seidemann Giesecke+Devrient Currency Technology GmbH, Munich, Germany

Kyeyoung Shin Said Business School, University of Oxford, Oxford, UK

Sebnem Elif Kocaoglu Ulbrich Contextual Solutions GmbH, Berlin, Germany

Hiromi Yamaoka Digital Currency Forum, Future Institute of Research, Tokyo, Japan

Victor Yaromin Morozzi Creative Lab, Phnom Penh, Cambodia

Selim Yazıcı Department of Business Administration, Faculty of Political Sciences, Istanbul University, Istanbul, Türkiye

List of Figures

Taler as a Synthetic Central Bank Digital Currency

Retail Central Bank Digital Currencies: An Inevitable Innovation for the Stability of the Monetary System in the Digital Age

Mapping the Stablecoin Ecosystem: Taxonomy, Stakeholders, and Systemic Interdependencies

Offline-Capable Central Bank Digital Currencies as a Key Enabler of a Resilient Digital Payment System

Will Tokenised Money Transform Wholesale and B2B Payments?

The "Productization" of Money and Its Impact at the Point of Sale

The Case for a Stablecoin Clearing System: Enabling Ubiquity Through Market Structure Evolution

Adoption by Design for Digital Currency Systems

The Pursuit of Resilience in European Retail Payments

Tokenization and the Future Monetary System: DCJPY as Tokenized Deposits in Japan

Blockchain and QR Codes: Revolutionizing Cross-Border Payments and Financial Inclusion in Southeast Asia – A Case Study of Cambodia's Bakong Project

Will Tokenised Money Overthrow Existing Financial Infrastructures? TradFi vs DeFi: Who Will Win?

List of Tables

Regulatory Approaches of Stablecoins

Will Tokenised Money Transform Wholesale and B2B Payments?

The "Productization" of Money and Its Impact at the Point of Sale

The Pursuit of Resilience in European Retail Payments

Introduction

Selim Yazıcı, C. Coşkun Küçüközmen, and Michael Salmony

Abstract The tokenisation of money has entered a pivotal phase, moving rapidly from experimental pilots to regulated deployments across multiple jurisdictions. This introductory chapter contextualises the emergence of central bank digital currencies (CBDCs), stablecoins, and deposit tokens within a broader narrative of monetary evolution, tracing the trajectory from the early "wild west" era of crypto-assets through landmark regulatory milestones such as the EU's MiCA framework and the US GENIUS Act. Against a backdrop marked by both transformative promise and high-profile failures, including the collapse of Terra/Luna and the FTX exchange, the editors articulate the rationale for a comprehensive, fact-based compendium on tokenised money. The chapter outlines the book's purpose: to serve as a practical and conceptual guide for governments, regulators, financial institutions, fintech firms, businesses, and academia navigating the complex digital money landscape. The five-part structure of the volume is introduced, organised around the fundamental questions of why new forms of money are needed, what forms they take, how they are implemented, where they are emerging geographically, and what critical perspectives remain essential for a balanced assessment. Drawing on contributions from more than thirty distinguished experts spanning major regions and disciplines, the book aspires to offer rigorous yet accessible insights into a rapidly evolving field whose implications for payments, banking, trade, and society remain profound and far-reaching.

S. Yazıcı (✉)
Department of Business Administration, Faculty of Political Sciences, Istanbul University, Istanbul, Türkiye
e-mail: selim@istanbul.edu.tr

C. C. Küçüközmen
Faculty of Business, Izmir University of Economics, Izmir, Türkiye
e-mail: coskun.kucukozmen@ieu.edu.tr

M. Salmony
Payments Innovation Consulting, Heidelberg, Germany
e-mail: salmony@payments-innovation.com

S. Yazıcı et al. (eds.), *Tokenisation of Money*, Contributions to Finance and Accounting, https://doi.org/10.1007/978-3-032-22946-5_1

Keywords Tokenisation · Tokenised money · CBDC · Stablecoin · Deposit token · Digital currency · Digital money · Financial regulation

Tokenisation of money has followed a steep, near-exponential trajectory in recent years. Several central banks have issued digital currencies (including the Bahamas, Nigeria, and Jamaica in the early 2020s, followed by initiatives or advanced pilots in India, China, Brazil, and Kazakhstan). Early-mover jurisdictions have introduced regulatory frameworks (such as the EU's MiCA in 2023 and the US GENIUS Act in 2025). At the same time, pilot projects, often coordinated through international institutions such as the BIS, have explored practical use cases, while the market has expanded rapidly with an increasing variety of digital currencies, issuers, exchanges, and supporting ecosystems.

Following the "wild west" phase of crypto-assets, demand for more stable and regulated forms of tokenised money, potentially issued by banks and overseen by public authorities, has grown steadily. Yet the space remains characterised by confusion (for example, Facebook's Libra/Diem initiative) and high-profile failures (such as the Mt. Gox and FTX collapses, which together resulted in losses exceeding €7 billion, and the collapse of the so-called "stablecoins" Terra/Luna). Nevertheless, the promise of tokenised money, which can be transferred instantly, efficiently, and globally remains compelling, as it has the potential to transform payments, banking, trade, and beyond.

Against this background, the three of us decided that it was time to provide not an exhaustive or definitive work (which is impossible) but essential guidance across the many dimensions of this rapidly evolving space. We initially focused on central bank digital currencies (CBDCs), particularly in light of the significant momentum at the time, notably in China and in Europe around the ECB. However, as interest in CBDCs cooled and global attention shifted increasingly towards stablecoins, we broadened the scope to encompass all forms of tokenised money.

Across these developments, we observed a clear gap: there was no handbook addressing the fundamental questions of "what is hype, what is real, and how will this new industry unfold?". As a result, we: a professor (Selim), a former central banker now professor (Coşkun), and a practitioner (Michael) decided to develop a book that brings together the perspectives of leading voices on the most important issues in this field. We submitted our proposal to a select number of global publishers and were pleased that Springer immediately recognised both the need and the potential of the project. The book you now hold in your hands (or on your tablet) is the result of these efforts.

1 Purpose of the Book

The global financial services industry is undergoing a profound transformation driven by technological advancements, with tokenised money, including Central Bank Digital Currencies (CBDCs), stablecoins, and deposit tokens at the centre of this shift. As the world moves toward a digital-first economy, these innovations are poised to revolutionise how consumers, businesses, and financial institutions transact. While some forms of digital money are already being deployed at a remarkable scale, there remains substantial confusion regarding taxonomy, business models, and the associated risks and opportunities. Developments vary significantly across regions; regulators are adopting distinct approaches, banks are experimenting with alternative models, and new service providers are entering the market to support emerging ecosystems.

This book serves as both a practical and conceptual guide to the rapid evolution of money. It provides an in-depth examination of the economic, technical, regulatory, and societal impacts of tokenisation. By exploring the potential and risks inherent in these new financial forms, it offers crucial insights for:

- *Governments and Regulators* navigating distinct policy approaches,
- *Banks and Fintech Firms* experimenting with new service propositions,
- *Businesses and End Users* seeking to understand how these changes affect daily transactions,
- *Universities and Research Centres* exploring the theoretical and practical limits.

Understanding these developments is essential for any stakeholder looking to navigate the increasingly complex digital landscape in future. Given the rapid proliferation of initiatives and the associated complexity we felt it was important to provide a comprehensive, fact-based compendium drawing on the insights of leading thinkers from around the world. The chapters examine multiple dimensions of current developments: the different types of tokenised money, implementation models, emerging regulatory frameworks, evolving alliances and ecosystems, and the geographies that are most active and the ways in which they are engaging.

Our aim is to address the most essential questions surrounding tokenised money: *why* it is needed, *what* forms it takes, *how* it works, and *where* it is being implemented. In particular, we explore which problems these innovations seek to solve, how they are designed and deployed, and the contexts in which they are emerging.

Unlike most other books on digital currencies and blockchain, the *Tokenisation of Money: From Fiat Currencies to Stablecoins* aims for comprehensive coverage of both public and private forms of tokenised money. It offers a deep dive into the economic, legal, and technical aspects of digital money, backed by case studies and practical insights. The book also provides a balanced perspective, presenting both the opportunities and challenges associated with these emerging financial systems.

The contributing authors have been selected for their forward-looking perspectives and expertise, spanning regulators, banks, fintech firms, service providers, academia, and all major regions of the world. Our ambition is for each chapter to be grounded in facts and analytical rigour, while remaining accessible and engaging to a broad readership. We therefore believe this book will be essential reading for regulators seeking to understand policy options and inform future decisions; for banks aiming to position themselves within emerging ecosystems; for fintech firms exploring new services and opportunities; for consumers and business professionals wishing to deepen their understanding of this transformative field; and for researchers and academics seeking to contribute to a still-maturing body of scholarship.

2 Structure of the Book

The book is structured into five parts, each focusing on key themes in the study of digital money. These parts are designed to provide a comprehensive understanding of the evolution of money, the need for new forms of money, the technical and governance challenges of tokenisation, and the global landscape of developments in digital money.

The first part addresses the question of *"why"* a new form of money is needed and examines the current and future evolution of tokenisation in finance overcoming the limitations of traditional money and payment systems in meeting the demands of a digital, global economy. It begins with a brief history of money, leading up to its modern digitisation, before introducing the main forms of contemporary tokenised money. The part then expands the discussion to broader developments in tokenisation, beyond the tokenisation of money alone.

The second part focuses on *"what"* by describing the various forms of tokenised money that are currently emerging. It first examines the different models of, and debates surrounding, central bank digital currencies (CBDCs). This is followed by a discussion of the main forms of non-CBDC tokenised money and their defining characteristics.

The third part addresses the question of *"how"* tokenised money can be implemented and delves into the practicalities of implementing tokenised money. It explores key implementation choices, including business models, ecosystem design, governance structures, regulatory approaches, infrastructure, innovation, and communication. In addition, it provides deeper analyses of several important application areas such as business-to-business (B2B) payments and point-of-sale (POS) use cases going beyond the more familiar retail, peer-to-peer, and cross-border applications.

The fourth part examines *"where"* tokenised money is developing across different geographies. It provides a global perspective on digital money developments. It begins with a global overview and then considers developments in Europe, China, Japan, and Southeast Asia.

Finally, in the fifth part, following the enthusiasm and optimism surrounding tokenised money, we present a range of more critical perspectives. These include discussions on the future of traditional finance versus decentralised finance (TradFi vs. DeFi), geopolitical considerations, and the tension between decentralised ideals and emerging forms of re-intermediation.

During the editorial process, we had the honour and great satisfaction of collaborating with more than 30 contributing authors, each recognised as a distinguished authority within their respective domains of expertise. We extend our deepest gratitude to all contributing authors for their expertise, dedication, and invaluable contributions to this volume.

We believe this book examines the topic of tokenisation across its many dimensions including geographic, regulatory, technical, legal, economic, societal, and operational. We acknowledge that the subject is vast and highly diverse, and that it is not possible to cover every aspect within a single volume. Nevertheless, we have sought to address the major themes across the most important dimensions. We also recognise that developments in this field are occurring at a rapid pace, and that some details may change between publication and readership. For this reason, we have focused on presenting core concepts, structures, and fundamental insights that we expect to remain broadly relevant over time.

We hope that practitioners, researchers, and regulators will find this book useful, and we welcome feedback and dialogue from experts and readers engaged in this evolving field.

Selim Yazıcı
C. Coşkun Küçüközmen
Michael Salmony
(Editors)
Istanbul/Izmir/London
February 2026

Follow Us:
- The Book Website: https://tokenisationofmoney.com/
- LinkedIn: https://www.linkedin.com/company/tokenisation-of-money/
- X: https://x.com/TokenisationofM

Why Do We Need Another Form of Money?

The Main Stages in the History of Money

Jean-Michel Godeffroy

Abstract Money was first invented over 5000 years ago, at the beginning of the Bronze Age, when economic activities began to diversify beyond agricultural self-sufficiency. While its functions have remained largely the same, the forms of money have evolved significantly—from physical commodities to digital data.

For more than two millennia, money was anchored to precious metals. However, as mineral discoveries proved insufficient to support expanding economies, rulers began to supplement metallic money with representative money—paper notes or coins made of base metals—redeemable in gold or silver. This First Age of Money came to an end in the twentieth century, following a prolonged decline that began with the outbreak of World War I in 1914 and concluded in 1971, when the US definitively severed the link between the dollar and gold.

The Second Age of Money, dominated by "fiat money," emerged gradually and is now the global standard. In this era, currency issuance is no longer constrained by gold reserves but is instead governed by central bank monetary policy. The rise of distributed ledger technologies in the early twenty-first century gave birth to crypto-assets. While many of these serve as speculative instruments rather than true currencies, stablecoins backed by fiat currencies have the potential to become a new form of money.

Keywords Money · Seigniorage · Fiat money · Crypto-assets

This chapter summarizes the sections on the history of money from the author's book *The Evolution of Money and Payments: From Commodity to Digital*, published in June 2025 on Amazon-Kindle Direct Publishing.

J.-M. Godeffroy (✉)
Independent consultant, former Director General at the European Central Bank (1998–2014), Paris, France
e-mail: info@jmgconsulting01.com

S. Yazıcı et al. (eds.), *Tokenisation of Money*, Contributions to Finance and Accounting, https://doi.org/10.1007/978-3-032-22946-5_2

1 Introduction

Money has taken many forms throughout history—sometimes physical, such as coins and banknotes, and sometimes immaterial, such as the balances held in bank accounts. This is why it so difficult to define. The simplest and most effective approach is to view it as a very special kind of asset that enables buyers to offer sellers a universally accepted counterpart in any circumstance. This highlights money's first and most fundamental function: to serve as a medium of exchange.

Money offers another important benefit: it enables transactions even when one of the parties does not have an immediate need to fulfil or wishes to delay spending to make larger purchases in the future. In this way, money also makes saving possible. This is its second function: to act as a store of value. Money provides yet another key advantage: it allows prices of goods and services to be expressed in terms of a single standard measure, rather than relying on relative prices between goods and services, which are too complex to manage. Therefore, money also fulfils a third function: to serve as a unit of account.

Hence, the definition of money proposed here is as follows: money is an asset that serves as a medium of exchange, a store of value, and a unit of account. This functional definition is not original; similar formulations appear in virtually all introductory economics textbooks. It is deeply rooted in history, as it applies to all forms of money used by humans for at least 5000 years. The Greek philosopher Aristotle was, nearly 2500 years ago, the first to identify these three fundamental functions of money.[1]

2 Primitive Commodity Money

According to current knowledge, money first appeared in Mesopotamia at the beginning of the Bronze Age, in the second half of the fourth millennium BC—at the same time that writing and permanent armies were being developed. Between the Tigris and Euphrates rivers, and soon in the fertile valleys of the Nile and Indus, economies that had previously been based largely on self-sufficiency began to diversify within growing cities ruled by increasingly powerful kings. Some city

[1]Aristotle's perspective was fundamentally philosophical: he sought to oppose usury and, more broadly, the charging of interest. In his view, money was created for a single, specific purpose—to serve as a medium of exchange. As he writes, "*From the primitive form of barter there developed exchange by means of money*" (*Politics* I.9, 1257a30–b10). Money also functions as a unit of account—"*All things must therefore be measured by some one thing; and this thing is money*" (*Nicomachean Ethics* V.5, 1133a19–b10)—and as a store of value—"*And because money endures, it is not easy to find anything else that could take its place*" (*Nicomachean Ethics* V.5, 1133b6–9). However, Aristotle regarded these latter functions as secondary: consequences of the invention of money rather than purposes that justified its existence.

dwellers specialized in artisanal trades (potters, shoemakers, millers, etc.), while others served kings or emperors as soldiers, priests, or administrators.

In such diversified economies, barter—the direct exchange of goods or services—was impractical. For barter to succeed, both parties had to want exactly what the other was offering, at the same time. Economists refer to this as the unlikely "coincidence of wants." Money solved this problem: it allowed buyers to offer sellers a universally acceptable means of exchange. Sellers could then use the money received to purchase other goods or services from different economic actors.

The first goods used as money were agricultural commodities that could be stored or preserved: grain and livestock in Mesopotamia, cocoa beans in Central America, for example. Commodity money was both a *monetary asset*, fulfilling the three essential functions of money, and a *non-monetary asset*, since it could also serve other purposes—for example, as food or jewelry. As a result, the value of commodity money was equal to its *intrinsic value*, i.e. the market value of the underlying non-monetary asset. For example, the value of a gold coin was, in principle, equivalent to the market value of the gold it contained.

In principle, any commodity could become a form of money. However, across different civilizations, a kind of "natural selection" took place, favouring goods that were non-perishable, easy to store, divisible, and widely accepted. In practice, precious metals gradually displaced other forms of commodity money. The Code of Hammurabi, written around 1750 BC and now preserved in the Louvre, bears traces of this transition: in the Code, while the wages of agricultural workers were still expressed in cereals, doctors' fees were already denominated in small amounts of silver.

3 Metallic Money and the Origins of Seigniorage

Over the centuries, gold and silver gradually supplanted other forms of commodity money. Gold does not oxidize, and silver corrodes very slowly. In ancient Mesopotamia, silver was often melted into ingots from which pieces of varying size could be cut. Their value depended on both weight and purity, since precious metals in nature are often mixed with non-precious metals. To facilitate trade between Anatolia and the Iranian plateau in the second millennium BC, Assyrian kings began stamping silver ingots with a seal to certify their purity.

In the mid-seventh century BC, the kings of Lydia in western Anatolia were the first to strike small ingots of electrum, a naturally occurring alloy of gold and silver, with their royal seal. Initially oval and thick, these ingots evolved into flatter, rounded shapes. These first coins were essentially pieces of metal whose weight and composition were guaranteed by the king. Unlike modern coins, they bore no denomination because their value corresponded directly to their weight in precious metal.

Coinage spread rapidly into the Greek and Persian worlds and later into the Roman Empire, not only because of its convenience but also because of the *seigniorage* it generated. Seigniorage refers to the financial gain derived from issuing money. In the case of coins, seigniorage is the difference between their "face value" and the actual market value of the metal they contained (their "intrinsic value"). Rather than reducing the size of coins, rulers typically decreased their precious-metal content, a less conspicuous alteration. Seigniorage acted as a form of hidden taxation, one little noticed by the general public. Because of the revenue at stake, governments reserved for themselves the exclusive right to mint coins, often punishing counterfeiters with death.

By the first century AD, Rome faced shortages of precious metals—and therefore of money. As a result, Augustus, the first Roman emperor (27 BC–14 AD), introduced low-value coins made of brass or copper, whose intrinsic value was far below their face value. He declared that four copper coins were equivalent to one silver sesterce, and, crucially, he permitted taxes to be paid in copper coins. This official guarantee made the fixed parity credible. In doing so, Augustus effectively created what would later be called *representative money*: money that could circulate only because the public trusted it could be exchanged, on demand and at face value, for "real" money in gold or silver.

No written accounts survived to witness public reactions to this innovation, suggesting that Romans accepted the new coins with little resistance. Archaeological evidence, however, tells a revealing story: gold and silver coins are often found as hoards, hidden or forgotten by their owners, while copper and brass coins are more frequently discovered scattered across everyday sites. This indicates that precious-metal coins were hoarded as stores of value, while base-metal coins were used in daily transactions. The phenomenon reflects what would later be formulated as *Gresham's Law*: "*bad money drives out good*." When two forms of currency circulate together at a fixed exchange rate, people tend to hoard the one with higher intrinsic value and spend the one of lower quality. For emperors, issuing representative money was doubly advantageous: it closed the money supply shortage and generated generous seigniorage, since coins were sold at face value, far above their production cost.

For Nero, who was emperor in the mid-first century AD, this was not enough. He resorted to large-scale currency debasement as a fiscal tool, irrespective of the needs of the economy. When Nero received ten gold or silver coins in taxes, he melted them down and reissued eleven coins of the same appearance and face value, each containing 10% less precious metal.

His successors, facing ever-worsening budgetary pressures, expanded this practice. By 268 AD, the "silver" coins issued in the Roman Empire contained only about 4% silver; the rest was base metal, with so much iron that the coins rusted. The debasement became impossible to conceal and gradually destroyed public confidence. Inflation was the inevitable result: between 256 and 280 AD, prices increased tenfold. A measure of wheat that had cost half a denarius under Augustus rose to 100 denarii under Gallienus (253–268 AD). Finally, Emperor Constantine (306–337 AD) restored stability through a major monetary reform, using gold confiscated from pagan temples.

4 Paper Money and the Rise of Credit Money

Paper money is another form of representative money, first appearing in China around 800 AD. Facing a shortage of gold and silver, China relied on bronze coins as commodity money. However, because bronze was far less valuable than precious metals, very large quantities were needed for trade, making the coins heavy and cumbersome. To overcome this, merchants began depositing their bronze coins with trusted individuals, who issued *deposit certificates* known as *jiaozis*. These certificates could then be used as a lighter and more convenient means of payment.

Two centuries later, in 1024, Chinese emperors assumed control of this system, issuing the certificates themselves and quickly monopolizing their production. Crucially, they abandoned the practice of backing paper notes with an equivalent quantity of metal, turning issuance into a source of seigniorage and a valuable fiscal resource. But as with Roman emperors in the third century, over-issuance proved fatal. By the fourteenth century, Chinese rulers were printing far more notes than the economy could absorb. To slow the drain of metallic reserves, they first restricted, then abolished, the right to exchange paper money for coins. They also decreed that merchants could not refuse payment in state-issued notes, effectively inventing what would later be called *legal tender*. Refusal to accept the emperor's money could even be punished by death. Nevertheless, these measures failed: over-supply of paper money triggered high inflation and destroyed confidence, contributing to the fall of the Yuan dynasty in 1368.

In Europe, paper money developed differently. From the late Middle Ages, it evolved into a form of *credit money*, circulating as a claim against its issuer. The process began with *bills of exchange,* acknowledgments of debt (IOUs) used among wholesale merchants. These allowed buyers to delay payment until they had resold the goods and secured the funds. Bills of exchange could be *"endorsed"*, meaning transferred to third parties, who in turn could use them as means of payment. From this emerged the *promissory note*, a written promise to pay a specified sum in gold or silver, at maturity to whoever held the note. When issued by banks, promissory notes resembled modern banknotes, since they entitled the bearer not only to claim precious metal on deposit, but alternatively to easily reuse them for payment purposes. It was in fourteenth-century Italy that the expression *nota di banco* ("bank note") first appeared, designating such claims.

The transition from metallic to paper money was temporarily interrupted in the sixteenth century, both in China and Europe, due to the massive influx of gold and silver from the Americas, which saturated the economy with coinage. Paper money innovations reemerged in Europe during the following century. From the mid-seventeenth century onward, banknotes were increasingly issued in round sums, which facilitated their circulation as payment instruments. Moreover, in Amsterdam, Hamburg, Stockholm and London, bankers recognized that much of their metallic reserves remained idle, since depositors did not withdraw funds simultaneously. Exploiting this, banks began issuing paper worth more than the metal they actually held. Thus, banknotes ceased to function as mere deposit certificates and instead became claims against the issuer—still redeemable for gold or silver coins, on demand, but exceeding the banks' actual reserves. Increasingly, banks issued banknotes to borrowers in place of delivering coins, and banknotes therefore began to emerge as by-products of credit operations. On banks' balance sheets, loans (earning interest) appeared on the asset side, while banknotes (bearing no interest) appeared on the liability side. Therefore banknote issuance generated significant seigniorage and was highly profitable for banks.

Today, only central banks issue "banknotes"—which might more precisely be called "central bank notes," although the traditional term has persisted in most languages. The central bank monopoly on banknotes issuance became universal during the nineteenth century, with the United States being the last major economy to adopt it, following the establishment of the Federal Reserve in 1913. The reasons for concentrating the issuing privilege in a single institution varied by country and period. In Sweden, the creation of the Royal Bank in 1668 was motivated by the government's desire to capture seigniorage revenue. In England and France, central banks received the banknotes' privilege in exchange for acting as bankers to the state. In the United States, the main concern was efficiency. Indeed, by the late nineteenth century, some 5000 different types of banknotes were in circulation. Only the notes of the most reputable banks were widely accepted, while those of lesser institutions circulated only locally. Far from their place of origin, such notes could sometimes be exchanged, but only at steep discounts.

5 Book Money and Digital Money

Book money refers to assets recorded in ledgers held by account-keeping institutions, which can be used for making payments. It is a very ancient form of money since traces of book money can be found in Mesopotamian clay tablets engraved more than 5000 years ago. As soon as humans mastered writing, they used it to record debts and maintain account balances. In principle, book money was born the day a debtor instructed an account-keeper to transfer part of his claim to a third party in order to settle a purchase or repay a debt. Evidence shows that book money was in use during the Roman era and the Middle Ages, though it remained limited in scope since both payer and payee needed to hold accounts with the same institution. The invention of the "cheque" in England in the eighteenth century helped to overcome this limitation and expanded the use of book money.

Over time, bankers came to dominate book money. Italian bankers in the fourteenth century and London's goldsmith-bankers in the seventeenth century enabled their clients to transfer balances between accounts without recourse to coins or banknotes. Book money thus became synonymous with *bank money*. Like banknotes, it was created as a by-product of bank lending and therefore also qualifies as "*credit money*".

Today, the term "book money" has become somewhat anachronistic, since money is no longer recorded in physical ledgers of cardboard and paper. Even when payments are initiated on paper—such as cheques—the processing, between and within banks, is entirely electronic. For this reason, book money is more accurately described today as *digital money*, i.e. monetary balances represented as digits in the databases of banks and other account-keeping institutions. The term "digital," however, is sometimes used in a narrower sense. For example, "digital currency" is often employed to refer specifically to cryptocurrencies (or crypto-assets). Similarly, the "digital euro" that the European Central Bank envisages to issue, creates some confusion, since commercial bank issued euros are already digital in nature.

A distinct category within digital money is *electronic money (or e-money)*, which emerged at the end of the twentieth century. The term is somewhat misleading, since all forms of digital money rely on electronic systems. Under EU legislation, electronic money is defined as *"electronically, including magnetically, stored monetary value as represented by a claim on the issuer which is issued on receipt of funds for the purpose of making payment transactions ... and which is accepted by a natural or legal person other than the electronic money issuer."* The key element in this definition is the third one: electronic money is always issued in exchange for already existing money. Indeed, unlike traditional bank money, which can be created (and issued) through lending activities, the issuance of electronic money does not expand the overall money supply but instead diversifies it, enabling individuals to hold balances in digital wallets rather than solely in traditional bank accounts.

When issued by banks, electronic money is simply a new distribution channel for existing bank money. The real innovation lies in permitting non-banks to issue electronic money, provided they comply with prudential requirements. The most important of these requirements is the obligation to maintain reserves equal to the funds collected, ensuring that customers can redeem their balances on demand, in whole or in part. Electronic money issuers are profit-seeking private entities whose revenue derives from the revenue spread between the non-interest-bearing electronic money they issue, and the interest earned on the reserve assets. After covering operating costs, this spread generates seigniorage, which provides the incentive for launching e-money schemes.

In practice, electronic money has not achieved widespread adoption in developed economies. In the European Union, for instance, it represents only about 0.15% of money in circulation. Its impact has been far greater in developing countries, particularly in Africa, through the rise of *mobile money*. In these systems, subsidiaries of mobile phone companies establish networks of local agents who act as intermediaries between mobile money providers and customers. The best-known model is *M-Pesa*, launched in Kenya in 2007, which has since inspired similar initiatives across the continent. Mobile money has become a powerful driver of financial inclusion, especially in regions where access to traditional banking services is difficult.

6 The Final Demise of Commodity Money

Until the outbreak of the First World War, all circulating forms of money were either commodity money or assets convertible into commodity money, most often gold or silver. Only a few exceptions have existed, when rulers issued paper money not backed by precious metals and used it directly to finance public spending. Notable examples include China in the fourteenth century and the United States during the War of Independence (*continental dollars*) and during the Civil War (*greenbacks*). However, these experiments were short-lived, primarily because there was no mechanism to prevent governments from issuing excessive amounts of money.

During the last quarter of the nineteenth century and up to 1914, major currencies were defined by their gold content and were freely convertible into gold, whether in the form of banknotes, base-metal coins, or book money. This gold standard system provided both internal stability (low inflation) and external stability (fixed exchange rates), and at the time it appeared likely to last indefinitely.

Everything changed after 1914. The First World War created unprecedented financial demands. Tax revenues proved insufficient to cover military expenses, so governments initially turned to public borrowing through large-scale war loans. When that still fell short, they relied heavily on their central banks for "advances." Before the war, such advances existed as short-term cash management tools—for example, bridging seasonal gaps before tax revenues were collected. Advances created money when issued but extinguished it upon repayment, leaving no lasting impact on the money supply. During the war, however, governments repeatedly rolled over and expanded these advances instead of repaying them. Central bank loans to governments function much like bank loans to private borrowers: they generate new money, and excessive money creation inevitably fuels inflation.

To prevent citizens from converting banknotes into gold on a large scale, belligerent governments suspended convertibility. This was essential to preserve dwindling gold reserves, which were needed to pay for imports of food and weapons. The suspension was meant to be temporary.

In France, between 1914 and 1920, both the money supply and the price level quadrupled. Returning to the 1914 gold parity would have required a 75% reduction in the money supply, which in turn would have necessitated equally drastic cuts in nominal wages and prices. Historically, however, such adjustments have proven politically difficult, as economic agents strongly resist reductions in nominal income. A large devaluation would have been a more realistic option, but the governments of the victorious powers resisted it, unwilling to penalize savers who had lent their gold through war loans. Ultimately, speculative pressures forced France to devalue its currency by 80% in 1928, relative to the Germinal franc of 1803. In 1931, Britain suspended gold convertibility for the pound sterling and allowed its value to fall.

The United States was in a comparatively stronger position. Between 1914 and 1919, U.S. prices rose by only 75%, while gold reserves increased from 2500 tonnes in 1914 to 6500 tonnes by 1933. As a result, the dollar's parity of $20.67 per ounce was not under immediate threat. Domestic convertibility (U.S. citizens exchanging dollars for gold) was never suspended during the war, although external convertibility (foreign claims on gold) was briefly halted. However, after the 1929 stock market crash Americans sought to protect their savings by massively converting dollars into gold, pushing the banking system toward collapse. In response, President Franklin Roosevelt in 1933 required U.S. citizens to deposit their gold with the Treasury. External convertibility was maintained but the dollar was officially devalued to $35 per ounce in 1934 to restore the competitiveness of American products on international markets. On the eve of World War II, the dollar was the sole major currency backed by gold, and only for official international use. The classical gold standard was effectively dead.

Before WW2 ended, the Allies and several neutral countries convened at *Bretton Woods* in 1944 to design a new monetary system that would avoid the instability of the interwar years. At the time, the United States held over 20,000 tonnes of gold—around three-quarters of global gold reserves. The system agreed upon was a *gold exchange standard*: Member-state currencies were pegged to gold, directly or indirectly via the dollar, itself fixed at $35 per ounce. Central banks were required to defend their currency's parity within a 1% margin, though adjustments were permitted to reflect economic conditions. Inflation-prone countries like France and Italy devalued several times, while low-inflation economies like Germany occasionally revalued.

The Bretton Woods system functioned well during the 1950s. In the 1960s, however, it began to unravel as the United States financed both President Lyndon Johnson's "Great Society" social programs and the Vietnam War. The resulting fiscal deficit was financed by foreign central banks purchasing U.S. Treasuries to build foreign-exchange reserves. The French economist Jacques Rueff called this "the deficit without tears." President Charles de Gaulle, alerted by Rueff, anticipated that U.S. gold reserves could not sustain unlimited dollar convertibility. France began converting large amounts of dollars into gold, soon followed by other European countries. U.S. gold holdings plunged from 20,000 tonnes to 8000, with an average outflow of 750 tonnes per year between 1955 and 1971.

The inevitable occurred on 15 August 1971, when President Richard Nixon announced the "temporary" suspension—effectively permanent—of foreign central banks' right to convert dollars into gold at $35 per ounce. In 1976, the Jamaica Accords formally ended the Bretton Woods system, abolishing the monetary role of gold and endorsing floating exchange rates. This not only marked the termination of the Bretton Woods system but also the definitive end of the link between currencies and commodities. In its place arose fiat money.

7 Fiat Money

Fiat' is a Latin word used in the late Middle Ages and the Early Modern period, meaning 'it shall be so because the ruler has so decreed.' "*The term fiat money emerged during the 1870s, when the Greenback Party was active in the United*

States."The "greenbacks" were banknotes issued directly by the U.S. government during the Civil War to finance military operations. These notes were backed neither by silver nor gold. After the war, the government gradually withdrew the excess supply it had created, with the aim of restoring the pre-war gold definition of the dollar. This deflationary strategy worked against the interests of indebted farmers and other borrowers, who therefore rallied behind the Greenback Party which demanded the continued issuance of government paper money, unconstrained by the gold standard. For them, the value of money—and its supply—was to be determined by political authority alone.

Central bank money is the core of modern fiat money systems. It is created when central banks lend to commercial banks, generating bank reserves kept in accounts at the central bank, used by banks for monetary policy operations and for settling interbank payments. These reserves are also used when banks purchase banknotes from the central bank for distribution to their customers. For the public, banknotes have so far been the only form of central bank money directly accessible. In a strict sense, "*fiat money*" covers only banknotes and coins, i.e. the forms of money which have been declared "legal tender".[2] However, in the economic literature, "*fiat money*" generally also includes private forms of money (e.g., bank deposits and electronic money), provided they are legally exchangeable at par with central bank money. In modern economies, therefore, the value of money is no longer anchored in gold or any other commodity. Instead, the value of all forms of fiat money is tied to the value of central bank money.

Central banks manage the money supply—the total quantity of money available—through monetary policy, which influences bank lending, the primary source of money creation. After the Second World War, many governments believed they could exploit a trade-off between inflation and unemployment, as suggested by the Phillips curve. Monetary and fiscal policies were therefore seen as complementary tools to optimize this balance. However, in the 1970s, the simultaneous occurrence of high inflation and high unemployment ("stagflation") discredited this view. Empirical evidence subsequently showed that countries with the most stable prices also tended to enjoy strong labour markets, and these countries were often those with the most independent central banks, such as Germany, Switzerland, and, to a lesser extent, the United States.

By the 1980s, "central bank independence" had become the prevailing doctrine. This independence was formalized in legislation: Governments could not instruct central banks or dismiss governors, whose mandates were deliberately long and often non-renewable. Officially, independence was justified as a safeguard for stable monetary policy and low inflation expectations. But the deeper rationale lay in experience: Elected governments had a clear inflationary bias, often preferring lower interest rates to boost short-term growth and re-election prospects. Independent central banks, by contrast, built a credible track record of keeping inflation low

[2] *Retail CBDCs* 'Central Bank Digital currencies) have also been added to the list in countries where they are available.

without pushing economies into deflation. Since 2000, inflation in major advanced economies has averaged close to 2%, the level generally targeted to balance price stability with economic flexibility (1.9% in the euro area, 2.1% in the United Kingdom, and 2.2% in the United States).

Nevertheless, fiat currencies face new challenges. Bitcoin and other "unbacked" crypto-assets, which rely on distributed ledger technology (DLT) but are not linked to fiat money, have been promoted as alternatives to state-backed currencies. However, their extreme volatility prevents them from fulfilling the three classical functions of money defined by Aristotle: medium of exchange, store of value, and unit of account. As a result, they are rarely used for everyday payments, except in illicit markets that value the anonymity they provide. For most people, Bitcoin is a speculative asset. By contrast, stablecoins—crypto-assets backed by fiat currencies (also called "electronic money tokens")—can be considered new forms of fiat money.

8 Conclusion: A Few Lessons from the History of Money

Money, invented more than 5000 years ago, is one of humanity's most enduring institutions. Once adopted, no society has ever abandoned it. Its forms, however, have continually evolved, shaped by human ingenuity. For instance, mobile money, stable coins and central bank digital currencies (CBDCs) did not exist at the start of this century—even as concepts.

Forms of money compete and undergo a process of natural selection, with those best adapted to their environment—and capable of providing substantial seigniorage to their issuers—surviving. Bank money competes with banknotes as banks seek to capture seigniorage from central banks; non-banks aim to issue electronic money to claim part of the seigniorage traditionally earned by banks; and banks, in turn, resist the introduction of CBDCs, fearing the loss of their seigniorage revenues.

When several forms of currency coexist within a territory, they tend to be tied to one that serves as an anchor. For most of the past two millennia and until 1914, this anchor was a commodity—first silver, then gold. Today, in the era of fiat money, it is the currency issued by the central bank that provides the anchor for all other forms of money.

The stability of an economy depends on the balance between money supply and money demand. An excess of money inevitably fuels inflation, as illustrated by the Roman Empire in the third century AD, the Age of Discoveries in the sixteenth century, and the First World War. Milton Friedman captured this principle in his famous dictum: "*Inflation is always and everywhere a monetary phenomenon.*[3]" Conversely, an insufficient money supply leads not only to falling prices but also to recession, since the rigidity of wages and prices constrains adjustment—an

[3] Friedman (1970), p. 11.

outcome observed both in ancient Rome and during the interwar period of the twentieth century.

Fiat currencies, when managed by independent central banks, seem uniquely capable of striking the delicate balance between excess and shortage of money. Unlike commodity-based currencies, they can adjust flexibly to economic needs while preserving credibility against inflation. In this sense, the gradual abandonment of commodity-based currencies—accelerated by the turbulences of the twentieth century—was probably inevitable. The future may still bring new forms of money, such as CBDCs or regulated stablecoins. But a rigid, algorithm-based asset like Bitcoin, detached from both state authority and economic adaptability, cannot provide a sustainable foundation for a smoothly functioning monetary system.

References

Friedman M (1970) The counter-revolution in monetary theory, *occasional paper no. 33*. Institute of Economic Affairs, London

Godeffroy JM (2025) The evolution of money and payments: from commodity to digital. Amazon-Kindle Direct Publishing

Tokenised Deposits: The Commercial Bank Money Upgrade in a Digital Economy

Haluk İnanmış

Abstract Tokenised deposits—also referred to as Commercial Bank Money Tokens (CBMTs)—represent the digital evolution of traditional commercial bank money issued on distributed ledger technology (DLT). They preserve the legal and economic characteristics of deposits while adding programmability, interoperability, and instant settlement capabilities. Functioning as regulated liabilities of licensed banks, tokenised deposits maintain the stability of the two-tier banking system and extend trust-based intermediation into programmable financial environments. This paper examines their core benefits, including efficiency gains, atomic settlement, and compliance automation, as well as their key design architectures across operational, governance, and infrastructure dimensions. It also analyses their primary use cases—ranging from domestic and cross-border payments to securities settlement, trade finance, treasury management, and FX transactions—demonstrating their potential to bridge traditional banking with decentralized ecosystems. Finally, the paper explores associated challenges in regulation, interoperability, financial stability, and technology governance, highlighting the need for harmonized standards and public-private collaboration. Tokenised deposits are positioned not as a replacement for stablecoins or central bank digital currencies (CBDCs), but as the most natural upgrade of commercial bank money in a digital economy.

Keywords Tokenised deposits • Commercial Bank money tokens • Programmable money • Distributed ledger technology • Two-tier banking system • Digital finance ecosystem

H. İnanmış (✉)
Inted Ltd., İstanbul, Türkiye
e-mail: haluk.inanmis@inted.com.tr

S. Yazıcı et al. (eds.), *Tokenisation of Money*, Contributions to Finance and Accounting, https://doi.org/10.1007/978-3-032-22946-5_3

1 Introduction

A *Tokenised Deposit* (also referred to as *Commercial Bank Money Token (CBMT)* or *Deposit Token*) is a digital representation of traditional commercial bank deposits, issued by regulated financial institutions like commercial banks on a distributed ledger technology (DLT) or blockchain. It is designed to function within regulated finance, offering new capabilities while retaining the trust and reliability associated with traditional banking. While the core economic and legal substance of the deposit remains unchanged—it's still a claim on a bank, backed by the bank's balance sheet—the format is transformed into a programmable, transferable digital token. This makes Tokenised Deposits distinct from other digital money forms like stablecoins and central bank digital currencies (CBDCs) (Visa 2024; Swiss Bankers Association 2023; Roland Berger 2023; Global Finance and Technology Network 2025).

2 Key Benefits and Characteristics of Tokenised Deposits

In an increasingly digital financial landscape, the demand for secure, efficient, and programmable forms of money is accelerating. Tokenised deposits have emerged as a promising innovation that bridges the gap between traditional banking and the opportunities enabled by distributed ledger technology. By transforming conventional bank deposits into digital tokens issued on secure, regulated platforms, they combine the reliability and trust of commercial bank money with the new capabilities for instant settlement, automation, and interoperability. This fusion of established safeguards with cutting-edge technology positions tokenised deposits as a foundational building block for the future of payments, asset transactions, and financial market infrastructure—making it essential to understand their core benefits and defining characteristics.

Issuing Only regulated deposit-taking institutions (commercial banks) are permitted to issue Tokenised Deposits. This ensures alignment with banking regulations and builds on established public trust in banks (European Banking Authority (EBA) 2024).

Backing and Liability Unlike stablecoins that are often 100% backed by high-quality liquid assets (HQLA), Tokenised Deposits are *fractionally backed* by the bank's entire balance sheet, similar to traditional deposits. This design aims to *preserve the fractional reserve banking model and the bank's role in credit creation*, which is vital for financial stability and economic growth. They represent a *liability of the issuing commercial or savings bank* (Digital Euro Association 2023).

Regulatory Oversight and Protection Tokenised Deposits retain their status as regulated bank deposits and are therefore subject to prudent regulations like capital, liquidity, and risk management rules. They typically fall under deposit insurance in the respective jurisdiction (e.g., Deposit Guarantee Scheme (DGS) in the EU, Federal Deposit Insurance Corporation (FDIC) in the US). Tokenised Deposit transactions must also comply with *Know-Your-Customer (KYC), Anti-Money Laundering (AML), and Countering the Financing of Terrorism (CFT) requirements*. DLT can enable novel and more effective means of compliance through features like tamper--proof digital identities, transparent transaction records, and automated screening (Digital Euro Association 2023).

Fungibility Tokenised Deposits are generally *fungible with traditional deposits* at the same bank and are designed to be easily converted at par value to and from conventional (non-tokenized) bank money. A crucial aspect is *fungibility between tokenized money issued by different participating commercial and savings banks*. This ensures that a Tokenised Deposit from one bank is considered equivalent to that from another, preventing the emergence of exchange rates between them. Solutions for fungibility include fully collateralized stablecoins or commercial bank tokens with interbank credit lines and central bank money settlement (Oliver Wyman, JPMorgan Chase, and Co 2023).

Programmability A core advantage of Tokenised Deposits is their *programmability through smart contracts*. This enables *automated, conditional transactions* where payments can be triggered automatically when predefined conditions are met, such as upon delivery of goods or services. This automation *reduces manual processes and human error*, leading to increased efficiency in payments, liquidity, and collateral management, as well as reconciliation processes. Programmability also facilitates the creation of *innovative financial products and services*, opening new revenue streams for banks (Oliver Wyman, JPMorgan Chase, and Co 2023; European Banking Authority (EBA) 2024).

Enhanced Efficiency and Speed Tokenised Deposits offer *near-real-time and instantaneous settlement* of transactions. This includes *atomic settlement*, where the exchange of securities and payment occurs simultaneously, significantly *reducing counterparty and settlement risks*. They can *dramatically reduce transaction costs and times*, including for cross-border payments, by streamlining processes and reducing intermediaries. Their 24/7 availability enables continuous transactions and settlement, bypassing traditional operating hours (Oliver Wyman, JPMorgan Chase, and Co 2023).

Preservation of the Two-Tier Banking System Tokenised Deposits are designed to integrate seamlessly into the *existing two-tier monetary system*, preserving the crucial role of commercial banks in *fractional reserve banking and credit creation*. Unlike some stablecoins, they are *backed by the bank's entire balance sheet*, which avoids locking up liquidity in fully-backed reserves, thereby sustaining the bank's lending capacity that drives economic growth (Digital Euro Association 2023).

Business Model and Use Cases Tokenised Deposits are particularly suitable for *Business-to-Business (B2B) applications*, including Industry 4.0, Machine-to-Machine (M2M) payments, and digital asset transactions. They can facilitate *digitalization of foreign trade transactions* and *trade finance automation*, significantly reducing counterparty risk in step-by-step transactions. They enable the *tokenization of illiquid assets* like real estate, allowing them to be traded on liquid markets and in fragments. They also support *treasury cash management optimization* and *liquidity management* for corporations, allowing for instant cash movement between subsidiaries and constant liquidity optimization without third-party facilitators (Federation of German Industries 2024; Roland Berger 2023; Die Deutsche Kreditwirtschaft 2021).

3 Design Architectures of Tokenised Deposits

The architecture of tokenised deposits determines how they are issued, recorded, governed, and integrated into existing financial infrastructures. While the underlying economic nature of the deposit—a liability of a regulated bank—remains constant, the technical and governance architecture defines the operational, regulatory, and interoperability characteristics of each implementation. Four interrelated design dimensions shape this architecture: operational design, issuance and governance model, infrastructure type, access and verification model.

3.1 Operational Design

Native Tokenised Deposits A native tokenised deposit is a form of commercial bank money whose primary record exists directly on a distributed ledger (DLT), making the ledger itself the authoritative source of ownership and value. This design allows deposits to be issued, held, and transferred entirely on-chain, enabling instant, peer-to-peer settlement and full programmability through smart contracts without reliance on off-chain reconciliation (Oliver Wyman, JPMorgan Chase, and Co 2023).

Non-native (Mirrored) Tokenised Deposits The definitive record of the deposit remains on the bank's traditional (off-chain) core banking system. The token on the blockchain mirrors the balance, and transfers are ultimately settled by updating the off-chain records, typically with reconciliation between the systems (Oliver Wyman, JPMorgan Chase, and Co 2023).

3.2 *Issuance and Governance Model*

Single Bank Ledger Issued by one financial institution for its customers, typically enabling intra-bank transfers. An example is JPM Coin, which settles payments between clients within the issuing bank itself (Bank of Japan 2024; Oliver Wyman, JPMorgan Chase, and Co 2023).

Shared Ledger Consortium Multiple banks collaborate on a shared ledger platform where each participant either issues its own issuer-specific tokens (often referred to as coloured tokens) or contributes to a jointly branded token structure with identifiable issuer attribution. This architecture enables efficient interbank transactions within a unified ecosystem, enhances liquidity management, and improves transparency of credit exposures. While tokens typically retain issuer-specific risk, the common infrastructure facilitates atomic or near real-time settlement and significantly reduces reconciliation overhead. Projects like Partior, USDF Consortium, and the Regulated Liability Network (RLN) use this model (UK Finance 2024a, b; Oliver Wyman, JPMorgan Chase, and Co 2023; Partior 2023; USDF Consortium 2024).

Universal Ledger This concept, explored by the BIS Innovation Hub through initiatives like Project Agorá, envisions combining tokenised deposits, tokenized assets, and central bank money on a single, programmable platform. The aim is to enhance the global financial system by enabling efficient, atomic settlement across multiple asset types and issuers. Project Agorá, involving the BIS and several major central banks, seeks to preserve the two-tier monetary system while enabling interoperability and programmability across public and private money. While not a BIS initiative, the private-sector project Partior—launched by DBS Bank, JP Morgan, and Temasek—pursues similar objectives by facilitating cross-border settlement using tokenized commercial bank money on a shared DLT infrastructure. This approach simplifies interoperability, supports real-time or atomic settlement, and reduces reconciliation overhead across financial institutions (Partior 2023; Bank of International Settlement (BIS) 2024).

3.3 *Infrastructure Type*

Public DLTs While less common for the core issuance due to regulatory and KYC concerns, some initiatives, like Project Guardian by the Monetary Authority of Singapore (MAS) and JPMorgan's Singapore dollar-denominated deposit token, have explored the use of *public blockchains.* The Swiss Bankers Association also suggests the Deposit Token (DT) should be based on public blockchain technology with additional protocols. However, transferring liabilities on a public blockchain raises KYC compliance challenges if the token can be transferred to individuals outside the issuer's KYC boundary (Swiss Bankers Association 2023; Bank of Japan 2024).

Private/Permissioned DLTs There is a strong preference among credit institutions for permissioned DLT platforms to ensure regulatory compliance, particularly with Anti-Money Laundering (AML) and Countering the Financing of Terrorism (CFT) requirements, by restricting access to known and authorized users. This choice allows for greater control over participants and transactions, which is crucial for regulated financial institutions. Many initiatives, including JPM Coin and the German Commercial Bank Money Token (CBMT), operate on private or permissioned blockchains (Federation of German Industries 2024; Bank of Japan 2024; Hong Kong Monetary Authority (HKMA) 2025; Die Deutsche Kreditwirtschaft 2021).

3.4 Access and Verification Model

- *Account-Based Model:* These tokenised deposits are represented digitally on a blockchain/DLT, but the ownership and transferability are tied explicitly to the identity of the account holder, similar to how funds sit in a traditional bank account. Account-Based tokenised deposits are used in a majority of current pilots and projects like UK Regulated Liability Network or German Banking Industry Committee (GBIC)‘s CBMT project (UK Finance 2024a; Federation of German Industries 2024; European Banking Authority (EBA) 2024; Die Deutsche Kreditwirtschaft 2021).
- *Token-Based Model:* Deposits exist as tokens that may be freely transferred (subject to regulatory controls), potentially functioning like bearer instruments or digital cash. These can enable direct peer-to-peer value exchange with programmability but raise additional regulatory and legal complexities. For instance, Project Guardian tested the issuance of a token-based tokenised deposit on a public blockchain, where the token, representing the issuer's deposits, was governed by a permissioned smart contract, allowing only whitelisted and KYC-verified users to hold it (Monetary Authority Singapore (MAS) and Banking International Settlement (BIS) 2023).

4 Key Use Cases for Tokenised Deposits

Tokenised deposits are rapidly emerging as the practical bridge between regulated banking and the digital asset economy, enabling new forms of settlement, liquidity, and automation. By embedding commercial bank money directly onto distributed ledger technology (DLT), they allow payments and financial transactions to occur in programmable, real-time, and compliance-assured environments. Their versatility spans multiple domains—from domestic and cross-border payments to securities settlement, trade finance, treasury management, and foreign exchange (FX) transactions—each leveraging the inherent strengths of tokenised deposits: instant settlement finality, interoperability, programmability and the preservation of regulatory safeguards. Collectively, these use cases illustrate how tokenised deposits extend the reach of traditional bank money into digital ecosystems while maintaining the trust, stability, and credit intermediation functions central to the existing banking system.

4.1 *Domestic Payments and Settlement*

Tokenised Deposits enable 24/7 instant payments by removing traditional banking delays and batch processing. They support atomic settlement, eliminating counterparty risk and the need for reconciliation. Transactions are transparently recorded on DLT, enhancing auditability and reducing manual errors. AML/CFT compliance and reporting can be automated. Interbank transfers become near-instant, especially when combined with wholesale CBDCs. Tokenised Deposits also support micropayments, opening new models like pay-per-use and streaming. Their programmable, always-on nature enhances financial accessibility, especially in underserved markets. Here are some examples.

In the Hong Kong e-HKD pilot involving Visa, HSBC, and Hang Seng Bank, Tokenised Deposits were tested in two key use cases. For property purchase settlement, they enabled end-to-end instant transfers of the buyer's deposit and final payment between banks, eliminating reliance on cheques, manual escrow, and multi-day settlement processes. Smart contracts enforced payment conditions, reducing settlement risk and shortening completion time to under 90 s (Boston Consulting Group 2024; Visa 2024).

UK Finance, through the UK Regulated Liability Network (RLN) pilot, demonstrated that Tokenised Deposits can be integrated with e-commerce and Point-of-Sale (PoS) systems, enabling programmable payments and enhanced settlement finality. Simulated card transactions confirmed compatibility with existing infrastructure, highlighting potential benefits such as fraud reduction, simplified settlement, and lower costs. Although latency was not tested, the design allows for future scalability and performance validation (UK Finance 2024a, b).

In the CBMT proof of concept, monitored by the German Banking Industry Committee (GBIC) and Federation of German Industries (BDI), a *streaming money use case* was tested to simulate automated, recurring payments. A predefined amount of tokenized commercial bank money (CBMT) was locked in a smart contract and programmed to be disbursed incrementally based on specific conditions—such as time intervals, usage levels, or production output. This setup enabled *real-time, usage-based micropayments* without manual intervention, allowing payees to receive funds instantly as contractual conditions were met. The use case demonstrated the potential of CBMT to support *subscription-like billing models*, pay-per-use scenarios, and recurring payments in sectors like utilities, digital services, or industrial machine operations (Federation of German Industries 2024; Die Deutsche Kreditwirtschaft 2021).

4.2 Cross-Border Payments

Real-Time, Low-Cost International Transfers: Tokenised Deposits can circumvent the frictions, costs, and delays of correspondent banking networks, enabling 24/7 cross-border transactions with atomic (simultaneous) settlement, reduced FX risks, and improved transparency. Projects like JPM Coin and Citi Token Services have already demonstrated these benefits for corporate clients.

Citi's Token Services for Cash has enabled institutional clients to move liquidity instantly and seamlessly across Citi branches worldwide by leveraging Tokenised Deposits on a private, permissioned blockchain. Fully embedded into Citi's existing global infrastructure, the service operates 24/7—eliminating delays caused by time zones, holidays, and banking cut-off times. Clients use their existing Citi accounts and interfaces without needing to manage tokens directly, as Citi handles the minting and burning processes behind the scenes. The solution delivers real-time settlement, enhanced transparency, and improved cash flow control, representing a major innovation in global treasury and liquidity management (Mastercard and Avalabs 2025).

JPM Coin's programmable payments feature enables institutional clients to automate fund transfers using Tokenised Deposits on J.P. Morgan's blockchain infrastructure. Rather than relying on manual instructions or static schedules, clients can define conditions—such as time triggers, balance thresholds, or external events—that automatically initiate payments once met. By using JPM Coin, a tokenized representation of fiat deposits, these payments can be executed instantly and around the clock across borders. *Siemens*, one of the early adopters, has leveraged this capability to enhance global treasury operations—improving liquidity control, reducing idle balances, and ensuring real-time, event-driven cash movement across jurisdictions (Treasury Management International (TMI) n.d.).

4.3 Securities Settlement and Trading

Tokenised Deposits play a crucial role in modernizing securities settlement and trading by enabling atomic delivery-versus-payment (DvP) on shared ledgers, reducing counterparty risk and settlement times. By serving as the cash leg in tokenized asset transactions, they support 24/7 settlement, programmable collateral management, and real-time liquidity optimization. Integrated into platforms like Visa's e-HKD pilot, and the Regulated Settlement Network (RSN), tokenised deposits have facilitated the settlement of tokenized securities, treasuries, and real estate transactions.

In the RSN PoC's Client-to-Client IG Bond DvP use case, tokenized commercial bank deposits represented clients' funds on each bank's partition and were essential for settling the client-side leg of the transaction. When the bond trade was executed, the seller's tokenized IG bonds and the buyer's tokenized commercial bank deposits were exchanged simultaneously, while interbank settlement occurred via tokenized central bank deposits. These commercial bank tokens enabled real-time tracking of client liabilities and allowed clients to move funds between their traditional and tokenized accounts, supporting 24/7, programmable, and auditable settlement (Regulated Settlement Network (RSN) 2024).

In the property purchase use case of the e-HKD Pilot Programme, Visa, HSBC, and Hang Seng Bank tested how tokenized commercial bank deposits could streamline high-value real estate transactions. The pilot showcased how smart contracts and tokenised deposits allowed the buyer's deposit and final payment to be settled instantly and atomically across banks, removing the need for cheques, manual escrow services, and multi-day settlement processes. The transaction was completed in under 90 seconds, demonstrating the potential for real-time settlement, enhanced efficiency, and reduced counterparty risk in property transactions (Boston Consulting Group 2024; Visa 2024).

4.4 *Treasury and Liquidity Management*

Tokenised Deposits on DLT enable corporates to instantly and securely transfer funds across entities, bypassing traditional banking limitations like cut-off times or time zones. Smart contracts automate treasury functions—such as liquidity management, scheduled investments, and conditional disbursements—with real-time execution and transparent audit trails. This allows for real-time global cash visibility, reduced transfer costs, instant data sharing with auditors, and precise on-chain collateral management, enhancing intraday liquidity and overall cash efficiency. By operating on shared ledgers, tokenised deposits facilitate cross-bank liquidity pooling and seamless cash positioning, enhancing efficiency, transparency, and control. Pilot projects by institutions like HSBC and Mastercard have demonstrated these benefits in real-world treasury workflows.

In a pilot conducted within the HKMA Fintech Supervisory Sandbox, HSBC tested a tokenised deposit prototype with Ant International, which acted as HSBC's treasury client, focusing on intragroup treasury operations. HSBC issued tokenised deposits on a proprietary network, backed by real bank deposits, enabling instant, 24/7 fund transfers across corporate entities within the group. This approach streamlined treasury workflows by removing cut-off time constraints and enhancing liquidity efficiency. Looking ahead, HSBC aims to expand the solution to interbank settlement by leveraging HKMA's interoperability layer, with potential future applications in cross-border payments (Hong Kong Monetary Authority (HKMA) 2025).

Mastercard, Standard Chartered Bank (Hong Kong), Mox, and Libeara partnered under the Hong Kong Monetary Authority's fintech sandbox to execute a proof-of-concept pilot using the Mastercard Multi-Token Network (MTN). The pilot showcased how a client's deposit at Mox Bank was tokenized and used to purchase a tokenized carbon credit issued via Libeara, with Standard Chartered supporting the issuance. The transaction was executed through a smart contract on MTN, enabling atomic settlement between the tokenised deposit and the tokenized asset. This demonstrated how tokenised deposits can enable real-time, programmable, cross-institutional settlement—potentially supporting efficient treasury workflows, including ESG-aligned asset allocation (Mastercard n.d.).

4.5 Trade Finance

Tokenised Deposits enhance trade finance by automating complex, multi-party transactions through smart contracts on distributed ledger technology. They enable automatic payments tied to trade milestones, convert paper-heavy processes into streamlined digital workflows, and support on-chain delivery-versus-payment models that allow simultaneous exchange of goods, documents, and funds, eliminating settlement risk. This reduces reliance on intermediaries while improving access to financing for suppliers, especially SMEs, by linking deposits to invoices as instant collateral. Overall, Tokenised Deposits bring faster settlement, greater transparency, reduced costs, and improved liquidity management across jurisdictions, modernizing and making global trade finance more efficient and secure. Here are some examples:

Citi has launched Citi Token Services, integrating tokenised deposits and smart contracts into its institutional offerings, including trade finance. In a pilot with Maersk and a canal authority, Citi digitized processes equivalent to bank guarantees and letters of credit, enabling programmable, instant payments using tokenised deposits. The solution operates on a private, permissioned blockchain managed by Citi, allowing clients to access real-time, automated settlement without needing their own blockchain infrastructure. This innovation significantly reduces settlement times from days to minutes and demonstrates the value of tokenised deposits in streamlining global trade operations (Citigroup n.d.).

In Project Guardian (Case Study 2), Tokenised Deposits were used to settle transactions involving tokenized trade and working capital loans represented as asset-backed security tokens. The pilot demonstrated how smart contracts could automate the execution of payment and asset transfers, enabling atomic Delivery-versus-Payment (DvP) and real-time settlement. By using tokenized commercial bank money as the settlement asset, the project enhanced efficiency, reduced counterparty risk, and showcased the potential for regulated tokenised deposits to support the origination and secondary trading of trade finance assets within decentralized capital markets (Monetary Authority Singapore (MAS) and Banking International Settlement (BIS) 2023).

4.6 Global FX Transactions

FX transactions, whether for corporates or bank-to-bank, represent one of the most compelling use cases for tokenised deposits, offering faster, more secure, and programmable cross-border settlement. By enabling atomic Payment-versus-Payment (PvP), reducing pre-funding needs, and supporting interoperability across currencies and institutions, tokenised deposits are transforming how value moves globally. Several global initiatives and pilots like Project Guardian, Partior, RLN are actively testing how tokenized commercial bank money and central bank money can improve FX workflows (UK Finance 2024a; Partior 2023; Monetary Authority Singapore (MAS) and Banking International Settlement (BIS) 2025). Here are some examples:

As part of Project Guardian, Ant International piloted a cross-border, cross-currency payment solution using tokenised deposits to enable instant 24/7 transfers between its internal entities. The initiative tested a token exchange model where a liquidity provider (Ant itself, in the pilot) facilitated the swap between tokenized SGD and USD deposits issued by different banks. The FX pricing was sourced off-chain via banking partners and injected into the system through a price oracle, while the actual exchange was executed using a Multi-Token Swap (MTS) smart contract on a shared ledger. Project Guardian provided the experimental sandbox to explore how programmable, interoperable, and settlement-final tokenised deposits could address traditional frictions in cross-border FX, such as delays, pre-funding, and limited market hours. This use case demonstrated how features like programmability, atomic settlement, 24/7 operability, and oracle integration can transform treasury and liquidity management (Monetary Authority Singapore (MAS) and Banking International Settlement (BIS) 2025).

In an FX PvP pilot conducted as part of Project Partior, the viability of atomic settlement for cross-border spot FX trades using tokenised deposits was successfully validated. By executing real-world USD/JPY and USD/SGD transactions between DBS, J.P. Morgan, and Mizuho, the project demonstrated how smart contracts can automate the matching of settlement instructions and ensure simultaneous delivery of both currency legs. This proof-of-concept showed that Partior's DLT-based infrastructure can eliminate settlement risk and function reliably beyond conventional market hours, laying the foundation for broader adoption of PvP settlement across the FX market (Partior 2024).

In the RLN pilot, Tokenised Deposits enabled more efficient, programmable, and risk-reduced cross-border FX payments between the UK and US. By allowing smart contracts to orchestrate pre-agreed transactions and ensuring atomic settlement of different currencies (e.g. GBP and USD), tokenised deposits removed the need for multiple intermediaries and mitigated settlement and FX risk. Their use facilitated real-time or near real-time delivery of funds across jurisdictions, reduced costs, and enabled 24/7 liquidity—overcoming time zone mismatches and operational limitations of traditional correspondent banking models (UK Finance 2023).

5 Understanding the Key Challenges and Considerations in Tokenised Deposits

Tokenised Deposits represent a significant evolution in the digitization of banking and payment systems, offering the potential to bridge traditional finance with DLT-based digital ecosystems. While maintaining the fundamental legal nature of a deposit, their DLT-based form introduces both transformative potential and complex challenges across regulatory, operational, and financial stability domains. The primary benefits of tokenised deposits also enhanced compliance with anti-money laundering (AML) and countering the financing of terrorism (CFT) requirements (UK Finance 2024a; Federation of German Industries 2024; European Banking Authority (EBA) 2024).

However, the deployment of tokenised deposits is not without its complexities. Core challenges involve navigating definitional ambiguities and regulatory fragmentation across jurisdictions, ensuring the legal certainty of DLT-based claims and smart contracts, and managing inherent operational and cybersecurity risks. Furthermore, significant considerations arise in addressing liquidity management complexities, fostering interoperability across diverse technological infrastructures, and protecting consumer interests in an increasingly digital financial landscape.

The strategic imperatives for the successful and responsible integration of tokenised deposits into the global financial system necessitate clear regulatory guidance and harmonization, the development and adoption of robust technical standards, and sustained collaborative engagement between public authorities and the private sector. Such concerted efforts are crucial to unlock the full potential of tokenised deposits while simultaneously safeguarding financial stability and consumer trust (Digital Euro Association 2023; European Banking Authority (EBA) 2024; Bank of International Settlement (BIS) 2023b).

5.1 Regulatory and Legal Considerations

Regulatory and legal considerations for tokenised deposits centre on ensuring they are clearly defined and classified within existing financial law, distinguishing them from e-money or stablecoins to avoid misapplied regulations. Their legal status must guarantee the same enforceability, settlement finality, and deposit insurance protection as traditional bank deposits. Compliance frameworks need to embed

AML/CFT, data protection, and operational resilience requirements from inception, while cross-border use raises challenges due to differing legal definitions, supervisory expectations, and consumer-protection rules. Clear regulatory alignment is essential to maintain trust, legal certainty, and interoperability across jurisdictions (Digital Euro Association 2023; European Banking Authority (EBA) 2024; Bank of International Settlement (BIS) 2023a).

5.2 *Operational and Technological Challenges*

Technological and operational challenges for tokenised deposits stem from the inherent risks of Distributed Ledger Technology, including vulnerabilities such as network attacks, protocol flaws, and smart contract bugs, as well as performance constraints like scalability, throughput, and energy efficiency. Banks generally favour permissioned DLTs to control access, meet regulatory requirements, and maintain operational resilience, but this creates a governance trade-off by introducing centralised oversight within a decentralised framework. Interoperability with other systems, reliance on shared or third-party infrastructures, and the need for rigorous security audits further complicate risk management. Ensuring robust, scalable, and regulator-trusted infrastructure is therefore essential to safely realise the key benefits of tokenised deposits (Digital Euro Association 2023; Hong Kong Monetary Authority (HKMA) 2025; European Banking Authority (EBA) 2024).

5.3 *Financial Stability and Monetary Policy Implications*

The financial stability and monetary policy implications of tokenised deposits centre on their potential to reshape liquidity dynamics, credit intermediation, and run risk. While tokenised deposits preserve the credit-creation role of commercial banks within the existing monetary system, their programmability and 24/7 transferability can reduce "deposit stickiness" and accelerate outflows under stress, heightening liquidity pressures. This effect may be amplified if early adopters are wholesale clients or tech-savvy users more prone to rapid withdrawals, and by the real-time transparency of on-chain flows that can fuel self-reinforcing panic. Although tokenised deposits inherit strong stability mechanisms—capital and liquidity requirements, deposit insurance, lender-of-last-resort access, and resolution planning—the digital speed of withdrawals could overwhelm traditional buffers, requiring enhanced stress testing and limits on programmability. Strategically, they can bolster monetary sovereignty and policy transmission by offering a regulated, credit-creating alternative to foreign or non-bank digital monies, but adoption must be managed to prevent fragmentation, contagion from shared DLT infrastructure failures, and systemic liquidity shocks (Digital Euro Association 2023; European Banking Authority (EBA) 2024; Bank of International Settlement (BIS) 2023a).

5.4 *Interoperability and Standardization Challenges*

Challenges around interoperability and standardization for tokenised deposits stem from the lack of common technical, legal, and operational frameworks across banks, networks, and jurisdictions. Without agreed standards for settlement processes, messaging formats, identity verification, and programmability, implementations risk becoming fragmented "walled gardens" that limit fungibility and network effects. Cross-ledger and cross-border transactions are particularly difficult, as differences in legal definitions, compliance requirements, and technical protocols can hinder seamless value transfer. Achieving true interoperability requires coordinated industry standards and governance models to ensure tokenised deposits can be used reliably and consistently across diverse platforms and markets (Digital Euro Association 2023; European Banking Authority (EBA) 2024; Bank of International Settlement (BIS) 2023b).

6 A Comparative Analysis of Digital Money Alternatives

The landscape of digital money is rapidly evolving, characterized by a diverse array of instruments designed to meet the demands for stable and liquid value in digital environments. Tokenized deposits (TDs), Central Bank Digital Currencies (CBDCs) and Stablecoins (SCs) represent the primary forms of digital money and money alternatives currently under development or in circulation (Table 1). While all aim to leverage technology, particularly Distributed Ledger Technology (DLT), because of their key benefits and characteristics, they differ significantly in their issuers, underlying claims, backing mechanisms, regulatory oversight, and broader implications for financial stability and monetary policy (Digital Euro Association 2023; European Banking Authority (EBA) 2024; Bank of International Settlement (BIS) 2023a).

Tokenised deposits are not a universal substitute for every form of digital money, but they are the most natural upgrade path for commercial-bank money in a tokenised economy. They:

- keep credit creation within regulated banks,
- maintain singleness of money through reserve-backed burn/issue settlement,
- reduce adoption and legal-certainty frictions relative to stablecoins, and
- offer programmability on a par with public-chain assets.

Table 1 Comparative analysis of digital money

Attribute	Tokenised Deposits	Stablecoins	CBDCs
Issuer type	Commercial bank	Private issuer (FinTechs, sometimes banks)	Central bank
Risk profile	Bank credit risk (deposit insured)	Issuer/reserve risk	Sovereign risk-free
Settlement asset	Commercial bank money	Private money (fiat-pegged)	Central bank money
Programmability	High (smart contracts, conditional payments)	High (DeFi integration)	Moderate–high (policy-driven)
DLT use	Yes (private/permissioned)	Yes (public or private DLT)	Optional (centralised or DLT)
Regulatory status	Ordinary deposit; covered by deposit insurance; existing bank rules apply	New regimes (EU MiCA, MAS SCS framework, US genius..)	Issued under central-bank law
Key challenges	Interoperability across banks still limited	Regulatory uncertainty, de-pegging risk	Political, privacy & adoption challenges
Backing assets	Entire bank balance sheet (fractional reserve)	1:1 HQLA/fiat/mixed assets	Central bank balance sheet

Source: Adapted from (Boston Consulting Group 2024; Visa 2024; Swiss Bankers Association 2023; Roland Berger 2023; Digital Euro Association 2023; Oliver Wyman, JPMorgan Chase, and Co 2023; Monetary Authority Singapore (MAS) and Banking International Settlement (BIS) 2023; Global Finance and Technology Network 2025; Bank of International Settlement (BIS) 2023a, b)

Stablecoins will remain useful where global, bank-agnostic bearer settlement is desired; CBDCs where public money is policy-optimal. For most wholesale settlement, conditional B2B payments and compliant DeFi use-cases, however, tokenised deposits currently provide the strongest blend of trust, functionality and regulatory fit. They aim to preserve the existing two-tier monetary system and the central role of commercial banks while embracing the efficiencies and functionalities offered by DLT (Digital Euro Association 2023; Oliver Wyman, JPMorgan Chase, and Co 2023; Bank of International Settlement (BIS) 2023a).

7 Conclusion

Tokenised Deposits represent a crucial evolution of commercial bank money, poised to become a strong foundation for the future digital economy. By embodying the inherent trust and regulatory safeguards of traditional banking within a DLT framework, tokenized deposits offer unparalleled benefits with their key characteristics, particularly for high-value payments, cross-border transactions, and capital market operations. They are uniquely positioned to preserve the vital role of fractional reserve banking and ensure the "singleness of money" in a rapidly digitizing world.

While significant challenges remain—from navigating complex regulatory ambiguities and integrating with legacy systems to managing new operational risks and ensuring consumer protection—the momentum from global pilot programs and strong institutional interest indicates an inevitable trajectory towards widespread adoption. The future digital money landscape will likely be one of coexistence, where tokenized deposits complement CBDCs and regulated stablecoins, each serving distinct purposes within a layered ecosystem.

To unlock this potential, a concerted effort is required. Regulators must prioritize clarity and international harmonization. Financial institutions must proactively invest in robust technology, interoperability standards, and talent, shifting their focus to revenue-generating use cases. Crucially, public and private sectors must collaborate to build the necessary infrastructure and foster an environment of responsible innovation. By embracing these strategic imperatives, tokenized deposits can stabilize and mature the digital money landscape, bridging traditional finance with the digital economy and ushering in a new era of efficiency, transparency, and trust.

References

Bank of International Settlement (BIS) (April 2023a) Bulletin 73: Stablecoins versus tokenised deposits: implications for the singleness of money, https://www.bis.org/publ/bisbull73.pdf. Accessed 10 Aug 2025

Bank of International Settlement (BIS) (June 2023b) Innovation Hub, Project Dynamo CBDCs, Stablecoins, and Deposit Tokens: Wholesale Adoption Explorations and Challenges, https://www.bis.org/innovation_hub/dynamo_study.pdf. Accessed 10 Aug 2025

Bank of International Settlement (BIS) (2024) Project agora: call for participation. Bank of International Settlement. https://www.bis.org/innovation_hub/projects/agora_application_package.pdf. Accessed 6 Aug 2025

Bank of Japan (2024) Bank of Japan Review: deposit tokenization: survey of overseas initiatives. Bank of Japan. https://www.boj.or.jp/en/research/wps_rev/rev_2024/data/rev24e09.pdf. Accessed 6 Aug 2025

Boston Consulting Group (2024) Reimagining a Future Empowered by e-HKD, Tokenised Deposits and Stablecoins, Hong Kong. https://www.bcg.com/publications/2024/china-reimagining-a-future-empowered-by-e-hkd-tokenised-deposits-and-stablecoins. Accessed 6 Aug 2025

Citigroup (n.d.). https://www.citigroup.com/global/news/press-release/2023/citi-develops-new-digital-asset-capabilities-for-institutional-clients. Accessed 8 Aug 2025

Die Deutsche Kreditwirtschaft (2021) Europe needs new money—an ecosystem of CBDC, tokenised commercial bank money and trigger solutions. Die Deutsche Kreditwirtschaft, Berlin

Digital Euro Association (2023) Banking on tokens: tokenized commercial Bank deposits -a primer. Digital Euro Association, Frankfurt. https://digital-euro-association.de/working-groups. Accessed 6 Aug 2025

European Banking Authority (EBA) (2024) Report on tokenised deposits. European Banking Authority, Brussels. https://www.eba.europa.eu/sites/default/files/2024-12/4b294386-1235-463f-b9b5-08f255160435/Report%20on%20Tokenised%20deposits.pdf. Accessed 7 Aug 2025

Federation of German Industries (2024) Commercial Bank money token: proof of concept report - new forms of money in an era of evolving industrial needs. German Banking Industry

Committee (GBIC) and Federation of German Industries (BDI), Berlin. https://english.bdi.eu/publication/news/commercial-bank-money-token. Accessed 5 Aug 2025
Global Finance & Technology Network (March 2025) The Future Belongs to Those Who Prepare Today - Readying for Tokenised Money, https://gftn.co/insights/the-future-belongs-to-those-who-prepare-today-readying-for-tokenised-money. Accessed 10 Aug 2025
Hong Kong Monetary Authority (HKMA) (2025) Distributed ledger Technology in the Financial Sector: a study on the opportunities and challenges. Hong Kong Monetary Authority. https://www.hkma.gov.hk/media/eng/doc/key-functions/banking-stability/DLT_Research_Paper.pdf. Accessed 6 Aug 2025
Mastercard (n.d.). https://www.mastercard.com/us/en/news-and-trends/Insights/2024/tokenizing-real-world-assets-and-currencies-is-essential-for-the.html. Accessed 8 Aug 2025
Mastercard and Avalabs (2025) Asset Tokenization: A comprehensive report and why you should start caring about the technology, Mastercard, https://b2b.mastercard.com/news-and-insights/report/asset-tokenization-a-comprehensive-report-and-why-you-should-start-caring-about-the-technology/. Accessed 8 Aug 2025
Monetary Authority Singapore (MAS) and Banking International Settlement (BIS) (2023) Project Guardian: Enabling Open and Interoperable Networks, Singapore, https://www.mas.gov.sg/publications/monographs-or-information-paper/2023/project-guardian-open-interoperable-networks. Accessed 7 Aug 2025
Monetary Authority Singapore (MAS) and Banking International Settlement (BIS) (2025) Project Guardian: Foreign Exchange: Use of Tokenised Bank Liabilities for Transaction Banking, Singapore, https://www.mas.gov.sg/-/media/mas-media-library/development/fintech/guardian/project-guardian-fx-workstream-transaction-banking.pdf. Accessed 7 Aug 2025
Oliver Wyman, JPMorgan Chase & Co (2023) Deposit tokens: a foundation for stable digital money. Oliver Wyman, JPMorgan Chase & Co. https://www.jpmorgan.com/kinexys/documents/deposit-tokens.pdf. Accessed 6 Aug 2025
Partior (2023) Transforming financial market infrastructure. Partior, Singapore. https://assets--global.website-files.com/651f6f739e2ae9f5c55af1cb/658440c48965a43ad358322c_Transforming_Financial_Market_Infrastructure_with_Partior.pdf. Accessed 6 Aug 2025
Partior (2024) Risk-free, 24x7 and efficient post-trade settlement with Partior's global FX settlements solution. Partior, Singapore. https://www.partior.com/news-and-insights/partior-publishes-paper-on-the-role-of-payment-vs-payment-in-fx-settlement. Accessed 6 Aug 2025
Regulated Settlement Network (RSN) (2024) Proof of Concept Business applicability report, https://www.sifma.org/wp-content/uploads/2024/12/RSN-Business-Applicability-Report-FINAL.pdf. Accessed 8 Aug 2025
Roland Berger (2023) The future of payments: how stablecoins and tokenized deposits innovate the financial services industry. Roland Berger, Dubai. https://www.rolandberger.com/publications/publication_pdf/Roland_Berger_The_Future_of_Payments.pdf. Accessed 6 Aug 2025
Swiss Bankers Association (2023) The deposit token: new money for digital Switzerland. Swiss Bankers Association. https://www.swissbanking.ch/en/media-politics/news/the-deposit-token-sba-white-paper-on-a-digital-swiss-franc. Accessed 6 Aug 2025
Treasury Management International (TMI) (n.d.). https://treasury-management.com/news/j-p-morgan-launches-programmable-payments-using-jpm-coin. Accessed 8 Aug 2025
UK Finance (2023) Regulated liability network UK discovery phase. UK Finance. https://www.ukfinance.org.uk/system/files/2023-09/Regulated%20Liability%20Network%20-%20UK%20Discovery%20Phase%20report%20.pdf, Accessed 7 Aug 2025
UK Finance (September 2024a) UK RLN experimentation phase summary report, UK Finance., https://www.ukfinance.org.uk/system/files/2024-09/UK%20Finance%20RLN%20Summary%20Report.pdf. Accessed 5 Aug 2025

UK Finance (2024b) UK RLN experimentation phase technical report. UK Finance. https://www.ukfinance.org.uk/system/files/2024-09/UK%20Finance%20RLN%20Technical%20Report.pdf Accessed 5 Aug 2025

USDF Consortium 2024, Tokenizing banking: tokenization of traditional assets holds potential to transform banking., https://usdfconsortium.com/wp-content/uploads/2024/05/USDF-Tokenization-White-Paper-1.pdf. Accessed 6 Aug 2025

Visa (2024) Tokenization of Money: e-HKD and the future of global money movement. Visa, https://corporate.visa.com/content/dam/VCOM/regional/na/us/Solutions/documents/e-hkd--and-the-future-of-global-money-movement.pdf. Accessed 5 Aug 2025

Tokenization of Securities

Michael Juul Rugaard

Abstract Building on a contested initiative by the trading platform Robinhood—which illustrates the growing interest in tokenized securities and underscores the need for vigilance and transparency—this chapter defines, analyzes, and discusses the tokenization of pre-securitized financial assets. It examines both the historical and ongoing developments in the field, outlines the advantages and barriers, enumerates the asset classes falling within this domain, and identifies the principal market participants, primarily financial institutions. Furthermore, the chapter explores the link between the tokenization of financial assets and wholesale CBDCs, highlighting the latter as a key prerequisite for realizing the full potential of securities tokenization.

Keywords Tokenized securities • Stocks • Bonds • ETFs • CBDCs • Digital wrappers • Security tokens

1 Intro: The Robinhood Case, Part 1

The fact that the topic of 'Tokenization of Securities' is more relevant than ever has clearly been illustrated by a recent debate following the controversial announcement by trading platform Robinhood of their so-called 'Stock Tokens'.

At a posh event in Cannes, France, on June 30, 2025, Robinhood's Chairman and CEO Vlad Tenev announced the company's new stock token product, which in the accompanying press release was described as follows:

> We've launched US stock and ETF tokens in the EU, giving eligible customers exposure to US equities with Robinhood Stock Tokens - featuring zero commissions or added spreads from Robinhood (other fees may apply), dividend support, and 24/5 access. With tokenized stocks,

M. Juul Rugaard (✉)
Independent author and creator of TVAC - Tokenization Value-Add Calculator, Copenhagen, Denmark
e-mail: michael@tvacai.com ; https://linkedin.com/in/michaeljuulrugaard

S. Yazıcı et al. (eds.), *Tokenisation of Money*, Contributions to Finance and Accounting, https://doi.org/10.1007/978-3-032-22946-5_4

> our European app transitions from being a crypto-only app to an all-in-one investment app powered by crypto. European customers will have access to 200+ US stock and ETF tokens. Stock token holders will also receive dividend payments directly in their app.[1]

What made this announcement truly unique—but in a controversial manner—was that the list of 200+ companies now 'represented' by Robinhood's new tokens not only included publicly listed companies such as NVIDIA, Microsoft, and Apple, but also the two unlisted, privately owned companies OpenAI and SpaceX. While Robinhood presented the new stock tokens as a revolutionary step forward for tokenization enabling European investors—even retail investors—to enrich their portfolio with exposure toward highly attractive US company shares, critics reviewed the stock tokens as anything but a positive contribution to the development of the token economy.

Should investors in OpenAI and SpaceX stock tokens fail to thoroughly read and comprehend the structural details of this new product, and instead rely primarily on Robinhood's messaging that it constitutes a significant step toward a democratized investment market - 'giving eligible customers exposure to US equities'—they could reasonably be led to believe that, by investing in an OpenAI Stock Token, for instance, they are in fact acquiring OpenAI shares and thereby obtaining an ownership stake in OpenAI. However, the OpenAI stock tokens are not equity tokens, but synthetic derivatives with no direct connection whatsoever to OpenAI. In fact, OpenAI reacted harshly on X to the Robinhood announcement, stating that[2]:

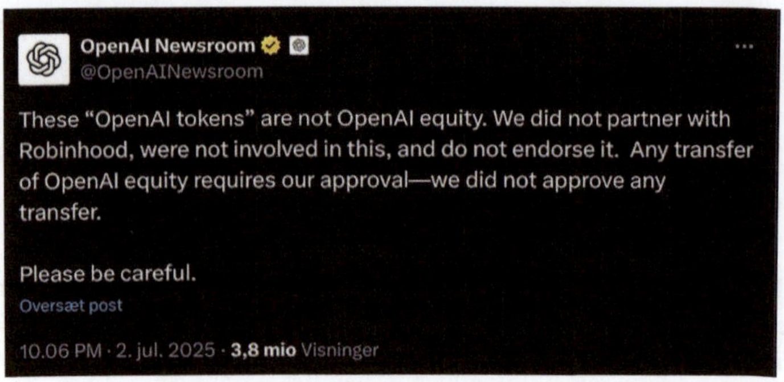

Let us leave the Robinhood debate for now and return later after a proper introduction to the topic of this chapter, tokenization of securities. The Robinhood case is interesting—and somewhat worrying—in several ways, but first of all it goes to show that the interest in tokenization of securities is heating up, and that developments—good or bad—are now happening rapidly within the realm of tokenization.

---

[1] https://via.ritzau.dk/pressemeddelelse/14480797/robinhood-markets-inc?publisherId=90446&lang=en.

[2] https://x.com/OpenAINewsroom/status/1940502391037874606?ref_src=twsrc%5Etfw%7Ctwcamp%5Etweetembed%7Ctwterm%5E1940502391037874606%7Ctwgr%5Ee387f47d59aecf96186a567ae1d568ce5565fe76%7Ctwcon%5Es1_&ref_url=https%3A%2F%2Fcrypto.news%2Fopenai-rejects-robinhoods-stock-tokens-warns-of-unauthorized-equity-claims%2F.

2 The Essence and Potential of Tokenization

Tokenization is a technology that allows ownership rights and other types of rights, in theory, of any type of asset to be represented digitally on a blockchain in the form of tokens. Furthermore, tokenized assets can be divided into smaller pieces, allowing for fractional ownership, with each token representing a portion of the asset.

The raison d'être of tokenization is usually expressed through a series of concrete improvements and advantages compared to the existing fundamental structure and modus operandi of investment and capital markets, which the token economy, at least in theory, enables. In many cases advantages through tokenization encompass both asset owners/token issuers and investors. The most significant advantages include:

2.1 *Increased Liquidity*

In a report from April 2024, Moody's stated the following on tokenization's ability to increase liquidity of otherwise illiquid assets:

> One of the most significant advantages of tokenization is the enhancement of liquidity for traditionally illiquid assets. By breaking down large assets into smaller, tradable tokens, investors can buy and sell their stakes in dedicated secondary markets with much greater ease, creating opportunities for investment and divestment that were previously limited by the illiquidity of these assets. This increased liquidity not only makes these investments more attractive but also more accessible to a broader range of investors.[3]

2.2 *24/7 Global Trading*

While traditional securities are mainly traded on centralised exchanges[4] within specific time zones and during limited hours, the vision for the future of tokenized assets is that the trading of these tokens happens on a global, cross-border 24/7/365 market accessible to, in principle, anyone. While this is theoretically possible, there are a number of regulatory challenges that still need to be addressed.

---

[3] https://events.moodys.com/2024-miu23545-smart-contracts-roundtable/sector-in-depth-tokenization-could-boost-liquidity-for-alternative-assets.

[4] Securities may also be traded on other platforms like ATS, OTC markets, or via cross-border listings.

2.3 *Enhanced Post-trading Efficiency*

Optimization of post-trading processes in the securities market through faster settlement times (ideally a reduction from T + 2 and T + 1 down to real-time settlement), reduction of resources and time spent on reconciliation, and partial elimination of various intermediaries such as brokers, clearinghouses and custodians.

2.4 *Compliance Through Smart Contracts*

Programmable security tokens enable the integration of self-executing smart contracts to automatically handle compliance requirements concerning investments in and trading of tokenized assets. This may include requirements such as KYC/AML checks, accreditation verification, and purchase controls based on the buyer's jurisdiction.

2.5 *Investment Democratisation Via Fractionalisation*

One of the grand visions of asset tokenization is to open up and democratise the global investment and capital market through fractionalisation. Significantly reducing the ticket size on attractive investment opportunities could potentially make large parts of the private and currently relatively illiquid investment market accessible for additional groups of investors—which, depending on applicable law in the jurisdiction concerned, could include retail investors.

Provided that asset tokenization continues to accelerate globally and the above-mentioned advantages materialises in large scale, tokenization could become a massive global and highly valuable megatrend. The Total Market Value of the asset tokenization industry has grown approximately fivefold over the last 5 years,[5] and according to data from RWA.xyz,[6] the total value of Real-World Assets (RWA) on-chain as of July 18, 2025 (time of writing) is $25.89B, up 7.59% from 30 days ago. The total number of Asset Issuers is 255. The total number of Asset Holders is 315,729, up 55.77% from 30 days ago. The RWA overview includes private credit,

[5] These numbers are estimations based on the following reports; https://www.marketsandmarkets.com/Market-Reports/tokenization-market-76652221.html https://www.fortunebusinessinsights.com/tokenization-market-107201 https://www.mckinsey.com/industries/financial-services/our-insights/from-ripples-to-waves-the-transformational-power-of-tokenizing-assets https://www.rolandberger.com/en/Insights/Publications/Tokenization-of-real-world-assets-unlocking-a-new-era-of-ownership-trading.html.

[6] https://app.rwa.xyz/.

US treasury debt, commodities, institutional alternative funds, stocks, corporate bonds, and non-US government debt.

3 Suitability for Tokenization

While it is technically possible—and legally likely not *im*possible—to tokenize almost any type of asset, not all asset classes are equally suitable for tokenization, at least not yet, and tokenization does not offer the same level of added value to all assets. Each asset class has its own prerequisites, advantages and limitations and must be assessed individually.

Moreover, the asset classes currently most suitable for tokenization may offer less added value from tokenization in the long term than other asset classes which today are less ripe for tokenization. Not least, a higher degree of regulatory maturity within and across jurisdictions is likely to minimize or even eliminate existing barriers for asset classes which today, for instance, cannot be tokenized directly but only via special purpose vehicles (SPVs). In the future, the ability for direct registration on blockchain (without parallel dual records like paper-based off-chain contracts) and, for instance, the management of ownership records via smart contracts could, and likely will, provide a significant boost to the tokenization of asset classes that are currently burdened, particularly by regulatory complexity.

The *Global Private Equity Report* 2023 by Bain & Company discussed the differences of tokenization suitability between asset classes and concluded that private equity, private debt, and private real estate in the longer term likely have a large tokenization potential:

> Theoretically, any asset class can be tokenized, but some are better suited than others. Inefficient, illiquid markets with easy-to-authenticate assets, like private equity, private debt, and private real estate, probably have the most to gain. Compared with public markets, these three fund classes have relatively manual and costly processes. Yet they have massive pools of AUM that are currently off limits to most investors. Tokenizing these markets could introduce a step change in efficiency and access.[7]

An analysis conducted by blockchain researcher Arnaldur Skorri Jónsson[8] shows that due to the still premature secondary markets for security tokens representing private equity, private debt, and private real estate, in reality a not insignificant part of the current secondary market transactions for these asset classes happens in the shape of buy-back clauses where investors choose to utilise a contractual buyback option and not actual investor to investor transactions. Obviously, this unsustainable situation needs to change and eventually it likely will, but realistically it could take some years still.

---

[7] https://www.bain.com/globalassets/noindex/2023/bain_report_global-private-equity-report-2023.pdf, p. 53.

[8] https://www.linkedin.com/in/addijonss/

However, this current situation is different to other asset classes which are already ripe for tokenization. Not least, tokenization of pre-securitized financial instruments garners significant attention, as we will see in the following.

4 Tokenizing Pre-securitised Assets

For financial assets as securities, the relevant legal frameworks for the US are the Securities Act of 1933, the Securities Exchange Act of 1934, and the 1946 SEC vs. Howey case with the still relevant interpretation of a security as an 'investment of money in a common enterprise with an expectation of profits derived from the efforts of others.' In the EU the relevant legal framework is MiFID II with its definition of Transferable Securities in Article 4(1) (44). Financial assets such as stocks, bonds, and ETFs all fall under these frameworks—also in a tokenized form.

In the following paragraphs—contrary to the Robinhood versus OpenAI dispute regarding privately held securities—focus will be on tokenization of listed securities, such as listed stocks, listed bonds, and ETFs, and roles and interests of financial institutions within this field.

Initially, asset tokenization as a technology grew from the bottom-up, driven by an undergrowth of primarily small, enthusiastic startup teams with a belief that the collapse of the ICO market in 2018 was not the end, but a new beginning of something much bigger. Only around 2022 did a top-down adoption of asset tokenization kick in with fast-increasing numbers of prominent financial institutions starting to pay attention to the technology and the emerging industry.

Today, tokenization of these securities are increasingly captivating the interest of the big capital market players looking for cost reductions tied to post-trading activities such as shorter settlement times, increased trading volumes, fewer intermediaries, 24/7 trading (where operationally feasible), partly compliance automation via smart contracts, reduction or elimination of intermediaries, decrease of reconciliation resources, and democratisation through fractionalisation (subject to regulatory constraints).

Examples of tokenized listed stock-like products include xStocks by Backed Finance including Alphabet xStock, Apple xStock, and Meta xStock. However, although "each xStock is backed 1:1 by the underlying stock,"[9] these tokens are not equity tokens, but tend to fall in the category of derivative-like financial products.

Examples of tokenized listed bonds include the Singaporean company ICH Genesis Pte. Ltd.[10] issuing tokenized bonds on iSTOX already in 2018. A 375 million Swiss franc-denominated bond was dual-listed on the traditional SIX Swiss Exchange and the SIX Digital Exchange (SDX) in November 2022. UBS stated:

---

[9] https://eu.kraken.com/xstocks.

[10] https://addx.co/en/investments/genesis/index.html and https://addx.co/en/about-us/index.html "2019, November: Listed our first issuance, ICH Genesis — the first ever digitised bond on a regulated blockchain-based exchange."

"Settlement via SDX CSD [DLT-based] is instant and automatic and does not require a central clearing counterparty."[11]

Furthermore, several exchange-traded funds (ETFs) have been tokenized over the last 2 years. Not least the world's largest asset manager, BlackRock, has led the way in this development. The first tokenized bond ETFs appeared in early 2023, including Ondo Finance's launch of OUSG (Ondo Short-Term US Treasuries Fund), referencing the BlackRock U.S. Treasuries ETF.

Citigroup asked rhetorically in a 2023 report if blockchain and tokenization had any role to play in the financial industry and answered partly through this description of the countless inefficiency challenges in the financial market's incumbent infrastructure:

> Today, different parts of the financial market infrastructure run on different rails, some built in the days of COBOL and Telex. Payment runs on its own tech stack, as does asset discovery and pre-trade matching, while clearing and settlement is on yet another stack. The financial industry has multiple layers of intermediaries working on the same data, but they do so in their own silos and require a lot of back-and-forth reconciliation. Cross-border payments go through multiple hoops on the correspondent banking infrastructure. Post-trade settlement on funds and bonds goes through a sequential process flow of Central Security Depositories (CSDs) and Central Counterparty Clearing Houses (CCPs), all introduced to reduce counterparty risk and settlement failures in traditional workflows.[12]

As the quote exemplifies, there is ample room for process optimisation of the incumbent financial infrastructure. For tokenized pre-securitised financial assets tokenization functions as a 'digital wrapper' which does not alter the structure or legal status of the securities but adds an additional layer of digitisation. In principle, all stocks, bonds, and other securities that have ever been issued and are still in existence can be tokenized via digital wrappers. Furthermore, new securities can be issued through traditional methods and wrapped in a digital layer as tokens.

The added digitisation layer allows the securities to interact with blockchain infrastructure, and can open up new markets through fractionalisation. Furthermore, it can potentially enable new features, for instance on DeFi platforms where tokenized shares may be used as collateral in smart contracts. Regulatory compliance and various API solutions and middleware are still required to ensure interoperability between the traditional financial industry's infrastructure and blockchain infrastructure.

However, pre-securitised financial assets can be tokenized and traded via digital wrappers without requiring a radical overhaul of the existing financial world's incumbent infrastructure. That said, the digital wrapper has limitations, particularly in leveraging opportunities such as those offered by smart contracts regarding token programmability, automated compliance, dividend distribution, and governance mechanisms. At its core, instead of reducing complexity, digital wrappers introduce dual off-chain and on-chain records, and with settlement finality still remaining off-chain.

---

[11] https://www.ubs.com/global/en/media/display-page-ndp/en-20221103-digital-bond.html.

[12] https://www.citifirst.com.hk/home/upload/citi_research/rsch_pdf_30143792.pdf, p. 59.

Nevertheless, tokenized securities could likely dominate the tokenization of the financial industry during a transitional phase, the duration of which will depend on factors such as developments in regulation, infrastructure, interoperability, and market adoption. During this transitional phase, the financial industry will simultaneously see projects that go beyond merely wrapping traditional securities and instead aim to fully leverage blockchain-based asset tokenization by issuing financial products directly on the blockchain as security tokens without an underlying, traditionally issued copy of the respective security.

Experiments in the financial industry involving this direct issuance of 'blockchain-only registered' securities in the form of security tokens are taking place. An example is Project Venus, announced in November 2022 by the European Investment Bank (EIB) in collaboration with Goldman Sachs Bank Europe, Santander, and Société Générale. Project Venus was a 100 million EUR two-year bond "issued, recorded and settled using private blockchain-based technology, and represents the inaugural issuance on Goldman Sachs' tokenisation platform – GS DAPTM." EIB Vice-President Ricardo Mourinho Félix stated: "Innovation is part of the EIB's identity and issuing this fully digital bond is another important step in helping to develop a fully digital ecosystem."[13]

Other examples are BlackRock's BUIDL fund tokenized directly on-chain with Securitize as transfer agent,[14] and Galaxy Digital's launch of its ordinary shares tokenized on Solana with full shareholder rights—voting, dividends, and ownership.[15]

However, a full transition from traditional securities to tokenized securities and further to blockchain-only security tokens entails a radical technological and infrastructural shift in the financial sector, which is costly and involves a range of risk factors that need to be addressed.

Nevertheless, such a transition is expected to occur over a span of years, likely with traditionally issued securities being phased out. In January 2025, Larry Fink, CEO of BlackRock, expressed his enthusiasm for tokenization in an interview with Bloomberg in Davos, stating: "If we can tokenize bonds and stocks… it will democratise investing in ways we can't imagine. I want the SEC to rapidly approve the tokenization of bonds and stocks."

In April 2025, Larry Fink followed up with this statement in his Annual Chairman's Letter to Investors:

> Every stock, every bond, every fund—every asset—can be tokenized. If they are, it will revolutionize investing. Markets wouldn't need to close. Transactions that currently take days would clear in seconds. And billions of dollars currently immobilized by settlement

---

13 https://www.eib.org/en/press/all/2022-448-eib-innovates-further-with-project-venus-the-first-euro-denominated-digital-bond-on-a-private-blockchain.

14 https://securitize.io/learn/press/blackrock-launches-first-tokenized-fund-buidl-on-the-ethereum-network.

15 https://www.galaxy.com/insights/research/tokenized-glxy.

> delays could be reinvested immediately back into the economy, generating more growth. Perhaps most importantly, tokenization makes investing much more democratic.[16]

The significance of the growing interest in tokenization by the world's largest institutional players cannot be overstated. JP Morgan, Goldman Sachs, Société Générale, and Deutsche Bank, to mention a few, have all made statements in favour of tokenization over the previous few years. However, every time one of these giants makes a move, it creates waves. And like some independent force of gravity, it pulls smaller players along and moves the market.

5 Tokenized Securities and CBDCs

To fully realise the advantages of securities tokenization in terms of optimisation of post-trading processes for financial institutions, a comprehensive infrastructural modernisation over time is inevitable. Reaching the goal of a token based instant Delivery versus Payment (DvP) two leg securities settlement process not only requires the delivery leg—transferring the ownership of the securities—to be optimised for a blockchain or DLT infrastructure, but the money or payment leg as well. This is where Central Bank Digital Currencies (CBDCs) and especially wholesale CBDCs in the coming years are expected to play a critical role.

The first CBDC test projects go back to around 2016, and as of today more than 130 countries, representing 98% of the global economy, are experimenting with CBDCs. Among the earliest wholesale CBDC projects were Canadian Project Jasper,[17] Project Stella, a collaboration between the ECB and the Bank of Japan,[18] and Project Ubin[19] from Singapore. The Monetary Authority of Singapore (MAS) described Project Ubin as "a collaborative project with the industry to explore the use of Blockchain and Distributed Ledger Technology (DLT) for clearing and settlement of payments and securities."[20]

Yet another project established jointly by the Swiss National Bank, BIS (Bank of International Settlement), and SIX is Project Helvetia.[21] This project is running until at least 2027 and piloting settlement of tokenized securities using wholesale CBDCs. BIS wrote the following about Helvetia in October 2024:

> The experiments showed that tokenisation can reduce the complexity of securities settlements by facilitating simpler and automated processes. They also confirmed that a wholesale CBDC (wCBDC) (understood as wholesale tokenised central bank money) can play a

---

[16] https://www.blackrock.com/corporate/investor-relations/larry-fink-annual-chairmans-letter.

[17] https://payments.ca/sites/default/files/2022-09/jasper_report_eng.pdf.

[18] https://www.boj.or.jp/en/paym/digital/index.htm.

[19] https://www.mas.gov.sg/news/media-releases/2016/mas-experimenting-with-blockchain-technology.

[20] https://www.mas.gov.sg/schemes-and-initiatives/project-ubin.

[21] https://www.bis.org/publ/othp35.pdf.

> critical role as a safe and neutral settlement asset for international financial transactions. The Swiss National Bank has taken forward the Helvetia investigation to a pilot stage, offering wCBDC for the settlement of commercial transactions with digital bonds.[22]

While private stablecoins serve a wide range of purposes for various user groups, CBDCs—and especially wholesale CBDCs—are specifically aimed at high-volume transactions and financial institutions. Concerns about CBDCs among proponents of private stablecoins revolve around potential loss of privacy through risks of centralized data collection, control, and surveillance. However, institutional financial actors, on the other hand, highlight the superior security and transparency of state-backed CBDCs as decisive advantages over private stablecoins. In 2024 The CFA Institute wrote the following about how and why wholesale CBDCs fit the task of settlement for institutional players:

> CBDCs come with privacy challenges that may make them less attractive for consumer use. But that same level of transparency could make them ideal for settlement between financial institutions. And if the projections for adoption prove correct, a wholesale CBDC could serve as the rails for a future financial system where trillions of dollars of tokenized assets flow seamlessly and securely between market participants each day.[23]

The role of CBDCs in the tokenization of securities establishes a solid link to monetary tokenization and the subtitle of this book—*From Fiat Currencies to Stablecoins*—since CBDCs, despite clear differences, may be viewed as the central banks' equivalent of the private crypto and token industry's stablecoins.

6 Outro: The Robinhood Case, Part 2

Now, let us return to the beginning of this chapter and conclude the discussion of the Robinhood case concerning the new so-called 'Stock Tokens'. As outlined in the preceding sections, the tokenization of a broad range of securities is accelerating, and with a growing number of major international financial institutions already involved, this development is likely to continue in the near future. Given this momentum, why not embrace and support Robinhood's new initiative—including private company 'Stock Tokens'—which ostensibly aims to further democratize securities tokenization?

There are at least three reasons why Robinhood's initiative is unlikely to benefit the broader development and adoption of asset tokenization.

First, investors in these Stock Tokens may be led to believe that they are purchasing equity tokens and thereby acquiring ownership in, for instance, a private company such as OpenAI. I do not wish to suggest that Robinhood intentionally seeks to mislead investors; however, it would not be surprising if some investors fail to fully understand what they are actually buying. Regardless of intent, this is

[22] https://www.bis.org/cpmi/publ/d225.pdf.

[23] https://www.cfainstitute.org/insights/articles/cbdcs-towards-a-tokenized-future.

problematic. The fact remains that Robinhood's tokens are synthetic derivatives, not equity.[24]

Second, by associating its tokens with private companies such as OpenAI—without having any formal agreement with those companies—Robinhood's actions risk resembling a kind of unsolicited or even adversarial intervention. Tokenization of private equity holds enormous potential and should be promoted and supported. But such efforts must take place on the companies' own terms. Only the companies themselves can tokenize their own shares and offer investors genuine equity tokens with the same rights as traditional shares. If Robinhood—intentionally or not—contributes to confusion about what constitutes a legitimate equity token, this could potentially harm the future development of private equity STOs.

Finally, transparency and honesty are absolutely essential for building trust in a still young and emerging industry such as asset tokenization. Any initiative that generates uncertainty or obscures rather than informs and educates investors on a truthful basis is potentially toxic to the industry's future. It is imperative that the asset tokenization industry operate with the highest possible levels of clarity, openness, and integrity - and offering tokens that resemble equity in private companies but are, in fact, synthetic derivatives are not conducive to that goal.

References

Bain & Company (2023) Global Private Equity Report 2023. https://www.bain.com/globalassets/noindex/2023/bain_report_global-private-equity-report-2023.pdf. Accessed 17 Aug 2025

Bank for International Settlements, SIX Group AG and Swiss National Bank (2020) Project Helvetia - Settling tokenised assets in central bank money. https://www.bis.org/publ/othp35.pdf. Accessed 17 Aug 2025

Bank of International Settlements (2024) Tokenisation in the context of money and other assets: concepts and implications for central banks. https://www.bis.org/cpmi/publ/d225.pdf. Accessed 17 Aug 2025

CFA Institute (2024) CBDCs: Towards a tokenized future. https://www.cfainstitute.org/insights/articles/cbdcs-towards-a-tokenized-future. Accessed 17 Aug 2025

Citigroup (2023) Money, Tokens, and Games. https://www.citifirst.com.hk/home/upload/citi_research/rsch_pdf_30143792.pdf. Accessed 17 Aug 2025

EIB (2022) EIB innovates further with Project Venus, the first euro-denominated digital bond on a private blockchain (press release). https://www.eib.org/en/press/all/2022-448-eib-innovates--further-with-project-venus-the-first-euro-denominated-digital-bond-on-a-private-blockchain. Accessed 17 Aug 2025

Fink L (2025) Larry Fink's 2025 Annual Chairman's Letter to Investors. https://www.blackrock.com/corporate/investor-relations/larry-fink-annual-chairmans-letter. Accessed 17 Aug 2025

Golub A (2025) Sam Altman slams Robinhood's "stock tokens" (LinkedIn post). https://www.linkedin.com/posts/antongolub_sam-altman-slams-robinhoods-stock-tokens-activity-

[24] See also Anton Golub's sharp post on LinkedIn: https://www.linkedin.com/posts/antongolub_sam-altman-slams-robinhoods-stock-tokens-activity-7346604773032259587-GDDD/?utm_source=share&utm_medium=member_desktop&rcm=ACoAAAAutZ4BYlE7iqRJ3nvcGI0ZCJOSZe_OMfU.

7346604773032259587-GDDD/?utm_source=share&utm_medium=member_desktop&rcm=ACoAAAAutZ4BYlE7iqRJ3nvcGI0ZCJOSZe_OMfU. Accessed 17 Aug 2025

MAS (2016) MAS, R3 and Financial Institutions experimenting with Blockchain Technology (press release). https://www.mas.gov.sg/news/media-releases/2016/mas-experimenting-with--blockchain-technology. Accessed 17 Aug 2025

MAS (2024) Project Ubin: Central Bank Digital Money using Distributed Ledger Technology. https://www.mas.gov.sg/schemes-and-initiatives/project-ubin. Accessed 17 Aug 2025

Moody's Investors Service (2024) Tokenization could boost liquidity for alternative assets https://events.moodys.com/2024-miu23545-smart-contracts-roundtable/sector-in-depth-tokenization--could-boost-liquidity-for-alternative-assets?profile_completed=1. Accessed 17 Aug 2025

OpenAI (2025) OpenAI Newsroom (X). https://x.com/OpenAINewsroom/status/1940502391037874606?ref_src=twsrc%5Etfw%7Ctwcamp%5Etweetembed%7Ctwterm%5E1940502391037874606%7Ctwgr%5Ee387f47d59aecf96186a567ae1d568ce5565fe76%7Ctwcon%5Es1_&ref_url=https%3A%2F%2Fcrypto.news%2Fopenai-rejects-robinhoods-stock-tokens--warns-of-unauthorized-equity-claims%2F. Accessed 17 Aug 2025

Payments Canada, Bank of Canada and R3 (2017) Project Jasper. https://payments.ca/sites/default/files/2022-09/jasper_report_eng.pdf. Accessed 17 Aug 2025

Robinbook Markets, Inc (2025) Robinhood Launches Stock Tokens, Reveals Layer 2 Blockchain, and Expands Crypto Suite in EU and US with Perpetual Futures and Staking (press release). https://via.ritzau.dk/pressemeddelelse/14480797/robinhood-markets-inc?publisherId=90446&lang=en. Accessed 17 Aug 2025

Rwa.xyz (2025) Global Market Overview. https://app.rwa.xyz/. Accessed 17 Aug 2025

The European Parliament and the Council (2022) Regulation (EU) 2022/858, 2022. https://eur--lex.europa.eu/legal-content/EN/TXT/PDF/?uri=CElex:32022R0858&from=EN. Accessed 17 Aug 2025

UBS (2022) UBS AG launches the world's first digital bond that is publicly traded and settled on both blockchain-based and traditional exchanges (press release). https://www.ubs.com/global/en/media/display-page-ndp/en-20221103-digital-bond.html. Accessed 17 Aug 2025

Tokenization of Liquid Investable Assets: Equities, Bonds and Funds

Emrah Ahi

Abstract Tokenization is changing capital markets by recording ownership of equities, bonds, and investment funds as programmable tokens on distributed ledgers. This chapter explains how this technology is transforming market structure and reducing the role of traditional intermediaries. It describes the main ideas and technical setup of tokenization and outlines its key benefits, including faster settlement, fractional ownership, programmability, and transparency. Case studies such as Banco Santander's 2019 blockchain bond, Hong Kong's green bond, and tokenized money-market funds show how on-chain issuance and settlement can lower costs and barriers for both issuers and investors. The chapter also links tokenization to the future of money, discussing how settlement through stablecoins, tokenized bank deposits, and central bank digital currencies (CBDCs) may affect monetary policy and financial stability. Although tokenization offers efficiency and innovation, its growth depends on strong legal frameworks, sufficient liquidity, and smooth integration with existing financial systems. The chapter concludes that tokenization complements traditional finance when supported by trusted settlement assets and clear regulation.

Keywords Tokenization · Digital securities · Programmable money · Stablecoins · Central bank digital currency · Financial stability

1 Introduction

The transition from paper certificates to electronic book entries revolutionized securities markets by dematerializing ownership and reducing settlement delays. Tokenization represents the next step in this long evolution: it encodes claims on real-world assets as programmable tokens on distributed ledgers. This chapter

E. Ahi (✉)
Özyeğin University, Istanbul, Türkiye
e-mail: emrah.ahi@ozyegin.edu.tr

S. Yazıcı et al. (eds.), *Tokenisation of Money*, Contributions to Finance and Accounting, https://doi.org/10.1007/978-3-032-22946-5_5

examines why and how issuers are tokenizing liquid assets—equities, bonds and investment funds—and situates these developments within the broader theme of money. By digitizing securities at the ledger level, tokenization promises not only operational efficiencies but also new features such as fractional ownership, automated corporate actions and seamless integration with decentralized finance protocols. These innovations blur the traditional boundary between "money" and "assets" because tokenized securities settle against on-chain cash tokens such as stablecoins or emerging CBDCs. The central argument of this chapter is that tokenization can enhance market efficiency and inclusiveness without undermining the fiat-denominated monetary system, if settlement relies on regulated digital cash and that appropriate safeguards protect investors. The chapter proceeds as follows: Sect. 1 explains the rationale for tokenizing liquid assets; Sect. 2 describes the core technical architecture; Sect. 3 outlines the benefits and market impact; Sect. 4 reviews tokenization across equities, bonds and funds; Sect. 5 discusses market infrastructure; Sect. 6 links tokenized securities to the evolution of money; and the conclusion reflects on prospects.

2 Rationale of Tokenizing Liquid Assets

The tokenization of liquid investable assets—broadly encompassing stocks, corporate bonds, sovereign debt and pooled investment vehicles—marks a significant evolution in how capital markets are organized and accessed. Unlike earlier waves of financial innovation that grafted new instruments onto existing infrastructure, tokenization rewrites market microstructure by recording ownership claims and transactional rules directly on programmable ledgers. Tokens representing real financial instruments are governed by smart contracts that embed the economic rights of holders and the obligations of issuers, enabling near-real-time settlement, automated servicing and continuous global access (Aldasoro et al. 2025).

The fundamental rationale is to address persistent inefficiencies in today's markets: multiday settlement periods expose parties to counterparty risk and tie up collateral; complex clearing and custody chains inflate costs; high minimum investments exclude retail investors; and fragmented systems restrict cross-border participation. Digitizing ownership into programmable units aims to reduce or eliminate these frictions. Notably, the OECD (2020) identifies efficiency gains, increased transparency and enhanced liquidity as key theoretical benefits of applying tokenization to financial assets.

Market projections for the tokenization of liquid assets underscore both the opportunity and the uncertainty. Industry research anticipates that the total value of tokenized financial instruments could rise from approximately USD 3.1 trillion in 2025 and USD 16 trillion by 2030, depending on assumptions about regulatory clarity and institutional adoption (World Economic Forum 2025). Figure 1 depicts the

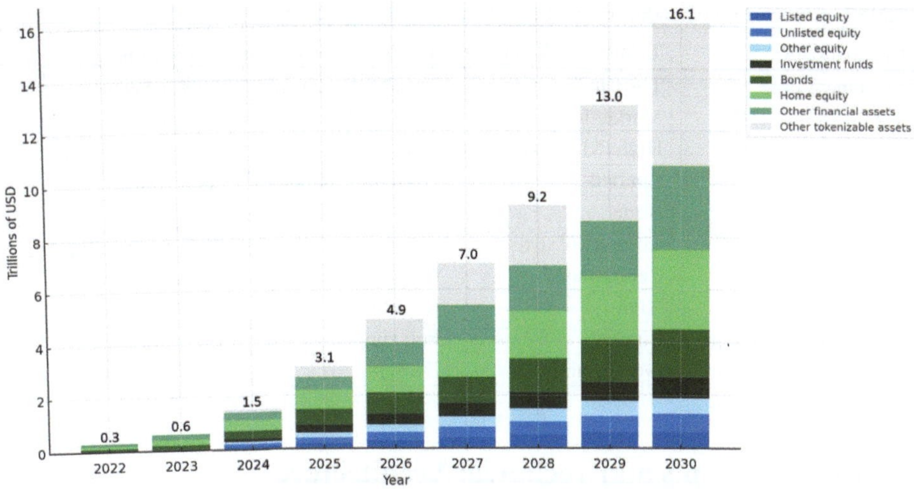

Fig. 1 Projection of Total Market Value of Tokenized Liquid Assets (*Source:* World Economic Forum 2025)

rapid growth in tokenized liquid asset value and the projected values illustrating accelerating momentum.

Tokenization can be viewed as part of the long trajectory of financial innovations that help complete markets, a role emphasized in Merton's (1990) seminal work on functional finance. By lowering barriers to participation and improving transparency, tokenization can be interpreted as a mechanism to enhance market efficiency in the sense defined by Fama (1970).

Tokenization does not simply replicate existing securities on a new substrate; it enables new functionalities such as fractionalization, algorithmic corporate actions and composable financial products. Fractional tokens lower minimum investments, permitting a broader investor base to participate in blue-chip equities, sovereign bonds or money-market funds. Programmability allows issuers to incorporate performance triggers, dynamic fees and governance rights directly into code. Transparency and auditability improve because every token transfer is recorded immutably on a shared ledger. These features have the potential to create more inclusive, efficient and innovative capital markets. At the same time, the adoption of tokenized instruments will depend on robust legal frameworks, operational resilience, market liquidity and investor protection. Table 1 provides a comparative overview of traditional versus tokenized assets, highlighting differences in settlement speed, transparency, accessibility and cost efficiency, which collectively underpin the rationale for rapid adoption.

Table 1 demonstrates the transformative potential of tokenization in financial markets by comparing traditional asset management with blockchain-based alternatives across nine key operational dimensions.

Table 1 Comparison of traditional and tokenized asset characteristics

Characteristic	Traditional Assets	Tokenized Assets	Improvement
Settlement time	T + 1 to T + 3 days	Near-instantaneous	99% + faster
Trading hours	Market hours only	24/7 availability	3x more access
Minimum investment	High ($1000+)	Low (any amount)	90% + reduction
Transparency	Limited	High (blockchain)	Real-time
Programmability	None	Smart contracts	Automated
Cross-border access	Complex/Expensive	Simplified	50% + cost reduction
Custody model	Centralized	Cryptographic	Enhanced security
Operational costs	High	Reduced	40–60% savings
Fractional ownership	Limited	Full support	Unlimited
Regulatory framework	Well-established	Evolving	In development

3 Core Concepts and Technical Architecture

3.1 *Tokenization Mechanisms*

At its core, tokenization involves expressing a claim on a real-world financial asset as a digital token on a blockchain. Three broad approaches have emerged. Native tokens are created directly on-chain and embody all rights associated with the underlying asset. An issuer programs a smart contract that represents a share of common stock or a bond, and the ledger becomes the authoritative record of ownership. Wrapped tokens represent off-chain securities held in custody; the token functions as a digital wrapper that inherits the rights of the underlying instrument but relies on off-chain legal documentation. Synthetic tokens provide economic exposure through derivatives or collateralized structures when direct tokenization is impractical; for example, a token may mirror the price of a high-yield bond index via swap agreements. In each case, the token contract encodes ownership rights, transfer restrictions, corporate actions and compliance conditions. For example, fully on-chain issuance is more straightforward for bearer instruments like bonds, whereas equity tokens often must represent off-chain shares under current legal regimes (OECD 2020).

3.2 *Smart Contracts and Automation*

Smart contracts—self-executing code deployed to a blockchain—are central to asset tokenization. They automate issuance, enable real-time transfer of ownership, and handle lifecycle events such as coupon payments, dividend distributions or redemptions. Conditional logic ensures that transfers comply with regulatory restrictions (e.g., preventing transfers to non-qualified investors) and that payments occur at predetermined dates. For example, a bond contract can automatically release coupon payments to token holders when due, eliminating manual processing and lowering operational costs. Smart contracts also support delivery versus payment (DvP) settlement, ensuring that securities and funds exchange simultaneously, thereby reducing counterparty risk. Despite these benefits, rigorous code auditing and security reviews are essential; vulnerabilities in smart contracts can lead to loss of funds, and upgrade mechanisms must balance flexibility with the immutability expected from blockchain systems (World Economic Forum 2025).

3.3 *Infrastructure Requirements and Interoperability*

Tokenized markets require both robust blockchain infrastructure and integration with legacy systems. Public blockchains like Ethereum offer global accessibility and transparency but may face scalability challenges and transaction-fee volatility. Permissioned or consortium blockchains provide more predictable throughput and compliance features; for instance, Switzerland's SIX Digital Exchange (SDX) operates on a regulated distributed ledger to support token issuance, trading and settlement within an institutional environment (SIX Digital Exchange 2024). Hybrid architecture combines public and permissioned layers, enabling open access while restricting sensitive processes. Interoperability across ledgers is critical because tokenized assets may reside on multiple chains. Portability frameworks and cross-chain protocols are being developed to allow tokens to move between different blockchains or to interact seamlessly, thereby avoiding market fragmentation (Barnes 2020).

4 Benefits of Tokenization and Market Impact

4.1 *Enhanced Efficiency and Cost Savings*

Tokenization promises substantial efficiency gains by streamlining post-trade processes. Traditional securities settle on a T + 2 or T + 3 basis, necessitating clearinghouses and custodians to reconcile transfers and maintain ledger entries. Smart contracts can execute DvP settlement within minutes. Capital is released more quickly, reducing margin requirements and counterparty exposure. Automation of corporate actions such as dividend payments, interest accruals, voting and regulatory reporting can reduce operational costs by up to 60% relative to manual processes (World Economic Forum 2025). Programmatic compliance checks embedded in tokens decrease the need for intermediaries to perform due diligence, thereby cutting transaction fees. The elimination of paper certificates and central depositories results in lower record-keeping expenses and fosters standardization of processes across jurisdictions. For instance, a blockchain-based bond system that removes centralized intermediaries can significantly decrease complexity and transaction costs by substituting a distributed trust infrastructure for traditional middlemen (Cisar et al. 2025). These efficiencies directly improve market liquidity and reduce issuance and servicing overhead.

4.2 *Democratization and Broader Access*

Fractional tokens lower investment thresholds and open previously exclusive markets to a wider range of investors. Whereas traditional bond issues may require minimum purchases of USD 100,000 or more, tokenized bonds can be divided into micro-units with purchase sizes below USD 100, granting retail investors participation in blue-chip corporate bonds, sovereign debt or private funds. This democratization can reduce home bias in portfolios and improve risk diversification. For example, the Hamilton Lane tokenized feeder fund on the Polygon blockchain allows investors to obtain exposure to private equity opportunities with minimum commitments of about USD 20,000 instead of several million dollars (Hamilton Lane 2022). Tokenization also enables global participation; investors in Asia can buy tokenized European government bonds at any time of day, bypassing geographical and time zone constraints.

4.3 *Programmability and Innovation*

Programmability enables features that are not feasible with paper or dematerialized securities. Tokens can incorporate performance-linked cash flows (e.g., adjusting coupon rates based on environmental performance metrics), automatic interest compounding, or built-in governance mechanisms that allow holders to vote on modifications to terms. Composite tokens can bundle several underlying assets—equities, commodities and currencies—into a single programmable instrument that rebalances automatically according to a predetermined algorithm. Decentralized finance (DeFi) platforms accept tokenized securities as collateral for borrowing or derivatives transactions, creating new liquidity channels and yield opportunities. For instance, the BlackRock BUIDL fund, a tokenized money-market fund on Ethereum, provides token holders with real-time settlement and the ability to pledge tokens in on-chain lending platforms for additional yield (BlackRock 2024). The composability of tokenized assets allows building complex financial products that interact seamlessly across protocols.

4.4 *Transparency and Auditability*

Blockchain records provide real-time, immutable histories of ownership and transfer, improving transparency relative to conventional record-keeping systems. Investors, regulators and auditors can trace the provenance of assets and verify outstanding supply at any time. On-chain transparency also facilitates real-time risk monitoring and compliance enforcement; suspicious activity patterns can be detected quickly, enabling improved anti-fraud and anti-money-laundering oversight. However, transparency must be balanced with privacy requirements; solutions such as zero-knowledge proofs or off-chain identity registries can help maintain confidentiality while proving compliance (García et al. 2022).

5 Tokenized Securities: Equities, Bonds and Funds

5.1 *Equities*

Tokenized equities replicate the economic and governance rights of shares while leveraging blockchain settlement. Issuers may deploy fully on-chain share tokens or tokenized depositary receipts that wrap existing securities. Early experiments such as Overstock.com's OSTKO preferred share demonstrated peer-to-peer trading and automated dividends but highlighted regulatory frictions (Overstock.com 2020). More recent initiatives include 21X in Germany, which facilitates wallet-based atomic settlement of shares using a regulated stablecoin and aims to reduce back-office costs (21X 2024). Empirical research suggests that tokenizing stocks can streamline clearing and enable direct interactions between issuers and investors while preserving compliance (Malinova and Park 2023). However, expanded retail access and continuous trading may amplify speculative behaviour, echoing Shiller's (2000) warnings about irrational exuberance.

5.2 *Corporate Bonds*

Corporate bond tokenization has moved from pilots to mainstream adoption. Banco Santander issued a US$20 million bond on the public Ethereum blockchain in 2019, with both the bond and the cash leg settled on-chain via smart contracts; the contract encoded coupon schedules and automatically executed payments, demonstrating the feasibility of end-to-end blockchain issuance (Banco Santander 2019). DBS Bank's 2021 SGD 15 million digital bond on the FIX Marketplace further illustrated how tokenization can lower minimum investments to around US$10,000, democratizing access to corporate debt (DBS Bank, 2021). Since these breakthroughs, more than sixty tokenized bond issues—roughly two dozen corporates and fifteen sovereigns—have been recorded, totaling about $8 billion (Bank for International Settlements 2024). Studies find that tokenized bonds exhibit similar yields, but tighter bid-ask spreads compared with conventional bonds, indicating improved liquidity without compromising pricing (Bank for International Settlements 2024). Issuers cite faster settlement, reduced administrative costs and broader investor reach as key benefits.

5.3 *Government Bonds*

Sovereign issuers are also experimenting with tokenization. Hong Kong's government issued the world's first tokenized green bond in 2023, raising US$102 million and providing real-time transparency on the use of proceeds; a larger US$200 million multicurrency tokenized bond followed in 2024 (Hong Kong Monetary Authority 2024). The European Investment Bank (EIB) launched a €50 million digital sterling bond on a DLT platform in 2023, achieving same-day settlement with digital cash (European Investment Bank 2023). Realize, a financial technology firm, tokenized U.S. Treasury bills in 2024 through its T-BILLS Fund, enabling global investors to access dollar-denominated risk-free assets via blockchain (Realize 2024). These initiatives signal growing sovereign adoption of tokenization, supported by legal reforms in Switzerland and Luxembourg that recognize security tokens as dematerialized instruments (Bank for International Settlements 2024). Pilot results suggest that tokenized government bonds can tighten bid-ask spreads and improve liquidity while maintaining credit quality (Aldasoro et al. 2025).

5.4 *Funds and Structured Products*

Pooled investment vehicles are natural candidates for tokenization because share registers and net asset value (NAV) calculations can be replicated on-chain. Franklin Templeton's OnChain U.S. Government Money Market Fund, launched in 2023, issues tokens on the Stellar and Polygon blockchains and automates dividend distributions (Franklin Templeton 2023). BlackRock's BUIDL fund, launched with Securitize in 2023, tokenizes money-market fund shares on Ethereum and had attracted over US$1.8 billion by mid-2025. Hamilton Lane's tokenized feeder funds provide retail investors access to private equity with much lower minimum commitments (Hamilton Lane 2022). WisdomTree offers a suite of tokenized funds across equities, commodities and bonds under its regulated Prime platform (WisdomTree 2024). Collectively, these examples show that tokenization can expand access to diversified portfolios, enable 24/7 trading and integrate with decentralized finance protocols, though adoption remains modest relative to traditional fund markets. Table 2 summarizes major tokenization initiatives across asset classes.

Data compiled by the author from multiple sources. Primary sources include official press releases from Santander (2019), European Investment Bank (2021), Hong Kong Monetary Authority (2023), BlackRock/Securitize (2024), Hamilton Lane (2022), WisdomTree (2025), Franklin Templeton SEC filings, and regulatory announcements from BaFin-regulated platforms 21X and 360X. Additional verification through Goldman Sachs insights, BIS Innovation Hub documentation, and financial news sources including CoinDesk, The Defiant, and LedgerInsights.

Table 2 Major tokenized asset implementations (2019–2025)

Project/Issuer	Asset type	Blockchain / Platform	Value (USD)	Launch year	Key innovations
Santander	Corporate bond	Ethereum	20 million	2019	First end-to-end blockchain bond issuance and settlement
EIB & Goldman Sachs	Supranational bond	Public blockchain	€50 million	2021	T + 0 settlement with CBDC pilot
Franklin OnChain	Government money fund	Stellar/ polygon	300 million+	2021	On-chain share registry with automatic dividend payments
HKMA	Sovereign green bond	Private DLT	102 million	2023	Real-time transparency on use of proceeds
BlackRock BUIDL	Money market fund	Ethereum	2 billion+	2024	Institutional-grade tokenized fund with DeFi integration
Hamilton lane	PE feeder fund	Polygon	50 million+	2022	Access to private equity via tokenized feeder
WisdomTree prime	Multi-asset funds	Ethereum	500 million+	2024	Suite of tokenized mutual funds and ETFs
21X	Tokenized equities	Permissioned DLT	Not public	2024	Atomic settlement of shares with stablecoin payment
360X	Digital bond trading	Permissioned DLT	300 million	2023	First secondary trading of Siemens digital bond
Realize T-BILLS	Tokenized T-bills	Ethereum	100 million+	2024	Global access to treasury-bill exposure via tokens

6 Market Infrastructure and Trading Venues

6.1 *Digital and Decentralized Infrastructure*

The growth of tokenized markets relies on both regulated and decentralized trading venues. Traditional exchanges are adapting their platforms to list security tokens and provide issuance, trading and custody services under existing regulatory frameworks; examples include Swiss and German digital exchanges that settle trades atomically using stablecoins or digital cash. Banks and specialized custodians safeguard private keys and offer insured storage, while stablecoins such as USDC facilitate on-chain payment of cash legs (Circle 2024). As trading volumes increase, coordination among exchanges, custodians and payment providers will determine market reliability and interoperability.

In parallel, decentralized protocols provide automated market making and peer-to-peer trading using liquidity pools and algorithmic pricing. These platforms demonstrate how tokenized assets could trade continuously without traditional intermediaries, but they face regulatory uncertainty and liquidity constraints. For example, despite over USD 25 billion in real-world assets being tokenized on public blockchains by 2025, many of these RWA tokens see very low secondary trading activity, with long holding periods and limited investor participation (Mafrur 2025). Structural factors such as regulatory gating, custodial concentration, valuation opacity and a lack of decentralized exchange venues have created liquidity bottlenecks even for tokenized assets that in theory enjoy 24/7 global markets. Hybrid models that combine permissioned access with decentralized execution seek to balance efficiency with compliance. Achieving deep and resilient liquidity for tokenized securities will require the participation of institutional investors and market-making services. However, the design of tokenized trading systems must avoid introducing new frictions. If traders are forced to reveal their ownership when transacting on-chain, intermediary market-makers can lose bargaining power—a potential *hold-up problem* that diminishes their incentive to provide liquidity (Lee et al. 2024). This underscores the need for careful market design so that the benefits of transparency and automation do not inadvertently deter traditional liquidity providers.

6.2 Settlement and Cash Leg Integration

Efficient settlement of tokenized assets requires a reliable on-chain cash component. Stablecoins such as USDC and USDT are widely used for settlement because they maintain parity with fiat currency and settle nearly instantly on-chain. For regulated securities, central bank digital currencies (CBDCs) or tokenized bank deposits may provide superior assurance. Pilot programs by the Banque de France, Swiss National Bank and the Monetary Authority of Singapore explore wholesale CBDC issuance to settle tokenized government bonds and commercial paper. Banks including JP Morgan and Standard Chartered have built tokenized deposit platforms that issue digital liabilities representing deposits in omnibus accounts; these tokens enable atomic settlement with securities tokens (Citi 2023). Integration of cash and securities settlement on a single ledger reduces operational complexity and eliminates the need for time-consuming bank transfers. Because wrapped tokens must be backed by off-chain securities, custodial brokers mint and redeem tokens and coordinate with registrars and clearinghouses, adding operational complexity and requiring robust reconciliation procedures.

6.3 *On-Chain Portfolio Management and DeFi Integration*

When financial assets exist natively on-chain, portfolio construction and maintenance can be embedded into autonomous programs. Smart contracts can rebalance portfolios based on momentum, volatility or calendar schedules and can automatically reinvest dividends or coupon payments. Decentralized protocols such as Index Coop and TokenSets enable investors to hold a single token that represents a basket of assets and rebalances according to transparent algorithms, reducing transaction costs while maintaining exposure to a desired index (Index Coop 2024). Real-time on-chain execution allows managers to respond to market conditions quickly, though algorithmic trading must be carefully designed to avoid front-running and market manipulation.

On-chain data also facilitates continuous analytics. Net asset values, exposures and performance metrics can be computed directly from ledger entries and off-chain pricing feeds, giving investors and regulators unprecedented transparency and enabling timely risk management (Watsky et al. 2024). Tokenized securities increasingly interact with decentralized finance: tokens representing bonds or fund shares can be pledged as collateral to obtain stablecoin loans or be used in on-chain derivatives and yield strategies. Protocols such as Maple Finance and Ondo Finance have created marketplaces for tokenized debt and treasury tokens, expanding liquidity but also raising governance and risk-management challenges (Tanveer et al. 2025).

7 Tokenized Securities and the Evolution of Money

The innovations discussed above extend beyond modernizing securities markets—they are reshaping the very link between financial assets and money. In conventional finance, securities settle against cash balances held in bank accounts. In tokenized markets, however, the cash leg is increasingly represented by digital tokens. On public blockchains, delivery-versus-payment (DvP) settlement typically relies on fiat-backed stablecoins such as USDC or USDT, whereas private networks are experimenting with tokenized bank deposits and wholesale central bank digital currencies (CBDCs).

The Bank for International Settlements (2025) argues that a future "unified ledger" could emerge from the integration of tokenized central bank reserves, commercial bank money, and government bonds—together forming a stable settlement foundation that preserves the *singleness of money*. Tokenized reserves would enable atomic settlement of securities and cash, while allowing monetary policy operations to occur within a programmable infrastructure. At the same time, the BIS cautions that most existing stablecoins perform poorly when tested against the principles of singleness, elasticity, and integrity. As bearer instruments that lack one-to-one convertibility with central bank money, they can fragment liquidity and undermine financial stability (Bank for International Settlements 2025).

Tokenized securities therefore interact with stablecoins and CBDCs in distinct ways. In permissionless markets, securities tokens often settle against stablecoins because regulated digital cash is not yet available. This arrangement enables 24/7 trading but introduces counterparty and redemption risk. Stablecoin regulation is evolving: the U.S. GENIUS Act of July 2025 requires payment stablecoins to be fully backed by U.S. dollar reserves and subjects issuers to capital and liquidity requirements; analysts expect this clarity to catalyze adoption and project that stablecoin market capitalization could exceed US$3 trillion by 2030 (Hentov et al. 2025). However, stablecoin flows reallocate liquidity from bank deposits into short-term Treasury securities and heighten the sensitivity of yield curves to redemptions (Hentov et al. 2025). They also risk accelerating dollarization in emerging markets and raise questions about monetary sovereignty (Hentov et al. 2025). CBDCs and tokenized deposits offer an alternative: central banks and commercial banks issue digital liabilities that maintain par convertibility with reserves, ensuring safe settlement and regulatory oversight. Pilots such as Project Pine demonstrate that central banks can implement monetary policy in tokenized markets by using smart contracts to conduct open-market operations; prototypes designed by the New York Federal Reserve and the BIS successfully executed liquidity injections and withdrawals under varying market conditions (Bank for International Settlements and Federal Reserve Bank of New York 2025). These experiments suggest that tokenized finance could make policy implementation nimbler while preserving central bank control.

Whether tokenization complements or challenges fiat-based monetary systems depends on the settlement asset. When tokens settle against regulated digital cash—tokenized deposits or wholesale CBDCs—tokenization enhances efficiency without altering the core two-tier structure (Bank for International Settlements 2025). Tokenized government bonds and central bank reserves can even strengthen the monetary system by enabling automated collateral management and faster policy transmission. By contrast, a system that relies on privately issued stablecoins as the primary settlement asset could fragment liquidity and erode the singleness of money. The BIS warns that stablecoins' failure on singleness, elasticity and integrity means they should play at most a subsidiary role in the monetary system (Bank for International Settlements 2025).

The implications for financial stability and monetary policy are multifaceted. Tokenization reduces settlement times and counterparty risk but could also accelerate the propagation of shocks. The IMF notes that highly interconnected tokenized markets might transmit disturbances more quickly (Agur et al. 2025). State Street analysts highlight that stablecoin flows can distort yield curves and that large-scale adoption may necessitate adjustments to macroprudential tools (Hentov et al. 2025). Conversely, prototypes from the New York Fed and BIS indicate that central banks could leverage smart contracts to conduct policy operations more rapidly (Bank for International Settlements and Federal Reserve Bank of New York 2025). Policymakers must therefore balance innovation with safeguards: integrating tokenized markets with regulated digital cash, enforcing investor protection and adapting liquidity management frameworks to this new environment.

8 Conclusion

Tokenization of liquid investable assets promises to reshape capital markets by reducing settlement times, lowering costs, broadening investor access, and enabling programmable innovations. Early pilots in equities, bonds, and funds show that tokenized instruments can replicate economic rights while integrating with decentralized finance. Market infrastructure is maturing, with regulated exchanges, stablecoin settlement, and custody solutions supporting institutional adoption, though technical and governance risks remain.

Importantly, tokenization does not eliminate inefficiencies; some may even intensify. The IMF warns that highly interconnected tokenized markets could transmit shocks more quickly, while complex smart contracts introduce new vulnerabilities (Agur et al. 2025). Regulation is adapting, but harmonization and legal certainty are critical for scale.

Looking ahead, tokenization extends classic finance insights—Markowitz (1952) and Sharpe (1964) on diversification, Fama (1970) on market efficiency, Fama and French (1992, 1993) on asset pricing factors, and Merton (1974, 1990) on credit risk and innovation—while Shiller's (2000) caution about speculative excess remains pertinent. If efficiency gains outweigh costs and confidence is secured, tokenization could move from pilots to a mainstream component of global markets within the next decade.

References

21X (2024) 21X exchange platform overview. 21X AG

Agur I, Villegas Bauer G, Mancini Griffoli T (2025) Tokenization and financial market inefficiencies. IMF Fintech notes 2025/001. International Monetary Fund

Aldasoro I, Cornelli G, Frost J, Wilkens PK, Lewrick U, Shreeti V (2025) Tokenization of government bonds: Assessment and roadmap. BIS Bulletin No. 107. Bank for International Settlements

Banco Santander (2019) Banco Santander issues first blockchain bond. Press release. https://www.santander.com/en/press-room/press-releases/santander-launches-the-first-end-to-end-blockchain-bond

Bank for International Settlements (2024) Tokenization of assets and market infrastructure. BIS Committee on Payments and Market Infrastructures Report

Bank for International Settlements (2025) BIS annual economic report 2025, chapter III: the next-generation monetary and financial system. Bank for International Settlements

Bank for International Settlements & Federal Reserve Bank of New York (2025) Project Pine: Exploring monetary policy in a tokenized financial system. Innovation Hub Report

Barnes R (2020) Factors in the portability of tokenized assets on distributed ledgers. arXiv preprint arXiv:2005.07370

BlackRock (2024) Annual chairman's letter to investors. BlackRock Inc.

Circle (2024) USDC integration with institutional trading platforms. Circle Internet Financial

Cisar D, Schellinger B, Stoetzer JC, Urbach N, Weiß FL, Guggenberger T (2025) Designing the future of bond markets: reducing transaction costs through tokenization. Electron Mark 35(1):1–22

Citi (2023) Citigroup introduces token services for institutional clients. Citi Treasury and Trade Solutions. https://www.citigroup.com/global/news/press-release/2023/citi-develops-new-digital-asset-capabilities-for-institutional-clients

European Investment Bank (2021) European Investment Bank. (2021, April 28). EIB issues its first ever digital bond on a public blockchain [Press release]. https://www.eib.org/en/press/all/2021-141-european-investment-bank-eib-issues-its-first-ever-digital-bond-on-a-public-blockchain

European Investment Bank (2023) European Investment Bank issues first digital sterling bond on blockchain. Press release

Fama EF (1970) Efficient capital markets: a review of theory and empirical work. J Financ 25(2):383–417

Fama EF, French KR (1992) The cross-section of expected stock returns. J Financ 47(2):427–465

Fama EF, French KR (1993) Common risk factors in the returns on stocks and bonds. J Financ Econ 33(1):3–56

Franklin Templeton (2023) Franklin OnChain U.S. government money fund annual report. Franklin Templeton Investments

García R, Cediel A, Teixidó M, Gil R (2022) Semantics and non-fungible tokens for copyright management on the metaverse and beyond. https://arxiv.org/abs/2208.14174

Hamilton Lane (2022) Hamilton Lane launches tokenized feeder fund. Press release. https://www.hamiltonlane.com/en-us/news/direct-equity-fund-on-securitize

Hentov E, Thiagarajan R, Gorshkov V, Im H (2025) The stablecoin moment, State Street Global Advisors. https://www.statestreet.com/web/insights/articles/documents/the-stablecoin-moment-paper.pdf

Hong Kong Monetary Authority (2023) Hong Kong Monetary Authority. (2023, August 24). Bond tokenisation in Hong Kong. https://www.hkma.gov.hk/media/eng/doc/key-information/press-release/2023/20230824e3a1.pdf

Hong Kong Monetary Authority (2024) HKMA issues multi-currency tokenized bond. Press release. https://www.hkma.gov.hk/eng/news-and-media/press-releases/2024/02/20240207-6/

Index Coop (2024) Index Cooperative annual report 2024

Lee MJ, Martin A, Townsend RM (2024) Optimal design of tokenized markets. Federal Reserve Bank of New York Staff Report No. 1121

Mafrur R (2025) Tokenize everything, but can you sell it? RWA liquidity challenges and the road ahead. https://arxiv.org/abs/2508.11651

Malinova K, Park A (2023) Tokenized stocks for trading and capital raising. *SSRN* Working Paper

Markowitz H (1952) Portfolio selection. *The*. J Financ 7(1):77–91

Merton RC (1974) On the pricing of corporate debt: the risk structure of interest rates. J Financ 29(2):449–470

Merton RC (1990) The financial system and economic performance. J Financ Serv Res 4(4):263–300

Organization for Economic Co-operation and Development (2020) The tokenization of assets and potential implications for financial markets. OECD Blockchain Policy Series. https://www.oecd.org/content/dam/oecd/en/publications/reports/2020/03/the-tokenisation-of-assets-and-potential-implications-for-financial-markets_370f9853/83493d34-en.pdf

Overstock.com (2020) Overstock.com announces completion of digital dividend distribution. Press release. https://www.forbes.com/sites/robertanzalone/2020/05/20/overstock-pays-ostko-over-4-million-shares-now-trading/

Realize (2024) Realize T-BILLS Fund: Tokenized U.S. Treasury bills. Press release. https://www.reuters.com/technology/abu-dhabi-firm-launch-tokenized-us-treasuries-fund-2024-10-31/

Sharpe WF (1964) Capital asset prices: a theory of market equilibrium under conditions of risk. J Financ 19(3):425–442

Shiller RJ (2000) Irrational exuberance. Princeton University Press

SIX Digital Exchange (2024) SDX platform development update. SIX Group Communications

Tanveer U, Ishaq S, Hoang TG (2025) Tokenized assets in a decentralized economy: balancing efficiency, value, and risks. Int J Prod Econ 282:Article 109554

Watsky C, Liu M, Ly N, Orr K, Seira A, Vida Z, Wu L (2024) Tokenized assets on public blockchains: How transparent is the blockchain? *FEDS Notes*. Board of Governors of the Federal Reserve System

WisdomTree (2024) WisdomTree digital funds annual report. WisdomTree Investments

WisdomTree (2025) WisdomTree. (2025, April 3). WisdomTree expands institutional tokenized fund platform to Arbitrum, Avalanche, Base and Optimism [Pressrelease]. WisdomTree, Inc.

World Economic Forum (2025) Asset tokenization in financial markets: the next generation of market infrastructure. World Economic Forum

Tokenisation of Illiquid Assets

Levent Güntay

Abstract Tokenisation of illiquid assets has moved from a futuristic promise to an increasingly tangible reality, fundamentally transforming how capital markets operate. This chapter explains how blockchain-based tokenisation can democratise access to traditionally exclusive investment opportunities through fractional ownership, reduce transaction costs and settlement times through smart-contract automation, and provide programmable liquidity while maintaining compliance with securities and property law. It surveys the major asset classes being digitised—commercial real estate, private credit, private equity, art and collectibles, and intellectual property—and assesses the benefits, challenges, and regulatory considerations associated with their tokenisation.

To place these developments within the broader evolution of money, the chapter demonstrates how tokenised payment systems and privately issued stablecoins make tokenised illiquid assets operationally viable by providing instant settlement, programmability, and interoperability. The analysis reveals critical complementarities between asset tokenisation and monetary innovation, showing how central bank digital currencies, stablecoins, and tokenised deposits together enable frictionless trading of digitised securities. Through illustrative cases and market examples spanning real estate, credit markets, and alternative investments, it is demonstrated that tokenisation is not merely a new technology but an institutional innovation reshaping capital markets. It integrates key lessons for investors, issuers, and regulators and reflects on the implications of illiquid-asset tokenisation for the future of finance and monetary policy.

Keywords Tokenisation · Illiquid assets · Blockchain · Fractional ownership · Private credit · Real estate · Art

L. Güntay (✉)
Department of International Finance, Özyeğin University, Istanbul, Türkiye
e-mail: levent.guntay@ozyegin.edu.tr

S. Yazıcı et al. (eds.), *Tokenisation of Money*, Contributions to Finance and Accounting, https://doi.org/10.1007/978-3-032-22946-5_6

1 Introduction: Rationale For and Benefits of Tokenising Illiquid Assets

An illiquid asset is an asset that cannot be easily and quickly converted into cash without a substantial loss in its value, primarily due to a lack of ready and willing buyers. This difficulty in selling means that the process can be lengthy and complex, making it hard to determine a precise market price. Examples of such assets include commercial real estate, private equity, private loans and unique collectibles like fine art.

The tokenisation of illiquid assets represents a paradigmatic shift in financial markets that fundamentally challenges notions of asset ownership, transfer mechanisms, and market accessibility (Tanveer et al. 2025; Liu and Chen 2025). This transformation extends beyond technological innovation to encompass a comprehensive reimagining of how capital markets can be structured to provide enhanced efficiency, transparency, and inclusivity while maintaining appropriate risk management and regulatory compliance standards. The application of blockchain technology to illiquid asset classes including real estate, mortgages, private equity, infrastructure, and credit instruments has created new possibilities for fractional ownership, automated governance, and global capital allocation that were previously uneconomical or technically infeasible (Xia et al. 2025).

A complete understanding of tokenising illiquid assets requires acknowledging that the digitisation of value includes money itself. The global push toward digital cash has generated three distinct forms of tokenised money: (i) central bank digital currencies (CBDCs), sovereign electronic notes issued by central banks; (ii) privately issued stablecoins, such as USDT and USDC, which are tokens backed by fiat reserves and circulate on public blockchains; and (iii) tokenised bank deposits, which represent customers' deposits as tokens on permissioned ledgers. Although stablecoin issuance has expanded rapidly to around USD 250 billion with daily on-chain transactions of USD 20–30 billion, this still represents less than 1% of global payment flows (Higginson and Spanz 2025). Nonetheless, tokenised cash offers instant settlement, programmability and 24/7 availability, making it an ideal settlement asset for tokenised securities (Higginson and Spanz 2025).

A critical insight is that tokenised assets and tokenised money are mutually reinforcing. Asset tokens rely on high-quality digital cash for settlement, while digital money finds compelling use cases in the trading and collateral management of illiquid assets. At the same time, the varieties of money tokens differ markedly in their issuers and trust models: stablecoins are issued by private companies and backed by reserves, tokenised deposits originate from regulated commercial banks, and CBDCs are issued exclusively by central banks (Paul 2025). Such differences have regulatory and risk implications. To ensure frictionless interactions, these tokens must be interchangeable at par value—maintaining the singleness of money (Paul 2025). Achieving this requires interoperable payment rails and coordination among issuers and regulators. Well-designed stablecoins and CBDCs could enable more efficient cross-border payments if regulators cooperate to regularise standards and limit regulatory arbitrage (Ernst and Young 2025). Interoperable, programmable payment systems thus sit at the heart of both illiquid asset tokenisation and the broader fiat-to-stablecoin transformation, providing the bridge between capital markets and monetary innovation.

The economic rationale for tokenising illiquid assets centers on addressing fundamental market inefficiencies including prohibitively high transaction costs, restricted investor access due to high minimum investment thresholds, pricing opacity creating information asymmetries, settlement delays increasing counterparty risk, and limited liquidity constraining portfolio management flexibility (Borjigin et al. 2025). These inefficiencies collectively create substantial deadweight losses in capital allocation and limit the ability of markets to efficiently price risk and allocate capital to its most productive uses. Tokenisation can thus be viewed as an effort to reduce real-world frictions (such as high transaction costs and information asymmetries) and move financial markets closer to the ideal conditions in the perfect capital markets framework of Modigliani and Miller (1958). Current market projections indicate substantial growth potential, with the global asset tokenization market valued at USD 2.08 trillion in 2025 and projected to reach USD 13.55 trillion by 2030 (Mordor Intelligence 2025).

Tokenisation enables fractional ownership of illiquid assets, allowing retail investors to participate in them with significantly lower capital requirements. This democratization via fractional ownership can reduce minimum investment thresholds from hundreds of thousands or millions of dollars to amounts accessible to retail investors, potentially expanding the investor base by orders of magnitude while providing diversification opportunities previously unavailable to smaller investors. The portability of tokenized assets across different blockchain networks further enhances their accessibility and utility (Barnes 2020). Operational efficiency improvements through smart contract automation can potentially reduce costs compared to traditional structures while eliminating manual processes, reducing settlement times from weeks to near-instantaneous transfers, and providing real-time transparency through immutable blockchain records (Deloitte 2024).

1.1 Enhanced Market Access and Democratization

One of the most significant benefits of illiquid asset tokenisation is the democratisation of investment opportunities that have traditionally been accessible only to institutional investors or high-net-worth individuals due to high minimum investment thresholds and complex legal structures. Tokenisation enables fractional ownership of illiquid assets and allows retail investors to participate in markets such as commercial real estate, private equity, and infrastructure investments with significantly lower capital requirements than traditional investment structures would permit.

The fractional ownership capabilities that tokenisation enables can reduce minimum investment thresholds from hundreds of thousands or millions of dollars to amounts that retail investors can access. This potentially expands the investor base for illiquid assets by orders of magnitude while it provides diversification opportunities that were previously unavailable to smaller investors. This democratization effect can improve capital allocation efficiency because it enables a broader range of investors to participate in asset classes that may offer attractive risk-adjusted returns but were previously inaccessible due to structural barriers rather than economic fundamentals.

The global accessibility that blockchain technology enables allows investors worldwide to participate in tokenised illiquid asset markets regardless of their geographic location or local banking relationships. This potentially creates more efficient global capital allocation and reduces the home bias that characterizes many traditional investment portfolios. This global accessibility can be particularly beneficial for emerging market investors who seek exposure to developed market assets or for investors in jurisdictions with limited local investment opportunities.

1.2 Operational Efficiency and Cost Reduction

Tokenisation can significantly reduce the operational costs associated with illiquid asset investment and management through the automation of routine processes, the elimination of intermediaries, and streamlined settlement procedures. Smart contracts can automate many administrative functions that fund administrators, transfer agents, and other intermediaries traditionally perform, such as investor onboarding, capital calls, distribution payments, and compliance monitoring. This automation reduces operational costs compared to traditional structures (Banerjee et al. 2024).

The elimination of paper-based processes and manual reconciliation procedures can reduce settlement times from weeks or months to near-instantaneous blockchain-based transfers. This improvement enhances capital efficiency and reduces counterparty risk while it enables more dynamic portfolio management strategies. The automation of compliance monitoring and reporting through smart contracts can reduce regulatory compliance costs while it improves the accuracy and timeliness of regulatory reporting. This potentially reduces the regulatory burden on both issuers and investors.

The standardization of legal documentation and operational procedures that tokenisation platforms enable can reduce the legal and administrative costs associated with the structuring of illiquid asset investments. This makes smaller transactions economically viable and enables the development of new investment products that would be uneconomical under traditional structures. This standardization can also improve market transparency and comparability, which makes it easier for investors to evaluate different investment opportunities and for regulators to monitor market developments.

1.3 Enhanced Liquidity and Price Discovery

While illiquid assets will likely remain less liquid than traditional securities even after tokenisation, the enhanced transferability enabled by blockchain technology can provide meaningful liquidity improvements that benefit both investors and asset values. The theoretical foundations for understanding liquidity and price discovery in financial markets start with Kyle (1985) demonstrating how private information gets incorporated into prices through continuous trading. Glosten and Milgrom (1985) provide the theoretical framework for bid-ask spreads and market making with asymmetric information. Amihud (2002) establishes the empirical relationship between illiquidity and expected returns and shows how liquidity constraints affect asset prices. O'Hara (2003) synthesizes this literature and demonstrates the role of liquidity in price discovery.

The ability to trade tokenised illiquid assets on secondary markets can provide investors with exit opportunities that may not exist in traditional structures, potentially reducing the liquidity premium required by investors and increasing asset values. The development of secondary markets for tokenised illiquid assets can improve price discovery by providing more frequent transaction data and enabling market-based valuation mechanisms that may be more accurate and timelier than traditional appraisal-based approaches. The transparency provided by blockchain technology can enhance price discovery by making transaction data and ownership information publicly available, reducing information asymmetries that can lead to mispricing and market inefficiencies.

The programmable nature of tokenised assets enables the implementation of sophisticated liquidity mechanisms including automated market makers, periodic auction systems, and dynamic pricing models that can provide liquidity even in the absence of natural buyers and sellers. These mechanisms can help bridge the gap between the desire for liquidity and the fundamental characteristics of illiquid assets that make continuous trading challenging or inappropriate.

1.4 Transparency and Governance Improvements

Blockchain technology provides unprecedented transparency in asset ownership, transaction history, and performance data, enabling investors to monitor their investments in real-time and access comprehensive information about asset performance and management activities. This transparency can reduce agency costs and improve alignment between asset managers and investors by making management activities more visible and accountable.

Smart contracts can automate governance processes including voting, decision-making, and the implementation of governance decisions, potentially improving the efficiency and transparency of asset governance while reducing the costs associated with traditional governance mechanisms. The immutable nature of blockchain records can provide a complete audit trail of all governance activities, improving accountability and reducing the potential for disputes or conflicts of interest.

The programmable nature of smart contracts enables the implementation of sophisticated governance mechanisms that can automatically adjust management fees, performance incentives, and other terms based on asset performance or other predetermined criteria, potentially improving alignment between managers and investors while reducing the need for complex legal documentation and ongoing monitoring.

Table 1 provides a comprehensive comparison of the traditional and tokenized illiquid asset characteristics. The comparisons between traditional and tokenized illiquid assets are based on academic research (e.g., Geltner et al. 2013; Schwarcz 2004; Zetzsche et al. 2019; Joshi and Choudhury 2024; Angeris and Chitra 2020), legal and governance studies (Bogert et al. 2007; Shehu et al. 2022), and industry reports and case studies (Deloitte 2025; Aspen Digital 2019; Banerjee et al. 2024; SNS Insider 2024).

The subsequent sections examine the tokenization of distinct asset classes, outlining their theoretical foundations, potential advantages, implementation

Table 1 Comparison of traditional and tokenized illiquid asset characteristics

Characteristic	Traditional Illiquid Assets	Tokenized Illiquid Assets	Improvement
Minimum investment	$100,000–$1000,000+	$1000–$10,000	Sizable reduction
Settlement time	30–90 days	1–3 days	Significantly faster
Trading hours	Business hours only	24/7 availability	Continuous access
Transparency	Limited reporting	Real-time blockchain data	Complete visibility
Liquidity	Very limited	Enhanced secondary markets	Significant improvement
Geographic access	Local/regional	Global accessibility	Worldwide reach
Fractional ownership	Complex/expensive	Native support	Full fractionalization
Operational costs	High (5–15% annually)	Reduced (2–8% annually)	Large savings
Governance	Manual processes	Automated smart contracts	Streamlined operations
Compliance monitoring	Periodic reporting	Continuous monitoring	Real-time compliance
Price discovery	Infrequent appraisals	Market-based pricing	Enhanced accuracy
Exit flexibility	Lock-up periods	Secondary market options	Improved liquidity

The table integrates insights from academic research, legal and governance analyses, and industry case studies to illustrate how tokenization reshapes asset accessibility, transparency, and liquidity. It highlights that blockchain-enabled structures substantially reduce investment thresholds, operational frictions, and settlement delays while enabling real-time compliance and broader market participation

Table 2 Major tokenized illiquid asset implementations (2020–2025)

Asset type	Platform/ Issuer	Transaction value	Year	Completion status	Key innovation
Real estate	St. Regis Aspen resort	$18 million	2018	Successfully completed	First major luxury resort tokenization
Real estate	Manhattan luxury condos	$30 million	2018	Successfully completed	First major Manhattan property tokenization
Real estate	Berlin residential project	€2 million	2020	Successfully completed	German regulatory compliance
Real estate	Brickblock Wiesbaden	€2 million	2019	Successfully completed	One of the first EU property tokenization
Private credit	TrueFi protocol	$1.72 billion	2020–2024	Ongoing operations	Uncollateralized DeFi lending
Private credit	Maple finance	~$4 billion	2021–2024	Ongoing operations	Institutional DeFi lending
Private credit	Apollo ACRED fund	$100 million	2025	Successfully launched	Traditional PE firm tokenization
Private equity	KKR tokenized fund	Part of $4B fund	2022	Successfully launched	Major PE firm blockchain adoption
Infrastructure	Enel renewable energy	N/A (pilot)	2025	Pilot launched	Renewable energy tokenization pilot (Enel–Conio on Algorand)
Art/ collectibles	Masterworks platform	$941 million AUM	2020–2024	Ongoing operations	Blue-chip art fractionalization

This table compiles representative real-world cases across real estate, private credit, private equity, infrastructure, and art sectors, highlighting each project's scale, completion status, and technological innovation. Data were synthesized from platform documentation, regulatory filings, and industry reports, supported by academic, legal, and market analyses to provide a comprehensive overview of operational progress and institutional adoption of tokenization as of August 2025

challenges, and current market applications. Tokenization projects over the last 5 years have demonstrated the viability of blockchain technology across multiple asset classes including real estate, private credit, private equity, infrastructure, and art. Table 2 presents a comparative overview of representative tokenization transactions across real estate, private credit, private equity, infrastructure, and art markets. The dataset is compiled from multiple sources, including platform documentation, regulatory filings, and industry reports (Algorand 2025; Aspen Times 2018; Cointelegraph 2020; Markets Media 2025; Messari 2021; PR Newswire 2019; Securitize 2022; TrueFi 2024; U.S. Securities and Exchange Commission 2021; Wolfson 2018). All data are cross-verified through multiple independent sources, and the table reflects the operational status of these tokenization initiatives as of August 2025.

2 Real Estate Tokenization: Transforming Property Investment

Real estate tokenization is one of the most mature applications of blockchain to illiquid assets. The global tokenized real estate market was valued at $3.8 billion in 2024 and is projected to reach $19.4 billion by 2033, reflecting strong institutional and retail interest (Smith and Baur 2025). Real estate is well suited for tokenization because its standardized legal frameworks and valuation methodologies contrast with high transaction costs and limited liquidity in traditional property markets (Simons 2022). Blockchain-based tokenization addresses these frictions by enabling fractional ownership and reducing settlement and management costs.

As described in Sect. 1, such structures employ special purpose vehicles and smart contracts to represent economic rights in real estate and to automate key functions such as rent distribution, governance and compliance (Bogert et al. 2007; Shehu et al. 2022). This allows investors to access property markets retaining clear legal separation between digital tokens and the underlying physical assets.

Several early case studies illustrate this transformation. In 2018, a luxury resort in Aspen, Colorado was tokenized using security tokens, lowering the minimum investment from $1 million to $10,000 and enabling secondary trading (Aspen Digital 2019). That same year, a $30 million office building in Manhattan was tokenized via a regulated security token offering automated rent collection and investor communications (Geltner et al. 2013). Internationally, Black Manta Capital Partners tokenized a €2 million Berlin rental project in 2020, allowing cross-border participation while adhering to local regulations (Tokeny 2020).

2.1 *Market Examples and Valuation Considerations*

The real estate tokenization market has witnessed several high-profile implementations demonstrating viability and benefits of digitized property investment. A notable example is the tokenization of a luxury resort property in Aspen, Colorado, completed in 2018 for $18 million through security tokens representing fractional ownership interests. The transaction was structured through a Delaware statutory trust with smart contracts automating rental income distribution and enabling secondary market trading, reducing minimum investment thresholds from $1 million to $10,000 while maintaining appropriate investor protection measures (Aspen Digital 2019). The transaction involved issuance of "Aspen Coins" on the Ethereum blockchain representing interests in a $18 M resort held in a Delaware statutory trust.

Another significant implementation involved tokenization of a commercial office building in Manhattan, valued at $30 million and completed in 2018 through a regulated security token offering raising capital from institutional and retail investors. The transaction utilized blockchain technology to automate rent collection and distribution, property management oversight, and investor communications, reducing operational costs compared to traditional structures. The valuation methodologies for tokenized real estate draw from established real estate analysis frameworks (Geltner et al. 2013) while incorporating new considerations related to blockchain technology and fractional ownership structures.

International examples include tokenization of residential rental properties in Berlin, Germany, where residential project was successfully tokenized in 2020, with Black Manta Capital Partners completing a security token offering for €2 million (Tokeny 2020). The transaction enabled cross-border investment and automated compliance with local rental regulations. This demonstrated how tokenization can facilitate international real estate investment while maintaining compliance with diverse regulatory frameworks and providing investors with exposure to foreign real estate markets that may be difficult to access through traditional investment structures.

3 Credit and Private Debt Tokenization: Revolutionizing Fixed Income Markets

Tokenized private credit has emerged as one of the fastest-growing segments of the real-world asset landscape, with more than $15 billion in assets on-chain and decentralized lending protocols processing billions of dollars of loans since 2020. Private credit markets are naturally suited to tokenization because loans have standardized cash flows and legal frameworks; by pooling loans into blockchain-based securities, originators can tap broader funding sources and investors gain exposure to tranches tailored to different risk appetites. In essence, tokenized credit applies traditional securitization theory—where risk is transferred through tranching—to a decentralized environment, leveraging smart contracts to automate servicing, reduce information asymmetries and permit fractional participation (Fabozzi and Kothari 2007; Cohen et al. 2017).

While public-financing and infrastructure tokenization may eventually extend these benefits to large-scale physical assets, the current focus of most platforms is on trade finance, real-estate lending and corporate credit. Major protocols such as Figure, Tradable, Maple, TrueFi, Centrifuge and Goldfinch illustrate this transition. For example, Figure has originated more than $11 billion in on-chain loans, while Maple and Tradable support diverse borrower segments. These platforms show that tokenized private credit is moving from pilot projects to institutional-grade infrastructure, with participation from pension funds, insurers and retail investors alike. Their experiences highlight both the operational efficiencies and the regulatory considerations that must be addressed as the market matures.

3.1 *Implementation Examples and Market Development*

Leading tokenized credit platforms have facilitated over $15 billion in private credit investments since 2020, with institutional investors including pension funds, insurance companies, and asset managers participating in tokenized credit markets alongside retail investors. These platforms typically focus on specific credit segments including trade finance, real estate lending, and corporate credit facilities, enabling specialized expertise while maintaining diversification benefits through portfolio construction and risk management techniques adapted from traditional credit markets.

As seen in Fig. 1, the dominance of DeFi protocols in this ecosystem is exemplified by Figure's commanding position with $11 billion in total loans, followed by Tradable's $2 billion and Maple's $1 billion. These platforms demonstrate how blockchain-based lending protocols have evolved from experimental platforms to institutional-grade infrastructure capable of processing multi-billion dollar credit volumes across diverse market segments.

Major DeFi platforms have demonstrated the viability of tokenized credit markets through successful implementations across various credit types and market segments. TrueFi, Centrifuge and Goldfinch have each developed specialized approaches ranging from uncollateralized governance models to real-world asset tokenization and emerging market focus. These implementations have provided valuable insights into the technical, operational, and regulatory aspects of credit

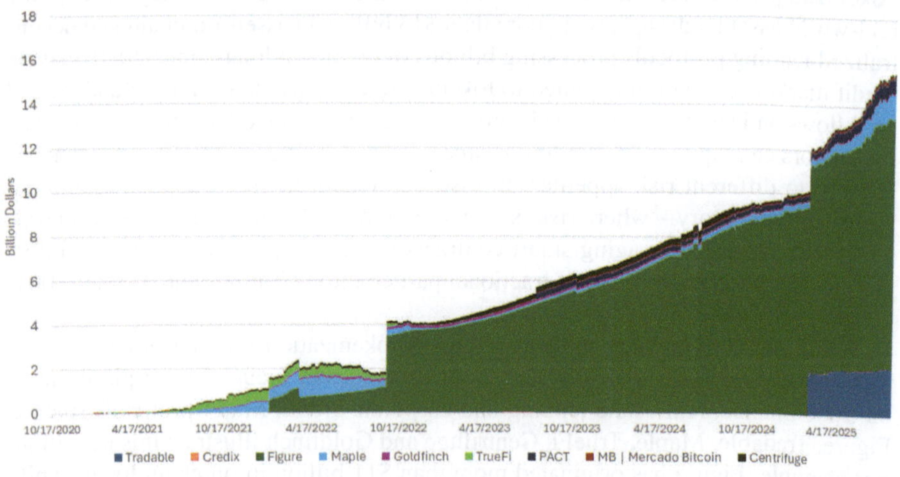

Fig. 1 Tokenized Private Credit Market Value Over Time (2020–2025) The figure illustrates the rapid expansion of the tokenized private credit market, showing cumulative transaction values across leading decentralized finance (DeFi) and institutional platforms such as TrueFi, Maple, Centrifuge, Figure, and Credix. Data are compiled and calculated by the author based on information from the RWA.XYZ database, incorporating cross-verified figures from platform analytics, regulatory disclosures, and industry market reports to reflect developments as of August 2025

tokenization while establishing market standards and best practices that are informing broader market development strategies. The success of these platforms has validated academic theories about the potential for blockchain technology to transform traditional credit markets.

4 Private Equity Tokenization: Democratizing Alternative Investments

Private equity tokenization represents an emerging frontier in illiquid asset digitization that addresses longstanding challenges in private equity markets including high minimum investment thresholds, limited liquidity, complex legal structures, and restricted investor access. The global private equity market, valued at over $10 trillion in assets under management (Ocorian 2025), has traditionally been accessible only to institutional investors and ultra-high-net-worth individuals due to minimum commitments typically ranging from $1 million to $25 million and complex partnership structures requiring sophisticated legal and operational infrastructure.

Private equity tokenization enables fractional ownership of private equity fund interests, direct company investments, and secondary market positions through blockchain-based digital securities that preserve essential characteristics of private equity investments while providing enhanced accessibility, transparency, and operational efficiency. The tokenization process typically involves creating special purpose vehicles that hold interests in private equity funds or direct investments and issue tokens representing beneficial ownership in these vehicles, enabling retail investors to participate in private equity markets with significantly reduced minimum investment requirements.

The implementation of private equity tokenization requires sophisticated legal structures that accommodate complex private equity investment terms including capital call mechanisms, distribution waterfalls, carried interest arrangements, and governance rights while ensuring compliance with securities regulations and maintaining alignment between general partners and limited partners. The legal framework for such structures builds upon established principles of investment fund organization and securities regulation, while incorporating new considerations related to blockchain technology and digital asset ownership.

Smart contracts can automate many operational aspects of private equity investments including capital call notifications and processing, distribution calculations and payments, performance reporting, and compliance monitoring, potentially reducing operational costs significantly to traditional private equity fund administration. The automation of routine administrative functions enables fund managers to focus on value creation activities while providing investors with real-time visibility into fund performance and portfolio company developments.

4.1 Regulatory Framework and Market Examples

The regulatory framework for private equity tokenization continues to evolve as authorities develop appropriate oversight mechanisms for blockchain-based private equity securities while balancing innovation promotion with investor protection and market integrity considerations. The Securities and Exchange Commission has provided guidance on the framework for investment contract analysis of digital assets (Securities and Exchange Commission 2020), which serves as a foundation for understanding the regulatory treatment of tokenized private equity interests.

Several leading platforms have facilitated private equity tokenization transactions, enabling accredited investors to purchase fractional interests in private equity funds and direct investments with minimum investments significantly lower than traditional structures. These implementations have demonstrated the viability of blockchain-based private equity investment structures across different private equity strategies and market segments, while providing valuable insights into the operational and regulatory challenges associated with tokenizing complex alternative investment structures.

Major private equity firms have explored tokenization of fund interests as a means of expanding investor access and improving operational efficiency, with pilot programs demonstrating how blockchain technology can streamline investor onboarding, capital call processing, and distribution management while maintaining the sophisticated investment management and value creation capabilities that characterize successful private equity investing.

5 Art, Collectibles, and Intellectual Property

Tokenization of art, collectibles, and other exotic assets represents a specialized application addressing unique challenges associated with valuing, trading, and managing alternative investments that often lack standardized markets or valuation methodologies. Recent academic research has explored the application of non-fungible tokens (NFTs) for copyright management and intellectual property protection, demonstrating how blockchain technology can provide new mechanisms for managing creative assets and intellectual property rights (García et al. 2022).

The authentication and provenance tracking capabilities of blockchain technology provide particular value for collectibles and luxury goods, where establishing authenticity and ownership history is critical for valuation and marketability. Smart contracts can automate verification of authenticity certificates, ownership transfers, and insurance coverage while providing immutable records of asset's complete ownership and transaction history, reducing fraud risk and enhancing market confidence in tokenized collectibles markets.

Patents and intellectual property assets represent another emerging area for tokenization, with blockchain technology enabling new models for IP licensing, royalty distribution, and collaborative innovation (Hosseini Bamakan et al. 2023). Tokenization can facilitate fractional ownership of patent portfolios, automated royalty payments to inventors and investors, and transparent tracking of IP usage and licensing agreements. This represents a significant advancement in intellectual property management and commercialization.

Leading tokenized art platforms have already fractionalized over a billion dollars' worth of blue-chip artworks: Masterworks reports more than US$941 million in assets under management across roughly 883,000 users (Brent 2025), while Yieldstreet's art funds hold paintings worth over US$600 million (Startup Stash 2025). Additionally, the Deloitte Art & Finance Report 2024 notes that regulated fractional-ownership initiatives exceeded US$1 billion in AUM by 2023 (Timeless 2024). For instance, Masterwork enables retail investors to purchase fractional ownership interests in paintings by renowned artists with minimum investments as low as $20. These platforms handle all aspects of art acquisition, storage, insurance, and eventual sale while providing investors with exposure to art market returns previously accessible only to wealthy collectors and institutional investors.

6 Technical Issues in Implementation and Future Outlook

The technical implementation of illiquid asset tokenization requires sophisticated integration of blockchain technology with traditional asset management and regulatory compliance systems, addressing challenges including asset custody, valuation mechanisms, and regulatory reporting requirements often more complex than those encountered in liquid asset tokenization. Development of robust technical infrastructure must balance efficiency and automation benefits of blockchain technology with security, reliability, and regulatory compliance requirements that institutional investors and regulators expect.

Recent developments in decentralized finance (DeFi) have provided new technical foundations for tokenized asset markets, with innovations in automated market making, liquidity provision, and price discovery mechanisms (Adams et al. 2021). These technical advances have enabled more sophisticated tokenization platforms that can support complex asset structures while maintaining the transparency and efficiency benefits of blockchain technology.

The development of comprehensive legal frameworks for tokenized assets has been crucial for market development, with specialized legal structures designed to accommodate the unique characteristics of different asset classes while ensuring compliance with applicable securities regulations (Antiersolutions 2024). These legal innovations have provided the foundation for institutional adoption of tokenized asset markets while maintaining appropriate investor protection standards.

Adoption of illiquid asset tokenization has accelerated significantly in recent years (Fig. 1), driven by improving regulatory clarity, technological maturation, and growing institutional acceptance of blockchain-based investment structures. Market developments indicate increasing sophistication in tokenization platforms, legal structures, and operational procedures enabling larger and more complex tokenization transactions while expanding range of asset types and investor segments that can participate in tokenized illiquid asset markets.

Integration of traditional financial institutions with tokenization platforms has been key driver of market development, with major banks, asset managers, and insurance companies developing capabilities to participate in tokenized asset markets while maintaining traditional risk management and regulatory compliance standards. Several major financial institutions have launched digital bond issuance platforms and tokenized investment products, demonstrating growing institutional acceptance of blockchain-based financial infrastructure.

The market outlook for tokenized illiquid assets remains positive, with continued growth expected across all major asset categories. Academic research suggests that tokenization can provide significant economic benefits through improved market efficiency, enhanced liquidity, and reduced transaction costs (Baltais et al. 2024). However, successful market development will require continued collaboration between technology providers, financial institutions, and regulatory authorities to ensure that tokenization enhances rather than complicates the management and trading of illiquid assets.

7 Conclusion

Tokenisation of illiquid assets represents a structural transformation in how value is stored, transferred, and governed. Across several asset classes, it shows a consistent pattern: the conversion of traditionally static, intermediated systems into programmable and interoperable networks. The central lesson is that tokenisation enhances market efficiency and inclusivity by lowering access barriers, embedding trust in code, and enabling continuous price discovery.

At a broader level, these developments are reshaping the architecture of money itself. As tokenised assets coexist and interact with stablecoins and central bank digital currencies, financial systems are converging toward a unified digital infrastructure where money and assets share the same technological substrate. This convergence point out to not only a new funding mechanism but a new monetary structure defined by interoperability, transparency, and programmable governance.

The rise of tokenised markets shows that money is entering a new stage and moving from systems based on bank accounts to digital assets where payments, investments, and ownership are closely connected.

References

Adams H, Zinsmeister N, Salem M, Keefer R, Robinson D (2021) Uniswap v3 core. Technical whitepaper. Uniswap Labs

Algorand (6 June 2025) Enel: Tokenizing renewable energy assets on Algorand. https://algorand.co/case-studies/enel-tokenizing-renewable-energy-assets-on-algorand

Amihud Y (2002) Illiquidity and stock returns: cross-section and time-series effects. J Financ Mark 5(1):31–56

Angeris G, Chitra T (2020) Improved price oracles: constant function market makers. In: Proceedings of the 2nd ACM conference on advances in financial technologies, pp 80–91. https://doi.org/10.1145/3419614.3423251

Antiersolutions (2024) Legal structures for tokenized assets: A comprehensive guide. Antier Solutions Legal Brief. https://www.antiersolutions.com/blogs

Aspen Digital (2019) The Aspen digital token offering: a case study in real estate tokenization. Aspen Digital Securities

Aspen Times (9 October 2018) In $18 million deal, nearly one-fifth of St. Regis Aspen sells through digital tokens. https://www.aspentimes.com/trending/in-18-million-deal-nearly-one-fifth-of-st-regis-aspen-sells-through-digital-tokens/

Baltais M, Sondore E, Putniņš TJ, Karlsen JR (2024) Economic impact potential of real-world asset tokenization. Stockholm School of Economics Riga Working Paper

Banerjee A, Sevillano J, Higginson M (2024) From ripples to waves: the transformational power of tokenizing assets. McKinsey & Company. https://www.mckinsey.com/industries/financial-services/our-insights/from-ripples-to-waves-the-transformational-power-of-tokenizing-assets

Barnes R (2020) Factors in the portability of tokenized assets on distributed ledgers. arXiv preprint, arXiv:2005.07461

Bogert GG, Bogert GT, Hess AM (2007) The law of trusts and trustees, 3rd edn. West Academic Publishing

Borjigin A, He C, Lee CCC, Zhou W (2025) Element and Everything Tokens: Two-Tier Architecture for Mobilizing Alternative Assets. arXiv preprint, arXiv:2508.11266

Brent (12 February 2025) Masterworks review: Best art investment platform of 2024/2025. Explore Alts. https://explorealts.com/masterworks-review/

Cohen LR, Samuelson L, Katz H (2017) How securitization can benefit from blockchain technology. J Struct Financ 23(2):51–60

Cointelegraph (14 April 2020) Berlin real estate worth $12M tokenized for everyday investors. https://cointelegraph.com/news/berlin-real-estate-worth-12m-tokenized-for-everyday-investors

Deloitte (2024) Risk management and governance of digital assets. Deloitte Financial Services

Deloitte (2025) Tokenized real estate. Deloitte Insights

Ernst & Young (2025) Stablecoins in focus: navigating the new digital financial landscape. EY-Parthenon. https://www.ey.com/content/dam/ey-unified-site/ey-com/en-us/insights/financial-services/documents/cs-eyp-stablecoin-survey.pdf

Fabozzi FJ, Kothari V (2007) Securitization: The tool of financial transformation. Yale ICF Working Paper No. 07–07

García R, Cediel A, Teixidó M, Gil R (2022) Semantics and Non-Fungible Tokens for Copyright Management on the Metaverse and Beyond. arXiv preprint, arXiv:2208.14174

Geltner D, Miller NG, Clayton J, Eichholtz P (2013) Commercial real estate analysis and investments, 3rd edn. OnCourse Learning

Glosten LR, Milgrom PR (1985) Bid, ask and transaction prices in a specialist market with heterogeneously informed traders. J Financ Econ 14(1):71–100

Higginson M, Spanz G (2025) The stable door opens: how tokenized cash enables next-gen payments. McKinsey & Company. https://www.mckinsey.com/industries/financial-services/our-insights/the-stable-door-opens-how-tokenized-cash-enables-next-gen-payments

Hosseini Bamakan SM, Nezhadsistani N, Bodaghi O, Qu Q (2023) Patents and intellectual property assets as non-fungible tokens: Key technologies and challenges. arXiv preprint, arXiv:2304.10490

Joshi S, Choudhury A (2024) Tokenization of real estate assets using blockchain. arXiv preprint, arXiv:2405.01852

Kyle AS (1985) Continuous auctions and insider trading. Econometrica 53(6):1315–1335

Liu X, Chen Y (2025) Blockchain-based asset tokenization: a comprehensive framework. J Financ Technol 12(3):45–67

Markets Media (23 June 2025) Apollo tokenized private credit fund reaches $100m. https://www.marketsmedia.com/apollo-tokenized-private-credit-fund-reaches-100m/

Messari (2021) Maple Finance. https://messari.io/project/maple-finance/profile

Modigliani F, Miller MH (1958) The cost of capital, corporation finance and the theory of investment. Am Econ Rev 48(3):261–297

Mordor Intelligence (2025) Asset tokenization market - growth, trends, COVID-19 impact, and forecasts (2025–2030). Mordor Intelligence Market Research

Ocorian (2025) Global private equity assets hit record $10.8 trillion following 2022 dip. https://www.ocorian.com/knowledge-hub/insights/global-private-equity-assets-hit-record-108-trillion-following-2022-dip

O'Hara M (2003) Presidential address: liquidity and price discovery. J Financ 58(4):1335–1354

Paul V (7 October 2025) Stablecoins, tokenized deposits, CBDCs: How banks are adopting and benefiting from the three corners of digital money. Fireblocks. https://www.fireblocks.com/blog/stablecoins-tokenized-deposits-cbdcs/

PR Newswire (28 March 2019) Brickblock tokenizes the first property in Europe. https://www.prnewswire.com/news-releases/brickblock-tokenizes-the-first-property-in-europe-300820582.html

Schwarcz SL (2004) The alchemy of asset securitization. Stanf J Law Bus Finance 1(1):133–154

Securities and Exchange Commission (2020) Framework for investment contract analysis of digital assets. SEC Strategic Hub for Innovation and Financial Technology

Securitize (13 September2022) Securitize launches fund for tokenized exposure to KKR. https://securitize.io/press-releases/securitize-kkr-tokenized-fund

Shehu AS, Pinto A, Correia ME (2022) A decentralised real estate transfer verification based on self-sovereign identity and smart contracts. arXiv preprint, arXiv:2207.04459

Simons RA (2022) Blockchain, cryptocurrency, and real estate. J Prop Invest Financ 24(1):72–85

Smith R, Baur DG (2025) Real estate tokenisation: Benefits, limitations and market dynamics. SSRN Working Paper, SSRN:5083787

SNS Insider (2024) Global asset tokenization market report 2024–2032. SNS Research

Startup Stash (3 March 2025) Top 15 physical art investment tools. https://startupstash.com/physical-art-investment-tools/

Tanveer U, Ishaq S, Hoang TG (2025) Tokenized assets in a decentralized economy: balancing efficiency, value, and risks. Int J Prod Econ 282:Article 109554

Timeless (15 April 2024) 5 things you should know about the art market in 2024. Timeless Magazine. https://www.timeless.investments/en/magazine/art-market-in-2024

Tokeny (15 April 2020) German real estate security token offering issued on the Black Manta investment platform. https://tokeny.com/german-real-estate-security-token-offering-issued-on-the-black-manta-investment-platform/

TrueFi (2024) TrueFi documentation: What is TrueFi? https://docs.truefi.io/

U.S. Securities and Exchange Commission (2 Nov 2021) Masterworks 075, LLC: Offering circular (Form 253G2). https://www.sec.gov/Archives/edgar/data/1876367/000149315221027020/form253g2.htm

Wolfson R (3 Oct 2018) A first for Manhattan: $30M real estate property tokenized with blockchain. Forbes. https://www.forbes.com/sites/rachelwolfson/2018/10/03/a-first-for-manhattan-30m-real-estate-property-tokenized-with-blockchain/

Xia N, Zhao X, Yang Y, Li Y, Li Y (2025) Exploration on real world assets and tokenization. arXiv preprint, arXiv:2503.01111

Zetzsche DA, Buckley RP, Arner DW, Fohr J-N (2019) The ICO gold rush: it's a scam, it's a bubble, it's a super challenge for regulators. Harv Int Law J 60(2):267–230

What Is Tokenised Money?

CBDC: A Solution Looking for a Problem?

Michael Salmony

Abstract Retail central bank digital currencies (CBDCs) such as the Digital Euro have become a prominent policy topic as central banks respond to declining cash usage, digitalisation of payments, and the growing influence of non-domestic payment platforms. However, despite extensive experimentation, retail CBDCs remain characterised by uncertain objectives, limited adoption, and unresolved tensions with existing financial intermediaries. This chapter critically examines the case for retail CBDCs, with particular focus on the proposed Digital Euro. It argues that the proliferation of policy rationales has diluted strategic clarity and that insufficient attention has been paid to the incentives of key stakeholders—consumers, merchants, and commercial banks—whose engagement is essential for success. Drawing on international experience, the chapter concludes that broad, online account-based retail CBDCs introduce severe risks without delivering commensurate benefits. Instead, it advances the case for a narrowly scoped, offline, token-based CBDC conceived as a modern evolution of physical cash. Such an approach aligns more closely with central bank mandates, preserves monetary stability, and addresses genuine gaps in resilience, privacy, and inclusion. In the context of advancing tokenisation of money and assets, this offline CBDC can serve as a public complement and backup to tokenised private money (such as stablecoins and tokenised deposits), providing a resilient public anchor rather than a direct substitute or competitor to the private sector.

Keywords Central Bank Digital Currency (CBDC) · Digital euro · Payment systems · Offline payments · Monetary policy · Financial stability · Tokenization · Stablecoins

M. Salmony (✉)
Payments Innovation Consulting, Heidelberg, Germany
e-mail: salmony@payments-innovation.com

S. Yazıcı et al. (eds.), *Tokenisation of Money*, Contributions to Finance and Accounting, https://doi.org/10.1007/978-3-032-22946-5_7

1 Introduction: Retail CBDC and the Question of Purpose

Retail central bank digital currencies (CBDCs) have emerged as one of the most debated innovations in monetary and payments policy. Initially framed as a response to declining cash usage and rapid technological change, CBDCs are now associated with a wide and expanding range of objectives, including safeguarding monetary sovereignty, enhancing payment resilience, fostering innovation, promoting financial inclusion, improving cross-border payments, and preserving the role of central bank money in an increasingly digital economy.

Despite substantial analytical work, pilot projects, and political momentum, a fundamental question remains insufficiently resolved: what concrete problem is a retail CBDC intended to solve that is not already addressed, or better addressed, by existing instruments and policy tools? This question is particularly salient in the European context. The proposed Digital Euro represents one of the most ambitious retail CBDC initiatives globally. At the time of writing, no formal decision to issue a Digital Euro has been taken, yet legislative proposals, technical experimentation, and institutional commitments suggest strong directional momentum. Empirical evidence from early retail CBDC deployments worldwide, however, reveals limited adoption, uncertain user value, and, in some cases, material risks to financial intermediation.

This chapter argues that much of the current debate suffers from two related weaknesses. First, the policy objectives assigned to retail CBDCs have proliferated to the point of incoherence (Salmony 2024), making it difficult to evaluate success or failure. Second, insufficient attention has been paid to the incentive structures of key stakeholders—consumers, merchants, and commercial banks—whose active engagement is essential for any retail payment instrument to function at scale (Salmony 2023b).

Against this background, the chapter advances a more constrained and institutionally grounded perspective. Many objectives currently associated with retail CBDCs—such as payment efficiency, innovation, and competition—are already being addressed through private-sector initiatives, regulatory reforms, and the rise of tokenised private money (e.g., stablecoins and tokenised bank deposits). By contrast, one area where a central bank possesses a clear mandate and comparative advantage is the provision of cash and cash-like instruments that ensure resilience, privacy, and universal access.

From this perspective, the most defensible case for a retail CBDC lies not in the creation of a broadly substitutive digital payment instrument competing with commercial bank or fintech solutions, but in the evolution of physical cash into a modern, offline-capable, digital bearer instrument. In the broader tokenisation landscape of the volume, such an offline, token-based CBDC would function as a public complement and backup to private solutions: stablecoins and tokenised deposits drive innovation and efficiency, especially in cross-border applications, while the public offline CBDC provides a resilient, privacy-preserving anchor and settlement asset.

This chapter is structured as follows. Section 2 reviews the range of policy rationales advanced for retail CBDCs and highlights the resulting lack of strategic focus. Section 3 examines the incentive constraints faced by consumers, merchants, and banks. Section 4 briefly reviews international experience. Section 5 develops the case for an offline, token-based Digital Euro. Section 6 discusses policy implications, and Section 7 concludes the argumentation proposed.

2 The Proliferation of CBDC Rationales and the Problem of Strategic Focus

Since the 2020s, central banks and international institutions have advanced an expanding set of justifications for retail CBDCs. Early discussions emphasised preserving access to public money, strategic autonomy, efficiency and innovation, access to digital financial services to everybody, resilience (Spaanderman 2023). Additional rationales have since been layered on, including declining cash usage, resilience against cyber risks, facilitation of fiscal transfers and 40 more (Fig. 1).

While each objective may be defensible in isolation, their cumulative effect has diluted strategic clarity. In Europe, initial Digital Euro communications focused on sovereignty and the monetary anchor role of central bank money. Subsequent statements have introduced additional objectives, creating uncertainty about primary purpose.

Fig. 1 (Too) many reasons are being put forward globally where CBDC is supposed to be the solution (Salmony 2023a)

Payment efficiency and innovation are already pursued through instant payments, open banking, and private tokenised solutions. Financial inclusion is often better addressed through targeted policies rather than new forms of money. Concerns about dependence on foreign payment schemes can be mitigated through competition policy and public–private partnerships [see Part 3 Chapter "From Stability Guardians to Innovation Architects: The Transformation of Monetary Authorities in the Digital Age" by Oxford in this book] without a retail CBDC.

Monetary sovereignty stands out as the most consistently articulated rationale. However, experience (e.g., India's UPI) shows that new public infrastructure can sometimes reinforce rather than reduce concentration on foreign platforms.

> UPI is dominated by Walmart's PhonePe and Google Pay with a combined market share of 83% - a de facto duopoly, leaving the national PayTM – which was supposed to assure sovereignty – far behind (Bartelt et al. 2024).

The proliferation of rationales obscures a more fundamental issue: whether a retail CBDC is the appropriate instrument. Without a clear hierarchy of goals, design choices risk inconsistency, and stakeholder support may erode.

3 Stakeholder Incentives and Adoption Constraints

Retail payment systems succeed only when they align with the incentives of users and intermediaries. This section thus examines consumers, merchants, and commercial banks.

3.1 Consumers

In advanced economies, the incremental value of a retail CBDC is often unclear. Existing instruments—bank transfers, cards, and mobile wallets—offer speed, convenience, and acceptance. Commercial bank deposits typically provide interest and deposit insurance without holding limits.

Proposed CBDC designs often impose holding caps, bear no interest, and introduce an additional category of money that consumers must manage (Fig. 2). Coexistence of commercial bank money and central bank digital money risks confusion without obvious benefits.

Pilot projects show limited organic uptake, often driven by heavy temporary commercial incentives rather than demand. Surveys must be interpreted cautiously: stated preferences in hypothetical scenarios diverge from actual behaviour, particularly for novel instruments (Table 1). Niche use cases, such as offline payments during outages, may resonate but are unlikely to drive widespread adoption alone.

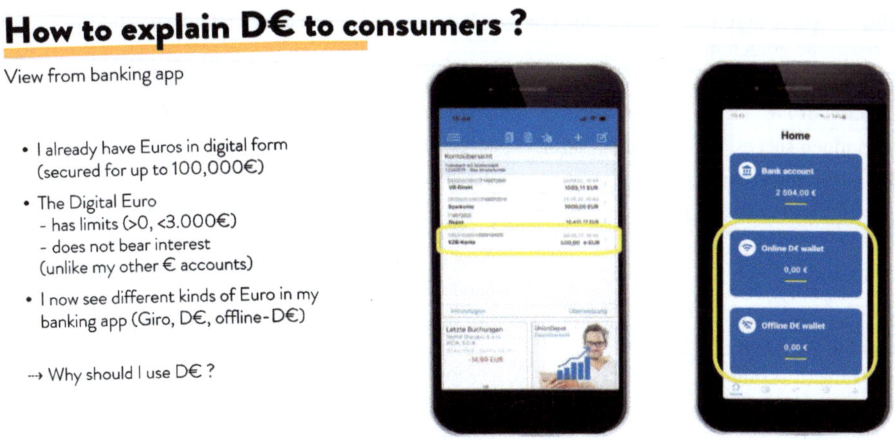

Fig. 2 Sample mockups of future banking apps showing balances in Euro, Digital Euro, Offline Digital Euro (Krüger and Busche 2023; Worldline 2023) … will consumers understand this?

3.2 *Merchants*

Merchants evaluate instruments on cost, reliability, ease of integration and customer demand. Lower fees, resilience and immediate settlement are potential advantages of CBDCs [see Part 4 Chapter "The Pursuit of Resilience in European Retail Payments" by ECB in this book]. However, mandatory acceptance obligations, integration costs, and uncertain consumer adoption complicate the value proposition (EuroCommerce 2025).

In jurisdictions with mature instant payment systems, marginal gains may be modest. Merchant support alone is unlikely to ensure success.

3.3 *Commercial Banks and Financial Stability*

Commercial banks are central to retail payments and indispensable for CBDC distribution in the envisaged 2-tier model. However, banks face risks from deposit substitution, reduced fee income, and implementation costs for the following services which they have to provide without direct remuneration (Bofinger 2023): Opening/closing a digital euro account, on/off-boarding and "Know Your Customer", Payment instrument management (provision and maintenance), Linking the digital euro account to a payment account, User life cycle management processes, (De-) Funding (manual and automated), (Reverse) waterfall, Transaction initiation (one-off transactions), Authentication, Payment confirmation/rejection notification, Refunds, Dispute/exception management, ATM services, etc.

Table 1 Many arguments on all sides in which direction D€ consumer adoption might go—will we reach the golden middle?

Arguments for high adoption of D€ ("too much success")	"Goldilocks" Zone (ideal adoption)	Arguments for low adoption of D€ ("too little success")
D€ is **100% secure** (state-backed)		Deposits already secured to €100,000—No need for another "secure" form of deposit
		Opening up debate that normal bank deposits are not fully secure may be harmful to banking system and financial stability
D€ is **as private as possible** (within the limits that it is online)		In practice consumers care more about convenience than privacy (see global success of Google's AndroidPay, see success of PayPal in Germany, …)
		Consumers do care about no yield on D€ (unlike interest-bearing normal deposits)
		Slippery slope (parameters may be changed with one stroke of the legislative pen):
		- privacy (reduction may be problem for consumers)
		- holding limit (increase/removal may be problem for banks)
		Even with 3000€ limit, the average European can keep/move all his monthly income in D€ - hence banks not motivated to support - hence banks will not encourage consumers to use D€
D€ (especially offline) is an attractive **modern digital form of cash**		People already have euro digitally in their existing bank accounts, can move them digitally, can spend them digitally - no value-add seen
		Having several electronic euro balances (in commercial bank account, D€, offline D€) will likely be very confusing
		Concerns in population about reduction/fear of abolishment/access to cash (see Sweden: Elderly, crime, handicapped,...) if only digital payments available
D€ provides a new **pan-European** means of payment		Consumers can already pay across the world (not only Europe) using Mastercard, Revolut, etc.
		Consumers are already overwhelmed by the number of (new) solutions
		Payments is already one of the most innovative, competitive domains of the economy
D€ increases **sovereignty** versus foreign providers		Foreign providers (ApplePay, GooglePay, PayPal, Amazon, social media, search, cards, cloud, …) are providing essential services which are unlikely to be replaced by EU services in the medium term - D€ may help only incrementally

(continued)

Table 1 (continued)

Arguments for high adoption of D€	"Goldilocks" Zone	Arguments for low adoption of D€
Consequences		
Disruption in banking system (danger of "state organised bank run")	Balanced roles between state and private sector	Waste of investments
Increased shift to state (vs private) infrastructure	Stability of financial system (esp. no bank runs)	Distraction of management from important topics
Scope creep of ECB mandate (online retail payment)	Advantages to *all* stakeholders in the ecosystem	Broken promises (see D€ goals)
		Reduced trust in Eurosystem
		Reputational damage

(*Source*: Author)

Even with holding limits, a CBDC could divert deposits, particularly in stress periods, raising liquidity (European Commission 2023) and bank-run concerns (Bofinger and Haas 2018; Bundesbank 2024). Banks are to bear significant operational burdens (onboarding, KYC, support) often without clear remuneration. Revenue opportunities from envisaged value-added services (e.g. notifications, management tools, information for merchants, etc) appear limited and may cannibalise existing income streams (Deloitte 2024).

These factors suggest misalignment between policy objectives and intermediary incentives. Public–private partnership models with transparent compensation are essential.

4 International Experience with Retail CBDCs

International experience highlights implementation and adoption challenges. Only a few jurisdictions have launched retail CBDCs, with most remaining in pilot or research phases.

China's e-CNY is the largest initiative but shows modest usage relative to existing platforms despite heavy government support (Nikkei 2026). Nigeria's eNaira has seen limited uptake despite policy push. India's e-rupee—the world's second largest CBDC—handles only fractions of a percent of the volumes seen in the successful UPI public–private partnership (Eximius 2025).

The United Arab Emirates pursues an ambitious multi-purpose Digital Dirham (having eight goals), including offline elements, with outcomes still emerging (UAE Central Bank 2025). Several advanced economies, including the UK and Canada, have adopted cautious stances or paused retail initiatives, wisely prioritising wholesale applications instead. Aggregate data (Atlantic Council 2026) confirm few full launches, many inactive projects, and growing scepticism in numerous jurisdictions: 11 launches promoted at the height of the CBDC hype in 2022 have now dwindled to only the three early adopters (Bahamas, Jamaica, Nigeria).

5 Offline CBDC as a Mandate-Consistent Solution

Against this backdrop, a narrowly scoped, offline, token-based CBDC warrants closer examination. Unlike account-based designs resembling bank deposits, an offline CBDC functions as a digital bearer instrument, analogous to physical cash.

It preserves cash attributes—peer-to-peer transferability, privacy, and finality—while leveraging digital technology for usability and resilience in multiple scenarios and use cases (ECB 2024) and leverages the advantages of tokenised money (Fig. 3). Offline functionality ensures operability during network outages or in low-connectivity environments, addressing genuine gaps as evidenced by central bank studies (Chen et al. 2023; BIS 2023) and since large proportions of the global population are unbanked (World Bank 2021) and offline (Intelpoint 2025) even in developed economies. These could benefit from a modern form of cash (stable, private, with no need for electricity or internet) such as an offline CBDC from Europe.

Institutionally, this aligns with central banks' traditional cash mandate. Rather than competing in deposit-taking or private payment solutions, the central bank here focuses on risk-free central bank money. Technological advances in secure hardware, cryptography and usability with smartphones overcome limitations of earlier e-purse failures, making robust solutions feasible today.

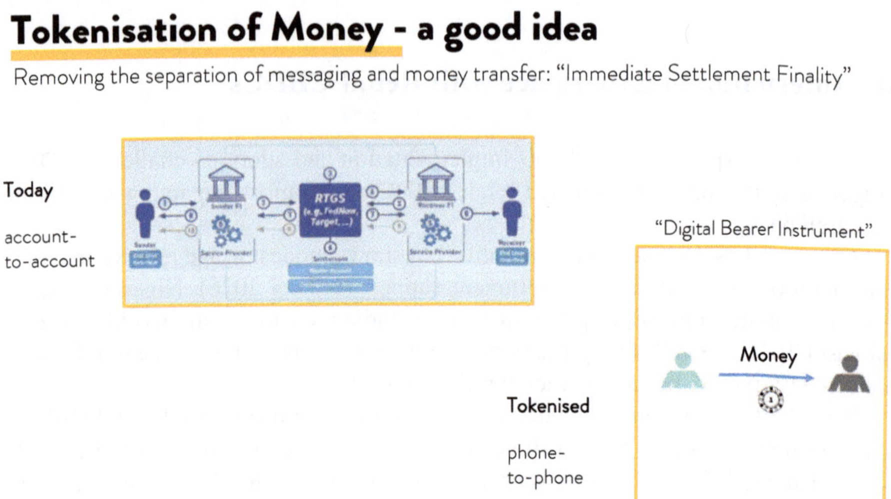

Fig. 3 Modern form of money—moving value directly between people/device/companies/machines using tokens/cryptograms to provide "Instant Settlement Finality" (*Source*: Author)

An offline CBDC could enhance financial inclusion domestically and internationally by enabling transactions without bank accounts or connectivity. In the tokenisation context of this volume, it serves as a public complement to tokenised private money: stablecoins and tokenised deposits offer innovation on private rails, while the public offline token-based CBDC provides a resilient, privacy-focused bearer instrument and potential settlement anchor. Banks could play a positive role in distribution, supporting business cases at the point of sale, in B2B and in IoT scenarios where prepaid models are preferred. Security remains critical and requires rigorous testing, but vendor assurances [see Part 3 Chapter "Offline-Capable Central Bank Digital Currencies as a Key Enabler of a Resilient Digital Payment System" by G+D in this book] and ongoing market experiences indicate feasibility. Resilience attributes have gained particular prominence following recent blackouts and should thus weigh heavily in policy choices.

6 Policy Implications and Design Principles

The analysis yields several implications. Clarity of purpose is essential: retail CBDCs should not address multiple heterogeneous problems simultaneously. Stakeholder incentives must drive design; regulation alone cannot ensure adoption.

Central banks should delineate their role carefully. Expanding into areas well-served by private providers risks crowding out innovation. Focusing on cash evolution leverages institutional strengths. Public–private partnerships remain critical, including transparent compensation for intermediaries.

In a tokenised monetary system, an offline CBDC can complement rather than substitute or directly compete with stablecoins and tokenised deposits, enhancing overall system resilience and public trust.

7 Conclusion

The interest in retail CBDCs reflects genuine challenges: declining cash usage, dependence on private platforms, and the need for resilient, inclusive infrastructures. However, experience suggests ambition alone is insufficient. Without clear objectives, coherent design, and credible incentives, retail CBDCs risk becoming costly solutions in search of well-defined problems.

This chapter has argued that many functions ascribed to retail CBDCs—efficiency, innovation, competition—can be more effectively addressed through existing infrastructures, regulatory interventions, market-driven initiatives, and tokenised private money. Broad account-based CBDCs risk unintended consequences for financial stability and intermediation.

At the same time, dismissing retail CBDCs entirely overlooks central banks' responsibility for cash. As physical cash usage declines, the absence of a digital equivalent preserving key attributes—offline usability, privacy, finality, and universal acceptance—creates a genuine gap. An offline, token-based CBDC designed as a modern form of cash offers a credible response.

This approach modernises cash without positioning central banks as competitors to commercial banks or private providers. It supports resilience, inclusion, and public trust while limiting risks to intermediation. It creates space for constructive public–private partnerships and complements the tokenisation of private money explored elsewhere in this book: stablecoins and tokenised deposits drive efficiency and innovation, while the public offline CBDC anchors the system with sovereign, resilient money.

The future of retail CBDCs depends less on technological sophistication than on institutional restraint. By defining clear boundaries, aligning incentives, and focusing on genuine public-good functions—particularly in a tokenised ecosystem—central banks can avoid pitfalls observed in early experiments and contribute meaningfully to monetary stability and resilience.

References

Atlantic Council (2026) Central Bank Digital Currency Tracker, Data from 2022 to today, https://www.atlanticcouncil.org/cbdctracker/

Bartelt N, Hommel U, Patel R, Ali S (2024) Payment service provision in times of accelerated market and regulatory change: the case of India. Published in Journal of Payment Strategy & Systems 17(3):271–290

BIS (11th May 2023) Project Polaris: Handbook for offline payments with CBDC, BIS, https://www.bis.org/publ/othp64.htm

Bofinger P (12 September 2023) Chair for Monetary Policy and International Economics at the Department of Economics at the University of Würzburg, The Digital Euro: An anchor of stability or a gigantic flop? at CBDC Conference, Istanbul

Bofinger P, Haas Th (June 2018) A simple microeconomic model for the analysis of Vollgeld, https://www.econstor.eu/bitstream/10419/179674/1/1024071626.pdf

Bundesbank (2024) CBDC and banks: Disintermediating fast and slow Deutsche Bundesbank Discussion Paper 15/2024, https://www.bundesbank.de/resource/blob/931090/be2be8b2c5324245e4147d6306689312/mL/2024-04-29-dkp-15-data.pdf

Chen S, Tirupam G, Han Q (2023) Beyond technology: considerations for rCBDC adoption. BIS, Journal of Payment Strategy & Systems 17(4):408–421. https://www.ingentaconnect.com/contentone/hsp/jpss/2023/00000017/00000004/art00006

Deloitte (2024) Maria Saenz de Buruaga Azcargorta, Monitor Deloitte, *Fee models for the CBDCs: the Digital Euro*, at Digital Euro Conference 2023, 29th February 2024, Frankfurt, https://www.youtube.com/watch?v=smOxfE3sVKg

ECB (2024) Progress on the preparation phase of a digital euro, European Central Bank, https://www.ecb.europa.eu/euro/digital_euro/progress/html/ecb.deprp202406.en.html

EuroCommerce (2025) Atze Faas, Head of Payments at EuroCommerce, Digital Euro Conference, Frankfurt, https://www.eurocommerce.eu/events/digital-euro-conference-2025-dec25/

European Commission (2023) *Bank profitability and central bank digital currency* 1 June 2023, https://publications.jrc.ec.europa.eu/repository/handle/JRC133796

Eximius Echo (22 October 2025) Beyond UPI: How CBDCs Could Redefine the Future of Money, https://eximiusecho.substack.com/p/beyond-upi-how-cbdcs-could-redefine

Intelpoint (2025) 54.3% of Nigeria's population — about 128.3 million people — are still unconnected, placing the country fourth in the world, Digital 2025 Global Overview Report, https://intelpoint.co/insights/54-3-of-nigerias-population-about-128-3-million-people-are-still-unconnected-placing-the-country-fourth-in-the-world/

Krüger N, Busche J (July 2023) Towards acceptance criteria for a digital euro, IU Discussion Papers—HSPV NRW, https://www.econstor.eu/bitstream/10419/273489/1/1853166162.pdf

Nikkei (4th February 2026) China starts paying interest on digital yuan in latest bid to extend its reach, Nikkei Asia, https://asia.nikkei.com/business/finance/china-starts-paying-interest-on-digital-yuan-in-latest-bid-to-extend-its-reach

Salmony M (25 September 2023a) Central Banks Rethinking CBDC, https://fintechistanbul.org/en/2023/09/25/central-banks-rethinking-cbdc/

Salmony M (2023b) Do we really need another dollar, euro, pound or yuan? How to create the right ecosystem for a successful central bank digital currency. J Payment Systems Strategy. https://ideas.repec.org/a/aza/jpss00/y2023v17i1p8-25.html

Salmony M (2024) Can the digital euro be made attractive to all key stakeholders? J Digital Banking 9(3) Winter 2024 by Henry Stewart Publications, https://www.ingentaconnect.com/content/hsp/jdb001/2024/00000009/00000003;jsessionid=o075oh0rdpci.x-ic-live-01

Spaanderman J (12 September 2023) The role of public money and the use of cash as a means of payment in a digital world, De Nederlandsche Bank (Dutch National Bank), CBDC Conference 2023 Istanbul, https://www.linkedin.com/posts/cbdc-conference_cbdc-fintech-centralbank-activity-7100365671602995200-lfRx

UAE Central Bank (2025) Digital Dirham—A Primer on the UAE's Central Bank Digital Currency, Policy Paper No. 1/2025, Central Bank of the UAE, July 2025, https://www.centralbank.ae/media/lczb23l4/cbdc-short-report_july.pdf

World Bank (2021) Global Findex Database 2021 (unbanked population and financial inclusion data), World Bank, https://www.worldbank.org/en/publication/globalfindex

Worldline (30 May 2023) Worldline delivers a front-end prototype for the digital euro, https://thepaypers.com/crypto-web3-and-cbdc/news/worldline-delivers-a-front-end-prototype-for-the-digital-euro

The Retail Central Bank Digital Currency (CBDC) Landscape

John Kiff

Abstract This chapter explores the global landscape of the 112 or more central banks that are exploring, or have explored, retail central bank digital currency (RCBDC). Emerging market and developing economy (EMDE) central banks are leading the way maybe because they see the benefits as more compelling than in advanced economies (AEs), where they perceive that risks may outweigh the potential benefits. The chapter explores how central banks navigate the trade-offs between offering RCBDCs that will be compelling digital payment instruments for users, while controlling the risks of banking sector disintermediation and use in illicit finance. However, so far, this has resulted in RCBDCs that offer nothing new and compelling to users, and all the RCBDCs that have been launched or piloted have met with underwhelming demand. This has not been helped by incomplete infrastructure (e.g., point of sale devices) and a lack of incentives for important partners (e.g., banks, payment service providers and merchants). Nevertheless, several central banks, most notably the European Central Bank, are considering moving outside the RCBDC design box, with remuneration and high levels of privacy being considered, which may result in a more compelling product.

Keywords Retail central Bank digital currency (rCBDC) • Emerging markets and financial inclusion • Future payment infrastructure • Banking disintermediation • Seigniorage • Privacy and anonymity • Offline payments • Programmable money • Adoption challenges

---

John Kiff with contributions from Jonas Gross.

J. Kiff (✉)
Kiffmeister LLC, Hillsboro, VA, USA
e-mail: john@kiffmeister.com

S. Yazıcı et al. (eds.), *Tokenisation of Money*, Contributions to Finance and Accounting, https://doi.org/10.1007/978-3-032-22946-5_8

1 Introduction

This chapter explores the global landscape of retail central bank digital currency (RCBDC). The Bank for International Settlements (BIS) defines a RCBDC as a broadly available general purpose digital payment instrument that is denominated in the jurisdiction's unit of account and that is a direct liability of the jurisdiction's monetary authority (BIS 2020). Note that this definition is agnostic as to the technology platform, so a RCBDC could be run on a traditional centralized ledger or on distributed ledger technology (DLT). According to CBDCTracker.org, at least 112 central banks have explored, or are exploring, RCBDC (Fig. 1).[1]

There is also a "wholesale central bank digital currency", which is limited to a set of predefined user groups, typically financial institutions. That is not the subject of this chapter. Also, the "direct liability" condition precludes national digital currencies not issued by central banks, and central bank-backed/run interbank payment platforms.[2]

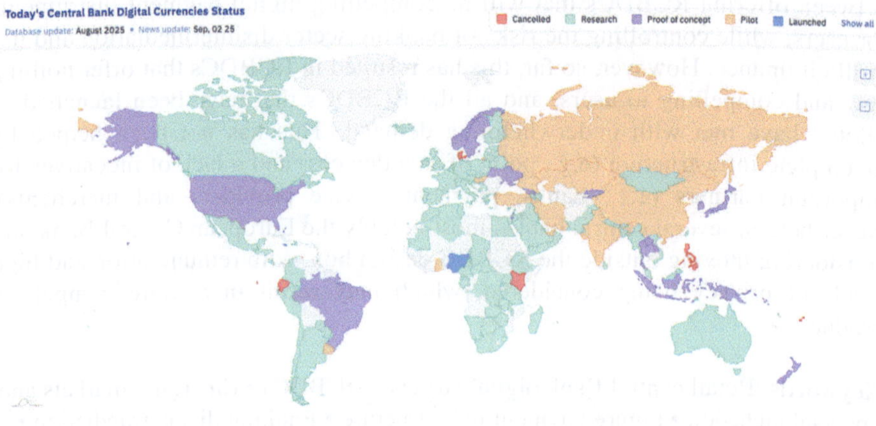

Fig. 1 The Retail Central Bank Digital Currency (RCBDC) Landscape (August 2025). *Source*: CBDCTracker.org

[1] It is "at least" because the CBDCTracker.org count is based on reliable public sources (almost all from the central banks themselves) and many central banks keep their central bank digital currency work undercover. However, according to the Bank for International Settlements (BIS), about 80% of the 93 central banks surveyed at the end of 2024 were exploring RCBDC (BIS, 2025). It should be noted that CBDCTracker.org does not count individual countries and national central banks that are in currency unions. For example, although several Eurozone central banks are exploring RCBDC, the Eurozone counts only as one, because the European Central Bank is the only central bank that would be legally authorized to issue a digital euro.

[2] An example of a national digital currency that is not a RCBDC is the U.S. dollar denominated stablecoin being tested by the Republic of Ministry of Finance Republic of Palau (2024). And central bank-backed interbank payment platforms like the Bank of Cambodia's Bakong do not meet the "direct liability" condition (Ueda and Hay 2024).

Getting back to the RCBDC landscape, while much attention focuses on the activities of China, Europe, India and the United States, emerging market and developing economy (EMDE) jurisdictions are leading the way. For example, the Bahamas, Ecuador, Finland, Jamaica and Nigeria have launched RCBDCs, and 13 other central banks, including China, India and Russia, have launched limited scale/time pilot tests.[3] In addition, 21 central banks have conducted proof-of-concepts (POCs), which differ from pilots in that they take place in a lab setting (e.g., among central bank staff). Most central banks are in the preparation phase (desk research and reaching out to technology platform providers).[4]

2 Motivations for Exploring/Issuing RCBDC

For EMDEs, some of the main motivations for exploring RCBDC are financial digitalization/ inclusion, reducing the costs/risks of managing physical cash, preserving seigniorage revenue as cash usage declines, and reducing currency substitution (e.g., dollarization).[5] Advanced economy (AE) central banks, faced with declining cash usage, are focused on ensuring access to universal low-cost digital payments, including reducing monopoly powers of private payment systems, maintaining central bank money relevance, and strategic autonomy from foreign payment service providers (PSPs). See Table 1 for other motivations for RCBDC exploration.

Table 1 Motivations Put Forward by Central Banks for Exploring/Issuing Retail CBDC

Emerging Market & Developing Economies	Advanced Economies
Financial digitalization/inclusion	Ensuring access to universal low-cost digital payments as cash usage declines
Reducing physical cash costs/risks	
Preserving seigniorage revenue	
Reducing currency substitution	Monetary sovereignty/Strategic autonomy
Improving payment system efficiency, competition, resiliency and safety	
Improving monetary policy effectiveness: targeted policy, accessing granular real-time payments data, breaking through lower zero bound on policy rates	
Fight tax evasion, money laundering and other illicit activities	
Distributing government payments	
Cross-border payments	

[3] Finland launched the Avant in 1992 but spun it off and sold it to commercial banks in1995 (Grym 2020). Ecuador launched the Dinero Electrónico in 2014 but shut it down in 2018 (Arauz et al. 2021).

[4] Tourpe et al. (2023) suggests a "5P" central bank digital currency decision-making framework (preparation, proof of concept, prototype, pilot, and production).

[5] Seigniorage is the profit that central banks make from the difference between the interest earned on non-monetary assets (e.g., government fixed-income securities) and the interest it pays (typically zero) on the monetary assets (i.e., currency) that it issues (Kahn et al. 2022).

3 Key RCBDC Design Characteristics

RCBDC design choices depend on policy objectives and country specifics, but among those RCBDCs that have launched or been piloted, there is much in common.

3.1 Operating Models and Private Sector Roles

In a single-tier operating model, the central bank performs all the tasks involved, from issuing and distributing the RCBDC to running user wallets. In multi-tier models, the central bank issues and redeems the RCBDC, but some or all the distribution and payment service functions are delegated to private-sector firms. Which model to adopt will depend on the breadth and depth of the country's financial sector, financial integrity standards, compliance, the availability of financial market infrastructure and supervision capacity.

All RCBDCs that have been launched or piloted run on two-tiered operating models of the "intermediated" variety (Fig. 2). In this variation, PSPs back the RCBDC they distribute in aggregated wholesale accounts at the central bank, which has access to the records of individual RCBDC holder balances (Auer and Böhme 2021). The central bank, however, maintains a backup copy of individual balances it would use to restart payments should a PSP fail. The PSP's RCBDC wholesale account is legally ring-fenced from the PSP's other operations and immediately available to the central bank in such an event. So far, no central banks have opted for a "hybrid" variant of the two-tier operating model, where the PSPs are merely agents on behalf of the central bank.

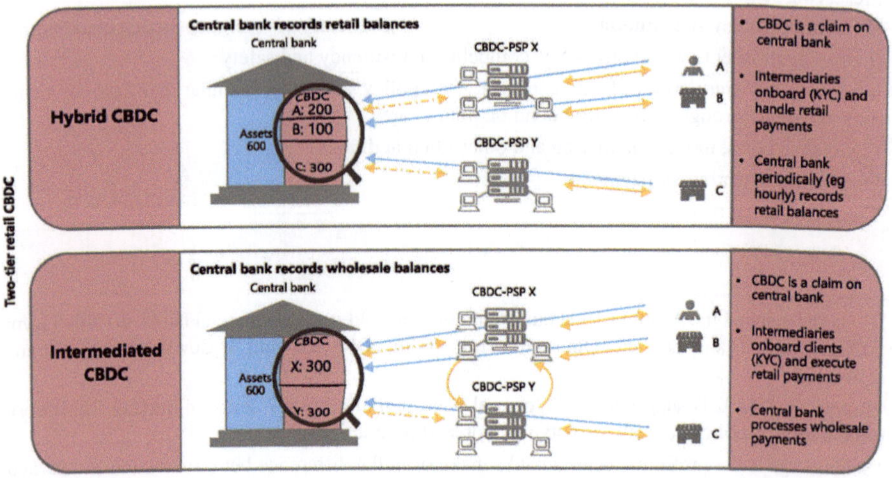

Fig. 2 Intermediated- vs Multi-Tier Operating Model. *Source*: Auer and Böhme 2021

Table 2 Distribution of RCBDC functions between the central bank and private sector

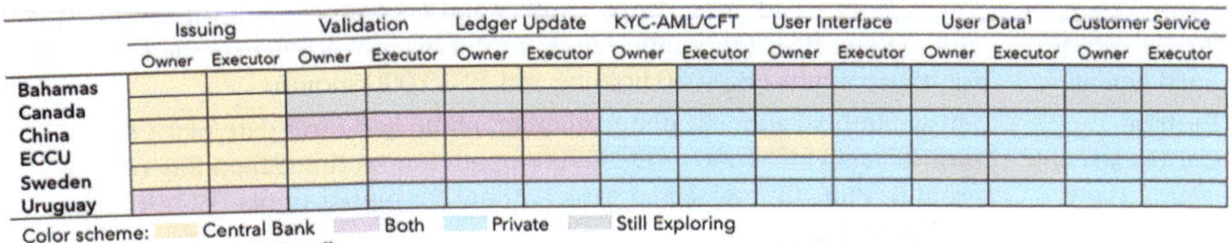

Source: Central banks and IMF staff.
Note: AML/CFT = anti-money laundering/combating the financing of terrorism; KYC = know your customer.
[1]One option is to grant central banks access to data stored by intermediaries. This is the practice in China.

Source: Söderberg et al. (2022)

The forms of intermediated models can vary depending on the distribution of functions between the central bank and private intermediaries. Also, sometimes the central bank is the owner of the technical system that carries out a specific function, but execution is delegated to a private intermediary. Table 2 summarizes how functions have been allocated in six RCBDC projects described in Söderberg et al. (2022).

3.2 *Remuneration and Transaction Fees*

Some academic research has advocated paying variable interest rates to RCBDC holders to modulate demand or provide a new monetary policy instrument (Bordo and Levin 2017). For example, an interest-bearing RCBDC could enhance the transmission of monetary policy by increasing the economy's response to policy rate changes. Such a RCBDC could be used to break the "zero lower bound" on policy rates to the extent that cash was made costly. Also, several theoretical papers have found positive macroeconomic effects of carefully calibrated RCBDC remuneration (Chiu et al. 2023; Paul et al. 2025). However, no central banks have launched or piloted remunerated RCBDC, typically because they want to promote the RCBDC as "digital cash" and limit RCBDC competition with bank deposits.[6]

None of the RCBDCs launched or piloted involve transaction fees to users, consistent with RCBDC being a public good, like physical cash. However, there is the question of how to compensate PSPs for the work they do in managing the distribution process. ECB (2023) suggests "basic usage" of a prospective digital euro would be free to users, but PSPs would be able to charge merchant fees, subject to regulatory caps, for providing digital euro-related services to offset operational costs. In the National Bank of Ukraine pilot project, P2P transactions were free of charge, but PSPs were able to charge up to one percent of the transaction amount on P2B

[6]The Bank of Israel is considering a remunerated RCBDC (Bank of Israel 2025). Bindseil (2019) has suggested a tiered remuneration system with relatively attractive interest rates on small RCBDC holdings, and lower rates on large ones, to mitigate the risk that the RCBDC disintermediates the private banking system.

Table 3 Holding/Transaction Limit Structures

Central Bank of the Bahamas Sand Dollar	Physical/email address, phone number and photo for low-limit access (B$500 holding and B$1500/month transaction). Plus, government-issued photo ID for higher limits (B$8000 holding and B$10,000/month)
Eastern Caribbean central Bank DCash	Physical/email address, phone number, photo and birth date/place for low limit access (EC$1000 to EC$2700/month transaction depending on risk profile). Plus, full name and bank account for higher limits (EC$3000 to EC$20,000/day)
Central Bank of Uruguay e-peso	Physical/email address, SIM card and national ID for low limit access (UYU30,000). No higher limits except for businesses (UYU200,000)
Central Bank of Nigeria eNaira	Physical/email address, phone number, passport photo and birth date/place for low limit access (N120,000 holding and N20,000/day). Plus, National Identity Number and bank account for higher limits (N50,000—N1,000,000/day and N300,000—N5,000,000 holding). No limits on businesses
People's Bank of China eCNY	SIM card for low limit access (¥10,000 holding, ¥2000/transaction and ¥5000/day). Plus, full name, address, phone number and bank account for higher limits (¥500,000 holding, ¥50,000/transaction and ¥100,000/day)
Bank of Jamaica Jam-Dex	Government-issued ID to activate a Lynk wallet but no holding limits. Person-to-person limit is J$100,000/day. Cash-out limit is J$100,000/day, cash-ins are limited to J$50,000/day from a bank account, J$50,000/month from a debit/credit card

Source: Noll (2024), Bergara and Ponce (2018), Ree (2023), Yang (2021) and JN Bank (2025)

and B2B transactions, which is slightly less than what is charged on other digital payment instruments and payment cards (NBU 2019).

3.3 Holding and Transaction Size Limits

All central banks that have launched or piloted RCBDC have applied holding and transaction size limits on users, to mitigate the risks of banking sector disintermediation discussed above, and the use of the RCBDC in illicit financial activities. Central banks are basing such limits on jurisdiction-specific empirical and theoretical studies of bank deposit to RCBDC substitution risk, and their interpretations of the relevant Financial Action Task Force (FATF) anti-money laundering and countering terrorist financing (AML/CFT) recommendations (Financial Action Task Force (FATF) 2012). Most central banks that have launched or piloted RCBDC have applied "proportionality" by assigning higher limits to users that present lower illicit finance risk (Table 3).[7]

China's eCNY users are identified only by their mobile phone SIM cards for the lowest tier of access (a holding limit of ¥10,000, and transactions are limited to ¥2000 up to ¥5000 per day). However, by providing full names, addresses and

[7] There are also design choices around central bank user data access. Central banks typically have access only to pseudonymous data, but in some cases can reveal data or a person's identity if they can show probable cause to do so (e.g., with a court order).

Table 4 Technology platforms used in RCBDC launches and pilots

Digital currency	Partner firm	Technology	Platform type
Bahamas sand Dollar	NZIA	NZIA cortex DLT	DLT private permissioned
China e-CNY	n/a	n/a	Centralized ledger
ECCB DCash and Nigeria eNaira	Bitt	Hyperledger fabric	DLT private permissioned
Ecuador dinero electrónico	n/a	Mobile money	Centralized ledger
Ghana	G + D	Filia	Centralized ledger
Jamaica	eCurrency	DSC[3]	Digital bearer instrument
Sweden e-krona	Accenture	R3 Corda	DLT private permissioned
Ukraine E-Hryvnia	Stellar	Stellar	DLT private permissioned
Uruguay e-peso	Roberto Giori	GSMT	Centralized ledger

Source: ITU (2025)

phone numbers, and by linking the RCBDC wallet with their bank accounts, users see their limits increase substantially (¥500,000 holding, ¥50,000 per transaction and ¥100,000 per day).

3.4 Centralized Versus Distributed Ledger Technology

A diversity of technical platforms, both centralized and distributed ledger-based, have been deployed, although those adopting the latter have opted for the private permissioned network variety (Table 4) (ITU 2025). They allow for control over platform participants and their access to the platform, and role-based oversight and visibility of transactions. Private permissioned platforms also ensure that the central bank retains full control over money issuance and monetary policy. Again, Jamaica is unusual in that its RCBDC doesn't use centralized or decentralized ledger technology. Instead, it is based on ledgerless digital bearer instruments.

No central banks are currently considering issuing RCBDC on public permissionless DLT platforms, as they are seen as falling short on scalability, settlement finality, and financial integrity risk management (BIS 2023).

3.5 Ensuring Access in Connectivity-Challenged Scenarios

Central banks are exploring RCBDCs that can operate across connectivity challenges ranging from cellular-only connectivity where mobile internet access is not available or affordable, to no connectivity at all (Tourpe et al. 2025). Several RCBDC projects have incorporated unstructured supplementary service data

(USSD) based mobile phone access.[8] These included the Banco Central del Ecuador Dinero Electrónico from 2014 to 2018, the Central Bank of Uruguay e-Peso pilot from 2017 to 2018, the Central Bank of Nigeria eNaira since 2022, and the Central Bank of Peru digital Sol pilot since 2024 (Arauz et al. 2021; Sarmiento 2022; Mohammed and Yusuf 2023; BCRP 2024).

Several central banks have explored RCBDC payment platforms that can operate when there is an absence or a prolonged breakdown of connectivity infrastructure, like during natural disasters, active conflicts, or in remote areas. The central banks of Australia, Ghana and Thailand have piloted RCBDC payments based on stored value cards that transfer value through intermediary devices, such as near field communication (NFC) or Bluetooth low-energy (BLE) enabled merchant point of sale (POS) devices or smartphones, while all devices are offline (RBA 2023; BOG 2024; BOT 2024).[9] The Reserve Bank of India has piloted direct device-to-device offline payment solutions that transfer funds between smartphones NFC connections and via quick-response (QR) codes (Crunchfish 2024).

3.6 *Privacy and Anonymity*

A RCBDC has the potential to give authorities information on users and their transactions, to facilitate detection, supervision, monitoring, and law enforcement efforts. However, this opens the central bank to criticisms that RCBDC could be used as a surveillance tool, and to censor users and transactions. Although complete anonymity could be supported by technologies such as blind signatures or zero-knowledge proofs, central banks must comply with FATF standards, so, in launches and pilots to date, central banks have opted for more nuanced privacy models (Table 5).[10,11]

Most central banks have applied variations of privacy threshold policies that allow higher degrees of privacy for low-value transactions, while large-value transactions are subject to standard customer due diligence checks. However, in most cases, all transaction and know-our-customer (KYC) data is visible to intermediaries, in the same way they are for other payments on their platforms, again to comply

[8] USSD creates a real-time, session-based connection between a mobile device and the mobile network, enabling two-way data exchange. USSD enables applications like mobile banking and access menus on feature phones.

[9] Finland's Avant card-based platform, launched in 1992, had offline capabilities that were never activated (Grym 2020)

[10] See DEA (2023) and Gross et al. (2021) for more on privacy-preserving technologies.

[11] European Central Bank (ECB) (2019) has suggested non-transferrable "anonymity vouchers" that allow users to anonymously transfer limited RCBDC amounts. Gross et al. (2022) have proposed a system that enables cash-like private RCBDC transactions up to specific monetary limits. If these limits are reached, transactions above the limit have similar degrees of privacy as existing digital payment platforms. Chaum et al. (2021) have proposed a system that allows central banks to issue tokens without knowing who owns them. The central bank ledger tracks coin identifiers, but transactions between wallets are not recorded.

Table 5 Central bank CBDC transaction data access

Central Bank of the Bahamas Sand Dollar	Transaction transparency to enable central bank (CB) to monitor suspicious transactions and stop accounts. Pseudonyms ensure user anonymity. CB maintains ledger and server is encrypted
Eastern Caribbean central Bank DCash	CB can see anonymized transaction data and outstanding CBDC in each digital wallet. Registered financial institutions can fully observe the identity of payers and payees and the purpose of transactions
Central Bank of Uruguay e-peso	User data is segregated across different databases. Transaction data per (anonymous) digital wallet can be decrypted to reveal the user's identity under very restrictive conditions—e.g., a competent authority prosecuting someone that has probable cause to access the transaction data
People's Bank of China eCNY	The CB is privy to the identity of its users as they are required to provide their real identities when they first sign up. However, users will have the ability to control what information they expose to counterparties
Bank of Jamaica jam-Dex	The CB does not maintain data on users. Wallet providers maintain the identities of their respective users and transactions in line with AML/CFT/CFP regulations

Source: ITU (2025), Noll (2024), Bergara and Ponce (2018) and PBOC (2021)

with FATF standards. But in most cases, central bank access is limited to data that has been anonymized and can be selectively decrypted only under very restrictive conditions, such as a court order.

3.7 *Programmability and Smart Contracts*

Smart contracts automatic execution of the terms of agreements and initiate related transactions without human intervention (Bechtel et al. 2023). Applications include paying sales taxes directly to tax authorities at point of sale, and integration with physical devices or internet-of-things (IoT) applications. Embedded smart contracts could also be used to implement targeted aid payments that can be spent only on predefined goods and services.[12] However, few central banks are planning to build programmability into their RCBDC, due to political pushback against the possibility that such "programmable money" could be used to exercise undue control over users (Emmer 2025).[13]

[12] "Programmable money" that embeds rules within the RCBDC that define or constrain its usage, should not be confused with "programmable payments" run by third parties that automate the execution of payments once pre-defined sets of conditions are met (Bechtel et al. 2023).

[13] MAS (2022) has proposed "purpose bound money" (PBM) by which RCBDC tokens are wrapped by removable programming logic. Once the conditions in the PBM wrapper are met, the underlying RCBDC token can be released and used without any constraints or functionality that may have been defined in the PBM wrapper.

4 Underwhelming Demand for RCBDCs

No central bank has fully launched a RCBDC since early 2022 (Jamaica's JAM--DEX) and among the five that launched, Ecuador and Finland have shut theirs down (Arauz et al. 2021; Grym 2020). Of the remaining three and the larger-scale pilots, uptake has been underwhelming, due to several factors (Table 6). The jurisdictions'

Table 6 Underwhelming Retail CBDC Adoption

Country and Launch Date	Motivation	Adoption	Adoption challenges
Ecuador dinero electrónico (2014–2018	• Reduce dependency on physical dollars • Financial inclusion	• 500, 000 wallets at peak, but there was little active usage	• Limited adoption incentives and cash-in networks. And insufficient public education • User concerns about privacy and government control • Opposition from commercial banks
Bahamas sand Dollar (Oct. 2020)	• High cost of cash distribution • Financial inclusion	• 133,481 wallets at end-2024 (out of a population of about 400,000) • Amount in circulation was \$2.6 million, less than 0.5% of cash in circulation.	• Banks, credit unions, and merchants are slow to participate in sand Dollar network. • Sand Dollar was not integrated with the traditional banking system regarding merchant accounts • Customer education was inadequate, failing to show users how and why to use sand dollars
Nigerian eNaira (Oct. 2021)	• High informality • Financial inclusion • Facilitation of remittances	• eNaira wallets grew to 13 million in 2023, representing 9% of active bank accounts in Nigeria, but almost all are inactive • Amount in circulation reported to be less than 0.4% of cash in circulation	• Under the current design, CBN would be able to see all eNaira transactions, making potential users concerned • Nigeria has a \$220 billion informal economy that thrives on cash. There are currently too few merchants and too little infrastructure for extensive eNaira use • A change of the technology provider after launch suggests that robust tech infrastructure was not in place
Jamaica Jam-Dex (July 2022)	• Financial inclusion	• Only 282,274 wallets have been downloaded (out of a population of 2.8 million, as of end-2024) • Amount in circulation was \$276 million, versus \$286 billion cash in circulation	• Slow merchant onboarding has been a big issue as retailers are required to upgrade their POS equipment to use jam-Dex • BOJ did not incentivize or mandate commercial banks to modify their ATMs to accept and convert Jam-Dex

Sources: Arauz et al. (2021), CBOB (2025), IMF (2024), Ree (2023), and BoJ (2025)

payments ecosystems may already be well served by digital payment instruments, making RCBDC redundant. Plus, navigating "knife edge" design challenges (e.g., no remuneration due to disintermediation concerns, and limited privacy due to FATF AML/CFT requirements) leads to RCBDCs that offer nothing new and compelling to users. And in some cases, the infrastructure (e.g., point of sale devices) is incomplete and important partners (e.g., banks, payment service providers and merchants) lack incentives. In other cases, central banks skip too quickly through the development phases and/or don't involve all stakeholders.

4.1 Narrow Use Cases as an Alternative Approach?

Tourpe et al. (2023) suggests a "5P" central bank digital currency decision-making framework (preparation, proof of concept, prototype, pilot, and production) in which users are not involved until the fourth phase. Such an approach is appropriate for "death star" RCBDCs aimed to be general-purpose payment instruments for all users since the stakes and risks are so high. If it is a failure, there could be reputational damage to the central bank and government. If it is too "successful" it would threaten existing PSPs and deposit-taking banks.

Kiff and Ostrowski (2024) suggest a "test and deploy" aimed at narrow use cases with an abbreviated preparation phase and rapid iterations through the next three phases (proof-of-concept, prototype and pilot) whereby RCBDC is issued to users in a safe and controlled manner to offer insight into user demand and experience. By focusing on narrow use cases, the risks associated with a death star RCBDC are absent, which allows for the more agile approach. Recent examples of such pilots include:

- *Hungary's Magyar Nemzeti Bank* issuing RCBDC to unbanked young people (MNB 2023).
- *The Reserve Bank of Australia* testing 16 use cases, many of which leverage programmable payments to facilitate multi-party, conditional or escrowed payments, or to enable atomic settlement of transactions in tokenized assets (RBA 2023).
- *The National Bank of Kazakhstan* testing various use cases, such as automating social support and student canteen subsidy payment distributions (NBK 2023).
- *The Hong Kong Monetary Authority (HKMA)* conducting 14 pilots that tested programmability, tokenization, and atomic settlement (HKMA 2023).

5 Conclusion: What's Next for RCBDCs?

There are more likely to be more EMDE central banks than AE ones testing and launching RCBDCs. That may be because the benefits of introducing RCBDCs in EMDEs are seen as more compelling than in AEs, where risks may outweigh the potential benefits. AE central banks, on the other hand, take a more cautious approach. They are mostly in the process of investigating the potential benefits of a RCBDC and studying risks carefully. They assess risks to the financial sector in detail, as central banks place a high priority on preserving financial stability. They will likely continue their more transparent, but slower, efforts, and it is no sure thing that many of the CDBCs will be put into circulation.

In this regard, more central banks are looking to fast payment systems (FPSs), stablecoins, and commercial bank deposit tokens to meet many of the objectives assigned to RCBDCs. In fact, several central banks that were running active RCBDC projects have put them on the backburner.[14] For example, Banco Central do Brasil (BCB) launched its Pix FPS in 2020 and by 2024 it was the most widely used payment method among Brazilians, being used by 76.4% of the population (BCB 2024). In the United States, the Federal Reserve has been ordered to cease its work on RCBDC, and legislation has been passed to encourage the use of stablecoins in contexts originally imagined for RCBDCs (White House 2025; U.S. Congress 2025). And South Korea has ceased its RCBDC experimentation and pivoted to tokenized commercial bank deposits. However, the ECB and Bank of Japan continue their RCBDC projects, and the Bank of Israel considers moving outside the RCBDC design box, with possible remuneration and high levels of privacy (BOI 2025).

Meanwhile, stay tuned!

References

Arauz A, Garratt R, Ramos DF (2021) Dinero Electrónico: the rise and fall of Ecuador's central Bank digital currency. Latin Am J Central Banking 2(2):100030. https://www.sciencedirect.com/science/article/pii/S2666143821000107

Auer R, Böhme R (21 June 2021) Central Bank Digital Currency: The Quest for Minimally Invasive Technology. BIS Working Paper No. 948. Bank for International Settlements, https://www.bis.org/publ/work948.htm

Banco Central de Reserva del Perú (BCRP) (15 July 2024) Resolución de Gerencia General No. RGG-0009-2024-BCRP. https://www.bcrp.gob.pe/docs/Transparencia/Normas-Legales/Resoluciones-Gerencia-General/2024/rgg-0009-2024-bcrp.pdf

Banco Central do Brasil (BCB) (4 Dec 2024) Pix Supera Dinheiro e já é o Meio de Pagamento mais Usado no Brasil. https://www.bcb.gov.br/detalhenoticia/20477/noticia

[14] Some central banks have publicly announced shutdowns of their RCBDC projects (e.g., Canada and Thailand), while others have simply gone quiet (e.g., Sweden).

Bank for International Settlements (BIS) (12 Dec 2023) High-level Requirements for a Retail Central Bank Digital Currency (CBDC) Architecture. Consultative Group on Innovation and the Digital Economy Technical Task Force Report. Bank for International Settlements, https://www.bis.org/publ/othp82.htm

Bank of Canada, Bank of England, Bank of Japan, European Central Bank, Federal Reserve, Sveriges Riksbank, Swiss National Bank, and Bank for International Settlements (9 Oct 2020) Central Bank Digital Currencies: Foundational Principles and Core Features. Bank for International Settlements, https://www.bis.org/publ/othp33.htm

Bank of Ghana (BOG) (22 Oct 2024) The eCedi Report. https://www.bog.gov.gh/wp-content/uploads/2024/10/The-eCedi-Report-221024.pdf

Bank of Israel (BOI) (March 2025) Preliminary Design for the Digital Shekel System. https://boi.org.il/media/54dpz1ew/initial-design-for-the-digital-shekel-system.pdf

Bank of Jamaica (BoJ) (April 2025) Annual Report 2024: Report and Statement of Accounts for the Year Ended 31 December 2024. https://boj.org.jm/wp-content/uploads/2025/04/2024-BOJ-Annual-Report-final.pdf

Bank of Thailand (BOT) (March 2024) Pilot Program - Retail CBDC Conclusion Report, https://www.bot.or.th/content/dam/bot/documents/en/financial-innovation/cbdc-digital-currency/rCBDC%20Conclusion%20Report.pdf

Bechtel A, Gross J, Sandner P, von Wachter V (12 April 2023) Programmable Money and Programmable Payments. Blog post, https://www.jonasgross.info/programmable-money-and-programmable-payments/

Bergara M, Ponce J (2018) Central Bank digital currency: the Uruguayan E-peso case. In: Gnan E, Masciandaro D (eds) Do we need central Bank digital currency? Economics, technology and institutions, pp 82–90. https://iris.unibocconi.it/retrieve/handle/11565/4014058/92065/Masciandaro%20SUERF%20book%20%2B%20SUERF%20book%20chapter.pdf

Bindseil U (January 2019) Tiered CBDC and the Financial System. ECB Working Paper 2351. European Central Bank, https://www.ecb.europa.eu/pub/pdf/scpwps/ecb.wp2351~c8c18bbd60.en.pdf

Bordo MD, Levin AT (August 2017) *Central Bank Digital Currency and the Future of Monetary Policy*. NBER Working Paper No. 23711. National Bureau of Economic Research, https://www.nber.org/system/files/working_papers/w23711/w23711.pdf

Central Bank of The Bahamas (CBOB) (22 May 2025) 2024 Annual Report & Statement of Accounts. https://www.centralbankbahamas.com/viewPDF/documents/2025-05-22-12-05-26-2024-CBOB-Annual-Report%2D%2DStatement-of-Accounts.pdf

Chaum D, Grothoff C, Moser T (2021) How to Issue a Central Bank Digital Currency. SNB Working Papers 2021–03. Zurich: Swiss National Bank. https://www.snb.ch/en/publications/research/working-papers/2021/working_paper_2021_03

Chiu J, Davoodalhosseini SM, Jiang J, Yu Z (2023) Bank market power and central Bank digital currency: theory and quantitative assessment. J Polit Econ 131(5) https://www.journals.uchicago.edu/doi/abs/10.1086/722517

Crunchfish (1 July 2024) Crunchfish and Tata Consultancy Services Enter Alliance Agreement to Offer Offline Payments for CBDCs. Press release, https://www.crunchfish.com/crunchfish-and-tata-consultancy-services-enter-alliance-agreement-to-offer-offline-payments-for-cbdcs

Digital Euro Association (DEA) (January 2023) *Privacy and Central Bank Digital Currencies*. DEA Public Digital Euro Working Group, https://7869715.fs1.hubspotusercontent-na1.net/hubfs/7869715/Privacy%20and%20CBDCs%20-%20Digital%20Euro%20Association%20Working%20Group.pdf digital-euro-association.de

Emmer T (17 July 2025) Majority Whip Tom Emmer's Flagship Legislation, the Anti-CBDC Surveillance State Act, Passes House of Representatives." Press release, https://emmer.house.gov/media-center/press-releases/majority-whip-tom-emmer-s-flagship-legislation-the-anti-cbdc-surveillance-state-act-passes-house-of-representatives

European Central Bank (22 February 2023) Compensation Model. For the Digital Euro. https://www.ecb.europa.eu/euro/digital_euro/timeline/profuse/shared/pdf/ecb.degov230222_item4compensationmodel.en.pdf
European Central Bank (ECB) (December 2019) Exploring Anonymity in Central Bank Digital Currencies. https://www.ecb.europa.eu/press/intro/publications/pdf/ecb.mipinfocus191217.en.pdf
Financial Action Task Force (FATF) (2012) The FATF Recommendations. Last updated June 2025. https://www.fatf-gafi.org/en/publications/Fatfrecommendations/Fatf-recommendations.html
Gross J, Sedlmeir J, Babel M, Bechtel A, Schellinger B (2021) Designing a Central Bank Digital Currency with Support for Cash-Like Privacy. https://ssrn.com/abstract=3891121
Gross J, Sedlmeir J, Seiter S (15 December 2022) How to Design a Compliant, Privacy-Preserving Fiat Stablecoin via Zero-Knowledge Proofs. Etonec (blog), https://www.etonec.com/post/how-to-design-a-compliant-privacy-preserving-fiat-stablecoin-via-zero-knowledge-proofs
Grym A (2020) Lessons learned from the world's first CBDC. BoF economics review no. 8/2020. Bank of Finland, Helsinki. https://hdl.handle.net/10419/224448
Hong Kong Monetary Authority (HKMA) (October 2023) e-HKD Pilot Programme: Phase 1 Report. https://www.hkma.gov.hk/media/eng/doc/key-information/press-release/2023/20231030e3a1.pdf
International Monetary Fund (IMF) (2024) Nigeria: 2024 article IV consultation—press release; staff report; staff statement; and statement by the executive director for Nigeria. Country report no. 2024/102. International Monetary Fund, Washington, DC. https://www.imf.org/en/Publications/CR/Issues/2024/05/08/Nigeria-2024-Article-IV-Consultation-Press-Release-Staff-Report-Staff-Statement-and-548726
International Telecommunication Union (ITU) (2025) Central Bank Digital Currency Reference Architecture. Architecture, Interoperability Requirements and Use Cases Working Group. https://www.itu.int/en/ITU-T/extcoop/dcgi/Documents/DCGI%20CBDC%20Reference%20Architecture%20Report-20-01-2025.pdf
JN Bank (2025) JN Wallet FAQs. Retrieved September 21. http://archive.today/2025.09.21-133239/https://www.jnbank.com/jn-wallet-faqs/
Kahn CM, Singh M, Alwazir J (2022) Digital money and central Bank operations. *IMF working papers* 2022/085. International Monetary Fund, Washington. https://www.imf.org/en/Publications/WP/Issues/2022/05/06/Digital-Money-and-Central-Bank-Operations-517534
Kiff J, Ostrowski C (17 January 2024) Test and Deploy: A New Era for CBDCs. *CoinDesk*, https://www.coindesk.com/opinion/2024/01/17/test-and-deploy-a-new-era-for-cbdcs
Magyar Nemzeti Bank (MNB) (12 May 2023) Conscious Money Management Digitally and Playfully—The MNB Student Safe Mobile Application Has Been Renewed. Press release, https://www.mnb.hu/en/pressroom/press-releases/press-releases-2023/conscious-money-management-digitally-and-playfully-the-mnb-student-safe-mobile-application-has-been-renewed
Ministry of Finance Republic of Palau (31 July 2024) National Government Payment Service Project: Phase 2a Report. Republic of Palau, https://www.palaugov.pw/wp-content/uploads/Palau-National-Payment-System-Phase-2a-Final-Report.pdf
Mohammed RS, Yusuf AO (2023) eNaira: The Journey So Far. In Obiora KI (2023) Economics of Digital Currencies: A Book of Readings. Central Bank of Nigeria. https://www.cbn.gov.ng/Out/2023/RSD/Economics%20of%20Digital%20Currencies.pdf
Monetary Authority of Singapore (MAS) (31 October 2022) Project Orchid: Programmable Digital SGD. https://www.mas.gov.sg/publications/monographs-or-information-paper/2022/project-orchid-whitepaper Monetary Authority of Singapore+1
National Bank of Kazakhstan (December 2023) Digital Tenge: Results of the First Implementation Phase. White Paper. https://nationalbank.kz/file/download/97556
National Bank of Ukraine (NBU) (2019) Analytical Report on E-hryvnia. https://bank.gov.ua/admin_uploads/article/Analytical%20Report%20on%20E-hryvnia.pdf

Noll F (10 Apr 2024) Observations from the Retail CBDCs of the Caribbean. *Payments System Research Briefings*, Federal Reserve Bank of Kansas City, https://www.kansascityfed.org/research/payments-system-research-briefings/observations-from-the-retail-cbdcs-of-the-caribbean/

Paul P, Ulate M, Wu JC (June 2025) A Macroeconomic Model of Central Bank Digital Currency. NBER Working Paper No. 33968. National Bureau of Economic Research, https://www.nber.org/papers/w33968

People's Bank of China (PBOC) (July 2021) Progress of Research & Development of E-CNY in China. PBOC Working Group on E-CNY Research and Development, http://www.pbc.gov.cn/en/3688110/3688172/4157443/4293696/2021071614584691871.pdf

Ree J (16 May 2023) Nigeria's eNaira, one year after. IMF working paper no. 2023/104. International Monetary Fund., https://www.imf.org/en/Publications/WP/Issues/2023/05/16/Nigerias-eNaira-One-Year-After-533487

Reserve Bank of Australia (RBA) (August 2023) Australian CBDC Pilot for Digital Finance Innovation: Project Report. https://www.rba.gov.au/payments-and-infrastructure/central-bank-digital-currency/pdf/australian-cbdc-pilot-for-digital-finance-innovation-project-report.pdf

Sarmiento A (2022) Seven lessons from the e-peso pilot plan: the possibility of a digital peso. Latin Am J Central Banking 3(2) https://www.sciencedirect.com/science/article/pii/S2666143822000175

Söderberg G, Bechara M, Bossu W, Che NX, Davidovic S, Kiff J, Lukonga I, Griffoli TM, Sun T, Yoshinaga A, et al (9 February 2022). Behind the Scenes of Central Bank Digital Currency: Emerging Trends, Insights, and Policy Lessons. *Fintech Notes* No. 2022/004, International Monetary Fund, https://www.imf.org/en/Publications/fintech-notes/Issues/2022/02/07/Behind-the-Scenes-of-Central-Bank-Digital-Currency-512174

Tourpe H, Lannquist A, Soderberg G (2023) A guide to central Bank digital currency product development: 5P methodology and Research and Development. IMF Fintech notes 2023/007. International Monetary Fund, Washington. September 8. https://www.imf.org/en/Publications/fintech-notes/Issues/2023/09/08/A-Guide-to-Central-Bank-Digital-Currency-Product-Development-538496

Tourpe H, Kiff J, Malaika M, Ostrowski C (2025) "Technology solutions to support central Bank digital currency with limited connectivity: review of existing approaches." Fintech note 2025/005. International Monetary Fund. August 7. https://www.imf.org/en/Publications/fintech-notes/Issues/2025/08/07/Technology-Solutions-to-Support-Central-Bank-Digital-Currency-with-Limited-Connectivity-A-569259

Ueda K, Hay C (2024) Design of a CBDC in a Highly Dollarized Emerging Market Economy: The Case of Cambodia. Asian Economic Policy Review, 19: 272–290. https://onlinelibrary.wiley.com/doi/full/10.1111/aepr.12464

U.S. Congress. Senate (2025) Guiding and Establishing National Innovation for U.S. Stablecoins Act. S. 1582. 119th Cong., 1st sess. https://www.congress.gov/bill/119th-congress/senate-bill/1582/text

White House (23 January 2025) Strengthening American Leadership in Digital Financial Technology. Executive Order. https://www.whitehouse.gov/presidential-actions/2025/01/strengthening-american-leadership-in-digital-financial-technology/

Yang P (11 June 2021) "Central Bank's Mu Changchun: Digital RMB Wallets Are Divided Into Different Levels According to the Strength of Customer Identity Recognition." *China Securities Journal*, https://www.cs.com.cn/xwzx/hg/202106/t20210611_6175187.html

Taler as a Synthetic Central Bank Digital Currency

Christian Grothoff, Mikolai Gütschow, and Valentin Seehausen

Abstract A synthetic Central Bank Digital Currency (sCBDC) is a privately issued payment instrument fully backed by central bank liabilities. GNU Taler is a token-based digital payment system that offers a range of unique features to its users, pairing ease-of-use with payment privacy and informational self-determination. As it is Free Software, any retail bank can easily adopt the technology to create an sCBDC, benefiting from its unique features and low operational costs, while receiving risk-free interest rates from central bank reserves. Our work introduces the concept and contrasts it with related payment instruments.

Keywords Self-custody • Privacy • Retail • sCBDC • Business model

1 Introduction

This chapter will first give a definition of "tokens" inspired from their use in information security. We will then give some background on GNU Taler, the free-software (Free software Foundation 1996) reference implementation of the Taler payment system, which uses digital coins, a special type of token representing fiat currency ownership. (Dold 2019) Next, we elaborate on the requirements on

C. Grothoff
Bern University of Applied Sciences, Biel, Switzerland

GNU Taler, Biel, Switzerland
e-mail: christian@grothoff.org

M. Gütschow (✉)
GNU Taler, Biel, Switzerland

TUD Dresden University of Technology, Dresden, Germany
e-mail: mikolai.guetschow@tu-dresden.de

V. Seehausen
Digital Euro Association, Frankfurt, Germany
e-mail: valentin.seehausen@digital-euro-association.de

S. Yazıcı et al. (eds.), *Tokenisation of Money*, Contributions to Finance and Accounting, https://doi.org/10.1007/978-3-032-22946-5_9

synthetic CBDCs and how GNU Taler could be used to implement one. Finally, we will discuss the advantages and disadvantages of this approach, and compare it with existing alternatives, including so-called stablecoins and the proposed design for the "Digital Euro".

2 Definitions: Tokens and Nonces

Tokens represent units of value or rights to use a resource. In information security, bearer tokens allow the "bearers", that is anyone with knowledge of the token's representation, access to certain resources. Paper tokens are commonly used to represent the value of a ride on a local public transport and stamping them grants the owner a single-use ride after which the token is void. Nonces are **n**umbers that are only used **once** in cryptographic protocols to prevent replay attacks or linkability. Tokens can also be nonces for the same reasons: the buyer of a ticket for some attraction (be it a movie, bus or rollercoaster ride) is supposed to only use the token once (no replay), but also no information should be retained that would link multiple rides to the rider's identity. Such nonce-tokens thus have a key advantage: they allow individuals to prove that they have a right to certain resources without necessarily linking these rights to a history of transactions or even their identity.

Checking one-time tokens requires validators to ensure that the token was issued by the proper authority and has not yet been used. For digital tokens, the former is straightforward by checking if the token carries a digital signature from an acceptable authority. Preventing double-spending requires an online check at the time of the transaction with a database that either tracks the numeric values of all tokens that remain in circulation, or the numeric values of all tokens that have already been spent. Our definition of tokens differs from the use of the term "token" as a unit of value for some non-fiat currency in the context of ERC-20 tokens (Vogelsteller and Buterin 2015) and similar technologies.

3 GNU Taler

GNU Taler is the Free/Libre Open-Source Software (FLOSS) implementing the Taler protocol. FLOSS licenses grant their users the irrevocable right to (1) execute the software for any purpose, (2) read the source code (defined as the preferred format for making modifications), (3) make modifications to the source code, and (4) to share the modified sources (and derived executables) with third parties. These conditions are necessary for informational self-determination as otherwise the owner of the software is put into a position to control the use of the software. In the context of critical infrastructures, the use of FLOSS is a decisive factor for maintaining sovereignty. (Rangel and Armando 2009) The Taler protocol uses *coins* stored in wallets by their owners in self-custody.

Such coins are both nonces and tokens: they are unique bit-strings, are used only in relation to a single transaction, and have a fixed value due to a digital signature. They are issued by the payment service provider called *exchange*. However, Taler coins are not random bit-strings but have a slightly more complex token structure: Each coin is made out of a public-private key pair, where the hash of the public key is signed by the exchange. The private key is generated by the coin's owner and never disclosed to any other party. It is used to sign messages that authorize spending the coin.

When a wallet *withdraws* digital cash, they ask an exchange to digitally sign coins. Tokens are signed by the exchange in return for an incoming wire transfer from the respective customer. The wire transfer subject is used by the wallet to authenticate for the withdrawal of the corresponding amount of digital coins (Fig. 1). The Taler protocol uses *blind signatures (*Dold 2019*)*: Here, the wallet first *blinds* the token before sending it to the exchange to be signed. The resulting signature is then *unblinded*, resulting in a valid signature on the unblinded coin. These cryptographic operations performed by the wallet prevent the exchange from learning the unique value of the coin being signed. As a result,

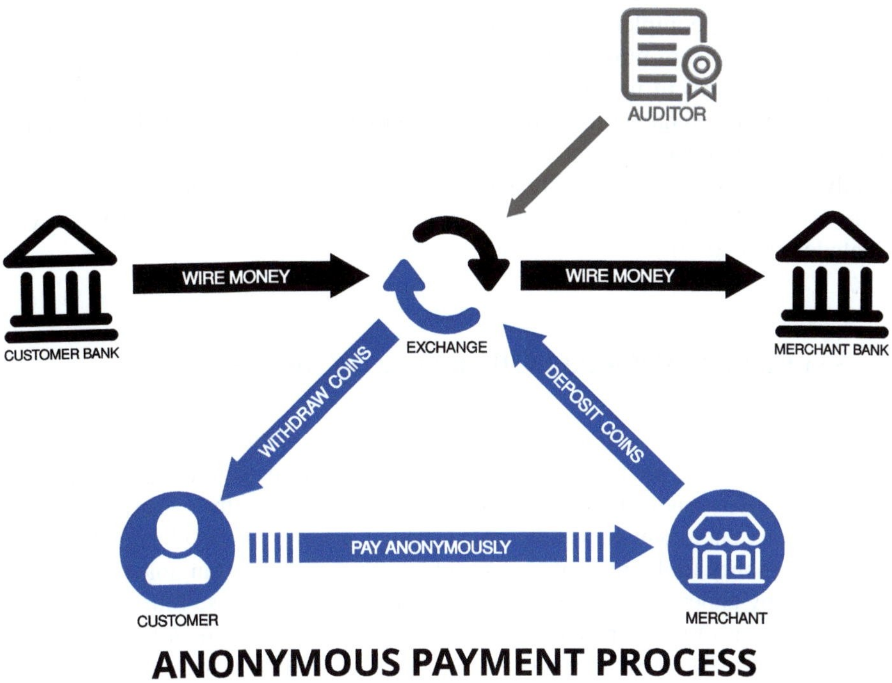

Fig. 1 Monetary flows in the Taler payment system. Value typically enters and exists the system through wire transfers. A customer *withdraws* blindly signed tokens from the *exchange*. During payments, they stay anonymous towards the payment provider. Merchants *deposit* the tokens instantly at the exchange and are thus identifiable

the exchange knows how many coins it issued, but does not know which customer has which coin. When coins are later *deposited*, the exchange can check its signature to determine that the coin is one that it issued, but it cannot link the deposited coin to the withdraw process. As a result, customers are identified when they withdraw funds, merchants are identified when they receive funds (enabling Anti-Money Laundering (AML) compliance), but customers can privately *spend* digital cash at merchants without these purchases being linkable to their identity.

A key difficulty with simplistic approaches to tokenizing assets is the need for giving change. If tokens have a fixed value and are used only in one transaction, it is not obvious how to ensure that buyers can pay arbitrary amounts with a small number of tokens. GNU Taler's *refresh* protocol provides a mechanism to efficiently give unlinkable change (Dold 2019) without negatively impacting other key properties of the protocol.

GNU Taler has shown to support more than 25′000 transactions per second on a single server with latencies dominated by a single network round-trip time with negligible costs per transaction. (Boss 2022) It can be safely used by merchants that are offline and is available on a broad range of platforms (Android, Chrome, F-Droid, Firefox, iOS, Ubuntu Touch, etc.). Integrations exist for various e--commerce solutions (Adobe E-Commerce, Drupal, Joomla!, Magento, Pretix, etc.). The code for the complete system and its integrations is publicly available under FLOSS licenses from https://git.taler.net/. Taler Operations is operating the GNU Taler payment system in Switzerland. The company issues digital coins denominated in CHF in exchange for wire transfers into its escrow account. The incoming funds are kept separate from the company's own assets and the business is not legally allowed to issue loans. The bank account is with PostFinance, which is also currently excluded from the credit and mortgage business by law (Swiss Confederation 2010).

4 Synthetic CBDCs and Other Types of Money

Money serves three basic purposes: unit of account, store of value, and medium of exchange (means of payment). While measuring the value of a certain good only needs commonly understood denominations irrespective of the concrete form of money, the extent to which the other two purposes are served may change. For most of history, money took physical forms such as coins, notes, or tangible goods, supplemented by paper-based account records. End-users would use fully anonymous cash as a means of payment and identifiable accounts as *commercial bank money* at retail banks mostly for savings and loans. Under a fractional reserve system, banks are not required to hold assets that would fully back all user deposits. Failed business strategies of retail banks, such as bad loans or investments, can thus put customer's savings at risk. Government policies often require retail bank deposits (commercial bank money) to be insured up to a certain limit, but insurance coverage is limited and state interventions are frequently used to bail out wealthy stakeholders when larger banks collapse. (Hu et al. 2023).

Regulated payment providers such as WeChat Pay, Alipay, M-Pesa or Taler Operations without banking licenses have started offering so-called *electronic money (e-money)*, where users hold a claim against the payment provider which promises convertibility at full face value to a certain (national) currency. (Adrian and Mancini Griffoli 2019) Such payment systems closely resemble traditional commercial bank accounts, including that they may only hold liquid assets sufficient to back regular net outflows with some safety margin. The key distinction between banks and e-money providers is that e-money providers are generally prohibited from giving out loans and investing in assets like stocks and equities. Furthermore, e-money, in contrast to commercial bank money, often cannot expect to benefit from government backing or deposit insurance.

Together, all such digital forms of money are increasingly displacing traditional cash controlled by the central bank, which is nevertheless presumed to anchor all of them. In face of this evolution, central banks have started investigating *Central Bank Digital Currencies (CBDCs)*: a digital form of money directly issued by a central bank instead of commercial banks or other financial intermediaries. Same as cash, a CBDC is a liability of the central bank, which entails that holders are not subject to insolvency risks of private financial institutes. Retail CBDCs, such as the envisioned Digital Euro (cf. Sect. 6.2), are available to the general public, i.e., private households and firms, while wholesale CBDCs are only offered to selected financial institutions, much like central bank reserves are usually only accessible to banks (Kumhof and Noone 2018).

Synthetic CBDCs (sCBDCs) are a middleground between these two options: Here, private financial institutions offer e-money to the general public, whose value is fully backed by the institution in central bank money (e.g., in the form of central bank reserves or a wholesale CBDC). While technically not a direct liability of the central bank (Cœure and Cunliffe 2020), such money is equivalent to a CBDC for most practical matters but has the advantage of possible competition between different operators. (Adrian and Mancini Griffoli 2019) From the perspective of asset backing, this is very similar to the concept of *narrow banks*, which back all their deposits by central bank reserves and sometimes government fonds. But while the focus of narrow banks lies on the store-of-value purpose of money, sCBDCs are rather meant to be used as a medium of exchange, as a potential competition to other forms of e-money that are backed in commercial bank money.

5 GNU Taler as sCBDC

To create an sCBDC with GNU Taler, one needs a private e-money operator who would issue digital cash of some fiat currency in return for incoming final wire transfers of the same currency. The operator would keep central bank money corresponding to the digital cash in circulation in an escrow account in the deposit facility of the respective central bank. By depositing 100% of the escrowed assets at the deposit facility, the operator would earn some modest risk-free interest from the central bank. Depending on the interest rate of the central bank, the resulting interest may even be sufficient to cover the cost of operating the payment system.[1]

However, the assets would still be at risk in cases where the operator were to go bankrupt, for example due to other business activities. To create an sCBDC that is risk-free in the same way that a CBDC would be, the operator would furthermore need to use asset segregation to ensure that the escrow account could not be used for other liabilities. Should the operator go bankrupt, GNU Taler's revocation mechanism could be used to notify wallets that their digital cash cannot be used for payments anymore. At that point, the wallets would deposit the digital cash back into each customer's bank account, erasing the remaining liability of the operator in a timely fashion. This would only reveal the remaining balance of each customer to the banking system; the transaction histories would remain private.

6 Alternative Approaches

This section discusses different forms of money that may serve a similar function as the sCBDC based on GNU Taler discussed above: Stablecoins, and the proposed design of the Digital Euro by the European Central Bank (ECB).

6.1 Stablecoins

Stablecoins are a distributed ledger-based payment instrument that is tied to assets in a fiat currency. They emerged as a variation on e-money promising to bridge highly volatile, unregulated and decentralized cryptocurrencies. In contrast to regulated e-money providers, early stablecoin operators often operated without any regard to regulation. As a result, the legal status of stablecoin assets was—and in some cases remains—unclear (Bullmann et al. 2019).

Most current implementations of stablecoins use an account-based model. They are smart contracts, which define the rules for alternations of account balances on a blockchain, for example ERC20 "tokens" on the Ethereum Virtual Machine (EVM).

In theory, the owner of the account can have full custody over the keys to spend money from the account. In practice, however, many users prefer the simplicity of custodial wallets where the keys are held by a fully trusted third party. In any case, there are no individual stablecoins and no tokens in the sense of our technical definition which have an inherent value.

---

[1] Should central bank interest rates be negative, the operator would have to charge fees including possibly holding fees from its customers. GNU Taler's *refresh fees* combined with expiration dates on coins in circulation could be used to implement a demurrage currency.

The term "stablecoin", apart from wrongly suggesting a bearer instrument similar to physical coins, also promises stability of the asset. However, many stablecoins that were said to be pegged to a fiat currency lost their "peg" after a certain amount of time. (Di Maggio 2024; Liu et al. 2023; Zack Abrams 2022) Some stablecoin issuers have pursued and received regulatory approvals, and some, like Gemini, subsequently ran into trouble for misrepresentation of their operations towards these regulators (Commodity Futures Trading Commission (CFTC) 2025).

Contemporary regulated stablecoins operations are designed like traditional e-money, often resembling a *narrow bank* (Kay 2009) with a reserve made up of high-quality liquid assets, which provides stability. These regulated operations mostly distinguish themselves from traditional e-money systems by their marketing and support for integration with distributed ledgers. The key difference between an sCBDC and the operation of a stablecoin is that the latter can include government securities in its backing. Given that interest rate changes on government securities can cause these assets to rapidly lose in value, this model is thus strictly less stable for investors (but possibly more profitable for operators) than what is required for an sCBDC.

Over the history of stablecoin development, diverse sets of user groups emerged, each with distinct motivations for adopting stablecoins. Initially, stablecoin users were mostly crypto-native actors: traders, liquidity providers, and early DeFi adopters. Their motivations include the desire to hedge volatility, park liquidity between trades, and maintain assets on-chain instead of exposing them to traditional banking. Stablecoins serve as a de facto unit of account and base currency for decentralized exchanges, lending markets, and yield farming protocols (Auer et al. 2023). This usage pattern reflects a preference for composability, and autonomy over traditional financial products.

In countries with unstable monetary systems, stablecoins became a tool to hold US dollar denominated assets without the need for a bank account. Individuals use stablecoins to preserve purchasing power, remit funds internationally, and circumvent capital controls. Particularly in regions with high inflation or limited access to foreign exchange markets, stablecoins represent a practical alternative to both local fiat currencies and formal financial institutions. Stablecoins bypassed the regulatory complexity and cost associated with foreign exchange conversions and international transfers. By easing the transfer of dollar-denominated assets globally without friction, stablecoins enable borderless payroll. Bypassing the traditional banking system also makes such income harder to trace for tax authorities and creates opportunities for tax evasion (Moura de Carvalho et al. 2024).

6.2 *The Digital Euro*

The most prominent and obvious alternative to a synthetic CBDC is a native retail CBDC: A digital form of central bank money that could be accessed by citizens and merchants. The Digital Euro, a CBDC proposed by the European Central Bank

(ECB), has been in the planning phase for several years at the time of this writing (European Central Bank 2024b).

The current design consists of two parts. The offline version is based on so-called "secure hardware" which is supposed to prevent double-spending while at the same time promising transitive anonymity subject to limits enforced by the hardware. However, given that hardware security modules under physical control of an adversary have a horrific track record (Grothoff and Dold 2021), we predict that the offline version will not be secure and thus does not warrant further discussion.

In the online version citizens are provided with a limited bank account at the central bank administered by private payment service providers (PSPs). Different to common bank accounts, these will be interest free and subject to a holding limit which is claimed to be necessary to ensure financial stability of the contemporary commercial bank system (European Central Bank 2024a), even though there are other options of mitigating the risk of bank runs (Groß et al. 2020). The holding limit for non-business users is discussed to be around 3000 euros (European Central Bank 2023), while business users will have a holding limit of zero.

As the Digital Euro becomes legal tender, merchants will be required to accept it. This mandate may entail significant adaptation costs, as businesses will need to update their payment systems, train staff, and implement additional measures to integrate the Digital Euro into their operations. Furthermore, banks and payment service providers (PSPs) must incorporate the new currency into their existing infrastructures and applications. These adjustments represent economy-wide costs—an unintended side effect of introducing the Digital Euro.

While economists debate whether there is any need for a Digital Euro (Navarrete 2025), concerns about privacy are prevalent among citizens. (ECB 2021) Some political actors have gone so far as to suggest that the Digital Euro could become a tool of surveillance and control. Not all actors share the European Central Bank (ECB)'s self-assessment as an eternally trustworthy custodian of a central database of financial transactions of all citizens. (d'Aligny et al. 2022) This is especially true as the current ECB design would enable linking transactions back to individuals (De Montjoye et al. 2015)—in sharp contrast to the Taler protocol, but similar to account-based stablecoins and commercial bank money.

7 Discussion

Table 1 provides an overview of the design choices made for the different types of money discussed in this chapter. Key questions for their viability and success are (1) why citizens should put their money into the respective asset category *(demand)*, and (2) what economic incentives exist for the profitable operation of such systems *(supply)*. The common selling point of CBDCs, sCBDCs and stablecoins is their promised value stability, either backed by central bank deposits, or government bonds and other high-liquidity assets. While several stablecoins have failed to hold up to this claim, both CBDCs and sCBDCs would only be subject to the volatility

Table 1 Comparison of different forms of money. From none to fully: ○, ◔, ◑, ◕, ●

Aspect	Design space	Cash	Comm. bank	Stable-coins	Digital Euro	GNU Taler (sCBDC)
Purpose	Store of value	◑	●	◑	◔	◔
	Medium of exchange	●	◕	◑	●	●
Backing	Central bank (reserves)	●	◔	○	●	●
	Government bonds	○	◔	●	○	○
Liability/Issuer	Private sector	○	●	●	○	●
	Central bank	●	○	○	●	○
Medium	Analog/hardware	●	◔	○	◔	○
	Digital/software	○	◕	●	●[b]	●
Privacy	Payer	●	○	◑	◔	●
	Payee	●	○	◑	◔[b]	○
Instrument	Account	○	●	◕[a]	◕	○
	Token	●	○	◔[a]	◔[b]	●
Architecture	Centralized	○	●	◑	●	●
	Decentralized	●	○	◕[c]	◔[b,c]	●[c]

[a] Both design choices are made, accounts are more common.
[b] The envisioned offline version suggests a form of tokenization which relies on trusted hardware and promises transitive anonymity.
[c] Tokens may be held under self-custody in a decentralized manner.

of the underlying currency that is arising from socio-economic factors including the monetary policy of the respective central bank, same as today's monetary anchor, cash. The demand for stablecoins is driven by their reduced regulatory or technical complexity for users who do not have a bank account in the respective currency or who need a fiat-currency to enter cryptocurrency trading. Stablecoins also enabled illegal activities including circumvention of capital-controls (Foley et al. 2019).

The proponents of the Digital Euro sometimes point to offline payments as a key unique sales proposition in terms of usability. However, as long as physical cash remains an option, its usability properties will remain hard to beat. That is especially true as cash avoids the regulatory compliance checks the European Central Bank (ECB) intends to impose on the Digital Euro. Instead of technical superiority to contemporary payment systems, the mandatory acceptance of the Digital Euro in virtually all points-of-sale across the Eurozone will be its most important advantage for citizens—at the likely very high cost of integration for merchants, indirectly covered by society at large. On the other hand, Taler as an sCBDC would offer a tangible improvement over the current payment system landscape by offering privacy-preserving one-click payments without customer traceability and identification at checkout. In addition, its account-less architecture with digital cash held in self-custody alleviates the burden of complex multi-factor account authentication. Compared to physical cash, the withdrawal of digital cash is possible anytime and from any place with Internet connectivity.

Apart from these benefits for users, pairing value stability with payer privacy and a frictionless user experience, offering an sCBDC based on Taler is also profitable for payment system operators: The reference implementation GNU Taler is Free Software, translating to low acquisition and maintenance costs. The centralized architecture allows for cost savings related to regulatory compliance compared to the distributed protocols at the base of stablecoins. It also enables higher transaction rates than distributed consensus algorithms. Self-custody of the token-based Taler payment system reduces the need for complex and costly user authentication as is the case for all account-based systems including most stablecoins and the Digital Euro. At the same time, the operator can earn risk-free interest with the users' deposits, as long as the central bank offers positive interest rates on reserves. In sharp contrast, banks would be legally required to distribute the Digital Euro without clear compensation for integration, onboarding, or support costs.

8 Conclusion

Payment instruments have historically emerged in response to practical needs: facilitating exchange, managing credit, supporting savings and lending, or adapting to political and regulatory constraints. As an example, the emergence of account-based e-money and stablecoins enabled efficient transactions at a global scale, but those systems fell short on payment privacy compared to cash. Today, the primary justification for introducing a Digital Euro appears to be reinforcing European monetary sovereignty, rather than advancing privacy, security, or usability. Given its limited technical innovation and proposed caps such as a €3000 holding limit, the Digital Euro offers few compelling reasons for widespread voluntary adoption, particularly considering the integration costs for merchants and payment providers.

In contrast, private and FLOSS-based initiatives like GNU Taler demonstrate how synthetic CBDCs can address both sovereignty and user demands. Fully backed by central bank reserves, a Taler-based synthetic CBDC could offer the same monetary stability while also providing privacy, self-custody, and operational efficiency—qualities that encourage voluntary adoption through genuine utility rather than through coercive mechanisms.

Tokenizing fiat currencies is just one possible application of the Taler protocol. Other fungible classes of assets could equally be used to back Taler tokens, including stocks, equities, precious metals or durable chemicals. Tokenized stocks in self-custody may lower costs by cutting out today's deposit and brokerage services. Tokenized precious metals would make payments in those assets easier because dealing with tiny amounts becomes practical. Furthermore, cryptographic signature validation would replace checking the substance of the asset in every transaction. Citizens in countries with disreputable central banks might prefer such asset-backed tokens over digital fiat. Regardless of the issuer or the backing asset they would benefit from the usability, scalabilty and payer anonymity guarantees enabled by tokenization.

Acknowledgements We thank Bernd Lucke and Özgür Kesim for constructive feedback on an earlier draft of this chapter. This work was supported by the German Federal Ministry of Research, Technology and Space under grant ConcreteContracts. This work was funded in part by the European Commission through the Horizon Europe program under project number 101135475 (TALER). It also has received funding from the Swiss State Secretariat for Education, Research and Innovation (SERI).

The opinions, findings, and conclusions or recommendations expressed are those of the authors and do not necessarily reflect those of any of the funding agencies or affiliated institutions.

References

Adrian T, Mancini Griffoli T (2019) The rise of digital money. FinTech notes. International Monetary Fund, Washington, D.C. https://doi.org/10.5089/9781498324908.063

Auer R, Doerr S, Frost J et al (2023) The Technology of Decentralised Finance (DeFi). BIS working papers no. 1066. Bank for International Settlements. https://doi.org/10.2139/ssrn.4431521

Boss M (2022) GNU Taler scalability: measuring and improving the performance of GNU Taler on Grid'5000. B.S. thesis. Bern University of Applied Sciences

Bullmann D, Klemm J, Pinna A (2019) In search for stability in crypto-assets: are Stablecoins the solution? ECB occasional paper no. 230. European Central Bank. https://doi.org/10.2139/ssrn.3444847

Cœure B, Cunliffe J (2020) Central Bank digital currencies: foundational Prin-ciples and Core features: report no. 1 in a series of collaborations from a Group of Central Banks. Bank for International Settlements, Basel

Commodity Futures Trading Commission (CFTC) (2025) Gemini Trust Ordered to pay $5 Million for Making False or Misleading Statements, Omissions to the CFTC. https://www.cftc.gov/PressRoom/PressReleases/9031-25

d'Aligny A, Benoist E, Dold F et al (2022) Who comes after us? The cor-rect mindset for designing a central bank digital currency. SUERF Policy Note 279:1–9

De Montjoye YA, Radaelli L, Singh VK et al (2015) Unique in the shopping mall: on the reidentifiability of credit card metadata. Science 347(6221):536–539. https://doi.org/10.1126/science.1256297

Di Maggio M (2024) Blockchain, crypto and DeFi: bridging finance and technology. John Wiley & Sons, pp 198–199

Dold F (2019) The GNU Taler system: practical and provably secure electronic payments. PhD thesis. University of Rennes, p 1

ECB (2021) Eurosystem report on the public consultation on a digi-tal euro. https://www.ecb.europa.eu/pub/pdf/other/Eurosystemreportonthepublicconsultationonadigitaleuro539fa8cd8d.en.pdf

European Central Bank (2023) Financial stability review. https://www.ecb.europa.eu/press/financial-stability-publications/fsr/html/ecb.fsr202311bfe9d7c565.en.html

European Central Bank (2024a) Progress on the preparation phase of a digital euro-first progress report. https://www.ecb.europa.eu/euro/digitaleuro/progress/html/ecb.deprp202406.en.html

European Central Bank (2024b) Timeline of the Digital Euro Project. https://www.ecb.europa.eu/euro/digitaleuro/progress/shared/pdf/241202-timeline-digital-euro-project.en.pdf

Foley S, Karlsen JR, Putnins TJ (2019) Sex, drugs, and Bitcoin: how much illegal activity is financed through Cryptocurrencies? Rev Financ Stud 32(5):1798–1853. https://doi.org/10.1093/rfs/hhz015

Free Software Foundation (1996) What is free software? https://gnu.org/philosophy/free-sw.html

Groß J, Klein M, Sandner P (2020) Digitale zentralbankw¨ahrungen: Chancen, risiken und blockchain-technologie. Wirtschaftsdienst 100(7):545–549. https://doi.org/10.1007/s10273-020-2702-7

Grothoff C, Dold F (2021) Why a digital Euro should be online-first and bearer-based. Tech. rep., The GNU Taler Project

Hu K, Tong A, Dastin J, et al (2023) Silicon valley exhales after us intervenes in SVB collapse. https://www.reuters.com/business/finance/silicon-valley-exhales-after-us-intervenes-svb-collapse-2023-03-13/

Kay J (2009) Narrow Banking: The Reform of Bank-ing Regulation. Center for the Study of Financial Innova-tion, https://bankunderground.co.uk/wp-content/uploads/2016/07/c8439-narrowbanking2cthereformofbankingregulation2cbyjohnkay.pdf

Kumhof M, Noone C (2018) Central Bank digital currencies - design principles and balance sheet implications. SSRN Electron J. https://doi.org/10.2139/ssrn.3180713

Liu J, Makarov I, Schoar A (2023) Anatomy of a Run: The Terra Luna Crash. NBER Working Paper w31160

Moura de Carvalho R, Inacio H, Marques RP (2024) An empirical analysis of tax evasion among companies engaged in Stablecoin transactions. J Risk Financial Manag 17:400. https://doi.org/10.3390/jrfm17090400

Navarrete F (2025) Do we really need a digital euro? a solution to what problem exactly? Tech. rep., C'ırculo de Empresarios

Rangel M, Armando E (2009) IT policies for development: analysis and rec-ommendations of free/libre open source software initiatives of the Bolivarian Republic of Venezuela. PhD thesis. Pennsylvania State University

Swiss Confederation (2010) Federal Act on the Organisation of Swiss Post. https://www.fedlex.admin.ch/eli/cc/2010/823/de, sR783.1; Stand — 19 Dec 2020

Vogelsteller F, Buterin V (2015) ERC-20 Token Standard: Interface for Tokens. https://eips.ethereum.org/EIPS/eip-20, ethereum Improvement Proposal 20

Zack Abrams (2022) Stablecoins can crash, too—why Neutrino USD's wild swings spell trouble. https://www.businessofbusiness.com/articles/stablecoins-can-crash-too-heres-why-neutrino-usds-wild-swings-spell-trouble-for-the-assets/

Retail Central Bank Digital Currencies: An Inevitable Innovation for the Stability of the Monetary System in the Digital Age

Inutu Lukonga

Abstract Central banks world wide are exploring the case for retail central bank digital currencies (CBDCs) as a complement to cash, but opinions on their necessity remain divided. Proponents emphasize CBDCs' potential to enhance financial inclusion and payment system efficiency, while skeptics contend that existing payment systems are already efficient and that the risks of CBDCs outweigh their benefits. This paper contends that currency issuance and payments are too critical to be left solely to profit-driven private actors, thus CBDCs are unavoidable if cash usage continues to decline and commerce continues to shift to online. It further suggests that skepticism about CBDCs stems from a narrow focus on their potential benefits rather than recognizing the potential role of CBDCs as an anchor of trust and stability in an increasingly digital monetary system. Given the complexity of CBDCs, the debate should shift from questinoning their necessity to focus on how to prepare for effective implementation.

Keywords Retail central bank digital currencies (CBDCs) · Payments · Technology · Monetary system · Financial stability

1 Introduction

The use of physical cash in transactions is declining globally, reflecting the combined effects of technological advancements, the digitalization of economies and evolving policy and regulatory frameworks. Mobile phones, particularly smart phones, have made digital transactions more accessible, facilitating the shift from paper-based payment methods to faster and more convenient digital

I. Lukonga (✉)
Lukonga Global Consulting LLC, Vienna, VA, USA

S. Yazıcı et al. (eds.), *Tokenisation of Money*, Contributions to Finance and Accounting, https://doi.org/10.1007/978-3-032-22946-5_10

alternatives.[1,2] The growth of e-commerce has further diminished the relevance of cash in transactions, a trend further accelerated by the COVID-19 pandemic. Many governments have also increasingly advocated for cashless societies to reduce informality and promote financial inclusion while regulatory changes, such as "open banking", facilitated the entry of new players, including technology companies, that have accelerated innovation in the payments industry.[3]

The decline in cash usage risks creating a monetary and payment system that is shaped and controlled by private actors. While private entities may offer innovative, convenient and efficient services, their dominance in payments could undermine the effectiveness of monetary policy, threaten monetary sovereignty and compromise public policy goals such as financial inclusion and consumer protection. Further, without central bank money to preserve the singleness of money, the proliferation of private currencies could lead to fragmentation in the payment system. As private issuers are driven by commercial motives, they can also exit markets abruptly, weakening payment system's overall resilience. Thus a balanced payment ecosystem, where public and private sectors play complementary roles, is needed to ensure stability, security, and equity.

A retail Central Bank Digital Currency (CBDC), hereafter referred to simply as a CBDC, offers central banks the opportunity to design money in a format that aligns with consumer preferences and the demands of the digital economy while also preserving their role in currency issuance and payments. Many central banks are, therefore, assessing the technical feasibility and policy implications of a CBDC as a complement to physical cash.[4] Even in economies where policy makers have stated that there is no immediate need to issue a CBDC, central banks are undertaking the technical groundwork to ensure that they are prepared, should conditions change.[5] International organizations such as the Bank for International Settlement (BIS) are also contributing to CBDC exploration through applied technology research, proofs of concept (POCs) and prototypes in collaboration with central banks around the world. Others, including the World Bank and the International Monetary Fund (IMF), provide support through capacity-building programs and analytical work.

[1] Paper-based payment methods include physical cash (notes and coins) and cheques, while digital payment methods encompass debit and credit cards, mobile money platforms (eg., M-Pesa, WeChat Pay), and digital wallets (such as PayPal, Google Pay, and Apple Pay) which facilitate digital transactions by storing and transferring electronic money (e-money).

[2] The convenience of cards, mobile applications (Apps), Quick Response (QR) codes, and digital wallet payment systems is further accelerating the use of electronic payments.

[3] Open banking regulations require banks to provide third-party providers with access to payment services and customer data through secure Application Programming Interfaces (APIs).

[4] According to the Atlantic council, by the end of February 2025, more than 130 jurisdictions were exploring CBDCs, of which 3 (The Bahamas, Nigeria and Jamaica) had fully launched CBDCs, 44 were conducting pilot programs, 29 were under development and 39 were undertaking research, 21 were inactive and 2 were canceled.

[5] For instance Canada, Japan, Korea, Singapore, Thailand, and the United Kingdom (UK).

But despite sustained research and pilot projects suggesting that CBDCs could become widespread, the future trajectory of CBDCs remains uncertain, as differing opinions persist regarding their necessity. Proponents often cite potential benefits such as promoting financial inclusion, reducing currency management costs, increasing competition, and improving payment efficiency as key motivations for considering CBDC issuance (BIS 2021). Skeptics, on the other hand, argue that cash remains widely available and accepted for payments, well-regulated stablecoins offer viable alternatives, retail payment systems are already efficient, financial inclusion can be achieved through other means, risks associated with CBDCs may outweigh the benefits and that a decline in cash alone may not pose substantial risks to monetary and financial stability.[6] Others (Michel and Anthony 2023) strongly oppose CBDCs, citing privacy risks and potential for government surveillance.

The paper argues that skepticism about the necessity of CBDCs is a result of conflating the core objectives of CBDCs with their potential benefits rather than recognizing CBDCs as a modern evolution of central bank money. The significant technological components of CBDCs have also resulted in technology companies driving the narrative about CBDCs, and the technocentric focus has overshadowed the foundational purpose of CBDCs, such as the singleness of money and stability anchor highlighted by central bank policy makers, such as Ingves (2018), Panetta (2022), Toronto Center (2023) and Bank of England (2023). Concerns among financial intermediaries about the potential impact of CBDCs on deposit bases, revenue streams, and their role in financial intermediation have also fueled resistance and further skewed the debate. CBDCs could, however, become unavoidable if the declining trend in cash usage and migration of commerce to online platforms continues. Currency issuance and payments are too important to leave solely to profit motivated private entities and the anchor role of central bank money will need to be maintained irrespective of technological innovations.

The paper further posits that because a CBDC is a novel and complex undertaking, the debate should shift from focusing on the necessity of a CBDC to how to implement CBDCs effectively. Implementing a CBDC is not an easy task and the challenge is compounded by the limited real-world experience, as CBDCs have only been operational in three countries for short durations. Further, while existing studies on CBDC related risks (Atlantic council 2022; BIS 2023a, c) have addressed specific concerns, there is a gap in studies that identify the full range of implementation challenges. Adequate preparations are, therefore, essential for a seamless integration of CBDCs into the current framework.

This paper focuses on a two-tiered retail CBDCs and adopts the following structure.[7] Section 2 discusses the role of CBDCs within the broader monetary system, distinguishing the core objectives from potential benefits. Section 3 outlines the

[6] For instance Australia, Denmark, Switzerland, Singapore, UK, and US, along with some industry associations in the US, Waller (2021), Independent Community of Bankers of America (2022) (Bowman (2023), Quarles (2021), Sultanum (2022) and Knogstrup (2023).

[7] A two-tiered, non-interest-bearing CBDC is the design of choice among countries (Box 1). Wholesale CBDCs are gaining traction but they are being covered in a companion paper.

rationale for CBDC adoption in the context of the ongoing digitalization and payment system modernization. Section 4 summarizes the findings of the study and emerging conclusions.

2 An Overview of CBDCs

A CBDC is a digital form of fiat money issued by the central bank in the national currency, intended for use by the public in everyday transactions. It is a liability of the central bank, carries legal tender status and functions as a unit of account, store of value, and medium of exchange. It is a third form of central bank money and an integral component of the monetary system, effectively serving as a digital bank note.

2.1 CBDCs and the Current Monetary System

The current monetary system is based on the co-existence of central bank and private money and on their convertibility at par. Central bank money consists of banknotes — currently the only form accessible to the general public and are in physical form only — and commercial bank reserves held at the central bank in digital form. Private money consists primarily of commercial bank deposits but technological advances and evolving regulatory changes have enabled non-bank entities to issue new forms of retail money, including electronic money (e-money), tokenized deposits and stablecoins (Fig. 1). The one-to-one convertibility between central bank and private money allows the two to be used interchangeably, enabling the smooth functioning of payment systems.

CBDCs, stablecoins, and tokenized deposits can be viewed as points along a continuum of tokenized monetary instruments, differentiated primarily by their issuers, governance arrangements, and risk characteristics. All three leverage distributed ledger or tokenization technologies to enable faster, programmable, and more efficient payments. The safety and liquidity of these instruments, however, varies considerably, with important implications for monetary sovereignty, financial stability, and payment system resilience depending on whether the underlying liability rests with a central bank, a commercial bank, or a private issuer.

- CBDCs are a direct digital liability of the central bank — the safest and most liquid form of money. As a liability of the central bank, CBDCs carry no credit or liquidity risk and derive their stability from the central banks' credibility as the issuer, supported by its mandate and track record in maintaining price stability through sound monetary policy.
- In the middle of the spectrum are commercial bank deposits and tokenized deposits, which are digital representations of claims on regulated commercial banks. These instruments remain fully integrated into the prudential and monetary

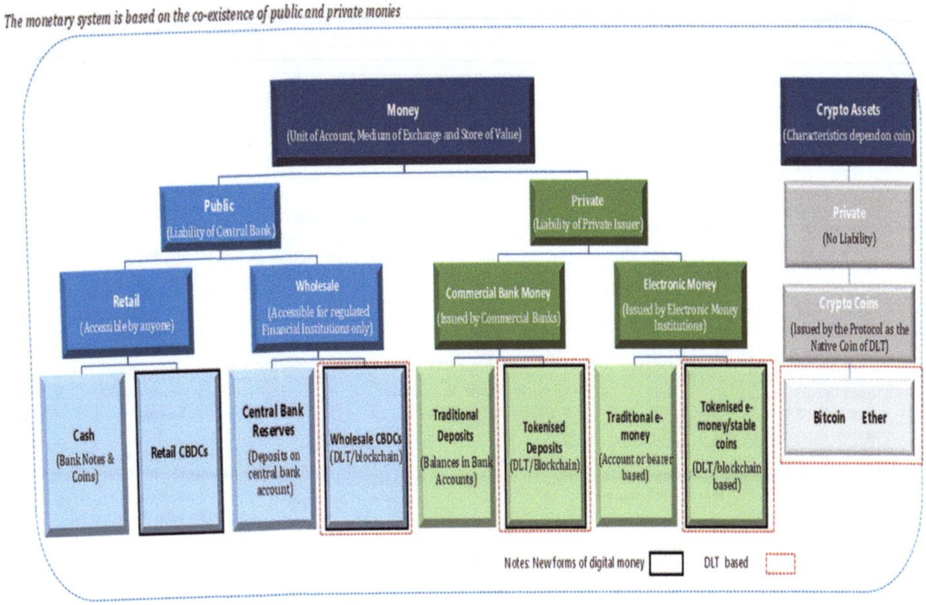

Fig. 1 The current monetary system

policy framework. Confidence in commercial bank money is reinforced by institutional safeguards, such as regulatory oversight, deposit insurance, the ability to move deposits across banks, access to lender of last resort (LoLR) facilities, and the guarantee that the deposits can be withdrawn in cash at par on demand.

- At the other end of the spectrum are stablecoins — privately issued tokens that may be pegged to sovereign currencies or commodities, or in some cases, rely on algorithmic mechanisms rather than collateral to stabilize their value. The value of stablecoins depends on the soundness of the stabilization mechanism, including the quality and liquidity of reserves and the issuers credibility, but these mechanisms may fail under market stress. Unlike bank deposits, stablecoins lack institutional safeguards such as prudential regulation, deposit insurance and LOLR access, making them more susceptible to runs.[8]

Central banks and commercial banks have traditionally played complementary roles (Fig. 2). Commercial bank money support economic activity by funding loans, investments, and day-to-day payments. Transactions are, however, ultimately settled in central bank money, which eliminates counterparty risk, ensures finality, and underpins trust in the financial system. This settlement function makes central bank money essential for both payment system integrity and overall monetary stability.

[8] The safeguards that commercial bank deposits enjoy also vary as not all countries have deposit insurance schemes. For stablecoins, convertibility to central bank money can vary and may not always be redeemable at par.

The roles of central bank and privately issued monies are complementary and not substitutable

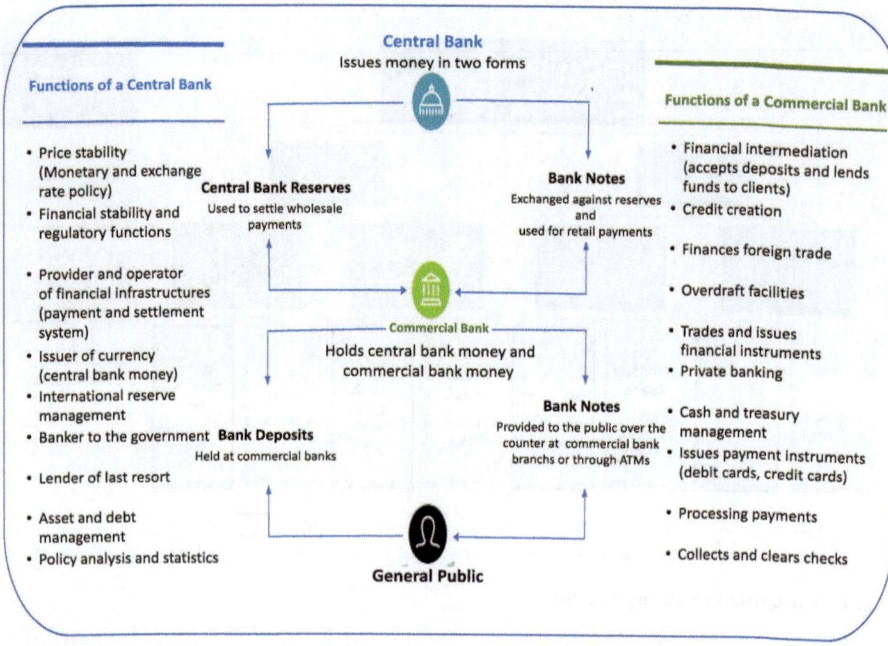

Fig. 2 The differential roles of central banks and commercial entities

Cash — the only form of central bank money directly accessible to the public — accounts for a small share of money supply in many countries, but it plays a critical role in anchoring trust in retail payments.[9] Cash is universally accepted, serves as the reference value for transactions, and underpins the convertibility of private money at par, thereby supporting the singleness of money.[10] The ability to convert private money — such as bank deposits or, where applicable stablecoins — into cash at Automatic Teller Machines (ATMs) or through the over the counter (OTC) withdrawals reinforces confidence in private issuers. Absent this convertibility, the public would have to continually assess the soundness of each issuer and might avoid holding some types of private money, leading to fragmentation in the payment system.[11][12]

[9] Cash as a share of money supply accounts for less than 10 percent in many countries (see Chart 3D).

[10] Commercial bank money is created through acceptance of deposits and lending activities in a fractional reserve system.

[11] Singleness of money is the principle that all different forms of money denominated in the same currency must be exchangeable with each other at par and is fundamental to monetary and financial stability.

[12] This explains why two banks may have different stock prices, but deposits held with them have the same value, allowing people to confidently open bank accounts without needing to scrutinize individual banks financial health.

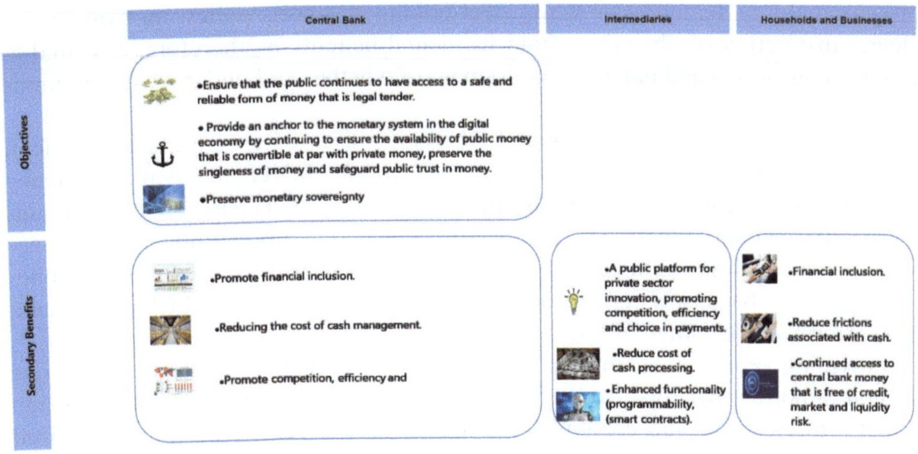

Fig. 3 Objectives of a CBDC versus its benefits

Historical experience shows that bank runs and financial crises often occur when confidence in an intermediary's capacity to convert deposits into cash is eroded. Similar dynamics are observed in stablecoin markets: when confidence in an issuer's capacity to maintain the peg weakens, investors rapidly redeem their holdings, triggering run-like behavior and destabilizing payment flows. These episodes underscore the unique stabilizing effects of cash (Panetta (2021), Cipollone (2024), Ingves (2018) and Jordan (2024)).

With consumers increasingly preferring digital payments, CBDCs would provide the public with a digital form of central bank money, thereby preserve the coexistence of central bank and private money in the digital era. CBDCs would be convertible at par with other forms of money and play the same stabilizing and unifying role as cash. Achieving these benefits, however, requires a careful design to ensure that CBDCs add value for users, complement rather than crowd out private innovation, avoid risks to financial intermediation and remain safe, secure and resilient to cyber risks and system failure (see Panetta 2022, Cipollone 2024).

2.2 *Objectives Versus Benefits of CBDCs*

A CBDC has clear and distinct policy objectives, alongside a set of complementary benefits that may materialize once it is introduced (Fig. 3). The current dialogue on CBDCs, however, often conflates objectives and benefits and this blurring of lines between these two concepts is contributing to skepticism about the necessity for a CBDC. Concerns about potential bank deposit disintermediation and related financial stability implications have further fueled private sector lobbying against CBDCs and reinforced institutional resistance. More broadly, debates sometimes elevate secondary or hypothetical advantages — such as operational efficiency or programmability features — while overlooking the core policy motivations. A clearer distinction of objectives from incidental benefits is, therefore, essential to enable an informed and balanced assessment of whether and under what conditions CBDCs should be pursued.

The primary objective of issuing CBDCs is to preserve the central bank's role in currency issuance and maintain public access to safe, universally available money in economies that are increasingly becoming digital. Even as payment technologies evolve, the "anchor" function of central bank money remains essential for monetary and financial stability. This anchor role must be preserved irrespective of technological change because a core attribute of money is trust without which money cannot perform its fundamental functions.

Providing central bank money to the public in digital form can also generate several important benefits. Advances in technology enable central banks to design CBDCs that can expand capabilities of money and support a range of localized public policy goals, such as financial inclusion, enhanced payment system efficiency, stronger resilience and enhanced financial integrity. A CBDC could improve financial inclusion by reaching populations without banking infrastructure[13]; enhance payment system efficiency through faster, 24/7 transactions, reduce the cost of cash issuance and distribution, bolster resilience by offering alternatives during network outages, and create transparent, auditable transaction trails that strengthen financial integrity frameworks.[14] While these benefits meaningfully influence design choices and timeline for CBDC issuance, they remain secondary advantages —and not the raison d'être — for issuing CBDCs.[15]

The relative importance of these benefits varies according to each country's economic, social, and technological conditions, which explains the diversity of motivations highlighted in national CBDC strategies. In economies such as Sweden, and Norway —where cash usage has significantly declined — concerns about payment system resilience and ensuring continued access to public money are driving interest in CBDCs. For Island economies like The Bahamas, the high cost of distributing and securing physical cash across dispersed populations was a major catalyst for early adoption. In jurisdictions with higher cash usage, such as in The Bahamas, Jamaica, and Nigeria, policy goals related to financial inclusion, reducing informality, and strengthening anti-money laundering and tax compliance frameworks have driven interest in CBDCs. Others, such as the European Central Bank (ECB), are further motivated by the need to safeguard monetary sovereignty and counter the influence of stablecoins and foreign providers' dominance.

---

[13] All digital payments make it easier to reach the underserved but CBDCs are uniquely positioned to do so because central banks have a policy objective to ensure that everyone has access to a safe means of payment.

[14] If cash usage declines, its effectiveness as a backup, its role as an anchor of stability in payments and the monetary system all diminish.

[15] Issuing treasury bills electronically introduces efficiencies in issuance and storage, but it does not alter their function as government short-term debt. Similarly, issuing a digital version of cash does not change the fundamentals of currency either.

Skepticism and resistance toward CBDCs arise both from a conflation of CBDCs core policy objectives with their broader, secondary benefits, and from concerns about their potential impact on the banking system. Traditionally, money and payments have been shaped by central banks, economists and financial institutions, but the technology-driven nature of CBDCs has brought technology firms more prominently into the discussion. These actors often approach CBDCs primarily through a technological lens, shifting the narrative away from CBDCs role in the broader monetary system. At the same time, apprehensions that CBDCs could weaken banks' revenue models or disrupt their intermediary function have amplified institutional resistance.

3 The Case for a CBDC

3.1 The Need for an Inclusive Payment System

The retail payment system—built on physical cash and private digital monies —continues to serve society well, but retail payments are witnessing a seismic shift from cash towards digital instruments.[16] Though a "*cashless society*" isn't on the immediate horizon nor desirable and cash remains essential in many economies,[17,18] the declining trend in the use of cash for transactions is unlikely to reverse given the migration of commerce to online, and the ease and convenience of digital means of payment.

Cash on Delivery (COD)—once an important mechanism for those without digital access or for consumers that are highly risk averse to digital fraud and cyberattacks—now represents a small and steadily shrinking share of retail payments. Merchants and delivery providers face higher costs and operational risks when handling cash, while an increasing number of consumers are opting for faster, integrated checkout experience. As a result, despite COD's advantages as a hedge against cyber and fraud risks and as an entry point for those without digital means of payments to participate in the digital economy, COD's use has been declining as the broader payments and e-commerce ecosystem increasingly favor digital prepayment (Fig. 4a–f).

[16] The share of cash in GDP remains increased during the COVID-19 pandemic as the store of value function and precautionary motive for holding cash outweighed the transaction motive in the face of economic uncertainty but use of cash in transactions is declining. The share of cash in M1 also shows a broad based decline (see Cabezas and Jara 2021).

[17] Cross country differences in the use of cash and noncash instruments remain significant, reflecting jurisdictions unique histories, culture, demographic set up, financial sector organization, digital infrastructure and laws and regulations.

[18] Some governments are advocating for the protection of the use of cash in payments for inclusion and resilience. See America's Payment Choice Act, Bank of Korea recent statement, Canadian campaigners, and regulations in Ireland, Norway and Spain.

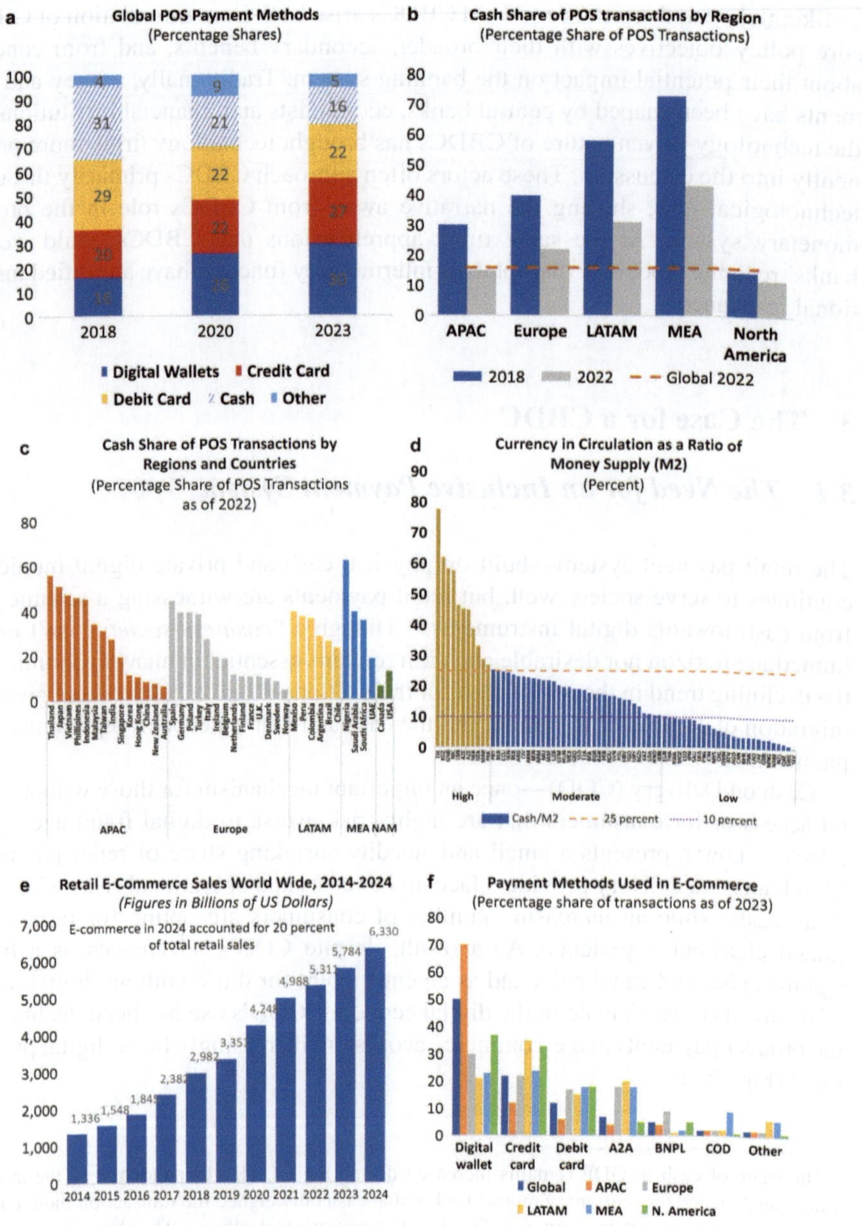

Fig. 4 Trends in the usage of cash in payment transactions

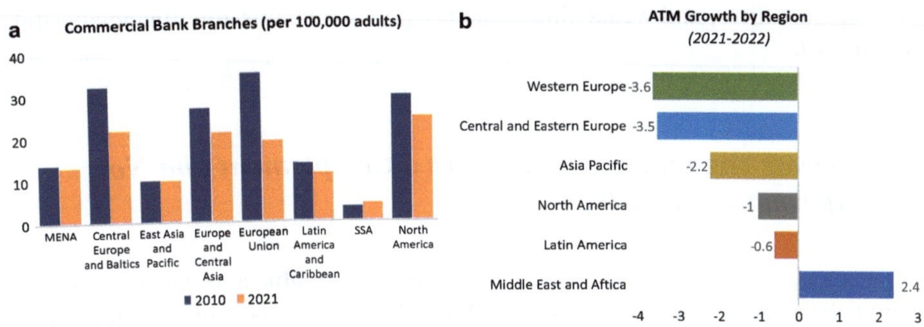

Fig. 5 Global and regional trends in bank branches and ATMs

Absent a public digital alternative, the decline in the use of cash and the shift to e-commerce, could exclude those without digital payment access from participating in the digital economy.[19] Financial exclusion risks are already materializing in some countries where private digital payments dominate. In Korea, Sweden, and UK, some businesses no longer accept cash while the decline in bank branches and ATMs across regions suggests that banks are scaling back cash services as digital payments rise (Fig. 5a–b).

Leaving the retail payment landscape entirely to private providers—without the safeguard of a universally accessible public digital money—creates structural vulnerabilities. Private issuers are profit-motivated and may not prioritize public interest objectives such as universal access, affordability and system-wide interoperability. They may favor closed systems thus a few dominant payment service providers (PSPs) could entrench their market power, creating concentration risk where the exit of a major player could disrupt payment flows. Private entities may even withdraw services altogether when business conditions change,[20] abruptly disrupting the retail payment system. Private sector instruments also carry issuer-specific risks, that vary in governance and resilience, and may not hold par convertibility in periods of stress and their currencies have been prone to confidence crises which, in the absence of public backstops, expose consumers to potential loss.[21] Without a neutral, publicly governed form of money anchoring the system, these dynamics risk fragmenting the payment landscape, concentrating critical payment functions in a

[19] Debit cards are only available to the public with bank accounts, credit cards are only issued if you meet certain eligibility criteria set by the issuer, and digital wallets are typically linked to bank accounts, debit or credit cards. CBDCs, by contrast, will be universally available, and can be used for e-commerce transactions.

[20] For instance, Mastercard and Visa immediately suspended operations in Russia over the invasion of Ukraine.

[21] Confidence crises have largely been attributed to opaque financial practices, inadequate regulatory oversight, and a lack of access to central bank liquidity support. See for example the experiences of Liberty reserve, E-Gold, the Icelandic Auroracoin, and algorithmic stablecoins Terra USD (UST), IRON stablecoin.

few dominant firms, and weakening monetary policy transmission, financial stability and trust.

3.2 *Private Digital Innovations Are a Complement and Not Alternative to CBDCs*

Private money such as stablecoins or e-money are not a viable alternative to CBDCs even if their regulation is made robust. A CBDC extends the trust and finality of central bank money into the digital realm, reinforcing the monetary system's integrity and providing a platform for innovation that aligns with public policy objectives. Even with regulation and insurance, private liabilities cannot fully replicate the safety and finality of central bank money—the foundation of trust in the monetary system. Currency issuance and payments are also too important to leave to the private sector. CBDCs also preserve the central bank's ability to transmit monetary policy directly in an increasingly digital economy.

Stablecoins promise par convertibility into central bank money, but this convertibility is not guaranteed. A loss of confidence can lead to deviations from par, fragment payment systems, disrupt payment chains, and undermine trust in digital payments.[22] Moreover, as stablecoin issuers are not part of the traditional monetary transmission architecture—reserve requirements, central bank remuneration of balances, and emergency liquidity backstops —large-scale adoption could weaken interest rate pass-through, shift liquidity creation to less regulated entities, and introduce new channels of credit and liquidity risks that bypass the central bank. While the current low adoption levels of stablecoins in payments limits the threat to monetary sovereignty, widespread use could complicate central banks' ability to assess the economy and implement effective policies.

Private digital innovations—including mobile money, digital wallets, and Fast Payment Systems (FPS)—have improved efficiency and accessibility in payment, but they do not eliminate the need for a universally accessible public digital money. E-money represents electronically stored funds used for making payments; digital wallets (Apple Pay, Google Pay, or PayPal), act as platforms to manage and transact those funds; and FPS enhance account-based bank transfers with near-instantaneous clearing. Despite these improvements, the underlying liabilities remain private, and these instruments cannot match the safety, stability or finality of central bank money.

Privacy concerns are important but not a sufficient reason to avoid issuing CBDCs as all digital payments leave a trail. PSPs are equally obligated to share personal information with law enforcement under legal frameworks and in fact,

[22] For example, stablecoins can be used for payments but also for trading thus their price can deviate from par value.

privacy risks can be greater with private digital payments when PSPs use transaction data for commercial purposes. Central banks, by contrast, prioritize public policy objectives, and a well-designed CBDCs could offer enhanced privacy while facilitating the necessary oversight (BIS 2021a).

Finally, although implementing a CBDC requires significant investment in infrastructure, IT expertise and public education, its broader economic benefits outweigh the costs. Resource constraints are, therefore, not a sufficient reason to delay, but highlight the need to prioritize and reallocate resources to meet the evolving needs of the digital payment ecosystem (Piero Cipollone 2024).

4 Conclusions

CBDCs are not merely a technological innovation in payments but a strategic instrument to preserve the central bank role in currency issuance and stability of payments and the broader financial system. Though CBDCs may utilize blockchain technologies that create the semblance of another innovation along a continuum of tokenized monetary instruments, CBDCs play a unique and more fundamental role in payments. As a direct liability of the central bank, CBDCs anchor trust, preserve the singleness of money, safeguard monetary sovereignty, and guarantee universal access to safe and stable digital money.

Payments are the lifeblood of commerce and economic transactions, and currency issuance has fundamental implications for monetary policy, financial stability and inflation control. Absent a public digital alternative, the declining use of cash risks creating a monetary system increasingly shaped by private actors. As commerce migrates online, individuals lacking access to digital payment options may be excluded from the digital economy.

Payments and currency issuance are also too important to be left entirely to profit-motivated private entities, whose decisions are not guided by public interest and who may exit the market based on commercial considerations which can abruptly disrupt the payment system. A system dominated by privately issued money could weaken monetary policy transmission, undermine monetary sovereignty, limit central banks' ability to achieve public policy goals like financial inclusion, reducing resilience and fragment the payment system. Dysfunction in payment systems can have system wide effects that propagate beyond national borders given the cross-border nature of payments.

A balanced payment ecosystem, where public and private sectors play complementary roles is, therefore, essential to ensure a stable, secure, and equitable financial system. Innovations in money and payments such as stablecoins, tokenized deposits can promote efficiencies but they are complements and not substitutes to CBDCs. Stablecoins, which aim to maintain a fixed value relative to a currency or commodity, are subject to market and confidence risks. Their value can deviate from par if reserves are insufficient or stabilization mechanisms fail, particularly under stress. Because stablecoins operate outside the traditional monetary system, widespread adoption could undermine monetary policy implementation by reducing central banks' ability to control liquidity, interest rates, and credit conditions. E-money represents pre-funded claims on private issuers and while they generally maintain par value relative to the underlying currency, they are exposed to issuer-specific risks—including insolvency, mismanagement, or operational failures—that could lead to consumer losses. Tokenized deposits and other private digital instruments also carry varying governance, resilience, and liquidity risks, that are only mitigated by deposit insurance and liquidity backstops. A neutral, universally accessible digital currency, like a CBDC, is therefore needed to anchor the system and mitigate these risks.

Fast Payment Systems (FPS) enhance the speed and convenience of digital transactions, allowing near-instantaneous account-to-account transfers between participating banks and payment service providers. FPS are, however, not a form of money, but rather it is infrastructure that facilitates the movement of private money. Their accessibility is generally limited to banked individuals and institutions, leaving unbanked populations excluded. Moreover, while FPS can provide rapid transfers, settlement may still rely on commercial bank reserves and clearing arrangements, which are subject to liquidity constraints and operational risks. FPS do not extend the safety, stability, or finality of central bank money to users, nor do they provide a neutral, universally accessible anchor in the digital payment ecosystem. Therefore, even in economies with advanced FPS, a CBDC is necessary to ensure that all segments of the population can access safe, central bank-backed digital money, preserving trust in payments and supporting effective monetary policy.

CBDCs, therefore, present a timely opportunity to modernize the provision of central bank money and maintain its relevance in a digital economy. While technology evolves, trust remains the cornerstone of effective and stable payments and central bank money is necessary to anchor that trust. There is no compelling reason why central bank money should not evolve in step with societal and technological changes.

The journey from CBDC innovation to integration into the payment system and eventual mainstream usage may be complex and not without challenges, but the economic advantages are profound and immeasurable. The question, therefore, should not be whether CBDCs are necessary, but how to implement them effectively. Analytical work must shift from testing hypothetical benefits to identifying the institutional, technological and policy conditions needed to realize the benefits that CBDCs promise. Central banks must proceed cautiously given the novelty and complexity of CBDCs but with clear resolve. The priority should not be to rush toward issuing a CBDC but to ensure a well-considered approach (Powell 2020). Collaboration with the private sector — especially on front-end design — and international engagement are critical. Innovation without stability erodes trust while stability without innovation would result in stasis.

References

Atlantic Council (2022) Missing key. The challenge of cybersecurity and Central Bank Digital Currency

Bank of England and HM Treasury (February 2023) The digital pound: A new form of money for households and businesses. Consultation Paper. UK

BIS (September 2021) Central bank digital currencies: financial stability implications. Report No. 4

BIS (2021a) Central bank digital currencies: system design and interoperability. Report no 2 in a series of collaborations from a group of central banks

BIS (May 2023a) Polaris. A handbook for offline payments with CBDC. BIS Innovation Hub

BIS (November 2023c) Central bank digital currency (CBDC) information security and operational risks to central banks

Bowman MW (2023) Considerations for a Central Bank Digital Currency. Speech given At the Georgetown University McDonough School of Business Psaros Center for Financial Markets and Policy, Washington, DC

Cabezas L, Jara A (December 2021) The demand for cash: stylized facts and substitution by electronic means of payment. CEPAL Review N° 135

Cipollone P (9 February 2024) Modernizing finance - the role of central bank money. Keynote speech at the 30th Congress of ASSIOM FOREX (the Italian financial markets association), Genoa

Independent Community of Bankers of America (2022) Comments on "Money and payments: The US dollar in the age of digital transformation" Paper for Consultation by the Board of Governors of the Federal Reserve. USA

Ingves S (6 November 2018) The e-krona and the payments of the future. Speech given at Di Framtidens betalningar

Jordan T (8 April 2024) Towards the future monetary system. Speech. Zurich

Knogstrup S (9 March 2023) New types of digital money. Speech. Danmarks Nationalbank

Michel N, Anthony N (2023) The risks of CBDCs: why central Bank digital currencies shouldn't be adopted. Visual feature. Cato Institute, Washington DC

Panetta F (2021) Central bank digital currencies: a monetary anchor for digital innovation. Speech. Elcano Royal Institute, Madrid

Panetta F (2022) Central Bank digital currencies: defining the problems, designing the solutions. Speech. US Monetary Policy Forum, New York

Powell J (2020) More important for U.S. to get digital currency right than be first. Reuters

Quarles RK (28 June 2021) Parachute pants and central bank money. Speech at the 113th Annual Utah Bankers Association Convention, Sun Valley, Idaho

Sultanum B (July 2022) Central Bank Digital Currencies and regulatory alternatives: the Case for Stablecoins. Economic Brief. Federal Reserve Bank of Richmond, No. 22–26

Toronto Center (2023) Central Bank Digital Currencies. Implications for supervisors. Canada

Waller CJ (5 August 2021) CBDC - A Solution in Search of a Problem? Speech by Mr Christopher J Waller, Member of the Board of Governors of the Federal Reserve System, Washington DC

Commercial Bank Money Token (CBMT)

Claus George

Abstract The Commercial Bank Money Token (CBMT) is a deposit token developed to support the transition to a more digitalized financial system. This insider perspective aims to elucidate the challenges and design considerations that led to the current development of the CBMT concept, addressing the initial problem of Distributed Ledger Technology (DLT) adoption and the absence of on-chain money. Without native digital currency, DLTs face challenges in automating transactions, relying on traditional systems that introduce inefficiencies. CBMT resolves this by tokenizing commercial bank money on a distributed ledger. Unlike stablecoins, CBMT is issued by banks and thereby backed by compliance with existing banking regulations.

Keywords Tokenised deposits · Deposit token · CBMT · DLT · Commercial Bank money

1 Benefits of DLT for Business Processes

Distributed Ledger Technologies (DLTs), can be used to automate supply chain management processes through smart contracts, potentially reducing manual errors and operational costs. Enhanced security, through decentralized and cryptographic measures, ensures data integrity and fosters trust among stakeholders without the need for a central trusted party. DLTs provide a shared platform for information exchange, which can improve coordination and decision-making among participants. Real-time inventory visibility aids in optimizing stock management and demand forecasting, reducing waste. Overall, DLTs can significantly transform supply chains, leading to more efficient, secure, and sustainable business operations.

C. George (✉)
DZ BANK AG, Frankfurt, Germany
e-mail: claus.george@dzbank.de

S. Yazıcı et al. (eds.), *Tokenisation of Money*, Contributions to Finance and Accounting, https://doi.org/10.1007/978-3-032-22946-5_11

1.1 *The Initial Problem: DLT Adoption and Lack of Money-on-Chain*

Without on-chain money, leveraging DLT for business processes becomes challenging. On-chain money is crucial for executing smart contract payments automatically, ensuring seamless and efficient transactions. Its absence means relying on traditional financial systems, which introduce intermediaries and delays, negating the swift, automated benefits DLTs offer. This reliance complicates real-time financial interactions, affecting liquidity and operational efficiency. Furthermore, without a native digital currency, transaction costs increase due to manual reconciliation and the complexity of integrating off-chain payment systems. These issues disrupt the streamlined processes DLTs are designed to facilitate, diminishing potential gains in transparency, cost reduction, and speed. Businesses may face difficulty in fully realizing DLT advantages, potentially requiring cumbersome hybrid solutions that compromise efficiency and increase implementation complexity. This gap challenges the transformative potential of DLTs, impacting how businesses optimize their operations and collaborate effectively across networks.

Hidden from the user's perspective is the interbank settlement process. While stablecoins and cryptocurrencies perfectly integrate with DLTs, it is still believed that "tokenised commercial bank money and digital central bank money bring the greatest functional benefit in terms of settling programmable payments." (BuBa 2020).

2 Existing Forms of Money: An Overview

Money exists in various forms, differentiated by their issuers—public or private. Central bank money is issued publicly by central banks and includes physical money and reserves, providing the most stable and widely accepted form due to government backing. Commercial bank money (CBM), issued privately, comprises deposits held in bank accounts, facilitating economic transactions via credit and debit mechanisms. Stablecoins, issued privately, are digital assets pegged to fiat currencies aiming to maintain stable value, serving as a bridge between traditional banking and digital currency realms.

Unpegged cryptocurrencies, although widely traded, are not classified as money since they are not a stable store of value and are used more as an investment than as a means of payment. Their private issuance and decentralized nature appeal to users seeking alternatives to conventional financial systems, yet their volatility limits mainstream acceptance.

Each form plays a distinct role in the financial ecosystem, balancing stability, accessibility, and innovation.

2.1 *From Commercial Bank Money to CBMT*

Traditional commercial bank money (CBM) and deposit token share common characteristics, such as being used for transactions, serving as a store of value, and being backed by bank reserves. Tokenized deposits are issued by regulated financial institutions, ensuring they are backed by the bank's balance sheet and subject to the same regulatory oversight as traditional CBM.

Both are essential components of the fractional reserve banking system, facilitating commerce and investment. The primary difference lies in their form and accessibility: traditional CBM exists as ledger entries within banks, typically accessed through bank accounts. Deposit token, however, are digital representations of such deposits on a distributed ledger, enabling increased transparency, quicker settlements, and potentially lower transaction costs. Tokenization provides enhanced interoperability with other digital assets, aligning with modern financial innovations.

CBMT is a form of on-chain CBM. The following text tries to unfold what the CBMT creators mean with "on-chain", the potential benefits CBMT brings to its users, the traits of CBM that distinguish it e. g. from stablecoins and how these traits got transferred into a token form.

2.2 *Distinguishing CBMT from Stablecoins*

In contrast to deposit tokens, stablecoins are a class of privately issued digital assets. They are designed to maintain a stable value by pegging them to fiat currencies, commodities, or a basket of assets. In contradistinction to deposit token, stablecoins are not inherently backed by direct bank deposits They rely on various mechanisms to maintain their value, such as collateralization or algorithmic adjustments. While stablecoins aim for stability, their value can fluctuate based on the issuer's reserve management and the collateral's integrity.

The key difference lies in issuer trust and regulatory frameworks. Deposit token are subject to regulatory oversight and operational disclosure requirements typical for banking systems. Stablecoins are generally designed for greater accessibility, but may be subject to different regulatory and risk considerations. Each serves distinct roles in digital finance, reflecting varying levels of stability, trust, and use cases.

2.3 *Sum Up: The Unique Value Proposition of CBMT*

After finishing the Proof of Concept, the association of the German industries "BDI The Voice of the German Industry" jointly published a report (BDI 2024) with the German Banking Industry Committee that starts with:

> The commercial bank money token, CBMT, represents a pioneering step towards a more digitalised financial system, achieved by placing commercial bank money onto distributed ledger technology, DLT. CBMT facilitates the seamless execution of money flows and business processes within the same systems, harnessing the flexibility and efficiency of DLT while retaining the trust and reliability associated with traditional banking.

The explanation why the BDI supports the CBMT closely matches what the Bank for International Settlement (BIS) calls “unified ledger” in the chapter “Blueprint for the future monetary system” of the World Economic Report 2023 (BIS 2023). These are the unabridged key take aways from BIS:

> Tokenisation of money and assets has great potential, but initiatives to date have taken place in silos without access to central bank money and the foundation of trust it provides.
>
> A new type of financial market infrastructure – a unified ledger – could capture the full benefits of tokenisation by combining central bank money, tokenised deposits and tokenised assets on a programmable platform.
>
> As well as improving existing processes through the seamless integration of transactions, a unified ledger could harness programmability to enable arrangements that are currently not practicable, thereby expanding the universe of possible economic outcomes.
>
> Multiple ledgers – each with a specific use case – might coexist, interlinked by application programming interfaces to ensure interoperability as well as promote financial inclusion and a level playing field.

The CBMT could be used as the asset for the money leg on unified ledgers, potentially supporting money flows and business processes with increased efficiency.

3 Design Principles

The following design principles have been grouped according to the following categories: economic, strategic, processual, and technological. These considerations guided the approach to developing the CBMT concept. The primary objective was to enable the seamless integration of well-established business practices with the novel technological solution known as DLT.

3.1 Economic Considerations

The overarching goal was to replicate CBM as accurately as possible. Individuals with a more technical background recognize that the CBMT may be missing opportunities provided by new technology. On the other hand, business users like treasurers see that they can apply the familiar legal and operational framework for CBM, such as in accounting and risk management.

The main limitation of CBM is that it is a restricted asset: to access this asset, one must have a banking relationship with a commercial bank, maintain a deposit with a specific bank, or a customer must have a claim against a particular bank.

CBM is the concept that enables bank customers to use their deposits at a chosen bank to settle a claim of a customer of another bank. This is possible only because banks participating in the "CBM" concept exchange claims of customers of other banks against these other banks into claims of their customers against themselves. This behaviour on the part of banks leads to what is known as "fungibility" and is the most notable characteristic of CBM.

This impacts the design of CBMT as follows:

Analogous to today's payment system, CBMT is open to all banks (multi-issuer). Each participating bank can issue claims in the form of tokens to its customers.

It is ensured that all participating customers have control over their tokens at any given time, issued by a bank with which they have a banking relationship.

Participating banks ensure, analogous to today's payment system, that tokens from various issuers are fungible and always maintain the same value. That is, a currency unit always holds the same value, regardless of which bank issued the token.

The conversion of CBM from the existing technological form to the new token-based form and back must be guaranteed by the banks.

The risk management of CBMT should not differ fundamentally for customers from that of today's CBM (liquidity management and counterparty default risk).

The initiation of a money transfer should be able to be programmed using the same technical means with which customers automate their core business processes. Contrary to today, the customer should be able to initiate the money transfer themselves.

It is essential to maximize overall benefits. This means exploiting the possibilities of new technology within the existing legislative framework while minimizing total costs. Multi-objective optimization implies the necessity of trade-offs and achieving an optimal result, or: several acceptable variants are possible.

3.2 *Strategic Considerations*

The primary focus of strategic considerations is the division of labor or the distribution of roles between banks and their customers. Today, banks not only provide money but also the payment systems and solutions used to transfer money. This is driven by both economic considerations and practical constraints.

The economic reasoning is straightforward: payment transactions can generate revenue. Practical constraints arise from the technology used. Currently, commercial banks must manage their money in isolated systems under their sole control. The fungibility of CBM is ultimately achieved through data exchange between the accounting systems of the participating banks.

These circumstances lead to the conclusion that banks also need to organize the data exchange and thus provide what is understood as payment systems.

Unified ledgers, however, offer the possibility of a different division of labor. Banks' money generates the greatest benefit where it is needed: on a technical platform that bank customers use to conduct their business processes. Any additional layer of abstraction would increase overall costs. Distributed ledger technology enables exactly this. Banks make their money available on DLTs, paving the way for a unified ledger where industrial customers process their transactions. In these ecosystems, there are no more payment systems for money flow; banks act as virtual asset service providers (VASP) for the asset "money".

It may appear counterintuitive that banks, which traditionally derive revenue from payment transactions, might reduce their direct involvement in segments of the value chain. CBMT has demonstrated the feasibility of substituting conventional payment transactions, at least in part, with tokenised money. Consequently, it is conceivable that specific components of the prevailing payment transaction business model will undergo substantial transformation. Therefore, financial institutions should proactively adapt their business models in anticipation of these structural changes.

3.3 *Processual Considerations*

The economic and strategic goals directly imply the support for unified ledgers, where the assets of banks and their customers coexist and are processed together.

Industrial DLTs will be shaped according to industry value networks. The core competence of banks lies in financial business, not in operating technical platforms. Therefore, CBMT supports the deployment of money on various DLTs formed in the industrial environment that require the asset of CBM. Nonetheless, banks reserve the freedom to choose whether to support a particular DLT ecosystem. A direct consequence of this is that CBMT should be fundamentally technology-agnostic.

In the 2023 proof of concept, the necessary functionality of CBMT was successfully demonstrated on systems implemented with Ethereum, R3, and Hyperledger Besu respectively. We are likely at the beginning of the technical development of DLTs. Compared to the lifespan of the concept of "bank deposit", the lifespan of specific DLTs is likely to be short. However, no functional regression is expected for DLTs. Since CBMT can be implemented on current DLTs, migration to future DLTs appears unproblematic. As a result, efficient on- and off-ramping processes become increasingly important. Since only banks issue the asset to be migrated and only bank customers use the asset to be migrated, existing bank accounts can be used for on- and off-ramping. Customers can also use these for transfers between different DLTs, should Hashed TimeLock Contracts (HTLCs) prove impractical as means of transferring money between different DLTs.

The concept depicts banks and users of CBM as entities. Interestingly, banks do not need to be semantically labeled as "banks," but only as issuers of the asset "money". Their role is not very different from an industrial user, such as a car rental service that issues tokens for hourly vehicle usage. The roles "bank" and "customer" are defined solely by the type of asset issued. Even a central bank would be represented in the CBMT concept by issuing money. The only difference would be that a central bank only had customers that also issue money (at least within the European legal framework).

However, different functionalities must be provided to customers and banks: Customers can transfer money, while banks, for example, can whitelist customers.

In order to archive fungibility the concept must allow access to all banks in principle. This multi-issuer and multi-DLT approach potentially induces a m*n complexity when trying to connect m banks and n DLTs. CBMT envisions a separate entity, the so-called Technical Service Provider. This serves as a point of contact for both DLT operators and banks, thereby reducing the complexity to m:1 and 1:n.

3.4 *Technological Considerations*

DLT is currently in its early stages, with anticipated advancements promising more functionality in future iterations compared to those available today. This evolution implies that products designed to operate successfully on the major current DLT platforms will likely remain viable and adaptable as technology progresses. The CBMT system was tested on leading DLT infrastructures.

These trials provided crucial insights, revealing that the main technological challenge lies not in the implementation of the CBMT itself but in achieving interoperability between different DLTs. Ensuring that varied DLT systems can communicate and function seamlessly together is critical for harnessing the full potential of distributed ledgers in financial transactions and beyond. The tests underscored the need for solutions that bridge diverse blockchain protocols, enabling cohesive integration and paving the way for more robust, efficient, and flexible digital ecosystems.

3.5 *The Core Design Principles*

The aforementioned considerations lead to the following design principles:

Multi-issuer The CBMT concept is open to any commercial bank wishing to join and issue its liabilities. Tokens issued by any issuer shall be as fungible as today's CBM.

Coloured Tokens Technically, there is only one token to prevent interoperability problems, but each pair (issuer/currency) gets a unique identifier (colour). Each user can recognise at any time which bank and which currency this token represents.

Technical Service Provider A third party besides banks and their customers is necessary. The TSP will technically deploy the token and act as a communication hub.

Programmable Payments That's why we are here. CBMT payments can be programmed in smart contracts, just like any other tokenised assets.

Multi-DLT Concept Banks are prepared to support multiple DLTs, which are probably set up by their customers to run business processes. Banks' role changes from 'vault' to VASP.

While the first three principles are intended to implement essential characteristics of CBM, the last two design principles will ensure that CBM is no longer a special good when it comes to accessing it.

4 Envisaged Usage

When developing a new product, the question of user experience cannot be avoided. CBMT is initially a concept, an idea. Unlike many other initiatives, CBMT does not want to build a new financial market infrastructure. The main goal is to make CBM available in a modern form on the infrastructures of corporate customers. The user experience therefore depends directly on these infrastructures and can vary greatly.

What should be consistent, however, is the experience that the tokens used are CBM. A description of the user experience must therefore focus on the procedural aspects or on one of many possible technical implementations.

4.1 The Core Processes

There are two very different target groups for the CBMT concept: technologists who want to implement supply chain processes on DLTs and accountants who want to represent assets in the company ledger.

As both target groups are necessary for the implementation of the CBMT concept in companies, it is important to describe the concept from their different perspectives.

4.1.1 An Accountants Perspective

The CBMT concept describes how the necessary functionality for accounting can be provided through a combination of a DLT, a specific token (the CBMT), and a wallet. Thus, the realization of the concept provides an accounting system based on a different technology than current accounting systems. Depending on the DLT used, there are subtle but important differences. The following explanation assumes an implementation of the CBMT based on an Etherum based network through an ERC1155 compatible token. The last sentence is unfortunately likely completely incomprehensible to accountants. It is needed, as terms from the DLT environment are used in the following section, making it necessary to commit to a specific DLT.

Key components of an accounting system include, among others, an operating platform, effective access protection, accounts, booking rules, and a booking journal. This is which parts CBMT can provide:

Operating Platform Current accounting systems, like most industry software, are operated either by the company itself or an IT provider. The accounting system relies on the functionality of a database and the operating system.

The CBMT system is operated on a DLT. Similar to an operating system, the DLT provides basic functionalities that allow a token to be processed.

Access Protection Current accounting systems are generally multi-client capable, meaning they can be used for various legal entities. Access protection grants access to the booking functionality of accounts of clients after user identification.

In the CBMT system, legal entities can register one or multiple addresses (similar to checking accounts) on a DLT. Similar to accounts, balances can be assigned to these addresses. Users must authenticate themselves to the DLT using cryptographic keys and then gain access to the booking functionality, especially transferring values managed under the associated addresses. Just like with bank accounts, before values represented by CBMT units can be associated with an address, this address must be authorized by an account-managing institution ("whitelisting"). In this process, the legal entity must first undergo the KYC process at the account-managing institution, where it is identified. A separate software, often referred to as a "wallet," is used to store/manage the cryptographic keys.

Account In current booking systems, each account has a unique identifier. Generally, there is at least one account per bank and currency (multi-currency accounts are possible) in financial accounting systems. The current balance of an account reflects the current claim against a specific bank in a currency. The balance results from the last booking cut and the transactions executed since then.

In the CBMT system, a CBM token maintains a list of all authorized addresses and their balance equivalents. Under an address, all claims against all counterparties in all currencies are recorded. Similar to the account balance in current booking systems, there is an entry per counterparty and currency representing the balance. The balance is shown in token units (in the literature "token units" are frequently abbreviated as "token"). Unlike current booking systems, there is no booking cut. The token units represent the current state after the last transaction recorded.

Booking Rules In current accounting systems, booking rules can be defined. The system's program code allows the regular execution of these rules, thereby providing users with booking functionality. A core functionality is value transfer: Book amount A from account Y to account Z. Besides the core functionality, users and administrators can define their own rules, enforcing company-specific accounting rules.

In the CBMT system, the CBM token provides token contracts named "transfer single" and "transfer batch" for one or multiple value transfers. Additional functionality, such as "escrow," can be provided by other smart contracts. Company-specific booking rules can potentially be realized by external off-chain software.

Booking Journal In current booking systems, parts of the program code are responsible for recording all relevant transactions in a journal. The creation of the journal is thus part of the booking system.

In DLT systems, all transactions are recorded cryptographically secure. The invocation of any token contract and the resulting state change are recorded. Therefore, a separate realization of a booking journal in the CBM token is not necessary.

4.1.2 A Supply Chain Technologists Perspective

The crucial processes are access to and transfer of money. As before, the processes are explained using the example of an implementation based on Ethereum. The CBM token adheres to the ERC1155 standard. It is accessible like any other asset that is represented by ERC1155 tokens, and the transfer of money occurs by invoking the transfer method, with the following described peculiarity.

4.1.3 The Process of Money Transfer

CBM is a restricted asset. It can and may only be held by entities for which, strictly speaking, the issuing bank maintains an account. This circumstance is fundamental to the nature of deposit money and must therefore also be replicated for the CBMT.

A customer will have at least two addresses: the convert address and the general address.

Convert address – The convert address is the inbound address of the customer. Tokens sent to the convert address will automatically be converted and forwarded to the associated general address.

General address – The general address is the outbound address of the customer. Sending tokens is always performed from the general address. (GBIC 2023).

From the user's perspective, this means that instead of one account, two different accounts must be specified and used for incoming and outgoing money. This circumstance is often perceived as a limitation by technologists. From our perspective, it is completely negligible for the target group, as they have (so far) worked with many accounts just to be able to assign incoming payments to corresponding business operations. Implementing unified ledgers and directly assigning payments to specific business operations may simplify processes and could reduce the number of accounts needed, even if separate addresses are used for incoming and outgoing transfers.

5 Further Reading

The main document is (GBIC 2021), which explains the motivation and basic design. (GBIC 2023) goes into detail about the processes and addresses specific technical implementations. (BDI 2024) presents the results of the proof of concept and is particularly valuable because it also includes customer evaluations of whether the CBMT lives up to its promises.

References

BDI, Bundesverband der deutschen Industrie e. V. (2024) Commercial Bank Money Token. https://english.bdi.eu/publication/news/commercial-bank-money-token

BIS, Bank for International Settlements (2023) Blueprint for the future monetary system: improving the old, enabling the new in: Annual Economic Report 2023 https://www.bis.org/publ/arpdf/ar2023e3.pdf

BuBA, Deutsche Bundesbank (2020) Money in programmable applications https://www.bundesbank.de/resource/blob/855148/ebaab681009124d4331e8e327cfaf97c/mL/2020-12-21-programmierbare-zahlung-anlage-data.pdf

GBIC, German Banking Industry Committee (2021) Europe needs new money—an ecosystem of CBDC, tokenised commercial bank money and trigger solutions. https://www.bvr.de/p.nsf/0/2081465F78445160C125870900507DFD/$file/20210625_DK_Ergebnisdokument_EN.pdf

GBIC, German Banking Industry Committee (2023) Working Paper on Commercial Bank Money Token, Version 1.51 https://die-dk.de/media/files/20230523_GBIC_Working_Paper_on_Commercial_Bank_Money_Token_V1.51_1_1.pdf

Stablecoin Use Cases and Adoption from the End-User Point of View

Sebnem Elif Kocaoglu Ulbrich

Abstract This chapter explores stablecoin use cases and adoption, with a focus on the end-user perspective, evaluating the topic using product adoption and marketing principles. While stablecoins were initially viewed as speculative instruments, they are increasingly positioned as integral components of future payment ecosystems, competing with and complementing Central Bank Digital Currencies ("CBDCs"). The chapter examines the drivers, barriers, and perceptions shaping stablecoin adoption, including regulatory clarity, institutional trust, and consumer education. Drawing on recent industry surveys and adoption studies, it analyzes the retail and institutional applications of stablecoins across payments, remittances, e-commerce, gaming, and corporate treasury. Special emphasis is placed on product adoption principles, from awareness to sustained use, and the importance of transparency, compliance, and strategic partnerships in building consumer confidence. Ultimately, the chapter argues that the long-term success of stablecoins depends not on speculative hype but on their ability to deliver tangible value, stability, and trust to everyday users.

Keywords Stablecoins · CBDCs · Fintech · Tokenized money · Digital payments · Financial inclusion · Cross-border transfers · Remittances · Consumer adoption · Blockchain · Regulatory compliance

1 Introduction

As financial institutions, fintechs, and regulators warm up to digital assets, stablecoins are increasingly viewed not just as speculative tools but as integral components of future payment ecosystems. The summer of 2025 turned out to be a breaking point for stablecoins. Many household tech companies and financial

S. E. Kocaoglu Ulbrich (✉)
Contextual Solutions GmbH, Berlin, Germany
e-mail: sebnemelif@contextuals.de

S. Yazıcı et al. (eds.), *Tokenisation of Money*, Contributions to Finance and Accounting, https://doi.org/10.1007/978-3-032-22946-5_12

institutions, including Stripe, Remitly, Société Générale, Visa, Mastercard, and Standard Chartered, laid out their plans for their stablecoins. The projects, at first instance, sound relevant enough to excite the tech communities around the world. However, the real-life use cases and the end-user relevance are still a black box. *Is there a concrete real-life scenario that will make stablecoins relevant for consumers? How do end-users define and understand stablecoins? Could stablecoins change the way they perceive money? If not, how will the adoption rates develop?*

This Chapter will discuss these questions in detail, analysing stablecoins from a product and market adoption point of view.

2 Stablecoins and CBDCs: Where Do We Stand on The Hype Cycle?

Stablecoins, digital assets pegged to stable reference values such as fiat currencies, are emerging as a transformative force in global payments and finance. Although they are often put in the same basket as cryptocurrencies, stablecoins are the market's response to making cryptocurrencies more "reliable" and "stable." They combine the efficiency and programmability of blockchain technology with the price stability traditionally associated with sovereign currencies.

Central Bank Digital Currencies ("CBDCs"), on the other hand, are the digital equivalent of a nation's official currency, issued and guaranteed directly by the central bank. While both CBDCs and stablecoins are forms of tokenized cash, their foundations differ significantly as CBDCs are sovereign money, whereas stablecoins are privately issued tokens designed to maintain a stable value by being pegged to assets such as fiat currencies (e.g., USD, EUR), commodities (e.g., gold), cryptocurrencies, or a basket of assets. The stability of stablecoins depends on the issuer's reserves, governance, and transparency, which makes them less secure than the state-backed nature of CBDCs. Conversely, CBDCs have a consistent theoretical value because they are directly tied to the issuing country's national currency.

When weighing CBDCs against stablecoins, the choice often reflects a trade-off between the institutional stability and legal certainty of a state-backed currency, and the potential currency and counterparty risks inherent in privately issued stablecoins.

CBDCs were initially planned to enhance the effectiveness of monetary policy transmission, modernize payment systems (and digital payments), financial inclusion, and transparency. They were also envisioned to offer an alternative to stablecoins, competing directly with the offers of BigTech and Co., which initially accelerated the development plans for many countries. They were seen as a public alternative to privately owned stablecoins and digital assets by politicians and regulators. The Bank of International Settlements ("BIS") surveyed 86 central banks around the world in 2024 and revealed that 94% of the participating institutions were exploring CBDCs.[1] Following the early announcements dating as early as 2017, a long research period and some pilot trials by some countries, the ambition around the (retail) CBDCs seems to have slowed down by Q3 2025,[2] contrary to expectations.

Why did national banks stop competing for (retail) CBDCs and eventually lose interest in the concept? The answer is not simple, and hidden behind many moving pieces, such as the privacy and financial stability risks, the technical and operational complexities, regulations (such as MiCAR[3]) decreasing the urgency, and China overtaking the competition. But most importantly, the public perception and enthusiasm levels could have had the biggest impact on the topic: most consumers were not enthusiastic and even clearly opposed the idea of a CBDC. For politicians, investing in projects that won't immediately boost their credibility, in the age of crude populism, might not be worth the political capital.

Numerous studies in the past 5 years are key to interpreting the public standpoint. For instance, one of the earlier surveys in Germany[4] revealed that CBDCs can become an attractive payment method only if they start offering novel payment functionalities, compared to other payment methods. This is a clear indication of low public awareness, which is a direct result of the lack of education by the public institutions. Other surveys conducted by the European Central Bank ("ECB") in 2023[5] and 2024[6] conclude a similar disinterest in CBDCs. Accordingly, despite a primary interest in the Digital Euro, consumer habits and preferences still overwhelmingly favor traditional forms of money.

Why should ordinary citizens switch from existing digital wallets or bank apps to CBDCs? In many advanced economies, consumers already have access to several fast, cheap, and reliable digital payment alternatives, including credit cards, P2P payment apps and wallets, and instant transfers. Since the consumers already have tools solving their "fast, cheap, efficient" payment problem, the "value-add" of a CBDC is less evident from their point of view. The results from the 2024 research

[1] Di Iorio (June 2024). https://www.bis.org/publ/bppdf/bispap147.pdf.

[2] The status quo of all active projects can be tracked via the CBDC Tracker: https://cbdctracker.org.

[3] Markets in Crypto-Assets Regulation ("MiCAR") is the European Union ("EU") regulation standardizing and harmonizing crypo-asset regulations across the member states, while ensuring market competition and investor protection. Link: https://eur-lex.europa.eu/eli/reg/2023/1114/oj/eng.

[4] The Bundesbank survey dated 2021 from Germany "What do households in Germany think about the digital euro? First results from surveys and interviews" reveal the low awareness levels of German households. Although Germany is not necessarily the digital finance pioneer in Europe, due to the adoption of digitalization to everyday life and consumer's digitalization related reservations in the historical context, the results are still striking and relevant in terms of consumer perception. Link: https://www.bundesbank.de/resource/blob/879312/807018037068359550e1d89a5dc366fe/mL/2021-10-digitaler-euro-private-haushalte-data.pdf

[5] Dimitris Georgarakos, Geoff Kenny, Luc Laeven, Justus Meyer, "Consumer attitudes towards a central bank digital currency," ECB Working Paper Series No 3035. Link: https://www.ecb.europa.eu/pub/pdf/scpwps/ecb~cde4bd616e.wp3035en.pdf.

[6] Nocciola and Zamora-Pérez (September 2024). https://www.ecb.europa.eu/press/research-publications/resbull/2024/html/ecb.rb240918~86165cbefc.en.pdf.

clearly point to *the CBDC design, the level of consumer awareness, and the growth of current new payment technologies* as the three key drivers of consumer demand, highlighting the fact that policymakers and regulators didn't inform the public sufficiently about potential CBDC use cases before committing to the project. Many pilot projects later, we have a more daunting question to answer: *Do they happen to know the answers to these questions? What are the real-life use cases and added values of a CBDC?*

Given the long-term commitments and substantial investments already made in the CBDC debate, this example inevitably prompts a broader question: *If central banks hesitate to push forward, why are private stablecoins advancing?* This divergence forces us to question the growing hype about another digital asset class: stablecoins. *Why are stablecoins relevant, and what can we expect of their adoption?*

3 Why Are Stablecoins Relevant?

3.1 *The Market Impact*

As of June 2025, the global stablecoin market is valued at over $286 billion,[7] and the supply has the potential to grow to $1.6 trillion by 2030 (base case),[8] with the overwhelming majority pegged to the U.S. dollar. While their early adoption was primarily driven by cryptocurrency traders seeking to hedge volatility, stablecoins are now moving beyond speculative use. They are increasingly embedded in retail payments, cross-border transfers, corporate treasury operations, and decentralized finance ("DeFi") ecosystems. However, as can be seen by the CBDC example, mere market value doesn't make the innovation or product relevant for consumers, nor does it have the potential to drive market adoption.

Stablecoins, when well-designed, can serve as efficient digital cash, offering speed, transparency, and cost savings in both traditional and emerging markets. Yet their promise is tempered by regulatory, operational, and systemic risks that must be addressed to safeguard financial stability.

3.2 *Risks and Challenges*

Initially, the rise of stablecoins has triggered concern among central banks and regulators. Institutions such as the BIS and the ECB warn that widespread private stablecoin use could undermine monetary sovereignty, disrupt the singleness of money,

[7] According to the CoinMarketCap data dated August 18, 2025.

[8] According to Citi Institute's "Digital Dollars, Banks and Public Sector Drive Blockchain Adoption" report, dated April 2025. Nevertheless, experts recommend approaching the market size topic cautiously.

and create new financial stability risks. If stablecoins reach scale without appropriate oversight, they could become parallel monetary systems beyond the control of public authorities.

From a technical perspective, stablecoins face vulnerabilities in their underlying smart contracts and oracles. Security breaches, coding errors, or data feed manipulations can lead to loss of funds or system outages. The collapse of algorithmic stablecoins such as TerraUSD in 2022[9] illustrated the fragility of poorly designed peg mechanisms, while more recent events, such as the temporary de-pegging of USDC after the collapse of one of its custodian banks, have shown that even fully backed stablecoins are not immune to shocks. These high-profile incidents underscore the importance of robust reserves and transparent operations.

Fraud and operational risks also remain significant. Because blockchain transactions are irreversible, fraudulent transfers can be difficult to detect and impossible to reverse once settled. Inadequate transparency in reserve holdings, as seen in the case of Tether's early operations, can erode user trust. Additionally, a significant portion of experts believe that stablecoins present anti-money laundering and counter-terrorism financing challenges, as their pseudonymous nature can facilitate illicit transfers without strong regulatory safeguards. However, pro-stablecoin experts challenge the nature of this scenario.

On a systemic level, a sudden wave of redemptions could force stablecoin issuers to liquidate reserves quickly, placing stress on traditional financial markets such as money-market funds or the U.S. Treasury market. Offering interest-bearing stablecoins could also invite classification as securities, triggering an entirely different set of regulatory obligations.

Regulators worldwide are now tightening rules for stablecoin issuers. The common thread across the U.S., EU, and Asia is clear: Asset-backing, transparency, and consumer safeguards are becoming non-negotiable. In the United States, the GENIUS Act[10] mandates all permitted stablecoin issuers to fully back their tokens on a one-to-one basis with cash or approved short-term government securities. Issuers must comply with strict Know Your Customer ("KYC") and Anti-Money Laundering ("AML") requirements and reporting standards and are regulated either at the federal or state level, depending on the size of their issuance. By prioritizing highly liquid reserves, this regulation is expected to channel significant stablecoin reserves into short-term U.S. Treasuries, injecting up to trillions into these markets.

[9] The U.S. Securities and Exchange Commission ("SEC") has charged Singapore-based Terraform Labs PTE Ltd. and its CEO, Do Hyeong Kwon, with orchestrating a multi-billion-dollar crypto securities fraud. The allegations center on an algorithmic stablecoin and other crypto-asset securities, which the SEC claims were offered and sold in violation of the registration and anti-fraud provisions of the Securities Act and the Exchange Act.

[10] The Guiding and Establishing National Innovation for US Stablecoins Act ("GENIUS Act") is the first-ever Federal regulatory system for stablecoins, signed into law on July 18, 2025, ensuring their stability and trust through strong reserve requirements, prioritizing "consumer protection, strengthens the U.S. dollar's reserve currency status, and bolsters our national security." Read the official White House Press Release: https://www.whitehouse.gov/fact-sheets/2025/07/fact-sheet-president-donald-j-trump-signs-genius-act-into-law/.

In the European Union, the MiCAR has been in force since mid-2024, introducing strict licensing requirements, public whitepapers, redemption obligations, and a ban on certain algorithmic stablecoins. Other jurisdictions, such as Hong Kong[11] and Bahrain,[12] have created licensing regimes that favor asset-backed stablecoins over experimental algorithmic designs.

To mitigate risks, issuers are first and foremost expected to adopt robust governance models with transparent and frequently audited reserve disclosures. Although the increasing regulatory oversight is making stablecoin issuers less nimble, forcing them to deal with increased operational burdens, the clear licensing frameworks are likely to boost consumer confidence in the market. In the light of this open innovation environment, stablecoin issuers should aim for full regulatory compliance and cross-border coordination between regulators to prevent regulatory arbitrage, ensure interoperability, and contain systemic spillovers. Only then can they create a product positioning and ecosystem encouraging new users to learn and test.

4 Use Cases and Adoption

4.1 Overview: Use Cases of Stablecoins

The versatility of stablecoins enables a wide range of use cases across multiple layers of the economy. In the retail sector, stablecoins can power instant, low-cost payments between individuals or between consumers and merchants, both online and at physical points of sale. For many in emerging markets, they provide a pathway to participate in the digital economy without the barriers of traditional banking. They are also increasingly used for cross-border remittances, allowing workers to send money home quickly and at a fraction of the cost charged by traditional remittance providers.

Enterprises may benefit from stablecoins in areas such as business-to-business transactions, liquidity management, and automated settlements. Stablecoins can be embedded into corporate treasury functions to facilitate programmable, real-time payments, reducing reliance on intermediary banks and improving cash flow efficiency. In the context of online marketplaces and platforms, they simplify payment flows, enabling faster settlement between buyers and sellers across different geographies.

---

[11] On May 2025, Hong Kong announced a licensing regime for fiat-referenced stablecoins ("FRS") issuers in Hong Kong, requiring FRS that purports to maintain a stable value with reference to Hong Kong dollars in or outside Hong Kong to obtain a license from the Monetary Authority ("MA").

[12] According to the press release dated July fourth, 2025, by the Central Bank of Bahrain, licensed stablecoin issuers are permitted to issue single currency stablecoins backed by Bahraini Dinar (BHD), United States Dollar (USD), or any other fiat currency acceptable by the CBB. Link: https://www.cbb.gov.bh/media-center/central-bank-of-bahrain-issues-framework-for-regulating-stablecoin-issuance/.

On the institutional side, stablecoins are emerging as a settlement layer for tokenized real-world assets such as securities, commodities, and real estate. Their ability to facilitate atomic settlement, where payment and asset delivery occur simultaneously, can reduce counterparty risk and settlement delays. Furthermore, hybrid monetary systems that blend private stablecoin issuance with central bank reserves are gaining attention as potential models for ensuring uniformity and resilience in digital payment infrastructures.

The growing interest from large corporates, financial institutions, and even governments suggests that stablecoins are moving toward mainstream adoption. Recent developments, such as Ripple's acquisition of the infrastructure firm Rail, demonstrate the infrastructure build-out underway to support enterprise-scale issuance and usage.

The appeal of stablecoins lies in their combination of speed, cost efficiency, and programmability. Transactions can settle in seconds, bypassing the delays and fees associated with legacy payment systems. This 24/7 availability is particularly valuable for businesses operating across time zones or for individuals who need to move funds urgently.

Programmability through smart contracts allows for automated, conditional payments, such as releasing funds when certain milestones are met, unlocking entirely new business models. The transparency of blockchain networks also offers traceability and auditability, enhancing compliance and enabling more effective monitoring for illicit activities. In underbanked regions, stablecoins can foster financial inclusion by giving people access to digital payments using only a smartphone, without requiring a traditional bank account.

When properly designed, stablecoins can also act as a store of value, offering protection against inflation or currency depreciation in countries facing monetary instability.

4.2 *Deep Dive: The Retail Use Cases*

Despite the many viable institutional and use cases of stablecoins, the retail use cases pose a similar dilemma to the CBDCs. In theory, stablecoins offer faster, cheaper, and more seamless local and cross-border payments. How do these features differ from the value propositions of the existing payment solutions, though?

Stablecoins have gained traction largely because private markets can move faster in deploying and experimenting with new payment solutions. But the critical question remains: what are their truly valuable use cases? Are stablecoins genuinely more efficient than existing digital payment infrastructures, or do they primarily serve as an alternative in markets where banking and payment ecosystems are slower to modernize?

In volatile markets with currency risk or high inflation, stablecoins could empower billions of underbanked individuals to access stable digital finance, especially in emerging markets facing monetary instability, enabling 24/7 instant payments without any location or institution-specific transaction limitations.

However, in more developed economies, where access to finance is the rule and not the exception, the end value could be less apparent from a customer's point of view. A consumer who has access to instant payment tools may find a new payment method confusing. Any new product, such as a stablecoin wallet, would be greeted with the question of "why," especially if the end-user doesn't understand the dynamics behind the product or if the product is challenging the widespread system (e.g., conventional wallets and banking apps). When focused on one of the most promising use cases around cheaper and faster cross-border payments, the customers will still need to be convinced when switching from their preferred payment providers (e.g., banking apps, Western Union, Wise, Remitly, etc.) to a new stablecoin wallet, even if the transaction is indeed cheaper and faster, as promised. An exception to this scenario would be due to the preferred payment providers issuing stablecoins or offering stablecoin wallets, which might not be too unlikely considering players like PayPal, Remitly, Moneygram, and other PayTech providers are steadily moving into the space. Nevertheless, unless these stablecoin wallets are offered as the go-to alternative for the required use cases, the adoption rates might remain the same, as converting new users is always the hardest.

4.3 *How Do End Users Perceive Stablecoins?*

McKinsey & Company's recent research[13] indicates that the stablecoin market transaction volume has risen sharply over the past 2 years, exceeding $27 trillion per year and likely to surpass legacy payment volumes in less than a decade. The growth is significant, but does the data actually signal a widespread and growing consumer adoption that could overshadow existing payment volumes?

The answer depends on two critical factors: **the user segmentation ("who" is using stablecoins), and the reasons they are using it ("why" are they using stablecoins).**

According to Kraken's user survey dated May 2025,[14] 70% of (participating) customers believe stablecoins unlock new financial opportunities or efficiencies, whereas stablecoins appear in 88% of U.S. crypto portfolios. Although a high number of participants indicate confidence in stablecoins, the fact that these users are already crypto holders indicates a high level of interest and expertise in the digital assets topic.

---

[13] Higginson and Spanz (July 2025). https://www.mckinsey.com/industries/financial-services/our-insights/the-stable-door-opens-how-tokenized-cash-enables-next-gen-payments.

[14] "Survey: Stablecoins appear in 88% of U.S. crypto portfolios," May 2025. Link: https://www.kraken.com/learn/stablecoin-crypto-survey.

The Motley Fool's 2025 Stablecoin Usage and Trends survey, dated August 2025,[15] on the other hand, paints a more realistic picture. The results indicate that half of the adults surveyed consider using stablecoins for everyday purchases. Accordingly, the number of consumers interested jumps to 71% among Gen Z and 60% among millennials, but plummets among older generations. The survey further highlights that knowledge and actual usage of stablecoins are uneven, with only roughly 1 in 5 participants saying they fully understand how stablecoins work; understanding drops significantly with older generations.

Individuals with deeper knowledge value stablecoins for instant cross-border payments, daily transactions, remittances, and as a hedge against local currency risk.

New users often show misunderstandings about reserve mechanisms and rely on the reputation of large issuers or perceived institutional backing, sometimes without a full grasp of the product's risks. In finance, trust is strongest when users see transparent reserves, regulatory compliance, and easy, seamless conversion between fiat and digital money. The ability to earn a yield (for example, on platforms like Coinbase) further incentivizes adoption in certain jurisdictions, but it isn't always possible.

Deutsche Bank's survey of over 3350 consumers dated March 2024[16] shows that the TerraUSD and Silicon Valley Bank incidents have left many questioning the stability of stablecoins, with only 18% of consumers expecting them to thrive, while 42% expect them to fade.

Knowledge gaps, worry about the algorithmic stability of some coins, and perceived risks of large, opaque issuers remain barriers to broader consumer trust, especially after high-profile incidents in the sector.

From a product point of view, only the number of recurring customers can clearly indicate if a product segment will reach high market adoption rates. Currently, despite a growing number of interested individuals and the number of stablecoin wallets increasing[17] by over 50% in one year, it could be too early to predict a stable, long-term market trend, due to similar patterns with the other digital asset classes in the past. After all, most consumer surveys accessible about stablecoin adoptions are currently run or backed by issuers and wallet providers, and might indicate a biased result or an unrepresentative test group (e.g., consisting only of users), not reflecting the broader population's views.

---

[15] The Motley Fool Stock Advisor 2025 Stablecoin Usage and Trends Survey, August fourth, 2025. Link: https://www.fool.com/research/stablecoin-usage-trends-survey/.

[16] Marion Laboure, Ph.D., Cassidy Ainsworth-Grace, Galina Pozdnyakova, "Stablecoins: Learning from 334 currency pegs since 1800," Deutsche Bank Research.

[17] According to "The State of Stablecoins 2025: Supply, Adoption & Market Trends," by Artemis and Dune, dated February 2025. Link: https://141496265.fs1.hubspotusercontent-eu1.net/hubfs/141496265/Dune_Artemis_Stablecoin_Report_March2025.pdf?utm_medium=email&_hsenc=p2ANqtz-8ShqO8TmycXloSONWRcpCdbCS0kPOxkZKYuvDd2d0G_MaoSqixten3GNIFmrI4L-_ZDhZGfuU0tNz2rPjAVjwU-EeVfidLY1K3ilM93u6xh5IZFuQ&_hsmi=106179118&utm_content=106179118&utm_source=hs_email.

Several sections rely on industry surveys that may over-represent crypto-savvy or self-selected user groups, inflating awareness, intent, and reported usage; this warrants a more systematic appraisal of evidence quality. At a minimum, studies should disclose the sampling frames (e.g., exchange or wallet customers versus population panels), recruitment channels (newsletters, X/Discord, in-app prompts), response rates, and any weighting used to address non-response bias. Key terms such as "use," "hold," and "payments" require operational definitions to avoid conflating custodial balances, speculative parking, and real-economy transactions. Cross-country comparisons should also account for differences in language, timing, and regulatory context. Without this evidentiary discipline, conclusions about mainstream stablecoin uptake risk overstating penetration and understating heterogeneity across segments and markets.

To overcome this cycle, potential retail use cases with daily-life responses, including micropayments, gaming, and cross-border e-commerce, should be emphasized. In micropayments and gaming ecosystems, stablecoins could enable seamless, programmable payments that are too costly or impractical with credit card rails. In cross-border e-commerce, stablecoins provide a universal settlement layer, eliminating currency conversion fees and enabling merchants to reach customers globally without relying on costly intermediaries. These niches demonstrate that, while stablecoins may not yet replace all retail payment options, they deliver tangible improvements where traditional solutions remain expensive, fragmented, or inaccessible.

5 Criteria for Successful End-User Adoption

In finance and banking, widespread product adoption is often driven by regulatory clarity, which provides an official stamp of approval and reduces uncertainty. This dynamic is particularly strong in the EU, where consumers tend to be more risk-averse. In this sense, the MiCAR framework of 2025 would play a decisive role in lowering risk perceptions among both consumers and institutions, ultimately encouraging broader adoption of stablecoins.

For issuers and institutional participants, however, regulation alone is not sufficient. They must prioritize robust reserve management, operational transparency, and compliance with emerging standards. Doing so not only minimizes legal and reputational risks but also strengthens credibility with partners and end users. Building alliances with custodians, payment processors, and technology providers can expand market reach and reinforce resilience. To ensure sustainable growth, issuers should focus on high-value use cases such as cross-border payments, remittances, and corporate treasury operations, rather than relying too heavily on speculative retail activity. Compliance with prudential requirements, AML, KYC, privacy, cybersecurity, and consumer protection, combined with independent audits, will be critical in fostering trust, particularly in the early stages of brand and market development.

Despite these measures, many consumers remain hesitant to use stablecoins, often because they associate them with volatile cryptocurrencies or lack a clear understanding of how they function. Even as regulatory frameworks provide greater security, wallet providers and issuers still face a pressing challenge: **explaining why consumers should use stablecoins at all, and which problems they meaningfully solve in today's economic, social, and political environment**. While stablecoins demonstrate strong advantages in cross-border payments and remittances, their adoption for everyday retail purchases is still limited; most merchants do not yet accept them. Therefore, articulating a tangible value proposition for everyday life remains essential.

Lessons can also be drawn from CBDC research. As revealed by the results of the ECB's CBDC analysis,[18] while consumers default to traditional payment methods, uptake of new digital forms of money depends on design tailored to user needs, clear communication, and network effects. The same principle applies to stablecoins: adoption will not happen organically unless providers actively guide consumers through the stages of product adoption.

The first step is **awareness**. Consumers need to understand that stablecoins differ from traditional cryptocurrencies clearly. Unlike Bitcoin or other volatile tokens, stablecoins are pegged to assets such as the U.S. dollar or the euro, which makes them far less prone to sudden price swings. Communicating this distinction clearly helps establish trust. Yet providers must also be transparent about risks; most stablecoins are not covered by deposit insurance. If consumers mistakenly assume bank-like protections or lose confidence in reserves, the result could be destabilizing redemption runs or issuer collapse. Transparent disclosure of governance, backing, and risks is therefore essential.

Next comes **interest**. Intermediaries can spark curiosity by explaining blockchain technology in simple terms, focusing on how it ensures transparency and protects transactions from fraud. By demystifying the technology, they reduce the sense of risk that many customers feel toward anything labeled "crypto."

The **evaluation** stage is where consumers weigh stablecoins against familiar payment methods like credit cards or instant transfers. Providers must emphasize practical advantages such as lower fees, real-time settlement, and global reach, while also addressing the trust gap. Unlike banks or established payment apps, most stablecoin issuers are not household names. Without validation from respected institutions, adoption may remain limited. Partnerships, certification schemes, and brand-building campaigns can help bridge this gap.

During the **trial** stage, users could be encouraged to experiment with low-risk use cases. Incentives such as small discounts or loyalty rewards for stablecoin payments can encourage firsthand experience, lowering psychological barriers to entry.

Finally, successful **adoption** depends on reinforcing positive experiences. Consumers need to see ongoing, practical benefits, such as faster refunds, seamless

---

[18] Nocciola and Zamora-Pérez (September 2024). https://www.ecb.europa.eu/press/research-publications/resbull/2024/html/ecb.rb240918~86165cbefc.en.pdf.

wallet integration, and consistent cost savings, explained clearly in comparison to existing solutions. Repetition and reliability can gradually transform stablecoins from a niche product into part of consumers' everyday financial routines.

Ultimately, adoption requires more than education: it must be underpinned by **transparent practices, regulatory compliance, operational stability, and a seamless digital experience**. Easy fiat on- and off-ramps, cross-platform compatibility, and intuitive interfaces will be non-negotiable for mass adoption. Without these foundations, stablecoins risk fading into yet another cycle of digital asset hype rather than achieving lasting integration into global finance.

6 Conclusion

Stablecoins make big promises in terms of payment system modernization and user experience. Nevertheless, despite the growing promise and market trends, stablecoins account for only a small part of the total crypto-asset market (predicted below 10% in 2022[19] and below 15% in 2025).[20] Furthermore, some experts expect most stablecoins to fail,[21] particularly "due to the lack of transparency in stablecoin operations and vulnerability to speculative sentiment." To fuel this growth and reverse the pessimistic predictions, market players would need to individually and collaboratively invest in awareness, risk mitigation, education, and transparency.

Ultimately, the future of stablecoins hinges not on hype but on trust. Without openness, resilience, and clear consumer value, they risk repeating the boom-and-bust cycle of earlier crypto experiments. With them, however, stablecoins could mature into a lasting pillar of the global payments system.

References

Adachi M, Da Silva PBP, Born A, Cappuccio M, Czák-Ludwig S, Gschossmann I, Pellicani A, Philipps SM, Plooij M, Rossteuscher I, Zeoli P (July 2022) Stablecoins' role in crypto and beyond: functions, risks and policy, ECB Macroprudental Bulletin, https://www.ecb.europa.eu/press/financial-stability-publications/macroprudential-bulletin/html/ecb.mpbu202207_2~836f682ed7.en.html

Deutsche Bundesbank (October 2021) What do households in Germany think about the digital euro? First results from surveys and interviews, Deutsche Bundesbank Monthly Report,

[19] Adachi et al. (July 2022). https://www.ecb.europa.eu/press/financial-stability-publications/macroprudential-bulletin/html/ecb.mpbu202207_2~836f682ed7.en.html.

[20] Adachi et al. (July 2022). https://www.ecb.europa.eu/press/financial-stability-publications/macroprudential-bulletin/html/ecb.mpbu202207_2~836f682ed7.en.html.

[21] Marion Laboure, Ph.D., Cassidy Ainsworth-Grace, Galina Pozdnyakova, "Stablecoins: Learning from 334 currency pegs since 1800," Deutsche Bank Research.

https://www.bundesbank.de/resource/blob/879312/807018037068359550e1d89a5dc366fe/mL/2021-10-digitaler-euro-private-haushalte-data.pdf
Di Iorio A, Kosse A, Ilaria M (June 2024) BIS Papers No 147, Embracing diversity, advancing together—results of the 2023 BIS survey on central bank digital currencies and crypto, https://www.bis.org/publ/bppdf/bispap147.pdf
Dimitris Georgarakos, Geoff Kenny, Luc Laeven, Justus Meyer, Consumer attitudes towards a central bank digital currency, ECB Working Paper Series No 3035. https://www.ecb.europa.eu/pub/pdf/scpwps/ecb~cde4bd616e.wp3035en.pdf
Ghose R, Bantanidis S et al (2025) Digital dollars, banks and public sector drive Blockchain adoption. Citi Institute. https://www.citigroup.com/rcs/citigpa/storage/public/GPS_Report_Blockchain_Digital_Dollar.pdf
Higginson M, Spanz G (2025) The stable door opens: how tokenized cash enables next-gen payments. McKinsey & Company. https://www.mckinsey.com/industries/financial-services/our-insights/the-stable-door-opens-how-tokenized-cash-enables-next-gen-payments
Marion Laboure, Ph.D. Cassidy Ainsworth-Grace, Galina Pozdnyakova, "Stablecoins: Learning from 334 currency pegs since 1800," Deutsche Bank Research
Nocciola L, Zamora-Pérez A (September 2024) Consumer demand for central bank digital currency as a means of payment, ECB Research Bulletin No. 122, https://www.ecb.europa.eu/press/research-publications/resbull/2024/html/ecb.rb240918~86165cbefc.en.pdf
The Motley Fool Stock Advisor (4 Aug 2025) Stablecoin Usage and Trends Survey, https://www.fool.com/research/stablecoin-usage-trends-survey/
The State of Stablecoins (2025) Supply, Adoption & Market Trends, by Artemis and Dune, dated February 2025. https://141496265.fs1.hubspotusercontent-eu1.net/hubfs/141496265/Dune_Artemis_Stablecoin_Report_March2025.pdf?utm_medium=email&_hsenc=p2ANqtz-8ShqO8TmycXloSONWRcpCdbCS0kPOxkZKYuvDd2d0G_MaoSqixten3GNIFmrI4L-_ZDhZGfuU0tNz2rPjAVjwU-EeVfidLY1K3ilM93u6xh5IZFuQ&_hsmi=106179118&utm_content=106179118&utm_source=hs_email

How to Implement Tokenised Money?

Mapping the Stablecoin Ecosystem: Taxonomy, Stakeholders, and Systemic Interdependencies

Selim Yazıcı

Abstract The stablecoin ecosystem has emerged as a critical bridge between traditional financial systems and the tokenized money market; however, "stablecoin" remains a "dangerously simple label" that obscures the complexity of fundamentally different financial products and risks. While existing literature extensively covers pricing mechanisms and regulatory frameworks, there remains a notable absence of research examining the ecosystem holistically, leaving regulators and financial institutions to "fly blind" regarding the true nature of their exposure. This chapter addresses this gap by establishing a comprehensive taxonomy and conceptual framework that transforms the stablecoin ecosystem from an abstract niche concept into a structured, analyzable part of the global financial system. By categorizing assets based on economic function, distinguishing between fiat-backed claims and algorithmic instruments, and mapping the functional roles of stakeholders ranging from issuers and custodians to oracles and infrastructure providers, this framework provides the "common language" necessary for effective risk assessment and policy formulation. The analysis further describes the complex interdependencies among these participants, such as the issuer-oracle dependency for collateral valuation and the liquidity feedback loops between exchanges and issuers. Ultimately, this chapter argues that a precise ecosystem definition is the prerequisite for mitigating systemic risk, enabling institutional business strategies, and fostering a transparent environment where users can accurately distinguish between secure assets and speculative instruments.

Keywords Stablecoin taxonomy • Stablecoin ecosystem • Ecosystem map • Stakeholders • Governance

S. Yazıcı (✉)
Istanbul University, Department of Business Administration, Faculty of Political Sciences, Istanbul, Türkiye
e-mail: selim@istanbul.edu.tr

S. Yazıcı et al. (eds.), *Tokenisation of Money*, Contributions to Finance and Accounting, https://doi.org/10.1007/978-3-032-22946-5_13

1 Introduction

Stablecoins are digital assets that aim to minimize price volatility relative to a reference (typically a fiat currency) and to combine fiat-like price stability with crypto--native programmability and settlement properties, making them useful as on-chain medium of exchange and unit of account. They are distinguished by their stabilization mechanism, custody model, and governance arrangements, which together determine trust, transparency, and resilience (Lipton et al. 2020). The stablecoin ecosystem is a rapidly evolving part of digital finance designed to bridge the gap between traditional financial systems and the tokenized money market by offering price stability, typically pegged to a fiat currency like the US dollar. Several jurisdictions have recently introduced legal and regulatory frameworks in response to stablecoins' growth, further intensifying global attention on the ecosystem and its technology, the blockchain.

The ecosystem approach, drawing from biological systems, has influenced management science through systems theory for decades. An ecosystem represents the environment sustaining organisms and the interconnected mechanisms ensuring continuity through dynamic relationships between living and non-living components. This system operates through equilibrium states maintained by reciprocal interactions among elements. Consistent with systems theory, disruption to any single element propagates throughout the entire system. Management scholars, inspired by biological frameworks, conceptualize businesses as "living organisms" within ecosystems, interpreting enterprises through an ecological-economic paradigm. Following this conceptual foundation, comprehending the ecosystem becomes essential for developing mechanisms that support ecosystem viability and growth (Yazici 2019).

Defining the "Stablecoin Ecosystem" is critically important because it moves stablecoins from an abstract, niche concept to a structured, analyzable, and manageable part of the global financial system. Also, there is a lot of confusion and a lack of agreed terminology. A clear definition is the foundation for regulations, risk management, strategic business development, and academic research. Without a common definition, regulators, banks, and researchers have the risk of "flying blind", unable to create effective rules, assess true risk, or build sustainable business models.

Academic literature on stablecoins extensively addresses pricing mechanisms, volatility patterns, and regulatory frameworks (Ante et al. 2023; Ito et al. 2020; Li et al. 2024; Moura de Carvalho et al. 2025); however, notable gaps persist regarding ecosystem-level architectures, participant interdependencies, and practical operational dynamics. A preliminary literature review across scholarly databases (WoS and Scopus, by using the keyword "stablecoin ecosystem", as of December 26, 2025) revealed an absence of dedicated research examining the stablecoin ecosystem holistically. This chapter aims to establish foundational knowledge of the stablecoin ecosystem by defining its structure, identifying key stakeholders, describing their roles, and mapping the interdependencies and interactions among participants.

The chapter begins by establishing the necessity for a stablecoin ecosystem taxonomy and develops a conceptual framework grounded in diverse stakeholder perspectives. It subsequently identifies the principal actors within the stablecoin ecosystem and clarifies their functional roles. This mapping provides an essential tool for risk assessment, regulatory framework development, and innovation strategies aimed at preserving stability and managing volatility.

2 Why Do We Need a Taxonomy for the Stablecoin Ecosystem?

We need a taxonomy (a formal classification system) for the "Stablecoin Ecosystem" because the term "stablecoin" is a dangerously simple label for a wide array of complex and fundamentally different financial products. Mixing them all together is like having a single category called "wheeled transport" that includes both a bicycle and a huge freight train. While both have wheels, they have entirely different purposes, technologies, and, most importantly, "risks" (Lebrun et al. 2024).

The lack of a common definition about the stablecoin ecosystem creates significant challenges across different stakeholder groups. For example, regulators lack the precision necessary for effective policy formulation, financial institutions cannot adequately quantify exposure, and researchers are constrained in their capacity to generate empirically sound analyses or sustainable strategic frameworks. That is why taxonomy is needed to allow regulators, investors, and the financial industry to disentangle this complexity. It provides a common language to accurately describe, compare, and regulate these assets based on their specific characteristics (Cengiz 2025).

3 The Importance of Taxonomy from a Multi-Stakeholder Framework

Each stakeholder approaches the challenge through a different lens: (1) *regulators* focus on identifying and mitigating systemic risks, (2) the *financial industry* seeks viable business architectures, (3) *investors and customers* require assurance and credibility, (4) *end users* need to understand and use it simply in their daily life, (5) while *academia* explores the theoretical and practical limits of research.

3.1 For Regulators and Policymakers (The "Risk" Problem)

Regulators are not concerned with a *label*; they are concerned with *economic function* and associated *risks*. The most pressing needs are regulatory clarity and adherence to compliance standards (Sood et al. 2023). Without well-defined parameters, effective oversight becomes impossible. Taxonomy serves as the essential foundation upon which all meaningful regulation is built. Effective regulatory oversight requires clearly defined boundaries, which are established by identifying the ecosystem's participants and activities (Catalini et al. 2022). Defining the ecosystem with precision clarifies which entities are involved and what activities fall under supervision. Some of the most critical functions for regulators and policy makers are:

- *Monetary Sovereignty:* The central bank's exclusive control over money issuance, supply, and policy faces challenges in the stablecoin ecosystem, where private issuers like Tether and Circle create fiat-pegged tokens that function as parallel currencies, potentially undermining state monetary monopolies. They introduce systemic risks if pegs fail, amplifying volatility in broader crypto and financial markets without sovereign backstops (Li et al. 2024).
- *Inclusiveness/Access to Finance:* Stablecoins enable instant, low-fee transactions via mobile wallets, reaching 1.7 billion unbanked adults globally without needing bank accounts or credit histories. Regulators see this as promoting equitable growth, especially in regions with limited infrastructure, while allowing oversight through reserve rules and AML compliance (Onufreiciuc and Stănescu 2023).
- *Apply the Right Rules:* A taxonomy addresses the regulator's fundamental question: "What exactly are we dealing with". For example, a fiat-backed stablecoin such as USDC operates similarly to bank deposits or money market fund shares, requiring regulatory oversight focused on banking-related concerns including reserve disclosure, liquidity management, and potential withdrawal pressures. In contrast, an algorithmic stablecoin behaves more like a high-risk, unsecured financial product (Catalini et al. 2022). These instruments present severe volatility and failure risks, as demonstrated by the Terra/Luna incident, demanding a correspondingly rigorous regulatory approach.
- *Define Jurisdictions:* "Which regulatory body holds jurisdiction over specific entities?" The classification of stablecoin issuers, whether they fall under banking regulations, money transaction rules, or constitute an entirely new category, directly determines the supervising authority, a question that emerging legislation such as the GENIUS Act seeks to resolve (Maex and Slavov 2025).
- *Manage Systemic Risk:* As the market grows, the failure of a major stablecoin could trigger a financial crisis. This is why regulatory bodies, and central banks must grasp the network of interdependencies within the system. A comprehensive classification framework enables authorities to chart the ecosystem and trace its connections to conventional finance, identifying critical points such as which banking institutions safeguard reserves and evaluating contagion risks (Catalini et al. 2022). Key questions emerge in crisis scenarios: If a leading issuer collapses,

which financial institutions are exposed through reserve holdings? Which payment infrastructures depend on that particular coin? By establishing clear definitions around reserve composition (whether cash or securities) and custodial arrangements (identifying the holding entities), stakeholders can accurately understand the likelihood and severity of a stablecoin run (like a traditional bank runs) (Cengiz 2025). Such risk assessment is unattainable without first establishing a well-defined ecosystem structure and mapping.

- *Apply Regulations Based on Activity:* A well-defined taxonomy enables regulators to assign regulations according to actual economic function. Does a wallet provider operate merely as a technology vendor, or does it assume custodial responsibilities with accompanying fiduciary obligations? When an issuer maintains reserves, does this constitute banking activity? Precise classifications prevent entities from exploiting gaps in the regulatory framework.
- *Prevent Illicit Finance:* A well-defined ecosystem structure enables regulators to pinpoint strategic enforcement nodes for Anti-Money Laundering (AML) and Countering the Financing of Terrorism (CFT) compliance, as well as consumer protection mandates, whether at the issuance, exchange, or wallet custody (Maex and Slavov 2025).

3.2 For the Financial Services Industry (The "Business" Problem)

For industry participants, precise definitions translate into managing risk, ensuring regulatory compliance, and capturing revenue opportunities. This classification framework serves as essential navigation through a promising but complex terrain. Financial institutions, including banks and fintechs, rely on taxonomy both for a strategic business instrument and a risk mitigation mechanism (Bains et al. 2022a). Some of the most critical functions for financial services industry are:

- *Identify Roles and Enables Business Strategy:* A taxonomy offers a strategic market framework that enables banks and firms to identify opportunities and operational approaches. For example, a financial institution can evaluate and select roles aligned with its business objectives:
  - *As an Issuer:* Creating its own stablecoin.
  - *As a Custodian:* Securely holding the reserve assets for other issuers.
  - *As an Infrastructure Provider:* Providing the on/off-ramps for converting cash to and from stablecoins.
- *Define Partners and Competitors:* It delineates the nature of market relationships, distinguishing collaborators from rivals and service providers. A financial institution might create partnerships with wallet providers, compete directly against stablecoin issuers, and engage blockchain networks as technology suppliers.

- *Allow Risk Management:* Undefined risks cannot be effectively managed by financial institutions. A structured classification system empowers risk management teams to develop tailored assessment frameworks. The risk profile of accepting a fully cash-backed stablecoin as collateral differs fundamentally from that of a cryptocurrency-backed variant.
- *Create Interoperability:* A common set of definitions is the starting point for building technical standards that enable different stablecoins and payment systems to communicate with each other, similar to how banks use common standards for wire transfers.

3.3 For Investors (The "Trust" Problem)

A classification framework delivers the clarity necessary to make well-informed choices and establish confidence in the system for investors (Fiedler and Ante 2023). Some of the most critical functions for investors are:

- *Enable True Risk Assessment:* A classification system enables users to comprehend the mechanics behind a stablecoin's stability, addressing the essential question: "What am I actually holding?"
  - *Category 1: Fiat-Backed (e.g., USDC):* The token represents a direct claim on equivalent reserves in cash and U.S. Treasuries, maintained at a regulated financial institution with monthly third-party audits.
  - *Category 2: Algorithmic (e.g., the former UST):* The token's value stability relies on algorithmic mechanisms tied to a separate, price-volatile cryptocurrency. This categorization distinguishes between a relatively secure asset and a high-risk speculative instrument.
- *Provide Clarity and Confidence:* Bank deposits come with understood protections through deposit insurance and regulatory oversight. A classification framework lays the groundwork for establishing equivalent transparent labeling for stablecoins, ensuring consumers understand both the nature of their holdings and the safeguards in place, so consumers know what they are getting and what protections they have.

3.4 For End Users (The "User Experience (UX)" Problem)

Like the investors, end users need to understand what they are holding and how to use it safely. Complexity brings distrust and user errors, on the other hand transparent, intuitive interfaces build confidence (Paul 2026). Some of the most critical functions for end users are:

- *UX and Design:* User Experience (UX) is critically important yet often overlooked in the stablecoin ecosystem. While much attention focuses on technical architecture, reserves, and regulation, UX determines whether stablecoins achieve mass adoption or remain a niche tool for crypto-native users. Poor UX (like onboarding, KYC/AML checks, wallet setup, transactions, or payments) creates barriers to entry, increases error rates, and undermines trust which can prevent stablecoins from fulfilling their promise of financial inclusion and efficient payments (Bains et al. 2022a).

- *Effective Public Relations:* People need to understand what they are holding, why they need it, and how to use it safely. Public Relations (PR) plays a critical yet underappreciated role in the stablecoin ecosystem, serving as the bridge between complex technical/financial infrastructure and public understanding, trust, and adoption. While UX determines *how* people interact with stablecoins, PR determines *whether* they choose to interact at all by shaping perceptions, building trust, managing crises, and translating complexity into accessible narratives. It provides the *narrative and trust infrastructure* that determines whether sophisticated technology becomes meaningful innovation.
- *Security:* Data privacy and cyber-crime are some of the most important issues for end users which are so critical in adoption
- *Simplicity:* Stablecoins can provide banking services to unbanked people. But current UX designs often exclude the very populations it claims to serve. They require technical knowledge most people don't have, they assume reliable internet connectivity, depend on smartphone ownership, lacks local currency integration, and require basic understanding of Blockchain concepts (Hardjono and Wiputra 2025).
- *Financial Literacy Gaps:* Most of the end users struggle to understand reserve backing, redemption mechanics, and risk differences between stablecoin types. They need to get an education and awareness building to understand and use it safely, confidently, and effortlessly.

3.5 For Academia (The "Research Model" Problem)

Precise definitions enable systematic classification, analytical modeling, and theoretical development for researchers. They establish the controlled conceptual environment necessary for studying emerging economic phenomena. Some of the most critical functions for researchers are:

- *Create a Clear Taxonomy for Research:* Research cannot begin without a clear agreement on a classification system (a taxonomy). Researchers must establish consensus on their subject of investigation. This system enables meaningful comparative analysis between fiat-collateralized stablecoins like USDC, crypto-collateralized variants such as DAI, and algorithmic models. Standardized terminology around concepts like "issuer", "reserve", and "redemption mechanism" ensures reproducibility and peer validation which are the fundamental principles of rigorous research methodology (Hoang et al. 2023).

- *Model Economic Impact:* Once the ecosystem is properly defined, it becomes possible to construct models examining its broader economic implications. Researchers can then pursue specific, empirically testable inquiries regarding:
  - *Monetary Policy:* How does a large, dollar-pegged stablecoin ecosystem affect the Federal Reserve's control over the money supply?
  - *Bank Disintermediation:* What happens to commercial bank deposits if millions of people and corporations choose to hold their "cash" in stablecoins instead of in bank accounts?
  - *Financial Inclusion:* Can a defined stablecoin ecosystem (including wallets and on-ramps) measurably reduce the cost of remittances for unbanked populations?
- *Inform Public Policy:* Academic research, particularly from legal and economic researchers, supplies the objective, evidence-based analysis that informs regulators in crafting more effective and well-grounded legislation about:
  - *Risk Analysis:* Researchers can simulate bank run scenarios and additional financial stress events to provide policymakers with impartial evaluations of genuine systemic vulnerabilities.
  - *Policy Effectiveness:* Researchers can compare alternative regulatory frameworks (such as Europe's MiCAR versus the U.S. GENIUS Act) to determine which approach better balances innovation with consumer protection.

A comprehensive stablecoin taxonomy serves as the essential foundation upon which all stakeholders can build a functional, sustainable ecosystem. For regulators, it transforms an opaque landscape into a mappable terrain where risks can be identified, jurisdiction clarified, and appropriate oversight applied. Industry participants gain the strategic clarity needed to navigate competitive positioning, manage risk exposure, and pursue revenue opportunities with confidence. Users benefit from the transparency required to make informed decisions and place trust in their holdings, understanding precisely what protections apply to their assets. Academia receives the structured framework necessary for rigorous research, reproducible studies, and evidence-based policy recommendations. Since we observe the needs from the different stakeholders' perspective now, we can define the key stakeholders in the stablecoin ecosystem.

4 Key Stakeholders of the Stablecoin Ecosystem

The stablecoin ecosystem comprises multiple distinct participant groups (stakeholders), each fulfilling specific roles in its creation, operation, and regulation. This complex network involves entities performing specialized functions across issuance, transfer, stabilization, custody, and access of digital assets. The primary actors within this infrastructure can be organized according to their functional responsibilities, spanning regulatory (Governance and Supervision Layer), technical

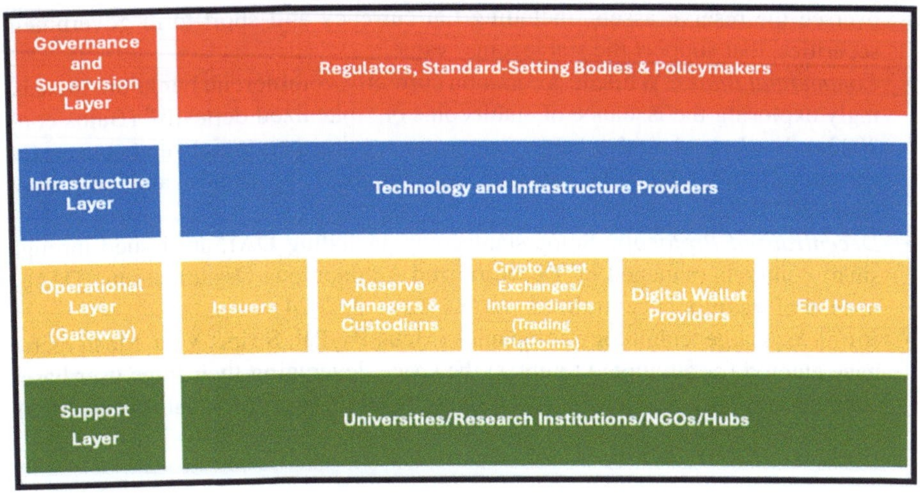

Fig. 1 Stablecoin ecosystem, *Source*: Author

(Infrastructure Layer), institutional (Operational Layer), and intellectual (Support Layer) dimensions (Fig. 1).

Core functions encompass (1) *issuance, redemption, and stability mechanisms* executed by issuers, reserve asset managers, custodians safeguarding reserves, market makers, and governance bodies; (2) *transfer operations* facilitated by blockchain networks, validators, and node operators; (3) *access points* provided through Payment Service Providers (PSPs), wallets and exchanges; and (4) intellectual and talent *support* is provided by universities, research institutions, NGOs, and through hubs (Bains et al. 2022a). A single entity may perform multiple functions or specialize in one area, with each role generating distinct risk profiles specific to its operational scope. Consequently, no single definitive framework exists for mapping this ecosystem. Our approach employs the most comprehensive model possible to encompass all participants within the system.

4.1 Issuers

These entities are responsible for creating and administering the stablecoin, including minting new tokens and burning them upon user redemption. Their primary responsibility involves managing the reserve assets (whether fiat currency, government securities, or alternative collateral) that underpin the stablecoin's value (Li et al. 2024). The issuer's governing body establishes and implements the operational rules for the stablecoin. They can be classified into distinct categories:

- *Non-Bank Financial Entities:* At present, the majority of stablecoins originate from non-bank entities such as Tether, Circle, and Paxos. These organizations oversee the reserve assets, including fiat currency and short-term government securities, that support the stablecoins' value.

- *Commercial Banks:* While less common currently, commercial banks are increasingly exploring the issuance of stablecoins or "tokenized deposits" (Bains et al. 2022a). In a hybrid model, banks may act as regulated endpoints that convert fiat currency into stablecoins, serving as compliant on-ramps and off-ramps (Ram 2025).
- *Decentralized Protocols:* Some stablecoins, including DAI, are issued through smart contracts managed by Decentralized Autonomous Organizations (DAOs) instead of traditional centralized entities (Li et al. 2024).
- *BigTechs:* Large technology companies (Meta, PayPal, Stripe, Visa, Mastercard) have entered (or attempted to enter) the space, leveraging their huge user bases to potentially scale stablecoins to a systemic level (Moura de Carvalho et al. 2025).

4.2 Reserve Managers and Custodians

These are the *financial institutions (often banks)* that are entrusted with holding and managing the actual assets in the stablecoin's reserve. Banks are playing an increasingly central and active role in the stablecoin ecosystem, moving from a cautious, supporting position to becoming key participants. These entities are responsible for the safe-keeping of the assets backing the stablecoins (Bains et al. 2022a).

Banks are increasingly viewed as essential endpoints that act as compliant on-ramps and off-ramps, facilitating conversion between fiat and stablecoins while ensuring adherence to regulations like AML/CFT. For example, a stablecoin issuer might store its U.S. dollar reserves in accounts at a partner bank or use a custodian to hold its U.S. Treasury bills. Banks' involvement is driven by growing regulatory clarity (such as the GENIUS Act in the U.S. and MiCAR in Europe) and the recognition of stablecoins as a major evolution in financial infrastructure (Mazza 2025). Banks play multiple roles in the stablecoin ecosystem as:

- *Stablecoin Issuer:* This is the most direct role. Instead of fintech companies like Circle or Tether, banks themselves are beginning to issue their own stablecoins (TRM 2025).
- *Reserve Managers and Custodians:* This is the most established and critical role banks play. For a stablecoin to be trusted, its reserves (the cash and other assets backing it) must be held securely. Banks provide this crucial trust and safety (Liang 2025).
- *Infrastructure and Service Provider:* Banks act as the essential bridge connecting the traditional financial system to the digital asset economy for their corporate and institutional clients (Safehorn 2025).
- *Agents of Compliance and Regulation*: As highly regulated entities, banks bring existing, robust compliance frameworks to the stablecoin space. Regulators often view bank participation as a way to make the ecosystem safer (Barr 2025).

4.3 Crypto Asset Exchanges/Intermediaries (Trading Platforms)

Exchanges function as trading hubs and liquidity providers, playing a critical role in facilitating stablecoin transactions for users. These marketplaces for crypto assets either match supply and demand or operate as market makers, serving as the principal gateway connecting the traditional fiat monetary system with the stablecoin ecosystem (Cerutti et al. 2025). They also act as Technology and Infrastructure Providers (see also Title 2.5 in this chapter).

- *Centralized Exchanges (CEXs):* Entities like Binance and Coinbase facilitate the exchange of fiat for crypto and vice versa (on-ramps/off-ramps). They often perform multiple functions, including custody, brokerage, and market-making, and play a crucial role in international stablecoin flows (Li et al. 2024).
- *Decentralized Exchanges (DEXs):* These platforms allow users to trade directly via smart contracts without an intermediary, often using stablecoins as a primary medium of exchange within the Decentralized Finance (DeFi) ecosystem (Makarov and Schoar 2020).

4.4 Digital Wallet Providers

Digital wallet providers supply the software or hardware solutions needed to store cryptographic keys for accessing and transferring stablecoins. These platforms enable users to securely hold, transmit, and receive stablecoins while integrating functionality for DeFi lending and payment transactions (Bains et al. 2022a). These digital wallets can be either user-controlled (unhosted) or managed by third-party providers such as dedicated wallet companies or cryptocurrency exchanges (hosted) (Cerutti et al. 2025).

- *Custodial/Hosted Wallets:* Third-party providers, typically exchanges, maintain custody of users' private keys. While this arrangement reintroduces centralization and counterparty exposure, it provides greater user convenience.
- *Non-Custodial/Unhosted Wallets:* Users maintain complete control over their private keys and assets. This approach embodies decentralization principles but shifts the entire security responsibility to individual users.

4.5 Technology and Infrastructure Providers

These are the technology firms and platforms that deliver the foundational infrastructure and tools, including blockchain technology, smart contracts, and protocols, essential for ecosystem operation:

- *Blockchain Networks:* The decentralized ledgers such as Ethereum, Solana, and Tron form the foundation upon which stablecoins are constructed and transactions are documented, alongside smart contracts that automate essential functions. These blockchain networks provide the shared execution and settlement infrastructure for stablecoin payments, maintaining the authoritative ledger, validating transactions, enforcing consensus protocols, and achieving settlement finality while supporting the network's consensus mechanism.
- *Critical Service Providers:* These are the cloud service providers and data centers that provide the hosting infrastructure for issuers, exchanges, and validators (Bains et al. 2022b).
- *Exchanges:* Platforms, both centralized and decentralized, that enable users to purchase, sell, and exchange stablecoins for fiat currency or alternative digital assets (see also Title 2.3 in this chapter).
- *Payment Processors:* Companies such as Stripe or PayPal that facilitate merchant acceptance of stablecoin payments.
- *Auditors:* Independent accounting and consulting firms that examine and verify the issuer's reserve holdings, ensuring transparency and confidence that the stablecoin maintains full backing. Most common ones are like Deloitte, KPMG, McKinsey, PwC, Grant Thornton, and Mazars.
- *Oracles/Data Providers:* Oracles are third-party services that provide *external data to smart contracts* on blockchain networks. Since blockchains are isolated systems that cannot natively access information outside their network, oracles act as trusted intermediaries that fetch, verify, and deliver real-world data to blockchain applications. Issuers rely on oracles for accurate crypto prices to avoid under-collateralization and liquidations during volatility. They provide real-time data for liquidations and smart contract execution in DeFi ecosystems (Agur et al. 2025). Their role is particularly crucial for crypto-collateralized and algorithmic stablecoins, where accurate, tamper-proof external data is essential for maintaining stability and preventing systemic failures (Hajek et al. 2024). As a result, their core functions are price discovery and valuation, liquidation mechanisms, smart contract execution, and risk management. Failure of oracle means failure of system, resulting inaccurate pricing which can trigger liquidations. For example, Oracles like Chainlink supply price feeds for collateral valuation and peg monitoring; Band Protocol is a decentralized oracle platform focusing on cross-chain data and aggregates data from multiple sources. Other examples of oracles are: API3, Pyth Network, Chronicle, and UMA (Universal Market Access).

4.6 Regulators, Standard-Setting Bodies and Policymakers

These are the governmental and international/supranational authorities that establish and implement regulatory frameworks for the stablecoin market. They aim to safeguard financial stability, ensure consumer protection, and combat illicit activities such as money laundering, while also defining the ecosystem's operational parameters (Moura de Carvalho et al. 2025).

- *Standard-Setting Bodies (SSBs):* Organizations like the Financial Stability Board (FSB), FATF, Basel Committee on Banking Supervision (BCBS), and CPMI-IOSCO develop global standards for regulation, supervision, and financial integrity (Cuervo et al. 2020).
- *National Regulators:* Central banks (like the U.S. Federal Reserve), financial regulators (like the SEC or FinCEN in the U.S.), authorities that license and supervise issuers and service providers, such as the NYDFS in the US, FINMA in Switzerland, or MAS in Singapore. They are responsible for implementing legislation like the Markets in Crypto-Assets (MiCA) regulation in Europe (Bains et al. 2022a).
- *International Economic and Trade Organizations (IETOs):* Like IMF, World Bank, WTO, OECD, UNCTAD, and G20 that play a *central role in setting norms and guiding policy coordination*. Many of the international economic and trade bodies have extensively analyzed stablecoins, recognizing their potential benefits while emphasizing significant associated risks and the need for robust regulatory frameworks.

4.7 End Users

This is the diverse group of individuals and organizations utilizing stablecoins for many purposes, including payments, trading, and value storage (Vatsa 2025):

- *Individuals (Retail):* They use stablecoins for remittances, particularly cross-border transfers, conducting payments, saving, or serving as a stable refuge to protect against cryptocurrency market volatility.
- *Businesses & Merchants (Wholesale):* These are institutional users leveraging stablecoins for expedited, cost-effective business-to-business (B2B) payments, corporate treasury management, and customer payment acceptance, typically through payment processor integration (Moura de Carvalho et al. 2025).
- *Traders & Exchanges:* Extensively utilize stablecoins as the primary trading medium on cryptocurrency platforms, commonly pairing fiat currencies, Bitcoin and other cryptocurrencies against stablecoins such as USDT or USDC, and vice versa.
- *DeFi Protocols:* Stablecoins serve as the essential foundation of Decentralized Finance (DeFi), playing a central role in lending, borrowing, and yield generation activities. DeFi protocols determine stablecoin usage parameters (such as collateral and liquidity provision), monitor and correct price peg deviations (through mechanisms like liquidity pool ratios and oracle pricing), and enforce liquidation procedures and borrowing limitations (Chemla et al. 2025).

4.8 *Universities/Research Institutions/NGOs/Hubs (FinTech, Blockchain, Innovation, etc.)*

As defined earlier, universities and research institutions enable systematic classification, analytical modeling, and theoretical development. They also function as the drivers of credibility, innovation, and analytical scrutiny within the stablecoin ecosystem. While issuers generate tokens and banks maintain reserves, academic institutions establish the intellectual foundation enabling secure system scalability. Additionally, universities may also operate as controlled testing environments (Sandboxes) for piloting stablecoins and Central Bank Digital Currency (CBDC) projects prior to broader implementation, of course by collaborating with the regulators. NGOs (Non-Governmental Organizations) play several important roles in the stablecoin ecosystem, though their involvement is still emerging as this space matures. Hubs like FinTech, Blockchain, Innovation, and Technology in many cities serve as nodes in the global financial network, facilitating the international nature of stablecoins, they also act as knowledge-sharing platforms of best practices between legislations, and access to VCs. The role of the universities, research institutions, NGOs (Non-Governmental Organizations), and Hubs can be broken down into different layers:

- *The Intellectual Layer (Research and Risk Modeling):* Universities and research institutions perform independent, empirical analysis that commercial entities may neglect. Academic researchers develop advanced mathematical models to simulate stablecoin behavior under severe market conditions, such as reserve bank failures or sudden liquidity crises. Economists at research institutions conduct economic impact assessments examining how stablecoins influence national monetary policy, inflation dynamics, and the U.S. Dollar's global standing (Moura de Carvalho et al. 2025). On the other side, NGOs contribute research on the social and economic impacts of stablecoins, particularly in developing economies. They also provide educational resources to help communities understand and safely use these digital assets.
- *The Governance Layer (Policy and Regulatory Advocacy):* Following the enactment of significant legislation such as the GENIUS Act in the U.S. and MiCAR in Europe, academic expertise has emerged as fundamental to policy formulation. Scholars regularly counsel central banks on crafting regulations that balance consumer protection with innovation promotion. Law academics examine stablecoin integration within existing property, contract, and securities frameworks, helping resolve regulatory ambiguities (Cengiz 2025). Some NGOs focus on advocating for responsible stablecoin regulation and consumer protection. They participate in policy discussions, helping to shape frameworks that balance innovation with safety, particularly regarding consumer rights, anti-money laundering measures, and systemic risk. They also have a "watchdog" function. Consumer protection and financial transparency organizations monitor stablecoin projects for compliance, misleading claims, or potential harm to vulnerable populations.

- *The Human Resource Layer (Talent and Workforce Development):* Universities servc as the principal source of specialized expertise needed to develop and oversee a financial services ecosystem. They graduate professionals skilled at the convergence of Computer Science (blockchain technology), Business and Finance (reserve management), and Law (regulatory compliance). Research centers such as Berkeley's Center for Digital Assets (CDA), Oxford, Cambridge, and Stanford's Center for Blockchain Research offer practical engagement with live stablecoin protocols, frequently supported by industry leaders including Ripple and Circle. These institutions also deliver technical education programs for central banks and regulatory supervisors (Schaubhut 2023). Hubs, on the other hand, concentrate technical talent, financial expertise, legal professionals, and blockchain developers in one location. This clustering effect accelerates innovation through collaboration, knowledge sharing, and easier access to specialized skills needed for building stablecoin infrastructure.
- *Practical Layer (Innovation Hubs/Incubators/Accelerators/Startup Funding):* Numerous technologies underpinning stablecoins originated in university research laboratories (Ling et al. 2025). University accelerators offer mentorship and early-stage support environments where students can develop next-generation stablecoin infrastructure providers, ranging from wallet services to specialized payment systems (Koonprasert et al. 2024). They can also work closely with the regulators to support their Sandbox initiatives with their expert knowledge. Fintech hubs also often operate as regulatory sandboxes where stablecoin projects can test their products under supervised conditions with relaxed regulations. This allows innovators to experiment while regulators learn about the technology, helping shape more informed and balanced policies. Fintech hubs provide proximity to venture capital, institutional investors, and traditional financial institutions. This ecosystem makes it easier for stablecoin projects to secure funding and establish partnerships with banks, payment processors, and other financial service providers.
- *Market Access and Legitimacy Layer:* Being based in established fintech hubs like London, Singapore, Hong Kong, or New York lends credibility to stablecoin projects and provides access to large markets. These locations offer better integration with existing financial infrastructure and clearer regulatory pathways to operate legally.

As a result of this detailed observation, we can map the ecosystem with key stakeholders as in Fig. 2 and define a taxonomy for the stablecoin ecosystem as a formal classification framework designed to resolve the ambiguity of the dangerously simple label of stablecoins by distinguishing between fundamentally different financial products and stakeholder functions. By mapping the complex network of participants such as issuers, custodians, infrastructure providers, and regulators, spanning across technical, institutional, and user dimensions, this framework transforms the ecosystem from an abstract niche concept into a structured, analyzable part of the global financial system. This common language enables regulators to mitigate systemic risk by applying rules based on actual economic

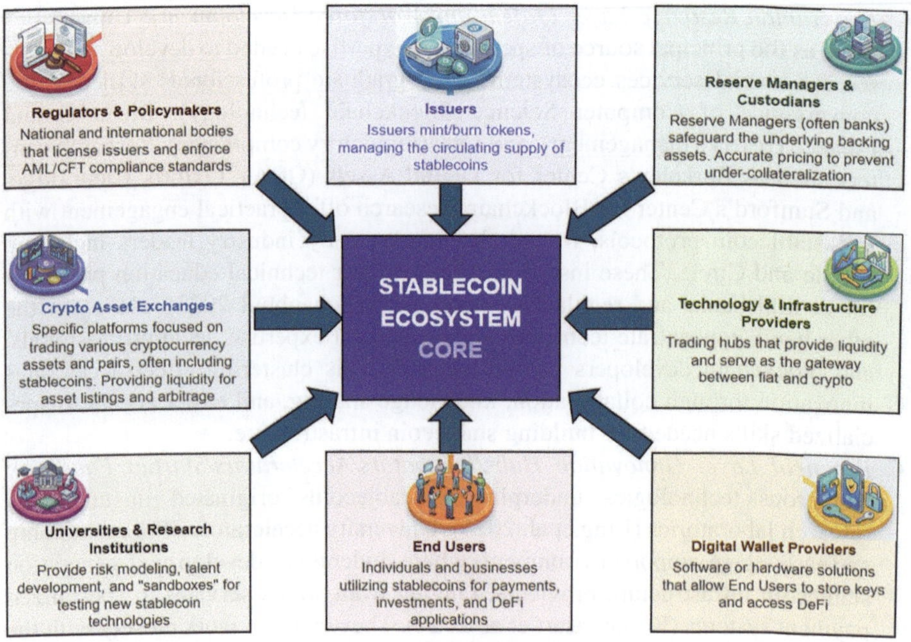

Fig. 2 Stablecoin ecosystem map with key stakeholders. *Source*: Author

function rather than broad labels, allows financial institutions to identify specific business architectures and liability exposures, and empowers users and investors to accurately assess the stability mechanisms behind their assets, such as distinguishing between secure fiat-backed claims and speculative algorithmic instruments.

5 Conclusion

The design of stablecoins presents significant challenges and controversies, particularly regarding regulatory compliance, operational transparency, and depegging risks. As explored in the other chapters of this book, each ecosystem function generates distinct risks and challenges inherent to its operations. The most critical challenges associated with issuance functions include liquidity mismatches and run risks, legal ambiguity, robust governance structures, consumer and investor protection, and the concentration of economic power among key service providers, and also across geographies. Additional relevant risks encompass operational resilience vulnerabilities, cybersecurity threats, and data privacy concerns (Bains et al. 2022a).

The governance of stablecoins represents one of the most complex and consequential challenges facing the ecosystem's maturation, with profound implications for the broader financial landscape. As stablecoins increasingly serve as critical infrastructure, like facilitating cross-border payments, enabling financial inclusion for unbanked populations, providing liquidity to decentralized finance protocols, and offering a stable store of value in volatile markets, their governance structures directly impact global financial stability and innovation. Unlike traditional financial instruments with well-established regulatory frameworks and accountability structures, stablecoins operate across a spectrum ranging from centralized corporate control to decentralized autonomous governance, each model presenting distinct risks and trade-offs. Given the stablecoin ecosystem's growing integration into both traditional finance and emerging digital economies, establishing robust, transparent, and accountable governance structures becomes essential not merely for regulatory compliance, but for maintaining user trust, protecting the millions who depend on these systems for their financial needs, and ensuring the ecosystem's long-term stability and legitimacy in supporting global economic activity.

As governments and regulatory authorities collaborate globally to develop frameworks governing stablecoin issuance and oversight, key areas of concern have crystallized around reserve management, anti-money laundering (AML) compliance, and consumer safeguards. The dynamic evolution of the stablecoin ecosystem demands continuous engagement between regulators and industry stakeholders to address risks and strengthen the dependability of these digital assets, as evidenced by legislative initiatives such as the GENIUS Act in the United States.

With the healthy developing of the stablecoin ecosystem, through a collaboration of all the stakeholders, it presents opportunities to transform financial transactions by offering a dependable medium of exchange resilient to market fluctuations. Nevertheless, the trajectory of stablecoins hinges on how effectively stakeholders navigate the regulatory, operational, and technological complexities inherent in their integration into the broader financial infrastructure. As examined in this chapter, significant interdependencies exist among ecosystem stakeholders. Issuers depend on oracles for precise cryptocurrency pricing to prevent under-collateralization and forced liquidations during market turbulence. Exchanges require issuer liquidity for asset listings and arbitrage opportunities, generating feedback mechanisms where peg failures trigger cascading effects through diminished trading activity. DeFi protocols are interconnected through stablecoin collateral networks, magnifying risks such as systemic deleveraging during crises, particularly evident in non-custodial frameworks.

As stablecoins evolve and become embedded within the global financial architecture, policymakers, regulators, industry participants, and academic institutions must collaborate to realize stablecoins' potential benefits while mitigating emerging risks. This cooperative framework will foster a more robust and accessible financial ecosystem, establishing foundations for innovative financial instruments capable of supporting sustained economic expansion.

References

Agur I, Bauer V, Mancini-Griffoli T, Peria MSM, Tan B (2025) Tokenization and financial market inefficiencies. International Monetary Fund

Ante L, Fiedler I, Willruth JM, Steinmetz F (2023) A systematic literature review of empirical research on Stablecoins. FinTech 2(1):34–47. https://doi.org/10.3390/fintech2010003

Bains P, Ismail A, Melo F, Sugimoto N (2022a) Regulating the crypto ecosystem: The case of Stablecoins and arrangements (Vol. 2022/008). International Monetary Fund

Bains P, Sugimoto N, Wilson C (2022b) BigTech in financial services: regulatory approaches and architecture (IMF, Ed. Vol. 2022). International Monetary Fund

Barr MS (2025) Exploring the Possibilities and Risks of New Payment Technologies. Retrieved 10.11 from https://www.federalreserve.gov/newsevents/speech/barr20251016a.htm

Catalini C, De Gortari A, Shah N (2022) Some simple economics of Stablecoins. Annual Review of Financial Economics 14(1):117–135. https://doi.org/10.1146/annurev-financial-111621-101151

Cengiz F (2025) Stablecoins and their regulation: a Hayekian approach. Journal of International Economic Law 28(2):204–223. https://doi.org/10.1093/jiel/jgaf014

Cerutti E, Forte S, Grinberg F, Gullo A, Hengge M, Jekabsone A, Kao K, Mancini T, Griffoli SMP, Miccoli M (2025) Understanding Stablecoins. International Monetary Fund. Washington DC

Chemla G, Knottenbelt W, Li Z, Xiong X, Delgado De Molina Rius A, Burnett AL (2025) Mind the Gap: How Stablecoins Can Secure the UK's Financial Future. Available at SSRN 5486386

Cuervo C, Morozova A, Sugimoto N (2020) Regulation of crypto assets. International Monetary Fund. Washington DC

Fiedler I, Ante L (2023) Stablecoins. In: Hugo KBB, Nikbakht E, Stein Smith S (eds) The emerald handbook on cryptoassets: investment opportunities and challenges. Emerald Publishing Limited, pp 93–105

Hajek B, Reijsbergen D, Datta A, Keppo J (2024) Collateral portfolio optimization in crypto-backed stablecoins. The International Conference on Mathematical Research for Blockchain Economy. pp. 93-111

Hardjono T, Wiputra R (2025) A Policy-Driven Ecosystem for an Indonesian Rupiah Stablecoin. Authorea Preprints

Hoang YH, Ngo VM, Bich V, N. (2023) Central bank digital currency: A systematic literature review using text mining approach. Research in International Business and Finance. 64:101889. https://doi.org/10.1016/j.ribaf.2023.101889

Ito K, Mita M, Ohsawa S, Tanaka H (2020) What is Stablecoin?: A survey on its mechanism and potential as decentralized payment systems. International Journal of Service and Knowledge Management. 4(2):71–86. https://doi.org/10.52731/ijskm.v4.i2.574

Koonprasert TT, Kanada S, Tsuda N, Reshidi E (2024) Central Bank digital currency adoption: Inclusive strategies for intermediaries and users (IMF Fintech note 2024/005, Issue). International Monetary Fund

Lebrun C, Leroux-Fankhauser O, Tovanich N, Vatter T, Gaudinat A (2024) Global taxonomy of stablecoins. The International Conference on Mathematical Research for Blockchain Economy

Li D, Han D, Weng T-H, Zheng Z, Li H, Li K-C (2024) On Stablecoin: Ecosystem, architecture, mechanism and applicability as payment method. Computer Standards & Interfaces 87:103747

Liang N (2025) Stablecoins: Issues for regulators as they implement GENIUS Act. Retrieved 10.01 from https://www.brookings.edu/articles/stablecoins-issues-for-regulators-as-they-implement-genius-act/

Ling S, Du Y, Zhou Y, Wu L, Wang C, Jia X, Yan H (2025) SoK: Stablecoin Designs, Risks, and the Stablecoin LEGO. *arXiv preprint arXiv:2506.17622*

Lipton A, Sardon A, Schär F, Schüpbach C (2020) From tether to libra: Stablecoins, digital currency and the future of money. *arXiv preprint arXiv:2005.12949*

Maex SA, Slavov S (2025) Initial evidence on the content and market implications of stablecoin reserve reporting. Journal of Accounting and Public Policy 51. https://doi.org/10.1016/j.jaccpubpol.2025.107309

Makarov I, Schoar A (2020) Trading and arbitrage in cryptocurrency markets. Journal of Financial Economics 135(2):293–319. https://doi.org/10.1016/j.jfineco.2019.07.001

Mazza R (20 Oct 2025) Why EU and US Banks Are Racing to Issue Stablecoins. Retrieved 20.01 from https://www.fintechweekly.com/magazine/articles/banks-racing-to-issue-stablecoins-us-europe-fintech

Moura de Carvalho R, Coelho Inácio H, Figueiredo Marques RP (2025) From instability to regulation: a systematic literature review on stablecoins. The International Journal of Digital Accounting Research 25:71–101

Onufreiciuc R, Stănescu L-E (2023) Financial inclusion through decentralized finance: A citizen perspective. European Journal of Law and Public Administration 10(2):117–127. https://doi.org/10.18662/eljpa/10.2/214

Paul B (2026) Regulatory considerations in decentralised finance. In: Business analytics in practice. Springer Nature, Cham, pp 83–99. https://doi.org/10.1007/978-3-032-06046-4_6

Ram R (2025) Bridging the Divide: The Hybrid Future of Stablecoins and Traditional Finance. Available at SSRN 5366106

Safehorn (2025) Top Banks Offering Crypto Custody Services in 2025. https://safeheron.com/blog/top-crypto-custody-banks-secure-digital-asset-storage-2025/

Schaubhut L (2023) Unleashing the Disruptive Potential of Stablecoins: An Analysis of Key Success Factors and Challenges in Shaping the Future of the Financial Industry. Universidade Catolica Portuguesa (Portugal)

Sood K, Singh S, Behl A, Sindhwani R, Kaur S, Pereira V (2023) Identification and prioritization of the risks in the mass adoption of artificial intelligence-driven stable coins: the quest for optimal resource utilization. Resources Policy 81:103235. https://doi.org/10.1016/j.resourpol.2022.103235

TRM (2025) Banking on Stablecoins: A Risk Mitigation Blueprint for Financial Institutions. Retrieved 10.01 from https://www.trmlabs.com/resources/blog/banking-on-stablecoins-a-risk-mitigation-blueprint-for-financial-institutions

Vatsa VR (2025) Stablecoins in the Modern Financial System. https://doi.org/10.2139/ssrn.5329957

Yazici S (2019) The Analysis of FinTech Ecosystem in Turkey. Journal of Business, Economics and Finance 8(4):188–197

Stablecoin Business Models: Current and Future Analysis

Haluk İnanmış

Abstract Stablecoins have transitioned from niche crypto instruments to core components of global financial infrastructure, reshaping how value is stored, transferred, and monetized. This paper examines the evolving business models of stablecoin issuers, banks, and electronic money institutions (EMIs), analysing how each participant captures value and manages regulatory, operational, and market risks. The findings show that despite structural and institutional differences, profitability across all models converges on three levers: yield from reserves, transaction-based revenues, and compliance-enabled trust. Issuers operate on a liquidity-and-yield logic, transforming reserve management into their principal profit source. Banks leverage their trust, capital, and regulatory status to monetize custody, compliance, and settlement infrastructure. EMIs, by contrast, build agility and connectivity into their models, acting as middleware between blockchain networks and traditional finance. Together, these models reflect a broader transformation in financial intermediation (from credit-based leverage to liquidity) and network-based value creation. The study concludes that sustainable development of the stablecoin ecosystem will depend on transparent reserve governance, interoperability, and coherent regulatory integration under frameworks such as MiCA, the GENIUS Act, and the Basel prudential standards.

Keywords Stablecoin business model • Issuers • Banks • Electronic money institutions • Regulatory frameworks • Digital finance ecosystem

---

H. İnanmış (✉)
Inted Ltd., İstanbul, Turkey
e-mail: haluk.inanmis@inted.com.tr

S. Yazıcı et al. (eds.), *Tokenisation of Money*, Contributions to Finance and Accounting, https://doi.org/10.1007/978-3-032-22946-5_14

1 Introduction

Stablecoins have shifted from niche crypto tools to core financial infrastructure, transforming both revenue generation and competitive dynamics. Issuers such as Tether and Circle now derive billions from interest on reserves, transaction fees, and liquidity deployment, making reserve management a profit center on par with traditional banking activities. Their scale demonstrates that stablecoins are not just a payments innovation, but a powerful business model built on trust, liquidity, and balance sheet optimization.

For financial institutions, stablecoins represent both opportunity and risk. By engaging early (through custody, compliance services, tokenization, FX spreads, or co-issuance) banks can capture new revenue streams and improve efficiency. Inaction, however, risks disintermediation as stablecoins increasingly dominate cross-border flows, remittances, and treasury management. With regulatory clarity lowering adoption barriers, the future business landscape will be defined by how issuers and institutions position themselves within an ecosystem that also includes tokenized deposits and CBDCs.

Stablecoin business models differ depending on the stakeholder's role—whether a dedicated stablecoin issuer, a financial institution issuing or using stablecoins, or an electronic money institute. Each type of participant emphasizes different revenue streams and strategic goals.

The following sections therefore focus not only on restating these business dynamics, but also on showing how each stakeholder translates them into distinct business logics: issuers pursue liquidity and yield efficiency, banks monetize trust and intermediation, and EMIs leverage connectivity and speed as their competitive advantage.

2 Business Model for Stablecoin Issuers

The business model of stablecoin issuers is fundamentally anchored in the yield generated from high-quality liquid assets (HQLA) held in reserve. These reserves (mainly short-term government securities such as U.S. Treasuries and cash deposits) constitute the backbone of issuer profitability. Because stablecoins are non--interest-bearing, issuers retain the entire return on these assets, effectively monetizing liquidity rather than intermediation. In 2024, Tether reportedly earned nearly USD 13 billion in profit from its reserve holdings. Circle, meanwhile, reported about USD 1.7 billion in revenue and USD 155–156 million in net income for the full year (Payments and Commerce Market Intelligence 2025; Roland Berger 2025; Digital Euro Association 2025).

Beyond reserve income, issuers derive complementary revenues. Transaction fees (applied to minting, redemption, and on-chain transfers) provide scalable income: for example, Tether reportedly earned around USD 87 million in fees in one week in early 2025 (Payments and Commerce Market Intelligence 2025). Lending and liquidity operations through credit markets and DeFi platforms such as Aave, Compound, and Nexo add incremental yield; Aave alone reported USD 18.4 million in weekly lending revenue (Payments and Commerce Market Intelligence 2025). Staking and liquidity provision activities (e.g., Maker, Curve, Lido Finance, Jito on Solana) further supplement returns (Jito generated USD 41.9 million in weekly fees and Lido USD 20.7 million) (Payments and Commerce Market Intelligence 2025). Additional institutional services, including custody, compliance frameworks, and liquidity provision for fintechs and payment processors, diversify income and enhance ecosystem embeddedness (Payments and Commerce Market Intelligence 2025).

The dominance of interest income makes issuers highly sensitive to interest-rate cycles: high-rate environments magnify profits, whereas low-rate periods compress margins. To mitigate cyclicality, issuers such as Circle have expanded into transaction-driven platforms (e.g., Circle Payments Network) to secure steadier fee income (BCG 2025; Digital Euro Association 2025; Austrian National Bank and BCG 2025). Unlike banks, which face prudential capital constraints, issuers operate with minimal regulatory buffers (amplifying both returns and exposure to policy shocks).

2.1 *Operational Efficiency and Profit Drivers*

Issuer operations exhibit extraordinary scalability and cost efficiency. Migration from expensive blockchains (e.g., Ethereum) to low-fee networks like Tron, Solana, and Base has reduced per-transaction costs from > USD 40 in 2016 to < USD 0.01 today (Roland Berger 2025). Tether achieved roughly USD 54 billion in operating profit in 2024 with ≈ 100 employees (around USD 535 million per FTE) while Circle earned USD 1.7 billion with ≈ 900 employees (BCG 2025). Maintaining reserves composed of ≈ 85% short-term Treasuries or repos and 15% cash ensures both yield and redemption liquidity (Roland Berger 2025; McKinsey and Company 2025). Transparency is critical: weak disclosure can trigger "shadow runs," as observed during USDC's temporary de-peg following the SVB collapse (BIS Innovation Hub and Bank of England 2024; FXC Intelligence 2025).

Because on-demand redemption for every user would be costly (particularly under KYC/AML checks) issuers restrict redemption rights to institutional clients who, in turn, supply liquidity to secondary markets (Roland Berger 2025; FXC Intelligence 2025; Innovate Finance 2025; Untitled Investment Expertise 2023). This model preserves convertibility while controlling compliance and transaction costs. By contrast, banks and EMIs rely on regulated payment infrastructures to handle redemptions directly through fiat systems.

2.2 *Regulation, Ecosystem Integration, and Risk Landscape*

Regulatory compliance constitutes both the largest cost center and a strategic necessity. Obligations span audits, reserve attestations, AML/KYC controls, and adherence to frameworks such as MiCA and the U.S. GENIUS Act (BIS Innovation Hub and Bank of England 2024). MiCA prohibits paying interest on stablecoins and mandates strict reserve composition and capital requirements (Innovate Finance 2025; Untitled Investment Expertise 2023; Austrian National Bank and BCG 2025). Issuers invest heavily in partnerships with exchanges, wallets, and payment processors to achieve network reach (costs absent for banks with established client networks or for EMIs operating under unified licences) (Fiftyone Insight and Fintech Blueprint 2025; Digital Euro Association 2025).

The broader risk environment is multi-layered.

Regulatory risk: fragmented jurisdictions (EU, U.S., Hong Kong) inflate compliance costs; bans and caps (China, India, EU USD limits) can abruptly restrict operations (Digital Euro Association 2025; Austrian National Bank and BCG 2025; BRN 2025).

Operational risk: interoperability gaps between blockchains raise costs and vulnerabilities; fiat on/off-ramps remain bottlenecks (Roland Berger 2025; FXC Intelligence 2025; BCG 2025; Digital Euro Association 2025; BRN 2025).

Market risk: profitability depends on interest-rate levels; dominant incumbents (USDT, USDC) create barriers to entry (BCG 2025; Digital Euro Association 2025; BRN 2025); traditional finance is developing rival "tokenized-deposit" instruments (Roland Berger 2023; Austrian National Bank and BCG 2025; BRN 2025).

Technological risk: reliance on foreign-controlled blockchains, smart-contract flaws, and weak custody procedures pose existential threats (Digital Euro Association 2025; McKinsey and Company 2025; Austrian National Bank and BCG 2025; BRN 2025).

In contrast to banks, which exchange margin for stability, and EMIs, which trade scale for agility, stablecoin issuers operate at the frontier of yield optimization (highly profitable but structurally exposed). Their sustainability depends on transparent governance, regulatory adaptability, and credible reserve management (BCG 2025; Digital Euro Association 2025; Austrian National Bank and BCG 2025).

3 Business Model for Financial Institutions

Banks participate in the stablecoin economy through service intermediation rather than direct yield extraction. Unlike independent issuers, they rarely profit from holding reserves themselves; instead, they monetize their regulatory position and infrastructure by supplying custody, settlement, and compliance services to stablecoin issuers and fintechs (Payments and Commerce Market Intelligence 2025; BCG 2025; Austrian National Bank and BCG 2025). Where banks co-issue their own stablecoins or tokenized deposits (examples include JPM Coin and EURI) they can also generate interest income on underlying reserves, but such exposure is constrained by prudential capital rules such as the Basel Committee's proposed 1250% risk weighting on public-chain assets (FT Partners 2025; McKinsey and Company 2025; WBS Gillmore Centre for Financial Technology 2025). This stands in sharp contrast to issuers, who internalize all reserve yield without capital requirements.

3.1 *Revenue Sources and Strategic Positioning*

Banks' revenue stack is therefore fee-based and relationship-driven. They earn from custody and safeguarding of fiat reserves (e.g., BNY Mellon for USDC), transaction and FX-spread income on cross-border stablecoin payments, and "Banking-as-a-Service" (BaaS) arrangements that license payment rails or compliance modules to fintechs (Payments and Commerce Market Intelligence 2025; BCG 2025). Through embedded-payment solutions and treasury platforms, banks also capture API-access and integration fees, mirroring EMI business models but at institutional rather than retail scale. Whereas EMIs depend on network connectivity and automation, banks leverage trust and regulatory credibility as competitive assets, converting what is a compliance cost for issuers into a compliance-as-a-service revenue line (Payments and Commerce Market Intelligence 2025; BRN 2025).

Their ability to cross-sell across established client relationships further differentiates them: integrating stablecoins into trade finance, payroll, and liquidity management allows banks to retain customers who might otherwise migrate to crypto-native providers (Payments and Commerce Market Intelligence 2025; Fiftyone Insight and Fintech Blueprint 2025; BCG 2025). Per-transaction margins are modest, yet total throughput and client stickiness deliver material profitability.

3.2 *Operational Efficiency and Technological Constraints*

Compared with lean issuers and digital-first EMIs, banks face structural efficiency limits. Legacy core-banking systems and batch-settlement processes restrict their capacity to exploit blockchain's real-time features (FT Partners 2025; Dynamic 2025). Nevertheless, large-scale infrastructure, robust risk controls, and 24/7 operational coverage provide resilience and reputational assurance valued by institutional clients. Several global banks have begun integrating permissioned or consortium blockchains to reconcile compliance needs with efficiency gains (a middle path between public-chain exposure and total exclusion from decentralized networks) (Austrian National Bank and BCG 2025; WBS Gillmore Centre for Financial Technology 2025). This hybridization defines banks' gradual modernization trajectory.

3.3 *Profitability Drivers and Risk Profile*

Bank participation yields moderate but stable profitability. Unlike issuers' interest-rate sensitivity, bank returns depend on transaction flow, client adoption, and pricing of value-added services. Their main cost pressures arise from prudential capital allocation, technology modernization, and legal compliance. However, unlike EMIs (whose compliance burden scales with each jurisdiction) banks benefit from supervisory continuity and established frameworks that reduce marginal compliance cost per transaction. The interplay of these factors turns regulatory infrastructure into a strategic moat rather than a constraint.

Key risks include deposit disintermediation as clients shift balances to stablecoins, capital inefficiency from restrictive risk weights, and third-party dependencies on external blockchain or oracle providers (BCG 2025; FT Partners 2025; Austrian National Bank and BCG 2025). Cybersecurity, reputational risk, and cross-jurisdictional sanctions compliance also remain material concerns (Austrian National Bank and BCG 2025; WBS Gillmore Centre for Financial Technology 2025). Still, the depth of governance, insured deposit frameworks, and diversified revenue base make banks less fragile than pure issuers in stress conditions.

4 Business Model for Electronic Money Institutions (EMIs)

Electronic Money Institutions occupy a hybrid position between stablecoin issuers and banks, combining the technological agility of the former with the regulatory grounding of the latter. Like issuers, EMIs focus on transactional and network-based revenues, but unlike issuers they cannot profit materially from reserve yields because client funds are typically held with partner banks (Payments and Commerce Market Intelligence 2025; BCG 2025; Dynamic 2025). And unlike banks, they lack access to central-bank money or large balance sheets, operating instead through digital platforms optimized for speed and integration.

4.1 *Revenue Model and Strategic Role*

EMIs generate income from transaction fees, API access, merchant-acquiring charges, and SaaS subscriptions derived from payment orchestration and infrastructure-as-a-service offerings (Payments and Commerce Market Intelligence 2025; Fiftyone Insight and Fintech Blueprint 2025; FT Partners 2025). This positions them as middleware providers linking banks, merchants, and blockchain networks. Examples include Orbital, which integrates fiat and stablecoin payments for corporates, and Bridge (acquired by Stripe for USD 1 billion), demonstrating the strategic value of controlling this integration layer (Payments and Commerce

Market Intelligence 2025; Fiftyone Insight and Fintech Blueprint 2025; FXC Intelligence 2025; FT Partners 2025). By comparison, issuers monetize liquidity and yield, and banks monetize custody and compliance; EMIs instead monetize access and connectivity.

EMIs can also offer wallet and custody solutions for SMEs and corporates, bundling insurance or premium support for additional fees (Payments and Commerce Market Intelligence 2025). However, reliance on partner banks for reserve custody and fiat settlement reduces profit margins and creates inter-institutional dependency absent in issuer models.

4.2 *Operational Efficiency and Regulatory Context*

EMIs benefit from lean, digital-first infrastructures built around APIs, modular payment engines, and blockchain integrations, enabling faster scaling than banks encumbered by legacy systems (Fiftyone Insight and Fintech Blueprint 2025; FT Partners 2025; Austrian National Bank and BCG 2025). Yet, unlike issuers who self-custody reserves, EMIs operate within regulated e-money frameworks that impose ring-fencing of client funds and regular supervision. Existing e-money or payment-institution licences give them relatively swift market entry and a foundation of regulatory trust (Fiftyone Insight and Fintech Blueprint 2025; Untitled Investment Expertise 2023; Austrian National Bank and BCG 2025). Under MiCA, however, EMIs issuing stablecoins cannot pay interest to holders, limiting their competitive flexibility (Innovate Finance 2025; Untitled Investment Expertise 2023; Digital Euro Association 2025; Austrian National Bank and BCG 2025).

Compared with issuers, whose compliance cost stems from building infrastructure de novo, EMIs extend already-embedded AML/KYC frameworks to stablecoin operations. Their marginal compliance cost is lower than that of new entrants but higher than that of banks operating under consolidated supervisory regimes.

4.3 *Profitability and Risk Profile*

EMIs' profitability depends primarily on transaction volume and network scale, not yield differentials. High automation and low fixed costs support solid unit economics, but aggregate profit potential remains limited by smaller balance sheets and revenue sharing with partner banks (Payments and Commerce Market Intelligence 2025; BCG 2025; Dynamic 2025). Their competitive edge lies in rapid innovation and integration speed (factors less accessible to highly regulated banks or yield-driven issuers).

Key risks differ accordingly. Partner-bank dependency exposes EMIs to liquidity bottlenecks or unilateral de-risking decisions (Payments and Commerce Market Intelligence 2025; Roland Berger 2025); AML/CFT exposure rises with the velocity of cross-border flows (FXC Intelligence 2025; Austrian National Bank and BCG 2025; WBS Gillmore Centre for Financial Technology 2025); and network-fragmentation costs hinder seamless interoperability across blockchains (BCG 2025; Digital Euro Association 2025; BRN 2025). While their compliance posture is stronger than that of most issuers, limited scale restricts resilience against technology failures or regulatory tightening.

5 Conclusion

The stablecoin ecosystem is shaped by three distinct yet interdependent business logics. Issuers operate on a liquidity-and-yield logic, transforming reserve management into their core profit engine. They monetize the spread between non-interest-bearing liabilities and returns on high-quality liquid assets, while supplementing income with network and transaction fees. Their model delivers exceptional scalability and profitability but is exposed to interest-rate cycles, peg stability risks, and fragmented regulatory oversight.

Banks, by contrast, follow an intermediation-and-trust logic. They monetize credibility, infrastructure, and regulatory depth through custody, settlement, compliance, and FX services rather than direct reserve yield. Their revenues are fee-based and relationship-driven, leveraging scale and prudential credibility but constrained by capital requirements, legacy systems, and deposit disintermediation. Electronic Money Institutions (EMIs) pursue an access-and-connectivity logic, acting as agile bridges between blockchain networks and traditional payment rails. They earn from transaction and API fees, monetizing speed and integration rather than balance-sheet yield, yet face dependence on partner banks and intense competition from larger issuers and incumbents. Together, these models redefine financial intermediation around liquidity, trust, and network connectivity as the core sources of value in the emerging tokenized-money landscape.

These evolving business dynamics signal a fundamental structural shift in financial intermediation, moving away from credit-based, balance-sheet-driven banking toward liquidity- and reserve-based digital money systems. Traditional intermediaries (banks, payment networks, and correspondent chains) are being replaced by blockchain-enabled networks that allow direct, near-instant value transfer without relying on credit creation. Profit generation increasingly depends on yields from High-Quality Liquid Assets and transaction-based fees, positioning reserve management as the new core of intermediation. Trust is maintained not through deposit insurance or regulatory guarantees but through transparency, proof-of-reserves, and technological credibility. As money becomes programmable and embedded within digital platforms, intermediation is being redefined around network participation, compliance capabilities, and liquidity governance rather than maturity transformation or balance-sheet leverage.

The rapid institutionalization of stablecoins amplifies these structural changes and introduces profound implications for regulators, policymakers, and the future architecture of tokenized money. As private issuers, banks, and EMIs increasingly perform quasi-monetary functions (holding reserves, settling transactions, and enabling programmable payments) regulators must extend prudential and conduct frameworks beyond traditional banking boundaries to ensure transparency, redemption integrity, and systemic resilience. Policymakers face the challenge of maintaining monetary sovereignty while supporting innovation, as stablecoins blur the distinction between public and private money. This evolution points toward a hybrid monetary order in which stablecoins, tokenized deposits, and central bank digital currencies coexist within interoperable, regulated infrastructures. The key policy priority will be to design governance frameworks that guarantee convertibility, interoperability, and supervision across these instruments, preventing regulatory arbitrage and fragmentation. Ultimately, the trajectory of tokenized money will hinge on whether this emerging system embeds trust, accountability, and resilience into its programmable foundations (ensuring that digital finance strengthens rather than destabilizes the global monetary framework).

References

Austrian National Bank & BCG (July 2025) Euro Money Tokens: Potential Economic Role of CBDCs and Euro-Denominated Stablecoins, Austrian National Bank & BCG, https://www.oenb.at/dam/jcr:542855f2-a5cf-40fc-b0dd-dfb1ddf7e8c4/Open-Forum-Euro-Denominated-Stablecoins-and-CBDC.pdf [Accessed 23 Aug 2025]

BCG (May 2025) Stablecoin: Five killer tests to gauge their potential. BCG, https://media--publications.bcg.com/Stablecoins-five-killer-tests-to-gauge-their-potential.pdf [Accessed 22 Aug 2025]

BIS Innovation Hub & Bank of England (July 2024) Project Pyxtrial: Monitoring the backing of Stablecoins, BIS Innovation Hub & Bank of England, https://www.bis.org/about/bisih/topics/suptech_regtech/pyxtrial.htm [Accessed 22 Aug 2025]

BRN (June 2025) The Stablecoin Revolution: Transforming Global Finance in the Digital Age, BRN, https://www.thebrn.co/ [Accessed 27 Aug 2025]

Digital Euro Association (2025) The Role of Stablecoins in Financial Sovereignty, Digital Euro Association, Frankfurt, https://digital-euro-association.de/blog/the-role-of-stablecoins-in-financial-sovereignty [Accessed 22 Aug 2025]

Dynamic (August 2025) The 2025 Stablecoin Playbook: A Strategic Guide for Fintechs and Builders Exploring Stablecoins, Dynamic, https://www.dynamic.xyz/2025-stablecoin-playbook [Accessed 27 Aug 2025]

Fiftyone Insight & Fintech Blueprint (July 2025), Money Movement 2.0: How Stablecoins Are Rebuilding Global Finance and Commerce, Fiftyone Insight & Fintech Blueprint, https://www.51insights.xyz/p/money-movement-20 [Accessed 22 Aug 2025]

FT Partners (May 2025) Stablecoin Payments: Crypto Finds its Killer App?, FT Partners, https://www.ftpartners.com/fintech-research/stablecoin-payments?ref=thisweekinfintech.com [Accessed 22 Aug 2025]

FXC Intelligence (July 2025) The state of stablecoins in cross-border payments: The 2025 industry primer, FXC Intelligence, https://www.fxcintel.com/research/reports/ct-state-of-stablecoins-cross-border-payments-2025 [Accessed 22 Aug 2025]

Innovate Finance (April 2025) Stablecoin: The UK Opportunity, Innovate Finance, https://www.innovatefinance.com/blogs/innovate-finance-uk-must-act-now-to-lead-the-global-stablecoin-economy/. [Accessed 22 Aug 2025]

McKinsey & Company (July 2025) The stable door opens: How tokenized cash enables next-gen payments, McKinsey & Company, https://www.mckinsey.com/industries/financial-services/our-insights/the-stable-door-opens-how-tokenized-cash-enables-next-gen-payments [Accessed 23 Aug 2025]

Payments and Commerce Market Intelligence (July 2025) Unlocking Revenue: How Banks Can Make Money with Stablecoins Through Strategic Partnerships. Payments and Commerce Market Intelligence, https://paymentscmi.com/how-banks-can-drive-revenues-with-stablecoins/. Accessed 22 Aug 2025

Roland Berger (2023) The Future of Payments: How stablecoins and tokenized deposits innovate the financial services industry. Roland Berger, Dubai, https://www.rolandberger.com/publications/publication_pdf/Roland_Berger_The_Future_of_Payments.pdf [Accessed 22 Aug 2025]

Roland Berger (2025) Stablecoins: The future of money?. Roland Berger, February. https://www.rolandberger.com/en/Insights/Publications/Stablecoins-The-future-of-money.html. Accessed 22 Aug 2025

Untitled Investment Expertise (December 2023) The Future of Euro Stablecoins: Playbook for a 100X Opportunity, Untitled Investment Expertise, https://www.jpmorgan.com/kinexys/documents/deposit-tokens.pdf [Accessed 22 Aug 2025]

WBS Gillmore Centre for Financial Technology (August 2025) Bridging the Divide: The Hybrid Future of Stablecoins and Traditional Finance, WBS Gillmore Centre for Financial Technology, https://warwick.ac.uk/fac/soc/wbs/subjects/finance/gillmore/publications/insightpapers/bridging_the_divide/ [Accessed 27 Aug 2025]

Offline-Capable Central Bank Digital Currencies as a Key Enabler of a Resilient Digital Payment System

Wolfram Seidemann, Lars Hupel, and Paula Martins

Abstract Central Bank Digital Currencies (CBDCs) support the creation of a resilient and inclusive digital payment ecosystem. We investigate the role of offline-capable CBDCs in ensuring universal access to financial services, especially in times of crisis when conventional digital systems are disrupted.

We assess technical feasibility of offline capabilities, following an approach by the Bank for International Settlements (BIS). We further discuss the token-based design of CBDCs and contrast it with traditional account-based systems. Such a CBDC design can preserve the two-tier distribution model known from the current cash cycle. Security requirements are addressed through a layered security architecture comprising hardware security, robust payment protocols, and double-spending protection by the central bank.

Practical experiences from various pilot studies demonstrate the operational effectiveness and user acceptance of offline CBDCs across different regions and use cases. We argue that such currencies will not only complement existing monetary systems but also foster a more equitable financial landscape. Finally, we put the proposed architecture into historical context, describing the evolution of digital payments, and illustrate their renewed relevance to global financial stability and inclusivity.

Keywords Central Bank digital currency (CBDC) • Offline CBDC • Digital money • Tokenisation

W. Seidemann · P. Martins
Giesecke+Devrient Currency Technology GmbH, Munich, Germany
e-mail: wolfram.seidemann@gi-de.com

L. Hupel (✉)
Giesecke+Devrient advance52 GmbH, Munich, Germany
e-mail: lars.hupel@gi-de.com

S. Yazıcı et al. (eds.), *Tokenisation of Money*, Contributions to Finance and Accounting, https://doi.org/10.1007/978-3-032-22946-5_15

1 Introduction

Integration of digital technologies into monetary systems has changed the way we carry out financial transactions. Over the past few decades, banks and businesses have streamlined cumbersome and time-consuming processes, making them more efficient and less time-consuming. With increasing digitalization in all areas of life, most people expect payments to be fast and convenient, above all else. According to a survey by Bitkom, Germany's digital association, 25% of internet users never read the terms and conditions of online services (Bitkom 2024). Many people take security for granted and might not realize that they are trading personal information for convenience with many payment service providers.

The transition towards digital payments creates significant risks. The major blackout in Spain and Portugal in April 2025, affecting tens of millions of people, illustrated this. It paralyzed all forms of electronic payment methods. Consumers and businesses were unable to conduct transactions, grinding the economy to a halt. This incident was a real-world stress test for our digital society, showing the fragility of our digital infrastructures.

In the absence of functional digital systems, cash typically serves as the sole reliable medium for transactions. There is a notable increase in demand for cash during periods of technological uncertainty—such as during the millennium change—, financial crises, and natural disasters like hurricanes or COVID-19 (Rösl and Seitz 2023; Spicer 2017).

Any disruption, whether caused by technical glitches or natural disasters, highlights the current digital payment systems' lack of resilience and the need for infrastructures that can withstand similar challenges in the future.

Moreover, payment services, which are largely driven by network effects and the benefits of widespread adoption, are a highly attractive business model. This fuels competition among providers, each seeking to grow their user base, which often leads to market fragmentation. In such an environment, various proprietary systems emerge, which limit interoperability and user choice.

A publicly provided platform based on common standards could counter this trend by serving as a neutral infrastructure layer. It would allow the private sector to build and offer innovative services while ensuring broad accessibility and compatibility. This open foundation would promote healthy competition focused on user--centric innovation rather than proprietary lock-in, ultimately fostering a more inclusive and efficient digital payment ecosystem.

2 The Evolution of Monetary Systems

The monetary system has evolved alongside societal developments. Changes in economic structures, political priorities, and technological innovations had a significant impact on the monetary system.

In its earliest form, goods and services were exchanged directly. However, there was neither a common measure of value nor a reliable way to store wealth.

Money is a convention. Communities defined conveniently exchangeable objects of value as money such as grain or shells. As a result of political and economic development, emerging sovereign entities established dedicated monetary systems which facilitated trade and economic expansion.

The rapid increase in population, coupled with urbanization and industrialization, further spurred trade and heightened the demand for money. Private banks, and later sovereign entities, introduced paper money as a type of bond backed by commodities.

The departure from the gold standard marked a significant move towards the abstraction of value. Over time, money has evolved from tangible assets to digital and abstract forms.

2.1 *From Physical to Electronic Transactions*

One of the earliest forms of digital payment dates back to the 1870s and the advent of telegraphy. Western Union offered to transfer money via telegraphic messages (Western Union 2025).

According to their own account, the first credit card payment occurred in 1950 with the introduction of the Diners Club card, 'the birth of the world's first multi-purpose charge card' (Diners Club 2024).

An even more remarkable event was the 'first legitimate online transaction', which occurred in 1994 (Fessenden 2015). This is because the modern concept of digital payments is closely linked to the development of computer and internet technologies. This significant milestone in e-commerce paved the way for the explosion of online shopping. The sector's robust worldwide growth is a major driver of cashless payments.

New technologies have significantly impacted the landscape of cashless payments. Chips based on *EMV (Europay, MasterCard, Visa)* standards have increased security for credit card payments and created a global standard for card payments. *NFC (Near Field Communication)* technology has cut down transaction times at the point-of-sale, allowing consumers to pay by simply tapping a card near a payment terminal. Recently, the proliferation of mobile payment apps and digital wallets—such as Apple Pay, Google Wallet, and Samsung Pay—lets users transact on card rails from their smart mobile devices.

As digital technology has expanded into most aspects of life, people increasingly expect a great user experience, including for financial transactions. This paved the way for the success of instant payment systems, which provide real-time, secure, and convenient app-based financial transactions. They address the demand for speed and efficiency. *A2A (account-to-account)* payments built on real-time payment rails are shaping the payment landscape in major emerging economies such as Brazil and India. This has led to a decline in cash usage at the point of sale. According to

McKinsey & Company (2024) 'global cash usage now stands at 80 percent of 2019 levels and continues to decrease at 4 percent a year'.

Yet, we can observe an increase of cash in circulation. According to official figures, the total cash circulation within the Eurozone amounted to € 1.578 trillion in April 2025 (European Central Bank 2025). This is almost 28% more than 6 years ago (€ 1.229 trillion in April 2019), growing at a faster rate than inflation would suggest.[1] Antti Heinonen, former Director of Banknote at the ECB, estimates that the number of banknotes in circulation globally is significantly higher than 900 billion pieces (Heinonen 2025). This 'paradox of banknotes' (Bailey 2009) can be explained by a shifting demand for cash: away from transactions, towards store of value (Zamora-Pérez 2021).

Presently, cash remains the only public payment method that can be used independently from the issuer. But electronic transactions typically involve third-party providers that may charge fees or use personal data. Payment providers often impose requirements—such as credit scores or a minimum age—that exclude large parts of the population. The COVID-19 pandemic exacerbated this problem and underscored the necessity for more resilient, accessible, and efficient payment systems.

A digital version of cash promises to complement existing means of payment and to extend universal access to everyone.

2.2 The Genesis of Digital Money

In the 1980s, David Chaum developed *DigiCash*, an electronic, anonymous payment scheme (Chaum 2025). But the concept of using cryptographic protocols to represent value only took off in the late 2000s with Bitcoin.

The global financial crisis of 2008 revealed significant vulnerabilities in the financial sector: excessive leverage, a lack of transparency, inadequate regulation, immense complexity, and the risks posed by institutions deemed 'too big to fail.' Public trust in established financial institutions eroded.

Cryptocurrencies, more specifically Bitcoin, emerged as a direct response to the crisis in 2008. In conjunction with blockchain technology, they were developed to address these perceived shortcomings. Nakamoto (2008) criticized that 'commerce on the Internet has come to rely almost exclusively on financial institutions serving as trusted third parties to process electronic payments.' In response, they outlined principles of a peer-to-peer electronic cash system operating independently of financial institutions.

While cryptocurrencies have proliferated largely unbothered by regulation, a combination of long-term trends and specific events has led to new developments.

[1] ECB statistics on banknotes and coins circulation: https://www.ecb.europa.eu/stats/policy_and_exchange_rates/banknotes+coins/circulation/html/index.en.html.

The increasing digitalization of the economy, coupled with the COVID-19 pandemic, accelerated the need for innovative, but resilient and stable financial solutions. This has catalyzed the development of *CBDCs (Central Bank Digital Currencies)*.

2.3 Towards a Tokenized Financial System

Tokenization—representation of value in digital format—is becoming increasingly prominent, with central banks, commercial banks, and multilateral organizations playing significant roles. Ravi Menon, former Managing Director of the Monetary Authority of Singapore and current Chairman at the Global Financial Technology Network, highlighted tokenization's transformative impact on finance in his keynote speech at the Point Zero Forum (Menon 2024). This is not a transient phenomenon; it's a structural change of financial market infrastructure that adds a new paradigm to the traditional, siloed architecture.

We can witness the tokenization of traditional instruments such as cash (in the form of CBDC), deposits and securities. This enables real-time, programmable, and interoperable value exchanges.

Central banks are spearheading a series of global experiments. Prominent initiatives such as *Project Agora, Project Rialto,* or *Project Meridian FX* address cross-border settlements, among other use cases. They enjoy support by the BIS to foster global exchange and standardization.

These efforts have not only offered technical insights but have recently culminated in the BIS' 'Finternet' concept: a cohesive, interoperable network of tokenized monies and assets, spanning the public and private sector. According to Carstens and Nilekani (2024), the 'Finternet would be designed to empower individuals and businesses by placing them at the centre of their financial lives.'

3 Why Central Bank Digital Currencies Matter

In a tokenized financial system, public money is not just an option, it is essential. The absence of a universally accepted, risk-free reference asset can leave the system vulnerable. Private digital currencies might struggle to maintain par, especially across various platforms and jurisdictions.

This discrepancy introduces exchange rate and counterparty risks. It also jeopardizes the fundamental concept of fungibility, crucial for a stable financial environment. Dominant private issuers have the potential to establish closed ecosystems that restrict user options and limit interoperability, thereby stifling competition.

A well-designed CBDC, issued as tokenized public money, directly mitigates these risks. Distributed through financial service providers—commercial banks and non-bank institutions—CBDCs stabilize the monetary and financial system. They would not only complement cash as a public means of payment, but also serve as a platform for innovation, forming the cornerstone of the digital economy.

3.1 Core Requirements of a Successful CBDC

Security A CBDC must adhere to a comprehensive security framework. This should include internal security protocols, external security assessments, and ongoing penetration testing (security by design). The BIS 'has leveraged the NIST cyber security framework but with two additional steps, namely prepare and adapt.' (BIS Innovation Hub 2023b). CBDCs also have unique requirements: Unlike traditional banking infrastructure, a CBDC would operate continuously, 24/7, allowing very little room for maintenance or downtime (Rafiee and Hupel 2024). To maintain the ongoing trust of all participants within the system, a strong and scalable *PKI (Public Key Infrastructure)* is essential.

Data Privacy CBDCs must prioritize users' privacy by safeguarding personal and transactional information against unauthorized access and breaches. They can offer greater privacy than commercial digital payment systems, which often rely on monetizing user data. Central banks have no (commercial or otherwise) interest in that, hence, they can design CBDC as public infrastructure with privacy safeguards. For example, operational, transactional, and administrative data can be separate. At the same time, CBDC must comply with rules on anti-money laundering and financial governance rules. Central banks should carefully balance transparency and anonymity to foster trust and acceptance among users.

Interoperability A CBDC system needs to integrate smoothly with current infrastructures (Hupel 2023). This allows financial institutions to seamlessly integrate digital currency into their ecosystems, which fosters the development of innovative applications. Cross-border interoperability would reduce costs and complexities, and significantly lower settlement and default risks for international transactions.

Offline Functionality Like cash, CBDC must function universally and without interruption. This allows it to achieve legal tender status, driving adoption. It should operate independently of network connectivity, bank accounts, or continuous access to electricity. It should not require high-end smartphones. CBDC promises a strong potential of financial inclusion to the many people left out of today's digital financial system. Offline functionality is a tangible example of strong privacy protection by design: it enables anonymous, cash-like transactions while still operating within a secure and regulated framework.

3.2 *The Importance of Offline CBDC*

Zooming in on the last requirement, offline functionality is central to achieve many central banks' policy objectives.

People should have access to a secure and reliable digital payment method. Offline functionality—through a well-designed CBDC and/or as an add-on to a national payment system—addresses this.

In a 2023 survey, 98% of central banks saw offline payment as either vital or advantageous for a retail CBDC (BIS Innovation Hub 2023a).

Resilience and universal acceptance of a national currency, whether physical or digital, are critical to its function and trustworthiness. Integrating offline functionality from the outset ensures that a CBDC remains functional without reliance on smartphones, network connections, internet access, or electricity.

Cash sets a high standard for its digital counterpart, which central banks intend to issue as legal tender. The European Central Bank (2020) notes that '[l]egal tender status would require that users be able to receive incoming payments through means that are as user-friendly as banknotes, for example by using a simple physical device that can also be used offline.'

By offering offline capabilities and simple, low-cost wallet formats like feature phones or chip cards CBDC helps ensure that everyone, regardless of their circumstances, has access to secure and convenient digital payments—anytime, anywhere.

4 Technical Feasibility

Many central banks have, or are currently, investigating CBDC designs that include some degree of offline capability. The BIS, in Project Polaris, distinguishes three types of offline capability, in increasing order of ambition (BIS Innovation Hub 2023a):

- *staged*, in which two parties can transact offline, but the receiving party cannot subsequently use funds received offline;
- *intermittently*, in which parties can transact offline without intervening online connection, but limited by risk parameters—such as a mandatory online integrity check after a fixed number of transactions—;
- *fully*, in which value circulates offline indefinitely and no online connection is ever required.

As an analogy, cash is in the last category with some aspects of 'intermittently' because—while there is no mandatory check on banknotes—they would typically return to the central bank after a certain period of use, particularly when becoming unfit for circulation. Payment cards, on the other hand, can be classified as 'staged,' because settlement is delayed and requires online connectivity (Hupel 2024).

Further, we assume that 'offline' means that both parties are not connected to the internet (sometimes referred to as 'dual offline').

The following details are based on design experiences gained in CBDC pilot projects. The approach—intermittently offline, re-spendable—has been tested intensively in Ghana, Thailand, and Hong Kong.

4.1 Use Cases for Retail CBDC

In its most basic form, retail CBDC should cater for everyday payment scenarios. In their eCedi design paper, Bank of Ghana (2022) describes the following user journeys:

1. Person-to-person transfers between unbanked people with hardware wallets
2. Purchases of goods and services with hardware wallets (point of sale)
3. Person-to-person transfers using bank-provided online wallets, possibly remotely
4. Purchases of goods and services using bank-provided online wallets, point of sale or e-commerce
5. Wallet funding (and redemption) with cash, e-money, or deposit accounts

If we consider the last point to be a 'special case' of a purchase, we can group the scenarios according to Fig. 1. All scenarios should support different form factors. Except for e-commerce, they should also work offline.

The eCedi pilot report confirms the need for the ability to re-spend funds received offline, 'providing opportunities for persons living in off-grid communities to access digital forms of payments and improve their livelihoods' (Bank of Ghana 2024). This is sometimes called 'consecutive offline,' to emphasize that a series of payments can happen without intervening online connection.

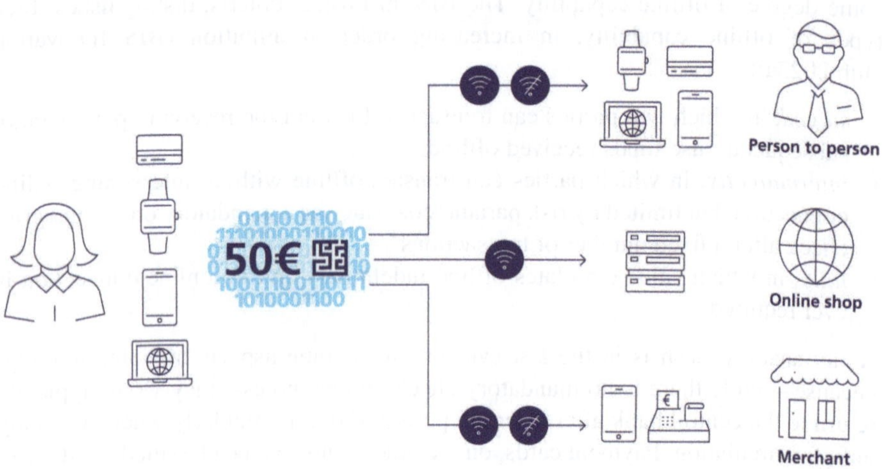

Fig. 1 Basic payment scenarios for retail CBDC (*Source*: Giesecke+Devrient)

But it would be wrong to assume that only emerging economies seek such features. The above scenarios, coupled with an intermittently offline model, also matches closely what the ECB envisions for the digital euro (European Central Bank 2024).

4.2 *An Offline-Capable Token Protocol*

In the world of credit (or debit) cards, payments are always based on identities. A customer uses a payment card as a credential to authenticate towards their bank, which then confirms the transaction. But as opposed to cash, settlement is delayed, which means that funds are not immediately transferred.

Consequently, it makes more sense to model CBDC based on cash. This is often referred to as a 'token-based system,' because money is represented as individual cryptographic tokens bearing a value.

Each token comprises a public-private keypair and a denomination. As opposed to banknotes, we are not confined to a fixed set of denominations. A wallet could—for example—hold three tokens worth € 5, € 9, and € 13 respectively.

As Bank of Ghana (2022) succinctly writes: 'Payment is done by transferring the [token] from one person to another. The concept is similar to cash payment transactions, where payment is done by transferring banknotes and/or coins from person A to person B.' Of course, the transfer is handled by the wallets, which abstracts away the implementation details from the user.

This contrasts with an 'account-based system,' in which value is tied to an account. Transactions work by debiting the payer account and crediting the payee account. Traditional banking uses this model, managing an assignment of account numbers to balances. But it has limits, which is why the Bank of Ghana and others opted for the token-based model (more details below).

Should a wallet not have the correct change available, tokens can be split into smaller denominations. In this, the input token is consumed and loses its validity, whereas two output tokens are freshly created. This is of course only admissible if the combined output values are equal to the input value.

For example, if the wallet holding € 5, € 9, and € 13 were to pay € 10 to another wallet, it could use the first two tokens, but split the € 9 first into 5 + 4, keeping the € 4. Each token receives an individual cryptographic keypair and can therefore be recognized by the central bank (more about this in Sect. 4.3).

Yet, the underlying token management is hidden from the user, who only sees an aggregate balance. Wallets can optimize holdings and split and merge tokens according to technical requirements. This does not rule out micro-payments: tokens can have an arbitrary precision as configured by the issuer.

This design has multiple advantages. Among them is increased **privacy**: while each token has a digital fingerprint, they are not associated with the wallet holder's identity. Tokens have a short life and are replaced quickly. This is a **cryptographic advantage**, because it shortens an attacker's time window during which they can

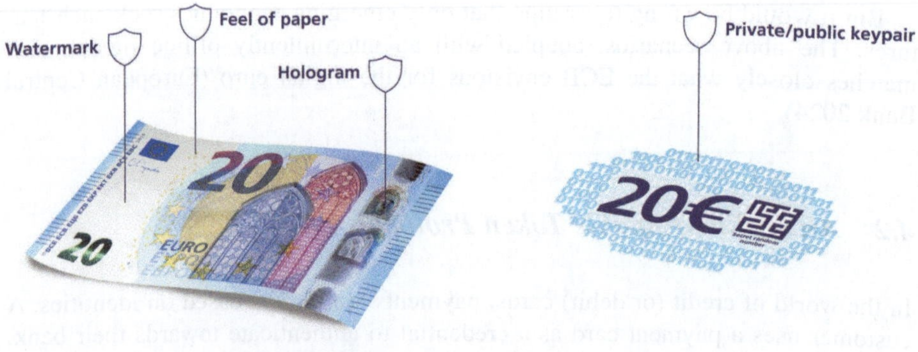

Fig. 2 Modelling digital cash after physical cash (*Source*: Giesecke+Devrient)

attack a particular piece of money. Finally, it allows to **ring-fence** compromised value. An invalid token can be isolated, without affecting many transactions, whereas a compromised account would need to be replaced entirely. Put simply, accounts unduly conflate 'identity' and 'value' (Fig. 2).

4.3 Two-Tier Distribution Model

Bringing CBDC into circulation mirrors the current two-tier financial system. It consists of *minting* and *distribution* and closely resembles the current cash cycle.

The central bank is the only entity that is allowed and able to mint CBDC. This cryptographic process is performed in an air-gapped, standalone environment. Freshly-minted tokens are physically transported to the central bank's digital vault.

FSPs (Financial Service Providers), including banks and other institutions, can request CBDC from the central bank against reserves. This would be part of their routine liquidity management, just like cash.

Finally, tokens are distributed to consumers' wallets on a variety of form factors. This can happen

- through existing mobile banking apps to which CBDC capability has been added through a SDK,
- on dedicated hardware devices such as chip cards, or
- online-only wallets hosted by an FSP of the consumer's choice.

From those wallets, consumers can transact CBDC for a range of use cases, for example, sending money between two smartphones using NFC (Fig. 3).

Merchants receiving CBDC at the point of sale can redeem them with their bank, which will credit the value to their bank account. The token stays with the bank and can be 'recycled'—i.e., distributed to another customer—or sent back to the central bank for monetary policy reasons. Any transaction, no matter whether it is large

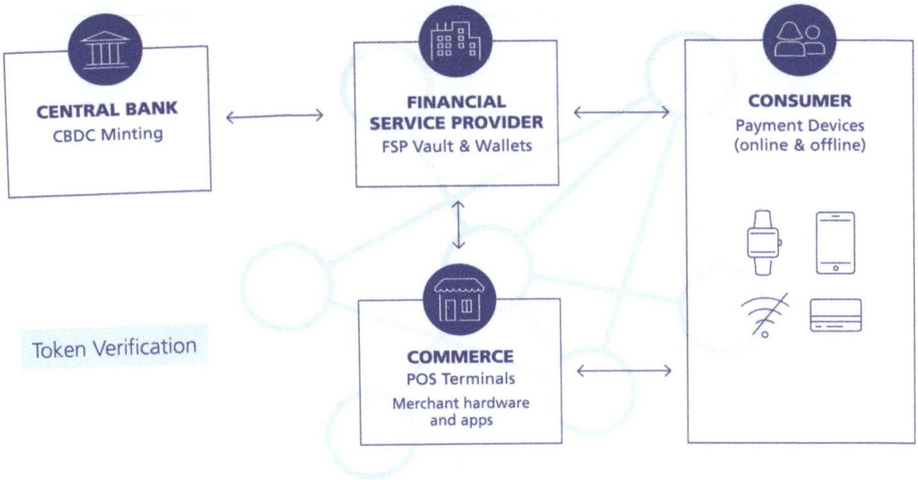

Fig. 3 Two-tier distribution model from minting to usage (*source*: Giesecke+Devrient)

value (e.g. between FSPs) or small value (e.g. between users), is end-to-end encrypted, protecting the tokens in transit.

Central banks should, as far as possible, enable FSPs to provide wallets on existing hardware and software platforms. For the former, the use of Secure Elements is state of the art (Sect. 4.4). For the latter, FSPs can integrate CBDC functionality into their apps and devices through SDKs.

Unbanked people can also participate in the system. For that, they need to obtain a hardware or software wallet, as specified by the issuing central bank. For example, the draft legislation on the digital euro envisions post offices or government authorities could act as non-bank intermediaries that provide basic CBDC services (European Commission 2023).

The core verification system allows all participants in the CBDC ecosystem to confirm that received tokens are valid. In the online scenario, this verification happens on the spot, while in offline mode, it is asynchronous: tokens from past offline transactions are checked as soon as any transacting party is online again.

4.4 Security Aspects in an Intermittently Offline Model

The European Central Bank (2024) states very clearly that the 'Eurosystem must maintain ownership and ensure integrity of its balance sheet,' which requires that (offline) CBDC must be protected '[a]gainst double-spending and undue money creation.' For that, they propose two key ingredients: a Secure Element in the wallet, whose 'tamper-resistant features protect the information stored on the device and allow mutual device authenticity checks;' and an occasional online integrity check that 'provides ultimate line of defence as the authenticity of […] offline digital euro is checked.'

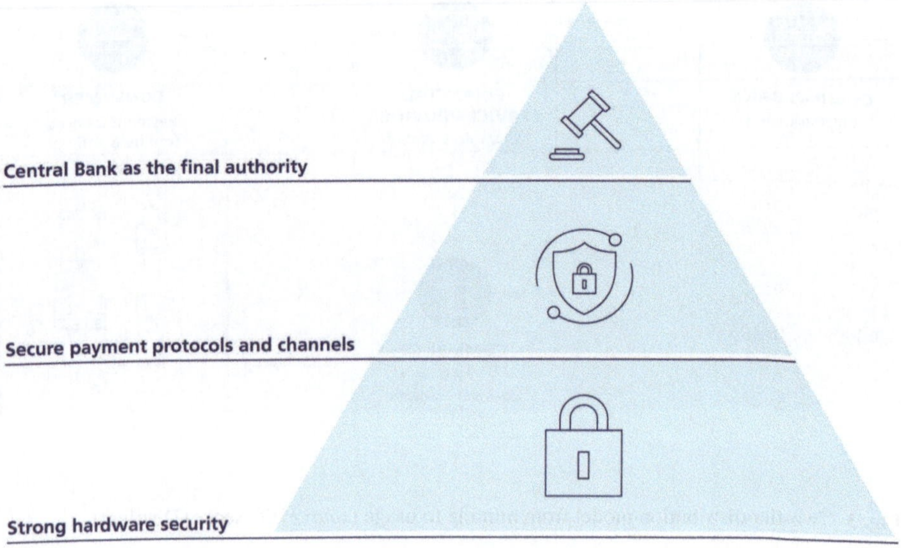

Fig. 4 A security architecture with three lines of defense (*source*: Giesecke + Devrient)

In the following, we elaborate on this model and insert an additional layer (Fig. 4), together forming a 'defense in depth' approach.

But let us first consider the main threat to digital currency—*double-spending*—which can be explained using an example attack on a wallet:

1. An attacker records the storage contents of the payer wallet.
2. The attacker performs a payment to an unsuspecting payee.
3. Now, the attacker resets the storage contents and performs a second payment.

If the payees are offline, they would be unable to detect this. Therefore, the security of offline CBDC payments hinges on stopping the attack from occurring in the first place. This is where the security model comes into play.

The model's bottom layer is **strong hardware security** based on *Secure Elements*. Those are standardized, tamper-resistant chips that protect against extraction, reset, manipulation, cloning, and other related attacks. For example, they have special shielding and coating and can detect physical attempts to break into the chip. The purpose of a Secure Element is to safely store cryptographic keys and other sensitive data, including the token keys (as described in Sect. 4.2). Software-only approaches, i.e., designs that do not incorporate hardware security, not only exclude offline use cases, but are also widely considered to be not secure enough (Christodorescu et al. 2020; Allen et al. 2020).

In the middle, **secure payment protocols and channels** provide protection against attacks when money is being moved. For example, wallets should always employ end-to-end encryption to prevent eavesdroppers from cloning tokens. The European Central Bank (2024) mentions this implicitly in the form of 'mutual device' authentication. But there also need to be mechanisms to resolve interrupted transactions which should not result in a situation where both payer and payee believe that they are in the possession of the money transferred.

Finally, the central bank must always be able to tell **authentic from counterfeit money**. This is very easy with a token system because every token can only be used once. In essence, this is the issuer acting as the final authority, just like for banknotes.

This final layer would not work in 'fully offline' mode (Sect. 4), because if value circulates offline indefinitely, by definition the central bank would be unable to act as the 'validator of last resort.' Yet, even if the transacting parties are offline—and therefore cannot reach the central bank—the other layers provide a high level of assurance.

Users need to be aware that with this approach, we cannot restore lost funds. This was proved by Kahn et al. (2021) in general for any payment system: out of the three desirable properties (i) protection against double-spending, (ii) offline capability, and (iii) loss recovery, only two are achievable simultaneously.

For example, debit cards compromise on offline capability. To avoid over drafting an account, transactions must be processed online. Paper cheques and credit cards work offline, but at the expense of potential double spending. But with CBDC being a central bank liability, this compromise is unacceptable.

The fact that tokens stored in a lost offline wallet cannot be recovered introduces an important aspect of user risk management. Users are unlikely to store large amounts of CBDC in offline wallets, knowing the potential for irreversible loss. This implies a natural differentiation in usage patterns: Offline CBDC will likely serve for smaller, everyday transactions, while online CBDC—with recovery mechanisms and stronger safeguards—will be prioritized for higher-value use cases.

In summary, this leaves a cash-like CBDC, supporting 'intermittently offline' payments while protecting against double-spending, to be the design sweet spot.

4.5 Practical Pilot Experiences

In this section, we describe experiences gathered in CBDC experimentations and pilot projects that encompassed both online and offline use cases.

In **Ghana,** the focus of the eCedi project was on 'financial inclusion, minimization of disruption to the financial service architecture, avoidance of financial disintermediation, safeguarding financial stability, ensuring regulatory certainty, system resilience and integrity and user-centric approach' (Bank of Ghana 2024). Field testing over 4 months in three regions—urban, peri-urban, and rural—was accompanied by user acceptance research. Of the 2923 total participants, 173 were offline (all in the rural region). Consumers and merchants received smartcards and POS terminals, respectively, to transact with each other. In this offline context, the report notes that 'technical feasibility was demonstrated,' and the utilized form factors were 'easy to use and intuitive.' Independent research by the Consultative Group to Assist the Poor corroborated the findings (Bank of Ghana 2024).

Shortly after a 2021 report on their vision for a retail CBDC, Bank of **Thailand** conducted a pilot project to 'to assess technological readiness and fundamental functions [...], evaluate the potential [...] in harnessing financial innovation beyond the existing payment infrastructure, explore whether CBDC infrastructure can safely enable open access for both banks and non-banks, and assess whether Retail CBDC can be an alternative payment infrastructure in the retail payment sector' (Bank of Thailand 2021, 2024). Besides testing a variety of standard payment use cases, the Bank also hosted an 'innovation track' to discover new applications through a public hackathon. This track enjoyed active industry participation, 'attract[ing] over 100 proposals.' In terms of offline functionality, the report attests 'the capability to handle hundreds of transactions during periods of disconnection before requiring synchronization with the core validation system' (Bank of Thailand 2024).

In these two projects, we could practically validate the above CBDC design, with the use cases set out in Sect. 4.1.

There is ample literature about experiments of other central banks around the world that investigate security architecture and user experience. For example, using various communication channels such as NFC, *BLE (Bluetooth Low Energy)* and QR codes (Bank of England 2025). The **British** study found that BLE can be used for transactions between phones[2] and NFC for transactions between a phone and a card. The Bank also employed Secure Elements to protect against double spending. They considered a similar security architecture as described in Sect. 4.4 as mitigation against security risks.

While the Bank was very conservative about possible security problems, the **ECB** is more confident in this state-of-the-art approach (European Central Bank 2024). Like banknotes, it is not 100% possible to prevent counterfeiting; however, individual counterfeits do not pose a systemic risk for the currency system. The ECB believes that the combination of secure hardware and online integrity checks helps the 'Eurosystem [...] maintain ownership and ensure integrity of its balance sheet.'

As part of their investigation, the ECB also examined card-to-card transactions, which requires special devices with two card slots (as tested in **Ghana**, see Fig. 5). This idea is not novel: in the 1990s, the 'Mondex' electronic cash system relied on smartcards and bespoke transfer devices. As Stalder (2002) describes, '[f]or a transaction, both Mondex cards were to be inserted in a card-reading device.' Top-ups and withdrawals required use of ATMs. Lack of infrastructure and cumbersome user experience were contributing factors to Mondex' lack of success.[3] But today, smartphones could fulfill all these functions. Attachable or wireless card readers even allow for card-to-card transactions (Fig. 6). This should greatly simplify deployment and user experience.

---

[2] NFC is also technically possible, but Bank of England considered it to be out of scope.

[3] Additionally, Mondex—an account based-system—provided unclear security guarantees (see also Sect. 4.4) and suffered from long transaction times, both problems that are solved now.

Fig. 5 Payment terminal with two card slots for card-to-card transactions; prototype device (source: Giesecke+Devrient)

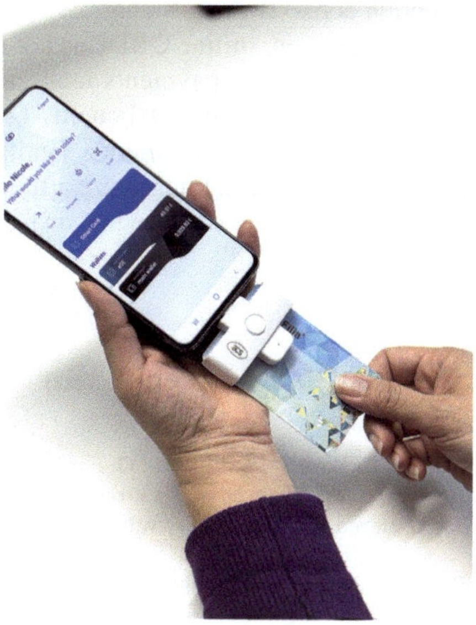

Fig. 6 Phone with attachable card reader, allowing for card-to-card payments without special devices (*source*: Giesecke+Devrient)

5 Towards a Resilient and Inclusive Future

The development of offline CBDC undoubtedly contributes to a resilient digital payment infrastructure. Past incidents—including blackouts and natural disasters—have already highlighted the weaknesses of (exclusively) online systems and the necessity for robust, offline-capable solutions.

CBDC, designed to be re-spendable offline, has undergone successful testing in pilots. The technology is mature for production deployment and satisfies all performance requirements.

The five 'A' framework—access, acceptance, availability, authenticity, and affection—serves as a useful basis for evaluation of payment systems in general (Seidemann 2023). We apply it to CBDC as follows.

Access is significantly broadened, as CBDC wallets can work without a bank account or advanced devices. This greatly enhances financial inclusion. Users can rely on cheap commodity hardware like a chip card. The lack of connectivity requirements fosters **acceptance,** by allowing transactions under any circumstances.

Similarly, **availability** is ensured because offline tokens enable transactions even in situations where digital systems might fail, such as during power outages. In an offline CBDC, use of tokens provides **authenticity.** The security approach eliminates single points of failure and mitigates risks effectively, ensuring operational integrity even if hardware is compromised. Finally, the offline functionality promotes **affection** for CBDC as a digital form of cash that is always accessible, in all places, and by all individuals. It supports privacy, increases the number of use cases, and allows users to transact independently of the issuer. This positions offline CBDC as a versatile and widely acceptable medium of exchange, facilitating its adoption across diverse scenarios.

In conclusion, offline CBDC is not merely an alternative to, but a necessary evolution of the digital payments landscape, mirroring the resilience and ubiquity of cash while harnessing the benefits of digital technology. Its readiness for widespread deployment could mark a significant shift towards a more inclusive and resilient financial system. Integrating offline functionalities from the inception of system design is crucial for achieving a digital payment system that is truly equitable and robust.

References

Allen S, Capkun S, Eyal I, Fanti G, Ford B, Grimmelmann J, Zhang F (July 2020) Design choices for Central Bank Digital Currency. Global Economy & Development Working Paper, 140. Retrieved from https://www.brookings.edu/wp-content/uploads/2020/07/Design-Choices-for-CBDC_Final-for-web.pdf

Bailey A (2009) Speech: banknotes in circulation: still rising: what does this mean for the future of cash. In: Banknote conference. Bank of England, Washington

Bank of England (2025) Digital pound experiment report: Offline payments. Retrieved from https://www.bankofengland.co.uk/report/2025/digital-pound-experiment-report-offline-payments

Bank of Ghana (2022) Design paper of the digital Cedi (eCedi). Retrieved from https://www.bog.gov.gh/wp-content/uploads/2022/03/eCedi-Design-Paper.pdf

Bank of Ghana (2024) A report on Bank of Ghana's Central Bank Digital Currency Pilot Project. Retrieved from https://www.bog.gov.gh/wp-content/uploads/2024/10/The-eCedi-Report-221024.pdf

Bank of Thailand (2021) The Way Forward for Retail CBDC in Thailand. Bank of Thailand. Retrieved from https://www.bot.or.th/content/dam/bot/documents/th/financial-innovation/cbdc/20210402_BOT_RetailCBDCPaper.pdf

Bank of Thailand (2024) Retail CBDC Conclusion Report. Retrieved from https://www.bot.or.th/content/dam/bot/documents/en/financial-innovation/cbdc-digital-currency/Update_Release_ENrCBDC%20Conclusion%20Report.pdf

BIS Innovation Hub (2023a) Project Polaris, Part 1: A handbook for offline payments with CBDC. https://www.bis.org/publ/othp64.pdf. Bank for International Settlements

BIS Innovation Hub (2023b) Project Polaris, Part 2: A security and resilience framework for CBDC systems. Bank for International Settlements

Bitkom (2024). https://www.bitkom.org/Presse/Presseinformation/AGB-meist-weggeklickt

Carstens A, Nilekani N (2024) BIS Working Papers No 1178 Finternet: the financial system for the future. Bank for International Settlements

Chaum D (2025). Retrieved from https://chaum.com/

Christodorescu M, Gu WC, Kumaresan R, Minaei M, Ozdayi M, Price B, Zamani M (2020) Towards a Two-Tier Hierarchical Infrastructure: An Offline Payment System for Central Bank Digital Currencies. https://doi.org/10.48550/arXiv.2012.08003

Diners Club (2024) 75 Years of Diners Club History. Retrieved July 16, 2025, from https://www.dinersclub.com/about-us/history/

European Central Bank (2020) Report on a digital Euro. European Central Bank. Retrieved from https://www.ecb.europa.eu/pub/pdf/other/Report_on_a_digital_euro~4d7268b458.en.pdf

European Central Bank (2024) State of play on offline digital euro. Retrieved from https://www.ecb.europa.eu/euro/digital_euro/timeline/profuse/shared/pdf//ecb.degov240411_item3updateofflinedigitaleuro.en.pdf

European Central Bank (2025) ECB statistics on banknotes and coins circulation. Retrieved from https://www.ecb.europa.eu/stats/policy_and_exchange_rates/banknotes+coins/circulation/html/index.en.html

European Commission (28 June 2023) Retrieved from Proposal for a regulation of the European Parliament and of the Council on the establishment of the digital euro: https://eur-lex.europa.eu/resource.html?uri=cellar:6f2f669f-1686-11ee-806b-01aa75ed71a1.0001.02/DOC_1&format=PDF

Fessenden M (2015) What Was the First Thing Sold on the Internet? Smithsonian Magazine. Retrieved from https://www.smithsonianmag.com/smart-news/what-was-first-thing-sold-internet-180957414/

Heinonen A (10 June 2025) Does the Number of Banknotes in Circulation Already Exceed 900 Billion? CashEssentials. Retrieved from https://cashessentials.org/does-the-number-of-banknotes-in-circulation-already-exceed-900-billion/

Hupel L (2023) Interoperability aspects of CBDC across ecosystems and borders. J Payments Strategy Syst. https://doi.org/10.69554/MBDJ6710

Hupel L (2024) A conceptual model for point-of-sale payment with retail CBDC. J Payments Strategy Syst. https://doi.org/10.69554/ETQK2745

Kahn CM, Van Oordt MR, Zhu Y (2021) Best before? Expiring central bank digital currency and loss recovery. Bank of Canada Staff Working Paper, 2021(67). https://doi.org/10.34989/swp-2021-67

McKinsey&Company (2024) Global Payments in 2024: Simpler interfaces, complex reality. Retrieved from https://www.mckinsey.com/industries/financial-services/our-insights/global-payments-in-2024-simpler-interfaces-complex-reality

Menon R (2024) Asset Tokenisation, Artificial Intelligence, Quantum Computing - Point Zero Forum 2024. Retrieved from https://gftn.co/insights-pzf/asset-tokenisation-artificial-intelligence-quantum-computing-pzf-2024

Nakamoto S (2008) Bitcoin: A Peer-to-Peer Electronic Cash System. https://bitcoin.org/bitcoin.pdf

Rafiee M, Hupel L (2024) How to design a Public Key Infrastructure for a Central Bank Digital Currency

Rösl G, Seitz F (2023) Uncertainty, politics, and crises: The case for cash. Frankfurt: IMFS Working Paper Series, No. 186, Goethe University Frankfurt, Institute for Monetary and Financial Stability (IMFS). https://doi.org/10.1016/j.latcb.2024.100128

Seidemann W (2023) *Building a resilient cash Infrastructure.* Currency News

Spicer J (2017) Cash Demand Doubled for Fed in Hurricane-hit Florida. Reuters. Retrieved from https://www.reuters.com/article/business/cash-demand-doubled-for-fed-in-hurricane-hit-florida-idUSKCN1BQ2L0/

Stalder F (2002) Failures and successes: notes on the development of electronic cash. Inf Soc 18(3). https://doi.org/10.1080/01972240290074968

Western Union (2025). https://www.westernunion.com/corporate/about-us.html

Zamora-Pérez A (2021) The paradox of banknotes: understanding the demand for cash beyond transactional use. ECB Economic Bulletin 2021(2)

The Legal and Governance Framework of Stablecoins: International Standards and Jurisdictional Divergences

Feride Hilal İmal

Abstract Entering the regulatory landscape amid concerns and risk-based warnings, stablecoins [Khan and Goodell (Libra: is it really about the money? https://ssrn.com/abstract=3441707, 2019); Zetzsche et al. (Oxford J Legal Stud 41:80–113, 2021)], despite the market crashes experienced in 2022 and 2023, have now reached a point where they can no longer be overlooked as a means and system of payment, particularly due to the support-oriented policies of major economies and a regulatory approach grounded in utility and oversight [Aldasoro et al. (Stablecoin growth—policy challenges and approaches. BIS Bulletin No 108. https://www.bis.org/publ/bisbull108.pdf, 2025)]. Nonetheless, the swift proliferation of stablecoins has not been paralleled by a commensurate regulatory response in terms of speed or effectiveness. The cross-border nature of stablecoins and the inability to confine their underlying technology within the limits of a single jurisdiction necessitate international regulatory coordination. That being said, each jurisdiction has opted to adopt approaches tailored to its specific needs. Consequently, formulating a universally applicable regulatory framework for stablecoins remains a significant challenge [Lehmann (Oxford J Legal Stud 37:406–434, 2017)]. This article examines the international regulatory perspective on stablecoins as both a global and national means of payment, weighing their risks and benefits, while assessing the work of international institutions and the applicability of existing global standards to stablecoins. The second section offers a comparative analysis of the regulation of payment stablecoins in two major economies, the European Union and the United States.

Keywords Stablecoin · Payment · Stablecoin regulation · MiCA · GENIUS act

---

F. H. İmal (✉)
İstanbul Bar Association, İstanbul, Türkiye
e-mail: feride.imal@universalhukuk.com

S. Yazıcı et al. (eds.), *Tokenisation of Money*, Contributions to Finance and Accounting, https://doi.org/10.1007/978-3-032-22946-5_16

1 Introduction

When stablecoins first emerged in 2014 as a class of crypto-assets combining the technological advantages of DLT networks, such as disintermediation, transparency, and security—with the low volatility of traditional, state-backed currencies, it was difficult to foresee the scale they would eventually reach. Before their potential benefits could be fully appreciated, Facebook's Libra[1] project and the category of "Global Stablecoins" (GSCs),[2] as termed by the FSB, swiftly became the focal point of criticism, being cast as a "threat to global financial stability", a reaction that can hardly be deemed unjustified.[3]

The rapid growth momentum of non-bank financial intermediaries (NBFIs), particularly technology companies,[4] the entry of major corporations into crypto-asset investments, and the emergence of global technology firms possessing vast customer bases and unparalleled datasets, offering financial services, have made it clear to regulators that the traditional financial system is on the brink of a fundamental transformation at the global level. Undoubtedly, the paradigm shift triggered by DLT within the financial system marks the advent of a new era in the restructuring of global monetary regulation—an era comparable to the 1970s, when the U.S. dollar was decoupled from gold and the age of floating fiat currencies began (Zetzsche et al. 2021, p. 80).

At this pivotal juncture, stablecoins, by virtue of their potential, rapidly transcended the confines of the DeFi ecosystem and became central to a wide array of critical issues, ranging from global finance to the sovereignty of nations. Due to

[1] Announced in 2019 by Facebook (now Meta), Libra—later renamed Diem—was introduced as a simple global currency and financial infrastructure capable of empowering billions of people. It was presented as an initiative led by the Libra Association, a consortium of independent private-sector members, with the declared aim of creating an inclusive, low-cost, and rapid ecosystem that would extend financial access to a significant portion of the world's population excluded from the global financial system. In its initial version, Libra was designed as a collateralized stablecoin, backed by a reserve of assets consisting of a basket of bank deposits and short-term, highly rated government securities held in a secure depository. See: Libra Association (2019); Under the intense pressure of regulators, who consistently underscored the risks and criticisms surrounding the project, several key members withdrew from the Libra Association. Despite the change of name and structure in December 2020, the project entered the liquidation phase on 2 February 2022. See: Statement by Diem CEO Stuart Levey on the Sale of Diem Group's Assets to Silvergate (2022).

[2] Global Stablecoins (GSCs) are stablecoins with the potential to achieve significant scale, coupled with the capacity for cross-jurisdictional access and adoption. See: FSB (2020a).

[3] For the reactions and statements following the announcement of the Libra project, see: Imal et al. (2024, p. 235).

[4] Comprising primarily pension funds, insurance companies, and other financial intermediaries, the NBFI sector has grown at a faster pace than the banking industry over the past decade, including the year 2019 when stablecoins first emerged. The financial assets of the NBFI sector rose from 42% in 2008 to nearly half of the global financial system by 2019, reaching USD 200.2 trillion. See: FSB (2020b); In 2023, the NBFI sector expanded by 8.5%, more than twice the growth rate of the banking sector (3.3%), raising its share of total global financial assets to 49.1%. See: FSB (2024).

their associated risks and potential benefits, stablecoins have assumed a position of particular significance in regulatory discussions, both as a global and national means of payment. As the currency of the DeFi ecosystem, stablecoins are emerging as a promising player within a maturing landscape, increasingly intertwined with traditional finance through numerous projects. Consequently, they have become a focal point of regulatory efforts, addressed by international regulatory and supervisory bodies, key jurisdictions, and various regions worldwide, independently of crypto-assets.

2 Regulatory Recommendations, Guidelines, and Standards

The initial international regulatory efforts addressing stablecoins—viewed with significant concern regarding their potential impact on the stability of the global financial system—have primarily focused on the risks they pose in cross-border payments. In particular, it has been emphasized that globally significant stablecoins (GSCs) entail risks in areas such as monetary sovereignty, financial stability, the existing global currency framework, AML/CFT compliance, multi-jurisdictional oversight, and fair competition, and that these areas require targeted regulatory measures (Arner et al. 2020).

Regardless of scale, stablecoins are identified to pose governance risks, risks associated with money laundering, terrorist financing, and other illegal financial activities, as well as risks to the security, efficiency, and integrity of payment systems, including concerns regarding cybersecurity and operational resilience—areas that must be central to the regulatory focus. Indeed, in 2022, the ecosystem experienced firsthand the risks posed by stablecoins, even those not classified as globally significant, providing a stark illustration of the consequences of scale-independent risks. The collapse of the algorithmic stablecoin pair TerraUSD/Luna inflicted substantial damage[5] within an unregulated ecosystem, triggering renewed regulatory alarm and generating intense pressure to implement comprehensive regulations that address stablecoins in a scale-independent manner without delay.

Despite all these risks that must be addressed, international regulators and supervisory authorities, albeit to varying degrees, acknowledge that stablecoins possess the potential to facilitate numerous financial system transactions more rapidly, efficiently, and securely, offer improvements in cross-border payment services, and enable broader participation in the financial system (Bank of England (BoE) 2021; G7 Working Group on Stablecoins 2019; Financial Stability Board (FSB) 2022a).

Irrespective of scale, there exists an imperative for stablecoins to provide market participants and users with a robust legal foundation that ensures legal certainty

[5] At the time of its collapse, TerraUSD was the third most valuable stablecoin with a market capitalization of USD 41 billion, on track to become a global payment instrument within DeFi markets. The total cost of its collapse to the entire stablecoin ecosystem is estimated at approximately USD 36 billion.

(Cœuré 2019). Stablecoin regulations must address a spectrum of legal and supervisory challenges and associated risks. Moreover, such regulations must be harmonized with existing legal frameworks and the statutory regimes of jurisdictions on a global scale (G7 Working Group on Stablecoins 2019, p. 4). This harmonization constitutes an absolute prerequisite for recognizing both scale-independent and systemically significant stablecoins beyond their roles within the DeFi ecosystem, enabling their adoption as retail or global payment systems (G7 Working Group on Stablecoins 2019, p. 5).

However, a stablecoin can only serve as an appropriate payment option for enhancing cross-border transactions if it qualifies as a *Properly Designed and Regulated* (PDR) stablecoin, as defined by the BIS. PDR stablecoins, as referenced by the BIS, are those that are properly designed and regulated to adhere to relevant international standards, guidelines, and recommendations established by bodies such as the FSB, CPMI, IOSCO, and FATF, as well as to comply with all applicable regulatory risk management requirements in the relevant jurisdictions for each of their functions, including, where applicable, systemically important stablecoins (BIS, CPMI 2023)). Accordingly, compliance with the recommendations, standards, and guidelines outlined below is a prerequisite for the acceptance and sustained function of stablecoins as a means of payment.

2.1 FSB Recommendations

The FSB,[6] mandated by the G20 to examine stablecoins, is engaged in identifying the global financial risks posed by stablecoins and in developing a regulatory framework, as well as ensuring its coordinated implementation.

The FSB began its work by analyzing the vulnerabilities within the existing regulatory regime and the financial stability risks posed by GSCs, subsequently issuing ten recommendations (commonly referred to as the "Ten Recommendations").[7] In October 2020, the FSB reviewed these recommendations and published a final report (FSB 2020c). This report emphasized that GSCs must comply with existing legal frameworks. However, it also noted that the scope and effectiveness of current regulatory and supervisory oversight mechanisms would become insufficient in terms of scope and efficiency if GSCs became significant and systemic across one or more jurisdictions. Highlighting that these recommendations should apply not only to GSCs but to all stablecoins to safeguard financial stability, the FSB, following a subsequent review, published them on 11 October 2022 as a proposed framework for establishing a regulatory regime (FSB 2022b).

Highlighting the associated risks, the FSB has reintroduced key questions surrounding the finalization and application of the Ten Recommendations, particularly

[6] FSB, https://www.fsb.org/about/, Last Accessed: 27.08.2025.

[7] FSB Global Stablecoin Consultative Document 14 April 2020.

in relation to the equality and enforceability of redemption rights vis-à-vis the issuer, the resilience of the stabilization mechanism, the composition of reserves, investment policies concerning reserves, disclosure obligations of issuers regarding reserve assets, and the governance of stablecoins. The FSB has further stated that countries should undertake substantial enhancements to ensure compliance with high-level recommendations when existing stablecoins are, or could potentially be, classified as GSCs.[8] As planned, on 17 July 2023, the FSB finalized the regulatory framework concerning the Ten Recommendations (FSB 2023)).

The FSB's recommendations constitute a comprehensive effort aimed at minimizing the financial stability risks posed by stablecoins and ensuring that they are regulated according to a consistent set of standards across all jurisdictions, thereby mitigating the risks of regulatory fragmentation and arbitrage.

2.2 *Standards of the Basel Committee on Banking Supervision (BCBS)*

As experienced during the market collapse commonly referred to as the "crypto winter,[9]" the risks associated with crypto assets can indeed spill over into the banking sector. In light of these concerns, it is critical to include crypto-assets within a strict global regulatory framework to safeguard the banking system against potential risks arising from banks' direct or indirect exposure to crypto-assets (Crypto-assets: A New Standard for Banks 2023).

In line with this approach, the BCBS[10] finalized its standards regarding the prudential treatment of banks' exposure to crypto-asset risks in a report issued on December 16, 2022 (Basel Committee on Banking Supervision 2022). Under the

---

[8] FSB Global Stablecoin Arrangements Consultative Report, 11 October 2022, p. 7.

[9] In the United States, the 2022 collapse of the cryptocurrency exchange FTX within the crypto-asset ecosystem, followed by the consecutive failures of Silvergate Capital, Signature Bank, and Silicon Valley Bank in March 2023, triggered a banking crisis. One of the primary causes identified was the devaluation of Treasury securities held in these banks' portfolios following the Federal Reserve's interest rate hikes, compounded by the exposure of assets held in the crypto market, which suffered declines during the same period. This crisis also impacted the three largest non-bank, asset-backed stablecoins. USDT, whose banking relationships were less transparent, broke its peg and rose to approximately USD 1.03, while BUSD fluctuated—falling to USD 0.9956, rising to USD 1.0095, and then dropping again to USD 0.9934. The stablecoin most affected was USDC, which held its reserves in the banks that failed; news of the crisis caused its value to drop to USD 0.901. However, following intervention by the Federal Deposit Insurance Corporation (FDIC), which extended deposit guarantees to all depositors, USDC rapidly regained its reference value. Facing the prospect of a significant redemption event, USDC subsequently moved all its assets to the Bank of New York Mellon, taking measures to mitigate potential risks arising from the crisis (CNBC n.d.).

[10] It is the primary global standard-setting body for the prudential regulation and supervision of banks, composed of central banks and banking supervisors. See: The Basel Committee – Overview (n.d.).

relevant regulation, crypto-assets, including stablecoins, comprise tokenized traditional assets and stablecoins with effective stabilization mechanisms. Provided that such crypto-assets meet the four classification criteria set forth by the BCBS, they will be deemed to present a lower risk profile than those in the second category. The second category of crypto-assets, on the other hand, encompasses all other crypto-assets that fail to meet the four classification criteria, including unbacked crypto-assets, tokenized traditional assets, and stablecoins with ineffective stabilization mechanisms. Given their higher risk profile, crypto-assets in this category are subject to additional and more stringent prudential requirements. Accordingly, crypto-assets in this category are subject to newly introduced conservative capital treatment. Additionally, they are subject to an exposure limit under the BCBS standards.

Additionally, banks are expected to implement other elements of the BCBS standard, such as requirements related to operational risk, liquidity, leverage, and large-scale exposures. Furthermore, banks intending to engage in activities involving crypto-assets are expected to minimize the risks associated with crypto-assets by establishing governance frameworks, implementing effective risk management practices, and conducting stress-testing analyses specific to crypto-assets.

In July 2024, the BCBS published an update (Basel Committee on Banking Supervision 2024a)) to the composition of reserve assets, including requirements regarding their credit quality, maturity, and liquidity, accompanied by an explanatory framework (Basel Committee on Banking Supervision 2024b). Scheduled to take effect on 1 January 2026, this targeted update includes revisions aimed at ensuring a consistent understanding of the criteria under which stablecoins may qualify for the privileged Group 1b regulatory treatment, as well as various technical amendments.

2.3 *Principles for Financial Market Infrastructures (PFMI)*

The PFMI principles establish international criteria for determining whether payment and market infrastructures are systemically important. As highlighted by the FSB, the risks posed by systemically important stablecoins to global financial stability are substantial.

Systemically important stablecoins are those designated based on certain criteria, such as scale and interconnectedness with the financial system, and are deemed to have systemic importance. These stablecoins generally manifest as GSCs. Given that stablecoins with systemic impacts fall within the highest risk category, they must be subject to more stringent regulatory requirements considering the risk-based approach (Bank of England (BoE) 2021, p. 86). Indeed, the failure of a systemically important stablecoin or the emergence of financial instability has the potential to affect the entire real economy (President's Working Group on Financial Markets (PWG) 2021, p. 14). In light of these principles, the systemic importance of a GSC is determined based on several criteria, such as the number of users, volume and type of transactions (e.g., wholesale or retail, domestic or cross-border, public or private sector, investment or payment-related), transaction value, the degree of interconnectedness with the real economy, traditional financial systems or other digital networks, and the availability of substitutes.[11]

Following a preliminary analysis[12] by the FSB suggesting that the PFMI principles could be applied to determine the systemic importance of global stablecoins, the *Committee on Payments and Market Infrastructures* (CPMI) published guidance affirming that the PFMI principles apply to global stablecoins, given that they constitute, or have the potential to constitute, systemically important payment infrastructures. This guidance did not establish new principles for stablecoins but clarified that the existing PFMI standards are equally relevant to them.

2.4 *Financial Action Task Force (FATF) Standards*

Since their inception, crypto-assets have been exploited by fraudsters, terrorist organizations, and other illicit actors for purposes such as money laundering and the proliferation of weapons of mass destruction (FATF 2025, p. 7). Tasked by the G20 with developing frameworks for crypto-assets, the FATF commenced its work in October 2018 by issuing an update to Recommendation No. 15 (FATF 2018). Pursuant to the second paragraph of Recommendation No. 15, titled New Technologies, the FATF advised member states to ensure that any regulations concerning *Virtual Asset Service Providers* (VASPs) are aligned with anti-money laundering and countering the financing of terrorism (AML/CFT) rules. Furthermore, it was recommended that compliance with these requirements be monitored through a licensing regime or alternative supervisory mechanism. In subsequent years, through further updates and issued statements, the FATF has continued to refine its guidance, specifically addressing the risks posed by stablecoins (FATF 2019a).

In its work, the FATF has emphasized that global stablecoins must comply with existing legal frameworks, remain subject to AML controls, and adhere to FATF standards (FATF 2019b, 2020). The FATF has noted that, due to features such as anonymity, global accessibility, and the potential for layering illicit funds, stablecoins carry the same risks as other crypto-assets, and that their widespread adoption could exacerbate vulnerabilities in AML/CFT compliance.

In 2023 and beyond, in response to the increasing adoption of stablecoins and their intensified use by illicit actors, the FATF has advised jurisdictions to monitor market developments, assess the associated risks of illicit finance, and implement appropriate risk-mitigation measures (FATF 2024). FATF found that the use of stablecoins by various illicit actors continued to increase since 2024, to the extent that a significant portion of on-chain illicit activity now involves stablecoins. In response, the FATF called for enhanced cooperation to ensure the effective implementation of

[11] PWG Reports on Stablecoins November 2021, p. 14.

[12] FSB Global Stablecoin Arrangements Consultative Report, 11 October 2022.

relevant FATF Standards to safeguard the integrity of the financial system (FATF 2025).

3 Regulations in Two Major Jurisdictions

The rise of stablecoins as both a means of payment and a component of financial infrastructure has rendered it indispensable for jurisdictions to adopt independent regulatory frameworks, both in the interest of investor protection and the preservation of financial stability. Within a payments ecosystem dominated by the U.S. dollar and U.S.-based infrastructures, the European Union, seeking to promote the Euro and European payment infrastructures while reducing dependency, emerged as the first major jurisdiction to enact a comprehensive regulation. Following the MiCA Regulation, designed to secure a first-mover advantage, several jurisdictions introduced stablecoin regulatory frameworks. However, the United States, with the dual objective of safeguarding its dominance in the stablecoin ecosystem and consolidating the leadership of the U.S. dollar and related infrastructures, enacted the GENIUS Act on July 18, 2025, regulating payment stablecoins. In these two major jurisdictions, the European Union and the United States, each adhering the distinct legal traditions and institutional structures, there exist discernible differences in regulatory approach. Nonetheless, these frameworks are of critical importance, both in terms of their regulatory reach and their role as reference points for other jurisdictions. Accordingly, this section of the article will provide a detailed examination of the EU's MiCA Regulation and the USA's GENIUS Act, with a particular focus on the payments dimension, shedding light on their convergences and divergences.

3.1 EU Regulation on Markets in Crypto Assets (MiCA)

3.1.1 General Overview

In December 2019, the EU committed to establishing a regulatory framework (The Council and the European Commission 2019), which it subsequently presented to the Parliament on 24 September 2020 (EU Regulatory Proposal for a Regulation of the European Parliament and of the Council on Markets in Crypto-Assets, and Amending Directive (EU) 2019). Following various amendments, the MiCA Regulation was finalized and published on 31 May 2023 (European Commission Regulation (EU) 2023), coming into full effect on 31 December 2024. Unlike directives, which can create regulatory arbitrage risks, the MiCA Regulation was established as a regulation, rendering it directly applicable across all EU member states.

The MiCA Regulation is highly significant because it provides a comprehensive framework for crypto-assets, with a particular focus on stablecoins. Indeed, it would not be wrong to state that the essence and primary impetus behind the MiCA

Regulation is stablecoins (Lehmann 2024). Although the Regulation does not explicitly define the term "stablecoin", the EU states in the explanatory memorandum of MiCA with emphasis on stablecoins that MiCA incorporates safeguard mechanisms aimed at mitigating the risks faced by financial stability and monetary policy.[13]

Under MiCA, crypto-assets that fall within the scope of existing financial regulations—such as financial instruments or deposits—are categorized by the European Commission into two specific groups: stablecoins pegged one-to-one to a single fiat currency are classified as *Electronic Money Tokens* (EMTs), while stablecoins pegged to one or more fiat currencies or to a basket of assets are classified as *Asset-Referenced Tokens* (ARTs). Additionally, MiCA establishes a category of significant stablecoins, including global stablecoins, subject to stricter rules if they meet certain criteria and achieve a substantial scale.

The MiCA Regulation distinguishes EMTs as a distinct category of stablecoins, aligning with the recommendations of international bodies by classifying these stablecoins as electronic money.[14] While the MiCA Regulation excludes crypto-assets that fall within the scope of existing financial instruments, deposits, or similar regulations, it specifically provides an exception for EMTs. Under the regulation, electronic money is already subject to its own legal framework under the *Electronic Money Directive 2* (EMD2) (European Parliament Council Directive of 2009/110/EC 2009); if the technology used to represent and support it is based on DLT, both MiCA and EMD2 will apply concurrently. In other words, MiCA regulates the characteristic features of EMTs while referring to EMD2 for other aspects of their oversight.[15] Consequently, the issuance of EMTs to the public or their acceptance for trading within the EU can only be carried out by institutions authorized either as credit institutions under the *Capital Requirements Directive* (EU Capital Requirement Directive 2013) or as electronic money institutions under EMD2.[16]

On the other hand, the issuer of an EMT, which is issued by referencing the currency of an EU member state, whether within or outside the EU, shall be required to be authorized as a credit institution or electronic money institution. This is because, in such cases, the EMTs in question are deemed to have been offered to the public in the EU.[17]

The MiCA Regulation introduces a graduated regulatory framework based on the risk potential of different categories of crypto-assets (Ostercamp 2022). In addition, the MiCA Regulation sets forth various obligations applicable to different

---

[13] Proposal for Regulation of MiCA, Explanatory Memorandum, Art. 3.

[14] MiCA, Art. 48/ para. 2.

[15] MiCA, Art. 8.

[16] MiCA Art. 48/para. 1; Under this regulation, issuers of EMTs referencing a non-EU currency—both within and outside the EU—and issuers of EMTs issued outside the EU are not required to be credit institutions or electronic money institutions, and therefore do not need authorization, so long as they have not yet offered these EMTs to the public in the EU or invited their trading within the EU. Authorization becomes necessary once a public offer or invitation to trade is requested.

[17] MiCA Art. 48/ para. 2.

business models such as crypto-asset service providers, crypto-asset trading platforms, custody of crypto-assets, crypto-asset order transmission, crypto-asset transactions, and crypto-asset consulting services, etc. and makes each one of them subject to minimum capital requirements.[18] No licensing requirement is imposed on the issuers of other crypto-assets including utility tokens not classified under EU financial regulations.[19] Nevertheless, it introduces certain governance and business conduct requirements applicable to such issuers.

Furthermore, in alignment with the recommendations of international bodies, the MiCA Regulation allows stablecoins with potential systemic significance to be designated as Significant ARTs or Significant EMTs, either on the initiative of the EBA or at the request of the issuer, based on criteria such as the value of the crypto-asset, its cross-border relevance, its connection to the financial system, and the size of its customer base. In such cases, Significant EMTs and ARTs will be subject to additional obligations, including stricter capital requirements and more rigorous liquidity policies.[20] Where a crypto-asset is classified as a significant ART, the EBA is designated as the supervisory authority on these crypto-assets to prevent regulatory arbitrage among member states.[21]

Moreover, the MiCA Regulation requires that significant stablecoins maintain at least 60% of their reserves in bank deposits to ensure integration with the banking system and safeguard liquidity. While this measure helps mitigate the risk of "euro/dollarization," it may also diminish the competitive capacity of euro-backed stablecoins.

While prior approval of the crypto-asset white papers is not required for EMTs, it is regulated that issuers shall notify their competent authority of their crypto-asset white paper at least 20 working days before the date of their publication.[22] Holders of assets have the right to make claims on EMTs at any time and at nominal value,[23] as is the case with the provisions applicable to ARTs; likewise, the accrual of interest is prohibited.[24]

3.1.2 Relationship Between the MiCA Regulation and PSD2

The relationship between the MiCA Regulation and Payment Services Directive 2 (PSD2) (Directive (EU) 2015/2366 of the European Parliament and of the Council 2015), the forthcoming payment services framework amendment, is pivotal in shaping the role of stablecoins as payment tokens and the EU strategy. This is

[18] MiCA, Art. 59.

[19] MiCA, Art. 4.

[20] MiCA, Art. 43–45.

[21] MiCA, Art. 43/ para. 2; MiCA, Art.56–58.

[22] MiCA, Art. 51.

[23] MiCA, Art. 49.

[24] MiCA, Art. 50.

because users of stablecoins, which have gained increasing popularity as a means of payment, should benefit from legal protections applicable to payment services, as required by the principle of technological neutrality (Parra 2025, s. 203). To this end, the EU—through MiCA Regulation's broad definition of crypto-assets that reflects the principle of technological neutrality—aims to cover all assets recorded on a DLT or similar technologies, not regulated under any EU financial services legislation, within the scope of the financial services legislation and to ensure that the legal acts applicable to financial services remain fit for the digital age.

Among other matters, the MiCA Regulation governs the provision of crypto-asset services within the EU and the authorization of Crypto Assets Service Providers (CASPs), whereas PSD2 regulates the provision of payment services within the EU.

Since PSD2 governs only payment transactions involving funds, it is necessary to assess whether EMTs and ARTs fall within the definition of "funds" in the context of PSD2. This is because only those crypto-assets that qualify as funds may be the subject of payment services covered by PSD2. It is stated in Preamble 40 of MiCA Regulation that ARTs could be widely adopted by holders to transfer value or as a means of exchange, and their capability to qualify as a means of payment is referred to in various articles.[25] In other words, MiCA Regulation explicitly underlines that ARTs may also be used as a means of payment, although not explicitly as in the case of EMTs. Accordingly, it should be noted that two categories of stablecoins covered by the MiCA Regulation, namely EMTs and ARTs, are regarded as crypto-assets with a payment function (payment tokens). Considering that Libra, which was initially introduced as a global means of payment and financial infrastructure, would also have qualified as an ART, ARTs clearly have a payment function.

Article 4(25) of PSD2 defines funds as banknotes and coins, scriptural money, or electronic money. As outlined in MiCA Regulation Art. 48(2), EMTs shall also be deemed to be electronic money. Therefore, it is beyond dispute that EMTs constitute funds that may be subject to the PSD2 activities. Nevertheless, ARTs are not defined under MiCA as instruments that qualify as electronic money or as funds. On the other side, neither the current definition of "funds" under PSD2 nor the draft PSD3, proposing a broader definition for funds, includes provisions that would encompass ARTs. Even if ARTs are recognized as potential means of exchange, they currently fall outside the scope of PSD2, and they are not addressed in the proposed PSD3/PSR (Proposal for a Directive of the European Parliament and of the Council 2023). Based on this, the crypto-asset services under the MiCA Regulation may fall within the scope of PSD2 only if they involve EMTs, and

[25] For instance, Art. 43(1) of MiCA Regulation lists ART as one of the significant classification criteria, namely "the significance of the activities of the issuer of the asset-referenced token on an international scale, including the use of the asset-referenced token for payments and remittances."

transactions involving ARTs or other crypto-assets shall not be subject to any payment services under PSD2.

While the MiCA Regulation broadly defines the scope of payment services involving EMTs, it leaves several critical issues unresolved. In order to apply the EU payment services regime to EMTs, it is necessary to clarify the definition of payment service provides to whom the rights, obligations, consumer protection and transparency regime will apply, and to determine how key concepts under the payment services regime—such as the payment account used to hold electronic money and payment instrument—correspond in the context of EMTs (Herrera 2025, s. 393).

Nevertheless, while payment services involving crypto-assets may exhibit parallels with PSD2, the technological structures of crypto-assets and the activities related thereto also differ. Since PSD2 was not designed with crypto-assets in mind, applying it to payment transactions involving crypto-assets brings about some challenges. The EBA has assessed that the uncertainties in the interaction between PSD2 and the MiCA Regulation could be resolved through the proposed PSD3/PSR frameworks, thereby aligning the EU payments market with contemporary requirements and enhancing its competitiveness (EBA 2025).

Despite various uncertainties it entails, the MiCA constitutes, as of today, the most comprehensive, articulated, and advanced discipline in the world for markets in crypto-assets (Annunziata 2023, s. 12). As underlined by the international regulatory authorities, based on the principle of "same risk, same regulation", the EU regulator has aimed to regulate crypto markets, adapting the concepts, rules, models, and structures set out in the MiCA Regulation from the regulatory and supervisory framework of core EU financial law provisions. With regard to the issuance of crypto-assets and their offer on the market, the model followed is the Prospectus Regulation. As for the regime applicable to crypto-asset service providers and trading platforms, the most obvious reference mode is, instead, MiFID. Similarly, the reference models for crypto-assets with a payment function are the regulations applicable to credit institutions and electronic money institutions (Annunziata 2023, s. 16).

3.2 Guiding and Establishing National Innovation for US Stablecoins (GENIUS) Act

Since 2020, crypto-assets have established a presence within the existing financial system at the federal level in the United States. The *Office of the Comptroller of the Currency* (OCC) has been granting charters to crypto banks. In addition to traditional banking activities, crypto banks offer deposit accounts in both U.S. dollars and crypto-assets, custodial solutions, and brokerage services. In the United States, where stablecoins are accorded particular significance, various efforts have been undertaken at the federal level to establish a regulatory framework, resulting in the introduction of multiple stablecoin legislative proposals.[26]

It would not be an exaggeration to describe 2025 as the "year of stablecoins" in the United States from the perspective of government policy. Upon taking office, the Trump administration revoked Executive Order dated March 9, 2022, issued by former President Joe Biden, and issued a new executive order. In this new executive order dated January 13, 2025, the Trump administration declared that the digital asset sector plays a vital role not only in innovation and economic development within the United States, but also in maintaining the U.S.' leadership on the global stage, and that it supports the growth of digital assets, blockchain technology, and related technologies. The administration further stated its intention to promote and preserve the sovereignty of the U.S. dollar—including by encouraging the development and expansion of lawful and legitimate U.S. dollar-backed stablecoins worldwide. Within this framework, the National Economic Council the President's Working Group on Digital Asset Markets (Working Group) was established within the body of the National Economic Council.

At the same time, it was decided to ban Central Bank Digital Currencies (CBDC) because they pose a threat to the stability of the financial system, individual privacy, and national sovereignty. Through the executive order, the administration declared that U.S. dollar-pegged stablecoins constitute a national priority and pledged to implement, without delay, a regulatory framework designed to promote and strengthen the sovereignty of the U.S. dollar (The White House 2025).

Indeed, U.S. dollar-pegged stablecoins are highly significant financial instruments for the United States. Indeed, 99% of all stablecoins in circulation are pegged to the U.S. dollar (Aldasoro et al. 2025, p. 3). In response to the growing trend of various countries implementing policies aimed at reducing their reliance on the U.S. dollar, the United States views the U.S. dollar-pegged stablecoins as a new financial instrument of strategic importance. In parallel to the Government's policy aiming to make the U.S. a hub for crypto-asset innovation and preserving the dominance of the U.S. dollar to combat inflation, the government enacted the Guiding and Establishing National Innovation for US Stablecoins (GENIUS) Act (US Congress n.d.-a) on July 18, 2025. This federal legislation, which was initially introduced on January 5, 2025, establishes the first regulatory framework for payment stablecoins (PSC), namely stablecoins fully pegged 1:1 to the U.S. dollar. The Act provides a legal definition for PSCs and assigns primary regulatory oversight to banking regulators. Concurrently, the *Anti-CBDC Surveillance State Act*, which aims to prohibit CBDCs, passed the House of Representatives on July 17, 2025, and it is about to be enacted (US Congress n.d.-b).

Under the GENIUS Act, the term PSC means a digital asset that is or is designed to be used as a means of payment or settlement, and the issuer of which is obligated to convert, redeem, or repurchase for a fixed amount of monetary value, and

[26] For a detailed comparison of stablecoin legislative proposals introduced in the United States, see: Awrey et al. (2025).

represents it will maintain or creates the reasonable expectation that it will maintain a stable value relative to the value of a fixed amount of monetary value.[27]

In the GENIUS Act, as in the EU's MiCA Regulation, stablecoins pegged one-to-one to a single currency have been designated for payment purposes. By contrast, stablecoins pegged to multiple currencies, to an asset, or to a combination thereof—such as the Libra project—have been excluded from the realm of payments, much like the ARTs under MiCA.

The GENIUS Act defines PSCs by reference to the reasonable expectation or belief of stability they are likely to create in the public. In light of this definition, the United States has treated the stability of stablecoins not as an objective feature but as a subjective element, deeming the intention or belief that a stablecoin is stable sufficient, rather than requiring actual stability. Similarly, the EU's payment instrument EMT, under the MiCA Regulation, is regarded as a category of crypto-asset intended to maintain a stable value by reference to the value of an official currency, thereby recognizing the aim of stability as sufficient. However, unlike the EU's EMT, the PSC is also defined by the issuer's obligation to convert, redeem, or repurchase at a fixed monetary value. This formulation entails the risk that a PSC may circumvent such an obligation and thereby fall outside the regulatory scope of the GENIUS Act. Indeed, it is for this very reason that the MiCA Regulation defines EMTs in terms far broader than the definition of electronic money to which they refer, while relegating the other conditions for classification as electronic money to the realm of legal obligations rather than definitional criteria. From the standpoint of preventing regulatory arbitrage, it must be said that MiCA's approach to defining EMTs is sounder.

While the GENIUS ACT allows PSC issuers to earn returns on the investment of reserve assets, it explicitly prohibits the distribution of such returns to users. Also, PSC issuers—given that their role in providing a payment instrument—are prohibited from offering interest or earnings to PSC holders.[28] However, incentives or promotional rewards offered by parties other than the issuer do not fall within the scope of this prohibition.

While the MiCA Regulation explicitly classifies EMTs as electronic money, thereby bringing them within the regulatory scope of EMD2 and, as a means of payment, PSD2, the United States—though it has structured PSC regulations in a manner resembling banking law and imposed on issuers prudential standards akin to those applicable to traditional banks—has made no explicit reference to the regulatory framework of any existing financial instrument. Under the GENIUS Act, the authority to issue PSCs is reserved exclusively to banks at both the federal and state levels, as well as to duly authorized entities that meet the prescribed requirements. By contrast, regulatory recommendations and legislative proposals advanced under the previous administration treated stablecoins as insured deposits falling within the scope of existing banking regulation. The GENIUS Act, however, expressly

[27] GENIUS Act, 2(22).

[28] GENIUS Act, 4(11).

provides that stablecoins are not deposits,[29] will not be protected by deposit insurance,[30] and prohibits PSC issuers from representing that such assets are federally insured or guaranteed by the state.[31]

In line with recent actions taken by the SEC (Securities and Exchange Commission 2025), the regulation affirms that PSCs are not investment products but are fundamentally payment instruments. The Act clearly distinguishes PSCs from securities, commodities, and investment contracts.

The GENIUS Act establishes a licensing regime by stipulating that, subject to certain exceptions, only permitted issuers may issue PSCs to U.S. citizens. Accordingly, permitted issuers may be subsidiaries of insured depository institutions, federally approved non-bank PSC issuers, or state-approved PSC issuers. These permitted issuers shall be audited by the relevant federal or state regulatory authority. Additionally, the Act provides that foreign PSC issuers may be allowed to offer PSCs in the United States through digital asset service providers, subject to certain requirements, including a determination by the Department of the Treasury that such issuers are subject to similar foreign regulations.

On the other side, in parallel with the MiCA Regulation and in order to safeguard redemption rights, issuers are prohibited from pledging, encumbering, or rehypothecating their reserve assets. PSC issuers are also obliged to submit monthly reports on reserves. In the event of a PSC issuer's insolvency, claims by PSC holders shall take precedence over those of other creditors against the issuer. The Act establishes a regulatory regime for PSC issuers that mirrors traditional banking standards, encouraging federal and state regulators to issue rules imposing capital, liquidity, and risk management standards.

The GENIUS Act takes effect on the earlier of the date that is 18 months after the enactment of the Act or the date that is 120 days after the date on which the primary Federal payment stablecoin regulators issue any final regulations implementing the Act. Additionally, a transitional period of 3 years is granted to digital asset service providers, and upon the expiration of this period, only PSCs issued by permitted PSC issuers may be offered to U.S. customers.

Giving recommendations to foster crypto-asset innovation and declaring that cryptocurrency will become a symbol for the new American Golden Age, the Working Group published a report titled Strengthening American Leadership in Digital Financial Technology on July 30, 2025. The report describes stablecoins as one of the most promising DLT solutions for payments, and characterizes the GENIUS Act as a milestone for stablecoins and digital payments. It is also stated in

29 GENIUS Act, 2(22) B, ii.

30 For criticisms suggesting that this Act would enable big tech firms and other commercial enterprises to acquire non-bank stablecoin issuers and utilize stablecoins in banking activities -thereby turning stablecoins into a form of "shadow deposits" and potentially triggering a major systemic financial crisis- and that, in such a scenario, the absence of federal deposit insurance and the protections afforded to FDIC-insured banks could compel the government to offer costly bailout packages, resulting in significant economic losses, see: Wilmarth (2025).

31 GENIUS Act, 4(e).

the report that the GENIUS Act lays the regulatory foundation for the financial rails of a new U.S. dollar system—one designed to support the U.S. economy and reinforce the global dominance of the dollar.

4 Conclusions

Recognizing stablecoins—whether irrespective of scale or as systemically significant instruments—as retail or global payment systems beyond their role within the DeFi ecosystem will only be possible if legal certainty is established. Ensuring such legal certainty constitutes an absolute prerequisite before stablecoins may be permitted for use on a global scale.

The cross-border use of stablecoins and the impossibility of confining their underlying technology within any single jurisdiction render international regulatory coordination indispensable. In this regard, numerous international standard-setters, including the BIS, the G20, and the G7, have concluded that the establishment of a global framework is necessary and have approached stablecoin regulation through the principle of "same risks, same rules," which has traditionally guided financial regulation. Indeed, international bodies have conducted studies on the applicability of existing international standards, recommendations, and principles such as the BCBS, FATF, CPMI, and IOSCO, primarily those designed to safeguard financial stability, to stablecoins. Bringing stablecoins within the scope of existing regulatory frameworks is, in fact, a prudent approach for legislators, as it enables reliance on rules that have been shaped through experience in addressing comparable risks.

Furthermore, international organizations such as the FSB seek to ensure consistency in regulatory implementation by focusing on the effective use of authority, tools, and resources necessary for enforcing existing legal frameworks, as well as on the functional application of international standards. Nonetheless, regulatory authorities across the globe operate under divergent legal and economic requirements, varying regulatory parameters, and differing political circumstances. Indeed, in its report issued in October 2021 on the implementation of its recommendations, the FSB expressed concern over the significant disparities in the progress and manner of stablecoin regulation across the 48 jurisdictions it had examined. While the FSB reiterated its recommendations aimed at eliminating the risks of regulatory fragmentation and arbitrage by ensuring that stablecoins are regulated in accordance with consistent sets of standards across all jurisdictions; the April 2024 report prepared by the Financial Stability Institute (FSI) of the Bank for International Settlement (BIS) revealed striking divergences in the regulatory frameworks applicable to in-scope stablecoins, the type of stablecoin with the highest potential for use as a means of payment. The referred report covered frameworks established by 11 authorities across seven jurisdictions, and found substantial differences in regulatory regimes that could lead to a lack of consistency and coordination in the oversight of stablecoins across jurisdictions. In this context, the two major jurisdictions under review have each approached stablecoins with distinct financial and geopolitical strategies.

It should be noted that the fundamental distinction between MiCA and the GENIUS Act lies in their respective regulatory approaches. While the European Union has adopted a more comprehensive and preventive regulatory model, the United States has opted for a market-based and incremental approach. MiCA's objective of establishing a homogeneous framework at the Union level ensures predictability for both investors and entrepreneurs.

Similarly, the enactment of the GENIUS Act in the United States represents a highly significant step toward achieving federal clarity. However, unlike MiCA, which as a regulation is directly applicable across all EU Member States, the U.S. remains subject to regulatory fragmentation under the GENIUS Act. This is because issuers are allowed to choose the regulatory framework to which they will be subject up to a certain issuance volume. Owing to the divergent regulatory regimes across states, such fragmented oversight may generate uncertainty for stablecoin issuers.

In the United States, the federal system gives rise to a multilayered regulatory structure, whereas at the EU level, the implementation of MiCA is carried out through a defined division of responsibilities between the European Securities and Markets Authority (ESMA) and national regulatory authorities. The EU's centralized framework is consistent with the principle of the single market.

MiCA has the potential to ensure trust and stability within the crypto-asset market in Europe. However, if interpreted too rigidly from the perspective of innovative ventures, it may constrain innovation. Conversely, while the GENIUS Act theoretically offers an innovation-friendly framework, questions remain regarding its practical enforceability and the coordination between institutions.

MiCA applies traditional financial regulatory principles to crypto-assets. This approach may, in certain respects, be seen as constraining innovation. In particular, there is a lack of clarity regarding how decentralized finance (DeFi) applications will be treated under the MiCA framework. The GENIUS Act was developed with a discourse supportive of innovation and adopts a technology-neutral regulatory approach. However, the lack of regulatory clarity may cause entrepreneurs to perceive themselves as operating within a gray area in practice.

Investor protection is one of MiCA's primary objectives. Through disclosure obligations, transparency principles, and corporate governance standards, it aims to enable consumers to make informed decisions. MiCA also contains specific provisions to guard against market abuse. In contrast, the GENIUS Act adopts a more market-based approach. While consumer protection remains important, it is not addressed with the same level of detail as under MiCA.

MiCA will also be effective for crypto firms outside the EU, as all companies wishing to operate within the Union are required to comply with its provisions. This positions the EU as a potential norm-setting actor in terms of global regulatory standards. The regulatory impact of the GENIUS Act has yet to materialize; however, given the United States' prominent role in the global financial system, the enactment of this legislation is expected to play a significant role in shaping regulatory standards. Both regulatory frameworks will be decisive for the future of the stablecoin economy, with the evolution of regulatory standards shaped by the interaction between these two models.

Despite their gaps and differences, it is essential that stablecoins, which have assumed a comprehensive regulatory role in the two major economies, are properly integrated into the financial system. Stablecoins will be integrated as national and global means of payment, provided they are regulated through a risk-based, proportionate approach that is technology-neutral and balanced between international cooperation and domestic requirements.

Stablecoins are a class of crypto-assets that most closely resemble the cryptographic embodiment of money, which has undergone numerous transformations over time. Therefore, the year 2025 has witnessed a multitude of projects in which stablecoins and traditional finance have become deeply intertwined in the mainstream. Nevertheless, despite existing gaps and divergences, stablecoins, which have secured a comprehensive regulatory role in two major economies, must be properly integrated into the financial system. Stablecoins will be integrated into the financial system as both national and global means of payment, provided they are regulated through a risk-based, proportionate approach that balances international cooperation with domestic requirements, irrespective of the underlying technology.

References

Aldasoro I, Aquılına M, Lewrıck U, Lım SH (2025) Stablecoin growth—policy challenges and approaches. BIS Bulletin No 108. https://www.bis.org/publ/bisbull108.pdf. Accessed 01 Aug 2025

Annunziata F (2023) An overview of the markets in Crypto-Assets Regulation (MiCAR). European Banking Institute working paper series no. 158. https://ssrn.com/abstract=4660379. Accessed 09 Jul 2025

Arner D, Auer R, Frost J (2020) BIS working papers No 905 stablecoins: risks, potential and regulation. https://www.bis.org/publ/work905.pdf. Accessed 27 Jul 2025

Awrey D, Jackson, HE, Massad T (2025) Stable foundations: towards a robust and bipartisan approach to stablecoin legislation. Harvard public law working paper 25–19. https://ssrn.com/abstract=5197044. Accessed 01 Aug 2025

Bank of England (BoE) (2021) New forms of digital money. https://www.bankofengland.co.uk/paper/2021/new-forms-of-digital-money. Accessed 27 Jul 2025

Basel Committee on Banking Supervision (2022). https://www.bis.org/bcbs/publ/d545.pdf. Accessed 08 Aug 2025

Basel Committee on Banking Supervision (2024a) Cryptoasset standard amendments. https://www.bis.org/bcbs/publ/d579.pdf. Accessed 27 Jul 2025

Basel Committee on Banking Supervision (2024b) Disclosure of cryptoasset exposures. https://www.bis.org/bcbs/publ/d580.pdf. Accessed 27 Jul 2025

BIS, CPMI (2023) Considerations for the use of stablecoin arrangements in cross-border payments, pp. 9–12. https://www.bis.org/cpmi/publ/d220.pdf. Accessed 27 Jul 2025

CNBC (n.d.). https://www.cnbc.com/2022/12/12/ftx-founder-sam-bankman-fried-arrested-in-the-bahamas-after-us-files-criminal-charges.html. Accessed 30 Aug 2025

Cœuré B (2019), Update from the Chair of the G7 working group on stablecoins. https://www.bis.org/cpmi/speeches/sp190718.pdf. Accessed 20 Aug 2025

Crypto-assets: A New Standard for Banks (2023) Supervision newsletter. https://www.banking-supervision.europa.eu/press/publications/newsletter/2023/html/ssm.nl230215_1.en.html. Accessed 08 Aug 2025

Directive (EU) 2015/2366 of the European Parliament and of the Council (2015) Payment services in the internal market, amending directives 2002/65/EC, 2009/110/EC and 2013/36/EU and Regulation (EU) No 1093/2010, and Repealing Directive 2007/64/EC. https://eur-lex.europa.eu/legal-content/EN/TXT/?uri=CELEX%3A02015L2366-20250117. Accessed 15 Jul 2025

EBA (2025) Opinion of the European Banking Authority on the interplay between Directive EU 2015/2366 (PSD2) and Regulation (EU) 2023/1114 (MiCA) in relation to crypto-asset service providers that transact electronic money tokens. https://www.eba.europa.eu/sites/default/files/2025-06/e2958c99-a1b0-4b07-9d31-bcba0a28dbe7/Opinion%20on%20the%20interplay%20between%20PSD2%20and%20MiCA.pdf. Accessed 13 Jul 2025

EU Capital Requirement Directive (2013) Directive 2013/36/Eu of the European Parliament and of the Council. https://eur-lex.europa.eu/LexUriServ/LexUriServ.do?uri=OJ:L:2013:176:0338:0436:En:PDF. Accessed 30 Jul 2025

EU Regulatory Proposal for a Regulation of the European Parliament and of the Council on Markets in Crypto-Assets, and Amending Directive (EU) (2019) 2019/1937, COM/2020/593 final (proposal for regulation of MiCA). https://eur-lex.euro-pa.eu/legal-content/EN/TXT/?uri=CELEX%3A52020PC0593. Accessed 02 Aug 2025

European Commission Regulation (EU) (2023) 2023/1114 of the European Parliament and of the Council of 31 May 2023 on markets in crypto-assets, and Amending Regulations (EU) No 1093/2010 and (EU) No 1095/2010 and Directives 2013/36/EU and (EU) 2019/1937 (MiCA). https://eur-lex.europa.eu/legal-content/EN/TXT/?uri=CELEX%3A32023R1114. Accessed 30 Jul 2025

European Parliament Council Directive of 2009/110/EC (2009). https://eur-lex.europa.eu/legal-content/en/TXT/?uri=CELEX%3A32009L0110. Accessed 30 Jul 2025

FATF (2018) Report to G20 Finance Ministers and Central Bank Governors. https://www.fatf-gafi.org/content/fatf-gafi/en/publications/Fatfgeneral/Report-g20-fm-cbg-july-2018.html. Accessed 27 Jul 2025

FATF (2019a) Guidance for a risk-based approach to virtual assets and virtual asset service providers. https://www.fatf-gafi.org/content/fatf-gafi/en/publications/Fatfrecommendations/Guidance-rba-virtual-assets.html. Accessed 27 July 2025

FATF (2019b) Money laundering risks from "stablecoins" and other emerging assets. https://www.fatf-gafi.org/publications/fatfgeneral/documents/statement-virtual-assets-global-stablecoins.html. Accessed 27 Jul 2025

FATF (2020) Report to the G20 Finance Ministers and Central Bank Governors on so-called stablecoins. https://www.fatf-gafi.org/media/fatf/documents/recommendations/Virtual-Assets-FATF-Report-G20-So-Called-Stablecoins.pdf. Accessed 27 Jul 2025

FATF (2024) Targeted update on implementation of the FATF standards on virtual assets and virtual asset service providers. https://www.fatf-gafi.org/content/dam/fatf-gafi/recommendations/2024-Targeted-Update-VAVASP.pdf.coredownload.inline.pdf. Accessed 27 Jul 2025

FATF (2025) Targeted update on implementation of the FATF standards on virtual assets and virtual asset service providers. https://www.fatf-gafi.org/content/dam/fatf-gafi/recommendations/2025-Targeted-Upate-VA-VASPs.pdf.coredownload.pdf. Accessed 27 Jul 2025

FSB (2020a) Addressing the regulatory, supervisory and oversight challenges raised by "global stablecoin" arrangements consultative document (FSB Global Stablecoin Consultative Document 14 April 2020). https://www.fsb.org/wp-content/uploads/P140420-1.pdf. Accessed 16 Aug 2025

FSB (2020b) Global monitoring report on non-bank financial intermediation. https://www.fsb.org/wp-content/uploads/P161220.pdf. Accessed 08 Aug 2025

FSB (2020c) Regulation, supervision and oversight of "global stablecoin" arrangements final report and high-level recommendations. https://www.fsb.org/wp-content/uploads/P131020-3.pdf. Accessed 06 Aug 2025

FSB (2022a) Assessment of risks to financial stability from crypto-assets. https://www.fsb.org/wp-content/uploads/P160222.pdf. Accessed 26 Jul 2025

FSB (2022b) Review of the FSB high-level recommendations of the regulation, supervision and oversight of "global stablecoin" arrangements consultative report. https://www.fsb.org/wp-content/uploads/P111022-4.pdf. Accessed 06 Aug 2025

FSB (2023) High-level recommendations for the regulation, supervision and oversight of global stablecoin arrangements final report. https://www.fsb.org/wp-content/uploads/P170723-3.pdf. Accessed 06 Aug 2025

FSB (2024) Global monitoring report on non-bank financial intermediation. https://www.fsb.org/2024/12/global-monitoring-report-on-non-bank-financial-intermediation-2024/. Accessed 20 Aug 2025

G7 Working Group on Stablecoins (2019) Investigating the impact of global stablecoins (G7 Working Group n stablecoins, investigating the impact of global stablecoins, October 2019). https://www.bis.org/cpmi/publ/d187.pdf. Accessed 28 Jul 2025

Herrera LA (2025) PSD3 and the regulation on payment services in the context of crypto assets as a means of payment, governance and control of data and digital economy in the European single market. In: Sempere PL (ed) Governance and technology series, vol 71. Springer. https://doi.org/10.1007/978-3-031-74889-9_16

Imal FH (2024) Hukuki Açıdan Stablecoin, 1st edn. Adalet, İstanbul

Khan V, Goodell G (2019) Libra: is it really about the money? https://ssrn.com/abstract=3441707. Accessed 26 Jul 2025

Lehmann M (2017) Legal fragmentation, extraterritoriality and uncertainty in global financial regulation. Oxf J Leg Stud 37(2):406–434. https://doi.org/10.1093/ojls/gqw028

Lehmann M (2024) MiCAR—Gold standard or regulatory poison for the crypto industry? European Banking Institute Working Paper Series 160, https://ssrn.com/abstract=4692743. Accessed 30 Jul 2025

Libra Association (2019) Introducing libra: a simple global currency and financial infrastructure that can empower billions of people. https://www.diem.com/en-us/updates/introducing-libra/. Accessed 26 Jul 2025

Ostercamp P (2022) Stablecoin regulation: EU, UK and US perspectives. https://doi.org/10.2139/ssrn.4038843. Accessed 30 Jul 2025

Parra AM (2025) Electronic money tokens under the MiCA regulation, governance and control of data and digital economy in the European single market. In: Sempere P (ed) Law, governance and technology series, vol 71. Springer. https://doi.org/10.1007/978-3-031-74889-9_9

President's Working Group on Financial Markets (PWG) (2021) Reports on stablecoins (PWG Reports on Stablecoins, November 2021). https://home.treasury.gov/sys-tem/files/136/StableCoinReport_Nov1_508.pdf. Accessed 27 Jul 2025

Proposal for a Directive of the European Parliament and of the Council (2023) Proposal for a directive of the European Parliament and of the Council on payment services and electronic money services in the internal market amending directive 98/26/EC and repealing directives 2015/2366/EU and 2009/110/EC (proposal for PSD3). https://eur-lex.europa.eu/legal-content/EN/TXT/?uri=CELEX:52023PC0366. Accessed 30 Jul 2025

Securities and Exchange Commission (2025) Statement on stablecoins. https://www.sec.gov/newsroom/speeches-statements/statement-stablecoins-040425. Accessed 31 Jul 2025

Statement by Diem CEO Stuart Levey on the sale of Diem Group's assets to silvergate (2022). https://www.diem.com/en-us/#Modal. Accessed 26 Jul 2025

The Basel Committee – Overview (n.d.). https://www.bis.org/bcbs/. Accessed 07 Aug 2025

The Council and the European Commission (2019) Joint statement by the Council and the Commission on stablecoins. https://www.consilium.europa.eu/pt/press/press-releases/2019/12/05/joint-statement-by-the-council-and-the-commission-on-stablecoins/. Accessed 30 Jul 2025

The White House (2025) Strengthening American leadership in digital financial technology. https://www.whitehouse.gov/presidential-actions/2025/01/strengthening-american-leadership-in-digital-financial-technology/. Accessed 01 Aug 2025

US Congress (n.d.-a) HR1919 anti-CBDC surveillance state ACT. https://www.congress.gov/bill/119th-congress/house-bill/1919/all-actions. Accessed 08 Jan 2025

US Congress (n.d.-b) S.1582-genius act (GENIUS Act). https://www.congress.gov/bill/119th-congress/senate-bill/1582/text. Accessed 01 Aug 2025

Wilmarth AE (2025) The looming threat of uninsured nonbank stablecoins. GWU Legal Studies Research Paper 2025–33. https://ssrn.com/abstract=5272859. Accessed 01 Aug 2025

Zetzsche DA, Buckley RP, Arner DW (2021) Regulating LIBRA. Oxf J Leg Stud 41:80–113. https://doi.org/10.1093/ojls/gqaa036

Regulatory Approaches of Stablecoins

John Ho

Abstract This chapter examines the purpose and use cases of stablecoins, including the emergence of global stablecoins and the Financial Stability Board's recommendations for the regulation, supervision and oversight of such arrangements. It analyses regulatory approaches across key jurisdictions, highlighting issuer obligations, reserve and redemption requirements, custody standards, and areas of convergence or divergence in regulatory trends. The chapter also explores how stablecoins may coexist with other forms of digital money, including CBDCs and tokenised deposits. It concludes by assessing the future trajectory of stablecoins and the implications for financial stability, innovation and cross-border coordination.

Keywords Stablecoins · Global stablecoins · Cross-border payments · Payments · Financial regulation · Digital assets · Cryptoassets · Asset referenced tokens · Emoney tokens · GENIUS Act · MiCA · Monetary sovereignty

1 Introduction

Rapid technological change is increasingly spurring private—and often Big Tech-promoted—initiatives throughout the world of finance, particularly in the payments domain. As a result, the global financial system has arrived at a potentially game-changing moment.

Recent developments include so-called stablecoins, which avoid the volatility of their higher-profile crypto cousins, like Bitcoin, because their value is supported by a pool of assets. These private stablecoins have flourished as they have delivered value as a source of liquidity in the crypto ecosystem, often providing a "safe haven" for investors during times of heightened volatility by obviating the need to enlist a regulated venue to convert cryptocurrency holdings back into fiat deposits. Indeed,

J. Ho
StanChart, Singapore, Singapore

S. Yazıcı et al. (eds.), *Tokenisation of Money*, Contributions to Finance and Accounting, https://doi.org/10.1007/978-3-032-22946-5_17

the emergence and growth of supply of the prominent stablecoin Tether first coincided with the rapid increase in cryptocurrency transaction volume.

Some stablecoins have sought to replicate the convertibility to central bank money that underpins the existing system of private money. Some do so without the attendant safeguards—prudential regulation and supervision—for the same risks. Others purport to do away with the risks altogether by essentially foregoing the useful credit creating role of private (bank) money, and the benefits of—and for—the banking system.

'Global' stablecoins issued by large technology companies are a particular concern, given their considerable existing market power globally. These can pose additional systemic risks and cause anti-competitive and other undesirable outcomes if such schemes also came to monopolise the issue of private money, or to challenge our monetary sovereignty.

2 What Are Stablecoins and What Are They Being Used For?

Stablecoins are digital assets that are designed to maintain a stable value relative to a national currency or other reference assets.[1] Stablecoins are typically issued by private entities rather than central banks, although in some jurisdictions they may be issued or facilitated by regulated banks or other licensed financial institutions.

A "stablecoin" is a relatively new form of digital asset. Stablecoins are designed to have a value that is more stable than cryptocurrencies like Bitcoin, which are notoriously volatile. The price of cryptocurrencies is very volatile. In 2020 and 2021, the volatility of cryptocurrencies dwarfed the volatility of the diversified [United States] stock and bond markets. This high volatility associated with cryptocurrencies means that cryptocurrencies cannot perform the three functions of money: a store of value, a means of payment and a unit of account.

Stablecoins are a type of settlement asset used in the majority of crypto transactions, and are digitally native crypto-assets that purport to peg their value to a fiat currency, predominantly US dollar.

Stablecoins have developed as both an entry and exit point to the crypto ecosystem, providing a way to transact on blockchains without the extreme volatility seen in other cryptocurrencies. They are used to buy and sell crypto assets on platforms as they avoid the costly 'off-ramps' and 'on-ramps' from fiat to crypto, can be integrated into smart contract protocols and can be held as a store of value within the crypto eco-system. The purported peg can be effected in a variety of way—by backing with real economy assets, by backing with crypto assets or by an algorithm intended to guarantee stable value.[2]

---

[1] U.S. President's Working Group on Financial Markets ("PWG"), Stablecoin Report, 1 November 2021, https://home.treasury.gov/system/files/136/StableCoinReport_Nov1_508.pdf.

[2] ECB Crypto-asset TaskForce, Stablecoins: Implications for monetary policy, financial stability, market infrastructure and payments, and banking supervision in the euro area", September 2020, https://www.ecb.europa.eu/pub/pdf/scpops/ecb.op247~fe3df92991.en.pdf.

In simple terms, they are digital tokens recorded on decentralised ledgers that aim to maintain a fixed value tied to a fiat currency (such as one US dollar). Unlike unbacked cryptocurrencies, most stablecoins are issued by a central entity, which promises redemption at par value based on its reserve assets. The credibility of this promise depends on the quality and size of the issuer's reserve pool.

This continued growth reflects both user needs and certain stablecoin features: ease of access, relative privacy, their positioning as an alternative to traditional finance, the ability to gain.

3 Project Libra

What captured the attention of the public and financial regulators in 2019 was the announcement by Meta (then Facebook) of the announcement of the vision of a stablecoin under Project Libra. Diem Coin (previously called Libra Coin) exemplified the vision of a global stablecoin, though it did not take off ultimately due to lack of regulatory approval.

In October 2019, Libra Association (later renamed Diem Association) announced its establishment with the participation of the following organisations, who had signed onto its charter: Anchorage, Andreessen Horowitz, Bison Trails Co., Breakthrough Initiatives, L.P., Novi Financial, Coinbase, Inc., Creative Destruction Lab, Farfetch UK Limited, Iliad, Kiva Microfunds, Lyft, Inc., Mercy Corps, PayU, Ribbit Capital, Spotify AB, Thrive Capital, Uber Technologies, Inc., Union Square Ventures, Vodafone, Women's World Banking, Xapo Holdings Limited.[3] The Association was eager to pursue its mission of building a better payment network, broadening access to essential financial services, and lowering costs for billions of people who need it the most.

Since the Libra project was announced on June 18, 2019, it has generated excitement around the world. However, it also prompted central banks and policymakers to come out with guidelines and proposals to regulate global stablecoins (GSCs). This prospect of global stablecoins that may challenge the global financial system has intensified calls for central bank digital currencies (CBDCs) to maintain the sovereign currency as the anchor of the nation's payment systems. The GSCs could have significant effects, both domestically and internationally, on the transmission of monetary policy, as well as financial stability, in addition to cross-jurisdictional efforts to combat money laundering and terrorist financing. They could also have implications for the international monetary system more generally, including currency substitution, and could therefore pose challenges to monetary sovereignty. GSCs also raise concerns around fair competition and antitrust policy, including in relation to payments data. These risks, which are of a systemic nature, merit careful monitoring and further study. Both benefits and risks of GSCs may affect some

[3] Ledger Insights, 15 May 2020, https://www.ledgerinsights.com/libra-adds-singapores-sovereign-fund-temasek/.

countries more significantly than others, depending on the state of development of their existing financial and payment systems, the stability of their currencies and their level of financial inclusion, among other factors.

In November 2021, the U.S. President's Working Group released the much-anticipated 'Report on Stablecoins'.[4] The group, comprised of the Federal Deposit Insurance Corporation and the Office of the Comptroller of the Currency, gave recommendations to Congress on new legislation to regulate stablecoins which challenges the feasibility of Diem's model. Given regulatory pushback, Libra could not obtain regulatory approval in the USA to move forward. On 31 January 2022, Diem announced the sale of its intellectual property and other assets related to the running of the Diem Payment Network to a U.S. bank holding company Silvergate Capital Corporation.[5]

4 Global Stablecoins (GSC)

A stablecoin that gains wide adoption and operates across multiple jurisdictions—known as a *global stablecoin (GSC)*—has the potential to become systemically important within and across financial systems. The activities of GSC arrangements, and the risks they may create, can cut across regulatory frameworks governing banking, payments, and securities or investments, both domestically and internationally.

GSCs are stablecoins that achieve global scale, with the potential to reshape payment systems and financial intermediation. While they promise faster and cheaper cross-border transactions and greater financial inclusion, their widespread use could undermine monetary policy and the stability of financial systems. If adopted as a store of value, GSCs could weaken the transmission of central bank policies by removing significant volumes of transactions from the traditional monetary system. By creating closed ecosystems or "walled gardens," GSCs risk fragmenting payment systems that currently revolve around central bank money, thereby diminishing the influence of central banks over domestic interest rates and credit conditions.

The expansion of GSCs also poses potential threats to financial stability and the integrity of the international monetary system. Although stablecoins currently have limited links to traditional finance, their rapid growth and increasing participation from both retail and institutional investors heighten the urgency of robust oversight. Poor management of liquidity, credit, or market risks could trigger contagion into the broader economy, especially if GSCs become deeply interconnected with banks and payment systems.

---

[4] U.S. Treasury, Report on Stablecoins, November 2021, https://home.treasury.gov/system/files/136/StableCoinReport_Nov1_508.pdf.

[5] https://www.bloomberg.com/news/articles/2022-01-31/meta-backed-diem-association-confirms-asset-sale-to-silvergate.

Beyond financial and monetary stability, GSCs raise concerns about fair competition and national monetary sovereignty. Widespread adoption could lead to currency substitution, eroding the ability of smaller economies to conduct independent monetary policy. Moreover, large technology firms behind many stablecoin projects could leverage their existing platforms to achieve rapid market dominance, providing similar services to regulated entities but without equivalent compliance obligations. This would create an uneven playing field and concentrate economic power further in the hands of a few global players.

In 2019 the G20 tasked the Financial Stability Board (FSB) with assessing regulatory challenges posed by GSCs and advising on coordinated global responses. In October 2020, the FSB released *High-level Recommendations for the Regulation, Supervision and Oversight of Global Stablecoin Arrangements*. Following further review, the FSB issued a final version in July 2023, forming part of its broader global regulatory framework for cryptoasset activities.

The term "*stablecoin*" does not have a universally accepted legal or regulatory definition, nor does it guarantee that the asset is truly stable in value. The FSB continues to use the term because it is widely adopted by both market participants and regulators.

In its 2023 final report, the FSB set out the following definitions:

- **Stablecoin**: a cryptoasset designed to maintain a stable value relative to a specific asset, or to a pool or basket of assets.
- **Stablecoin arrangement**: the broader framework of functions and activities that support the issuance and operation of a stablecoin and aim to maintain its value.
- **Global Stablecoin (GSC)**: a stablecoin with existing or potential use across multiple jurisdictions, which could become systemically important within and across financial systems—for example, as a means of payment or as a store of value.

Key factors in determining whether a stablecoin qualifies as a GSC include:

1. Whether disruptions or failures in its arrangement could materially affect crypto markets, the global financial system, or the broader economy.
2. Its potential for widespread cross-border use.

Additional considerations may be drawn from criteria typically used to assess financial market infrastructures and global systemically important banks. Of particular importance is whether a stablecoin could achieve significant scale, adoption, and cross-jurisdictional reach.[6]

[6] BIS, Recommendations for the Regulation, Supervision and Oversight of Global Stablecoin Arrangements—Executive Summary, Feb 2024, https://www.bis.org/fsi/fsisummaries/global_stablecoins.htm.

4.1 The High-Level Recommendations for GSC Arrangements

The high-level GSC recommendations aim to address financial stability risks posed by GSCs, both at the domestic and international level, while supporting responsible innovation and providing sufficient flexibility for jurisdictions to implement domestic approaches. They seek to promote consistent and effective regulation, supervision and oversight of GSCs and stablecoins with the potential to become GSCs across jurisdictions. In addition, these recommendations emphasise a technology-neutral approach that prioritises underlying activities and risks (Table 1).

The GSC recommendations are intended to be flexible so that they can be incorporated into the wide variety of regulatory frameworks potentially applicable to stablecoins around the world.

Table 1 The high-level recommendations for GSC arrangements[a]

Recommendation	Definition
1. Authorities' readiness to regulate and supervise global stablecoin arrangements	Authorities should have and utilise the appropriate powers and tools, and adequate resources, to comprehensively regulate, supervise and oversee a GSC arrangement and its associated functions and activities, and enforce relevant laws and regulations effectively.
2. Comprehensive oversight of GSC activities and functions	Authorities should apply comprehensive and effective regulatory, supervisory and oversight requirements consistent with international standards to GSC arrangements on a functional basis and proportionate to their risks insofar as such requirements are consistent with their respective mandates.
3. Cross-border cooperation, coordination and information sharing	Authorities should cooperate and coordinate with each other, both domestically and internationally, to foster efficient and effective communication, information sharing and consultation in order to support each other in fulfilling their respective mandates and to ensure comprehensive regulation, supervision and oversight of a GSC arrangement across borders and sectors, and to encourage consistency of regulatory and supervisory outcomes.
4. Governance structures and decentralised operations	Authorities should require that GSC arrangements have in place and disclose a comprehensive governance framework with clear and direct lines of responsibility and accountability for all functions and activities within the GSC arrangement.
5. Risk management	Authorities should require that GSC arrangements have effective risk management frameworks in place that comprehensively address all material risks associated with their functions and activities, especially with regard to operational resilience, cyber security safeguards and anti-money laundering/countering the financing of terrorism (AML/CFT) measures, as well as "fit and proper" requirements, if applicable, and consistent with jurisdictions' laws and regulations.

(continued)

Table 1 (continued)

Recommendation	Definition
6. Data storage and access to data	Authorities should require that GSC arrangements have in place robust frameworks, including systems and processes for the collecting, storing, safeguarding and timely and accurate reporting of data. Authorities should have access to the data as necessary and appropriate to fulfil their regulatory, supervisory and oversight mandates.
7. Recovery and resolution of the GSC	Authorities should require that GSC arrangements have appropriate recovery and resolution plans.
8. Disclosures	Authorities should require that GSC issuers and, where applicable, other participants in the GSC arrangements provide all users and relevant stakeholders with comprehensive and transparent information to understand the functioning of the GSC arrangement, including with respect to the governance framework, any conflicts of interest and their management, redemption rights, stabilisation mechanism, operations, risk management framework and financial condition.
9. Redemption rights, stabilisation and prudential requirements	Authorities should require that GSC arrangements provide a robust legal claim to all users against the issuer and/or underlying reserve assets and guarantee timely redemption. For GSCs referenced to a single fiat currency, redemption should be at par into fiat. To maintain a stable value at all times and mitigate the risks of runs, authorities should require GSC arrangements to have an effective stabilisation mechanism, clear redemption rights and meet prudential requirements.
10. Conformance with regulatory, supervisory and oversight requirements before commencing operations	Authorities should require that GSC arrangements meet all applicable regulatory, supervisory and oversight requirements of a particular jurisdiction before commencing any operations in that jurisdiction and adapt to new regulatory requirements as necessary and as appropriate.

[a]Ibid
Source: https://www.bis.org/fsi/fsisummaries/global_stablecoins.pdf

5 Regulatory Approaches to Stablecoins

The rapid expansion of stablecoins has prompted policymakers to explore how existing financial rules should apply and where new frameworks are needed triggered a wave of regulatory responses worldwide.

The key reasons oft cited for the need to have regulation around stablecoins are:

5.1 *Financial Stability*

Global regulators are concerned that unregulated stablecoins could weaken local currencies, disrupt monetary policy, or create financial instability in a crisis. By operating outside existing financial frameworks, stablecoins could introduce unforeseen systemic risks. To counter this, frameworks like the EU's MiCA impose usage limits and supervisory oversight.

5.2 *Anti-Money Laundering and Consumer Protection*

Because stablecoins can move quickly and across borders without intermediaries, they can slip through the cracks of traditional compliance systems. To reduce these risks, regulators require stablecoin issuers and platforms to follow anti-money laundering (AML) and know-your-customer (KYC) rules, just like banks and payment processors.

5.3 *Reserve Backing and Redemption Assurance*

Stablecoin users need confidence that their tokens can be redeemed at full value at any time. To support this, regulations require issuers to maintain one-to-one reserve backing, offer clear redemption rights, and publish regular attestations.

The passage of the U.S. GENIUS Act in July 2025 has opened a path for stablecoins to be adopted in the U.S. under a regulatory framework and this has also propelled other jurisdictions to consider implementing appropriate framework to regulate the issuance, redemption and transfer of such stablecoins.

Jurisdictions such as the European Union (EU), Hong Kong, Japan, South Korea, Singapore, the United Arab Emirates (UAE), the United Kingdom (UK), and others are now actively developing or implementing dedicated regulatory regimes. While some of these initiatives have been underway since 2023, the U.S.—driven by strong momentum under the Trump administration's push for new GENIUS Act—has accelerated global policy debates and hastened implementation efforts.

Across the jurisdictions reviewed, regulators are broadly converging on three core requirements for stablecoin issuers[7]:

- **Full reserve backing** to ensure solvency and stability
- **Clear redemption rights** to protect users and maintain trust
- **Robust custody and safeguarding of client assets** to mitigate operational and counterparty risks

Yet, despite this convergence, regulatory details diverge significantly. For example, what constitutes "eligible reserves" or how redemption timelines are defined varies across jurisdictions. Some regulators apply a more bank-like prudential approach, while others lean toward securities or payments frameworks.

---

[7] EY, Global Approaches to Stablecoin Regulation, (July 2025), https://media.licdn.com/dms/document/media/v2/D4E1FAQH-2Y986dvwgg/feedshare-document-pdf-analyzed/B4EZgtbU.FHoAY/0/1753108804195?e=1756944000&v=beta&t=PsxjgC78ZG2hOvdQkSWzMqWnLhuJkynFvcPCiD0jVVg, at p. 5.

Table 2 Global regulatory landscape of stablecoins[a]

Jurisdictions	Stablecoins regime
USA	GENIUS Act passed in July 2025
EU	EU MiCA implemented since June 2023
Hong Kong	Stablecoin Ordinance effective August 2025
Singapore	Stablecoin Regulatory Regime effective August 2023
Japan	Stablecoin Regulatory Regime effective June 2023
UAE	Payment Token Services Regulation (UAE Stablecoin Regulation) effective August 2024
Thailand	Bank of Thailand Stablecoin Regulation Policy effective March 2021
Switzerland	Regulatory framework developing
United Kingdom	Regulatory framework developing
Bahrain	Central Bank of Bahrain Stablecoin Issuance and Offering Module effective July 2025

[a]GFTN (2025). GFTN global digital assets report 2025, at p. 12, https://media.licdn.com/dms/document/media/v2/D4D1FAQGWYHukqzFtNQ/feedshare-document-pdf-analyzed/B4DZpulKOaIAAg/0/1762791880196?e=1765411200&v=beta&t=cUGUiqolsAPBKGsg_VKyHXyDDi0_GWUjKCm9D9UET4Q

These divergences reflect differences in legal frameworks, market structures, and policy priorities. They also highlight the influence of international standard setters such as the Financial Stability Board (FSB) and the International Organization of Securities Commissions (IOSCO). Both bodies have issued principles and recommendations on global stablecoins, focusing on financial stability, consumer protection, and cross-border consistency. However, because these standards are non-binding guidance rather than prescriptive rules, jurisdictions interpret and adapt them differently based on their domestic contexts.

As a result, the regulatory landscape for stablecoins is becoming fragmented. This opens the door to regulatory arbitrage—where issuers may choose jurisdictions with more favourable rules—and creates uneven impacts on business models, risk management, and adoption rates across markets. Over time, this patchwork approach may complicate cross-border interoperability, even as global regulators strive to balance innovation, financial stability, and investor protection (Table 2).

Stablecoins have rapidly become a foundational element of the digital asset ecosystem, with transaction volumes reaching tens of trillions of US dollars annually. Nonetheless, such figures should be contextualised, as much of the activity reflects financial market usage rather than end-user payment flows.[8]

The passage of the GENIUS Act in July, 2025 established a U.S. regulatory framework for stablecoins, providing greater legal clarity and setting the stage for wider adoption. The GENIUS Act creates a uniform, prudential framework for "payment stablecoins" used as means of payment or settlement, clarifies which entities

[8] Ibid.

may issue them, sets reserve, redemption, disclosure, AML/CFT and operational requirements, and assigns federal and state supervisory roles. It also carves payment stablecoins (issued by permitted issuers) out of "security" and "commodity" status, channelling primary oversight to banking regulators rather than the SEC/CFTC.[9]

The EU's Markets in Cryptoasset Regulations (MiCA) create a consistent, risk-focused framework for all EU member states. In Asia, jurisdictions such as Japan, Singapore and Hong Kong have also introduced or are implementing regulatory regimes for stablecoins. Meanwhile, other markets, including Saudi Arabia, Qatar and India are still observing the space and have yet to introduce comprehensive stablecoin-specific frameworks.

As GENIUS Act and EU MiCA are covered in other chapters in this publication, this chapter would focus on comparative regulatory approaches in other key jurisdictions, covering some of the key GSC requirements such as issuer requirements, reserve rules, redemption rights, eligible issuers, custody and areas of convergence and/or divergence trends.

6 Key Regulatory Dimensions

The following sections will provide a comparative deep dive across these jurisdictions, focusing on key regulatory dimensions such as legal classification, issuer requirements, reserve asset rules, custody, and redemption rights. The aim is to highlight both areas of convergence and jurisdiction-specific approaches that shape the evolution of compliant stablecoin ecosystems. Jurisdictions like Saudi Arabia, Brazil, India, and Qatar are excluded from this comparison, as stablecoin regulation in these markets is either in very early stages with no public announcements or is explicitly excluded from the current digital asset regulatory framework.

6.1 Legal Classifications

Across major jurisdictions that have legislative framework for fiat-pegged stablecoins, the legal treatment of stablecoins has shifted toward a functional, payment-focused perspective. In the United States, the GENIUS Act classifies them as "payment stablecoins," which must be issued by regulated financial institutions. The European Union provides one of the most structured frameworks through MiCA, which distinguishes stablecoins as either e-money tokens (EMTs) or asset-referenced tokens (ARTs) based on how their value is maintained.

EMTs are stablecoins that preserve their value by referencing a single official currency, such as the euro or U.S. dollar, and are regulated in line with traditional electronic money under EU payment rules. In contrast, ARTs are tied to a basket of

[9] S.394-GENIUS Act of 2025, https://www.congress.gov/bill/119th-congress/senate-bill/394/text.

Table 3 Stablecoin legislative regime

Jurisdiction	Definition/Classification
USA	Payment stablecoins (GENIUS Act)
EU	E-money tokens or asset referenced tokens under MiCA
Japan	Electronic payment instruments under the Payment Services Act
United Kingdom	A form of Digital Settlement Assets under FSMA 2023
Switzerland	Proposed bill for a single currency fiat stablecoin issued in Switzerland
Singapore	Single currency stablecoin
UAE	Stablecoins regulated as payment tokens
Hong Kong	Fiat referenced stablecoins

assets—ranging from multiple fiat currencies to commodities or other crypto assets—and fall under a separate, more tailored regulatory regime due to their added complexity and potential use as investment or value-storage instruments. MiCA's dual categorisation enables the EU to clearly separate stablecoins intended for payments and monetary activity (EMTs) from those designed for investment-oriented or alternative financial functions (ARTs).

Japan places stablecoins within its existing framework for electronic payment instruments, signalling its intent to integrate them directly into established payment law. The United Kingdom refers to them as Digital Securities Assets (DSAs), aligning them with its systemic payments regulatory structure. Singapore defines stablecoins as Single Currency Stablecoins (SCSs) based on specific criteria that apply to fiat-backed instruments.

Switzerland adopts a broader definition of value-stable tokens, focusing on their role as payment instruments designed to reduce price volatility. The UAE classifies stablecoins as "payment tokens" under its 2024 Central Bank regulation, treating them strictly as stored-value tools for payments and remittances while excluding investment or speculative uses. Hong Kong, meanwhile, recognises only fiat-referenced stablecoins and explicitly prohibits algorithmic models.

Together, these regulatory approaches reflect each jurisdiction's distinct philosophy and risk tolerance in incorporating stablecoins into their financial and monetary frameworks (Table 3).

6.2 *Licensing and Authorisation*[10]

Across jurisdictions with established stablecoin rules, issuers typically need either a dedicated stablecoin licence or a banking licence. In many places, banks may issue stablecoins directly, though some require issuance through a

[10] FSB, 16 October 2025, Thematic Review on FSB Global Regulatory Framework for Crypto-asset Activities, pp. 37–40, https://www.fsb.org/uploads/P161025-1.pdf.

non-deposit-taking subsidiary. Bermuda requires banks to obtain an additional licence for single-currency-pegged stablecoins. The EU, Japan and Singapore allow banks to issue balance-sheet-backed stablecoins without setting aside a separate reserve.

Beyond banks, electronic money institutions and payment service providers can also issue stablecoins in several jurisdictions. The EU limits EMT issuance to banks and EMIs, while Armenia follows a similar model. In Japan, only banks, trust companies and funds transfer service providers may issue stablecoins.

Many jurisdictions also permit non-bank issuers subject to licensing. Bermuda and The Bahamas use principles-based frameworks, and Hong Kong allows non-bank issuance with proof of adequate capabilities. In the US, non-banks may obtain an OCC licence for payment stablecoins. Singapore, the UK and the EU all allow non-bank issuers under specific conditions, including ART issuance in the EU. In Australia, issuance depends on whether the stablecoin qualifies as a financial product.

Rules on permitted activities differ: Singapore plans to restrict issuers to stablecoin business only, while Hong Kong requires approval for business expansion. The EU and Bermuda allow broader activities but retain supervisory intervention powers. The EU has additional requirements where multiple entities issue the same token, including a unified reserve and coordinated recovery plans.

Switzerland currently allows certain issuers to operate under bank guarantees without a banking licence which carries potential risks, particularly in terms of regulatory visibility, depositor protection, and prudential oversight. As such reforms are underway to strengthen the framework.

Overall, global regulatory approaches differ widely in maturity and strictness. Tighter regimes provide stronger safeguards but raise compliance costs, while looser approaches risk regulatory arbitrage. These divergences pose challenges for global issuers and highlight the need for greater international coordination to support both innovation and financial stability.

6.3 Reserve Asset Requirements[11]

Most jurisdictions that have introduced stablecoin regulations insist that issuers maintain full reserve backing at all times, meaning the pool of reserve assets must at least equal the total value of stablecoins in circulation. This core safeguard is intended to preserve price stability and ensure holders can redeem their tokens at par. Regulatory frameworks in Singapore, Hong Kong, Japan, the United States, and the UK (for both systemic and non-systemic stablecoins under its proposed regime) all embed this requirement.

[11] FSB, 16 October 2025, Thematic review on FSB global regulatory framework for crypto-asset activities, pp. 52–53, https://www.fsb.org/uploads/P161025-1.pdf.

A number of regulators go beyond simple 1:1 backing by imposing supplementary capital requirements, creating a financial buffer to protect users from market swings, credit deterioration, and operational risks. The EU's MiCA regime is a prime example: while it mandates 1:1 reserves, it also obliges issuers—particularly of 'significant' tokens—to hold additional 'own funds' (capital) calculated as a percentage of their reserve assets. The UK is also weighing similar expectations for systemic issuers, together with additional capital resources to cover operational losses and wind-down needs. Hong Kong's proposed framework likewise emphasizes that reserve assets must always equal the par value, while requiring issuers to maintain adequate paid-up capital calibrated to the specific risk profile of their operations. These additional layers of protection are designed to reinforce financial stability, especially where stablecoins could have system-wide significance.

Other jurisdictions take a lighter approach. In Canada, reserve assets must fully support virtual-currency-referenced tokens, but adequacy is only assessed on a once-daily fair value basis rather than continuously. Bermuda's principles-based Digital Asset Business regime obliges issuers to maintain reserves but does not specify real-time or over-collateralisation requirements. The Bahamas adopts a disclosure-centric model, requiring issuers to set out their stabilisation mechanisms in offering materials without expressly mandating full or excess collateral backing.

Such periodic or disclosure-based regimes fall short of the standard set out in GSC Recommendation 9, which calls for reserve assets to match outstanding stablecoins at all times. As a result, they may provide a lower level of assurance compared with frameworks that enforce continuous or over-collateralised reserve requirements.

6.4 Custody of Reserve Assets[12]

GSC Recommendation 9 calls for reserve-backed stablecoin arrangements to ensure secure custody, proper record-keeping, and continuous protection of ownership rights, including segregation of reserves from the assets of issuers, group entities, and custodians. Most jurisdictions follow this model by requiring segregation, bankruptcy-remoteness, and the use of qualified custodians. Armenia, the EU, Hong Kong, Singapore, the US, and the UK all mandate or propose legal or operational ring-fencing, achieved through statutory trusts or contractual structures—for example, Hong Kong's trust requirements backed by legal opinions, the UK's proposed statutory trusts for systemic coins, and the EU's operational segregation with licensed custodians. Many frameworks also require reserve assets to be held with regulated custodians such as banks or investment firms, with places like the EU and Canada imposing due diligence obligations to ensure custodians have adequate controls and expertise.

[12] FSB, 16 October 2025, Thematic review on FSB global regulatory framework for crypto-asset activities, pp. 55–57, https://www.fsb.org/uploads/P161025-1.pdf.

Despite broad alignment, jurisdictions differ on whether custody must be held onshore. Local-custody requirements—seen in Hong Kong, Armenia, Nigeria, and the EU—aim to strengthen oversight and user protection, though Hong Kong allows limited offshore arrangements subject to safeguards. The UK allows offshore custody for non-systemic coins with strict safeguarding and third-party custodian requirements, but for sterling-denominated systemic stablecoins, it proposes that issuers, capital, and backing assets be based in the UK. Others, including Singapore, Canada, and Bermuda, permit offshore custody if specific conditions or legal protections are met.

There is a growing regulatory trend against allowing issuers to self-custody reserves. Japan and Singapore explicitly prohibit it. The EU's MiCA effectively restricts it by mandating that reserves be held by independent, licensed credit institutions or investment firms. While some jurisdictions like the Bahamas take a more flexible approach, the prevailing view is that allowing self-custody without robust, independent oversight creates conflicts of interest that could undermine FSB Recommendation 9.

Finally, approaches to bankruptcy-remoteness vary. The EU, Hong Kong, and the UK require explicit legal protections to ensure reserve assets remain unencumbered and available for redemption even if the custodian or issuer becomes insolvent. Other jurisdictions, such as Bermuda and Brazil, rely on operational segregation and common-law principles. While these provide significant protection, regulators continue to debate whether a lack of explicit statutory "carve-outs" for stablecoin holders might face challenges in complex, cross-border insolvency proceedings.

6.5 *Redemption Rights*[13]

Regulatory approaches to stablecoin redemption at par value fall broadly into two camps: those that expressly require 1:1 redemption and those that stop short of doing so. Armenia, The Bahamas, the EU, Hong Kong, Japan, Singapore, the UK, and the US all mandate—or plan to mandate—that issuers redeem stablecoins at a one-to-one rate with the relevant reference asset. Under the EU's MiCA, for example, holders can claim redemption directly from the issuer at par value for EMTs or at market value for ARTs, with fees barred except in recovery scenarios. The UK also intends to enforce par-value redemption, treating it as essential for confidence in systemic stablecoins used as money. Singapore's upcoming regime similarly requires redemption at par within a prescribed timeframe, while Japan's Payment Service Act ensures redemptions occur at face value. The Bahamas likewise obliges issuers to redeem on a 1:1 basis.

[13] FSB, 16 October 2025, Thematic Review on FSB Global Regulatory Framework for Crypto-asset Activities, pp. 50–51, https://www.fsb.org/uploads/P161025-1.pdf.

Other jurisdictions do not define redemption at par value as a strict requirement. Canada relies on disclosures to ensure users understand their redemption rights, without specifying exact terms. Bermuda's principles-based regime assesses redemption arrangements holistically rather than imposing a par-value rule.

Timeliness of redemption is another area where regulatory practice diverges. Some jurisdictions set explicit deadlines, while others simply require prompt processing. Singapore obliges issuers to satisfy valid redemption requests within five business days. Hong Kong requires redemption within the following business day. The UK is considering even tighter rules: T+1 for non-systemic issuers, and same-day—or real-time where feasible—for systemic stablecoins, reflecting the importance of maintaining trust in instruments that may function as money.

These differing redemption expectations may create frictions for stablecoins issued across multiple jurisdictions and amplify run dynamics. Institutional users able to move quickly across borders might redeem first in jurisdictions with faster timelines, while issuers could face operational strain rebalancing reserves and meeting varying redemption standards simultaneously.

7 Key Jurisdictions Introducing Regulatory Frameworks

Apart from discussions on the GENIUS Act and EU MiCA in other chapters, the following section offers a concise overview of key jurisdictions that have introduced, or are in the process of introducing, regulatory frameworks for stablecoins.

7.1 Hong Kong

7.1.1 Regulatory Framework

- Hong Kong has enacted the Stablecoins Ordinance (Cap. 656), which provides a regulatory regime for fiat-referenced stablecoin issuers.
- The Legislative Council passed the bill on 21 May 2025[14]; the Ordinance commenced on 1 August 2025, the same day the Hong Kong Monetary Authority (**HKMA**) opened licensing applications and released its core rulebook (supervisory & AML/CFT guidelines plus explanatory notes).[15]

[14] HKMA, 21 May 2025, Government welcomes the passage of the Stablecoins Bill, https://www.hkma.gov.hk/eng/news-and-media/press-releases/2025/05/20250521-3/.

[15] HKMA, 29 July 2025, Implementation of regulatory regime for stablecoin issuers, https://www.hkma.gov.hk/eng/news-and-media/press-releases/2025/07/20250729-4/.

7.1.2 What the Stablecoins Ordinance Aims To Do?

- The Stablecoins Ordinance establishes a licensing and supervisory regime for fiat-referenced stablecoins (**FRS**) issuers in Hong Kong, to further enhance Hong Kong's regulatory framework on virtual-asset (**VA**) activities.
- The Stablecoins Ordinance adopts the principle of "same activity, same risks, same regulation", ensuring alignment with international standards while adapting to local circumstances.[16]
- It provides proper safeguards against financial stability risks and money laundering, promotes investor protection, and lays a solid foundation for the sustainable development of the industry.
- It initially focuses on issuers (not trading venues) and sets rules for reserves, redemption, governance, disclosures, AML/CFT, and operational resilience.
- Algorithmic or unbacked "stablecoins" are outside scope because of strict reserve rules.

7.1.3 Key Provisions of the Hong Kong Stablecoin Regime

(a) **Issuance, Offer & Sale of Payment Stablecoins**

- **Licensing required**: Under the Stablecoins Ordinance (Cap. 656) ("SO"), the HKMA is the authority responsible for the licensing of persons who conduct regulated stablecoin activities in Hong Kong.[17] Any person who, in the course of business, issues an FRS in Hong Kong, or issues an FRS that purports to maintain a stable value with reference to Hong Kong dollars in or outside Hong Kong will need to obtain a licence from the HKMA.[18] According to the Ordinance, it will be illegal for any person to offer any unlicensed FRS to a retail investor, or actively market the issue of unlicensed FRS to the public of Hong Kong.[19] Advertising of regulated stablecoin activities is restricted.[20]
- **Scope limited to FRS**: The framework applies to coins referenced to one or more official (fiat) currencies.[21] The current scope excludes non-fiat-referenced stablecoins, such as those referencing gold or other precious metals, crypto-collateralized stablecoins and algorithmic stablecoins, and

[16] HKMA, 23 June 2025, Robust and Sustainable Development of Stablecoins, https://www.hkma.gov.hk/eng/news-and-media/insight/2025/06/20250623/.

[17] HKMA, 29 July 2025, Stablecoins Ordinance – Explanatory Note on Licensing of Stablecoin Issuers, https://www.hkma.gov.hk/media/eng/doc/key-functions/ifc/stablecoin-issuers/Explanatory_Notes_on_Licensing_of_Stablecoin_Issuers_eng.pdf.

[18] Stablecoins Ordinance, https://www.elegislation.gov.hk/hk/cap656?xpid=ID_1438402726674_003.

[19] HKMA, 23 July 2025, The Steadfast and Sustainable Development of Stablecoins, https://www.hkma.gov.hk/eng/news-and-media/insight/2025/07/20250723/.

[20] Ibid.

[21] Stablecoins Ordinance, https://www.elegislation.gov.hk/hk/cap656?xpid=ID_1438402726674_003, see Section 4 (Definition of Specified Stablecoin).

stablecoins issued outside Hong Kong that do not reference Hong Kong dollars.[22]

- **No interest to holders**: Issuers **must not pay interest or interest-like returns** on the stablecoin.[23]
- **Transitional path**: Pre-existing operators have a limited transition window and must engage the HKMA early. As of the time of this publication, parties interested in applying for a licence are encouraged to contact the HKMA, by 31 August 2025**,** so that the HKMA may communicate regulatory expectations and provide feedback as appropriate. While licensing will be an ongoing process, interested parties that consider themselves sufficiently ready and wish to be considered early should submit the application to the HKMA by 30 September 2025.[24]
- According to HKMA, considering the novelty and potential risks of stablecoin, the need for user protection, market capacity and long-term development, it expects to set a high bar for licensing. It is envisaged that only a handful of licences will be granted initially.[25] The first licences are expected in early 2026 under a cautious rollout.

(b) **Regulation and Supervision of Permitted Issuers**

- **Primary supervisor**: The **HKMA** licenses and supervises issuers, with powers to set conditions, inspect, require information, and take enforcement action in the interests of holders and stability. The **SFC** coordinates on market-wide and conduct matters when relevant.[26]
- **Guidelines and expectations**: The HKMA has issued a "Guideline on Supervision of Licensed Stablecoin Issuer" detailing minimum criteria tied to governance, fit-and-proper, risk management, systems, and controls.[27]

(c) **Regulatory Requirements for Issuers**

- **Full backing (with buffer)**: Reserve assets' market value must at all times be equal or above par value of outstanding stablecoins, with appropriate over-collateralisation expected.[28]

---

[22] Ditto.

[23] Stablecoins Ordinance, https://www.elegislation.gov.hk/hk/cap656?xpid=ID_1438402726674_003.

[24] HKMA, 29 July 2025, Implementation of regulatory regime for stablecoin issuers, https://www.hkma.gov.hk/eng/news-and-media/press-releases/2025/07/20250729-4/.

[25] HKMA and SFC, 14 August 2025, Joint Statement by the HKMA and SFC of the stablecoin related market movements, https://apps.sfc.hk/edistributionWeb/gateway/EN/news-and-announcements/news/doc?refNo=25PR123.

[26] Stablecoins Ordinance, https://www.elegislation.gov.hk/hk/cap656?xpid=ID_1438402726674_003.

[27] HKMA, July 2025, Guideline on Supervision of Licensed Stablecoin Issuer, https://www.hkma.gov.hk/media/eng/doc/key-functions/ifc/stablecoin-issuers/Guideline_on_supervision_of_licensed_stablecoin_issuers_eng.pdf.

[28] Stablecoins Ordinance, https://www.elegislation.gov.hk/hk/cap656?xpid=ID_1438402726674_003.

- **Segregation and custody**: Reserve assets must be segregated from the issuer's own assets and held under robust custody arrangements to protect holders.[29]
- **Redemption rights and disclosures**: Holders must have clear, timely redemption to par and access to regular public reporting on reserve composition, valuation, and risk controls. Misleading claims (e.g., implying government guarantees) are prohibited.[30]
- **Governance, risk, and resilience**: Issuers must maintain strong governance, operational resilience, **cybersecurity**, and **AML/CFT** controls consistent with Hong Kong standards and international expectations.[31]

(d) **Additional Rule-Making or Considerations**

- **Market communications discipline**: Following rapid price moves tied to "licensing rumours," HKMA and SFC jointly reminded firms on 14 August 2025 to avoid **speculative or misleading statements** about licence applications.[32]

7.1.4 Prospects for the Industry

- **Institutional entry likely**: Clarity on 1:1 reserves and redemption should pull in banks and large fintechs; several established players have already signalled intent to apply. First approvals are expected early 2026, implying staged adoption.
- **Higher compliance bar**: Strict reserve, disclosure, and governance rules raise costs and will likely concentrate issuance among well-capitalized firms. Smaller or algorithmic projects may remain outside the retail Hong Kong market.
- **HKD and USD focus, CNH interest**: Early applications are expected to target HKD- and USD-pegged coins; this may be followed by the introduction of offshore-RMB **(CNH)** design stablecoins at a later stage depending on market demand.
- **Regional positioning**: With a live licensing regime and RMB/HKD infrastructure, Hong Kong strengthens its position as a testing ground for Asia's regulated stablecoins and cross-border payment pilots.

---

[29] Ibid.

[30] HKMA, July 2025, Explanatory Notes on Licensing of Stablecoin Issuers, https://www.hkma.gov.hk/media/eng/doc/key-functions/ifc/stablecoin-issuers/Explanatory_Notes_on_Licensing_of_Stablecoin_Issuers_eng.pdf.

[31] Ibid.

[32] HKMA and SFC, 14 August 2025, Joint Statement by the HKMA and SFC of the stablecoin related market movements, https://apps.sfc.hk/edistributionWeb/gateway/EN/news-and-announcements/news/doc?refNo=25PR123.

7.1.5 Takeaways

- **First in Asia Pacific (ex Japan)**: Hong Kong is one of the earliest jurisdictions in Asia to launch a licensing and supervisory framework for FRS issuers.
- **Risk-based flexible regulatory regime**: The Stablecoins Ordinance has established a risk-based, pragmatic, and flexible regulatory regime.
- **Digital asset ecosystem**: HKMA believes that a robust and fit-for-purpose regulatory environment would provide favourable conditions to support the healthy, responsible, and sustainable development of Hong Kong's stablecoin and the broader digital asset ecosystem.[33]
- **Orderly rollout**: A measured timetable (transitional period; first licences in 2026) aims to control risks and build public trust while enabling innovation by regulated institutions.
- **Financial centre for digital assets**: HKM.
- A aspires for Hong Kong to be a digital asset financial centre hub. Following the implementation of the stablecoins issuers regulatory regimes, the Hong Kong Government intends to launch consultations on virtual assets (VAs) over-the-counter and custodian services, and promulgate the second policy statement on the development of VAs.[34]

7.2 *Singapore*

7.2.1 Existence and Passage of Specific Legislation

Singapore has established a regulatory framework for stablecoins under the Payment Services Act (PS Act) 2019. On 15 August 2023, the **Monetary Authority of Singapore (MAS)** announced the finalization of a new regulatory framework specifically for **single-currency stablecoins (SCS)** pegged to the Singapore Dollar or any G10 currency, issued in Singapore.[35]

7.2.2 Objectives of the Legislation

The primary objectives of the MAS's stablecoin regulatory framework are to:

- Ensure a **high degree of value stability** for stablecoins regulated in Singapore.
- Establish clear guidelines for the issuance, offer, and sale of stablecoins.

---

[33] HKMA, 21 May 2025, Government welcomes the passage of the Stablecoins Bill, https://www.hkma.gov.hk/eng/news-and-media/press-releases/2025/05/20250521-3/.

[34] Ibid.

[35] MAS, 15 August 2023, MAS finalises stablecoin regulatory regime, https://www.mas.gov.sg/news/media-releases/2023/mas-finalises-stablecoin-regulatory-framework.

- Enhance **consumer protection** and **market integrity** in the digital asset ecosystem.
- Provide a clear distinction between **MAS-regulated stablecoins** and other digital payment tokens.[36]

7.2.3 Key Provisions of the Stablecoin Regime

(a) **Issuance, Offer, and Sale of Payment Stablecoins**

- **Eligibility**: Only stablecoins pegged to the Singapore Dollar or any G10 currency and issued within Singapore are eligible to be recognized as MAS-regulated stablecoins.[37]
- **Issuance service**: The act of issuing stablecoins is categorised as a regulated activity under the PS Act.[38]
- **Consumer labelling**: Issuers must label their stablecoins as "MAS-regulated stablecoins" to help consumers distinguish them from other digital payment tokens.

(b) **Regulation and Supervision of Permitted Payment Stablecoin Issuers**

- **Regulatory oversight**: Issuers of MAS-regulated stablecoins are subject to supervision by the MAS to ensure compliance with the established framework.
- **Public consultation**: The MAS conducted a public consultation in October 2022 to gather feedback on the proposed regulatory approach, which was considered in finalizing the framework.

(c) **Regulatory Requirements for Payment Stablecoin Issuers**

- **Reserve assets**: Issuers must maintain a portfolio of reserve assets denominated in the currency of the stablecoin peg to provide a high degree of assurance of value stability.
- **Redemption timeline**: Clear timelines must be established for the redemption of stablecoins to ensure liquidity and consumer confidence.
- **Capital and prudential requirements**: Issuers are required to meet specific capital and prudential standards to ensure financial stability and resilience.

(d) **Additional Rule-Making or Considerations**

- **Legislative amendments**: The MAS is working on the necessary legislative amendments to implement the stablecoin framework and has indicated plans to consult on those amendments in due course.

---

[36] Ibid.

[37] MAS.

[38] MAS, April 2024, FAQs on Payment Service Act, https://www.mas.gov.sg/-/media/mas-media-library/regulation/faqs/pd/faqs-on-payment-services-act-2019/payment-services-act-faq%2D%2D19-april-2024.pdf.

- **Consumer protection**: The MAS has emphasized the need for issuers and their intermediaries to adhere to guidelines that ringfence customers' cryptocurrency assets and enhance customer protection.

7.2.4 Prospects for the Industry

- **Regulatory clarity**: The finalisation of the stablecoin regulatory framework in Singapore provides clear guidelines, fostering a more secure and predictable environment for issuers and consumers.
- **Market confidence**: The emphasis on value stability and consumer protection is likely to enhance trust in Singapore's digital asset ecosystem.
- **Innovation encouragement**: The regulatory framework aims to support innovation while ensuring financial stability, potentially positioning Singapore as a leading hub for digital asset development in Asia.

7.2.5 Key Takeaways

- **Regulatory evolution**: Singapore has evolved its regulatory approach to include specific provisions for stablecoins under the PS Act.
- **Consumer assurance**: The introduction of the "MAS-regulated stablecoin" label aims to provide consumers with assurance regarding the stability and reliability of the stablecoins they use.
- **Ongoing developments**: The MAS continues to refine the regulatory framework, with upcoming legislative amendments and consultations to further enhance the stablecoin ecosystem.

7.3 Japan

7.3.1 Regulatory Framework

Japan's regulatory framework for stablecoins was established through amendments to the **Payment Services Act (PSA)**, which came into effect on **June 1, 2023**. These amendments were based on the **Act Partially Amending the Payment Services Act**, promulgated on **June 10, 2022**.

The legislation officially recognizes fiat-pegged stablecoins as "electronic payment instruments" and introduces a licensing regime for their issuance and distribution.

7.3.2 Objectives of the Legislation

The primary objectives of Japan's stablecoin legislation are to:

- **Ensure financial stability**: By regulating stablecoins, Japan aims to maintain the stability of its financial system and prevent systemic risks associated with unregulated digital assets.
- **Protect consumers**: The legislation seeks to safeguard consumers by ensuring that stablecoins are backed by sufficient reserves and are redeemable at par value.
- **Promote innovation**: While regulating stablecoins, Japan also aims to foster innovation in the digital payment sector by providing a clear legal framework for their use.
- **Enhance market integrity**: The legislation aims to enhance the integrity of the digital asset market by establishing clear rules and standards for stablecoin issuers and intermediaries.

7.3.3 Key Provisions of the Stablecoin Regime

(a) **Issuance, Offer, and Sale of Payment Stablecoins**

- **Authorized issuers**: Only licensed entities, including banks, trust banks, and registered funds transfer service providers, are permitted to issue stablecoins.[39]
- **Reserve requirements**: Issuers must back their stablecoins with high-quality, liquid assets such as bank deposits and government bonds to ensure stability and redeemability.
- **Redemption rights**: Holders of stablecoins have the right to redeem them at face value, ensuring consumer protection and confidence in the system.

(b) **Regulation and Supervision of Permitted Payment Stablecoin Issuers**

- **Licensing**: Issuers must register with the **Financial Services Agency (FSA)** as funds transfer service providers, subjecting them to regulatory oversight.[40]
- **Ongoing supervision**: The FSA conducts regular inspections and audits to ensure compliance with regulatory requirements and to assess the financial health of issuers.

(c) **Regulatory Requirements for Payment Stablecoin Issuers**

- **Capital adequacy**: Issuers are required to maintain adequate capital reserves to absorb potential losses and ensure operational resilience.
- **Transparency and reporting**: Regular reporting to the FSA is mandated, including disclosures about reserves, liabilities, and operational activities.
- **Consumer protection measures**: Issuers must implement measures to protect consumer funds, including segregation of customer assets and clear communication about risks.

---

[39] TKILaw, 27 February 2024, Regulatory landscape for stablecoins and related payment services, https://www.tkilaw.com/en/7053.

[40] Finolab, 2 April 2025, Amendment to the Payment Services Act (2025), https://finolab.tokyo/finolabresearch/fr-fintech-topics/summary-amendment-to-the-payment-services-act-2025-summary-of-key-points-fintech-topics-114/.

(d) **Additional Rule Making or Considerations**

- **Algorithmic stablecoins**: The legislation does not recognise algorithmic stablecoins as electronic payment instruments; thus, they are not subject to the same regulatory framework.
- **Cross-border operations**: Foreign entities wishing to issue stablecoins in Japan must comply with local regulations, including obtaining necessary licenses and adhering to reserve requirements.
- **Future reforms**: The FSA continues to monitor developments in the stablecoin market and may introduce further amendments to the PSA to address emerging risks and opportunities.[41]

7.3.4 Prospects for the Industry

- **Market expansion**: The clear regulatory framework is expected to encourage both domestic and international entities to enter the Japanese stablecoin market, fostering competition and innovation. On 19 August 2025, Reuters reported that Japanese startup JPYC said it will issue the first stablecoin pegged to the yen later in the year after receiving a licence. The stablecoin, which will be called "JPYC", will be fully convertible to the yen and backed by domestic savings and Japanese government bonds (JGBs), the company's CEO Noritaka Okabe told a news conference.[42]
- **Institutional adoption**: With the introduction of regulated stablecoins, institutions may increasingly adopt digital assets for payments, settlements, and other financial services.
- **Economic implications**: The issuance of yen-backed stablecoins could influence the demand for Japanese government bonds, as these assets may be used as collateral or held in reserve.
- **Technological integration**: The regulatory clarity provides a foundation for integrating stablecoins into various technological platforms, including blockchain-based applications and decentralized finance (DeFi) systems.

7.3.5 Key Takeaways

- **Regulatory clarity**: Japan has established a comprehensive legal framework for stablecoins, providing clear guidelines for issuance, operation, and supervision.
- **Consumer protection**: The legislation emphasises consumer rights, including redemption guarantees and transparency requirements.

---

[41] Financial Services Agency (FSA), April 2025, https://www.fsa.go.jp/en/news/2025/20250425/20250425.html.

[42] Reuters, 19 August 2025, Japanese startup to issue the first JPY-pegged stablecoin, https://www.reuters.com/sustainability/boards-policy-regulation/japan-startup-issue-first-yen-pegged-stablecoin-2025-08-19/.

- **Market opportunities**: The regulatory environment is conducive to innovation and growth in the digital payment sector, attracting both domestic and international players.
- **Ongoing oversight**: The FSA maintains active supervision to ensure compliance and to adapt to the evolving landscape of digital assets.

7.4 *United Arab Emirates (UAE)*

7.4.1 Regulatory Framework

In June 2024, the Central Bank of the UAE (CBUAE) approved the **Payment Token Services Regulation** (Circular No. 2/2024),[43] marking a significant step in the regulation of stablecoins within the country. This regulation came into effect on June 2025, with a potential extension at the discretion of the CBUAE.

7.4.2 Objectives of the Legislation

The primary objectives of the Payment Token Services Regulation[44] are to:

- **Ensure financial stability**: By regulating stablecoins, the UAE aims to maintain the stability of its financial system and prevent systemic risks associated with unregulated digital assets.
- **Protect consumers**: The regulation seeks to safeguard consumers by ensuring that stablecoins are backed by sufficient reserves and are redeemable at par value.
- **Promote innovation**: While regulating stablecoins, the UAE aims to foster innovation in the digital payment sector by providing a clear legal framework for their use.
- **Enhance market integrity**: The regulation aims to enhance the integrity of the digital asset market by establishing clear rules and standards for stablecoin issuers and intermediaries.

7.4.3 Key Provisions of the Stablecoin Regime[45]

(a) **Issuance, Offer, and Sale of Payment Stablecoins**

- **Authorised issuers**: Only licensed entities, including banks and registered funds transfer service providers, are permitted to issue stablecoins.

[43] Central Bank of UAE, Rulebook on Payment Token Services Regulation, https://rulebook.centralbank.ae/en/rulebook/payment-token-services-regulation.

[44] Ibid.

[45] Ibid.

- **Reserve requirements**: Issuers must back their stablecoins with high-quality, liquid assets such as bank deposits and government bonds to ensure stability and redeemability.
- **Redemption rights**: Holders of stablecoins have the right to redeem them at face value, ensuring consumer protection and confidence in the system.

(b) **Regulation and Supervision of Permitted Payment Stablecoin Issuers**

- **Licensing**: Issuers must register with the CBUAE as funds transfer service providers, subjecting them to regulatory oversight.
- **Ongoing supervision**: The CBUAE conducts regular inspections and audits to ensure compliance with regulatory requirements and to assess the financial health of issuers.

(c) **Regulatory Requirements for Payment Stablecoin Issuers**

- **Capital adequacy**: Issuers are required to maintain adequate capital reserves to absorb potential losses and ensure operational resilience.
- **Transparency and reporting**: Regular reporting to the CBUAE is mandated, including disclosures about reserves, liabilities, and operational activities.
- **Consumer protection measures**: Issuers must implement measures to protect consumer funds, including segregation of customer assets and clear communication about risks.

(d) **Additional Rule Making or Considerations**

- **Algorithmic stablecoins**: The regulation does not recognise algorithmic stablecoins as electronic payment instruments; thus, they are not subject to the same regulatory framework.
- **Cross-border operations**: Foreign entities wishing to issue stablecoins in the UAE must comply with local regulations, including obtaining necessary licenses and adhering to reserve requirements.
- **Future reforms**: The CBUAE continues to monitor developments in the stablecoin market and may introduce further amendments to the regulation to address emerging risks and opportunities.

7.4.4 Prospects for the Industry

- **Market expansion**: The clear regulatory framework is expected to encourage both domestic and international entities to enter the UAE stablecoin market, fostering competition and innovation.
- **Institutional adoption**: With the introduction of regulated stablecoins, institutions may increasingly adopt digital assets for payments, settlements, and other financial services.
- **Economic implications**: The issuance of dirham-backed stablecoins could influence the demand for UAE government bonds, as these assets may be used as collateral or held in reserve.

- **Technological integration**: The regulatory clarity provides a foundation for integrating stablecoins into various technological platforms, including blockchain-based applications and decentralized finance (DeFi) systems.

7.4.5 Key Takeaways

- **Regulatory clarity**: The UAE has established a comprehensive legal framework for stablecoins, providing clear guidelines for issuance, operation, and supervision.
- **Consumer protection**: The regulation emphasizes consumer rights, including redemption guarantees and transparency requirements.
- **Market opportunities**: The regulatory environment is conducive to innovation and growth in the digital payment sector, attracting both domestic and international players
- **Ongoing oversight**: The CBUAE maintains active supervision to ensure compliance and to adapt to the evolving landscape of digital assets.

7.5 *Thailand*

7.5.1 Regulatory Framework

Thailand's regulatory framework for stablecoins is evolving through a combination of enacted laws, policy and ongoing consultations:

- **Currency Act B.E. 2501 (1958)**: This Act prohibits the issuance of any currency other than the Thai baht. The Bank of Thailand (BOT) has interpreted this to mean that baht-pegged stablecoins intended for use as a means of payment violate this Act.
- **Payment Systems Act B.E. 2560 (2017)**: This Act governs electronic money (e-money) and payment systems in Thailand. The BOT has indicated that baht-backed stablecoins intended for use as a means of payment may be classified as e-money under this Act, subjecting them to regulation by the BOT.
- **Emergency Decree on Digital Asset Businesses B.E. 2561 (2018)**: This Decree regulates digital asset businesses in Thailand, including cryptocurrency exchanges and brokers. It provides a legal framework for the operation of digital asset businesses but does not specifically address stablecoins.

The BOT has also issued policy guidelines on stablecoins, indicating that while baht-backed stablecoins may be subject to regulation under the Payment Systems Act, other forms of stablecoins, including foreign currency-backed and algorithmic stablecoins, are currently unregulated.[46]

[46] Bank of Thailand, 2021, Stablecoins Regulation Policy, https://www.bot.or.th/en/news-and-media/news/news-20210319-2.html.

7.5.2 Objectives of the Legislation

The primary objectives of Thailand's stablecoin legislation are:

- **Preventing currency substitution**: To prevent the issuance and use of stablecoins that could be perceived as competing with the Thai baht, thereby undermining confidence in the national currency system.[47]
- **Regulating electronic money**: To ensure that baht-backed stablecoins used as a means of payment are regulated as e-money under the Payment Systems Act, subjecting them to oversight by the BOT.[48]
- **Monitoring emerging technologies**: To monitor developments in stablecoins and other digital assets, with the possibility of introducing regulations as necessary to address risks and ensure financial stability.[49]

7.5.3 Key Provisions of the Stablecoin Regime

(a) **Issuance, Offer, and Sale of Payment Stablecoins**

- **Baht-backed stablecoins**: Stablecoins pegged to the Thai baht intended for use as a means of payment may be classified as e-money under the Payment Systems Act and are subject to regulation by the BOT.[50]
- **Other stablecoins**: Stablecoins pegged to foreign currencies or other assets, including algorithmic stablecoins, are currently unregulated. The BOT is studying these types of stablecoins and is open to receiving comments and feedback before deciding whether and how they should be regulated.[51]

(b) **Regulation and Supervision of Permitted Payment Stablecoin Issuers**

- **Licensing**: Issuers of baht-backed stablecoins intended for use as a means of payment must consult with the BOT before commencing operations.[52]
- **Oversight**: The BOT oversees risks associated with e-money, such as settlement, money laundering, cybersecurity, and consumer protection risks.[53]

---

[47] Ibid.

[48] Tilleke and Gibbins (2021). Stablecoin Policy Guidelines Issued by the Bank of Thailand, https://www.tilleke.com/insights/stablecoin-policy-guidelines-issued-by-bank-of-thailand/30/.

[49] Bank of Thailand, 2021, Stablecoins Regulation Policy, https://www.bot.or.th/en/news-and-media/news/news-20210319-2.html.

[50] Tilleke & Gibbins, 5 April 2021, Stablecoin Policy Guidelines Issued by the Bank of Thailand, https://www.tilleke.com/insights/stablecoin-policy-guidelines-issued-by-bank-of-thailand/30/.

[51] Ibid.

[52] Bank of Thailand, 2021, Stablecoins Regulation Policy, https://www.bot.or.th/en/news-and-media/news/news-20210319-2.html.

[53] Ibid.

(c) **Regulatory Requirements for Payment Stablecoin Issuers**

- **Compliance with E-money regulations**: Issuers of baht-backed stablecoins intended for use as a means of payment must comply with regulations governing e-money, including requirements related to settlement, money laundering, cybersecurity, and consumer protection.[54]
- **Reserve requirements**: The BOT has not specified reserve requirements for stablecoin issuers. However, it is expected that issuers would need to maintain sufficient reserves to back the stablecoins issued, similar to requirements for e-money issuers.

(d) **Additional Rule Making or Considerations**

- **Regulation of other stablecoins**: The BOT is studying the regulation of stablecoins pegged to foreign currencies or other assets and is open to receiving comments and feedback before deciding whether and how these stablecoins should be regulated.[55]
- **Development of a Central Bank Digital Currency (CBDC)**: The BOT is developing a retail-type CBDC to meet the needs of the general public, improve service efficiency in the business sector, and increase access to financial services.[56]

7.5.4 Prospects for the Industry

- **Innovation and adoption**: The development of a retail-type CBDC and the issuance of baht-backed stablecoins could drive innovation in the digital payments sector and increase adoption of digital currencies in Thailand.
- **Regulatory clarity**: The BOT's policy guidelines provide clarity on the regulatory treatment of baht-backed stablecoins, which could encourage investment and development in this area.
- **Global alignment**: Thailand's approach to stablecoin regulation aligns with international practices, such as those in Singapore and the UK, which could facilitate cross-border transactions and cooperation.

---

[54] Bank of Thailand, 2021, Stablecoins Regulation Policy, https://www.bot.or.th/en/news-and-media/news/news-20210319-2.html.

[55] Tilleke & Gibbins, 5 April 2021, Stablecoin Policy Guidelines Issued by the Bank of Thailand, https://www.tilleke.com/insights/stablecoin-policy-guidelines-issued-by-bank-of-thailand/30/.

[56] Bank of Thailand, 2021, Stablecoins Regulation Policy, https://www.bot.or.th/en/news-and-media/news/news-20210319-2.html.

7.5.5 Key Takeaways

- **Regulatory framework**: Thailand's regulatory framework for stablecoins is evolving, with clear guidelines for baht-backed stablecoins intended for use as a means of payment.
- **Licensing requirements**: Issuers of baht-backed stablecoins must consult with the BOT before commencing operations and comply with regulations governing e-money.
- **Unregulated stablecoins**: Other forms of stablecoins, including those pegged to foreign currencies or other assets, are currently unregulated, with the BOT studying the need for regulation.
- **CBDC development**: The BOT is developing a retail-type CBDC to meet the needs of the general public and improve access to financial services.
- **International alignment**: Thailand's approach to stablecoin regulation aligns with international practices, which could facilitate global cooperation and adoption.

7.6 Switzerland

7.6.1 Regulatory Framework

Switzerland does not have a standalone law specifically dedicated to stablecoins. Instead, the Swiss Financial Market Supervisory Authority (FINMA) provides regulatory clarity through guidance documents.

The most recent of these is **FINMA Guidance 06/2024**, published on July 26, 2024. This guidance addresses the regulatory treatment of stablecoins under existing Swiss financial market laws, including the Banking Act and the Anti-Money Laundering Act.[57]

7.6.2 Objectives of the Guidance

FINMA's Guidance 06/2024[58] aims to:

- **Clarify regulatory classification**: Provide a framework for determining whether stablecoins require a banking license or fall under other financial market regulations.

---

[57] FINMA, 26 July 2024, FINMA Guidance 06/2024, https://www.finma.ch/en/~/media/finma/dokumente/dokumentencenter/myfinma/4dokumentation/finma-aufsichtsmitteilungen/20240726-finma-aufsichtsmitteilung-06-2024.pdf?sc_lang=en&hash=03D675C1247EAFAE0C391.

[58] Ibid.

- **Enhance Legal Certainty**: Offer guidance to stablecoin issuers and financial institutions on compliance with Swiss financial market laws.
- **Address risks**: Highlight potential risks associated with stablecoins, including money laundering, terrorist financing, and circumvention of sanctions.

7.6.3 Key Provisions of the Stablecoin Regime

(a) **Issuance, Offer, and Sale of Payment Stablecoins**
FINMA emphasizes a "substance over form" approach, meaning that the regulatory classification of a stablecoin depends on its specific features rather than its labeling. Stablecoins may require a banking license if they involve[59]:

- A claim against the issuer that is redeemable at par.
- Backing by fiat currency or precious metals.
- Management of underlying assets for the account and risk of token holders.

Issuers must assess their stablecoin's structure to determine applicable regulatory requirements.[60]

(b) **Regulation and Supervision of Permitted Payment Stablecoin Issuers**
Issuers may be exempt from banking license requirements if they obtain a **default guarantee** from a Swiss bank. This guarantee must[61]:

- Cover the total amount of all deposits (i.e., claims of stablecoin holders).
- Provide an individual claim for each customer in the event of the issuer's bankruptcy.
- Be transparent to customers, who must be informed about the guarantee.

Banks providing such guarantees must manage associated legal, reputational, and operational risks.

(c) **Regulatory Requirements for Payment Stablecoin Issuers**
Stablecoin issuers are considered financial intermediaries under the Anti-Money Laundering Act (AMLA). They are required to[62]:

- Verify the identity of all persons holding their stablecoins, including those acquiring them on secondary markets.

---

[59] GLI, 25 October 2025, Blockchain and cryptocurrency laws and regulations in Switzerland, https://www.globallegalinsights.com/practice-areas/blockchain-cryptocurrency-laws-and-regulations/switzerland/.

[60] FINMA, 26 July 2024, FINMA Guidance 06/2024, https://www.finma.ch/en/~/media/finma/dokumente/dokumentencenter/myfinma/4dokumentation/finma-aufsichtsmitteilungen/20240726-finma-aufsichtsmitteilung-06-2024.pdf?sc_lang=en&hash=03D675C1247EAFAE0C391.

[61] PWC, 29 July 2024, FINMA issues stablecoin guidance, https://www.pwc.ch/en/insights/regulation/finma-stablecoin-guidance.html.

[62] Schellenberg Wittmer, 30 July 2024, FINMA Guidance 06/2024 on Stablecoins, https://www.swlegal.com/de/insights/newsletter-detail/finma-guidance-062024-on-stablecoins/.

- Implement measures to prevent anonymous transfers, such as whitelisting addresses or restricting transfers to other regulated entities.

Compliance with AMLA is mandatory to mitigate risks associated with money laundering and terrorist financing.

(d) **Additional Rule Making or Considerations**

FINMA's guidance is not legally binding but reflects its supervisory practice. The authority may update its guidance as the stablecoin landscape evolves. Furthermore, the Swiss Bankers Association has highlighted the need for a stablecoin backed by the Swiss franc to ensure widespread acceptance and mitigate risks related to monetary policy and financial stability.[63]

On 22 October 2025, the Federal Council initiated the consultation on an amendment to the Financial Institutions Act.[64] Under the proposed regulatory framework:

- **New license**: The Federal Council is proposing a new license category for "payment instrument institutions" to issue certain stablecoins.
- **Stablecoin requirements**: Stablecoins issued under this new license must be:
  - Fully backed by segregated assets.
  - Fully redeemable at par value.
  - Published via a whitepaper.
- **Enhanced protections**: The new rules would improve customer protection by segregating customer funds in case of bankruptcy and removing the previous CHF 100 million deposit cap.
- **AML**: The new rules will provide more detail on AML obligations for stablecoin issuers.
- **Consultation**: The consultation process is scheduled to continue until 6 February 2026. After this period, the Federal Council is expected to prepare a report summarising the feedback from relevant stakeholders and to submit its final dispatch, along with the draft bill, to Swiss Parliament.

7.6.4 Prospects for the Industry

- **Innovation-friendly environment**: Switzerland's regulatory clarity fosters an environment conducive to innovation in the stablecoin sector.
- **Global competitiveness**: The country's approach positions it as a competitive hub for stablecoin projects, attracting international interest.

[63] Swiss Banking, April 2025, Stablecoins in Switzerland, https://www.swissbanking.ch/_Resources/Persistent/0/5/0/1/0501708bb8d749954729879c52024ab0cb65d2d7/SBA%20Expert%20report%20stablecoins.pdf.

[64] Federal Council, 22 October 2025, Federal Council moves forward with stablecoins and crypto: consultation launched, https://www.news.admin.ch/en/newnsb/x4TMWQ1SWofNoFx7XyHhY.

- **Integration with traditional finance**: The requirement for default guarantees and adherence to AMLA facilitates the integration of stablecoins into the traditional financial system.[65]

7.6.5 Key Takeaways

- **Growing digital economy**: Stablecoins have the potential to strengthen the digital economy in Switzerland as they represent efficient, potentially low-cost and secure means of payment. Switzerland could benefit from the introduction of a Swiss franc stablecoin.
- **Regulatory clarity**: FINMA's guidance provides clear criteria for determining when a stablecoin requires a banking license in Switzerland.
- **Risk management**: Issuers must assess and manage legal, reputational, and operational risks, especially when utilizing default guarantees.
- **AML compliance**: Strict adherence to anti-money laundering regulations is essential for stablecoin issuers.
- **Evolving landscape**: The regulatory framework in Switzerland may evolve in response to developments in the stablecoin market.

7.7 *United Kingdom*

7.7.1 Regulatory Framework

The United Kingdom has not yet enacted a standalone law specifically dedicated to stablecoins. However, significant steps have been taken to integrate stablecoins into the UK's financial regulatory framework.

As of 28 May 2025, the Financial Conduct Authority (FCA) had published **Consultation Papers**: Issued CP25/14 and CP25/15, seeking feedback on proposed rules for stablecoin issuance and cryptoasset custody.[66]

On 10 November 2025, the Bank of England (Bank) launched a consultation paper on its proposed regulatory regime for sterling-denominated systemic stablecoins. It sets out the Bank's policy positions for a proposed regulatory regime for sterling-denominated systemic stablecoins for UK payments, issued by non-bank.[67]

---

[65] PWC, 30 July 2024, FINMA publishes guidance on stablecoin supervisory practice, https://www.pwc.ch/en/insights/regulation/finma-stablecoin-guidance.html.

[66] FCA, 28 May 2025, FCA seeks further views on stablecoins and crypto, https://www.fca.org.uk/news/press-releases/fca-seeks-further-views-stablecoins-and-crypto-custody.

[67] Bank of England, 10 November 2025, Consultation Paper on proposed regulatory regime forsterling-denominatedsystemicstablecoins,https://media.licdn.com/dms/document/media/v2/D4D1FAQHRGcZmukBcpA/feedshare-document-pdf-analyzed/B4DZpucVz7JUAc-/0/1762789521719?e=1765411200&v=beta&t=AYL76bNYArpg2FZ-ax2WBQRqLbtjhql8wlNoLSNpuXI.

Under the UK stablecoin regime, both the Prudential Regulation Authority (PRA) and the Financial Conduct Authority (FCA) have distinct but complementary roles, reflecting their respective remits over financial stability and market conduct. The PRA, part of the Bank of England, is responsible for prudential supervision i.e., ensuring the financial safety and soundness of firms issuing stablecoins, especially those that may pose systemic risks. The FCA focuses on conduct regulation, i.e., ensuring consumer protection, market integrity, and transparency.

7.7.2 Objectives of the Legislation and Regulatory Approach

The UK's regulatory initiatives aim to[68]:

- **Integrate stablecoins into the financial system**: Ensure that stablecoins are subject to the same regulatory standards as traditional financial instruments.
- **Enhance consumer protection**: Implement safeguards to protect users from potential risks associated with stablecoin transactions.
- **Promote financial stability**: Address concerns related to the impact of stablecoins on monetary policy and financial systems.
- **Align with international standards**: Ensure that the UK's regulatory approach is consistent with global best practices.

7.7.3 Key Provisions of the Stablecoin Regime[69]

(a) **Issuance, Offer, and Sale of Payment Stablecoins**

- **Regulated activity**: Issuing fiat-referenced stablecoins will be classified as a regulated activity under the Financial Services and Markets Act 2000 (Regulated Activities) Order 2001.
- **Authorization requirement**: Firms wishing to issue stablecoins must obtain authorization from the Financial Conduct Authority (FCA).
- **Consumer disclosure**: Issuers must provide clear information to consumers regarding the redemption policy and backing assets.

(b) **Regulation and Supervision of Permitted Payment Stablecoin Issuers**

- **Prudential standards**: Issuers will be subject to prudential requirements, including capital adequacy and liquidity standards.
- **Custody requirements**: Stablecoin custodians must segregate client assets and hold them in trust.

[68] HMT, 29 April 2025, Future financial services regulatory regime for cryptoassets (regulated activities)—Policy Note, https://www.gov.uk/government/publications/regulatory-regime-for-cryptoassets-regulated-activities-draft-si-and-policy-note/future-financial-services-regulatory-regime-for-cryptoassets-regulated-activities-policy-note-accessible.

[69] Ibid.

- **Operational oversight**: Firms must maintain robust governance and operational controls.

(c) **Regulatory Requirements for Payment Stablecoin Issuers**

- **Asset backing**: Stablecoins must be 100% backed by high-quality liquid assets.
- **Redemption rights**: Holders must have the right to redeem stablecoins at par value.
- **Anti-money laundering (AML) compliance**: Issuers are required to implement measures to prevent money laundering and terrorist financing.

(d) **Additional Rule Making or Considerations**

Stablecoins Cohort Sandbox: On 26 November 2025, the FCA launched a special cohort within its Regulatory Sandbox for firms issuing stablecoins. This is a unique chance for innovative companies to test their stablecoin products and services under the UK's evolving regulatory regime.[70]

This cohort is part of FCA's commitment to supporting growth and innovation in UK financial services. It complements broader innovation initiatives such as the Digital Securities Sandbox.

- **Market abuse framework**: The draft legislation includes provisions to address market abuse related to cryptoassets.[71]
- **Cross-border activities**: The regime considers activities of overseas firms targeting UK consumers.
- **Decentralised finance (DeFi)**: The approach distinguishes between decentralized and centralized entities, with decentralized models potentially exempt from certain regulations.

7.7.4 Prospects for the Industry

- **Regulatory clarity**: The establishment of a clear regulatory framework is expected to foster innovation and attract investment in the stablecoin sector in United Kingdom and enable the government to provide policy framework to establish United Kingdom as the crypto hub.
- **Consumer confidence**: Enhanced consumer protection measures are likely to increase trust in stablecoin products.
- **Market integration**: Stablecoins are anticipated to become more integrated into mainstream financial services, including payments and investment products.
- **Global competitiveness**: The UK's regulatory approach positions it to compete with other jurisdictions in the global stablecoin market.

---

[70] FCA, 26 November 2025, Regulatory Sandbox_ Stablecoins Cohort, https://www.fca.org.uk/firms/innovation/regulatory-sandbox/stablecoins-cohort.

[71] Ibid.

7.7.5 Key Takeaways

- **Regulatory framework**: The UK is moving towards a comprehensive regulatory regime for stablecoins, integrating them into existing financial regulations.
- **Authorisation process**: Firms wishing to issue stablecoins must obtain authorization from the FCA and adhere to prudential and operational standards.[72]
- **Consumer protection**: The regime emphasizes transparency, redemption rights, and AML compliance to protect consumers.
- **International alignment**: The UK's approach aligns with global best practices, ensuring consistency in the regulation of stablecoins.
- **Implementation timeline**: Final rules are expected to be published in 2026, with the regime becoming operational thereafter.[73]

7.8 Bahrain

7.8.1 Regulatory Framework

Bahrain has introduced a comprehensive regulatory framework for stablecoins. In July 2025, the Central Bank of Bahrain (CBB) launched the Stablecoin Issuance and Offering (SIO) Module under Rulebook Volume 6.[74]

This framework establishes licensing and regulatory requirements for entities wishing to issue and offer stablecoins within or from the Kingdom of Bahrain. It permits the issuance of single-currency fiat-backed stablecoins pegged to the Bahraini Dinar, US Dollar, or other approved fiat currencies.

7.8.2 Objectives of the SIO Framework

The SIO framework[75] aims to:

- **Provide legal clarity**: Offer a clear and structured approach to the issuance and offering of stablecoins, enhancing regulatory certainty for market participants.
- **Ensure financial stability**: Implement safeguards to maintain the stability of the financial system, particularly concerning digital assets.

---

[72] Norton Rose Fulbright, June 2025, The UK regime for cryptoassets: draft rules and legislation, https://www.nortonrosefulbright.com/en/knowledge/publications/8d8b8337/the-uk-regime-for-cryptoassets-draft-rules-and-legislation.

[73] FCA, 28 May 2025, FCA seeks further views on stablecoins and crypto, https://www.fca.org.uk/news/press-releases/fca-seeks-further-views-stablecoins-and-crypto-custody.

[74] Central Bank of Bahrain (CBB), July 2025, CBB Rulebook on Stablecoins, https://cbben.thomsonreuters.com/rulebook/sio-stablecoin-issuance-offering.

[75] Ibid.

- **Promote innovation**: Foster innovation in the digital finance sector by providing a conducive environment for the development and deployment of stablecoins.
- **Enhance consumer protection**: Establish measures to protect consumers engaging with stablecoins, ensuring their rights and interests are safeguarded.

7.8.3 Key Provisions of the Stablecoin Regime

(a) **Issuance, Offer, and Sale of Payment Stablecoins**

- **Licensing requirement**: Entities must obtain a license from the CBB to issue and offer stablecoins.[76]
- **Eligible stablecoins**: Only single-currency fiat-backed stablecoins are permitted, with backing in the Bahraini Dinar, US Dollar, or other fiat currencies approved by the CBB.[77]
- **Reserve asset management**: Issuers must manage and safeguard reserve assets backing the stablecoins, ensuring they are sufficient to meet redemption requests.[78]

(b) **Regulation and Supervision of Permitted Payment Stablecoin Issuers**

- **Regulated activities**: The CBB oversees activities related to the issuance, offering, controlling supply, minting and burning operations, and ancillary services such as reserve asset management and custody arrangements.[79]
- **Ongoing compliance**: Issuers are required to adhere to the CBB's regulations and guidelines, ensuring continuous compliance with established standards.

(c) **Regulatory Requirements for Payment Stablecoin Issuers**

- **Fit and proper criteria**: Issuers must meet the CBB's "Fit and Proper" requirements, demonstrating competence, integrity, and financial soundness.
- **Anti-money laundering (AML) and countering the financing of terrorism (CFT)**: Issuers must comply with AML and CFT regulations, implementing necessary measures to prevent illicit activities.
- **Audit and reporting**: Regular audits and reporting are mandated to ensure transparency and accountability in operations.

---

[76] Central Bank of Bahrain (CBB), July 2025, CBB Rulebook on Stablecoins, https://cbben.thomsonreuters.com/rulebook/sio-stablecoin-issuance-offering.

[77] Ibid.

[78] Ibid.

[79] Central Bank of Bahrain (CBB), July 2025, CBB Rulebook on Stablecoins, https://cbben.thomsonreuters.com/rulebook/sio-stablecoin-issuance-offering.

(d) **Additional Rule Making or Considerations**

- **Yield-bearing stablecoins**: Issuers are allowed to offer yield-bearing stablecoins, provided the yield is derived from interest or rewards earned from the investment of reserve assets.[80] The yield rate must be reasonable and not adversely affect the stability of the stablecoin or the financial health of the issuer.
- **Prior approval for new services**: Issuers must seek prior written approval from the CBB before offering new services not included in their original license application.[81]

7.8.4 Prospects for the Industry

- **Regional leadership**: Bahrain's proactive approach positions it as a regional leader in the Middle East in digital asset regulation, attracting international crypto firms and investors.
- **Economic diversification**: The stablecoin framework supports Bahrain's efforts to diversify its economy, reducing reliance on oil revenues by fostering growth in the digital finance sector.
- **Enhanced financial inclusion**: By providing a regulated environment for stablecoins, Bahrain can enhance access to financial services, particularly for underserved populations.

7.8.5 Key Takeaways

- **Comprehensive regulatory framework**: Bahrain has established a detailed and structured approach to regulating stablecoins, covering issuance, offering, and ancillary services.
- **International alignment**: The SIO framework aligns with global standards, drawing from best practices to ensure robust regulation.
- **Support for innovation**: The framework balances regulatory oversight with support for innovation, allowing for the development of new financial products like yield-bearing stablecoins.
- **Attractive destination for crypto firms**: Bahrain's regulatory clarity and supportive environment make it an attractive destination for international crypto firms seeking to operate in the Middle East.

In conclusion, Bahrain's stablecoin regulatory framework represents a significant step towards integrating digital assets into the financial system, providing a balanced approach that promotes innovation while ensuring stability and consumer protection.

---

[80] CBB, SIO 6.6.1, https://cbben.thomsonreuters.com/rulebook/sio-661.

[81] CBB, CBB Rule Book, SIO 2.2.7, https://cbben.thomsonreuters.com/rulebook/sio-227.

8 Stablecoins Co-existence

The growth of stablecoins carries significant implications for cross-border regulatory coordination, risks of regulatory arbitrage, and how they may eventually coexist alongside central bank digital currencies (CBDCs).

First, stablecoins highlight the urgent need for stronger cross-border regulatory coordination. These instruments can be issued in one country, traded globally, and used for services offered by firms operating across multiple jurisdictions. This creates complexity in supervision, enforcement, and oversight. Without coordinated standards, one regulator's efforts to enforce strong reserve backing, risk controls, and redemption rights may be weakened if users can simply shift to foreign-issued stablecoins operating under weaker oversight. Global alignment on key principles—such as transparency of reserves, redemption mechanisms, operational resilience, and consumer safeguards—will help ensure that stablecoins do not become channels for contagion or systemic instability. The work of international bodies like the FSB, BIS, and IOSCO is helping to build convergence, but significant gaps remain across regions and regulatory philosophies.

Second, the rise of stablecoins increases the risk of regulatory arbitrage. If rules differ significantly across jurisdictions, issuers may choose to base themselves in countries with weaker requirements, lower compliance burdens, or unclear legal definitions. This can undermine the regulatory goals of major financial centres and create a "race to the bottom." For example, jurisdictions that delay establishing stablecoin rules may find themselves hosting issuers whose operations are risky or opaque. Similarly, countries with overly restrictive frameworks may unintentionally push innovation offshore. A balanced, risk-based, and internationally consistent approach can help avoid these unintended outcomes. As regulations mature, the challenge will be to maintain high standards without driving activity into unregulated spaces.

Third, stablecoins raise important questions about the long-term coexistence of private digital money and CBDCs. Many central banks are exploring CBDCs to improve payment efficiency, enhance monetary sovereignty, and support financial inclusion. Stablecoins, however, already provide digital money that is widely used in crypto markets and increasingly in real-world payment applications. The two forms of digital currency need not compete directly. Instead, they may evolve in complementary ways. CBDCs could become the safest settlement asset for domestic payments and wholesale financial markets, while stablecoins could serve as programmable instruments used in global commerce, tokenised asset markets, and cross-border payments. Well-designed regulation will be crucial to ensure that stablecoins remain securely backed and interoperable with CBDC systems, rather than undermining monetary stability or creating parallel, opaque payment networks.

Whilst stablecoins offer significant potential benefits, but their cross-border nature means they cannot be regulated effectively by countries acting alone. Stronger international coordination, credible rules that reduce opportunities for regulatory arbitrage, and a thoughtful approach to their coexistence with CBDCs will be essential. With well-aligned policies, stablecoins and CBDCs can reinforce one another, supporting safer, more efficient, and more innovative global payments.

9 Conclusion: The Future of Stablecoins

While it is impossible to predict what the future has in store in the constantly changing world of blockchain, stablecoins could help bring cryptocurrencies as a whole to the mainstream. Already, financial services players—from bank incumbent JPMorgan to payments network Visa—are giving nods to stablecoin technology through partnerships and internal R&D.

The year 2025 marks a turning point in global digital finance, as stablecoins evolve from niche crypto instruments into the backbone of international commerce. As of 3 December 2025, the market capitalisation of global stablecoins has exceeded US$300b,[82] a meteoric rise from a decade ago. With growing adoption across world, the landmark U.S. legislation with the passage of the GENIUS Act, and rapidly shifting market dynamics, stablecoins are reshaping how money is created, moved, and trusted.

Each form of stablecoins comes with its own unique set of benefits and drawbacks, and none of them are perfect. Yet the value and stability they could provide to businesses and individuals globally—by enabling universal access to established national currencies, streamlining payments and remittances, and supporting emerging financial applications—could be disruptive.

The defining features of stablecoins, their cryptographic security and programmability, support the robust use cases that are currently driving the usage of existing public and institutional stablecoins.

Regulation is defining the rules of the rail. Liquidity is deepening across corridors and currency pairs. Interoperability is moving from aspiration to reality as issuers, payment networks, and domestic systems connect. And programmability, the ability to embed compliance, governance, and logic into the payment flow itself, is turning stablecoins into financial software.

Banks and fintech companies must work together to address key issues in the industry; the challenges range from technology and market and payment infrastructure to legal and compliance requirements.

Governments worldwide are exploring the use of central bank-backed digital currencies and other forms of stablecoin as they recalibrate monetary policies and modernise their financial systems. However, with central bank digital currencies (CBDCs) emerging as a major contender, will CBDCs displace stablecoins. It will be a long time before CBDCs are wide available in major economies and widely used locally and on a cross-border basis.

---

[82] CoinGecko, Stablecoins by Market Capitalization, 3 December 2025, https://www.coingecko.com/en/categories/stablecoins.

Stablecoins are entrenched in the crypto ecosystem and likely to co-exist with public forms of money such as CBDCs. Greater regulatory certainty over the status of stablecoins and their issuers could create market opportunities for the operating entities as well as for other financial institutions, many of which have so far been deterred from engaging with stablecoin operators due to regulatory risk.

Stablecoins are gaining real traction as clearer regulations open the door for banks and fintechs to work more closely together. The stablecoin revolution is more than technological shift—it represents a fundamental reimagining of money itself. Stablecoins are poised to become a core financial infrastructure by 2030.

References

Bank of England (November 2025) Consultation paper on proposed regulatory regime for sterling-denominated systemic stablecoins. https://media.licdn.com/dms/document/media/v2/D4D1FAQHRGcZmukBcpA/feedshare-document-pdf-analyzed/B4DZpucVz7JUAc-/0/1762789521719?e=1765411200&v=beta&t=AYL76bNYArpg2FZ-ax2WBQRqLbtjhql8wlNoLSNpuXI

Bank of Thailand (2021) Stablecoins regulation policy. https://www.bot.or.th/en/news-and-media/news/news-20210319-2.html

BIS (February 2024) Recommendations for the regulation, supervision and oversight of global stablecoin arrangements - executive summary. https://www.bis.org/fsi/fsisummaries/global_stablecoins.htm

CBB CBB Rule Book, SIO 2.2.7. https://cbben.thomsonreuters.com/rulebook/sio-227

CBB SIO 6.6.1. https://cbben.thomsonreuters.com/rulebook/sio-661

Central Bank of UAE (2024) Rulebook on payment token services regulation. https://rulebook.centralbank.ae/en/rulebook/payment-token-services-regulation

CoinGecko (December 2025) Stablecoins by market capitalization. https://www.coingecko.com/en/categories/stablecoins

ECB Crypto-asset TaskForce (September 2020) Stablecoins: implications for monetary policy, financial stability, market infrastructure and payments, and banking supervision in the euro area. https://www.ecb.europa.eu/pub/pdf/scpops/ecb.op247~fe3df92991.en.pdf

EY (July 2025) Global approaches to stablecoin regulation. https://media.licdn.com/dms/document/media/v2/D4E1FAQH-2Y986dvwgg/feedshare-document-pdf-analyzed/B4EZgtbU.FHoAY/0/1753108804195?e=1756944000&v=beta&t=PsxjgC78ZG2hOvdQkSWzMqWnLhuJkynFvcPCiD0jVVg, at p 5

FCA (November 2025a) Regulatory sandbox: stablecoins cohort. https://www.fca.org.uk/firms/innovation/regulatory-sandbox/stablecoins-cohort

FCA (May 2025b) FCA seeks further views on stablecoins and crypto. https://www.fca.org.uk/news/press-releases/fca-seeks-further-views-stablecoins-and-crypto-custody

Federal Council (October 2025) Federal council moves forward with stablecoins and crypto: consultation launched. https://www.news.admin.ch/en/newnsb/x4TMWQ1SWofNoFx7XyHhY

Financial Services Agency (FSA) (April 2025. https://www.fsa.go.jp/en/news/2025/20250425/20250425.html

FINMA (July 2024) FINMA guidance 06/2024. https://www.finma.ch/en/~/media/finma/dokumente/dokumentencenter/myfinma/4dokumentation/finma-aufsichtsmitteilungen/20240726-finma-aufsichtsmitteilung-06-2024.pdf?sc_lang=en&hash=03D675C1247EAFAE0C391

Finolab (April 2025) Amendment to the Payment Services Act (2025). https://finolab.tokyo/finolabresearch/fr-fintech-topics/summary-amendment-to-the-payment-services-act-2025-summary-of-key-points-fintech-topics-114/

FSB (October 2025) Thematic review on FSB global regulatory framework for crypto-asset activities, pp 37–40. https://www.fsb.org/uploads/P161025-1.pdf

GENIUS (2025) Act of 2025. https://www.congress.gov/bill/119th-congress/senate-bill/394/text

GFTN (2025) GFTN global digital assets report 2025, p 12. https://media.licdn.com/dms/document/media/v2/D4D1FAQGWYHukqzFtNQ/feedshare-document-pdf-analyzed/B4DZpulKOaIAAg/0/1762791880196?e=1765411200&v=beta&t=cUGUiqolsAPBKGsg_VKyHXyDDi0_GWUjKCm9D9UET4Q

GLI (October 2025) Blockchain and cryptocurrency laws and regulations in Switzerland. https://www.globallegalinsights.com/practice-areas/blockchain-cryptocurrency-laws-and-regulations/switzerland/

HKMA (May 2025a) Government welcomes the passage of the stablecoins bill. https://www.hkma.gov.hk/eng/news-and-media/press-releases/2025/05/20250521-3/

HKMA (July 2025b) The steadfast and sustainable development of stablecoins. https://www.hkma.gov.hk/eng/news-and-media/insight/2025/07/20250723/

HKMA (July 2025c) Implementation of regulatory regime for stablecoin issuers. https://www.hkma.gov.hk/eng/news-and-media/press-releases/2025/07/20250729-4/

HKMA (July 2025d) Stablecoins ordinance – explanatory note on licensing of stablecoin issuers. https://www.hkma.gov.hk/media/eng/doc/key-functions/ifc/stablecoin-issuers/Explanatory_Notes_on_Licensing_of_Stablecoin_Issuers_eng.pdf

HKMA (July 2025e) Explanatory notes on licensing of stablecoin issuers. https://www.hkma.gov.hk/media/eng/doc/key-functions/ifc/stablecoin-issuers/Explanatory_Notes_on_Licensing_of_Stablecoin_Issuers_eng.pdf

HKMA and SFC (August 2025) Joint Statement by the HKMA and SFC of the stablecoin related market movements. https://apps.sfc.hk/edistributionWeb/gateway/EN/news-and-announcements/news/doc?refNo=25PR123

HMT (April 2025) Future financial services regulatory regime for cryptoassets (regulated activities) – policy note. https://www.gov.uk/government/publications/regulatory-regime-for-cryptoassets-regulated-activities-draft-si-and-policy-note/future-financial-services-regulatory-regime-for-cryptoassets-regulated-activities-policy-note-accessible

Ledger Insights (May 2020). https://www.ledgerinsights.com/libra-adds-singapores-sovereign-fund-temasek/

MAS (August 2023) MAS finalises stablecoin regulatory regime. https://www.mas.gov.sg/news/media-releases/2023/mas-finalises-stablecoin-regulatory-framework

MAS (April 2024) FAqs on payment service act. https://www.mas.gov.sg/-/media/mas-media-library/regulation/faqs/pd/faqs-on-payment-services-act-2019/payment-services-act-faq%2D%2D19-april-2024.pdf

Norton Rose Fulbright (June 2025) The UK regime for cryptoassets: draft rules and legislation. https://www.nortonrosefulbright.com/en/knowledge/publications/8d8b8337/the-uk-regime-for-cryptoassets-draft-rules-and-legislation

PWC (July 2024a) FINMA issues stablecoin guidance. https://www.pwc.ch/en/insights/regulation/finma-stablecoin-guidance.html

PWC (July 2024b) FINMA publishes guidance on stablecoin supervisory practice. https://www.pwc.ch/en/insights/regulation/finma-stablecoin-guidance.html

Reuters (August 2025) Japanese startup to issue the first JPY-pegged stablecoin. https://www.reuters.com/sustainability/boards-policy-regulation/japan-startup-issue-first-yen-pegged-stablecoin-2025-08-19/

Schellenberg Wittmer (July 2024) FINMA guidance 06/2024 on stablecoins. https://www.swlegal.com/de/insights/newsletter-detail/finma-guidance-062024-on-stablecoins/

Stablecoins Ordinance. https://www.elegislation.gov.hk/hk/cap656?xpid=ID_1438402726674_003

Swiss Banking (April 2025) Stablecoins in Switzerland. https://www.swissbanking.ch/_Resources/Persistent/0/5/0/1/0501708bb8d749954729879c52024ab0cb65d2d7/SBA%20Expert%20report%20stablecoins.pdf

Tilleke & Gibbins (April 2021) Stablecoin policy guidelines issued by the Bank of Thailand. https://www.tilleke.com/insights/stablecoin-policy-guidelines-issued-by-bank-of-thailand/30/
TKILaw (February 2024) Regulatory landscape for stablecoins and related payment services. https://www.tkilaw.com/en/7053
U.S. President's Working Group on Financial Markets ("PWG") (November 2021) Stablecoin Report. https://home.treasury.gov/system/files/136/StableCoinReport_Nov1_508.pdf

Will Tokenised Money Transform Wholesale and B2B Payments?

Erin McCune

Abstract While retail payments have undergone successive waves of digitization wholesale and B2B transactions—representing over $1200 trillion annually—remain plagued by manual reconciliation, fragmented systems, and operational inefficiencies. This chapter develops a framework specifically tailored to evaluate tokenised money (stablecoins, tokenised deposits, and CBDCs) for business payments, grounded in five operational imperatives: data integration, interoperability, fund quality, settlement infrastructure, and governance. Applying this framework reveals four adoption archetypes already emerging: dollarisation in unstable currencies, programmable settlement for capital markets, bank-led tokenised deposits, and convergence infrastructure bridging traditional and tokenised systems. The analysis demonstrates that no single tokenised instrument satisfies all business requirements, and technical capabilities have dramatically outpaced institutional readiness. Through scenario analysis, the chapter identifies critical dependencies for transformation: privacy-preserving identity frameworks, mutualized acceptance mechanisms, and orchestration layers that abstract complexity while preserving institutional relationships. The research provides actionable guidance for banks, enterprise software providers, fintechs, regulators, and businesses navigating this evolving landscape, emphasising that transformation of economically critical wholesale payment requires purpose-built solutions that respect commercial relationships and enable automation while maintaining trust.

Keywords Wholesale payments · Business-to-business (B2B) payments · Tokenised deposits · Smart contracts · Payment interoperability · ISO 20022 · Treasury management

E. McCune (✉)
Forte Fintech LLC, San Francisco, CA, USA
e-mail: erin@fortefintech.com

S. Yazıcı et al. (eds.), *Tokenisation of Money*, Contributions to Finance and Accounting, https://doi.org/10.1007/978-3-032-22946-5_18

1 Introduction

While retail payments have undergone successive waves of digitization business-originated transactions remain plagued by inefficiency. Wholesale payments,[1] and in particular business-to-business (B2B) payments, are characterized by manual reconciliation, an intensely fragmented provider ecosystem, and unwieldy interfaces across solutions. These inefficiencies impose substantial costs: strained working capital, unpredictable settlement timing, and operational complexity for businesses of all sizes.

Tokenised money—whether stablecoins, tokenised commercial bank deposits, or central bank digital currencies—has attracted significant policy, academic, and private sector attention. Yet most literature emphasizes interbank settlement and cross-border consumer remittances,[2] overlooking the structural requirements of business payments. This gap matters because wholesale and B2B flows exhibit distinct needs that retail analyses fail to capture: complex data requirements, many-to-many relationships, embedded credit terms, and safeguards that reinforce trust.

This chapter develops a framework specific to wholesale payments and associated workflows. Applying this framework reveals how current tokenised money uses cluster into archetypes—from dollarization in unstable currency markets to programmable interbank settlement for capital markets. The analysis shows that no single form of tokenised money addresses all business payment requirements. This discussion is not merely diagnostic. By identifying drivers of current use and impediments to widespread transformation, the framework provides actionable guidance for banks, enterprise software providers, fintechs, regulators, and businesses themselves.

The chapter proceeds as follows: Sect. 2 develops the evaluation framework, Sect. 3 applies it to identify adoption archetypes, Sect. 4 explores future scenarios, and Sect. 5 suggests enablers and design choices necessary to realize the promise of tokenised money for business transactions. Throughout, the analysis maintains focus on a central insight: technical capabilities have outpaced institutional and industry readiness. Over time, as technology evolves, partnerships coalesce, cooperation develops, and new entrants learn more about wholesale and B2B payments this framework should provide enduring relevance as a roadmap for the industry.[3]

---

[1] See Fig. 1 for a description of core wholesale payment flows.

[2] The term "remittance" is ambiguous in payments. In retail and policy contexts, it usually means a migrant worker's cross-border transfer back home. In corporate accounting contexts, however, remittance information refers to data that explains what a payment is for: a list of invoices paid, the amount paid for each, and explanation for any deductions. The sources cited here overwhelmingly use the former sense, but several also touch on the latter in discussing reconciliation, ISO 20022 data, and payment messaging.

[3] Regulatory, technology, and competitive dynamics are evolving quickly. This chapter was written in August 2025 and specific evidence cited here may already be out of date, but the framework and assessment approach is meant to endure. Please refer to the author's Substack *Forte Fintech Field Notes* for more recent evidence and analysis: https://fortefintech.substack.com/.

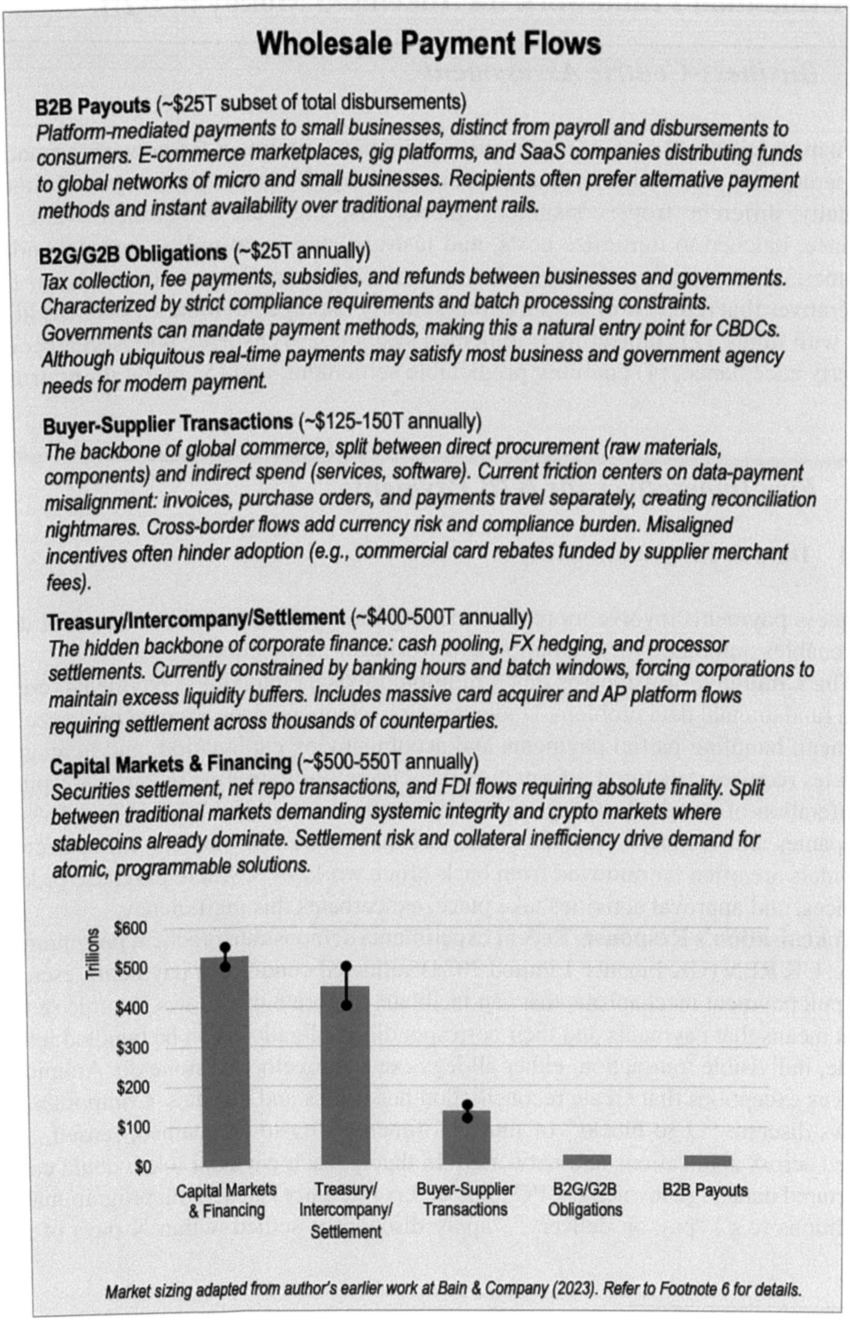

Fig. 1 Wholesale payment flows: scale and characteristics

2 Evaluation Framework for Tokenised Money in B2B

2.1 *Business-Centric Assessment*

Evaluating tokenised money for business payments requires a framework grounded in operational realities rather than monetary theory. Business payments are fundamentally different from consumer transactions; they are scheduled weeks in advance, batched to minimize costs, and just one step in complex, interdependent commercial relationships between buyers and suppliers. Success depends on five imperatives that reflect how corporations actually manage payments: (1) embedding data with funds, (2) connecting fragmented systems, (3) ensuring widespread counterparty acceptance, (4) enabling predictable settlement, and (5) maintaining trust.

2.2 *Five Imperatives for B2B Payments*

2.2.1 Data & Programmability

Business payments involve more than moving money; they require contextual data that enables automatic reconciliation and workflow automation.

The Challenge: Businesses batch multiple invoices into single payments, creating a fundamental data problem. Understanding which invoices are paid by a specific payment, handling partial payments and accompanying explanation, and managing disputes requires structured information that current rails struggle to carry. Despite a proliferation of standards, Capgemini, Microsoft, and AutoRek (2025) find 56% of companies still reconcile manually. The fact that banks and financial infrastructure providers are often far removed from back-office workflows, where purchase orders, invoices, and approval activities take place, exacerbates this inefficiency.

Tokenisation's Response: Recent experiments demonstrate practical programmability. UK RLN (UK Finance Limited 2024) validated conditional payments, escrow, and pull payment mechanisms that can facilitate corporate workflows. Atomic settlement means that payments and their corresponding obligations can be bundled into a single, indivisible transaction: either all legs execute together, or none do. Atomicity reduces exceptions that create reconciliation headaches and disputes. Composability allows discrete "Lego blocks" of financial functionality to be chained, reused, and scaled across applications and networks.[4] In theory, each payment token could carry structured data (e.g., invoice ID, PO number, tax reference) along with programmable conditions (e.g., "pay on delivery," "apply discount if settled within X days of the

[4] The author is indebted to Josh Solesbury at ParaFi Capital for this effective Lego block analogy. Refer to his Medium post *Getting to the Crux of Stablecoin Utility* (December 26, 2024). Source URL: https://medium.com/letters-from-the-savannah/getting-to-the-crux-of-stablecoin-utility-7e53fea29286.

invoice"). The MIT Digital Currency Initiative and J.P. Morgan's Kinexys project emphasise the importance of narrowly scoped standards for payment tokens that include components that can be adapted by jurisdiction and financial institution and aligned with existing standards such as ISO 20022 (MIT/Kinexys 2025). The focus is on mandatory payment-control information to support AML and sanction screening, but could be applied to contextual data (invoice reference, purchase orders, customs codes, remittance data) at the token level.

2.2.2 Interoperability

The many-to-many nature of B2B relationships demands solutions that work across fragmented ecosystems without requiring universal adoption.

The Challenge: One manufacturer may have 10,000 suppliers, but only integrates electronically with its most strategic partners. Each business uses multiple banks, various payment providers, and different enterprise software. Atomicity and programmability are valuable, but only if they work across the fragmented landscape of banks, fintechs, corporates, and jurisdictions; otherwise, adding tokenisation risks creating yet another integration burden or manual intervention.

Tokenisation's Response: Widespread adoption requires abstraction layers that preserve each individual business' ability to work with its preferred software vendors and financial providers. Retail payment service providers like Stripe are already demonstrating this model—merchants accept stablecoins without directly using crypto infrastructure. UK RLN's orchestration layer and Canton's network-of-networks architecture show how technical interoperability can preserve institutional autonomy and control (Digital Asset 2024).

2.2.3 Quality of Funds

Buyers and suppliers are not concerned with abstract monetary theory. For businesses, quality of funds equals practical acceptance by counterparties, predictable value, and accounting treatment as cash.

The Challenge: While economists debate "singleness" and "elasticity," corporate finance and accounting teams have more prosaic concerns. Treasurers view funds quality through the lens of liquidity, yield, and safety. Can I fulfill my obligations, e.g., will my suppliers accept this? What can I earn on these funds at rest? Is there counterparty risk? Accountants, finance leaders, and CFOs are concerned with mark-to-market volatility and cash equivalent status. Does my auditor classify it as cash or a financial instrument? Can I exchange this token at par? Accounting standards for stablecoins that vary by geography, and continue to evolve, create operational friction that theoretical purity does not resolve.

Tokenisation's Response: Different instruments serve different needs. Tokenised bank deposits (Citi Token Services, JPM's Kinexys) inherit existing prudential frameworks, processing billions daily while maintaining cash-equivalent status.

CBDCs are, by definition, quality money. The Bank for International Settlements (2025) has proposed a "unified ledger" that integrates CBDCs, tokenised deposits, and tokenised assets into a single programmable platform.

Stablecoins lack this assurance unless robust redemption frameworks exist. The SEC's "Covered Stablecoins" framework and the GENIUS Act create pathways for regulated tokens with clear redemption rights (U.S. Securities and Exchange Commission, Division of Corporation Finance 2025). The Ubyx proposal (McLaughlin 2025) addresses this by creating a mutualized acceptance network: any stablecoin from participating issuers could be deposited into existing bank accounts at par. This solves the "which stablecoin do I accept?" problem for corporates and enables consistent accounting treatment as cash equivalents. In the meantime, real world usage in emerging market and developing economies (EMDE) demonstrate that businesses pay a premium for stablecoins, prioritizing access to reliable funds over theoretical perfection.

In the two-tier banking system, deposits are elastic: banks extend credit, creating deposits backed by reserves. CBDCs could inherit elasticity through central bank policy tools. Stablecoins, by contrast, are typically fully prefunded and therefore lack elasticity, operating as "narrow money." Yet banks will likely offer products that enable businesses of all sizes to easily sweep funds in and out of stablecoin or tokenised deposits to support specific use cases and complement existing liquidity management tools.

2.2.4 Settlement Infrastructure

Wholesale settlement must handle massive volumes, enable conditional execution, and support frictionless foreign exchange for global trade.

The Challenge: Wholesale payment flows not only facilitate movement of funds between operating accounts that companies maintain with multiple banks in various jurisdictions, they also enable funding and settlement activity that underpin retail purchase transactions, payroll and payouts, and bunk payment of suppliers. Current payment choices force trade-offs: wire transfers provide finality but lack programmability, ACH offers low-cost but delayed settlement, instant payments are not yet universal, cards enable dispute resolution and earn rebates for buyers, but at cost that typically outweighs supplier benefits.

Cross-border adds complexity—only the most highly liquid currencies offer low spreads; time zones and operating cut-offs inhibit instant funds movement; and compliance checks introduce friction. Yet, according to Swift, the vast majority of traditional correspondent banking transaction value arrives at the destination within minutes via Swift gpi. However, that speed is mostly between money center banks, in liquid currencies, during banking hours. There's still a lot of inefficiency and unpredictability in the system, particularly when conducting business in low- and middle-income countries.

Tokenisation's Response: Experiments demonstrate that tokenised money can streamline these massive behind-the-scenes flows. The Guardian FX Workstream

(2025) shows tokenised bank liabilities enabling atomic PvP[5] beyond CLS coverage. Project Pine proves central banks can conduct programmable operations (BIS Innovation Hub [Swiss Centre] and New York Innovation Center [FRBNY] 2025). Yet implementation gaps remain: 24/7 infrastructure requires fundamental operational changes, liquidity management must adapt to continuous settlement, and legal finality across borders needs resolution. The technical capabilities exist; operational transformation lags.

2.2.5 Safety & Oversight

Driving wholesale payment improvement requires safety and oversight that balance innovation with the stability and trust businesses demand.

The Challenge: Businesses rely on data security and privacy provisions, predictable regulatory treatment, clear liability allocation, and dispute resolution mechanisms built over decades. Privacy is paramount—payment patterns reveal sensitive corporate intelligence. Compliance is non-negotiable, but current frameworks often assume retail use cases, missing B2B complexity where a single transaction might involve multiple jurisdictions and entities. Federated models that enable TradFI cooperation across jurisdictions and institutions typically exclude non-bank participants.

Tokenisation's Response: Project Pine built a toolkit of smart contracts that could enforce eligibility rules for collateral, counterparties, and reserve operations. The RLN prototype allowed funds to be locked or unlocked until regulatory or contractual checks were satisfied. In the stablecoin space, the Ubyx model makes redemption through regulated off-ramps mandatory, embedding AML, KYC, sanctions, and fraud checks in the redemption process.

Banks leverage existing frameworks and trusted correspondent relationships for tokenised deposits, preserving existing corporate customer relationships while adding programmability. Fintechs are layering familiar protections—chargebacks, dispute resolution—onto stablecoin rails for retail use cases; these safeguards will likely be embedded in SaaS and vertical-specific software used by SMBs that may do business with enterprises as well as consumers.

Critically, potential data privacy improvements like Stéphane Canon's (2025) decoupled architecture separate sensitive commercial details from ownership records, addressing the risk that public transparency would expose pricing strategies and payment terms.

Yet, regulatory clarity varies by jurisdiction: the U.S. signals support through proposed legislation, Europe emphasizes control through digital euro development. Businesses navigate this fragmentation pragmatically.

---

[5] PvP (Payment versus Payment): A mechanism that ensures that the final transfer of a payment in one currency occurs if and only if the final transfer of a payment in another currency or currencies takes place.

Table 1 Tokenised money instruments against B2B imperatives

Legend: *Tokenised money potential to address business payment imperatives*

None — *High*

Dimension / Criterion	*Stablecoins*	*Tokenised Deposits*	*CBDCs*
Data & Programmability	High flexibility on public chains, but fragmented standards; weak enterprise-grade controls.	RLN, Kinexys, ISO 20022 integration; strong orchestration potential.	Early tooling suggests limited programmability in pilots.
Interoperability	Global reach via public chains, but governance and AML fragmented.	RLN experiments show multi-issuer orchestration and API layers work.	Wholesale CBDCs promising, but limited pilots. Standards lagging.
Money Quality	Fail BIS singleness/integrity tests, yet GENIUS/SEC argue payment stables can meet standards. Emerging market SMBs and consumers willing to pay a premium for access to dollars anyway.	Bank prudential standards; singleness via central bank settlement.	Anchored in central bank money; strong on elasticity and integrity.
Settlement Infrastructure	Already delivers immediacy in cross-border B2B and crypto-trading settlement use cases.	Proven PvP/DvP atomic settlement in PoCs. But legal/standards gaps remain.	Wholesale pilots (Project Pine, Guardian FX) show feasibility. Retail CBDC plumbing less clear.
Safety & Oversight	Tiered redemption access, issuer risk, AML/CFT exposure, and privacy concerns. Systemic effects ambiguous.	Legally neutral, FMI alignment possible; prudential governance frameworks.	Public backstop. Systemic stability and monetary sovereignty.

These insights guide analysis of current adoption patterns and future scenarios in the following sections.
Source: Created by the Author

2.3 *Current State Assessment*

The evaluation framework reveals how tokenisation addresses fundamental business payment challenges across five critical dimensions. The imperatives also suggest that no single form of tokenised money can address all business payment requirements (see Table 1).

3 Applying the Framework: Archetypes and Use Cases

3.1 *B2B Payment Flows: Context and Scale*

An understanding of the scale and nature of business-originated payment flows is necessary to ground the archetype analysis. Five major categories represent over \$1200 trillion[6] in annual volume, each with distinct operational requirements that shape how tokenised money might gain traction.

[6] This sizing is adapted from the author's work while at Bain & Company. McCune, Erin. "Unsexy wholesale payments represent 94% of global transaction flows." LinkedIn, January 10, 2024 (Source: https://www.linkedin.com/feed/update/urn:li:share:7158520249879863296) citing research summarized in Bain & Company. "Fragmentation of Wholesale Payments." Bain &

This taxonomy reveals that the degree and nature of friction points varies by use case. The following discussion uses archetypes to understand how tokenised money is being deployed today and how it might shape the future of wholesale and B2B payments.

3.2 *Identifying Patterns: Archetypes of Tokenised Money Adoption*

Analysis of business payment flows and relevance of tokenised money attributes reveals recurring patterns, as demonstrated by pilots and early market use. These adoption archetypes defined by the intersection of trust requirements, data integration needs, and geographic factors help predict where different forms of tokenised money will naturally find adoption in the coming years.

Tokenised Money Adoption Archetypes:

- **Dollarisation:** Currency substitution where quality of funds dominates all other imperatives
- **Programmable Settlement:** Data-value integration where embedded logic is the primary driver
- **TradFI Tokens:** Preservation of existing relationships while adding programmability
- **Convergence Infrastructure:** Bridging TradFI and new approaches to expand relevance and drive impact

3.2.1 The Dollarisation Archetype: Currency Substitution in Unstable Markets

The dollarisation archetype manifests where currency instability drives digital dollar adoption. Reuter (2025) analysis reveals stablecoin flows equal 7.7% of GDP in Latin America and 6.7% in Africa/Middle East. Artemis (2025) identified $36 billion in annualized B2B stablecoin transactions. Guardian FX demonstrates that this pattern extends beyond B2B transactions to corporate treasury management, as multinationals funding EMDE subsidiaries increasingly bypass correspondent banking through tokenised flows.

Consumers and businesses have demonstrated their willingness to pay a "stablecoin premium"[7] to access dollars, and non-bank providers are rushing to intermediate these flows. These fintechs abstract the complexity of direct stablecoin handling

Company Insights, October 17, 2023 (Source: https://www.bain.com/insights/fragmentation-of-wholesale-payments/).

[7] BVNK. A Decade of Digital Dollars: The Rise of Stablecoins and Tokenised Money. London: BVNK 2024. https://www.bvnk.com/report/decade-of-digital-dollars.

while preserving the essential benefit: reliable USD value in unstable currency environments. Pragmatic rather than monetary policy considerations around "money quality" are driving emerging market retail and SMB use thus far. The risk is that central bankers in geographies where stablecoins are gaining traction and further eroding relevance of local fiat may respond by tightening regulation.

3.2.2 The Programmable Settlement Archetype: Binding Data to Value

Programmable settlement emerges where data-value integration drives efficiency gains at scale. UK RLN experiments demonstrated a 70% reduction in reconciliation errors through embedded ISO 20022 data, directly addressing an enduring business challenge. In capital markets, Project Pine showed wholesale CBDCs executing repos and collateral swaps through smart contracts, eliminating manual intervention. The archetype extends beyond pilots through production implementations. Major financial market infrastructures now employ programmable settlement for securities transactions, while tokenised trade finance platforms bind payment to shipment documentation.

Privacy concerns are paramount. Canton Network's selective disclosure framework prevents institutional transparency risk by enabling necessary regulatory access while protecting commercial confidentiality. Chainlink's Automated Compliance Engine enables permissioned access based on compliance and eligibility requirements, incorporating the GLEIF verifiable Legal Entity Identifier (vLEI) and the ERC3643 open-source suite of smart contracts (Chainlink Labs 2025). However, the data, decision logic, and workflows that drive smart contracts reside in enterprise software and SaaS solutions that drive back offices for businesses of all sizes. Thus, programmability will require solving both technical and industry cooperation challenges simultaneously.

3.2.3 The TradFI Token Archetype: Institutional Evolution

Banks are deploying tokenised deposits to modernize operations and preserve priority client relationships. Citi Token Services facilitates instant cross-border transfers (Payoneer 2024) and programmable trade finance for institutional clients, processing billions in tokenised deposits. J.P. Morgan's Kinexys handles over $10 billion daily in wholesale payments (dominated by repos/reverse repos but inter/intra-company transfers use is increasing), demonstrating that bank-issued tokens can achieve scale while maintaining prudential standards.

UK RLN experiments extend this model to multi-bank consortia, showing how tokenised deposits can interoperate while preserving monetary singleness through central bank settlement. Ubyx's nascent clearing network extends this model by creating fungibility across stablecoin issuers in anticipation of a proliferation of bank- and fintech-issued stablecoins operating side by side. While CLS only supports 18 currencies, as referenced above Guardian FX indicates tokenisation could enable 24/7 PvP and atomic settlement across more currencies significantly reducing FX settlement risk.

This archetype addresses treasury and intercompany flows where batch processing constraints limit efficiency. Banks maintain their central role while offering enhanced capabilities: 24/7 availability, programmable liquidity management, and atomic settlement. The challenge lies in achieving interoperability—without which bank tokens risk creating new silos and intensifying fragmentation.

3.2.4 The Convergence Infrastructure Archetype: Bridging Worlds

Fintechs and payment service providers collapse boundaries by providing linkages between traditional and tokenised money. Visa and Mastercard partnerships with crypto platforms, combined with acquirer investments in stablecoin innovations, create infrastructure where payment type becomes irrelevant to merchants. Worldpay (in collaboration with BVNK) allows corporates to disburse funds as stablecoin without requiring direct crypto interaction. Stripe's unified API treats stablecoins, cards, and bank transfers as interchangeable from a supplier's perspective.

These industry developments demonstrate that widespread adoption need not require users to directly interact with tokenised instruments. Convergence infrastructure offered by these providers preserves familiar consumer-centric governance features—dispute resolution, chargebacks, consumer protections—while delivering tokenised efficiency to merchants. As fintechs expand their investment in stablecoin infrastructure (e.g., developing proprietary L1s), they will have greater capacity to address wholesale payment needs, particularly the $125–150 Trillion in global B2B AP/AR flows.

The convergence infrastructure archetype addresses all five imperatives simultaneously. This suggests widespread transformation may occur through abstraction rather than direct adoption.

3.3 *Implications for Design and Adoption*

These archetypes reveal how tokenised money capabilities are used to address specific friction points rather than to pursue universal solutions or drive interoperability across the wholesale payment ecosystem. Payment service providers and banks are converging on hybrid models that preserve the benefits of both TradFI and crypto-centric approaches. Geographic patterns persist, with EMDE markets embracing direct stablecoin adoption while developed markets prefer intermediated access. The evidence suggests transformation is occurring not through wholesale replacement of existing systems but through sophisticated abstraction layers that make the underlying technology invisible to end users.

4 Scenarios for Tokenised Business Payments

The archetypes identified in Sect. 3 reveal current adoption patterns, but their evolution remains uncertain. The following three potential scenarios demonstrate varying degrees to which the framework's five imperatives are satisfied and coordination challenges are overcome (refer to Table 2).

4.1 Potential Future Scenarios

1. **Transformation**: Tokenised money achieves widespread wholesale payment adoption. Regulatory frameworks converge globally through mechanisms like the GENIUS Act and coordinated MiCA implementation. Capital and liquidity requirements in key geographies align on treatment of permissioned and permissionless chains and stablecoins such that banks gain comfort in participating directly and indirectly. Privacy-preserving architectures solve institutional transparency concerns while multi-issuer consortia achieve critical mass enabling widespread interoperability. The largest banks lead transformation by issuing interoperable tokenised deposits, while payment service providers and enterprise software solutions abstract complexity and drive conditional logic. Archetype patterns mature and converge—programmable settlement becomes standard, convergence infrastructure makes instrument choice irrelevant, and geographic fragmentation yields to global standards.
2. **Incremental Progress**: Tokenised money gains traction in specific niches without transforming core wholesale flows. Banks deploy tokenised deposits selectively, maintaining traditional rails in parallel, eroding cost benefits. The imperatives achieve partial satisfaction: programmability succeeds in pilots, but fragmented standards and competing consortia prevent interoperability. Accounting treatment keeps stablecoins classified as financial instruments rather than cash equivalents, eroding corporate demand. Geographic divergence accelerates as Europe restricts dollar stablecoins to protect monetary sovereignty while the U.S. pursues "cryptomercantilism."[8] Archetypes evolve independently—dollarization continues in unstable currencies, but programmable settlement stalls in developed markets.
3. **Marginalization**: Tokenised money retreats to crypto-native use cases. The vulnerabilities identified by Financial Stability Board (2024)—liquidity mismatches and operational fragilities—materialize during market stress. Major redemption crises echo the USDC de-peg during Silicon Valley Bank's collapse, while pri-

[8] Éric Monnet coined the term cryptomercantilisme (in French) in his Le Grand Continent essay "Cryptomercantilisme: la doctrine économique de Donald Trump". It was subsequently published in English in "Cryptomercantilism vs. Monetary Sovereignty—Dealing with the Challenge of US Stablecoins for the EU" (June 2025), by Jens van 't Klooster, Edoardo D. Martino, and Eric Monnet.

Table 2 Industry participant implications & factor realization across scenarios

Actor/ Factor	Transformation (20% likelihood)	Incremental (60% likelihood)	Marginalisation (20% likelihood)
Actor strategies			
Buyers & suppliers	Corporates adopt tokenised deposits & stablecoins across procurement, payouts, treasury; Ubyx-style mutualized acceptance drives enterprise adoption. SMEs gain working capital access via programmable financing, both domestically and x-border. Stablecoin demand intensifies in high-friction/low-fiat confidence corridors, driving counterparties in other geos to adopt	Some adoption in platform payouts and emerging market corridors with currency instability. SMEs adopt tokenised USD, but large corporate procurement and treasury remains on traditional rails; a hybrid approach dominates	Minimal uptake; suppliers skeptical of stability after de-pegging events distrust redemption; buyers see no ROI over enhanced ACH/ RTP; privacy/cyber risks and fragmented standards deter businesses of all sizes
TradFI banks	Issue tokenised deposits at scale; monetize intraday liquidity and programmable FX; lead consortia to preserve client relationships; RLN/Canton governance models anchor "singleness" of money	Project Guardian experiments and two-layer advocacy support cautious innovation while preserving the traditional banking model. TradFIs hedge bets: join pilot consortia but favor conventional rails; position tokenisation as premium add-on for select institutional clients. Merely defensive innovation	Retreat: regulatory uncertainty and Basel III capital impacts drive withdrawal. Governance challenges preclude effective collaboration consortia. Banks focus instead on protecting deposits from stablecoin disintermediation
Enterprise software	ERP/treasury vendors embed tokenised settlement natively; programmability enhances reconciliation, dynamic discounting, and liquidity forecasting; tokenised rails are widely available in AP/AR suites generating new SaaS revenue streams	Limited integration via APIs for select workflows; tokenised payments remain separate from core AP/ AR modules and are used for niche supplier disbursements (emerging market corridors), thus majority of B2B transactions occur via ACH/RTP; wait-and-see approach prevails	Abandon Tokenisation; focus on ISO 20022 adoption, AI-powered reconciliation, and real-time payment instead

(continued)

Table 2 (continued)

Actor/ Factor	Transformation (20% likelihood)	Incremental (60% likelihood)	Marginalisation (20% likelihood)
Fintechs	Aggressively expand programmable supply chain finance, instant payouts, and tokenised FX; capture underserved SME and cross-border segments. Reduce reliance on traditional banks with native, proprietary tokenised infrastructure	Opportunistic plays in emerging market corridors and gig economy payouts where Tokenisation beats traditional rails; largely avoid regulated spaces	Business models constrained by compliance costs, security breaches, fragmentation, and lack of enterprise demand; pivot away from B2B to focus on crypto-native niches and agentic AI purchasing
Enabling/Preventative factors			
Policy & regulation	**Supportive frameworks:** GENIUS Act creates U.S. federal perimeter; MiCA provides clarity in EU; stablecoins achieve IAS7 cash-equivalent status; global coordination emerges. CBDCs become systemic in a small number of key geographies	**Fragmented:** U.S. permissive but unclear; EU defensive via digital euro; accounting treatment remains ambiguous; privacy standards diverge, siloed CBDC pilots create patchwork approach	**Adverse:** BIS "triple test" drives restrictive stance; stablecoins confined to crypto trading; CBDCs positioned as only acceptable innovation
Geopolitics	**Drive utility:** U.S. pursues "cryptomercantilism" (dollar stablecoins as reserve driver); EU builds digital euro; emerging-market businesses adopt tokenised USD and encourage buyers to pay with stablecoins	**Multipolar:** Coexistence of dollar stablecoins, euro CBDC, and RMB corridors without meaningful interoperability	**Restrictive:** China/ EMDEs ban foreign stablecoins to defend sovereignty
Risks/ Integrity	**Manageable:** Canton/RLN deliver selective privacy; effective governance enables unified ledgers to reduce systemic risks. Widespread issuance of vLEI fosters trust	**Latent:** fragmented standards persist; inadequate operational risk mitigation; off-ramp liquidity frictions	**Realized:** High profile de-pegs erode confidence in stablecoin; hacks and privacy failures undermine corporate expectations of privacy; cash displacement risks amplify caution

(continued)

Table 2 (continued)

Actor/ Factor	Transformation (20% likelihood)	Incremental (60% likelihood)	Marginalisation (20% likelihood)
Technology	**Supportive:** APIs and agentic AI in the back-office facilitate programmability; open banking (both regulatory-mandated and market-led) facilitates access to data. ISO 20022 emerges as a key enabler of interoperability across both TradFI and new entrants	**Somewhat useful:** ISO 20022 provides useful compatibility between TradFI and crypto-native solutions but is only used for a limited number of flows/ geographies. Open Banking proves useful for on-ramps and off-ramps in a subset of emerging market corridors	**Not a driver or adequate alternative:** ISO 20022 remains behind-the-scenes, limited to market infrastructure and bank operations rather than a key conduit for corporate date flows. Agentic AI and even RPA are adequate to address enough back-office automation such that tokenised money programmability becomes less compelling
Bottom line			
Adoption impact	**High:** adoption across all B2B archetypes (direct procurement, payouts, x-border trade corridors, capital markets settlement); tokenised money coexists with both stablecoins and CBDCs, albeit with geographic variation	**Medium:** concentrated in emerging market corridors, platform payouts, multinational liquidity; modest substitution risk	**Minimal:** RTP, ISO 20022, AI automation solve frictions without tokenisation; tokenised money relegated to niche use cases (e.g., capital market settlement)

Source: Created by the Author

vacy breaches expose commercial strategies, validating institutional transparency concerns. Banks retreat, enterprise software providers abandon Tokenisation, and fintechs pivot away from B2B use cases. Corporations achieve required efficiencies through AI-powered reconciliation and instant payments instead, rendering Tokenisation unnecessarily complex.

4.2 *Actor Strategies and Market Dynamics*

Table 2 below demonstrates how strategic choices by industry actors shapes potential outcomes for tokenised money and business-originated payments.

- **Buyers and suppliers** of all sizes will only be motivated to change long-standing back-office processes and try new solutions if they realise meaningful benefits: seamless automation, enhanced working capital, greater visibility into cash flow, and payment-related data to drive decision-making. Conversely, if tokenised money programmability is limited to non-strategic corridors, not widely available in enterprise software alongside familiar payment rails, and isolated to fringe use cases, businesses will not adopt it.

- **TradFI banks'** approach proves particularly decisive—proactive tokenised deposit issuance enables transformation, cautious pilots maintain incremental progress, while defensive retreat ensures marginalisation.
- **Enterprise software** providers act as amplifiers: native integration of tokenised settlement accelerates corporate adoption, while treating it as peripheral functionality limits impact.
- **Fintechs** vary from aggressive expansion capturing underserved segments in the transformation scenarios to a complete pivot away from B2B under marginalisation. If these industry participants do not realize strong demand (and associated revenues) they will quickly turn their focus to other opportunities such as agentic commerce.

The regulatory stance creates the foundation; supportive frameworks enable innovation while restrictive approaches confine tokenised money to trading rather than payments.

4.3 *Scenario Likelihood*

Thus far evidence supports differential probability weights for each scenario:

Transformation (20%) requires simultaneous satisfaction of all dependencies—historically rare in financial infrastructure. Even proven technology cannot overcome the coordination challenge of aligning governance, standards, and incentives across jurisdictions, institutions, and industry participants.

Incremental Progress (60%) aligns with the status quo, where regional variations and competing standards produce narrowly functional but fragmented outcomes. Current indicators—divergent regulatory approaches, isolated pilots, traditional rail persistence—reinforce this trajectory.

Marginalisation (20%) suggests concurrent failures across dependencies. While individual crises have occurred, systemic collapse remains unlikely given $26 trillion in current flows and expanding institutional commitment.

4.4 *Implications*

These scenarios reveal that technological capability is necessary but insufficient to drive meaningful improvement in wholesale payments and associated back-office automation. Approximately $2 trillion in stablecoin flows,[9] successful multi-bank

[9] The widely cited $2 trillion figure is from this IMF paper: Reuter, Marco. Decrypting Crypto: How to Estimate International Stablecoin Flows. IMF Working Paper WP/25/141. Washington,

pilots, and programmable monetary tools prove feasibility. Yet the gap between incremental and transformative adoption for business payments requires coordinated intervention across all five imperatives. Without such coordination, the status quo leads to fragmentation where efficiency gains concentrate in specific corridors and discrete use cases rather than transforming business payments comprehensively. This suggests practitioners should prepare for persistent heterogeneity—multiple instruments, varied regulatory regimes, and corridor-specific solutions. Section 5 examines specific interventions that would increase the likelihood of genuine transformation.

5 Making It Happen

5.1 *Preconditions and Design Choices*

The gap between current adoption patterns and the truly transformative potential of tokenised money depends on design choices and enabling conditions. The framework's five imperatives translate into concrete implementation requirements outlined below.

5.2 *Critical Enablers by Imperative*

5.2.1 Data & Programmability: From Standards to Implementation

- Standardized APIs and enterprise connectors beyond ISO 20022
- Selective disclosure mechanisms (Canton's "configurable privacy")
- Essential controls: suspend, seize, audit trails (Kinexys specifications)
- Decoupled architecture separating sensitive details from ownership (a la Canon)

5.2.2 Interoperability: Preventing New Silos

- Network-of-networks architectures preserving institutional sovereignty
- Portable identity credentials (vLEIs) reducing duplicate KYC/KYB and facilitating cross-chain connectivity
- Treasury and abstraction layers presenting unified interfaces
- Gateway solutions bridging traditional and tokenised systems

---

DC: International Monetary Fund, June 2025.

5.2.3 Quality of Funds: Regulatory Clarity and Practical Singleness

- U.S.: Covered stablecoin definitions with reserve requirements and bankruptcy protections
- Europe: Strict backing requirements with holding limits
- Tokenised deposits: Singleness through central bank settlement
- Market solution: Mutualized acceptance layers enabling par redemption (Ubyx)
- Unambiguous accounting treatment enabling cash-equivalent classification in key geographies

5.2.4 Settlement Infrastructure: Beyond Proof of Concept

- Continuous operating models (potentially agentic AI-enabled) that extend beyond batch processing
- Dynamic liquidity management for always-on settlement
- Orchestration layers for scheduling, netting, and liquidity allocation
- Enterprise software harnesses programmatic money to address persistent reconciliation challenges and automation gaps

5.2.5 Governance: Aligning Incentives Across Ecosystems

- Liability frameworks allocating risks across ecosystem
- Privacy regulations balancing confidentiality with compliance
- Economic incentives avoiding past failures:
  - Pricing precision liquidity and working capital, not default instant settlement
  - Collectively funding federated digital identity infrastructure
  - Reward software providers that must absorb integration costs and have means to drive programmatic logic

5.3 *Coordinated Action Required*

Moving from incremental to transformative adoption requires simultaneous progress across all five imperatives. This analysis points to three critical dependencies that determine whether tokenised money achieves its potential or fragments into incompatible silos.

1. Identity frameworks must enable portability across platforms while preserving privacy—a technical problem with governance implications.
2. Acceptance mechanisms must solve the many-to-many problem of B2B payments through mutualized frameworks or equivalent solutions.

3. Orchestration capabilities must abstract complexity while preserving the institutional relationships that underpin wholesale finance.

Technical experiments prove feasibility across multiple forms of tokenised money. The remaining challenge is institutional: aligning incentives, governance structures, and technical standards to realize the benefit of global programmatic money movement across the fragmented wholesale payment ecosystem.

6 Conclusion

This analysis examined tokenised money through the specific lens of wholesale payments, developing a framework grounded in operational realities rather than monetary theory. The five imperatives (data/programmability, interoperability, quality of funds, settlement infrastructure, and governance) reveal why current adoption clusters into distinct archetypes. No single tokenised money instrument satisfies all imperatives; instead, different forms of tokenised money naturally align with specific use cases. The framework also demonstrates that technological advances have dramatically outpaced institutional and industry readiness.

The scenarios explored (transformation, incremental progress, marginalization) are not predetermined. Current evidence favors incremental adoption (60% probability) where efficiency gains concentrate in specific corridors rather than transforming the $1200 trillion wholesale payment ecosystem. Achieving transformation requires simultaneous satisfaction of all five imperatives, particularly the governance and interoperability challenges that have historically constrained B2B payment innovation. Three critical dependencies are clear: privacy-preserving identity frameworks that work across platforms, mutualized acceptance mechanisms that solve the many-to-many problem of business relationships, and convergence layers that present unified interfaces while preserving institutional sovereignty.

The path forward demands that stakeholders abandon defensive postures in favor of coordinated action. Banks must move beyond cautious pilots to deploy interoperable tokenised deposits at scale. Regulators need frameworks that provide clarity without constraining innovation, drawing from both the U.S. pragmatism embodied in the GENIUS Act and European monetary sovereignty concerns. Technology providers should prioritise mundane but critical capabilities like portable vLEI credentials and enterprise system connectors. Most importantly, the industry must also address economic incentives—past B2B payment innovations failed by misallocating costs and benefits, rewarding buyers at suppliers' expense. Success requires recognising that wholesale payments are not simply retail payments at larger scale; they demand purpose-built solutions that respect commercial relationships, preserve privacy, and enable automation while maintaining the trust that underpins economically critical trillion-dollar flows.

References

Artemis, Castle Island, Dragonfly (2025) Stablecoin payments from the ground up

Bain & Company (2023) Fragmentation of wholesale payments. https://www.bain.com/insights/fragmentation-of-wholesale-payments/

Bank for International Settlements (2025) Annual economic report 2025: Chapter III – the next-generation monetary and financial system. https://www.bis.org/publ/arpdf/ar2025e3.htm

BIS Innovation Hub (Swiss Centre), New York Innovation Center (FRBNY) (2025) Project Pine: central bank open market operations with smart contracts

BVNK (2024) A decade of digital dollars: the rise of stablecoins and tokenised money. https://www.bvnk.com/report/decade-of-digital-dollars

Canon S (2025) A decoupled architecture for tokenised financial assets: enabling interoperability and digital transformation

Capgemini, Microsoft, AutoRek (2025) The future of payments operations: agentic AI and the rise of digital colleagues

Chainlink Labs (2025) Automated compliance engine. https://chain.link/automated-compliance-engine

Digital Asset (2024) Canton coin: a Canton-network-native payment application. https://www.digitalasset.com/

Financial Stability Board (2024) The financial stability implications of tokenisation. https://www.fsb.org/uploads/P221024-2.pdf

Guardian FX Workstream (Ant International, ISDA, MAS, HSBC, BNY Mellon, OCBC, et al) (2025) Tokenised bank liabilities and shared ledger in cross-border payments (Project Guardian FX Workstream)

McCune E (2024). Unsexy wholesale payments represent 94% of global transaction flows. https://www.linkedin.com/feed/update/urn:li:share:7158520249879863296

McLaughlin T (2025) Ubyx whitepaper: stablecoin ubiquity. https://ubyx.xyz

MIT Digital Currency Initiative, J.P. Morgan Kinexys (2025) Designing payment tokens for safety, integrity, interoperability and usability

Payoneer (2024) Payoneer leverages Citi's blockchain technology to enable 24/7 global payment services. https://investor.payoneer.com/news-releases/news-release-details/payoneer-leverages-citis-blockchain-technology-enable-247-global

Reuter M (2025) Decrypting crypto: how to estimate international stablecoin flows

Solesbury J (2024) Getting to the crux of stablecoin utility. https://medium.com/letters-from-the-savannah/getting-to-the-crux-of-stablecoin-utility-7e53fea29286 (ParaFi Capital)

U.S. Securities and Exchange Commission, Division of Corporation Finance (2025) Statement on stablecoins. https://www.sec.gov/newsroom/speeches-statements/statement-stablecoins-040425

UK Finance Limited (2024 September) UK Finance RLN experimentation phase: summary report. https://www.ukfinance.org.uk/system/files/2024-09/UK%20Finance%20RLN%20Summary%20Report.pdf

van't Klooster J, Martino ED, Monnet, É (2025) Cryptomercantilism vs. monetary sovereignty: dealing with the challenge of US stablecoins for the EU (Study 760274). European Parliament. https://www.europarl.europa.eu/RegData/etudes/STUD/2025/760274/ECTI_STU(2025)760274_EN.pdf

Further Reading

Bezemer D, Sanders M, Kramer B, Simic A (2025) Stablecoins and digital euro: friends or foes of European monetary policy?

Catalini C (2025) Stripe's Tempo and the ghost of Libra's past. https://www.forbes.com/sites/christiancatalini/2025/09/05/stripes-tempo-and-the-ghost-of-facebooks-libras-past

Citi Institute (2025) Digital dollars: banks and public sector drive blockchain adoption. https://www.citigroup.com/global/insights/digital-dollars

Global Legal Entity Identifier Foundation (GLEIF) (2024) Organizational identity: the missing link in digital assets and decentralized finance. https://www.gleif.org/en/newsroom/blog/organizational-identity-the-missing-link-in-digital-assets-and-decentralized-finance

Lee H (Swift) (2025) Nobody wins from fragmentation. https://flow.db.com/more/technology/nobody-wins-from-fragmentation#!

McNamara K, Marpu RP (2025) Banking 2.0: the stablecoin banking revolution — how digital assets are reshaping global finance. https://arxiv.org/abs/2508.11395v1

The "Productization" of Money and Its Impact at the Point of Sale

Thibault Pele

Abstract This chapter explores how the tokenization of money is reshaping payments, with a focus on stablecoin at the point of sale (POS), in retail and e-commerce. It states that money is no longer just a medium of exchange, but increasingly a product shaped by technology, user experience, and competition between private and public issuers. With the emergence of a new monetary stack, it introduces programmability, enabling payments to carry conditions such as discounts or loyalty. The analysis also considered a generational gap in the adoption, which highlights digital native and legacy infrastructure. The stablecoins are analysed through their impact on the commercial value chain, and the challenges that arise from this. It increases the importance of payment service provider, which require to adapt their target operating model to support a multi-rail future.

Keywords Central Bank digital currency (CBDC) · Digital euro (D€) · Stablecoins · Cryptocurrencies · Blockchain · Payment · Tokenization · POS

1 Money Is Becoming a Product

In today's digital economy, money itself is being "productized", meaning a customizable product or service rather than a utility. The productization of money in this chapter refers to the emergence of diverse forms of digital currencies, issued both by public institutions and private entities, with distinct features or branding.

Over the past few years, Central banks and Financial Institutions have introduced different types of tokenized money (Bank for International Settlements (BIS) 2023), including Central Bank Digital Currencies (CBDCs) (High-level Recommendations for the Regulation, Supervision and Oversight of Global Stablecoin Arrangements n.d.), private stablecoins (Central Bank digital currencies for cross-border payments

T. Pele (✉)
Worldline Financial Services, Paris, France
e-mail: thibault.pele@worldline.com

S. Yazıcı et al. (eds.), *Tokenisation of Money*, Contributions to Finance and Accounting, https://doi.org/10.1007/978-3-032-22946-5_19

Table 1 The different forms of Tokenized Money and their key characteristics

Layer	Issuer	Trust model	Programmability	Use cases
CBDC	Central Bank	Legal tender, no credit risk	Limited	Offline payment, universal acceptance
Tokenized deposit	Commercial Bank	Deposit insurance, regulated banks	High	Retail payment
Stablecoins	Private entity	Reserved-back Regulated (GENIUS ACT, MiCA)	Very high on the Blokchain	Cross-border, embedded finance, retail

n.d.), and tokenized deposit (issued by banks) (Blueprint for the future monetary system: improving the old, enabling the new n.d.). Those new forms of money bring new capacities through programmability and are often tied to ecosystem. It's not about the money itself; it's about the creation of a whole ecosystem. For example, major non-financial companies like Amazon, Walmart, or Meta have reportedly explored issuing their own branded stablecoin.[1] This trend is in reality a shift towards money as a differentiated product, which has unique attributes or roadmap, and which is customer based.

Make no mistake, the productization of money is built upon the privatization of money trend, as commercial bank money (CoBM) is gaining traction. What's different now is the technology. Tokenization is leveraging Distributed Ledger Technology (DLT) such as the Blockchain to operate. It brings the so called "Smart Contract" which enables automation of task but also brings interoperability "by design". I like to describe blockchain as the "universal language" as it allows systems to share information, in complete security, and therefore reduces the reliance on APIs.

Yet, if money becomes a product, it also requires a new architecture to support it (Table 1).

2 The New Monetary Stack: Interoperability?

The emergence of tokenized money is not a simple innovation. It goes beyond by transforming the monetary stack. This new stack is reshaping the architecture of payment itself, especially for the merchants, at the point of sale. Each money should co-exist, with its own purpose (Fig. 1).

For merchants the stack offers optionality, and choices.

- CBDC ensure finality and lower fees
- Tokenized deposit enables instant settlement, in the existent payment infrastructure of the banks
- Stablecoins open new customers segments, and new use cases.

[1] https://www.wsj.com/finance/banking/walmart-amazon-stablecoin-07de2fdd

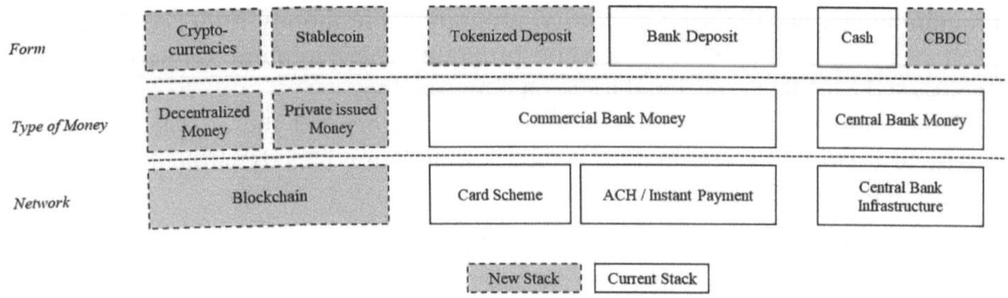

Fig. 1 Overview of the monetary stack: forms of money (cryptocurrencies, stablecoins, tokenized deposits, bank deposit, cash, CBDC) are linked to their type of money (decentralized, privately issued, commercial bank, or central bank money), and supported by different network infrastructures (blockchain, card schemes, instant payments, central banks infrastructure)

For Consumers, the stack should remain transparent. While more choices mean more complexity, a huge work is being done on the user facing interface to abstract the complexity.

However, multiple new forms of money raise the critical issue of interoperability. A fundamental principle is the singleness of money, which mean that different forms of money should all exchange at par value. On a tokenized environment it means to ensure that a CBDC, tokenized deposit, or stablecoin are all equal, and convertible on demand. But behind this relies technological challenge as different network should be connected. Beyond the stack itself, the change comes when money is no longer a mere exchange of value, but programmable.

3 Introducing Programmability at the Point of Sale

Programmability at the point of sale is the ability for merchants and developers to customize and extend checkout systems. In the late 1970's we already saw smart POS system introduce by Gene Mosher's Old Canal Café,[2] who could receive customer orders and print complete preparation detail in the kitchen. Later, the system evolved to become PC-based, gaining even more capabilities. Nowadays, the POS terminals are evolving with 40% of terminals sold in 2023 are running on Android OS (Connected POS Terminal Market Report 2025), the "Smart POS". It brings even more flexibility for the merchants to install custom application. Not limited to payment, but POS terminals are now being used for loyalty, connected to CRM, and even more.

While programmability was always limited to POS software or terminal, now the digital currency brings new capacities with the money and/or payment itself being

[2] https://www.posmatic.com/point-of-sale/what-is-point-of-sale.php#:~:text=The%20programmability%20of%20such%20systems,labor%20and%20food%20cost%20reports

programmable. For the sake of clarity, programmable money refers to the money itself carrying executable logic, while programmable payment keeps the money passive and execute conditional logic on a transaction.

Programmable money brings new interactions, beyond the simple transfer of funds. In retail and e-commerce, it means transaction can dynamically adjust to context and trigger automated action.

- **Automated Discount & Promotions:** Smart Contracts linked to a stablecoin can automatically apply discounts or promotional offers when predefined condition are met. Non exhaustive list include priority to use voucher and deducts the corresponding amount. Another example could come directly from the retailer which would apply discount for payments made on off-peak days.
- **Real time tax handling:** Maybe one of the most studied and cited benefit of programmable money is the ability to handle taxes and compliance within the transaction. One good example is with the VAT where during the payment, the appropriate amount of VAT would be sent to authority. It would bring simplicity for the accounting of the merchants and improve tax efficiency for governments.
- **Loyalty and rewards:** Loyalty programs can be reimagined, rewarding the customers in the form of programmable tokens that customers earn and spend like cash. Based on an open protocol such as blockchain, the token could be not limited to one store but mutualized. It also brings modularity for merchants, making it easier to programme their assets.
- **Escrow Payment:** It enables conditional release of funds without relying on third party escrow service. One of the use case looked-at is the "pay-on-delivery", or automated refunds. For instance, a marketplace could use a stablecoin to transfer the payment to the seller only when the package is reported as delivered. Not only limited to stablecoin, but CBDC are also exploring this use case. The ECB launched an experimentation call for the market to explore the benefit of conditional payment, based on Digital Euro (Call for expressions of interest in innovation partnerships for the digital euro n.d.).

While programmability at the POS bring benefit for merchants and consumers, and could redefine how they interact together, the transition is not without challenges. Privacy is a central concern that could lead to a distrust of the consumer. Interoperability is another hurdle again as with multiple currencies, ledger, and wallets, the absence of standards could lead to increased complexity. Finally, questions remain around governance, control, and security: who writes the rules, or the smart contract? And is the smart contract secured enough?

For programmability to realize its promise, it will require more than technology. It needs first a coordinated approach across regulators, payments provider, and merchants. And second, merchants and consumers to adopt it, to embrace it.

4 A Matter of Generation

In today’s market, a generational shift is evident among people. We can’t look at the question of payment user experience, or payment habits, without taking in consideration the gap between the new generation of the older one. And that apply both to consumers and merchants. Academic studies highlight a generational divide in how people consume and how businesses operate.

Young consumers (Gen Z and Millennials) grown-up as Digital Native. They interact mainly online through their smartphone as an interface. A recent study found that half of Gen Z and Millennials are using digital payments, like Apple Pay or Google Pay (Paper, Plastic or Pixels: Payment Preferences by Generation n.d.). In comparison that’s only 35% for Gen X and 18% for boomers. Another example of that in the exponential increase of Tiktok-Shop who’ve been a seism on the market and pushing more social media as a distribution channel. More than digital payment means or channel, it’s about human interaction. Older generations are valuing more face-to-face services, and are concerned about the digitization, while the feeling is lower for the new generation. Not only the young consumer and the older use different payment mean but also don’t have the same feeling about cryptocurrencies and stablecoins. In a survey for Motley Fool’s, 71% of Gen Z and 60% of millennials would use stablecoins for shopping. That’s only 31% of Gen X and 18% of baby boomers. The gap is real (Younger Americans lead the charge on stablecoin adoption, but baby boomers are skeptical n.d.).

The shift is not visible only for the consumers, but also from the businesses themselves. When surveying small businesses in the US, a large majority of youngers owner are already adopting new technologies such as AI. More than two times compared to older one (Millennial and Gen Z small-business leaders aren’t just embracing AI. They’re using it differently n.d.). The intent is clear: Going to a cashless society.

The general shift in payment is not just about digital native versus elder consumers. It’s about preventing a conflict, where only part of society benefits from innovation. Stablecoin, or CBDC, will not replace existing methods overnight. They will and should co-exist, at least for a long term, because payments are not only about efficiency, but also about trust, and inclusion. The challenge is not technological, but social: how to ensure new form of money enhances choice rather than creatin inequity. Adoption will be over time, and success will come from our ability to create bridges and not cutting ties.

5 Stablecoin and the Commercial Value Chain: Frictions and Opportunities

Stablecoin in circulation as of today are worth more than 250 Billion €. In the next few years, analyst disagree among them, where Citi estimated it could increase up to 500 Billion in 2030, and even up to 3.8 Trillion (GPS Report Blockchain Digital

Dollar n.d.). Yet, even with a traction, volume still represent less than 1% of daily payment. Reasons for that are some challenges that arise with the stablecoin.

- **Regulatory & Compliance:** There is a lack of clear and unified regulatory framework. Things are going better, with the GENIUS ACT (n.d.) in US, signed in July 2025, and MICA in place for months in Europe. But still, there are concern regarding AML, getting the licence, etc. For merchants, it's still a barrier to entry as it's not clear to them.
- **Liquidity & Conversion Cost:** In stablecoin hold the promise of instant settlement. However, one of the major issues is the conversion between the stablecoin and fiat. If stablecoin to stablecoin is instant, merchants are still interested to be settle in fiat, and therefore, introduce new fees, remove the instant settlement. As of today, the stablecoin is still an intermediary, that your off-ramp. PSPs are developing services for merchants to facilitate this, but merchants are still hesitant. On the consumer side also, it requires an on-ramp phase. The promise of the stablecoin transaction is here, but currently, we are on-ramping from fiat to stablecoin, and then off-ramping stablecoin to fiat. If the transaction itself is faster and cheaper, the whole process could even increase the costs compared to today's payment methods.
- **Volatiliy & Trust:** By design, stablecoin eliminate the risk of volatility from cryptos. However, public perception (especially with the collapse of terra-luna (Crypto crash: Stablecoin collapse sends tokens tumbling n.d.)) associate stablecoin with crypto risks. The stablecoin issuers made great work to become more transparency on their holding, but still, they don't provide the same guarantee than fiat. Few people know precisely that assets backing the stablecoin, or the bank where the reserve are hold.
- **Merchant Acceptance & Integration:** Stablecoins are working well. But that's not enough. Develop a functional product is not the hardest part. It's how to scale it. And when it comes to scale, Stablecoin need to fit the current payment infrastructure. As of today, few merchants have what it takes to accept stablecoin. Wallets, on-chain fraud, integration on cashier, accountability… All of those things are required to scale. This full-scale development can only be done with the support of existing PSPs, and stablecoin treated just like any other new rail.
- **Privacy:** As stablecoin operate on public blockchain, it raises privacy concerns, because transaction detail are visible by anyone. It poses challenges as either consumers or merchants might be reluctant to adapt a payment mean that expose payment flows. Some technical explorations are being done, such as the Zero Knowledge Proof (ZKP) that would enable full private transaction on the blockchain. ZKPs are cryptographic protocols that allow one part to prove the validity of a statement without revealing details (amount, or recipient). As a user, you could use this protocol during the payment to hide the amount or receiver wallet address. Despite this potential, it remains limited today, as performance due to more complex computation might affect the user-experience at the POS.

Beyond regulatory and operational considerations, an important question is around the "user experience". Todays' card and mobile payments are extremely smooths and hard to beat: tap and go. In comparison, stablecoin payments today can feel cumbersome: consumers need to on-ramp into stablecoins, and merchants off-ramp back into fiat. The process represents a burden at the check-out. Then it is fair to ask if stablecoins bring a genuine innovation for the consumers.

However, it's good to explain it as a transitional stage. The situation is similar to the move from 3G to 4G to 5G in telecoms resulting in an improvement of the infrastructure (in speed, resiliency,...). At first consumers did not perceive a difference as they could still browse internet the same way. For the consumers, the real difference came later, when the industry developed new applications enabled by the upgraded infrastructure.

The current stage we are, is a necessary step to achieve the transformation. In the long run, the vision is that stablecoin become invisible: payroll in stablecoins, wallets as everyday payments and identity app. But all of that, in a more resilient, open, innovative payment ecosystem, and turning stablecoin in an opportunity.

6 Assessing the Opportunities

Understanding the role of stablecoin at POS require a structured framework that capture both the timing (and adoption) and the impact on the chain. We propose three adoptions phases:

- Short term incremental gain
- Medium term strategic lever
- Long term transformation model

In the short term, stablecoin will mainly deliver incremental efficiency: Processing fees. While traditional payments often incur merchants' fees between 2% and 3% of transactions, stablecoin-based rails can operate below 1%, with the reduction of intermediaries. In addition to processing fees, near instant settlement allow for a better management of the treasury. A third area of improvement is cross-border, reducing once again the fees due to the reduction of intermediaries.

In the medium term, stablecoin become strategic enablers of customer engagement, through programmability. Discount or reward are embedded directly in the payment flow, triggered by custom conditions. In comparison with existing system, relying on close loop, tokenized reward can be interoperable on different platform. It is to be noted that today, 28% of consumers drop the loyalty program without redeeming any points (Six Step Approach to building sustainable customer loyalty n.d.).

In the long term, stablecoin may enable a shift in the retail industry. In some year, the stablecoin would become systemic, as the payroll are distributed directly in stablecoin. No more on-ramp, or off-ramp. Some models would be included by design, such as BNPL (buy-now-pay-later). Finally, we should consider also the rise of AI, and agentic. In a few years, the e-commerce might be perform by AI agents (autonomous software capable of doing actions). This will even more require

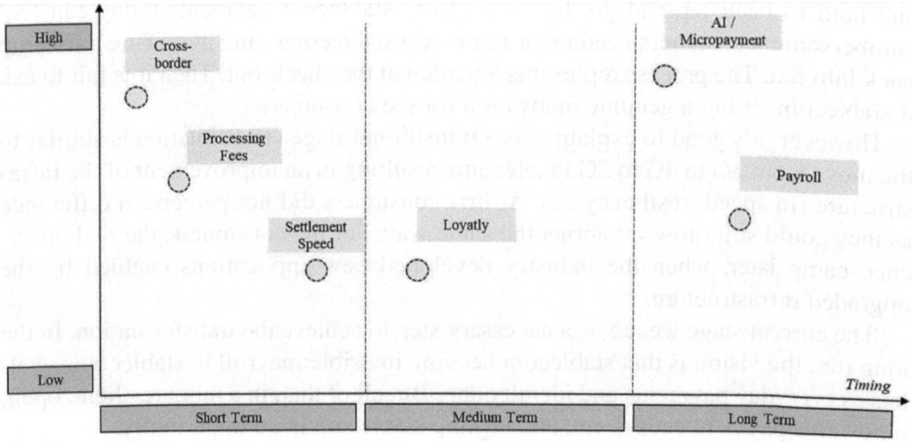

Fig. 2 Potential stablecoin use case over time: short-term focus on cross-border payments, processing fees, and settlement speed. Medium term on loyalty. Long-term on payroll and AI/Micropayment with expected impact from low to high

efficient infrastructure. This will be the era of micro-payment, and machine-to-machine economy. The nature of stablecoin, on the blockchain technology, which is open, fast, and programmable is the perfect infrastructure. AI agent could operate their own wallet, have their own identity on the blockchain, and trigger payment, using smart contracts.

Assessing opportunities is only the first step. To make them real, vision must align with operation changes, with PSPs as an essential part (Worldpay to Enable Stablecoin Payouts for Global Businesses in Collaboration with BVNK n.d.) (Fig. 2).

7 The Role of Payment Service Providers in a Multi Rail Tokenized Future

In todays' industry, multi-rail refers to the coexistence of cards, account to account, wallets, and other payment methods. Here, we focus on the extension of this concept to the "tokenized money": how legacy rails will co-exist and interoperate with new forms of tokenized money.

The payment landscape is transforming, with new form of digital money emerging, PSPs are playing a critical role. They have the responsibility to bridge legacy payment rails with new one, whether it's blockchain based, or CBDCs. The PSPs challenge is to integrate these new options into existing POS system without adding fiction to the user. In the perfect world, consumers remain conscious of the complexity behind the scenes, but with an intuitive and seamless user experience.

The tokenized future is about interoperability, not replacing one system overnight. PSPs will evolve in the future becoming even more this bridge connector between rails, ensuring that a payment in any form can be accepted and settled in the merchant's preferred form. PSPs are orchestrator across multiple payment networks, hiding complexity behind a unified service for merchants and consumers.

From aggregator to orchestrator is not an easy run. Each transaction should be route over the optimal rail, with the same security and controls, and guarantees for the consumers and merchants. The routing, is a smart engine, ensuring the best processing outcome for the merchant.

To fulfil this orchestrator role, PSPs should develop new capabilities:

- **Integrating new rails:** Connect new rails, with the legacy one. Some have already move forward, like Worldpay in collaboration with BVNK. With this, PSPs support stablecoin transactions within its existing system, without the merchant handling the cryptographic keys.
- **Custody:** Merchants accepting stablecoin payments will need a wallet to receive and manage funds. Many will not want to handle that themselves. PSPs can then provide custody services by offering secure wallets, managing private keys through technology like HSM or MPC (multi-part computation), and ensuring back-ups/recovery process.
- **Liquidity & Conversion Management:** PSPs take the capacity to convert stablecoins and fiat. The PSPs might partner with market maker, liquidity pools, or stablecoin issuers
- **Unified Interface at the POS:** Update the POS or terminal software to include QR Code management. It should be as generic as possible, compatible with multiple wallets. It includes also the capacity to detect the blockchain being used, without adding new complexity for the merchant.
- **Unified Interface for e-commerce:** Adding stablecoin as a payment method at the check-out that would either generate a QR Code to be scan by the smartphone or open the wallet in your browser to execute the transaction.
- **Regulatory compliance:** One of the most significant shifts for PSPs is the need to meet bank-level compliance and regulatory standards. In Europe, PSPs are responsible to perform a KYC at the onboarding, both for merchants, and consumers. Also to comply with the AML regulation, which mandate PSP to ensure that wallets are not linked to any sanctions. Finally, the Transfer of Fund Regulation (TFR) mandate CASP to verify ownership and control of self-hosted wallet above a €1000 (Fig. 3).

As we see, the payment flow is not very different to what PSP are used to provide, because while having its own specificities, stablecoin is a rail at the end. That's why PSPs adaption go through a mix of adapting existing system but also enable new opportunities for them.

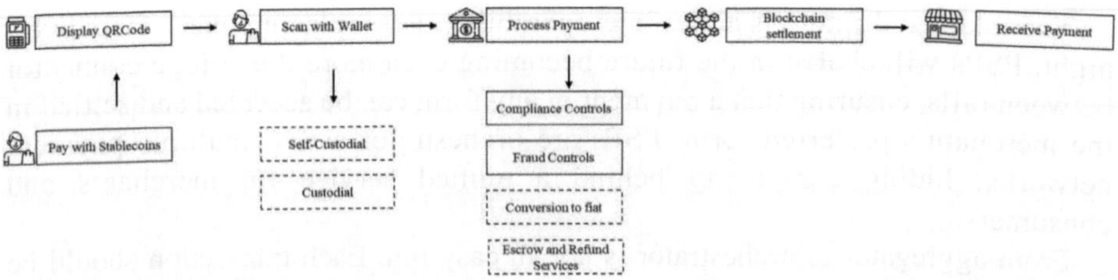

Fig. 3 Illustration of a stablecoin payment flow, from QRCode and wallet scan to payment processing, compliance, and fraud controls, conversion of required, blockchain settlement, and final receipt of payment by the merchant

8 Conclusion: Money as a Modular Invisible and Strategic Asset

The evolution from fiat to tokenized money show that payments are no longer a monolithic process by a dynamic ecosystem. The productization of money explored through this chapter reveal how stablecoin, CBDC, or tokenized deposit add new capabilities to the monetary system and its impact at the point of sale, for merchants and consumers.

In a legacy system, money follow a linear journey from issuer to merchant, processed by network and acquirers. Tokenized money breaks this model. It introduces modularity: multi form of currency, co-existing, and interoperating. The consumer will have more choice than ever and adapt its payment with the use case and his needs. Each of this new module come with specific rules, governance, and controls.

If modularity defines the infrastructure, invisibility define the user experience. Consumers and merchants cannot expect to manage the complexity of this. At the POS, or online, money must remain invisible and convenient. A good payment mean is a payment mean that is adopted. If we look at previous innovation such as contactless card or mobile wallet, it succeeds because they reduce friction.

Finally, more than ever money is a strategic asset. Payment no longer stops at value transfer, but extend to loyalty, treasury, and other services. With Tokenization, money can be designed, programmed, and embedded. It's a choice of efficiency, of features, and even competitive advantage.

The payment industry is at the edge of a structural shift. Tokenized money is moving from pilot to adoption at a pace we've never seen before, forcing both merchants and PSPs to rethink their role. For merchant, success will depend on seeing payments not only as cost, but as competitive edge and lever to enhance customer experience. For PSPs, the challenge is to shift from processor to orchestrator of value among multi-rails. Those who embrace this transformation will not only keep-up with technological changes, but also shape the next generation of commerce, and build a greater ecosystem.

References

Bank for International Settlements (BIS) (2023) Annual economic report. https://www.bis.org/publ/arpdf/ar2023e3.htm

Blueprint for the future monetary system: improving the old, enabling the new (n.d.) https://www.bis.org/publ/arpdf/ar2023e3.pdf

Call for expressions of interest in innovation partnerships for the digital euro (n.d.) https://www.ecb.europa.eu/press/intro/news/html/ecb.mipnews241031.en.html

Central Bank digital currencies for cross-border payments (n.d.) https://www.bis.org/publ/othp38.pdf

Connected POS Terminal Market Report (2025) https://finance.yahoo.com/news/connected-pos-terminals-market-report-083800323.html

Crypto crash: Stablecoin collapse sends tokens tumbling (n.d.) https://www.bbc.com/news/technology-61425209

GENIUS ACT (n.d.) https://www.congress.gov/bill/119th-congress/senate-bill/394/text

GPS Report Blockchain Digital Dollar (n.d.) https://www.citigroup.com/rcs/citigpa/storage/pulic/GPS_Report_Blockchain_Digital_Dollar.pdf

High-level Recommendations for the Regulation, Supervision and Oversight of Global Stablecoin Arrangements (n.d.) https://www.fsb.org/uploads/P170723-3.pdf

Millennial and Gen Z small-business leaders aren't just embracing AI (n.d.) They're using it differently. https://www.fastcompany.com/91172546/millennial-gen-z-business-owners-adopt-ai-use-tools-differently-than-baby-boomers

Paper, Plastic or Pixels: Payment Preferences by Generation (n.d.) https://www.kantar.com/north-america/inspiration/research-services/payment-preferences-by-generation-pf#:~:text=Digital%20payment%20types%20like%20Apple,of%20these%20modern%20payment%20technologies

Six Step Approach to building sustainable customer loyalty (n.d.) https://www.capgemini.com/insights/expert-perspectives/six-step-approach-to-building-sustainable-customer-loyalty/

Worldpay to Enable Stablecoin Payouts for Global Businesses in Collaboration with BVNK (n.d.) https://corporate.worldpay.com/news-releases/news-release-details/worldpay-enable-stablecoin-payouts-global-businesses

Younger Americans lead the charge on stablecoin adoption, but baby boomers are skeptical (n.d.) https://www.fool.com/research/stablecoin-usage-trends-survey/

The Case for a Stablecoin Clearing System: Enabling Ubiquity Through Market Structure Evolution

Tony McLaughlin and Michael Salmony

Abstract Stablecoins will reach their full potential as peer-to-peer, digitally-native money when the option to redeem them at par value on demand is ubiquitous. A clearing system Ubyx is proposed that solves the many-to-many problem between issuers and accepting institutions, enabling anyone to deposit stablecoins into existing financial accounts (held at banks and regulated non-banks) at full value.

This helps stablecoins make the transition from crypto use-cases into universal digital cash. Stablecoins can achieve IAS7 cash equivalent status, opening the door to mainstream corporate adoption. It helps stablecoins to exhibit singleness of money (between issuers, and with reference to other form factors of fiat currency), and promotes redemption through regulated channels subject to AML, KYC, sanctions, and fraud checking.

The stablecoin ecosystem will be multi-currency, pluralistic, collaborative where it needs to be, competitive where it should be and provide the foundation for the next wave of permissionless innovation. An original goal of cryptocurrency will be achieved—mass market peer-to-peer digital money conducted over public-permissionless blockchains. By solving the many-to-many network problem, achieving cash equivalence and aligning economic incentives, the stablecoin epoch will be ushered in—Stablecoins will become ubiquitous, general-purpose methods of digital payment.

Keywords Stablecoin clearing system · Redemption · Accounting

---

T. McLaughlin
Ubyx, Wilmington, DE, USA

London, United Kingdom
e-mail: Tony@ubyx.xyz

M. Salmony (✉)
Payments Innovation Consulting, Heidelberg, Germany
e-mail: salmony@payments-innovation.com

S. Yazıcı et al. (eds.), *Tokenisation of Money*, Contributions to Finance and Accounting, https://doi.org/10.1007/978-3-032-22946-5_20

General-purpose stablecoins	Special-purpose stablecoins
IAS 32 financial instruments	IAS 7 cash equivalents
Non-bank issuers	Bank and non-bank issuers
100% backed	Varied methods of backing
Sold through exchanges	Redeemed at par value on demand
No interest payable to end users	Interest can be paid to end users
Cash-like bearer instrument	Superset of features that go beyond lagacy payment types
Bilateral issuer-acceptance network	Mutualized acceptance network

Fig. 1 Stablecoins as We Understand Them Today vs. General-Purpose Stablecoins (Source: Ubyx Whitepaper (McLaughlin 2025), p. 37)

1 Introduction

Stablecoins represent a significant innovation in the digital asset ecosystem, (Adrian and Mancini-Griffoli 2021), offering price stability against national currencies while exhibiting many of the benefits that public blockchain networks provide. These digital assets have demonstrated remarkable growth and resilience, expanding from specialised crypto use cases to addressing broader financial needs. However, despite their potential as efficient, borderless payment mechanisms, stablecoins remain trapped in a limited ecosystem, unable to achieve the ubiquity necessary to serve as general-purpose digital money.

To illustrate the current state and the potential future of stablecoins, see Fig. 1.

This chapter examines the current market structure limitations preventing stablecoins from achieving their full potential and makes the case for a fundamental ecosystem state change: the establishment of a unified clearing system for stablecoins. By drawing parallels with the evolution of traditional payment systems and analyzing the network effects required for widespread adoption, we present a comprehensive argument for why such infrastructure is not merely beneficial but necessary for stablecoin ubiquity. Stablecoins have been the subject of increasing research interest, as evidenced by systematic literature review (Ante and Fiedler 2023).

2 Current Market Structure Limitations

The stablecoin ecosystem today faces several critical constraints that collectively restrict widespread adoption beyond crypto-specialised use cases. These limitations stem from the market's current structure and inhibit stablecoins from becoming truly ubiquitous digital money.

2.1 The Universal Redemption Problem

Unlike traditional payment methods, stablecoins lack universal redemption capabilities (Gorton and Zhang 2022). When receiving a check, credit card payment, or bank transfer, recipients can deposit these instruments at any financial institution for 100% of their stated value, irrespective of the issuer. This universal redemption does not yet exist for stablecoins, creating a significant barrier to adoption. Businesses and individuals receiving stablecoins face uncertainty about how to convert them back to traditional currency efficiently and at full value.

The current ecosystem offers limited entry points (on-ramps) to acquire stablecoins, typically through cryptocurrency exchanges or direct relationships with issuers—the latter being an option available only to large players. More problematically, when users want to convert stablecoins back to traditional money, their options (off-ramps) are few, inconsistent across different stablecoins, and unavailable in many jurisdictions.

This redemption uncertainty forces stablecoin recipients to individually assess the creditworthiness of both the issuer and their available off-ramp options—a level of due diligence unrealistic for everyday transactions. The resulting friction pushes many potential users away from stablecoins entirely, particularly corporate entities that require predictable treasury operations.

2.2 The Many-to-Many Network Problem

The stablecoin ecosystem faces a classic network coordination problem concerning redemptions. In a healthy ecosystem, there will be many issuers and many accepting institutions. Actors who seek to create competitive advantages through bilateral acceptance arrangements are ultimately working against themselves and the wider ecosystem's health.

This situation mirrors the early days of other payment networks (Rochet and Tirole 2003), where the lack of standardised clearing mechanisms created inefficiencies. Consider the historical development of check clearing or card payment processing—initially fragmented systems that eventually required centralised clearing mechanisms to achieve scale. In a pluralistic network of issuers and accepting institutions, the same logic that drove the creation of clearing systems for checks, cards, and ACH applies to the emerging stablecoin ecosystem.

Figure 2 illustrates this concept, showing the complexity of bilateral arrangements compared to a centralised clearing system.

The inefficiencies of bilateral arrangements in payment systems have been studied in the context of traditional banking, where network effects play a crucial role in the adoption of shared infrastructure (Milne 2006).

To be clear, this clearing requirement applies only to the redemption process—not to the transfer of stablecoins between users, which should remain peer-to-peer

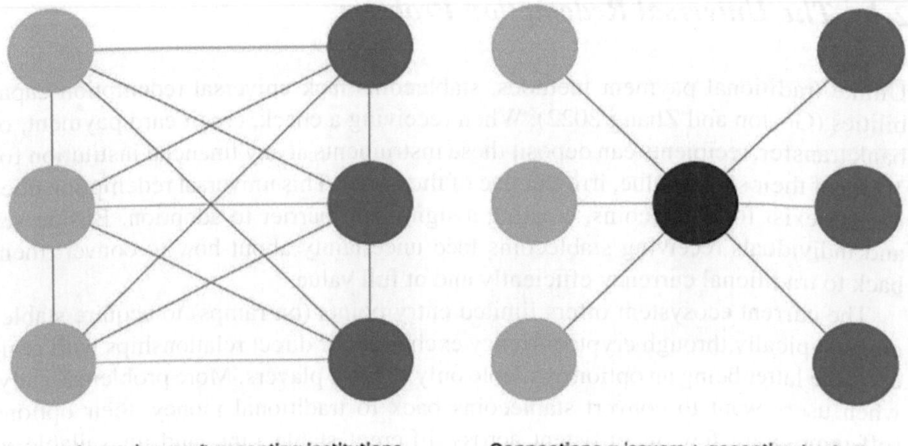

Fig. 2 Rational for Clearing Arrangements (Source: Ubyx Whitepaper, p. 6)

according to blockchain's founding principles. The need for a clearing system arises specifically when recipients wish to redeem stablecoins at par value through their existing financial institutions, and those institutions need a mechanism to collect the fiat currency from multiple issuers efficiently.

2.3 *The Accounting Treatment Barrier*

For stablecoins to achieve mainstream corporate adoption, they must clear a critical hurdle: qualifying as "cash equivalents" under international accounting standards (IASB 2010). This is not merely a technicality but a fundamental requirement for corporations to use stablecoins in everyday operations, as operational liquidity is managed with cash equivalents.

Currently, when businesses hold stablecoins, they are classified as financial instruments under IAS32. This classification creates significant operational and compliance burdens. Companies do not want their operating cash tied up in financial instruments—they need it classified as cash or cash equivalents to efficiently manage liquidity and satisfy reporting requirements.

The IAS7 standard requires that for an instrument to qualify as a cash equivalent, it must be "readily convertible to a known amount of cash and be subject to an insignificant risk of changes in value." Meeting this standard requires more than regulatory declarations; it demands a practical redemption infrastructure that creates the factual evidence accounting bodies need to recognise stablecoins as cash equivalents.

2.4 *The Network Effect Challenge*

The limitations described above create a chicken-and-egg problem that has trapped stablecoins in a specialised niche. The network effects that would drive universal adoption cannot take hold because the current market structure inhibits them.

For stablecoins to achieve ubiquity, they require a level of indifference among recipients—the confidence that regardless of which stablecoin is received, it can be easily redeemed at full value or held as needed. This indifference is the core principle behind universal acceptance of checks and cards. When recipients stop worrying about which stablecoin they are receiving or how to off-ramp, adoption can accelerate exponentially (Prasad 2021).

However, the current bilateral arrangements between issuers and off-ramps create an unscalable model. Just as the credit card system would never have achieved universal adoption if each card issuer needed to establish direct relationships with every merchant, stablecoins cannot achieve ubiquity if each issuer must build its own redemption network through bilateral agreements.

The mathematical reality is stark: in a system with N issuers and M accepting institutions, bilateral arrangements would require $N \times M$ connections. A clearing system reduces this to $N + M$ connections, creating dramatically more efficient scaling as the network grows. This is not merely theoretical efficiency; it represents the difference between a niche payment system and a ubiquitous one.

3 The Case for a Stablecoin Clearing System

A stablecoin clearing system would resolve the limitations described above and create the conditions for ubiquity. Such a system would not replace existing stablecoin off-ramps but would add a critical new channel enabling users to accept a variety of stablecoins while being relatively indifferent to the issuer.

3.1 *Enabling Universal Redemption*

A clearing system makes redeeming stablecoins as simple as depositing a check. Recipients could deposit any participating stablecoin at their existing financial institution and receive credit for its full value in their account. The financial institution would then use the clearing system to route the stablecoins back to the issuer and collect the underlying fiat currency.

This universal redemption mechanism transforms stablecoins from specialised crypto instruments into widely accepted digital cash, addressing the primary barrier to adoption. When users can confidently accept any stablecoin knowing it can be easily converted to traditional currency, the entire value proposition changes.

3.2 *Solving the Many-to-Many Problem*

A clearing system efficiently connects issuers and financial institutions through a standardised infrastructure with clear rules. Rather than each stablecoin issuer negotiating separate relationships with hundreds of potential off-ramp providers, a single connection to the clearing system provides global reach. Similarly, receiving institutions gain the ability to process stablecoins from any participating issuer through one integration.

This mutualization of acceptance dramatically reduces the infrastructure burden for all participants while exponentially increasing network reach. The technical standardization also creates efficiency, as institutions follow the same process regardless of which stablecoin is being redeemed, similar to how banks process checks drawn on different institutions through a shared clearing system.

3.3 *Achieving Cash Equivalence*

A clearing system creates the factual basis for stablecoins to achieve cash equivalent status under accounting standards. By homogenizing the redemption process across issuers through standardised rules, pre-funded settlement accounts, and established redemption patterns, the clearing system provides the evidence accounting bodies need to classify stablecoins appropriately.

This reclassification would unlock stablecoins for:

- Business-to-business (B2B) payments
- Consumer-to-business (C2B) transactions
- Business-to-consumer (B2C) disbursements
- Complex multi-party transactions
- International cash and liquidity management for corporations
- Interbank settlements currently conducted through correspondent banking
- Wholesale financial market settlements

Without cash equivalence, stablecoins will remain specialised crypto tools, unable to fulfill their transformative potential in the broader financial system.

Definitions:

- **"General purpose stablecoin":** a token transacted on a public-permissionless network that can be converted on demand at par value against a range of regulated issuer types through a ubiquitous acceptance network.
- **"Stablecoin Singularity":** the day that stablecoins are granted IAS7 cash equivalence, after which stablecoins rapidly become ubiquitous forms of peer-to-peer digital money and the stablecoin epoch commences in full force.

IAS 32: Financial Instruments	IAS 7: Cash Equivalent
"A financial instrument is any contract that gives rise to a financial asset of one entity and a financial liability or equity instrument of another entity."	*"For an investment to qualify as a cash equivalent it must be readily convertible to a known amount of cash and be subject to an insignificant risk of changes in value."*

3.4 Reinforcing Peer-to-Peer Payments

Bitcoin introduced a revolutionary concept: digital money that moves directly between people without intermediaries (Allen et al. 2020). While Bitcoin itself has become more of a store of value than everyday money, stablecoins now fulfill this original vision—but only if people can trust them enough to keep and use them as readily as they trust traditional financial products.

A clearing system preserves the core peer-to-peer nature of stablecoin transactions while adding redemption assurance. This creates true recipient indifference—users can either keep stablecoins in native digital form for future use or convert them to traditional account balances at full value. This neutrality between holding and redeeming is essential for stablecoins to compete with existing payment methods on a level playing field.

Figure 3 shows the peer-to-peer payments system with few intermediaries.

3.5 Alignment with Regulatory Objectives

A well-designed stablecoin clearing system would not only benefit market participants but would also align with key regulatory objectives:

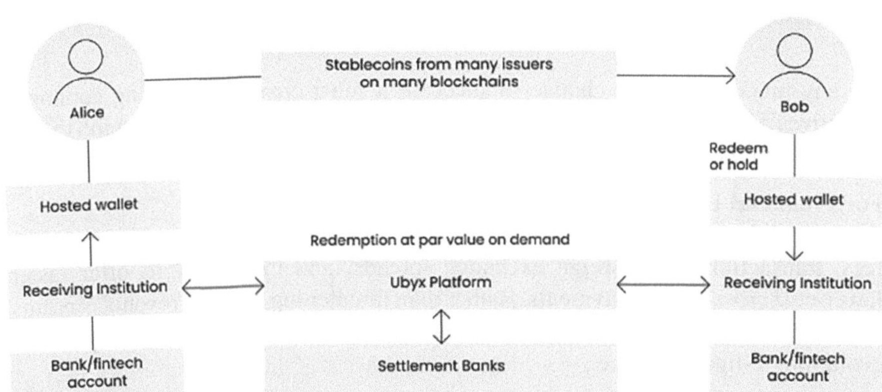

Fig. 3 Peer-to-peer payments (Source: Ubyx Whitepaper, p. 9)

Monetary Coherence
Regulators and central banks are rightfully concerned with maintaining "singleness of money" (FSB 2020)—ensuring that different forms of the same currency maintain consistent value (BIS 2022). A clearing system establishes standardised redemption processes and mandates issuer pre-funding, ensuring full-value redemption. This addresses regulatory requirements for monetary stability and coherence between traditional and digital forms of money, a key concern highlighted by global bodies (G7 Working Group 2019).

Controlled Innovation
By channeling stablecoin activity through regulated financial institutions with established compliance frameworks (IOSCO 2021), a clearing system provides a structured pathway for innovation. The system embeds stablecoins within existing KYC, AML, and anti-fraud processes, utilizing rigorous procedures that are already trusted by regulators. This aligns with the Financial Stability Board's call for robust governance and risk management in global stablecoin arrangements (FSB 2023).

System Resilience
A clearing system operating across multiple independent blockchain networks creates payment redundancy and resilience (BIS 2023). If one blockchain network experiences disruption, payments can continue on others, creating a more robust overall financial infrastructure than exists today. Such a system would be designed in accordance with the established Principles for Financial Market Infrastructures, ensuring it meets the highest standards for safety and efficiency (CPMI-IOSCO 2012).

The regulatory framework for stablecoin payment systems is actively in analysis, with (Bank of England 2023) proposing a regime for systemic payment systems using stablecoins.

3.6 *Economic Incentives for Adoption*

For any market structure change to succeed, it must create compelling economic incentives for all participants. A stablecoin clearing system would establish balanced economic models that drive adoption:

For Financial Institutions
Banks and fintechs gain new revenue opportunities through stablecoin acceptance fees, transaction fees, foreign exchange spreads, and the ability to offer faster, lower-cost cross-border payments. Rather than threatening existing revenue streams, these new services expand them while positioning institutions strategically for the evolution of digital finance.

Economic opportunities
With a $1 trillion supply of stablecoins circulating globally and 0.5% redeemed daily, the economics of acceptance are compelling. At a 100bps redemption fee and 100bps FX spread, the potential gross revenue is significant:
• *A country capturing 5% of global redemption flow could generate* ***$1.825 billion*** *per year in gross revenue for its local financial institutions.* • *A single bank or non-bank with 5% market share in that country stands to earn* ***$91.25 million*** *annually—from accepting overseas stablecoins and redeeming them at par value through Ubyx.*

For Stablecoin Issuers

Issuers currently rely heavily on interest income from reserve assets, a model vulnerable to interest-rate fluctuations. A clearing system introduces alternative revenue streams, potentially including redemption fees paid directly by receiving institutions. This creates more predictable and sustainable business models while dramatically expanding distribution reach.

For End Users

Businesses and individuals benefit from increased competition and choice in payment methods, driving down costs and improving service quality. The ability to seamlessly move between stablecoin and traditional balances reduces friction and increases financial flexibility.

4 The Path to Implementation

Implementing a stablecoin clearing system requires coordinated action among ecosystem participants:

1. Establishing clear governance frameworks that define access criteria, operational standards, and settlement processes
2. Developing standardised APIs for submitting redemption requests, routing stablecoins, and settling fiat transfers
3. Creating pre-funded settlement mechanisms that ensure receiving institutions obtain full value from issuers
4. Building compliance layers that satisfy regulatory requirements across jurisdictions

The technology underpinning such a system should be designed for progressive decentralization—starting with proven, trusted infrastructure that builds confidence with regulators and traditional financial institutions, then evolving toward greater decentralization as the system matures.

5 The Market Opportunity

The potential economic opportunity from a unified clearing system is substantial. In a hypothetical scenario with $1 trillion in stablecoin supply and 0.5% redeemed daily, the potential gross revenue from redemption fees and FX spreads could reach tens of billions annually. This represents a significant opportunity for financial institutions to capture new value.

More importantly, a clearing system would enable stablecoins to address the entire global payments market—estimated at over $2 trillion in annual revenue. By solving the common acceptance challenge, a clearing system would allow stablecoins to fulfill their promise as the digital economy's native peer-to-peer payment system.

6 Conclusion: The Necessary State Transition

For stablecoins to achieve their full potential, they require a common framework for universal redemption, liquidity, and acceptance. This is not merely a technical improvement but a fundamental ecosystem state change—a transition from today's fragmented landscape of bilateral connections to a mutualised network where universal redemption underpins confidence and drives adoption.

Figure 4 presents the envisioned general-purpose stablecoin ecosystem, highlighting how a clearing system enables a mutualised network for universal redemption and acceptance.

The development of such infrastructure requires collaborative action from issuers, financial institutions, technology providers, and regulators. While challenging to coordinate, this ecosystem state change offers tremendous benefits to all participants, creating powerful network effects that drive stablecoin adoption from specialised crypto applications to ubiquitous digital money.

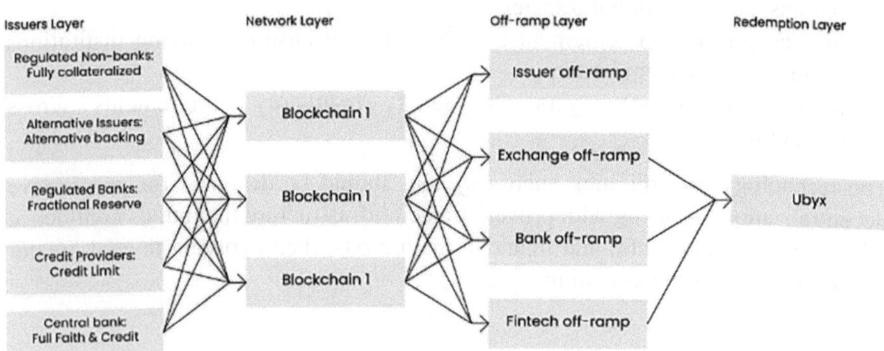

Fig. 4 General-Purpose Stablecoin Ecosystem (Source: Ubyx Whitepaper, p. 38)

In a world where financial institutions provide hosted wallets connected to multiple public blockchains, a new level of financial system resilience will emerge. Even during disruptions to national payment systems, users would retain the ability to transact via public blockchains with cash-equivalent stablecoins redeemable at par value through trusted financial institutions.

The transition to stablecoin ubiquity is not merely desirable (Arner et al. 2022)—it is inevitable. The question is whether the industry will proactively build the necessary clearing infrastructure or allow fragmentation to persist, delaying the benefits of this transformation. Those who recognise this necessity and act first will shape the future of digital money, while those who resist risk missing a historic opportunity in the evolution of global payments.

Prepare for the Stablecoin Epoch

In the age of paper payments, was there any financial institution that could not serve its customers' needs for cash and cheques? In the era of financial messaging, was there a bank that could not make or receive electronic payments? In the time of cards, is there an institution on the planet that cannot issue debit or credit cards? So it shall be in the Stablecoin Epoch: every bank and non-bank financial institution will enable customers to receive stablecoins—from many issuers, in many currencies, across many public blockchains—and to hold and pay with stablecoins. Those who choose not to participate will see their clients migrate to those who do. Choosing not to act is a choice, because the process has already begun.

References

Adrian T, Mancini-Griffoli T (2021) The rise of digital money. IMF

Allen F, Gu X, Jagtiani J (2020) A survey of Fintech research and policy discussion. Federal Reserve Bank of Philadelphia

Ante L, Fiedler I (2023) A systematic literature review of empirical research on stablecoins. FinTech 2(1):34–55. https://doi.org/10.3390/fintech2010003

Arner DW, Auer R, Frost J (2022) Stablecoins: risks, potential and regulation. Bank for International Settlements

Bank for International Settlements (BIS) (2022) The future monetary system. In Annual economic report 2022 (Chapter III)

Bank of England (2023) Regulatory regime for systemic payment systems using stablecoins and related service providers. Available at: https://www.bankofengland.co.uk/paper/2023/dp/regulatory-regime-for-systemic-payment-systems-using-stablecoins-and-related-service-providers

BIS (2023) The future monetary system. Bank for International Settlements annual economic report

Committee on Payments and Market Infrastructures (CPMI) & International Organization of Securities Commissions (IOSCO) (2012) Principles for financial market infrastructures. Bank for International Settlements

Financial Stability Board (FSB). (2023). FSB global stablecoin arrangements: final guidance, recommendations and report
FSB (2020) Regulation, supervision and oversight of global Stablecoin arrangements. Financial Stability Board
G7 Working Group on Stablecoins (2019) Investigating the impact of global stablecoins. Bank for International Settlements
Gorton G, Zhang J (2022) Taming wildcat stablecoins. University of Chicago
International Accounting Standards Board (IASB). (2010). IAS 7 statement of cash flows. Available at: https://www.ifrs.org/issued-standards/list-of-standards/ias-7-statement-of-cash-flows/
IOSCO (2021) Recommendations on Stablecoin arrangements. International Organization of Securities Commissions
McLaughlin T (2025) Ubyx white paper— Stablecoin Ubiquity. https://www.ubyx.xyz/whitepaper. Accessed 22 Jul 2025
Milne A (2006) What is in it for us? Network effects and bank payment innovation. J Bank Financ 30(6):1613–1630. https://doi.org/10.1016/j.jbankfin.2005.09.006
Prasad ES (2021) The future of money: how the digital revolution is transforming currencies and finance. Harvard University Press
Rochet JC, Tirole J (2003) Platform competition in two-sided markets. J Eur Econ Assoc 1(4):990–1029

Adoption by Design for Digital Currency Systems

Gabriel R. Bizama

Abstract Digital currency represents a transformative form of money, potentially issued and regulated by central banks or other entities, offering inherent benefits such as programmability, enhanced security, and privacy features. However, the architectural design of a functional digital currency ecosystem, including but not limited to Central Bank Digital Currency (CBDC), involves significant technical and socio-economic challenges. This chapter documents the design process and resulting prototype of a non-custodial wallet: a physical or software device enabling users to securely store and spend digital currency across various transactional contexts. To effectively navigate the complex design challenges inherent in a digital currency system, an iterative and user-centred approach was adopted. This involved conducting a series of intensive workshops with a broad spectrum of internal and external stakeholders, employing innovative methods such as storytelling, metaphorical analogy, and 'provotypes'. These techniques were instrumental in effectively communicating complex digital currency concepts, eliciting critical user feedback, and integrating fundamental normative values into the technical specifications. The research successfully derived a set of foundational guidelines for designing digital currency systems that balance technical feasibility with social considerations, ensuring alignment with genuine user needs and values. This work on significantly contributes to the extant digital currency discourse by providing a tangible, practical example of the potential use of digital currency in everyday life and by emphatically underscoring the vital importance of a human-centred design methodology in this emerging field.

Keywords Payments · Digital currencies · Non-custodial wallet · Socio-technical design

G. R. Bizama (✉)
Institute for Civil Law, University of Bern, Bern, Switzerland
e-mail: gabriel.bizama@unibe.ch

S. Yazıcı et al. (eds.), *Tokenisation of Money*, Contributions to Finance and Accounting, https://doi.org/10.1007/978-3-032-22946-5_21

1 Introduction: Contextualising Digital Currency Design

Design frameworks applied to the sector are currently required in the development of comprehensive digital currency systems. This study adopts physical cash as a foundational reference point, drawing from its established values, transactional practices, and inherent user familiarity. This approach facilitates the development of a coherent set of design guidelines intended to support future endeavours in the digital currency sector. Key recommendations emphasise anchoring the design in existing monetary concepts, fostering engagement with diverse stakeholders through inclusive and accessible communication, and ensuring that any new system complements, rather than replaces, the existing payments system. The overarching goal is the creation of systems that are intrinsically adaptable, interoperable, and fully responsive to the everyday financial behaviours and preferences of end-users.

To explore the practical storage and expenditure of a digital currency, a non-custodial wallet prototype was developed and tested. The methodology prioritised inclusive design, employing tools such as storytelling and provotypes, a portmanteau of 'provocation' and 'prototype', to render complex digital finance concepts more relatable and to actively explore the social, ethical, and cultural implications of the technology.

This research underscores a crucial balance: preserving the utility of legacy systems like cash while simultaneously expanding future possibilities. By integrating technical design with essential social factors, including privacy, usability, and access, digital currency systems can be effectively developed to enhance user autonomy and accurately reflect diverse financial needs and contexts.

This chapter is based on a joint research project that involved the work from scholars from the University of Bern, University College London, Royal Melbourne Institute of Technology University, Fallow Earth and the Scottish Government and published in the *Journal of Payments Strategy & Systems in Volume 19, Number 3 (DOI: 10.69554/KRMP9840)*. It could be deemed as a starting point on the work required in the development of a well-designed digital currency systems. It also identifies future areas of work to achieve a robust digital currency ecosystem. The research contributes to the digital currency literature and it could assist central banks, financial entities, academia, policymakers and standard setting bodies on the design and implementation of digital currency systems.

1.1 The Socio-Technical Nature of Money

The concept of a socio-technical system provides a vital lens for designers to examine the intricate interaction between society—from individuals to large institutions—and technology (Baxter and Sommerville 2011). Money itself functions as a form of social technology, its meaning and function profoundly shaped by the social relationships that underpin it (Ingham 1996). Such systems evolve dynamically in response to shifting social, cultural, and political conditions (Kling and Lamb 1999). As society progresses, the forms and uses of money inevitably change.

Crucially, cash remains a significant barrier to purely digital design approaches. It is preferred by older generations who rely on established routines (Vines et al. 2012) and is essential for individuals who do not have access to the digital infrastructure or well-developed digital skills (Dai et al. 2023; Bon and Akkermans 2020). Consequently, cash retains pivotal properties, such as instant settlement for merchants and offline functionality, often rendering it preferable to digital cashless payments that can involve significant processing delays (Kameswaran and Muralidhar 2019).

Designers have previously utilised approaches such as inclusive design to address user requirements within a technical framework (Clarkson et al. 2013), and have applied various methodologies to deepen this understanding (Courage and Baxter 2005). However, a recognised lack of a dedicated design framework for money narratives (Elsden and Speed 2022) has made user-centric design in this area a novel and complex field. The consequences of this omission are evident, for instance, in the low adoption and trust issues faced by Nigeria's eNaira implementation, largely attributed to insufficient consideration of user needs, daily financial practices, and existing public comprehension of money.

2 Designing a Non-custodial Wallet: Challenges and Framework

The development of a novel digital currency system requires navigating distinct challenges that span conceptualisation and design implementation.

2.1 Challenges in Digital Currency System Creation

1. **Incorporating normative values into technical design:** The primary challenge is integrating social, cultural, or political values into the technical requirements. Given that money is fundamentally a social relation (Halloluwa et al. 2018), its design involves more than just its physical or digital form; it requires designing the very values that people associate with money's function. While design researchers have developed methods for socio-technical systems (Dardenne et al. 1993; Bryl et al. 2009; Maguire 2014), these often fail to fully translate to abstract concepts like money and value, creating a lack of frameworks for generating shared understanding between designers and stakeholders (Pommeranz et al. 2013). This research addressed this by formulating guidelines based on key cash principles: diverse payment options, individual asset ownership, and privacy by design. This was grounded in the

established value placed on cash's inherent properties, including anonymity, security (Krueger and Seitz 2018), fungibility, accessibility, non-discrimination and direct ownership (Vines et al. 2012; Kameswaran and Muralidhar 2019; McAndrews 2020).
2. **Addressing the complexity of a digital currency system:** Digital currency is inherently complex, often inaccessible to the everyday public due to its novelty, technical terminology, and entanglement with complex existing payment infrastructures. To forge a shared understanding and vision among a diverse group of stakeholders, the project employed techniques inspired by design methods that use metaphors to boost creativity with non-experts (Ylipulli et al. 2017) and communicate technical terms through analogical reasoning in disciplines such as computer science (Van Dyke 1988).
3. **Effectively demonstrating system specifications:** The third challenge involved finding effective means to demonstrate the system's technical specifications, benefits, and drawbacks to potential users. The proposed design model was structured around three interconnected strands:
    - **Meta-design:** Focusing on working practices, knowledge exchange, and stakeholder engagement (Bauer and Herder 2009; Fischer and Scharff 2000; Fischer et al. 2004).
    - **Technical systems design:** Focusing on system functionality and development (Bacon 2005; Goodman et al. 2011; Cockton 2019).
    - **Interaction design:** Focusing on the system's interface with the wider world (Fischer 2007; Herrmann 2014; Thornton et al. 2022; Schütz and Gomez 2020).

2.2 *Design Requirements and Technical Prerequisites*

Inspired by the essential values of cash, the following technical prerequisites were established for the digital currency system:

- **Ownership:** The system must be token-based (not account-based), with tokens (analogous to banknotes) being unforgeable by design (Goodell et al. 2023).
- **Possession and control:** Users must have the option to store tokens directly in non-custodial wallets that are non-identifiable, not third-party issued or registered, and do not require trusted computing.
- **Privacy:** The payer's identity must be unlinked from the recipient, transaction value, and metadata (e.g., time, location). This requires privacy by design in the system architecture.
- **Legal:** The system must be compatible with Anti-Money Laundering (AML) requirements, while allowing authorities a mechanism to identify the recipient of the money.

- **Interoperability and two-tier distribution:** The design must respect the existing two-tiered banking system, with central banks issuing the currency and private-sector organisations (banks, payment services providers, digital wallets) handling clearing and settlement, all under the central bank oversight. The system must interoperate with today's financial infrastructure.

These requirements led to the identification of blind signatures as a suitable technical component. As suggested by Chaum (1983; Chaum et al. 2021), blind signatures enable measurable anonymity while upholding legality by disguising the transaction content from the signing authority, thus maintaining the payer's privacy during transaction validation.

3 Human-Centred Design Methodology and Stakeholder Engagement

To ensure a human-centred perspective, the project's design phase heavily emphasised interaction aspects through structured workshops.

3.1 Human-Centred Digital Currency Workshop

A workshop titled 'Human-centred digital currency' was held, inspired by the socio-technical walkthrough method (Herrmann et al. 2004; Herrmann 2009) which uses step-by-step system diagram discussions. Conducted twice with 15 participants (including the central bank, national authorities, commercial banks, and fintechs), the workshop aimed to: (1) facilitate team member interaction, (2) align understanding of the system, (3) refine the digital currency customer journey, and (4) explore human factors from various user perspectives.

In this internal workshop, participants were assigned stakeholder roles (e.g., central bank, financial entity, customer) and used an interactive Miro board to simulate the process of creating, validating, and spending a digital currency. Post-step discussions allowed for critical reflection, clarification of mechanics, and the consideration of alternative approaches.

A critical gap identified was the need for a visual representation of everyday usage scenarios. Visual narrative-driven tools, specifically comics, were adopted to address this. Comics are effective for facilitating communication and conveying complex ideas in a familiar format (Wang et al. 2019; Kang et al. 2021; Haughney 2018), grounding the technical system in a relatable story, such as buying coffee. This story-driven approach successfully shifted the focus toward human-centric issues: the roles of the central bank and vendors, and the process of token minting. The workshop successfully enhanced participants' comprehension of the asset life cycle and stakeholder roles, yielding valuable insights that refined both the technical design of the non-custodial wallet and the overall system.

3.2 *Storytelling and Provotypes Workshop*

The human-centred approach was extended in a second, larger workshop: 'Stories of Central Bank Digital Currency'. Twenty-two participants, encompassing public sector, private sector, and academia, engaged in a multi-stakeholder evaluation. The core goal was to gather feedback on human factors and end-user journeys, specifically gathering requirements for user interaction devices. The workshop was divided into two stages: 'Mapping present-day transaction journeys' and 'Provotypes to elicit user insights and critique'.

3.2.1 Mapping Present-Day Transaction Journeys

The user journey mapping method was employed, which is a creative technique that quickly provides a multi-dimensional understanding of user processes and helps prioritise design concepts (Endmann and Keßner 2019; Marquez et al. 2015; Howard 2014). Participants, divided into six groups, mapped present-day payment scenarios (e.g., supermarket, bureau de change, charity donation) using Post-it notes.

This activity revealed the intricate entanglement of payments with social, political, economic, and personal circumstances. For instance, one scenario involved splitting a supermarket payment between credit card and cash to maintain privacy from a partner. This exercise built shared knowledge and provided deep user insight into complex, everyday payment decisions, bolstering the understanding of the digital currency proposal's contextual requirements.

3.2.2 Provotypes to Elicit User Insights and Critique

Following journey mapping, participants engaged with provotypes (Boer and Donovan 2012), a large-format comic strip illustrating the digital currency user journey and a 3D-printed model of the debit card-style hardware wallet featured in the comic. By applying their insights from existing payment systems to these tangible, narrative-driven representations, participants engaged in self-led, critical discussions, capturing their conversations on Post-it notes applied to the relevant parts of the payment journey. This user-focused approach, integrating technical aspects into a narrative, proved effective in eliciting deep and actionable design insights that guided the refinement of the system's technical requirements and helped identify flaws in initial framing.

4 Designing the Non-custodial Wallet Prototype

Moving from user insights to system delivery, the design drew inspiration from the concept of a wallet as a device historically associated with money. The exploration focused on the distinction between custodial (externally stored, intermediary-handled assets) and non-custodial wallets (stored directly on a user's device, with no intermediation) (Gomzin 2022).

4.1 *Security and Trust Requirements*

As cash is trusted by users, a digital currency must do the same. While traditional payments rely on institutional protections, decentralised digital currency system generally lack these (Borio 2019). Therefore, the digital currency wallet design must provide uncompromising security, privacy, and identity protection, while concurrently supporting regulatory frameworks (like AML) similar to centralised methods.

Achieving privacy by design requires a transaction paradigm shift away from typical four-point pull payments. The goal is to unlink the transacting parties' identities. This can be achieved through blind signatures or zero-knowledge proofs (as used in Zcash and Monero). Crucially, to adhere to legal requirements, the system suggests that the payee (merchant), being more subject to tax and business regulations, should be the party who communicates with the third party for fair exchange, rather than the payer (consumer), who is more susceptible to transaction profiling harm.

The non-custodial approach was chosen because it allows users to transact without an intermediary, supporting core design principles: the wallet must store digital currency information, perform cryptographic functions, and send/receive data.

4.2 *Wallet Design Concepts*

Four distinct non-custodial wallet concepts were developed to explore the balance between security, convenience, and affordability:

1. **The 'I can't believe it is not a phone' wallet:** A phone-like, lightweight, independent device running a light operating system (OS) for core cryptographic functions. **Pros:** Simplifies sophisticated operations (token selection), customisable user interface (UI). **Cons:** High cost (display, computation), requires charging, larger attack surface due to complex OS.
2. **The 'card plus' wallet:** A thin device with no UI, requiring a trusted companion device (e.g., a phone) for operation. **Pros:** Thin, card-portable, can leverage

companion device accessibility features. **Cons:** Requires a companion device, may involve more steps.

3. **The 'final check' wallet:** A hybrid featuring a simple numerical UI for transaction verification when physically plugged into a device. **Pros:** Better security than the 'card plus' (user validates payment on hardware they control), thin, minimal power consumption. **Cons:** Interaction limited to value check and final authorisation.
4. **The 'minimum standalone' wallet:** An upgrade of the 'final check' with a more capable UI, numerical pad, and buttons for verification, allowing payers to select amounts and manage (Fig. 1). **Pros:** Allows choice of payment amount, token selection, recipient identity verification, PIN protection. **Cons:** Larger display requires more thickness and power, potentially necessitating charging.

Experimentation showed the 'minimum standalone' wallet to be the closest match to the requirements, offering the best overall balance of security and user-friendliness, despite a higher cost than the 'card plus'. A simulation of this wallet was created using the Next.js frontend JavaScript framework to test functionality, including withdrawing assets and making a payment. The research stresses that a variety of viable wallet designs is necessary to meet diverse user needs.

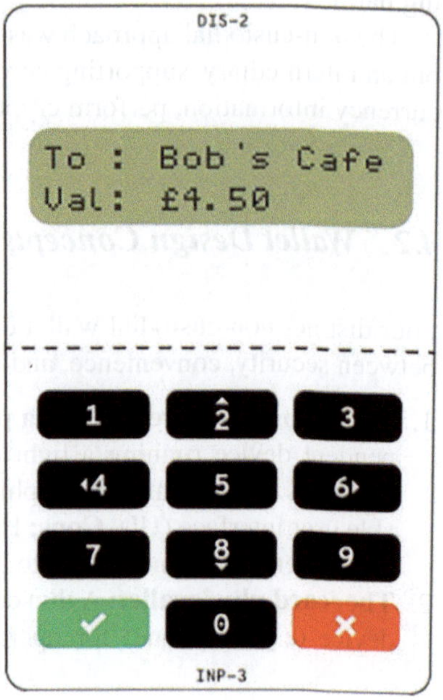

Fig. 1 The 'minimum standalone' wallet. Source: Author

5 Design Takeaways and Future Direction

The exploration of cash provided an essential and crucial starting point for designing a digital currency system in the absence of pre-existing frameworks. The insights gathered are valuable for others entering this space. The following are foundational guidelines derived from this study for establishing a starting point for digital currency systems:

- **Foundation in existing monetary concepts:** Utilise existing concepts of money, particularly the established values and practices of cash, as the initial basis for design requirements.
- **Inclusive stakeholder engagement:** Incorporate the views of a diverse set of stakeholders. Acknowledge the expert-oriented nature of digital currency discourse and employ narrative-driven tools (e.g., comics, metaphors) to convey complex information, ensuring an inclusive design process where experts and non-experts can engage confidently.
- **Envisioning everyday use:** Design should help users envision the technology in everyday scenarios. Focus on the human factors of a digital currency system to ensure the resulting system reflects user values.

6 Future Areas of Work

An aspect that was not included in the scope of the research project was a potential offline capability of a non-custodial wallet. A relevant element of cash is that it can be used without access to the digital infrastructure. Access to mobile and internet connectivity is one of the main shortcomings of current fast payment systems, specifically in emerging economies. Users in remote and dense urban areas face challenges to make payments. This is the case of mobile money in Africa, Pix in Brazil or UPI in India which could be deemed as the most developed and advanced fast payment systems globally. Offline is an area of future work to ensure that a well-designed and robust digital currency system could possess similar capabilities as cash.

A further aspect should be addressed in the design model of a digital currency system is embedding fraud mitigation tools into the customer experience. Emerging technologies such as artificial intelligence could contribute to balance usability, privacy and security, considering the increasing level of fraud, particularly through social engineering, that fast payment system are facing worldwide. Addressing the lack of connectivity and privacy-related security issues challenges of well-adopted fast payment systems is a significant task for central banks and regulators designing and supervising digital currency systems. This is an area that public and private sector collaboration is required to achieve robust and well-designed payment systems.

7 Conclusion

This chapter examined the design of a non-custodial wallet which enables users to store and transact digital currency, including but not limited to CBDC. The design process was informed by established values and practices associated with existing forms of money, particularly cash. To support an inclusive and reflective approach, perspectives from a diverse set of stakeholders, both internal and external to the project team, were incorporated throughout the design process. Narrative-driven methods, including storytelling and the use of metaphors, were employed to enhance the accessibility and intelligibility of digital currency for users. In addition, provotypes were used to elicit user feedback and critical reflection on the proposed digital currency system.

The findings provide a set of foundational design guidelines for digital currency systems, including the need for compatibility with other forms of money, the promotion of accessibility and inclusion, and a careful balancing of technical and social considerations. The study further underscored the importance of safeguarding established forms of money, particularly cash, as a means of preserving flexible payment options and mitigating their potential marginalisation.

Overall, the research demonstrates the innovative potential of digital currency system design to enhance user privacy and security while maintaining usability and expanding the range of payment choices available to individuals. The chapter concludes by encouraging designers to engage critically with the design of money, recognising its significant capacity to shape everyday life.

References

Bacon E (2005) Defining interaction design. Interactions 12(3):34–35

Bauer JM, Herder PM (2009) Designing socio-technical systems. In: Philosophy of technology and engineering sciences. Elsevier, North-Holland, pp 601–630

Baxter G, Sommerville I (2011) Socio-technical systems: from design methods to systems engineering. Interact Comput 23(1):4–17

Boer L, Donovan J (2012) Provotypes for participatory innovation. In: *Proceedings of the designing interactive systems conference*, Madeira, Portugal, from July 5–9, 2025, pp 388–397

Bon A, Akkermans H (2020) Digital (in)equality, digital inclusion, digital humanism: summary of the web science workshop. In: *12th ACM conference on web science companion*, 6–10 July, online, pp 3–5

Borio C (2019) On money, debt, trust, and central banking. Cato J 39:267. Available at: Borio, CEV (2019, January 11) On money, debt, trust and central banking. BIS Working Paper No. 763, Available at SSRN: https://ssrn.com/abstract=3329729

Bryl V, Giorgini P, Mylopoulos J (2009) Designing socio-technical systems: from stakeholder goals to social networks. Requir Eng 14:47–70

Chaum D (1983) Blind signatures for untraceable payments. Adv Cryptol Proc Crypto 82(3):199–203

Chaum D, Grothoff C, Moser T (2021) How to issue a central bank digital currency. Swiss National Bank Working Paper, No. 3/2021. https://www.snb.ch/en/publications/research/working-papers/2021/working_paper_2021_03
Clarkson PJ, Coleman R, Keates S, Lebbon C (2013) Inclusive design: design for the whole population. Published online by the Association for Computing Machinery
Cockton G (2019) Balancing interaction design. In: *Extended abstracts of the 2019 CHI conference on human factors in computing systems*, paper C13, Association for Computing Machinery, New York, NY
Courage C, Baxter K (2005) Understanding your users: a practical guide to user requirements methods, tools, and techniques. Gulf Professional Publishing, San Francisco
Dai J, Miedema J, Hernandez S, Sutton-Lalani A, Moffatt K (2023) Cognitive accessibility of digital payments: a literature review. In: *Proceedings of the 20th International Web for All Conference*, 30 Apr.–1 May 2023, Austin, Texas, United States, pp 116–121
Dardenne A, Van Lamsweerde A, Fickas S (1993) Goal-directed requirements acquisition. Sci Comput Program 20(1–2):3–50
Elsden C, Speed C (2022) Designing new money: creative transactions on twitch. In: *Proceedings of the 2022 design research society conference*, June 25 to July 1, 2022, Bilbao, Spain
Endmann A, Keßner D (2019) User journey mapping — a method in user experience design. I-Com 15(1):105–110
Fischer G (2007) Designing socio-technical environments in support of meta-design and social creativity. In: *Proceedings of the 8th international conference on computer supported collaborative learning*, International Society of the Learning Sciences, Rhodes, Greece, from June 8–13, 2009, pp 2–11
Fischer G, Scharff E (2000) Meta-design: design for designers. In: *Proceedings of the 3rd conference on designing interactive systems: processes, practices, methods, and techniques*, New York City, USA, from August 17–19, 2000. Association for Computing Machinery, New York, NY, pp 396–405
Fischer G, Giaccardi E, Ye Y, Sutcliffe AG, Mehandjiev N (2004) Meta-design: a manifesto for end-user development. Commun ACM 47(9):33–37
Gomzin S (2022) How to choose the wallet. In: Crypto basics: a nontechnical introduction to creating your own money for investors and inventors. Springer, pp 165–182. Apress
Goodell G, Toliver DR, Nakib HD (2023) A scalable architecture for electronic payments. Lect Notes Comput Sci 13412
Goodman E, Stolterman E, Wakkary R (2011) Understanding interaction design practices. In: *Proceedings of the SIGCHI conference on human factors in computing systems*, Boston, Massachusetts, 1983. Association for Computing Machinery, New York, NY, pp 1061–1070
Halloluwa T, Bandara P, Usoof H, Vyas D (2018) Value for money: co-designing with underbanked women from rural Sri Lanka. In: *Proceedings of the 30th Australian Conference on Computer-Human Interaction*, December 4–7, 2018, Australia, pp 63–73
Haughney E (2018) Using comics to communicate qualitative user research findings. In: *CHI '08 extended abstracts on human factors in computing systems*, pp 2209–2212
Herrmann T (2009) The socio-technical walkthrough (STWT): a means of research-oriented intervention into organizations. Sprouts at AIS electronic library (AISeL)
Herrmann T (2014) Revisiting socio-technical system design. In: *Proceedings of the 2014 European conference on cognitive ergonomics*, Vienna, Austria, from September 1st to 3rd, 2014, Association for Computing Machinery, New York, NY
Herrmann T, Kunau G, Loser KU, Menold N (2004) Socio-technical walkthrough: designing technology along work processes. In: *Proceedings of the eighth conference on participatory design: artful integration: interweaving media, materials and practices — volume 1*, July 27–31, 2004, Toronto, Canada, pp 132–141
Howard T (2014) Journey mapping: a brief overview. Commun Des Q Rev 2(3):10–13
Ingham G (1996) Money is a social relation. Rev Soc Econ 54(4):507–529

Kameswaran V, Muralidhar SH (2019) Cash, digital payments and accessibility: a case study from metropolitan India. Proc ACM Hum-Comput Interact 3(CSCW):1–23

Kang D, Ho T, Marquardt N, Mutlu B, Bianchi A (2021) ToonNote: improving communication in computational notebooks using interactive data comics. In: *Proceedings of the 2021 CHI conference on human factors in computing systems*, May 8–13, 2021, online virtual conference (originally Yokohama, Japan) Association for Computing Machinery, New York, NY

Kling R, Lamb R (1999) IT and organizational change in digital economies: a socio-technical approach. ACM SIGCAS Computers and Society 29(3):17–25

Krueger M, Seitz F (2018) Pros and cons of cash: the state of the debate. Credit Capital Mark 51(1):15–40

Maguire M (2014) Socio-technical systems and interaction design—21st century relevance. Appl Ergon 45(2):162–170

Marquez JJ, Downey A, Clement R (2015) Walking a mile in the user's shoes: customer journey mapping as a method to understanding the user experience. Internet Ref Serv Q 20(3–4):135–150

McAndrews JJ (2020) The case for cash. Latin Am J Central Bank 1(1–4):100004

Pommeranz A, Detweiler C, Wiggers P, Jonker C (2013) Elicitation of situated values: need for tools to help stakeholders and designers to reflect and communicate. Ethics Inf Technol 14(4):285–303

Schütz J, Gomez JM (2020) Towards collaborative technical debt management in systems of systems. In: *Proceedings of the 3rd International Conference on Technical Debt*, Seoul Republic of Korea June 28–30, 2020. Association for Computing Machinery, New York, NY, pp 87–91

Thornton L, Knowles B, Blair G (2022) The alchemy of trust: the creative act of designing trustworthy socio-technical systems. In: *Proceedings of the 2022 ACM conference on fairness, accountability, and transparency*, Seoul, South Korea on June 21–24 2022. Association for Computing Machinery, New York, NY, pp 1387–1398

Van Dyke C (1988) Binary jargon: the metaphoric language of computing. ACM SIGCSE Bull 20(3):34–41

Vines J, Blythe M, Dunphy P, Monk A (2012) Eighty something: banking for the older old. In: *Proceedings of the designing interactive systems conference*, July 6–10, 2020, Eindhoven, Netherlands, pp 11–20

Wang Z, Wang S, Farinella M, Murray-Rust D, Riche NH, Bach B (2019) Comparing effectiveness and engagement of data comics and infographics. In: *Proceedings of the 2019 CHI conference on human factors in computing systems*, Glasgow, Scotland, UK, May 04–09, 2019. Association for Computing Machinery, New York, NY, pp 1–12

Ylipulli J, Luusua A, Ojala T (2017) On creative metaphors in technology design: case "magic". In: *Proceedings of the 8th international conference on communities and technologies*, Troyes France, June 26–30, 2017, pp 280–289

From Stability Guardians to Innovation Architects: The Transformation of Monetary Authorities in the Digital Age

Kamila Nigmatulina, Kyeyoung Shin, and Pinar Ozcan

Abstract This chapter delves into how monetary authorities are redefining their traditional roles amid the digital transformation of money. The rise of privately issued digital currencies has reshaped the conventional architecture of monetary systems and challenged the long-term authority of central banks. In response, monetary authorities have begun to transform from stability-oriented regulators into innovation-oriented institutions. Drawing on the cases of the National Bank of Georgia, the National Bank of Kazakhstan, and the Hong Kong Monetary Authority, the chapter shows how central banks have engaged with digital finance experimentation, infrastructure transformation, and institutional redesign. It identifies three distinct strategic responses—maintenance, adaptation, and transformation—through which central banks balance their mandates for monetary stability with the demands for technological modernization. These cases illustrate that innovation within public financial institutions is not only about technology, but also about organizational learning and coordination. By experimenting with central bank digital currencies, digital identity frameworks, regulatory frameworks, and tokenization systems, central banks are not only reacting to disruption but proactively shaping the future monetary order. The chapter thus argues that central banks are becoming key architects of digital financial ecosystems, blending governance, regulation, technology, and trust in novel ways.

Keywords Digital money • Central banks • Institutional change • Financial innovation • Central bank digital currencies (CBDCs) • Stablecoins

K. Nigmatulina (✉) · K. Shin · P. Ozcan
Saïd Business School, University of Oxford, Oxford, UK
e-mail: Kamila.Nigmatulina@sbs.ox.ac.uk; Kyeyoung.Shin.DPHIL@said.oxford.edu; Pinar.Ozcan@sbs.ox.ac.uk

S. Yazıcı et al. (eds.), *Tokenisation of Money*, Contributions to Finance and Accounting, https://doi.org/10.1007/978-3-032-22946-5_22

1 Introduction

Technological advances in cryptography, blockchain architecture, and distributed systems—collectively forming a new layer of digital infrastructure—have opened the way for private sector actors to create novel forms of digital currency. Among the most prominent are highly volatile cryptocurrencies, such as Bitcoin and Ethereum, alongside more value-stable instruments known as stablecoins. A striking illustration is the proposed global stablecoin Libra (later renamed Diem), announced by Facebook but ultimately abandoned in the face of intense regulatory scrutiny.

These innovations have begun to reshape the monetary landscape, disrupting the traditional architecture of money and payments in at least two significant ways. First, they introduce alternative units of account and exchange that compete with state-issued currencies. Second, and more fundamentally, they call into question the institutionalized roles of central banks and other incumbent money issuers, thereby challenging long-standing safeguards for monetary sovereignty and macroeconomic stability. Central banks, which are institutions historically endowed with high legitimacy and a mandate for gradual, stability-oriented change, now find themselves compelled to respond to these external pressures with unprecedented speed and experimentation.

Central banks' traditional mandates to ensure monetary stability and financial safety, coupled with the legitimacy derived from their exclusive authority to issue legal tender, are increasingly being tested by the growing adoption of digital money. Operating largely outside established regulatory regimes, privately issued digital money offers alternative, decentralized mechanisms for the storage and transfer of value. Their rapid diffusion challenges the ability of central banks to safeguard monetary sovereignty and maintain control over payment infrastructures. As digital assets and tokenized forms of value proliferate, central banks have been forced to reconsider their institutional boundaries and technological capabilities. In response, central banks around the world have adopted markedly different approaches. While some have reinforced existing institutional arrangements through prohibition or strict regulation, others have pursued controlled experimentation and innovation. These different responses reflect variation in how central banks interpret and act upon the disruptive rise of private digital money.

In this chapter, we analyze three monetary authorities—the National Bank of Georgia, the National Bank of Kazakhstan, and the Hong Kong Monetary Authority—that have adopted the digital transformation of money as a tool for experimentation and transformation, leading to not only innovative financial products but also new roles, mandates, and functions for central banks. Although central banks in large economies tend to receive more attention in global discussion on digital money, the three cases examined here, which emerged inductively from our broader field study, demonstrate that central banks in small and medium-sized economies can also leverage digital transformation not only to respond to the rise of cryptocurrencies but also to accelerate financial innovation with the aim to strengthen their position within the global monetary system.

Our analysis draws on a multi-year, field-level study examining how central banks around the world have responded to the rise of digital currencies. Drawing on more than 70 in-depth interviews with central bankers, policymakers, technology providers, and industry experts, complemented by extensive field observations at international conferences and closed-door events as well as analyses of hundreds of pages of secondary data from industry report, news articles, blog posts, policy and regulatory documents, compiled over 3 years, we examine the mechanisms through which central banks interpreted and acted upon the emergence of digital currencies. This inductive approach, supported by triangulation across interviews, observations, and archival materials, enabled us to identify distinct patterns in how central banks made sense of a common legitimacy disruption. We show that while the disruption was global, central banks' responses varied markedly and that experimentation and transformation are key examples of strategies that will lead to the long-term transformation of the roles different stakeholders play within financial services.

2 Responding to the Rise of Private Sector-Issued Digital Money

For central banks, the rapid growth of cryptocurrencies, stablecoins, and other forms of privately issued digital money was more than about technical novelty; they represented the emergence of a privately issued, borderless form of money operating outside established regulatory frameworks, serving as a wake-up call to many. This new form of economic activity, typically being outside the control of a central bank, posed a direct threat to central bank authority. The concern emerged that if these new instruments predominated, central banks would risk losing control, undermining the effectiveness of their monetary policy. Such concerns spurred central banks to act, as many realized that they could not remain on the sidelines for long without jeopardizing their relevance and authority in an increasingly digital financial system.

Nonetheless, despite this common threat, central banks varied in how they acted upon it. Our analysis shows that there were three distinct ways in which central banks responded to the rise of cryptocurrencies.

1. *Institutional Maintenance*: reinforcing existing arrangements and actively delegitimizing the source of disruption.
2. *Institutional Adaptation*: selectively incorporating disruptive elements through structured experimentation.
3. *Institutional Transformation*: transforming mandates, roles, and infrastructures to pursue new opportunities and global leadership.

For central banks that engaged in institutional maintenance, cryptocurrencies were primarily a challenge to the moral and political foundations of central bank authority. Institutional maintenance unfolded through three key mechanisms. First, in the discursive realm, central banks engaged in sustained campaigns to delegitimize cryptocurrencies, framing them as inherently flawed and socially harmful. They consistently disseminated messages associating cryptocurrencies with illegality, fraud, and instability. Repeated across public forums and financial literacy campaigns, these narratives discouraged private experimentation and justified subsequent coercive measures. Second, coercive measures reinforced this discursive strategy. Central banks pursuing maintenance, imposed prohibitions or severe restrictions on cryptocurrency issuance, trading, and promotion to align rhetoric with enforcement. These legal boundaries defined the limits of legitimate financial practice, explicitly asserting that trading should be limited to official currencies approved by the central bank. Such prohibitions were aligned with anti–money laundering and counter–terrorism financing objectives and aimed to foreclose the emergence of parallel monetary infrastructures. Finally, boundary policing took the form of selective engagement and strategic exclusion. Central banks actively supported fintech and digital innovation while maintaining a strict "no crypto" stance. They framed CBDCs as a safe and stable alternative, reinforcing their exclusive authority over legitimate money and preserving their traditional role as guardians of stability.

By contrast, central banks characterized by institutional adaptation approached cryptocurrencies with ambivalence, seeing them not as existential dangers but as opportunities for controlled learning. Institutional adaptation often began with structured experimentation in tightly bounded arenas, typically formalized as regulatory sandboxes or technical pilots. Authorities adopted a "learning by doing" approach, authorizing limited trials of blockchain-enabled services within predefined restrictions. These sandboxes functioned as protective shells, enabling observation and learning without triggering systemic exposure. Experiments were structured to align with institutional identity, allowing targeted innovation while safeguarding monetary and regulatory stability. A second adaptation mechanism involved collaboration within deliberately narrow boundaries. Central banks formed partnerships with technology providers, financial institutions, and international bodies to access technical expertise while preserving control. These engagements were temporary and designed to build capacity without requiring a wholesale shift in authority. Such bounded collaborations enabled learning and experimentation while ensuring that central banks remained in the driving seat. Finally, central banks practicing adaptation relied on discursive hedging, explicitly framing pilots as exploratory, gradual, and reversible. This framing allowed central banks to demonstrate responsiveness and learning while ring-fencing their legitimacy and limiting exposure to unforeseen risks.

At the most transformative end of the spectrum, central banks pursuing institutional transformation framed disruption as a catalyst for organizational renewal. Their transformation efforts unfolded through three main mechanisms. First, expanding mandates involved formally redefining roles beyond traditional objectives of monetary and financial stability. Central banks with this approach viewed disruption as an opportunity to reshape central banking. Explicit commitments to financial innovation and ecosystem development legitimized investments in digital currencies and positioned central banks not only as regulators but as orchestrators of innovation ecosystems. Second, innovation was enacted through multilateral pilots that served as norm-shaping exercises. Global initiatives allowed central banks to demonstrate technical competence through iterative agile experiments—moving from prototype to pilot to minimum viable product—while influencing governance norms, interoperability standards, and emerging legal frameworks. These pilots functioned as platforms for translating technical experiments into normative authority and reinforcing leadership in global financial architecture. Third, building foundational infrastructures positioned central banks as indispensable hubs of digital ecosystems. Investments in digital identity systems, tokenization frameworks, and programmable settlement rails embedded their authority within the architecture of digital finance. By constructing publicly governed 'pipes and rails,' central banks ensured that future innovation would remain anchored in trusted public infrastructure.

This divergence in institutional responses shows that while some central banks have adopted defensive postures to preserve established arrangements, others have proactively pursued experimentation and transformation. The latter responses are particularly instructive because they reveal how high-legitimacy public institutions can engage in innovation without undermining their foundational mandate of stability. They highlight the practical dilemmas central banks face as they balance risk aversion with the need for technological renewal, and they offer rare insights into how conservative bureaucracies learn, adapt, and lead in contexts of rapid disruption. These forward-looking responses thus provide a valuable lens for understanding not only the transformation of monetary institutions but also the broader reconfiguration of authority and trust in digital finance.

Achieving such transformations, however, is not without risks or challenges. Innovation can introduce new operational, financial, and governance trade-offs that must be carefully managed:

Operational and Technological Risks The implementation of CBDCs or other innovative infrastructures requires advanced, secure, and highly scalable technological systems. Cybersecurity threats such as hacking incidents or insider breaches could compromise the integrity of national monetary systems. Scalability challenges further complicate issuance and adoption, particularly in large economies where payment volumes and transaction speeds must be compatible with the existing systems. Dependence on private-sector technology providers for key technologies, such as distributed ledger platforms, cloud services, or cryptographic solutions, can create vendor dependency. This dependency may undermine sovereignty and create monetary stability issues.

Risks for the Financial System Central bank innovation is inevitably at the crossroads with societal debates over privacy, market structure, and the role of the state. A CBDC, for instance, can create tension between privacy and surveillance. While citizens may demand anonymity, policymakers and regulators may focus on traceability to combat illicit finance. The introduction of a central bank retail platform could also disrupt the commercial banks. The potential disintermediation may occur if households shift deposits away from private banks toward CBDCs.

Governance Challenge Interoperability between different digital currencies and payment infrastructures remains a technical and regulatory challenge. In addition, digital currencies may provoke stronger geopolitical competition, potentially reshaping the balance of monetary power.

In the following section, we examine three central banks that interpreted the rise of cryptocurrencies as an opportunity for institutional change. These cases are particularly instructive because they show how high-legitimacy public institutions can navigate technological disruption in ways that build new capabilities and reshape their roles. As technological disruptions intensify, public institutions increasingly face systemic risks such as the ones outlined above yet must still safeguard stability and trust. While there may be many possible responses to such pressures, the three cases we focus on offer especially insightful lessons, highlighting how other high-legitimacy public institutions, such as regulators and public agencies, can respond to emerging technologies in ways that remain anchored in their core mandates while also advancing innovation in the public interest.

3 Case 1: National Bank of Georgia

3.1 *The Middle Corridor, Fintech Strategy, and the National Bank of Georgia*

The National Bank of Georgia (NBG) demonstrates an illustrative case of a central bank—a key decision-maker and regulator of the financial system—that has embraced the digital transformation of financial services as an opportunity to create a platform for digital finance experimentation. The NBG is the central bank of Georgia, which was created in 1991, though the first central bank, the State Bank of Georgia, existed in 1919(National Bank of Georgia, n.d.-a). The NBG works across eight key areas: ensuring price stability, supervision for financial stability, issuance of money, management of international reserves, protecting consumer rights, promoting the development of the securities market, and fostering the development of payment systems(National Bank of Georgia, n.d.-b). The NBG also represents Georgia in international financial arenas. In addition to these traditional roles, NBG plays a unique role as a generator of innovative projects and ideas, enabling competition within the local financial sector. The Georgian commercial banking sector is highly concentrated, creating high barriers to entry for smaller players, such as fintech organizations, which makes competition with large traditional banks challenging. Georgia has 14 commercial banks, three digital banks, and two microbanks, all of which are privately owned. After a period of consolidation, the two largest banking groups make up more than three-quarters of total assets. That is why, in the era of rapid digitization of financial services, the NBG became a facilitator of digital finance experimentation, enabling diversity among stakeholders.

Another strategic driver behind NBG's strategy of digital finance experimentation is the unique position of Georgia within the Middle Corridor—a key transport route connecting Europe and Asia through Kazakhstan, Azerbaijan, Georgia, and Türkiye (National Bank of Georgia, 2025). The key efforts of the NBG within the Middle Corridor expansion are, first, to facilitate trade as a major trade route by increasing economic ties between Asia and Europe. Second, expand the country's role as a financial hub by positioning it as a fintech regional hub for the Middle Corridor countries, attracting investors to support the Middle Corridor's growth. These key efforts are the pillars of the NBG's Fintech Strategy of Georgia (National Bank of Georgia, 2025). That prioritizes the development of modern financial infrastructure, promotes responsible innovation and competition, and supports cross-border collaboration and integration.

The Digital Lari (D-Gel) experimentation pilot, which represents the Georgian retail CBDC, and the tokenized deposits project, which is part of the Regulatory Sandbox, are key examples of how the NBG facilitated digital finance experimentation in the country, onboarding other public and private sector organizations in the process.

3.2 *Digital Finance Experimentation: Digital Lari (D-Gel)*

The NBG has been actively researching CBDCs since mid-2020 as a technology-driven innovation in the digital money space, demonstrating how smart contracts, programmability, and tokenization can be applied in financial services. The Financial and Supervisory Technology Development, responsible for facilitating innovative projects within the NBG, led this pilot following a bottom-up, CBDC-as-a-platform approach to its implementation. The bottom-up approach to the CBDC pilot was chosen to address the local needs of the Georgian financial services sector; this approach also enabled the testing of use cases specific to local needs and those that will be relevant to the country in the longer term.

The NBG also understood from the very beginning that the complexity of CBDC implementation as a critical technology infrastructure project requires a modular, learning-by-doing approach to allow flexibility around design features and functionalities of local CBDC. Moreover, the team recognized that the complexity of this type of project also includes the legal aspects involving other public sector organizations, such as the Parliament, to initiate changes to the regulatory frameworks, thereby enabling the CBDC to be recognized as a legal tender. Therefore, after the research stage was finalized and potential areas for D-Gel pilot identified, the decision was made to find an external technology partner not only to provide the technology for the pilot but also to work on developing and advancing the locally focused use cases of D-Gel. This collaboration led to testing specific use cases with other stakeholders. These include payroll denominated in D-Gel, minting and releasing commemorative tokens, the acquisition of real estate using automated settlement with D-Gel, and tokenization of government retail bonds. With the payroll use case involving volunteer employees, the NBG aimed to test paying a fraction of the compensation using automated, event-triggered transactions when the NBG's payroll wallet automatically initiated a transaction. The tokenization of a government bond use case aimed to understand how this capital market instrument can be tokenized and stimulate growth in the P2P secondary market in the future. The role of D-Gel is to serve as the designated digital currency sent to bondholders, as yield is automatically distributed from the issuer's wallet. The pilot stage of D-Gel was finalized in February 2025, and a decision on the next steps will be announced after a detailed analysis of the pilot results.

Strategic Learnings: Internal Adaptation and External Coordination

The case of D-Gel demonstrates how the NBG balanced two main strategies, allowing the regulator to test and experiment with critical digital money infrastructure while minimizing the risks associated with this type of experimentation: internal adaptation and external coordination.

Internal adaptation is a strategic approach that enabled the NBG to interpret the digital transformation of money as an opportunity to experiment and, consequently, to transform itself in the first place. One of the key pillars of this approach is learning and knowledge capacity building within the central bank itself. The establishment of the Financial and Supervisory Technology Development as a special team dedicated to observing the technological transformation is an example of structural internal adaptation. Another example is the launch of the Innovation Office in 2020.

The process of capacity building varies from traditional desk research on new developments to constant knowledge transfer between teams (for example, an online group where Finance and Technology team members share their insights and answer questions about innovation and technology from other team members). Other mechanisms include the 'learning-by-doing' and modular approaches towards pilots, meaning that pilots are governance experiments, not only tech tests, and should be approached with an open mind to surface legal, operational, and supervisory questions, moving from small-scale and scoped use cases towards larger-scale projects without exposing the general financial system to systemic risks.

External coordination with critical stakeholders is the key strategy of the NBG to transition from the research phase of new technology-driven innovation to the testing and pilot phases. The stakeholders involved in the financial system are not always aligned in their motivations, interpretations, and levels of reward, particularly in cases where experimentation yields unclear outcomes. Therefore, the NBG played the role of a coordinator of these diverse stakeholders.

The coordination mechanisms include careful selection of a technology partner as a provider of key technology infrastructure and educator of how these technologies can be applied to financial services. The NBG's efforts to educate commercial banks, fintech providers, and other public sector organizations on how they can benefit from CBDC use cases are another example of external coordination. The NBG's educational efforts included presentations, workshops, and roundtables with stakeholders; they also involved constant collaboration and flexibility in approaching use cases to create the most positive impact for stakeholders, both in terms of increasing their revenue streams and improving the efficiency of their business models.

3.3 *Digital Finance Experimentation: Tokenized Deposits Project*

The experience of the D-Gel pilot inspired the NBG to launch in February 2025 the tokenized deposit and certificates of deposit project to allow financial institutions to test innovative products under supervision. This project was launched as part of the Regulatory Sandbox. For the NBG, it is an opportunity to leverage the strategies applied during the D-Gel pilot and to monitor, observe, and understand the key mechanisms, benefits for consumers, risks, and opportunities of tokenized deposits in a controlled environment. Additionally, this initiative may facilitate the development of new financial products, enhance the diversity of the local financial services ecosystem, and establish a secondary market for certificates of deposit. The initiative also aims to raise financial awareness, stimulate commercial banks to adopt new technologies, and optimize the costs and risks associated with the introduction of new technology. The current stage of the project is the invitation stage, which focuses on receiving applications from the brokerage companies and commercial banks.

While the Digital Lari pilot demonstrated how the central bank might transform its role into the issuer of a digital form of money while still playing a role of key regulator of financial services, the tokenized deposit project, in turn, is an initiative that makes the NBG a provider of a controlled environment for financial services providers, who in turn, will create new products. This project is also the next step towards a deeper exploration of blockchain technology under regulatory oversight. It will enable the refinement of insights gained from the CBDC pilot project, further enhancing the understanding of potential blockchain applications in financial services.

The NBG work extends beyond the supervision of these projects; the team from the Financial and Supervisory Department actively participates in spreading awareness of general fintech transformations and educating other stakeholders on more specific developments. For example, the department produced TV programs about current fintech trends and projects in Georgia, as well as partnered with 10 × 1000 Tech for Inclusion, a global educational platform (co-founded by the IFC and Ant Group) that focuses on training a new generation of tech specialists.

3.4 Key Takeaways

The case of the NBG's approach to the rise of digital money is an illustrative example of how a traditional and incumbent organization makes sense of the digital transformation of money as an opportunity to initiate digital finance experimentation. Two key projects from this experimentation strategy (the D-Gel pilot and the tokenized deposit project) illustrate how the NBG was able to balance its key mandate of financial stability provider with the role of experimentation facilitator. Through a careful *internal adaptation strategy* that included knowledge building, leadership support, and educational instruments, the NBG successfully aligned the different teams within the central banks to support experimentation with both D-Gel and the tokenized deposits project. Internal resistance within organizations is recognized as a critical factor that can hinder or completely halt innovation experimentation within organizations. Simultaneously, the NBG, leveraging its role as a trusted regulator and central bank, worked efficiently in coordinating with external stakeholders using a phased approach to onboarding them into the projects and educating them about the opportunities that experimentation with next-generation technologies can bring to their organizations. Additionally, the NBG recognized that digital currencies and their underlying technologies could be a key pillar to leverage their position within the Middle Corridor and transform into a regional financial hub.

4 Case 2: National Bank of Kazakhstan

4.1 The National Bank of Kazakhstan and the Formation of the National Payment Corporation

The National Bank of Kazakhstan (NBK) is a case of a central bank that approached the rise of digital currencies as an *opportunity* to transform financial services through testing and integrating digital currencies within the broader projects of the country's digitization of public infrastructure. The Digital Tenge—the country's local CBDC—is the key project of this experimentation.

The NBK is the Central Bank of the Republic of Kazakhstan and represents the upper (first tier) of the country's banking system. The NBK was established in 1993 with the key task to modernize how the interbank payment system worked, and the national currency (tenge) was introduced the same year[1](National Bank of Kazakhstan, n.d.-a). The NBK's key functions span across four areas: developing and conducting the monetary policy, contributing to the stability of the monetary system, ensuring the functioning of the payment system, and statistics

[1] https://nationalbank.kz/en/page/currency-history

activities[2](National Bank of Kazakhstan, n.d.-b). The NBK approach to fulfilling these tasks embraces the critical role of technology for financial system stability in the long term—a brief overview of the current numbers shows that the pace of digitization of financial services in Kazakhstan is rapid, the share of cashless payment in the total number of transactions reached 86–87% in 2024, and mobile banking is used by more than 81% of the population. The private sector digital payment systems (e.g., Halyk Bank super app) enable the platform for customers to make a variety of everyday payments.

The NBK understood the importance of researching new technological developments relevant to financial services a long time ago. In 2013, Kazakhstan established the Kazakhstan Interbank Settlement Center (KISC) to facilitate transactions between banks and enhance the overall efficiency of the banking system. Over time, the primary purpose of this entity shifted to research and development of payment system technologies, as well as prototyping. Additionally, being created as a separate entity, the teams were able to work in a fast-paced and agile environment, which allowed them to learn and prototype more quickly than they would have if they were part of the NBK, a larger and more bureaucratic entity. Therefore, the teams of this organization closely followed the growth of digital money and emerging use cases that they perceived as relevant to local settings (e.g., a large-scale CBDC pilot in China, Kazakhstan's trade partner). In 2023, the KISC was reorganized and transformed into the Joint Stock Company National Payment Corporation of the National Bank of the Republic of Kazakhstan (NPC or NPCK), which is owned by the NBK. This strategic move of reorganization and spinning out this entity is to facilitate more research and experimentation with digital finance. Being a separate entity enabled more financial and administrative freedom internally to implement fundamentally new projects. This organization became the national provider of payment systems and digital finance infrastructure in Kazakhstan, continuing the pathway of transformation through research and experimentation with digital money.

In addition, in 2020–2022, the NBK developed country-level strategies to promote digital payments and the national financial infrastructure, including the Development of the Financial Sector of the Republic of Kazakhstan until 2030, the Strategic Roadmap for Fintech and Innovation for 2020–2025, and the National Payment System Development Strategy. These strategies outlined the stages of digital financial infrastructure as a key step in implementing the national financial infrastructure. As part of this implementation, the NBK launched the biometric identification service, Identification Data Exchange Center (IDEC), in 2020 (during the COVID-19 pandemic). The primary purpose of IDEC is to facilitate proper customer due diligence procedures by financial market participants when providing services remotely, while ensuring the security of citizens' personal data. The system is unique compared to similar solutions in other countries because it verifies a client's biometric data (photo) against information stored in the State Databases (SDB) and enables financial institutions to conduct remote customer identification. The

[2] https://nationalbank.kz/en/page/o-nacionalnom-banke

SDB is directly connected to several government databases, ensuring the accuracy of data and maintaining regular updates. The IDEC enabled commercial banks to streamline the customer onboarding process and expedite the approval of not only small loans but also mortgages and car loans.

4.2 *Embracing Transformation: Digital Tenge*

The Digital Tenge project was announced by the NBK in 2021 as a potential third form of the national currency of Kazakhstan, alongside cash and its digital form. There were several motivations behind this project, similar to other countries, including payment system efficiency and financial inclusion; however, the NBK and the NPCK understood that the Digital Tenge's role is significant in the country's attempt to develop DPI and national digital financial infrastructure, which is far beyond just a cashless payment instrument.

While the NBK is the issuer of the Digital Tenge, the NPCK is the operator of the system, researching, developing, and testing use cases, as well as coordinating with internal and external stakeholders. In 2023, the NPCK conducted a limited pilot involving real transactions, including person-to-person transfers and merchant payments, with participation from commercial banks and major payment providers. One of the most interesting use cases was the launch of a pilot project of "digital vouchers" for free meals in schools and the world's first bank cards linked to a digital account in Digital Tenge with Visa, Mastercard, and local commercial banks[3](National Payment Corporation of Kazakhstan, 2025). In 2024 there was a shift of the focus to experiment with use cases with the involvement of the state, a shift that showed the broader strategy of incorporating Digital Tenge into the national digital finance infrastructure and test how Digital Tenge can be integrated with the government funds (the National fund) provision. Digital funds were used to finance infrastructure projects such as the construction of railways and gas pipelines. Digital VAT testing demonstrated how Digital Tenge integration can enhance the efficiency and transparency of VAT administration, as well as speed up the tax refund process.

Strategic Learnings: Organizational Segmentation and Adaptive Experimentation

The case of Digital Tenge demonstrates how two main strategies —*organizational segmentation* and *adaptive experimentation* —were balanced to test how digital currencies can become an integral part of digital infrastructure.

Organizational segmentation is a key strategy chosen by the NBK to balance responsibilities between the NBK and the NPCK. Given the previous positive experience with the KISC, it allowed the NBK to safeguard the agile, fast-paced culture of the NPCK, reduce the bureaucratic hurdles for new projects, attract more

[3] https://npck.kz/wp-content/uploads/2025/07/Digital_Tenge_Report_2024_ENG-2.pdf

financial resources, and attract the best talent and skills to initiate experimentation. While the NBK as a legal issuer of the Digital Tenge was actively involved in the general development of the key aspects of the project such as the model of CBDC, types of use cases and necessary future changes in the legislation, all other aspects of the testing phase such as onboarding of stakeholders, educational work, technological elements and operating of the CBDC platform were implemented by the NPCK's team.

Adaptive experimentation by the NPCK for the Digital Tenge project is a strategy based on three pillars. First, the phased onboarding of key stakeholders—one illustrative example is the careful selection of a technology partner to allow for flexible experimentation and avoid the lock-in effect. The phased approach also provides time and resources for continuous collaboration with stakeholders through workshops, meetings, sandboxes, and idea brainstorming. Second, a holistic approach to Digital Tenge as an integral part of the national digital infrastructure. Third, continuous knowledge creation of the Digital Tenge value proposition. As a shift in 2024 from use cases focused on retail payments to those relevant to government funds, it demonstrated that Digital Tenge was tested not as a final product with fixed characteristics but as a tool to address specific challenges that can evolve over time.

4.3 Key Takeaways

The NBK pursued the transformative pathway through the *strategic organizational segmentation* of roles and tasks with the NPCK, which preserved the innovation culture of the NPCK. In addition, the NBK's initiation of the IDEC project enabled the more holistic interpretation of Digital Tenge as an integral part of the national digital infrastructure. The NPCK, through *adaptive experimentation*, advanced Digital Tenge testing beyond early-stage pilots toward integration into the national financial infrastructure, exploring how digital currency can be used as both a policy tool and a technological and institutional innovation.

5 Case 3: Hong Kong Monetary Authority

The Hong Kong Monetary Authority (HKMA), operating in one of the world's most globally connected financial hubs, has faced both the opportunities and pressures of rapid fintech transformation. The growth of cryptocurrencies, stablecoins, and tokenized assets posed not only a technical challenge but also a legitimacy test for Hong Kong's financial architecture. In response, the HKMA began extending its role into digital finance experimentation and infrastructure development. The HKMA thus represents a case of institutional transformation, characterized by both internal reconfiguration and external orchestration.

5.1 *Internal Reconfiguration: Expanding Mandates and Institutional Renewal*

Internally, the HKMA sought to integrate innovation more explicitly into its mandate and organizational design. The "Fintech 2025" strategy (HKMA 2021), announced in June 2021, signaled a significant shift. Aimed at ensuring that all banks in Hong Kong 'go Fintech' by 2025 and at preparing the jurisdiction for CBDC development, the strategy broadened the Authority's objectives from regulatory oversight to facilitating technological modernization.

To operationalize this vision, the HKMA created the Fintech Facilitation Office (FFO) to coordinate initiatives across government, industry, and academia. The FFO's function as a central coordination unit enabled structured engagement with financial institutions and technology firms in controlled settings. Complementing this, the CBDC Expert Group brought together academics and industry experts to examine technical and policy issues surrounding digital currencies. These arrangements helped the HKMA build internal expertise and establish decision processes for assessing innovation-related risks.

This internal reconfiguration also served to mitigate several categories of risk identified earlier in the chapter. Pilot projects and research partnerships were used to test emerging technologies on a small scale before implementation, reducing technological and operational risks. The diversification of partnerships and the development of in-house knowledge reduced dependence on external technology vendors, thereby limiting vendor lock-in and preserving institutional autonomy.

5.2 *External Orchestration: Experimentation, Collaboration, and Ecosystem Building*

Externally, the HKMA has combined experimentation with international collaboration to engage with the digital finance transition while maintaining oversight and control.

Project mBridge illustrates this approach. Conducted jointly with the Bank for International Settlements (BIS) Innovation Hub, the People's Bank of China, the Bank of Thailand, the Central Bank of the United Arab Emirates, and the Saudi Central Bank, the project explores using multiple CBDCs on a shared platform for real-time cross-border payments. The HKMA chaired the project's legal subcommittee and contributed to the design of governance, compliance, and risk management frameworks. This emphasis on legal and regulatory design helped mitigate governance and interoperability risks by ensuring that the technical system incorporated jurisdictional safeguards and anti-money laundering standards. By participating in such multilateral projects, the HKMA engaged in the collective development of standards that may shape the emerging cross-border CBDC environment.

At the domestic level, Project Aurum, which is a collaboration between the HKMA, the BIS Innovation Hub, and the Hong Kong Applied Science and Technology Research Institute, examines the design of a potential retail CBDC (the e-HKD). The project's two-tier architecture separates wholesale settlement from retail distribution, which helps prevent financial system risks such as bank disintermediation. Privacy and traceability are balanced through tiered identity requirements that permit law enforcement access without eliminating user confidentiality. By conducting these tests in a controlled environment, the HKMA could evaluate operational resilience and cybersecurity issues before considering broader implementation.

The Authority's Project Ensemble, launched in 2024, extends this experimentation to the domain of tokenized assets. The initiative aims to develop a wholesale CBDC platform to support settlement of tokenized securities and to strengthen the region's financial-market infrastructure. The project's Architecture Community, which comprises commercial banks, technology firms, universities, and regulators, co-creates technical standards and workflows. This collaborative governance model disperses technological and operational responsibilities while maintaining the HKMA's supervisory role, thereby reducing systemic concentration risks and embedding oversight into the infrastructure itself.

These projects illustrate how the HKMA manages the trade-off between innovation and control. Cross-border initiatives such as mBridge address coordination and interoperability challenges, while domestic pilots like Aurum provide controlled settings for learning. Infrastructure programs such as Ensemble anchor experimentation within publicly governed rails. Each activity layer serves as a mechanism for managing the uncertainties associated with technological change while maintaining coherence with the Authority's statutory objectives.

5.3 *Key Takeaways*

The HKMA's journey shows how a monetary authority in a global financial hub can engage in digital money experimentation while preserving its traditional commitment to stability and trust. Its initiatives exemplify institutional innovation through the gradual extension of mandates, creation of new coordination structures, and participation in international standard-setting.

The monetary authority has used experimentation to clarify boundaries and develop institutional capacity. Its actions reveal a pragmatic orientation: learning through controlled pilots, embedding governance mechanisms early in technological design, and maintaining a clear division between exploratory projects and formal policy adoption. These measures help mitigate the operational, systemic, and governance risks associated with digital currencies.

At the same time, the HKMA's experience underscores the continuing tension facing monetary authorities globally: as they expand their roles into areas of development and oversight of frontier technologies and ecosystem coordination, they must continually balance the pursuit of innovation with the need to preserve public trust and monetary authority. The HKMA's case illustrates one possible configuration of this balance: an incremental yet coordinated approach that integrates innovation into the institutional fabric of central banking while preserving its fundamental role in maintaining stability.

6 Conclusion

Central banks are no longer merely reactive regulators seeking to preserve stability; they are increasingly proactive innovators shaping the architecture of the digital monetary future. The three cases examined in this chapter show that the rise of digital money is transforming their role from guardians of price stability to designers of new financial infrastructures. Across Georgia, Kazakhstan, and Hong Kong, we observed several common mechanisms at work, including building internal capabilities, experimenting in controlled environments, coordinating diverse stakeholders in the financial ecosystem, and embedding new governance frameworks in line with the evolving landscape. These cases show how institutional change takes place in practice.

The three cases illustrate that institutional responses to digital money are not discrete, one-off decisions but dynamic, multidimensional processes that unfold across both internal and external domains. Internally, central banks must build new organizational capabilities, which involve developing technical expertise, collaborating with cross-functional teams, and, when necessary, reshaping organizational structures to support experimentation and learning. These internal adjustments allow monetary authorities to reinterpret their mandates and innovate. Externally, central banks must coordinate with a broader range of stakeholders, including new actors such as stablecoin issuers, to align incentives, co-create foundational infrastructures, and ensure interoperability. Across the strategic pathways identified in this chapter (institutional maintenance, adaptation, and transformation), central banks' ability to navigate digital money disruption depends on how effectively they manage the dual processes of internal reconfiguration and external orchestration.

The three cases also show that the implications for monetary policy and financial stability surface through the choices that central banks make as they experiment with digital money. The pilots examined—such as Georgia's programmable retail CBDC, Kazakhstan's tokenized settlement rails, and Hong Kong's cross-border payment platforms—demonstrate that digital infrastructures can reshape monetary influence and oversight. As central banks gain greater direct visibility into how liquidity flows through payment systems, their capacity to read the economy and act on it is significantly enhanced. At the same time, new forms of money and new types of market participants expose new dimensions of financial stability. Programmable money changes how quickly funds move, and tokenized instruments blur the boundaries between markets and payments. Meanwhile, greater reliance on private-sector technology providers means they become part of the core financial plumbing, which could introduce a variety of operational and cybersecurity risks from a stability perspective. These shifts underscore that engaging with digital money requires monetary authorities to rethink how policy tools function and how systemic risks are monitored and mitigated in a programmable financial environment.

Ultimately, the long-term success of central banks' innovation efforts will depend on their ability to balance their traditional mandate of ensuring financial stability with the need to respond to rapid technological innovation. Money can be understood as a public good, whose credibility rests on trust, and innovation can either erode that trust if pursued prematurely or reinforce it if pursued with institutional clarity. How effectively central banks manage this balance will shape whether they remain passive observers of technological change or become central architects of the evolving monetary landscape.

References

Hong Kong Monetary Authority (2021, June 8). *The HKMA unveils "Fintech 2025" strategy*. Retrieved October 05, 2025, from https://www.hkma.gov.hk/eng/news-and-media/press-releases/2021/06/20210608-4/

National Bank of Georgia (2025, May). *Fintech development strategy*. Retrieved September 16, 2025, from https://nbg.gov.ge/en/page/fintech-development-strategy

National Bank of Georgia. (n.d.-a). *About the Bank*. Retrieved September 16, 2025, from https://nbg.gov.ge/en/page/about-the-bank

National Bank of Georgia. (n.d.-b). *What we do*. Retrieved September 16, 2025, from https://nbg.gov.ge/en/page/what-we-do

National Bank of Kazakhstan. (n.d.-a). *History of the national currency*. Retrieved October 01, 2025, from https://nationalbank.kz/en/page/currency-historynationalbank.kz

National Bank of Kazakhstan. (n.d.-b). *About the National Bank*. Retrieved October 01, 2025, from https://nationalbank.kz/en/page/o-nacionalnom-banke

National Payment Corporation of Kazakhstan (2025, July). Digital Tenge Report 2024 (2nd ed.). Retrieved October 02, 2025, from https://npck.kz/wp-content/uploads/2025/07/Digital_Tenge_Report_2024_ENG-2.pdf

Global Digital Money Landscape: Current Developments Over the World

Public and Private Developments Around the World

Mehmet Kerse

Abstract This paper examines the evolving landscape of tokenized money, focusing on public and private sector developments around Central Bank Digital Currencies (CBDCs), stablecoins, and tokenized deposits. It highlights how central banks across more than 130 countries are accelerating CBDC research and deployment, including in China and India, for diverse motivations including improving payment efficiency, monetary policy and financial inclusion.

In parallel, the rise of stablecoins has prompted new regulatory frameworks, including the European Union's Markets-in-crypto assets (MiCA) regulation, the proposed regulation of the Financial Conduct Authority (FCA) of the United Kingdom, and the GENIUS Act of the United States, each addressing consumer protection, asset backing, and reserve transparency, among others.

Furthermore, the study discusses the tokenization of assets and money, through initiatives like Project Agorá of Bank for International Settlements, JP Morgan's deposit token, and Singapore's Project Guardian —illustrating how tokenization has the potential to reshape cross-border payments and market infrastructures. The paper concludes that the convergence of CBDCs, stablecoins, and tokenized deposits signals a hybrid monetary future defined by interoperability, regulatory clarity, and public-private collaboration.

Keywords Stablecoins • CBDC • Tokenization • Digital currency • Tokenized deposits • Digital money • Financial regulation • Central banks • MiCA • GENIUS Act

M. Kerse (✉)
Regulation and Policy for Digital Innovation, Frankfurt, Germany

S. Yazıcı et al. (eds.), *Tokenisation of Money*, Contributions to Finance and Accounting, https://doi.org/10.1007/978-3-032-22946-5_23

1 Introduction

The concept of money is undergoing one of its most profound transformations since the advent of electronic payments. Technological innovation—driven by advances in distributed ledger technology (DLT), cryptography, and digital finance—has enabled the creation of new forms of money that exist natively in programmable, tokenized form. These innovations challenge traditional notions of value transfer and settlement, prompting both public and private sectors to explore new digital money instruments. Among these, Central Bank Digital Currencies (CBDCs), stablecoins, and tokenized deposits have emerged as the three forms of tokenized money having the potential to reshape the global financial landscape.

While cryptoassets first demonstrated the technical feasibility of digital currencies, their volatility and lack of regulatory oversight limited their use as reliable means of payment. In response, many policymakers, regulators and market participants have turned their attention toward tokenized representations of sovereign and regulated money. Central banks have intensified research and pilot programs for CBDCs, motivated by goals such as enhancing payment efficiency, preserving monetary sovereignty, and improving financial inclusion. Simultaneously, the private sector has accelerated the issuance of stablecoins and the development of tokenized deposit frameworks, each seeking to combine the efficiency of DLT with the stability of fiat-backed reserves or traditional bank liabilities.

The convergence of these developments reflects a broader shift toward the tokenization, where digital representations of money and assets can be exchanged seamlessly across interoperable networks. However, this transformation also raises critical policy questions regarding financial stability, regulatory consistency, consumer protection, and the future architecture of the monetary system. How should digital forms of money coexist and interoperate? What governance and compliance frameworks are required to safeguard trust and resilience in a tokenized economy?

This section examines these questions by analyzing global developments in CBDCs, stablecoins, and tokenized deposits. It explores how governments, regulators (e.g., central banks), and private institutions are approaching the tokenization of money through distinct yet increasingly interconnected pathways. By discussing regulatory initiatives such as the EU's Markets in Crypto-Assets (MiCA) regulation, the UK's proposed stablecoin regime, and the US GENIUS Act, alongside projects such as the BIS's Project Agorá, JP Morgan's Deposit Token, and Singapore's Project Guardian, the study situates these efforts within a broader context of digital money innovation. Ultimately, it argues that the future of money is likely to be hybrid—defined by interoperability, shared standards, and collaboration between the public and private sectors.

2 Developments on CBDC Around the Globe

CBDC is a new form of fiat currency. Unlike most innovations in the financial sector, it is not led by private-sector but is instead a central bank response to private--sector innovations—cryptoassets in particular. CBDCs are classified into two types: (i) wholesale CBDC and (ii) retail CBDC. A key difference between retail CBDCs and existing cashless payment instruments (e.g., e-money, credit transfer, direct debit, card payments) is that a CBDC represents a direct claim on a central bank, rather than a liability of a private financial services provider (FSP). Retail CBDCs can be further segmented into one-tier or two-tier models, depending on the role of intermediaries (e.g., banks, e-money issuers, payment service providers) in their distribution (Kerse et al. 2024).

According to Atlantic Council's CBDC tracker as of July 2025, more than 130 countries—representing 98% of global GDP—are exploring CBDCs. In May 2020, that number was only 35. Currently, 72 countries are in the advanced stages of exploration (i.e., development, pilot, or launch). Three countries have fully launched a digital currency—the Bahamas, Jamaica, and Nigeria. All three countries are focused on expanding the reach of their CBDCs domestically (Atlantic Council 2025).

When it comes to retail CBDC, many countries are piloting (e.g., Ghana, China, India), while others remain in the exploration phase (e.g., Indonesia, Peru, Thailand). Some jurisdictions have already conducted proofs of concepts or developed prototypes (e.g., Euro Area, UAE, Hong Kong). On the other hand, as of July 2025, 20 central banks have launched, piloted or done proof-of-concept work on DLT based wholesale CBDC (Kiff 2025).

One of the central banks working on CBDC is the Central Bank of the United Arab Emirates (CBUAE). It is developing the Digital Dirham for retail, wholesale, and cross-border payments. Operated through a two-tier model, the Digital Dirham will be distributed by licensed financial institutions such as banks, exchange houses, and payment service providers, as well as fintechs holding stored-value facility licenses. It will use a hybrid, wallet-based access system and operate as an unremunerated, tiered CBDC with appropriate user limits. The CBUAE will also develop bilateral and multilateral CBDC arrangements to facilitate cross-border payments and offshore holdings of the Digital Dirham. As part of the first phase of implementation, the CBUAE demonstrated that multi-CBDC platforms can improve the efficiency of cross-border payments. With increasing trade and capital flows between the UAE and other markets—particularly within the MENA region—the Digital Dirham's potential for facilitating cross-border transactions is gaining growing policy and market interest (CBUAE 2025). China's digital yuan (e-CNY) remains the world's largest CBDC pilot. By June 2024, total transaction volume reached 7 trillion e-CNY (US$986 billion) across 17 provincial regions and sectors such as education, healthcare, and tourism. This was nearly four times the 1.8 trillion yuan

(US$253 billion) recorded by the People's Bank of China in June 2023. India's e-rupee is now the second-largest CBDC pilot. The digital rupee in circulation rose to ₹10.16 billion (US$122 million) by March 2025, a 334% increase from ₹2.34 billion (US$28 million) in 2024. In 2025, the Reserve Bank of India is expanding both retail and wholesale CBDC pilots with new use cases, offline functionality, and broader participation.[1]

One major wholesale CBDC initiative is Project mBridge, a multi-CBDC platform designed to facilitate real-time, peer-to-peer cross-border payments and FX transactions using wholesale CBDCs. It operates on a purpose-built permissioned blockchain—the mBridge Ledger—which incorporates jurisdiction-specific legal, regulatory, and governance requirements. The project began in 2021 through collaboration between the BIS Innovation Hub, the Bank of Thailand, the Central Bank of the United Arab Emirates, the Digital Currency Institute of the People's Bank of China and the Hong Kong Monetary Authority. The Saudi Central Bank joined in 2024. The project seeks to address some of the key inefficiencies in cross-border payments, including high costs, low speed, and operational complexities. It also aims to improve financial inclusion, particularly in jurisdictions where correspondent banking has declined, leading to higher costs and delays. Multi-CBDC arrangements that connect different jurisdictions through a single common technical infrastructure have the potential to improve the current system and make cross-border payments immediate, low-cost, and universally accessible with final settlement (BIS 2024).

Several central banks are participating as observing members in Project mBridge, including the Bank of France, the Central Bank of Türkiye, the National Bank of Kazakhstan, the Federal Reserve Bank of New York (New York Innovation Center), and the Reserve Bank of Australia. Recently, the BIS handed operational responsibility for the platform over to the central banks of China, Hong Kong, Saudi Arabia, Thailand, and the UAE (BIS 2024b).

Many central banks considering CBDC issuance believe it could enhance payments efficiency, reduce costs, and improve financial inclusion. In emerging markets and developing economies (EMDEs), financial inclusion is often cited as the primary motivation for CBDC development (Auer et al. 2022). However, early retail CBDC launches—such as in Nigeria and the Bahamas—have seen limited adoption so far. Some countries (e.g., Kenya, the Philippines) have deprioritized retail CBDC development. Recently, the tone of the debate seems to be shifting toward skepticism regarding the need to issue a retail CBDC (Cook et al. 2023).

[1] See Atlantic Council CBDC Tracker for CBDC related work of countries around the globe.

3 Stablecoin Developments Around the Globe

The rapid rise in the use of stablecoins across both developed countries and EMDEs has prompted financial regulators worldwide to reevaluate how they approach cryptoassets. Stablecoins, which aim to maintain a stable value relative to traditional currencies or assets, are increasingly being used for payments, remittances, and as on-ramps to the broader crypto ecosystem. Their growing popularity and potential integration into mainstream financial systems have raised important questions around consumer protection, financial stability, and monetary sovereignty.

Many jurisdictions have developed or are in the process of developing regulatory frameworks for cryptoasset activities, including stablecoin issuance. Regimes are evolving quickly, alongside new use cases that increasingly interact with more traditional financial services. Below, we highlight three examples: the EU's Markets in Crypto-Assets (MiCA) regulation, the US GENIUS Act, the UK Financial Conduct Authority's (FCA) recent proposals, which aim to address the unique risks and functions associated with certain cryptoassets.

3.1 MiCA

MiCA classifies cryptoassets into three types, which is distinguished from one another and subject to different requirements depending on the risks they entail. The classification is based on whether the cryptoassets seek to stabilize their value by reference to other assets (MiCA Regulation 2023):

- The first type consists of cryptoassets that aim to stabilize their value by referencing only one official currency. The function of such cryptoassets is very similar to the function of electronic money (e-money) as defined in EU's Directive 2009/110/EC. Like e-money, such cryptoassets are electronic surrogates for coins and banknotes and are likely to be used for making payments. Those cryptoassets is defined in MiCA as 'e-money tokens'.
- The second type of cryptoassets concerns 'asset-referenced tokens', which aim to stabilize their value by referencing another value or right, or combination thereof, including one or several official currencies. That second type covers all other cryptoassets, other than e-money tokens, whose value is backed by assets, to avoid circumvention and to make MiCA regulation future-proof.
- Finally, the third type consists of cryptoassets other than asset-referenced tokens and e-money tokens, and covers a wide variety of cryptoassets, including utility tokens.

MiCA contains provisions that aim to provide appropriate protection to consumers and investors of cryptoassets. To ensure their protection, prospective retail holders of cryptoassets should be informed about the characteristics, functions, and risks of the cryptoassets they intend to purchase. When making an offer to the public of cryptoassets—other than asset-referenced tokens or e-money tokens—or when seeking their admission to trading within the EU, offerors or persons seeking admission to trading should draw up, notify to their competent authority, and publish an information document containing mandatory disclosures, known as a cryptoasset white paper. This white paper should include:

- General information on the issuer, offeror or person seeking admission to trading
- Details of the project to be funded with the capital raised
- Information on the public offer or admission to trading
- The rights and obligations attached to the cryptoassets
- The underlying technology supporting the cryptoassets
- The associated risks

However, it should not contain a description of risks that are unforeseeable and very unlikely to materialize. The information in both the white paper and related marketing communications—including advertising messages, promotional materials, and content disseminated through social media platforms—must be fair, clear, and not misleading. Furthermore, all promotional content should remain consistent with the information provided in the cryptoasset white paper.

To properly protect retail holders, issuers of asset-referenced tokens should always provide holders of such tokens with information that is complete, fair, clear and not misleading. Cryptoasset white papers for asset-referenced tokens should include details on:

- The stabilization mechanism
- The investment policy of the reserve assets
- The custody arrangements for the reserve assets
- The rights provided to holders

To safeguard holders of asset-referenced tokens against a decline in the value of the assets backing the value of the tokens, issuers should only invest the reserve assets in secure, low-risk assets with minimal market, concentration, and credit risk. Since asset-referenced tokens could be used as a means of exchange, all profits or losses arising from the investment of reserve assets must be borne by the issuer.

To cover their liability against holders of asset-referenced tokens, issuers should constitute and maintain a reserve of assets that reflects the risks associated with such liability. The reserve of assets should be used for the benefit of the holders when the issuer is unable to meet its obligations towards the holders, including in cases of insolvency. It must be structured and managed in a way that adequately covers market and currency risks. Issuers should ensure prudent management of the reserve of assets, in particular by:

- Maintaining a reserve value at least equal to the value of tokens in circulation; and managing changes in the reserve to avoid adverse effects on the markets for the reserve assets.

To achieve this, issuers of asset-referenced tokens must establish clear and detailed policies that describe, among other things:

- The composition of the reserve of assets
- The allocation of assets within the reserve
- A comprehensive assessment of the risks associated with the reserve assets
- The procedures for issuing and redeeming the asset-referenced tokens
- The procedures for increasing or decreasing the reserve; and
- The investment policy applied when reserve assets are invested.

Issuers of asset-referenced tokens that are marketed both in the EU and in third countries must ensure that their reserve of assets is available to cover their liability towards the EU holders. Accordingly, the requirement to hold the reserve of assets with firms subject to EU law should apply in proportion to the share of asset-referenced tokens that is expected to be marketed in the EU.

In addition, to reduce the risk asset-referenced tokens being used primarily as a store of value, issuers of asset-referenced tokens and cryptoasset service providers, when providing cryptoasset services related to asset-referenced tokens, must not grant interest to token holders related to the duration of their holding period.[2]

3.2 United Kingdom (UK)

In May 2025, Financial Conduct Authority (FCA) of the UK published Consultation Paper CP25/14 on the proposed regulation of stablecoin issuance and cryptoasset custody (FCA 2025). The paper states that these proposals align with the FCA's statuary objectives—consumer protection, market integrity and effective competition—and advance its secondary objective of international competitiveness and growth, as far as reasonably possible.

The FCA proposes to authorize the activity of issuing a "qualifying stablecoin". Qualifying stablecoins, as defined in the UK Treasury's draft legislation, are cryptoassets which seek or purport to maintain their value with reference to a fiat currency (a government-issued currency, such as pound sterling or US dollar) by the issuer holding, or arranging for the holding, of fiat currency or fiat currency and other assets.

Under the FCA's proposals, qualifying stablecoin issuers will be required to:

[2] See EU's MiCA Regulation for more details.

- Back the stablecoins with secure, liquid assets in a statutory trust for the benefit of qualifying stablecoin holders. These backing assets should be held with a third-party custodian who is not in the issuer's group.
- Offer redemption of qualifying stablecoins in exchange for money to all holders. Payment orders to transfer redeemed funds to qualifying stablecoin holders should be placed at the latest by the end of the next business day following receipt of a redemption request.
- Clearly disclose their policy for redemption and the composition of backing assets to consumers.

Issuers of qualifying stablecoins established in the UK will be required to obtain authorization from the FCA to carry on this activity by way of business in the UK. While stablecoins are similar in some respects to other financial instruments and specified investments, subject to finalized legislation, FCA intends to regulate them as money-like instruments rather than as investment products. This means that qualifying stablecoin issuers are expected to:

- Offer all holders the right to redeem at par value, and the redemption value should not fluctuate in line with the performance of the underlying backing assets as is the case with a fund
- Refrain from passing interest on the backing asset pool to qualifying stablecoin holders, further distinguishing qualifying stablecoins from funds or other investment products.

According to the proposal, issuers of qualifying stablecoins would be required to safeguard backing assets effectively. The planned regulatory requirements include:

- Holding backing assets on behalf of stablecoin holders under a statutory trust, with the issuer as trustee and a fiduciary duty between the issuer and stablecoin holders
- Promptly segregating backing assets upon receipt and placing them with an independent third party not connected with the issuer's group. FCA proposes that issuers can only accept money or qualifying stablecoins issued by FCA-authorized firms, in exchange for qualifying stablecoins they issue.
- Conducting reconciliations of backing assets at least daily, ensuring shortfalls are topped up and excesses removed, or that qualifying stablecoins are minted or burned to ensure parity is maintained.[3]

[3] For the details of the proposal, see FCA (2025).

3.3 *United States (US), GENIUS Act*

The US published Guiding and Establishing National Innovation for US Stablecoins Act (GENIUS Act, n.d) in July 2025. The Act introduces a licensing, regulatory, and supervisory framework for payment stablecoin issuers.

The Act defines a "payment stablecoin" as a digital asset that is, or is designed to be, used as a means of payment or settlement, and which the issuer is obligated to convert, redeem, or repurchase for a fixed amount of monetary value; and represents that such issuer will maintain, or create the reasonable expectation that it will maintain, a stable value relative to the value of a fixed amount of monetary value.

The Act clarifies that "payment stablecoin" does not include a digital asset that is a national currency, a deposit, or a security as defined under applicable laws. The GENIUS Act further provides only a permitted payment stablecoin issuer (PPSI) can issue payment stablecoins in the US.

A PPSI is defined as a person formed in the US that is -

- A subsidiary of an insured depository institution that has been approved to issue payment stablecoins under Section 5 of the Act;
- A Federal qualified payment stablecoin issuer; or
- A State qualified payment stablecoin issuer (GENIUS Act, n.d.)

According to the Act

- A subsidiary of an insured depository institution may issue payment stablecoins after receiving approval from the insured depository institution's appropriate federal banking agency.
- A federal qualified payment stablecoin issuer may be a nonbank entity, an uninsured national bank, or a federal branch of a foreign bank and must be approved by the Office of the Comptroller of the Currency (OCC) to issue payment stablecoins.
- A state-qualified payment stablecoin issuer is an entity established under the laws of a state that has been approved by a state payment stablecoin regulator to issue payment stablecoins and is not an uninsured national bank, federal branch, insured depository institution, or a subsidiary of any of the foregoing (Sidley 2025)

The GENIUS Act also establishes a procedure by which payment stablecoin issuers that are supervised by a regulator of a foreign country can issue payment stablecoins in the US without becoming a PPSI under the Act. In general, this procedure requires that the Secretary of the US Treasury determine that the regulatory regime of the foreign issuer's jurisdiction to be comparable to the requirements of the GENIUS Act. Also, the foreign issuer must register with the OCC and maintain reserves in a US financial institution sufficient to meet the liquidity demands to customers in the US.

If a foreign issuer is domiciled in a jurisdiction that has not been determined to be comparable by the Secretary of the US Treasury, the issuer may formally request such a determination under the procedure set forth in the Act (Morgan Lewis 2025).

Comparative analysis of certain regulations for single fiat-backed stablecoin issuers (from the EU's MICA, the UK's proposed regulation, the US GENIUS Act)

	European Union (MiCA)	United Kingdom (proposed regulation)	United States (GENIUS Act)
Definition of single fiat-back stablecoin	"e-money tokens," which are cryptoassets (i.e., digital representations of a value or right that can be transferred and stored electronically using DLT or similar technology) that purport to maintain a stable value by referencing the value of one official currency. CBDC is excluded. While cryptoassets qualifying as financial instruments under MiFID are also excluded, e-money tokens are explicitly treated as e-money and thus subject to the EU e-money regime as well as MiCA. Holders of e-money tokens have a claim against their issuers of those e-money tokens	"Qualifying stablecoins" are cryptoassets which seek or purport to maintain their value with reference to a fiat currency (a government--issued currency, such as pound sterling or US dollar) by the issuer holding, or arranging for the holding, of fiat currency or fiat currency and other assets.	"Payment stablecoin" is defined as a digital asset that is, or is designed to be, used as a means of payment or settlement that the issuer is obligated to convert, redeem, or repurchase for a fixed amount of monetary value; and represents that such issuer will maintain, or create the reasonable expectation that it will maintain, a stable value relative to the value of a fixed amount of monetary value.

(continued)

(continued)

	European Union (MiCA)	United Kingdom (proposed regulation)	United States (GENIUS Act)
Interest payments to stablecoin holders	Prohibited. Issuers of e-money tokens and cryptoasset service providers (CASPs) when they provide cryptoasset services related to e-money tokens, must not grant interest to holders, including interest not related to the length of time that such holders hold these e-money tokens.	Prohibited. Issuers may retain, but not pass to directly or indirectly consumers, interest or other benefits (e.g., dividends) received from the stablecoin's backing assets.	Issuers are prohibited from paying holders any form of interest or yield (whether in cash, tokens, or other consideration) solely in connection with the holding, use, or retention of such stablecoin
Composition of reserve assets	1:1 backing required with liquid reserves. At least 30% of received funds must be held in segregated accounts with a regulated EU credit institution (i.e., bank deposits). The remaining funds can be placed in low-risk, highly liquid financial instruments denominated in the same currency as the one referenced by the e-money token. This minimum amount of the reserves consisting of deposits is increased to 60% for e-money issuers issuing e-money tokens that are significant.	1:1 backing required with fiat currency and other permitted assets, i.e., short-term government treasury debt instruments issued by the UK or Zone A countries, and short--term cash deposits (and, subject to FCA permission and certain conditions, longer-term government debt instruments, units in a Public Debt Constant Net Asset Value Money Market Fund, and assets, rights, or money held under a repurchase agreement). Issuers must hold at least 5% of their backing assets in the form of on-demand UK bank deposits and must have a backing assets risk-management framework.	Issuers must maintain reserves backing outstanding payment stablecoins on at least a one-to-one basis. Reserves must comprise high-quality liquid assets such as US coins and currency or money standing to the credit of an account with a Federal Reserve Bank; demand deposits held at an insured depository institution; short-term Treasury bills, notes, or bonds; money received under certain overnight repurchase agreements and overnight reverse repurchase agreements; certain money market funds; or the tokenized form of any of these assets.

(continued)

(continued)

	European Union (MiCA)	United Kingdom (proposed regulation)	United States (GENIUS Act)
Safeguarding and segregation of reserve assets	Issuers must hold at least 30% of received funds in segregated accounts at EU credit institutions. Deposited funds must be in the form of deposits (sight or term deposits). Issuers of significant e-money tokens are subject to stricter safeguarding requirements.	Issuers must hold backing assets in a statutory trust (for the stablecoin holders' benefit), meaning that the issuers, as trustees, would have fiduciary duties to the holders as beneficiaries. Issuers must appoint third parties that are unconnected to them and their group to hold the backing assets in segregated accounts (but with the issuers, as trustees, remaining legally responsible), and issuers must procure the appointed third party to sign a letter acknowledging the assets are held on trust for the stablecoin holders.	Reserves must be segregated from and not be commingled with other assets of the issuer. Reserves required may not be pledged, rehypothecated, or reused by the permitted payment stablecoin issuer, either directly or indirectly

(continued)

(continued)

	European Union (MiCA)	United Kingdom (proposed regulation)	United States (GENIUS Act)
Disclosures and audits of reserves	Issuers must publish, and submit to the relevant national competent authority, a white paper on the stablecoin being issued, which includes the key characteristics, risks, rights of token holders and details of the issuer, and keep this updated with material changes. Additionally, issuers of significant e-money tokens must mandate an independent audit of the reserve of assets every 6 months and publish as soon as possible in a publicly and easily accessible place on their website a summary of the audit report.	Issuers must publish online, and keep updated, information allowing stablecoin holders to understand and make informed decisions when buying, selling, and redeeming stablecoins. The information that must be updated at least once in every three-month period includes (i) the value and percentage breakdown of the assets comprising the backing asset pool, (ii) the total number of stablecoins that have been minted and issued, and (iii) a statement that confirms that the issuer is meeting the requirement for the stablecoin pool to be backed 1:1 by assets in the backing asset pool. Issuers must also undertake an annual independent review to verify this remains accurate.	Issuers must publish the monthly composition of reserves on its website, containing— (i) the total number of outstanding payment stablecoins issued by the issuer; and (ii) the amount and composition of the reserves, including the average tenor and geographic location of custody of each category of reserve instruments.

Source: Compiled by the author using information from (i) Morgan Lewis 2025, (ii) MiCA Regulation, (iii) UK proposed regulation, and (iv) the GENIUS Act

3.4 *Government-Led Stablecoin Initiatives*

While stablecoins are typically defined as privately issued liabilities—distinct from CBDC—the digital currency landscape is evolving. Global research into CBDCs has accelerated in recent years, with many governments exploring digital money as a tool to modernize payments, enhance financial stability, and preserve monetary sovereignty. Yet, alongside this momentum, a smaller but growing category of government-led stablecoin initiatives is beginning to emerge. These projects are often experimental or limited in scale, with governmental bodies either sponsoring or directly issuing stablecoins, mark a departure from the traditional model of stablecoins where issued by purely private sector.

The rationale behind such initiatives varies, but several recurring motivations stand out. Compared with full-scale CBDC deployment, government-sponsored/supported stablecoins can sometimes be implemented more quickly and at lower cost, especially when they leverage existing public blockchain infrastructure or partner with established private-sector technology providers. They may offer a practical means to pilot digital currency use cases—such as improving cross-border remittances, expanding financial access, or generating new revenue streams—without committing the significant resources required for a nationwide CBDC rollout. Importantly, these models allow governments to capture some benefits of digital currency innovation while avoiding the balance sheet implications of issuing direct central bank liabilities, a step that can raise institutional, operational, or political challenges. Two examples below illustrate this trend:

- **Palau Stablecoin (PSC):** Launched as part of a public–private partnership between the Republic of Palau and Ripple, the Palau Stablecoin illustrates how small island nations can experiment with digital currency as a tool for economic resilience. Operating on the XRP Ledger, PSC is designed to reduce transaction costs and expand access to financial services for Palauan citizens, many of whom face challenges related to limited banking infrastructure and high remittance fees. Unlike a CBDC, PSC circulates on a public blockchain, yet government oversight is preserved through the Ministry of Finance, ensuring a degree of monetary control and legal clarity. It demonstrates how smaller nations can leverage digital currencies to strengthen financial sovereignty (Ministry of Finance, Republic of Palau, 2024).
- **Wyoming Stable Token:** Currently in testing across seven blockchains and expected to launch in 2025, this state-issued stablecoin is backed by U.S. Treasury securities at 102% overcollateralization. Interest generated from the reserves will fund Wyoming's education system, creating a novel revenue stream while reinforcing US dollar dominance in digital markets (DEA 2025).

4 Tokenization Developments Around the Globe

Across the globe, both private and public sector initiatives are exploring tokenization in financial services. Many of these efforts aim to reduce existing inefficiencies and frictions by streamlining various aspects of financial transactions, or in some instances, the entire end-to-end process. By doing so, tokenization can enhance the safety and efficiency of financial markets through greater transparency, lower transaction and information costs, increased speed, and stronger risk management. Also, it paves the way for new use cases and functions, such as those that support broader financial inclusion.

Tokenization not only has the potential to enhance existing systems, but also to enable innovations by creating new forms and possibilities of contracting. For instance, in cross-border payments, it could replace today's complex network of intermediaries and sequential account updates in correspondent banking with a single, integrated process. Combined with advanced compliance tools available on the platform, tokenization can reduce operational risks, costs, and delays.[4] Similarly, in capital markets, it could facilitate contingent execution of actions such as collateral management, delivery-versus-payment arrangements, and margin adjustments.

It is important to note that not all frictions present in financial transactions—including existing payment, clearing and settlement arrangements—can, or should, be fully addressed through token-based systems. Some frictions serve important policy and risk management objectives, such as central bank access policies or anti-money laundering / combating the financing of terrorism—AML/CFT compliance. And they will remain to some extent regardless of the technology and arrangement used. While the overall scale of token arrangements remains limited, projects that have reached the production stage are expanding both scope and scale. These initiatives vary in whether they are operated by individual firms or developed as joint projects, reflecting both the investment trade-offs faced by the private sector and the importance of network effects in supporting viable token arrangements. Private sector projects also differ in the types of assets involved, including the nature of the settlement asset used (e.g., commercial bank money, stablecoins). By contrast, public sector efforts have largely concentrated on central bank money as the settlement asset within in token arrangements. Several central banks are actively exploring how programmable platforms could be implemented in this context. The BIS Innovation Hub has also been leading a number of initiatives in this area (see Box 1).[5]

Box 1 BIS Innovation Hub Projects Involving Tokenization

	Helvetia[1]	Jura[2]	Dunbar[3]	Mariana[4]	Agorá[5]	Promissa[6]	Genesis[7]	Dynamo[8]
BISIH Centre	CH	CH	SG	CH and SG	Hub-wide	CH	HK	HK
Currencies	CHF	CHF, EUR	AUD, MYR, SGD, SAR	EUR, SGD, CHF	EUR, JPY, KRW, MXP, CHF, GBP, USD	CHF, USD, SDR	HKD	HKD
DLT used	Corda	Corda	Corda, Quorum	Ethereum	TBD	Canton	Stella, Hyperledger, Canton, RDOS	Ethereum
wCBDC	✓	✓	✓	✓	✓	X	X	X
Tokenised Deposits	X	X	X	X	✓	X	X	X
Tokenised digital assets	✓	✓	X	X	X	✓	✓	✓
AMM[9]	X	X	X	✓	X	X	X	X
PvP	X	✓	✓	✓	✓	X	X	X
DvP	✓	✓	X	X	X	✓	✓	X

✓ = tested; X = not possible/out of scope; PvP = Payment versus Payment, DvP = delivery versus payment, AMM = automated market-makers, RDOS = regulated DeFi operating system

Source: BIS Innovation Hub

[4] For more on the potential role of tokenization in the next-generation monetary and financial system, visit BIS (2025).

[5] For more, see BIS and CPMI (2024).

Many financial authorities closely monitor developments in tokenization within financial services to better understand emerging business models and assess whether regulation and supervision may be needed for these models and related products. For example, as part of the European Banking Authority's (EBA) 2024–2025 priorities on innovative applications, the EBA conducted an analysis on the tokenization of deposits by credit institutions. The aim was to identify existing cases, potential benefits and challenges, and possible actions that the EBA and competent authorities in Euro Area could take to address identified issues. According to the published report, the tokenization of deposits offers opportunities to improve the efficiency of fund transfers from on-chain deposit accounts, including through programmability functionalities. However, it also raises challenges, such as regulatory classification, operational risks, and implications for financial inclusion (EBA 2024). The development of tokenized deposits—along with their associated benefits, challenges, and regulatory considerations—requires continued attention in the broader context of the EU banking and payments sector's ongoing digitalization. Below are some other initiatives around the globe on tokenization:

4.1 Project Agora of BIS

More recently, central banks have joined forces with regulated financial services providers in Project Agorá to build on the unified ledger concept proposed by the BIS. The project is supported by seven central banks: Bank of France (for the Eurosystem), Bank of Japan, Bank of Korea, Bank of Mexico, Swiss National Bank, Bank of England, and the Federal Reserve Bank of New York (BISIH 2025).

Project Agora combines tokenized commercial bank money for payments with tokenized central bank money for settlement on a single programmable platform. This could enhance the functioning of the monetary system and provide new solutions using smart contracts and programmability while preserving its two-tier structure. Specifically, the design allows for the simultaneous tokenization of commercial bank deposits and wholesale central bank money, governed by programmable smart contracts on a shared ledger. This preserves the two-tier central bank–commercial bank relationship while enhancing compliance, speed, transparency, and cost-efficiency in correspondent banking. Agorá builds on existing correspondent banking models, making it both feasible and legally implementable today.

As a major public-private partnership, the project aims to address several technological, legal and regulatory inefficiencies in today's payments landscape. This includes improving pre-screening processes and enhancing the exchange of information for AML/CFT compliance checks.[6]

Convened by the Institute of International Finance, the private sector consortium includes over 40 regulated financial institutions—major global banks (e.g. Citi,

[6] For more see BIS 2024c.

HSBC, Deutsche Bank, BBVA), payment network operators (Visa, Mastercard), and financial market infrastructure providers (SWIFT, Euroclear, SIX Digital Exchange) (Ledger Insights 2024a).

The initiative intends to provide a credible, regulated alternative to private stablecoins for cross-border and institutional payments, potentially redefining how programmable money is used without relying on crypto-native infrastructure. In its 2025 Annual Economic Report, the BIS emphasizes that stablecoins lack key features of "sound money"—such as central bank backing (singleness), elastic supply, and regulated integrity. The unified ledger model, in contrast, embeds these features, potentially crowding out stablecoins in the institutional cross-border context (BIS 2025).

As of June 2025, the project concluded its conceptual phase and is moving towards the building phase of a prototype. While promising, participants have flagged operational challenges—specifically, **liquidity fragmentation** across currency pairs and balancing interoperability with T + 0 settlement requirements. These stem from the complexity of linking different jurisdictional subdomains and liquidity frameworks on a unified ledger (Popowicz 2025).

If successful, Project Agorá could lay the conceptual and technical groundwork for a new type of financial market infrastructure that enable seamless, programmable cross-border settlement using tokenized deposits. While still experimental, its broad public-private collaboration and multinational participation make it the BIS Innovation Hub's most ambitious initiative to date—and a potential inflection point in how regulated financial institutions approach programmable money and cross-border value transfer.

4.2 *JP Morgan Deposit Token*

J.P. Morgan has recently launched a proof of concept for its USD Deposit Token (JPMD), aimed at institutional clients and built on Base, an Ethereum Layer 2 blockchain developed within Coinbase (JP Morgan 2025a). This initiative marks the first time Kinexys, the JPM's blockchain business unit, is leveraging a public blockchain to support institutional payments.

JPMD is a permissioned USD deposit token intended to bring commercial bank deposits on-chain. It enables secure, near real-time peer-to-peer transfers between wallets on Base, giving JP Morgan's institutional clients the ability to move funds quickly and efficiently with minimal friction. The initiative is intended to enhance operational efficiency and support real-time financial decision-making.

Unlike stablecoins, which have historically dominated public blockchains for digital payments, JPMD integrates directly with traditional banking systems while offering the advantages of digital assets—such as 24/7 settlement, real-time liquidity, and the potential to pay interest to holders. This makes it an attractive alternative for institutions seeking reliable liquidity with seamless connection to their existing financial infrastructure.

By bringing commercial bank deposits into the digital asset ecosystem, JPMD intends to enhance the institutional digital payments landscape and supports broader industry adoption. It represents a first-of-its-kind innovation: a permissioned deposit token exclusively for institutional use, facilitating secure on-chain money transfers while aligning with regulatory and compliance expectations. Kinexys has been developing blockchain-based financial infrastructure since 2015, including onchain deposit accounts on its private networks (JP Morgan 2025b).

4.3 Regulated Liability Network

The Regulated Liability Network (RLN) is a proposed financial market infrastructure that leverages DLT to support an interoperable network of digital money, including central bank money, tokenized commercial bank deposits, and electronic money (RLN 2022).

Rather than limiting digital currency innovation to CBDC, RLN seeks to extend the legal concept of regulated liabilities to tokenized money issued by commercial banks and regulated nonbanks, allowing them to coexist on the same programmable platform. It is "always-on", supports programmability, enables multi-asset settlement, and aims to improve interoperability across issuers.[7]

RLN's core purpose is to enable a unified, multi-currency, multi-asset settlement network that maintains the existing two-tier financial system—public sector (central banks) and private regulated sector (e.g., banks, e-money issuers)—while reducing friction in both retail and wholesale payments. By bringing regulated liabilities onto a shared ledger, RLN offers on-chain finality, 24/7 settlement, and the possibility to embed smart-contract logic in regulated financial flows (e.g. conditional payments, escrow, automation of corporate treasuries).

In the **UK**, UK Finance led a Discovery Phase in 2023, followed by a successful Experimentation Phase involving 11 major banks—Barclays, Citi UK, HSBC UK, Lloyds, NatWest, Santander UK, Standard Chartered, Nationwide, Virgin Money—together with Mastercard and Visa, supported by technology vendors like R3 and Quant. The trial simulated five different use-cases, including property purchases and tokenized bond settlement, demonstrating greater settlement efficiencies, reduced failed-payment costs, stronger protection against authorized push payment fraud, and smoother customer journeys (Ledger Insights 2024b). The consensus was that RLN provides a viable innovation platform, with the next steps being regulatory engagement and exploration of scalability and business models.

In the US, the New York Innovation Center conducted a proof-of-concept in 2022–2023 that simulated on-chain settlement using tokenized commercial bank liabilities and wholesale CBDC for both domestic and cross-border U.S. dollar payments. The initiative demonstrated that a shared-ledger architecture could

[7] For more on the details of RLN, see (RLN 2022) and UK Finance, n.d.

realistically support real-time, interoperable payments between regulated institutions, while meeting technical, legal and business feasibility requirements (New York Fed, n.d.).

Building on the conceptual foundations of the RLN, *Ubyx* was launched in 2025. Ubyx reflects an attempt to apply similar design principles in practice. Founded by Tony McLaughlin—the original proponent of the RLN— Ubyx explores the development of multi-issuer clearing system for stablecoins and tokenized money that enables par-value redemption and interoperability between banks, fintechs, and blockchain networks (McLellan 2025, Ubyx 2025). Whereas RLN serves primarily as a reference architecture for shared-ledger settlement among regulated liabilities, Ubyx seeks to test these concepts within the context of stablecoin clearing and fiat on/off-ramps. In this sense, Ubyx can be viewed as an early practical instantiation of the RLN framework, experimenting with ways to promote "singleness of money" across digital and traditional payment instruments (Ledger Insights 2025).

4.4 *Project Guardian (Singapore)*

Project Guardian is a key initiative launched by the Monetary Authority of Singapore (MAS) in 2022. It brings major global financial services providers and financial authorities to pilot and structure the tokenization of traditional assets—such as bonds, funds, and commercial papers across interoperable blockchain networks (MAS and BIS 2023).

Guided by MAS's vision for open and interoperable networks, the project aims to prevent fragmentation by enabling tokenized assets to move seamlessly across different platforms and jurisdictions. A central element is the role of regulated institutions, which act as trust anchors for identity, compliance, and credential issuance. Core frameworks produced under Project Guardian include the Guardian Fixed Income Framework and Guardian Funds Framework, developed in collaboration with International Capital Market Association and other authorities (ICMA 2025). These frameworks set out standards for areas such as delivery-versus-payment settlement, custody, token taxonomy, governance, and cross-border compliance (Allen and Gledhill 2024).

To promote confidence in the settlement of tokenized assets in financial markets, regulated and credible forms of tokenized money are needed as common settlement assets. Such settlement assets would help reduce risks and decrease the level of market fragmentation. Therefore, MAS is enabling FSPs' access to such common settlement assets including a Singapore-dollar wholesale CBDC for market testing purposes. The initial test network is designed to support three main features:

- **Settlement facility**: Issuance, transfer, and redemption of Singapore-dollar wholesale CBDC, with potential extensions to other forms of central bank and commercial bank liabilities.

- **Programmability**: The use of automated and conditional triggers for tokenized transactions, including the use of Purpose-Bound Money.
- **Interoperability**: Linkages with existing financial market infrastructures[8]

In addition, live pilots have demonstrated the project's potential. For example, Swift, UBS Asset Management, and Chainlink successfully settled tokenized fund subscriptions and redemptions via the Swift network. This allowed digital asset transactions to settle off-chain in fiat currency using a payment system already adopted by more than 11,500 FSPs, across over 200 countries and territories. This collaboration illustrates how FSPs can leverage blockchain technology, the Chainlink Platform, and the Swift network to settle subscriptions and redemptions for tokenized investment fund vehicles, thereby allowing the straight-through-processing of the payment leg without requiring global adoption of an on-chain form of payment. This helps in the automation of the entire lifecycle of the fund redemption and subscription process.[9] Through Project Guardian, tokenized money—both wholesale CBDC or regulated tokenized bank liabilities—is envisioned as the foundational settlement layer supporting large-scale asset tokenization across borders and platforms.

5 Conclusion

The rapid emergence of tokenization projects raises important questions about the long-term role and relevance of stablecoins in global finance. Many tokenization initiatives—such as Project Agorá, the Regulated Liability Network (RLN), and tokenized deposit pilots— seek to bring regulated money directly into DLT. By leveraging bank deposits, central bank money, or regulated e-money as settlement assets, some of these projects aim to provide a safer and more compliant alternative to privately issued stablecoins. Unlike stablecoins, which often operate on the margins of regulatory frameworks and can present risks related to reserve management or operational transparency, tokenized liabilities from regulated institutions embed legal clarity and supervisory oversight from the outset. This positioning could limit the comparative advantage that stablecoins once held in providing blockchain-native settlement assets. However, it is also important to highlight that the ultimate outcome will also depend on future regulations governing stablecoins evolve.

If these tokenization initiatives mature into widely adopted infrastructures, they may reduce demand for stablecoins in institutional and cross-border use cases. For example, in wholesale payments and settlement, tokenized deposits or central bank money could displace stablecoins by offering the same programmability and interoperability without concerns about redemption risk or reserve adequacy. However, this does not necessarily imply the disappearance of stablecoins altogether. Instead, their relevance may shift toward retail-facing use cases, particularly

[8] For more, see Allen and Gledhill 2024.

[9] For more on the role of Swift and Chainlink, see Swift (2024) and Chainlink (2024).

in jurisdictions where access to regulated digital money lags or where stablecoins continue to offer advantages in cross-border remittances and integration with decentralized finance ecosystems.

In this sense, the trajectory of tokenization and stablecoins may not be one of direct substitution, but of differentiation. Tokenized deposits and CBDC-backed platforms are likely to dominate regulated, large-value, and institutional contexts, while stablecoins may retain relevance in more open, retail, or crypto-native environments. The degree of overlap will depend heavily on how interoperable tokenization platforms become and whether stablecoins can evolve to meet higher regulatory and operational standards. Rather than rendering stablecoins obsolete, tokenization may instead redefine their comparative role within a broader digital money ecosystem.

In conclusion, the evolving global digital money landscape reflects a dynamic interplay between public sector initiatives and private sector innovations. Central banks worldwide are advancing CBDC projects at an unprecedented pace, aiming to enhance efficiency, strengthen monetary sovereignty, and broaden financial inclusion, among others. At the same time, private sector contributions—through stablecoins, tokenization initiatives, and new settlement models—are challenging traditional infrastructures while creating fresh opportunities for innovation and competition. Together, these developments illustrate that the future of money will not be shaped by one dominant model, but rather by a constellation of interoperable systems, each tailored to the unique economic, legal, and technological contexts of its jurisdiction.

Yet, this rapid transformation also brings challenges that demand careful calibration. Adoption hurdles, regulatory uncertainties, and risks to financial stability remain significant. Governments and regulators must balance innovation with safeguards that protect consumers, preserve trust, and ensure resilience. The initiatives outlined both the promise and complexity of reimagining money in a digital era.

Ultimately, the convergence of public and private sector efforts marks a pivotal moment in financial history. Whether through global-scale projects like mBridge and Project Agorá, or more limited experiments such as Palau's stablecoin and JP Morgan's deposit token, the coming years will likely determine the extent to which digital money can deliver on its transformative potential. Success will depend not only on technology, but also on governance, cooperation, and the ability of institutions to build systems that are inclusive, interoperable, and trusted across borders.

References

Allen and Gledhill (2024, November 28) MAS announces plans to support commercialization of asset tokenization. https://www.allenandgledhill.com/sg/publication/articles/29424/mas-announces-plans-to-support-commercialisation-of-asset-tokenisation

Auer R, Banka H, Boakye-Adjei NY, Faragallah A, Frost J, Natarajan H, Jermy Prenio J (2022) Central Bank digital currencies: a new tool in the financial inclusion toolkit? FSI Insights No. 41. BIS. https://www.bis.org/fsi/publ/insights41.pdf

Bank for International Settlements (BIS) (2024) Project mBridge reached minimum viable product stage. https://www.bis.org/about/bisih/topics/cbdc/mcbdc_bridge.htm

BIS (2024b, October 31) The future of finance. Speech by Augustin Carstens. https://www.bis.org/speeches/sp241031.htm

BIS (2024c, April 03) Project Agora: central banks and banking sector embark on major project to explore tokenization of cross-border payments. https://www.bis.org/press/p240403.htm

BIS (2025, June 24) The next-generation monetary and financial system. Annual Economic Report. https://www.bis.org/publ/arpdf/ar2025e3.htm

BIS and Committee on Payments and Market Infrastructures (CPMI) (2024) Tokenization in the context of money and other assets: concepts and implications for central banks. Report to the G20, Joint Report. https://www.bis.org/cpmi/publ/d225.pdf

BIS Innovation Hub (BISIH) (2025) Project Agora—frequently asked questions. Retrieved October 28, 2025, from https://www.bis.org/innovation_hub/projects/agora_faq.pdf

CBDC Tracker (2025) Atlantic council. Retrieved October 28, 2025, from https://www.atlanticcouncil.org/cbdctracker/

Central Bank of the United Arab Emirates (CBUAE) (2025, July) Digital Dirham—a primer on the UAE's Central Bank Digital Currency. https://www.centralbank.ae/media/lczb2314/cbdc-short-report_july.pdf

Chainlink (2024, November 12) Chainlink powers 3 major use cases under the Monetary Authority of Singapore's Project Guardian. https://blog.chain.link/chainlink-project-guardian/

Cook W, Staschen S, Kerse M (2023) Inclusive CBDCs: inflated expectations or a new productivity? Blog. CGAP, Washington, DC. https://www.cgap.org/blog/inclusive-cbdcs-inflated-expectations-or-new-productivity

Digital Euro Association (DEA) (2025) The role of stablecoins in financial sovereignty. https://7869715.fs1.hubspotusercontent-na1.net/hubfs/7869715/DEA%20-%20The%20Role%20of%20Stablecoins%20in%20Financial%20Sovereignty-2.pdf

European Banking Authority (EBA) (2024) Report on tokenised deposits. https://www.eba.europa.eu/sites/default/files/2024-12/4b294386-1235-463f-b9b5-08f255160435/Report%20on%20Tokenised%20deposits.pdf

Federal Reserve Bank of New York (New York Fed) (n.d.) Facilitating wholesale digital asset settlement. Retrieved October 28, 2025, from https://www.newyorkfed.org/aboutthefed/nyic/facilitating-wholesale-digital-asset-settlement

Financial Conduct Authority (FCA) (2025) CP25/14: Stablecoin issuance and cryptoasset custody. https://www.fca.org.uk/publications/consultation-papers/cp25-14-stablecoin-issuance-cryptoasset-custody

Guiding and Establishing National Innovation for U.S. Stablecoins Act (GENIUS Act) (n.d.) Retrieved October 28, 2025, from https://www.congress.gov/bill/119th-congress/senate-bill/1582/text/enr

International Capital Market Association (ICMA) (2025, June 2) ICMA to lead Project Guardian fixed income workstream. https://www.icmagroup.org/News/news-in-brief/icma-to-lead-project-guardian-fixed-income-workstream

JP Morgan (2025a) Deposit tokens. Retrieved October 28, 2025, from https://www.jpmorgan.com/kinexys/content-hub/deposit-tokens

JP Morgan (2025b) JP Morgan launches USD deposit token, JPMD, proof concept for institutional clients on Base, a public blockchain built within Coinbase. https://www.jpmorgan.com/payments/newsroom/kinexys-usd-digital-deposit-tokens

Kerse M, Newbury LB, Staschen S (2024) Financial inclusion and disruptive innovation: regulatory implications. CGAP. https://www.cgap.org/research/publication/financial-inclusion-and-disruptive-innovation-regulatory-implications

Kiff J (2025) Jurisdictions where retail CBDC is being explored and Jurisdictions where DLT--based wholesale CBDC is being explored. Kiffmeister Chronicles. Retrieved October 28, 2025, from https://kiffmeister.com/category/special/page/2/

Ledger Insights (2024a) 41 institutions join BIS tokenized cross border payment Project Agora. https://www.ledgerinsights.com/41-institutions-join-bis-tokenized-cross-border-payment--project-agora/

Ledger Insights (2024b) 11 banks say regulated liability network experiments for tokenized deposits were a success. https://www.ledgerinsights.com/11-banks-say-regulated-liability-network--experiments-for-tokenized-deposits-were-a-success/

Ledger Insights (2025) Ubyx to launch stablecoin off-ramp network via banks. https://www.ledgerinsights.com/ubyx-bank-stablecoin-off-ramp-network-launches/

McLellan L (2025) The path to stablecoin ubiquity lies through banks. OMFIF, Blog. https://www.omfif.org/2025/03/the-path-to-stablecoin-ubiquity-lies-through-banks

Ministry of Finance Republic of Palau National Government Payment Service Project: Phase 2a Report, July 31, 2024 https://www.palaugov.pw/wpcontent/uploads/Palau-National-Payment-System-Phase-2a-Final-Report.pdf

Monetary Authority of Singapore (MAS) and BIS (2023) Project guardian: enabling open and interoperable networks. https://www.mas.gov.sg/-/media/mas-media-library/development/fintech/project-guardian/project-guardian-open-interoperable-network.pdf

Morgan, Lewis & Bockius LLP (Morgan Lewis) (2025) GENIUS Act passess in US Congress: a breakdown of the landmark stablecoin law. https://www.morganlewis.com/pubs/2025/07/genius-act-passes-in-us-congress-a-breakdown-of-the-landmark-stablecoin-law

Popowicz J (2025, May 7) Project Agora faces fragmentation challenges. Article. https://www.centralbanking.com/fintech/7972833/project-agora-faces-fragmentation-challenges?check_logged_in=1

Regulation (EU) 2023/1114 of the European Parliament and of the Council of 31 May 2023 on markets in crypto-assets, and amending Regulations (EU) No 1093/2010 and (EU) No 1095/2010 and Directives 2013/36/EU and (EU) 2019/1937 (MiCA Regulation 2023). https://eur-lex.europa.eu/legal-content/EN/TXT/PDF/?uri=CELEX:32023R1114

Sidley (2025) The GENIUS Act: a framework for US stablecoin issuance. https://www.sidley.com/en/insights/newsupdates/2025/07/the-genius-act-a-framework-for-us-stablecoin-issuance

Swift (2024) Swift, UBS Asset Management, and Chainlink successfully complete innovative pilot to bridge tokenized assets with existing payment systems. https://www.swift.com/news-events/press-releases/swift-ubs-asset-management-and-chainlink-successfully-complete-innovative--pilot-bridge-tokenized-assets-existing-payment-systems

The Regulated Liability Network (RLN), Digital Sovereign Currency (2022) Whitepaper. https://regulatedliabilitynetwork.org/wp-content/uploads/2022/11/The-Regulated-Liability-Network--Whitepaper.pdf

Ubyx (2025) Ubyx: stablecoin ubiquity. https://www.ubyx.xyz

UK Finance (n.d.) Tokenised sterling deposits. Retrieved October 28, 2025, from https://www.ukfinance.org.uk/tokenised-sterling-deposits

The Pursuit of Resilience in European Retail Payments

Paul Desprairies and Philipp Neubauer

Abstract In recent years, resilience in retail payments has evolved from a technical operational matter to a crucial component of European strategic autonomy. Currently, the euro area faces a dual vulnerability: a systemic reliance on non-European International Card Schemes (ICS)—which serve as the exclusive infrastructure for domestic card transactions in 13 of the 21 Euro Area Member States—and a fragmented European private sector unable to overcome a collective problem to build a unified alternative. This chapter adopts a resilience-focused perspective to evaluate potential solutions to this autonomy gap, conducting a comparative analysis between traditional payment systems, private stablecoin initiatives, tokenized deposits and the Eurosystem's proposed Digital Euro.

Our analysis reveals that while stable crypto-assets offer theoretical robustness through decentralized back-ends, their practical utility is compromised by structural bottlenecks at the consumer-facing front-end layer and by an ultimate dependency on network connectivity. In contrast, the Digital Euro introduces an architectural paradigm designed to maximize operational continuity. We examine the offline modality, which utilizes hardware-based secure elements to enable peer-to-peer settlement without third-party validation, effectively replicating the resilience of physical cash at the Point Of Sale (POS). Concurrently, we analyze the online infrastructure (Digital Euro Service Platform—DESP), which targets high availability and introduces "emergency switching" to decouple asset access from intermediary unavailability. The chapter concludes that the Digital Euro is designed to resolve structural failures and bring unique attributes of cash into the digital realm, thereby safeguarding the strategic autonomy and long-term stability of the European retail payment landscape.

Keywords Digital euro · Retail payments · Strategic autonomy · Operational resilience · Central Bank Digital Currency (CBDC) · Stablecoins · Tokenized deposits · Offline payments

---

P. Desprairies · P. Neubauer (✉)
Directorate Digital Euro, European Central Bank, Frankfurt, Germany
e-mail: paul.desprairies@ecb.europa.eu; philipp.neubauer@ecb.europa.eu

S. Yazıcı et al. (eds.), *Tokenisation of Money*, Contributions to Finance and Accounting, https://doi.org/10.1007/978-3-032-22946-5_24

1 Introduction

In recent years, retail payments have transitioned from a functional utility to a cornerstone of strategic priority for the resilience of the European financial ecosystem. Rising geopolitical tensions and the increasing risk of payment systems being leveraged as instruments of economic or political coercion—a phenomenon frequently termed the "weaponization of payments"—have necessitated a rethinking of Europe's roadmap for strategic autonomy and resilience in retail payments. This transformation is particularly pronounced in the euro area. Currently, 13 out of 21 Member States rely entirely on U.S.-based International Card Schemes (ICS) such as Visa and Mastercard because they lack domestic card schemes (European Central Bank (2025a). Furthermore, the increasing complexity of payment ecosystems has introduced new operational risks, amplifying the potential of single points of failure in critical market infrastructure.

To address this vulnerability, two divergent philosophical and technological paradigms have emerged that share the common goal of enhancing payment resilience. The first paradigm revolves around crypto-assets and their underlying infrastructures based on Distributed Ledger Technology (DLT), including stablecoins and tokenized deposits (hereafter referred to as "stable crypto-assets"). Proponents of these solutions argue that their decentralized architectures offer unprecedented levels of resilience and autonomy. The second paradigm centers on retail Central Bank Digital Currencies (CBDCs),[1] through which central banks aim to translate unique attributes of physical cash into a digital medium. On this journey they pursue key policy objectives such as enhancing the resilience of digital payments. In this vein, the Eurosystem is actively preparing the potential issuance of a Digital Euro to safeguard monetary sovereignty and fortify Europe's payment landscape.

This chapter adopts a resilience-focused perspective to conduct a comparative analysis of two approaches: blockchain-based stablecoins and stable crypto-assets on the one hand, and the Digital Euro on the other. By examining their respective technological foundations, operational frameworks, and architectural designs, this chapter seeks to contribute to the ongoing dialogue on the future of a sovereign and robust European retail payment landscape.

[1] Central banks are currently investigating two distinct forms of CBDC: retail and wholesale. Retail CBDC is a completely new means of payment designed for the general public. In contrast, wholesale CBDC refers to the evolution of existing interbank settlement infrastructures. These initiatives primarily investigate the application of DLT in inter-institution settlement to optimise the simultaneous exchange of securities with central bank money.

2 The Increasing Dependency on Foreign Market Players in European Retail Payments

Since the introduction of the single currency, and notwithstanding the objectives outlined in the Eurosystem retail payment strategy (European Central Bank 2023a), the European private sector has failed to offer a truly European-governed payment solution with pan-European reach. Today, approximately two-thirds of card-based transactions, encompassing both domestic and cross-border payments within the euro area, are processed by non-European providers such as Visa and Mastercard (European Central Bank 2025a). At the same time, wallet providers are increasingly dominated by foreign Original Equipment Manufacturers (OEMs) such as Apple and Samsung, alongside major digital platforms often categorized as "BigTechs", for example, PayPal and AliPay. While reliance on foreign intermediaries for local currency settlements may be considered as a benign efficiency in times of stability, rising geopolitical tensions have underlined the vulnerabilities inherent in this dependency. This shift has alarmed policy makers to proactively reinforce the resilience of the euro area's critical payment infrastructure.

This section investigates the root causes of Europe's increasing dependency on external infrastructure for retail payments. It begins by analyzing geopolitical vulnerabilities associated with this dependency, before transitioning to a critical assessment of the operational resilience deficit inherent in today's fragmented payment ecosystem.

2.1 *Geopolitical Vulnerabilities and Market Fragmentation in the European Retail Payments Landscape*

Over the past 25 years, ICS have solidified their position as key players in card payments, effectively defining the very rules governing how Europeans pay at the Point Of Sale (POS).[2] Building on these rules, OEMs—most notably smartphone providers—have further increased these geopolitical dependencies by establishing proprietary market standards for proximity payments at the POS. At the same time, BigTechs are starting to leverage the Instant Payments Regulation (IPR) (European Parliament and Council of the European Union 2024) to provide account-to-account payment services at the POS, directly challenging traditional card schemes (PayPal 2025). European players seek to realize the full potential of the Single Euro Payments Area (SEPA) by expanding from person-to-person to POS payments, but

[2] It is noteworthy that while the technical standards for Near Field Communication (NFC) and supporting protocols, such as the Host Controller Interface used in proximity payments, are influenced by European organizations like the European Telecommunications Standards Institute (ETSI) and the NFC Forum, the practical implementation of these technologies in mobile devices remain under the control of non-European OEMs.

the success of these initiatives remains heavily dependent on infrastructure and actors mainly located outside of Europe.

This structural reliance on non-European payment rails introduces vulnerabilities regarding Europe's strategic autonomy. The potential for payment infrastructures to be instrumentalized in geopolitical tensions has been demonstrated on several occasions in recent history. In 2010, following political pressure from the U.S. government, Visa and Mastercard stopped accepting payments to Sunshine Press, the media organization operating WikiLeaks (Greenberg 2010). Even though Visa Europe stated in official filings with the European Commission that it had *"not come under or reacted to pressure from any government"* (European Commission 2012), subsequent court documents contradicted this denial. Filings in the case *DataCell ehf. v. Visa Inc.* et al. (2015) revealed that key U.S. politicians had *"instructed their respective staffs to contact Defendants and request that Defendants stop payment processing on donations for Sunshine Press."*. It took DataCell, the Icelandic server hosting provider for Sunshine Press/WikiLeaks, about 2 years to win its court case against Valitor, the Icelandic partner of Visa and Mastercard, and thereby resume acceptance of card payments (Valdimarsson 2013). In 2019, the case was settled for 1.2 billion Icelandic Króna in damages due to Valitor's unlawful termination of payment processing (Daðason 2019). Most importantly, the European Commission was unable to act at the time and rejected initial complaints by DataCell despite the geopolitical gravity.

More recently, Visa and Mastercard ceased their activities in Russia because of the Russian invasion of Ukraine in 2022 (Visa 2022; Mastercard 2022). At the same time, SWIFT disconnected Business Identifier Codes (BICs) belonging to Russian banks (European Commission 2022). Although, ICS may only exercise ultimate control over transactions processed by payment processors they own, it must be noted that no publicly listed processor that operates across multiple EU Member States is completely owned by EU investors (European Central Bank 2025b). In other words, in an extreme scenario where dominant ICS would be pressured to stop operations in the euro area, consumers in countries without a domestic card scheme—such as Austria or Ireland—would be widely unable to pay electronically for their groceries in stores.

These developments raise the question of why a unified private-led pan-European payment solution and set of standards have failed to emerge in the digital age. This void persists, even though the direct contact of commercial banks with their customers through payments is weakened by the increasing spread of wallets provided by foreign players. While the private sector has undertaken substantial efforts to connect payment services across the euro area, these initiatives have largely resulted in regional clusters rather than a truly integrated single market. Currently, two main initiatives exist: (1) the European Payment Initiative (EPI) envisioning a unified payment scheme supported by a single front-end solution called "Wero Wallet" in Northern Europe, and (2) the European Payments Alliance (EuroPA) aiming to interconnect domestic solutions including Bancomat, Bizum and MB WAY in Southern Europe.

Concurrently, European Payment Service Providers (PSPs) and associations have attempted to counterbalance the dominance of OEMs and ICS. For example, the European Payments Council (EPC) defined a QR-code standard that allows merchants to accept payments via a QR-code displayed on the POS terminal. This initiative sought to bypass costly commercial agreements between distributing PSPs and OEMs to access the NFC antenna on smartphones, and between acquiring PSPs and ICS to accept and process transactions based on proprietary market standards such as EMV specifications.[3] This approach was particularly advantageous for European wallet providers such as MB Way in Portugal, allowing them to offer mobile payments at the POS while being technically restricted from the NFC interface on iOS devices. Yet, following the implementation of the Digital Markets Act (DMA) (European Parliament and Council of the European Union 2022)—which requires gatekeepers to grant third-party access to NFC technology—the competitive sustainability of QR-code based solutions against the superior user experience of NFC transactions at the POS remains an open question.

Europe is still awaiting a successful pan-European payment solution led by the private sector. The following section delineates the structural hurdles that European PSPs encounter in their pursuit of market integration.

2.1.1 Structural Barriers to European Market Integration

Historically, private European initiatives have failed to scale in geographical scope. This failure can be attributed to three structural market frictions:

1. PSPs face a collective action problem that hinders the coordination necessary to build a sovereign payment infrastructure. In game theory, establishing a new market standard requires collaboration to achieve the best collective outcome, yet individual self-interests conflict with group efficiency. For example, a PSP faces immediate commercial pressure to adopt solutions like Apple Pay or ICS to avoid losing customers to rivals who already provide such solutions. This pressure is reinforced by the "first mover advantage" pricing models offered by Apple Pay and ICS. In these models, early adopters are usually incentivized with lower fees, while late adopters need to calculate with higher costs. Therefore, individual rational choices prevail, locking the market into a prisoner's dilemma where PSPs rely on non-European providers even though this undermines the collective goal of establishing an independent European alternative.
2. The retail payment market is a two-sided market characterized by strong network effects. In this ecosystem, the utility of a payment instrument for consumers is directly correlated with its adoption by merchants and vice-versa. Hence, for a new European payment scheme to challenge dominant players, it must

[3] EMV specifications are an industry standard for secure card-based payments. They are owned by a consortium called EMVCo, currently consisting of American Express, Discover, JCB, Mastercard, UnionPay and Visa.

overcome the "chicken-and-egg" problem by achieving critical mass on both issuance and acceptance sides simultaneously. This is even more difficult when dominant players offer unmatched global reach. For example, a European cardholder is offered ubiquitous payment acceptance when travelling to the United States or Japan. This global interoperability acts as a significant market barrier, effectively obliging European PSPs to issue international cards to satisfy consumer demand.

3. The fragmentation of the European retail payment market creates substantial investment hurdles. European PSPs operate legacy infrastructures and domestic schemes that lack technical uniformity. Bridging these silos requires expensive acceptance layers and complex dispute management frameworks for cross-border transactions at the POS. When combined with the coordination failure and the network effects issues mentioned above, these factors leave little to no viable business case for private investment.

Hence, in the European retail payment market, which comprises several thousand PSPs, maintaining a cooperative equilibrium is structurally challenging due to the inherent incentive to defect. ICS exploit these dynamics by offering large fee discounts to issuing banks that choose to switch from domestic schemes to ICS (European Central Bank 2025c). Provided the reliance of payment systems on critical mass and network effects, the non-participation of even a single systemic European PSP can be enough to strongly undermine the economic viability of a pan-European payment initiative.

These market dynamics drove actors to pursue specialized roles to optimize operational efficiency and user experience, resulting in increased system fragility. The following section provides an analysis of the multi-layered complexity of today's regulated payment ecosystem.

2.2 The Operational Resilience Deficit in European Retail Payments

Operational resilience may be defined as *"the ability of individual financial firms, financial market infrastructures (FMIs) and the wider financial system to prevent, adapt and respond to, as well as recover and learn from, operational disruptions"* (Bank of England 2024). Given their systemic importance, complex payment systems are inherently vulnerable to risks ranging from cyberattacks, technical failures, and operational errors. In this context, the regulated payment landscape in Europe faces significant resilience challenges. It features a diverse range of actors and technologies distributed across three main levels: (1) the payment front-end, (2) PSPs, and (3) the payment back-end. When complemented with the end users—who initiate or receive payments—and the payment schemes that establish the governance rules, a complex, multi-layered payment chain surfaces (see below Fig. 1).

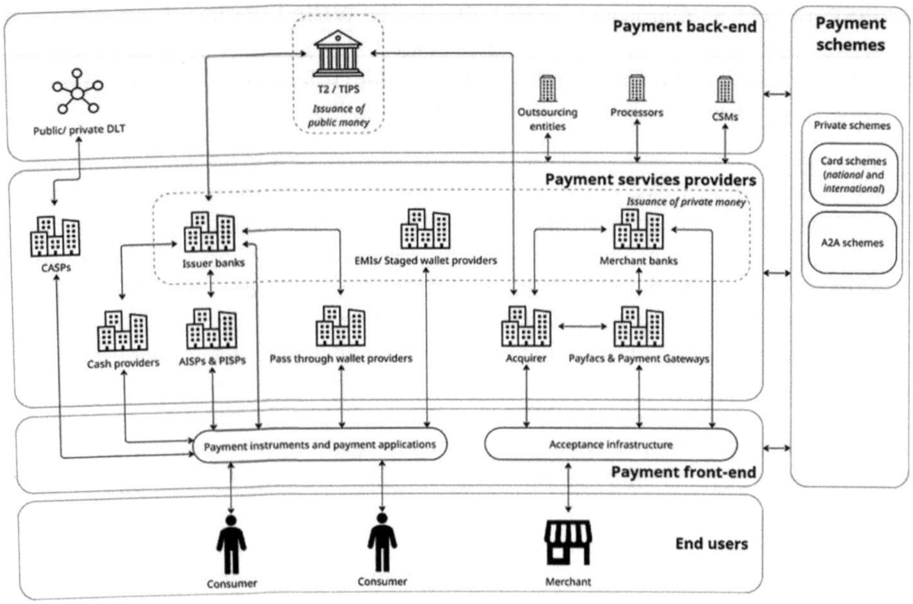

Fig. 1 Europe's regulated payment ecosystem: a complex, multi-layered payment chain (designed by the Authors)

The payment front-end enables the initiation of payments and the confirmation of receipt. It features a variety of payment instruments, such as debit and credit cards, as well as consumer payment applications such as Apple Wallet and Google Wallet. On the recipient side, merchants utilize payment acceptance infrastructure, including POS terminals and e-commerce checkout pages, to receive payments in exchange for goods or services. While the general public interacts almost exclusively with this front-end layer, the successful execution of a transaction requires coordination of multiple actors operating "behind the curtain", specifically within the PSP and payment back-end stages.

The PSP level encompasses all entities offering payment services to consumers and merchants via the payment front-end, effectively connecting end users to the payment back-end. While some PSPs specialize in specific roles, such as acquiring, others hold multiple licenses to offer a plethora of different services. Broadly, PSPs can be categorized into two distinct groups:

1. PSPs that *issue* private money based on their own liabilities. This includes credit institutions—covering issuer banks (e.g., Deutsche Bank) and merchant banks (e.g., BNP Paribas)—that issue commercial bank money (tokenized or not) and Electronic Money Institutions (EMIs), which are also staged wallet providers (e.g., PayPal).
2. PSPs that *do not issue* money but facilitate the transfer of private and public money. On the consumer side, this category ranges from cash providers, Account Information Service Provides/Payment Initiation Service Providers (AISPs/

PISPs)—such as Klarna and the EPI offering the WERO Wallet—to pass-through wallet providers (e.g., Apple Wallet) and Crypto-Assets Service Providers (CASPs) (e.g., Bitpanda). On the merchant side, it includes acquirers and gateways (e.g., Nexi, Adyen) as well as payment facilitators (e.g., SumUp).

The Payment back-end consists of the entities operating the underlying infrastructure used to process, clear and settle transactions. This includes Real-Time Gross Settlement (RTGS) systems such as T2 and TIPS which facilitate the final settlement of transactions in central bank money, DLTs enabling alternative settlement layers (e.g., Ethereum blockchain) and Clearing and Settlement Mechanisms (CSMs) (e.g., EBA clearing and STET). Furthermore, processors (e.g., VisaNet and Mastercard Switch) and outsourcing entities that manage technical operations such as Finanz Informatik, serving the German Savings Banks Finance Group are also part of this layer. Together with PSPs, these entities operate within the governance frameworks of payment schemes (e.g., SEPA Inst., SPAA, Girocard, Visa or Mastercard), which mandate the rules and standards for how transactions are executed along the payment chain.

This architectural complexity of the European payment landscape presents a trade-off between efficiency and robustness. While the fragmentation and specialization of actors have optimized efficiency and user experience, they also introduced systemic fragility. In contrast to a payment with cash, digital payments have evolved into a complex chain of sequential validations. Hence, the resilience of Europe's entire payment chain is defined by its weakest chain link. A disruption at a single stage, be it a technical outage at an acquirer, a cyberattack on a CSM or an internet failure, can halt the entire transaction flow, exposing the landscape to significant operational risk.

Against this backdrop of geopolitical vulnerability and structural fragmentation, the subsequent section analyzes and compares the multiple shades of resiliencies between tokenized forms of money and the Digital Euro.

3 Resilience in Digital Retail Payments: An Analytical Comparison Between Tokenized Forms of Money and the Digital Euro

3.1 The Valuable, But Partial Contribution of Tokenized Forms of Money to the Resilience of the Retail Payment Market

Crypto-assets pegged to a fiat currency (principally stablecoins and stable crypto-assets) are frequently cited as offering highly resilient payment mechanisms due to the distributed architecture of their underlying infrastructure. Indeed, DLT, such as blockchains, ensure that no single point of failure can compromise the entire network, making it robust against local outages or cyberattacks targeting specific participants (also called "nodes"). The Bitcoin network, for instance, has been operating without any outage since March 11, 2013 (Narayanan 2015).

However, resilience in retail payments is defined not only by the availability of the settlement ledger but also the reliability of the end-to-end transaction chain. When retail payments are made with stable crypto-assets (hereafter named "crypto-payments"), the overall resilience hinges on its weakest link. Two structural vulnerabilities question their superior resilience.

Firstly, while the settlement layer may be decentralized, the channels and protocols used to initiate crypto-payments are often operated or governed by centralized entities. For instance, payment cards for crypto-payments are typically issued by large exchanges such as Coinbase and Binance and require their authorization of transactions at the POS. Thus, if the authorization server fails the payment is rejected regardless of the availability of the underlying blockchain ledger. Moreover, the interaction between user wallets and the blockchain is often mediated by Remote Procedure Call (RPC) nodes to facilitate access. RPCs are software communication protocols used for reading data from or writing data to a blockchain. Hence, although resilient RPC node provider solutions exist, such as Chainstack with an uptime of over 99.99% (Chainstack 2025), RPC providers create centralized bottlenecks and represent a single point of failure, frequently being targeted by Distributed Denial-of-Service attacks (Gross 2025).

Secondly, unlike cash, owners of stable crypto-assets do not physically possess their funds without external dependencies. Although an end user may possess the private keys to control their crypto-assets, the ability to perform a transfer with final settlement[4] is intrinsically linked to the stability and reliability of the internet itself—a factor that is far from guaranteed. This vulnerability to physical infrastructure failures becomes quickly tangible when considering the massive power outage that struck Spain and Portugal in April 2025 (Henley et al. 2025). Similarly, an internet outage due to a Verizon network malfunction lasted approximately three hours in the USA in 2019 (Diaz 2019). The same year, the Indian government suspended internet access in Kashmir for nine days amid mass protests related to a controversial domestic law (Masih et al. 2019).

As a result, at the front-end layer, crypto-payments are structurally not more resilient than traditional card-based payment methods, because they are in practice also vulnerable to operational risks imposed by front-end dependencies and a fragile internet infrastructure. The following section examines the proposal of the European Central Bank (ECB) to maximize resilience in the European retail payment market through the introduction of a Digital Euro.

[4] There exist so-called Layer 2 solutions, which process transactions off the main blockchain (Layer 1) to increase speed and reduce costs. However, they entail liquidity risks and delayed finality due to the required online settlement verification and recording on the main blockchain.

3.2 Strengthening European Payment Resilience Through the Digital Euro

The Digital Euro would be a European digital payment solution built by Europeans for Europeans. The Eurosystem's strategy to enhance the resilience of the European retail payments landscape covers both the technical infrastructure and the very foundation of the monetary system. In other words, the Digital Euro is designed as a resilience mechanism for the currency itself. By introducing a digital equivalent to cash, the Eurosystem would aim to preserve the general public's access to central bank money. This ensures that the European payment system remains anchored by a sovereign, universally accessible public asset, regardless of operational failures or strategic redirection of private intermediaries.

The Digital Euro is designed to support a broad spectrum of use cases, including person-to-person, POS and e-commerce payments. The following sections evaluate how the Digital Euro is uniquely positioned to strengthen the resilience of European retail payments, with a specific focus on the physical POS and e-commerce environments.

3.2.1 Offline: Setting a Higher Resilience Standard at the POS

The ECB would issue a Digital Euro with offline functionality, allowing Digital Euro to be reused in multiple transactions without the need for internet connectivity. Today, in situations where there is no internet connectivity, for example during in-flight purchases, deferred authorization mechanisms are used where payment information is temporarily stored in POS terminals until internet connectivity is restored to authorize and settle a transaction. In such situations, the merchant bears a credit risk because it cannot verify a consumer's available balance to perform the transaction and it has to submit the deferred payment authorization to the merchant's bank (the acquiring bank) within a given timeframe, usually 24 hours (Visa 2021).

In contrast, just like physical cash, the offline Digital Euro itself is stored locally in an offline Digital Euro wallet and transacted on a peer-to-peer basis. Offline Digital Euro may be held on a device such as a smartphone, smart card or POS terminal. For smartphones, the storage relies on so-called "secure elements" (SE),[5] integrated by OEMs such as Apple and Samsung, which are designed to protect funds against the risk of double spending. Following the analogy of physical cash, payments with offline Digital Euro would offer immediate offline authorization, guaranteeing that the SE is genuine, and final settlement without involving any PSP (European Commission 2023, Art. 30). This means that the availability of funds is verified offline, and the funds move instantly between devices, for example via Near Field Communication (NFC). Hence, a payment with offline Digital Euro would

[5] A tamper-proof chip with pre-installed software that can store confidential and cryptographic data and run secure applications.

offer lower credit risk in comparison to transactions with private money (see simplified flow in below Fig. 2). To ensure a common user experience across the euro area, necessary business rules and technical standards for offline Digital Euro transactions would be defined within a Digital Euro scheme rulebook.

By removing the reliance on internet connectivity and third-party validation, the offline solution ensures that Digital Euro users would always have the ability to pay, even during network disruptions At the same time, banks are enabled to avoid the usual credit risks related to traditional offline payments. For example, on August 30, 2025, when the banking group Credit Mutuel experienced a critical failure of its authorization servers for 2 hours, the entire bank's payment acceptance services became unreachable (Le Monde 2025). An offline Digital Euro, functioning independently of authorization servers, would have allowed merchants serviced by Credit Mutuel to sustain payment acceptance throughout such an outage.

Despite the promising advantages of offline Digital Euro to bolster resilience at the POS across Europe, it is not a panacea for all infrastructure failures. While the transfer of offline Digital Euro between SEs would take place offline, the lifecycle of offline Digital Euro is constraint by limits imposed in the draft regulation of a digital euro. Theoretically, consumers could remain offline indefinitely, as long as they would fund and defund their offline Digital Euro wallets exclusively through offline transactions within allowed holding limits. However, system security and integrity would rely on synchronization (European Central Bank 2024). Online connectivity with the Digital Euro Service Platform (DESP) via PSPs is required to

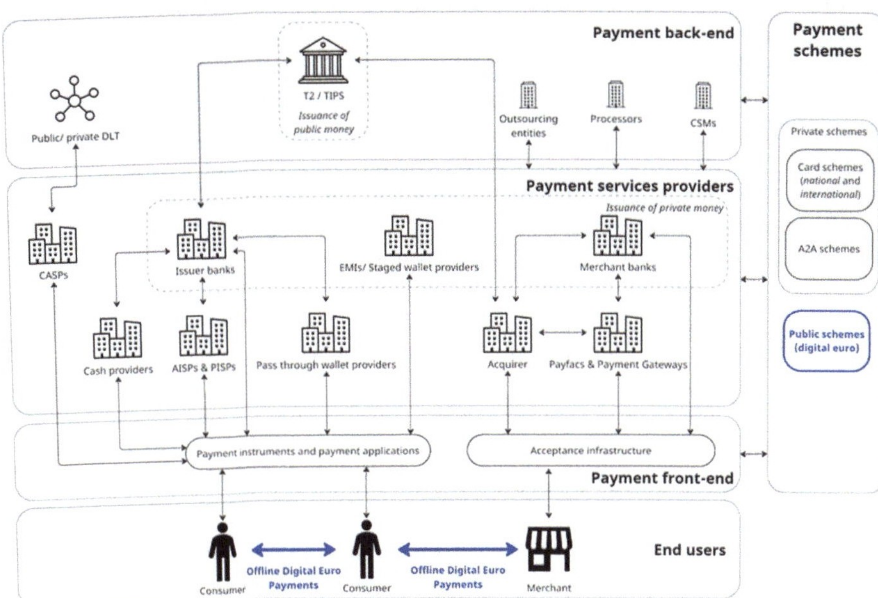

Fig. 2 Offline Digital Euro payments in Europe's regulated payment ecosystem (designed by the Authors)

perform critical checks to detect instances where hardware and software security were bypassed. The same online connectivity is also necessary to verify the authenticity of offline Digital Euro during the defunding process, ensuring accurate reconciliation with the Eurosystem ledger when offline Digital Euro funds are converted into cash or private money.

Another limitation is the reliance on non-European smartphone providers. Currently, major OEMs manufacturing devices capable of supporting offline Digital Euro do not have their headquarters located in Europe. From a geopolitical perspective, this dependence raises sovereignty concerns regarding the resilience of consumer-facing front-end services. However, the proposed regulation for a Digital Euro introduces safeguards to mandate access to smartphones, including their SE (European Commission 2023). In particular, Article 5.5 of the underlying DMA states that gatekeepers "*shall allow end users to access and use, through its core platform services, content, subscriptions, features or other items, by using the software application of a business user, including where those end users acquired such items from the relevant business user without using the core platform services of the gatekeeper*" (European Parliament and Council of the European Union 2022). Since this provision only partially mitigates dependency risks by ensuring fair access and interoperability, offline Digital Euro would also be made available via smart cards. This strategy not only mitigates the reliance on smartphones but also improves the overall accessibility of the Digital Euro, for example for the elderly.

Consequently, the architectural paradigm of offline Digital Euro fundamentally diverges from standard DLT models. In DLT environments, ownership of assets is recorded on a shared network state, which requires persistent connectivity for access and consensus. On the other side, the ECB's proposal for an offline Digital Euro leverages hardware-based local storage to become a digital bearer instrument. This architecture enables transaction finality in peer-to-peer transactions without requiring settlement verification and recording by a third party. By decoupling payment execution from network availability, the Digital Euro introduces a new layer of operational resilience, ensuring access to public digital money when traditional digital payment methods pause.

At this stage, it must be noted that consumers would be offered the choice to receive access to online Digital Euro, offline Digital Euro or both. Nonetheless, due diligence checks during onboarding to the Digital Euro environment would be standardized. The following section explores the potential benefits of online Digital Euro.

3.2.2 Online: Enhancing Resilience Both for POS and E-Commerce Payments

A resilient online Digital Euro must ensure high and consistent levels of robustness along all segments of its payment chain. Following the description of Europe's regulated payment landscape in Sect. 2.1.1, the payment chain can be conceptually separated into three distinct layers: the back-end infrastructure provided by the Eurosystem, the intermediary role of PSPs, and the front-end payment solutions available to consumers and merchants.

A Look at the Digital Euro Back-end

The back-end infrastructure of the Digital Euro, referred to as the Digital Euro Service Platform (DESP), forms the operational core of the payment system. The DESP consists of several modular components, each responsible for delivering specific core functions. These include settlement services for online transaction finality; risk and fraud management services designed to monitor and mitigate illicit activity; and alias look-up services, which facilitate the mapping of end user identifiers such as telephone numbers to specific Digital Euro Account Numbers (DEAN) (European Central Bank 2025d).

The ECB has clarified that the Digital Euro would be built by EU nationals controlled by EU nationals on European infrastructure (Cipollone 2025a). Furthermore, the Digital Euro infrastructure would not rely on DLT (European Central Bank 2025e). Instead, it would utilize a payment back-end architecture distributed across multiple geographical regions within Europe (European Central Bank 2023b). This multi-region distribution is a strategic requirement for robust fault tolerance, high availability, and guaranteed business continuity, even under stress conditions:

> The digital euro components should demonstrate a high degree of reliability enabling them to be available 24 hours every day of the year by ensuring an availability rate of at least 99.99% – allowing for a maximum tolerable downtime of 13.15 minutes – calculated on a quarterly basis. The digital euro components should tolerate hardware and/or software failures so that overall performance and availability is still provided as intended, thus ensuring resilience in the face of component failures and local and regional disasters. the digital euro components should be distributed between at least two operational sites in each geographical region and across at least three geographical regions (defined as at least 500km between two operational sites belonging to different geographical regions). The digital euro components should ensure a Recovery Time Objective of 45 seconds, even if a switchover to another operational site is required. (European Central Bank 2023c)

Hence, the DESP infrastructure would be distributed across at least three different regions in Europe, distant by at least 500 km each. Operational sites would not only be interconnected within individual regions but also between regions (see Fig. 3 below).

The Eurosystem has confirmed that it would perform settlement verification and recording of online Digital Euro transactions as well as manage the settlement ledger for all online Digital Euro balances (European Central Bank 2022). However, the internal governance framework, potentially involving various National Central Banks has remained publicly undefined. Therefore, it is too early to perform a complete comparative analysis between the resilience of DESP and a DLT infrastructure.

A Look at the PSP Level

PSPs, such as commercial banks, would play a key role in the distribution of the Digital Euro to end users. Under current regulatory frameworks, including PSD2 and AML/CFT regulations, PSPs are mandated to perform due diligence checks prior to offering payment services. In the context of the online Digital Euro, the successful completion of these due diligence checks translates into the issuance of a password called “technical proof” by PSPs to end users. This proof functions

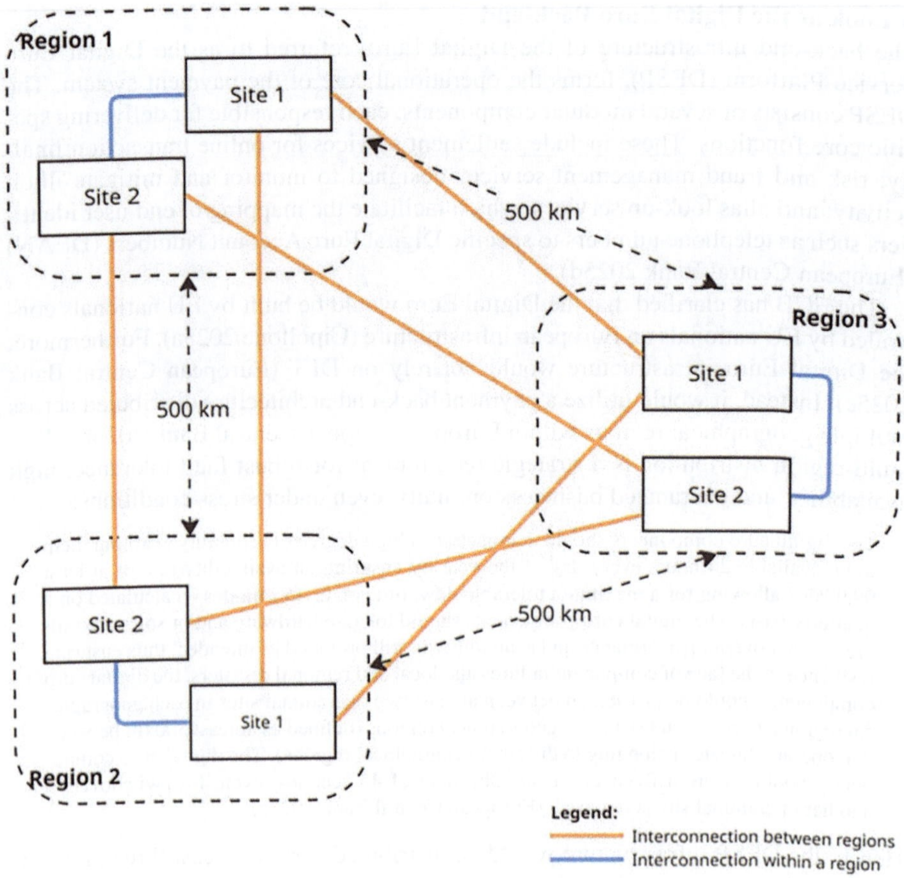

Fig. 3 Visualization of the geographical distribution of the DESP infrastructure (designed by the Authors)

analogously to a private key in the realm of crypto-assets. It provides cryptographic proof of ownership allowing end users to claim and access their online Digital Euro funds, which are recorded securely in the settlement ledger of the Eurosystem.

A notable feature of the online Digital Euro is its proposed "emergency switching" between PSPs, which significantly enhances system resilience. This functionality safeguards operational continuity by decoupling asset accessibility from the availability of any single intermediary. If a PSP becomes technically unavailable, end users can still access their online Digital Euro funds by sharing their technical proof with a functioning PSP. This switching process between PSPs mirrors the resilience offered by DLTs, where end users retain control over their assets independently of the status of any intermediary. In both the Digital Euro and DLT environments this robustness is achieved because funds are not held within a bank's infrastructure but are safeguarded in an independently governed infrastructure.

A Look at the Digital Euro Front-end

To ensure broad accessibility and foster consumer choice, the Digital Euro would support a diverse range of front-end payment solutions. Consumers would be able to initiate payments via a standalone Digital Euro app provided by the Eurosystem as well as through the proprietary interfaces of PSPs. While PSPs would be mandated to support the Digital Euro app, the integration of Digital Euro services into their own proprietary front-end solutions would be voluntary (European Commission 2023). To cater to modern consumer behavior these user interfaces would accommodate various payment initiation methods, including QR-code scanning for request-to-pay scenarios and integrated in-app payments for frictionless e-commerce transactions.

The Digital Euro app would serve as a critical resilience anchor for the European payment landscape (Cipollone 2025b). By providing a public-sector alternative to non-European payment applications such as Apple Wallet and Google Wallet, it mitigates strategic dependencies on foreign infrastructures. Furthermore, it would ensure continuity in the case of a significant cyberattack on one or multiple PSPs. For example, should a PSP's app suffer from an outage while its backend infrastructure remains intact, the end user could still access their online Digital Euro funds via the Digital Euro app. Also, in the event of a systemic failure where multiple PSPs within a specific geographic region become unreachable, end users could easily utilize the emergency switching functionality.

Notwithstanding the resilience advantages provided by a plurality of front-end solutions in the e-commerce domain, the payment front-end remains the most vulnerable segment of the payment chain. This structural fragility stems from the reliance on merchants' environments. Most e-commerce websites operate on traditional client-server architectures, which inherently include single points of failure. Such centralized frameworks expose e-commerce platforms to risks such as server outages, cyberattacks, or technical malfunctions, which can disrupt payment processing and hinder transactions regardless of the availability of payment rails themselves.

This dependency on merchant-operated infrastructure represents a significant boundary to the Eurosystem's ambitions of achieving end-to-end resilience. These limitations are not unique to a Digital Euro but are also faced by the crypto-payment industry, where decentralized settlement layers often remain dependent on centralized user interfaces for transaction initiation. Hence, the "last mile" challenge is a structural and shared vulnerabilities across both technological paradigms.

3.2.3 Comparative Analysis of Resilience Across Retail Payment Solutions

The Table 1 provides a comparison between payments based on "classic" payment systems (e.g., ICS or Apple Pay), stable crypto-asset payments, and online/offline Digital Euro across various dimensions such as sovereignty, payment back-end resilience, PSP level resilience, and end-user level resilience.

Table 1 Resilience of payment methods—A comparative analysis (designed by the Authors)

	Payment based on "classic" payment system (e.g. ICS or Apple Pay)	Stable crypto-asset payment	Online Digital Euro payment	Offline Digital Euro payment
Sovereignty (geopolitical resilience)	Standard	Enhanced (public blockchains could be seen as more sovereign infrastructures)	Enhanced (the DESP would be sourced from EU entities only)	Enhanced (no reliance on any payment back-end)
Payment back-end (operational resilience)	Standard	Enhanced (decentralized infrastructure)	Enhanced (decentralized infrastructure)	*n/a*
PSP level (operational resilience)	Standard	Enhanced (PSP switching possible via disintermediated stable crypto-asset payments)	Enhanced (emergency switching between PSPs)	*n/a*
End user level (operational resilience)	Standard	Standard	Standard	Enhanced (no internet connection required for payment)

Classic payment systems are described as providing standard levels of resilience and sovereignty, relying on traditional infrastructures and payment back-ends. In contrast, stable crypto-asset payments and online Digital Euro payments offer enhanced geopolitical and operational resilience. While stable crypto-asset payments increase geopolitical resilience by utilizing globally decentralized public blockchains, online Digital Euro payments rely on operational sites distributed across Europe. Both payment solutions provide PSP switching functionalities, allowing users to avoid having their funds locked in with their PSPs.

Offline Digital Euro, on the other hand, showcases an enhanced level of resilience across all dimensions. Paying with offline Digital Euro does not require a PSP or payment back-end to process the transaction. Funds are stored at the end user level and can be moved without any internet connection.

4 Conclusion

The evolution of European retail payments is defined by a critical need for operational resilience. Current reliance on global card schemes, BigTechs and complex supply chains creates structural vulnerabilities, yet private sector efforts to build an independent alternative have been stifled by market fragmentation and collective action problems (often modeled as a "Prisoner's Dilemma").

While stable crypto-assets offer decentralized back-end resilience, their practical utility is constrained by reliance on centralized gateways and continuous connectivity. In that context, the Eurosystem's Digital Euro proposes a hybrid solution. The offline modality utilizes hardware-based secure elements to enable peer-to-peer settlement without internet access, replicating the resilience of cash. At the same time, the online payment back-end infrastructure targets high availability with a decentralized set-up while PSPs are required to offer "emergency switching" between PSPs to their customers to decouple asset access from intermediary unavailability.

Ultimately, while merchant-operated infrastructure represents a significant boundary to Europe's ambitions of achieving end-to-end resilience in retail payments, the Digital Euro represents a vital policy intervention. By resolving structural coordination failures and bringing unique attributes of cash into the digital realm—for example offline functionality—it aims to safeguard the strategic sovereignty and long-term stability of the European retail payment landscape.

Acknowledgements We would like to thank Massimo Cappuccio, Charles-Enguerrand Coste and Lauren Del Giudice for helpful discussions and comments. All remaining errors are ours. This chapter was written independently by the authors and is not directly connected to the Eurosystem's Digital Euro project. It should not be interpreted as reflecting the European Central Bank's position on the design of the Digital Euro.

Disclaimer This chapter should not be reported as representing the views of the European Central Bank (ECB). The views expressed are those of the authors and do not necessarily reflect those of the ECB.

References

Bank of England (2024) Operational resilience in a macroprudential framework. Financial stability paper. Bank of England, London. https://www.bankofengland.co.uk/-/media/boe/files/financial-stability-paper/2024/operational-resilience-in-a-macroprudential-framework. Accessed 13 Nov 2025

Chainstack (2025) Chainstack global node. https://chainstack.com/global-nodes/. Accessed 7 Dec 2025

Cipollone P (2025a) The digital euro: a collective step forward for Europe. Introductory statement by Piero Cipollone, Member of the Executive Board of the ECB, at the Committee on Economic and Monetary Affairs of the European Parliament, Brussels, 17 Nov 2025. European Central Bank, Frankfurt am Main. https://www.ecb.europa.eu/press/key/date/2025/html/ecb.sp251117_1~e62f13b4dd.en.html. Accessed 18 Nov 2025

Cipollone P (2025b) The digital euro: ensuring resilience and inclusion in digital payments. Introductory statement by Piero Cipollone, Member of the Executive Board of the ECB, at the Committee on Economic and Monetary Affairs of the European Parliament, Brussels, 4 Sept 2025. European Central Bank, Frankfurt am Main. https://www.ecb.europa.eu/press/key/date/2025/html/ecb.sp250904~70ab593276.en.html. Accessed 14 Nov 2025

Daðason KT (2019) Valitor dæmt til að greiða 1,2 milljarða [Valitor ordered to pay 1.2 billion]. Vísir, 24 Apr 2019. https://www.visir.is/g/2019190429492/valitor-daemt-til-ad-greida-1-2-milljarda. Accessed 11 Nov 2025

DataCell ehf. v. Visa Inc. et al. (2015) No. 1:14-cv-1658. Memorandum opinion. U.S. District Court for the Eastern District of Virginia, 30 July 2015. https://law.justia.com/cases/federal/district-courts/virginia/vaedce/1:2014cv01658/311120/56/. Accessed 13 Nov 2025

Diaz J (2019) Verizon outages reported nationwide. *The New York Times*, 18 Dec 2019. https://www.nytimes.com/2019/12/18/business/verizon-outages.html. Accessed 14 Nov 2025

European Central Bank (2022) Progress on the investigation phase of a digital euro—second report. European Central Bank, Frankfurt am Main. https://www.ecb.europa.eu/euro/digital_euro/timeline/profuse/shared/pdf//ecb.degov221221_Progress.en.pdf. Accessed 11 Nov 2025

European Central Bank (2023a) The Eurosystem's retail payments strategy: priorities for 2024 and beyond. European Central Bank, Frankfurt am Main. https://www.ecb.europa.eu/pub/pdf/other/ecb.eurosystemretailpaymentsstrategy~5a74eb9ac1.en.pdf. Accessed 12 Nov 2025

European Central Bank (2023b) Market research on possible technical solutions for a digital euro. European Central Bank, Frankfurt am Main. https://www.ecb.europa.eu/press/intro/news/html/ecb.mipnews230113.en.html. Accessed 15 Nov 2025

European Central Bank (2023c) Digital euro market research – annex 1 – functional and non-functional requirements linked to the market research for a potential digital euro implementation. European Central Bank, Frankfurt am Main. https://www.ecb.europa.eu/euro/digital_euro/timeline/profuse/shared/pdf//ecb.dedocs230113_Annex_1_Digital_euro_market_research.en.pdf. Accessed 11 Nov 2025

European Central Bank (2024) State of play on offline digital euro. Presentation at the 11th ERPB technical session on digital euro, Frankfurt am Main, 11 April 2024. https://www.ecb.europa.eu/euro/digital_euro/timeline/profuse/shared/pdf/ecb.degov240411_item3updateofflinedigitaleuro.en.pdf. Accessed 18 Nov 2025

European Central Bank (2025a) Most EU countries rely on international card schemes for card payments, ECB report shows. Press release, 28 Feb 2025. European Central Bank, Frankfurt am Main. https://www.ecb.europa.eu/press/pr/date/2025/html/ecb.pr250228_1~7f0697af45.en.html. Accessed 12 Nov 2025

European Central Bank (2025b) Report on card schemes and processors. European Central Bank, Frankfurt am Main. https://www.ecb.europa.eu/pub/pdf/other/ecb.reportcardschemes202502~1614226b0a.cs.pdf. Accessed 13 Nov 2025

European Central Bank (2025c) Fit of the digital euro in the payment ecosystem: report on the dedicated Euro Retail Payments Board (ERPB) technical workstream. European Central Bank, Frankfurt am Main. https://www.ecb.europa.eu/euro/digital_euro/timeline/profuse/shared/pdf/ecb.deprep251030_digital_euro_fit_payment_ecosystem_report.en.pdf. Accessed 13 Nov 2025

European Central Bank (2025d) ECB selects digital euro service providers. European Central Bank, Frankfurt am Main. https://www.ecb.europa.eu/press/intro/news/html/ecb.mipnews251002.en.html. Accessed 12 Nov 2025

European Central Bank (2025e) FAQs on the digital euro. European Central Bank, Frankfurt am Main. https://www.ecb.europa.eu/euro/digital_euro/faqs/html/ecb.faq_digital_euro.en.html. Accessed 1 Dec 2025

European Commission (2012) Case COMP/39921—Datacell/Visa & MasterCard (provisional assessment). European Commission, Brussels. https://wikileaks.org/IMG/pdf/EUPreliminaryDecision1.pdf. Accessed 15 Nov 2025

European Commission (2022) Ukraine: EU agrees to exclude key Russian banks from SWIFT. Press release, 2 Mar 2022. European Commission, Brussels. https://ec.europa.eu/commission/presscorner/detail/en/ip_22_1484. Accessed 12 Nov 2025

European Commission (2023) Proposal for a Regulation of the European Parliament and of the Council on the establishment of the digital euro. COM (2023) 369 final. https://eur-lex.europa.eu/legal-content/EN/TXT/?uri=CELEX:52023PC0369. Accessed 10 Nov 2025

European Parliament and Council of the European Union (2022) Regulation (EU) 2022/1925 of the European Parliament and of the Council of 14 September 2022 on contestable and fair markets in the digital sector and amending Directives (EU) 2019/1937 and (EU) 2020/1828 (Digital

Markets Act). Official Journal of the European Union, OJ L 265, 12 December 2022. https://eur-lex.europa.eu/legal-content/EN/TXT/?uri=uriserv%3AOJ.L_.2022.265.01.0001.01.ENG. Accessed 18 Nov 2025

European Parliament and Council of the European Union (2024) Regulation (EU) 2024/886 of the European Parliament and of the Council of 13 Mar 2024 amending Regulations (EU) No 260/2012 and (EU) 2021/1230 and Directives 98/26/EC and (EU) 2015/2366 as regards instant credit transfers in euro. Official Journal of the European Union, OJ L, 2024/886. https://eur-lex.europa.eu/legal-content/EN/TXT/?uri=CELEX:32024R0886. Accessed 12 Nov 2025

Greenberg A (2010) Visa, MasterCard move to choke WikiLeaks. Forbes, 7 Dec 2010. https://www.forbes.com/sites/andygreenberg/2010/12/07/visa-mastercard-move-to-choke-wikileaks/. Accessed 12 Nov 2025

Gross J (2025) Amazon outage forces hundreds of websites offline for hours. The New York Times, 20 Oct 2025. https://www.nytimes.com/2025/10/20/business/aws-down-internet-outage.html. Accessed 17 Nov 2025

Henley J, Kassam A, Jones S (2025) Tens of millions across Spain and Portugal hit by huge power outage. The Guardian, 28 Apr 2025. https://www.theguardian.com/world/2025/apr/28/spain-portugal-power-outage. Accessed 13 Nov 2025

Le Monde (2025) Le Crédit mutuel touché par une panne qui a empêché ses clients de payer ou de retirer de l'argent. Le Monde, 30 Aug 2025. https://www.lemonde.fr/economie/article/2025/08/30/le-credit-mutuel-touche-par-une-panne-qui-a-empeche-ses-clients-de-payer-ou-de-retirer-de-l-argent_6637559_3234.html. Accessed 12 Nov 2025

Masih N, Irfan S, Slater J (2019) India's internet shutdown in Kashmir is now the longest ever in a democracy. The Washington Post, 15 Dec 2019. https://www.washingtonpost.com/world/asia_pacific/indias-internet-shutdown-in-kashmir-is-now-the-longest-ever-in-a-democracy/2019/12/15/bb0693ea-1dfc-11ea-977a-15a6710ed6da_story.html. Accessed 15 Nov 2025

Mastercard (2022) Mastercard statement on suspension of Russian operations. Press release, 5 Mar 2022. Mastercard, Purchase. https://www.mastercard.com/global/en/news-and-trends/press/2022/march/mastercard-statement-on-suspension-of-russian-operations.html. Accessed 14 Nov 2025

Narayanan A (2015) Analyzing the 2013 Bitcoin fork: centralized decision-making saved the day. CITP Blog, Princeton University. https://blog.citp.princeton.edu/2015/07/28/analyzing-the-2013-bitcoin-fork-centralized-decision-making-saved-the-day/. Accessed 13 Nov 2025

PayPal (2025) PayPal announces plans to revolutionize in-store payments in Germany. Press release, 5 May 2025. PayPal. https://newsroom.paypal-corp.com/2025-05-05-PayPal-announces-plans-to-revolutionize-in-store-payments-in-Germany. Accessed 12 Nov 2025

Valdimarsson OR (2013) Iceland's top court orders valitor to process WikiLeaks payments. Bloomberg, 24 Apr 2013. https://www.bloomberg.com/news/articles/2013-04-24/iceland-s-top-court-orders-valitor-to-process-wikileaks-payments. Accessed 13 Nov 2025

Visa (2021) Deferred authorization indicator reminder. Visa Business News, Article ID: AI10879, Mar 2021. https://usa.visa.com/dam/VCOM/global/support-legal/documents/deferred-authorization-indicator-reminder.pdf. Accessed 17 Nov 2025

Visa (2022) Visa suspends operations in Russia. Press release, 5 Mar 2022. Visa Inc., San Francisco. https://usa.visa.com/about-visa/newsroom/press-releases.releaseId.18871.html. Accessed 15 Nov 2025

China's e-CNY: From Wallet Wars to a National Payments Operating System

Zennon Kapron

Abstract China did not build the e-CNY to replace cash so much as to upgrade the operating system of its money. By introducing a programmable, state-issued payment rail that can run beneath commercial wallets and into devices, the PBoC (People's Bank of China) aims to harden resilience, reclaim visibility over a previously duopolistic payments stack, and open new pipes for industrial automation and cross-border settlement. This chapter argues that the e-CNY's real test is not retail hype, but whether it can quietly become the common layer under Alipay, WeChat Pay, and future machine-to-machine flows, while balancing privacy, liquidity, and global interoperability. We map the architecture, incentives, and geopolitics, and set out measurable milestones to demonstrate whether the "payments OS" vision is working.

Keywords CBDC · e-CNY China · Alipay WeChat Pay

1 Introduction

China did not set out to build another wallet. It set out to re-platform money. For a decade, Alipay and WeChat Pay defined the consumer experience of payments: fast, QR-native, and seamless. The e-CNY aims lower in the stack: a programmable, state-issued payment rail designed to be resilient in outages, precise for policy delivery, and observable for supervision, while remaining largely invisible to the user (People's Bank of China 2021; BIS 2020). In that sense, the digital yuan is less a product than an operating system: a kernel beneath existing front-ends that can run in phones, cards, wearables, terminals, and eventually machines.

Why go to this trouble now? There are three principal reasons. First, policy transmission: stimulus vouchers, disaster relief, fee holidays, and tax rebates work better

Z. Kapron (✉)
GL Insight, Cambridge, MA, USA
e-mail: zennon@glinsight.com

S. Yazıcı et al. (eds.), *Tokenisation of Money*, Contributions to Finance and Accounting, https://doi.org/10.1007/978-3-032-22946-5_25

when they are instant, precisely targeted, and challenging to game (People's Bank of China 2021). Second, system resilience: dual-offline transfers give cash-like redundancy in a world where networks fail (People's Bank of China 2022). Third, governance and competition: the QR duopoly of WeChat Pay and Alipay delivered convenience but concentrated data and pricing power; a public rail centralizes settlement while leaving the edge to private UX (BIS 2020; People's Bank of China 2021).

This chapter makes a simple claim: if the e-CNY quietly becomes the default settlement leg under the user interfaces (UI) people already love and powers the next wave of industrial and cross-border use cases, then Beijing will have succeeded. We start with the "why" behind a payments OS, define the architecture and guardrails that make it work, and then tackle the question most readers care about: coexistence and competition with Alipay and WeChat Pay. From there, we look beyond retail to machine-to-machine and B2B flows, assess cross-border implications, examine privacy and trust, and close with adoption KPIs and realistic success/failure markers.

2 Why China Needs a Payments OS

China did not need another digital wallet; it needed a way to re-platform money. After a decade in which the QR duopoly of Alipay and WeChat Pay delivered extraordinary convenience, policymakers were confronting three structural gaps that commercial rails could not fully close: policy transmission at machine speed, system resilience, including dual-offline payments in outages, and standardized supervisory visibility for AML/CFT and macro-prudential monitoring (People's Bank of China 2021; BIS 2020).

A state rail also addresses a governance problem created by success. Alipay and WeChat Pay stitched together a nation of consumers and merchants. Still, their advantages, including closed data loops, super-app engagement, and proprietary risk models, became single points of dependence in the retail stack. The e-CNY's two-tier design recenters the settlement layer with the central bank while preserving private-sector UX competition at the edge, consistent with global CBDC principles that stress coexistence and complementarity with existing forms of money (BIS 2020; People's Bank of China 2021).

Programmability is the second pillar: policy-bounded conditionality in the form of money that can expire, be steered to eligible merchants, or settle against verifiable events such as e-invoices and delivery milestones. That is how you make stimulus granular, reduce leakage in public spending, and automate B2B workflows without rewriting the commercial front end (People's Bank of China 2021). Hardware-backed dual-offline transfers, where both payer and payee can be disconnected, extend that logic to crisis scenarios (People's Bank of China 2022).

The third driver is strategic autonomy in the form of a pragmatic push to reduce friction and vulnerability in cross-border flows that matter to China. Domestic eCNY and wholesale CBDC workstreams are complementary here: at home, the retail rail standardizes data and resilience; abroad, projects like mBridge explore real-time cross-border settlement among participating central banks and commercial banks (BIS Innovation Hub et al. 2021; BIS 2024; HKMA 2024a, 2024b). Even if capital controls remain intact, being technically able to settle trade faster and with fewer correspondent layers is an option value Beijing wants (Carnegie Endowment 2021).

Finally, the design tries to square the circle on trust and privacy. The PBoC's doctrine of "controllable (managed) anonymity" promises small-value privacy with traceability for larger or suspicious activity, an approach designed to protect users while still meeting supervisory obligations (People's Bank of China 2021; DigiChina 2022). Whether that balance convinces both domestic and international users is partly a communications challenge and partly a UX one; either way, making privacy a design parameter, not an afterthought, is central to adoption (DigiChina 2022).

If the rationale is to restack money around resilience, programmability, and observability, the next question is what that stack looks like. The e-CNY's two-tier design, wallet taxonomy, and dual-offline mechanics are specific engineering choices that translate policy aims into day-to-day payments (People's Bank of China 2021; BIS 2020).

3 Architecture Snapshot (What It Is…and Isn't)

The PBoC was very deliberate in many of the design choices that it took for the e-CNY; indeed, it is a digital currency with Chinese characteristics. Some of the more salient attributes of the e-CNY include:

Two-tier Issuance and Distribution The PBoC issues e-CNY and sets the rulebook; operating institutions (commercial banks and licensed payment platforms) distribute wallets and provide onboarding, KYC, and day-to-day service. Settlement finality rests on the central bank liability. Still, the customer relationship remains with intermediaries, which helps limit disintermediation risk and aligns with what have become international CBDC design principles (People's Bank of China 2021; BIS 2020).

Wallet Taxonomy and Limits The e-CNY supports multiple wallet types with tiered KYC and holding/transaction caps. The spectrum runs from light wallets (mobile-number registration, low limits) to full-KYC wallets with higher limits for individuals and enterprises. This allows broad access to those that are un- or underbanked, while providing guardrails against large-scale deposit flight or illicit use (People's Bank of China 2021).

Form Factors: Software and Hardware Beyond the standard app-based wallets, the e-CNY supports hardware wallets embedded in IC cards, phone chips, and wearables (badges, bracelets, smart watches). These can enable tap-and-go payments, dual-offline transfers, and elderly-friendly UX (large fonts, tactile buttons). For devices and unattended terminals, the same hardware approach underpins machine-to-machine use cases (People's Bank of China 2022).

Offline and Dual-offline Offline mode allows a connected device to pay an unconnected one; dual-offline allows value transfer when neither is connected, with risk controls (secure elements, replay prevention, post-reconnection reconciliation). This is the resilience feature most unlike conventional QR payments and is core to the "payments OS" thesis: the rail must work in any situation or context (People's Bank of China 2022).

Programmability (Within Policy Bounds) The system supports conditional payments. For example, vouchers spendable only at specific merchant categories, or funds that unlock upon verified delivery. Crucially, programmability is scoped to policy and compliance, not open-ended public smart contracts. That keeps the central bank out of application-layer front-end innovation while allowing government, banks, and platforms to implement targeted flows (People's Bank of China 2021).

Data Governance: 'Controllable Anonymity' The PBoC positions the e-CNY as providing anonymity for small-value retail, increasing granularity of visibility with value and risk. Intermediaries collect and hold user data as needed for onboarding and compliance; authorities gain standardized access for lawful purposes. The goal is to limit private data monopolies without enabling excessive surveillance. How this is perceived in the end will depend on final regulations and audits. (People's Bank of China 2021; DigiChina 2022).

Interoperability: With Legacy Rails and Cross-border Pilots Domestically, the e-CNY is meant to coexist with cash, bank deposits, and private e-money, and to interoperate with existing retail payment infrastructure via operating institutions' front ends (BIS 2020; People's Bank of China 2021). Cross-border, China participates in Project mBridge, which moved to an MVP stage in 2024, exploring real-time, PvP settlement among participating central banks and commercial banks. While mBridge is wholesale and the e-CNY is retail, the technical and governance learnings are complementary (BIS Innovation Hub et al. 2021; BIS 2024; HKMA 2024a, 2024b).

What It Is Not The e-CNY is not a public blockchain; consensus and data are centrally governed. It is also not designed to displace the super apps' front ends; instead, it provides a rail that banks and platforms can surface through SDKs and mini programs. And it is not a magic wand for RMB internationalization; capital-account policy still dominates outcomes, even if better rails improve corridor efficiency (BIS 2020; People's Bank of China 2021).

Blueprint in hand, the practical issue is where this rail meets reality: at the front end. China does not need to rip out super-apps that already work; it needs them to ride the rail. The competitive equilibrium will be set by mandates, merchant math, and SDK depth more than by slogans.

4 Coexistence or Takeover? E-CNY vs. Alipay and WeChat Pay

Alipay and WeChat Pay remain the UIs of daily life; e-CNY restacks the rail beneath them. The pragmatic equilibrium is rail-under-UI: keep familiar front-ends, route settlement over e-CNY where resilience, traceability or policy-driven conditionality are required (People's Bank of China 2021). Mandates in public collections, subsidies and transit normalize balances and acceptance without forcing a front-end switch.

Economically, a central-bank rail can compress vanilla acquiring costs and shorten settlement for SMEs; at scale, a few basis points matter in China. Platforms will pivot harder to value-added services such as loyalty, marketing, BNPL, and working-capital, where engagement and proprietary data still differentiate (BIS 2020). Data governance recenters supervisory visibility at the rail while preserving the minimum data platforms need to manage risk (People's Bank of China 2021).

In practice this likely means that the UX will remain the same on the front end, while the payments will settle in e-CNY. The government will support policy-targeted flows that such as vouchers and rebates that only can be used at eligible merchants. Finally, large chain merchants will likely keep to super-app bundles for traffic, while micro-merchants lean into e-CNY for economics.

As the space develops, it will be important to watch for explicit acceptance mandates in public payments and transit, visible shifts in SME fees and settlement latency for e-CNY vs legacy QR and SDK depth that lets third-party front-ends expose offline and conditional features. If e-CNY becomes the invisible settlement default under popular UIs, Beijing will have achieved a payments OS without breaking the apps people live in.

5 Beyond Retail: Where the OS Metaphor Earns Its Keep

The most crucial test for the e-CNY may be the flows consumers never see. A payments operating system is successful when it can move money between devices, firms, and agencies with minimal human touch, reliably, cheaply, and with policy logic baked in. Three domains stand out:

First, Industrial and IoT Payments QR wallets are excellent for people, less so for machines. An OS-level rail with hardware wallets and secure elements makes unattended payments viable: EV charging posts that settle per kilowatt; vending and ticketing that clear in spotty connectivity; smart meters that reconcile micro-payments on reconnection. These rely on offline and dual-offline transfers with replay controls and post-event reconciliation, capabilities the PBoC highlights as core resilience features rather than UX novelties (People's Bank of China 2022).

Second, B2B and Supply-chain Automation China's digital invoicing and e-logistics backbone already captures delivery, acceptance, and tax events. The policy-bounded programmability in eCNY enables automatic fund release for specific events, including partial payments upon shipment, balance upon verified receipt, and escrow-like flows tied to a verified e-invoice. You do not need public smart contracts to get 80% of the benefit; you need conditionality scoped to compliance and business rules (People's Bank of China 2021). For SMEs, that means fewer days-sales-outstanding and less reconciliation; for banks, new fee pools around programmable disbursement and enterprise wallets.

Third, Government Rails The OS frame is most persuasive in public finance: disaster relief that clears in hours, not weeks; municipal consumption vouchers with time or merchant-category limits; targeted tax rebates and fee holidays that cannot leak into ineligible uses. By placing the constraint at the rail, rather than in coupons or platform rules, policy becomes specific and auditable (People's Bank of China 2021). For citizens, the front end can still be Alipay or WeChat Pay; the constraint logic just lives below the waterline.

All of this raises a practical design question: will the state build parallel front ends, or expose these functions via APIs/SDKs so banks and platforms can surface them inside the super-apps and corporate portals firms already use? The latter is the only scalable answer. A two-tier model that keeps customer relationships with intermediaries and caps/tiers retail balances to limit disintermediation is precisely how the PBoC and the BIS frame CBDC coexistence (BIS 2020; People's Bank of China 2021). That alignment matters for developer momentum: the more the rail behaves like an addressable system service (offline transfer, conditional payout, hardware wallet), the faster enterprise teams will embed it.

Risk Lives in the Plumbing Dual-offline value transfer requires device attestation, anti-replay protections, and rapid post-reconnect reconciliation to keep fraud contained (People's Bank of China 2022). Conditional payments need careful scoping so "programmability" doesn't mutate into opaque administrative controls. And merchant math must work: if acceptance requires new terminals but delivers no gain in fees or settlement latency, adoption will stall. That's why the KPI set for this domain is different: the count of offline-capable devices in the field, the share of public disbursements running with constraints, and the proportion of invoice-linked B2B payments are better success markers than app downloads.

The promise, if it works, is subtle: an OS that fades into the background while making the economy more machine-addressable, exactly where private QR rails reach their limits.

Domestically, the OS can harden resilience and sharpen policy. But money is global. China's wholesale work tests whether similar gains can emerge across borders without rewriting capital-account policy (BIS Innovation Hub et al. 2021; BIS 2024; HKMA 2024a, 2024b). The question is not "RMB vs. USD," but whether selected trade corridors can settle faster, cheaper, and with PvP finality.

6 Cross-Border Dimension

Cross-border is where ambitions meet policy. China's retail e-CNY is domestic by design; the wholesale track is where settlement logic jumps borders. Here, Project mBridge looms large: a multi-CBDC platform led by the BIS Innovation Hub's Hong Kong Centre with HKMA, the Bank of Thailand, the UAE's central bank, and the PBoC's Digital Currency Institute. The project moved to an MVP stage in 2024, aiming for real-time, PvP settlement among participating central and commercial banks (BIS Innovation Hub et al. 2021; BIS 2024; HKMA 2024a, 2024b). The goal is more efficient plumbing: fewer correspondent hops, lower FX frictions, and atomic settlement that natively embeds compliance.

That will not dissolve capital controls or replace correspondent banking overnight. Still, it will create corridor effects: faster settlement where RMB is already critical, such as trade with Greater Bay Area counterparties, parts of ASEAN, and Belt and Road projects. The connective tissue with retail e-CNY is pragmatic rather than direct: domestic standardization of data and resilience at home, plus wholesale rails abroad, lowers the operational cost of choosing to transact in RMB when it already makes sense (BIS 2020; BIS Innovation Hub et al. 2021). Meanwhile, Hong Kong's role as a sandbox has deepened: HKMA's work has gradually expanded e-CNY connectivity, for example, enabling easier top-ups via local infrastructure to support cross-boundary retail scenarios, signaling how consumer-facing use cases can be tested without rewriting the capital account (HKMA 2024a, 2024b).

The interoperability challenges are as much governance as code: who provides FX, how AML/CFT checks port across jurisdictions, what data is shared with whom, and what the escalation path looks like when rules conflict. Those are solvable in constrained corridors with strong supervisors; they are harder at a global scale. Hence, the likely path: an MVP-to-production arc focused on a few high-traffic lanes, while the domestic e-CNY keeps maturing in parallel.

Suppose the domestic OS quietly becomes the default settlement leg, and the wholesale rail delivers faster, safer corridor settlement where RMB demand already exists. In that case, Beijing will have bought option value: a future in which using RMB is technically easier, not a foregone conclusion, but a live choice (BIS 2024; HKMA 2024a, 2024b).

7 Privacy, Security, and Trust

Controllable anonymity is achieved through tiered KYC limits, limited data collection, and regulated supervisory access to balance privacy with necessary oversight for AML/CFT and macro-prudential monitoring (People's Bank of China 2021; BIS 2020; DigiChina 2022).

Dual-offline value transfer adds resilience but requires secure hardware, anti-replay measures, and reconciliation rules to avoid double-spending. Recovery processes should protect user identity and trust, especially for low-KYC wallets and vulnerable users (People's Bank of China 2022). The goal is cash-like usability with improved accountability.

Effective communication and governance depend on transparent disclosures in wallets, clear privacy controls, and regular audits. International cooperation on data localization and lawful access will be key to foreign adoption of e-CNY systems (People's Bank of China 2021; DigiChina 2022).

8 Banking-System Impact

A key concern with a retail CBDC is its potential to drain deposits from traditional banks, thereby raising funding costs and constraining credit supply. To mitigate this risk, China has implemented precautionary measures such as two-tier distribution, a non-interest-bearing design, and tiered caps and limits—all aimed at keeping balances transactional and reducing the likelihood of flight-to-quality during times of stress (BIS 2020; People's Bank of China 2021). It will be essential to observe how dynamically these caps are adjusted in response to financial shocks.

Turning to payment economics, the introduction of e-CNY can compress basic acquiring margins and accelerate settlement for SMEs. Banks and payment platforms will likely adapt revenue models toward VAS such as merchant analytics, cash-flow lending, BNPL offerings, loyalty programs, and mini-program storefronts. The payment rail itself becomes a cost-efficient pipe, while the competitive focus shifts to the margins available through VAS.

In addition, new roles and fee pools will emerge for intermediaries, including wallet issuance and management, SDK distribution, hardware wallet provisioning, corporate onboarding for enterprise wallets, and the design of programmable disbursements. For treasury and cash management teams, the benefits include streamlined reconciliation and reduced counterparty risk, especially when settlement finality is anchored at the central bank.

Finally, supervision and risk management stand to gain from the standardized transaction data at the infrastructure level, which will enhance fraud detection, strengthen AML/CFT investigations, and support stress-testing. For banks, real-time transaction visibility can reduce operational risks and minimize fraud losses, while for regulators, it sharpens the feedback loop for more accurate policy decisions (BIS 2020; People's Bank of China 2021).

With incentives aligned, execution comes down to mandate density, merchant math, and developer momentum.

9 Adoption Strategy and KPIs

Levers That Move Both Sides of the Market Public-sector anchors (taxes, fines, fees, subsidies, public payroll), transit and utilities, and targeted consumption vouchers normalize holding and acceptance. Merchant-side carrots include lower fees and faster settlement for SME ticket sizes. Citizen-side nudges include red-envelope campaigns, frictionless top-ups, and guaranteed acceptance at public-touchpoint merchants.

Developer and Hardware Strategy Treat core capabilities including offline transfer, conditional payout, and hardware wallets, as addressable system services exposed through SDKs and open documentation. Put certified secure elements into mainstream POS and consumer devices via OEM partnerships, and subsidize upgrades where resilience matters (transport, healthcare, disaster relief).

Phased timeline (indicative):

- 0–18 months: deepen mandates in public flows; expand SDK coverage; seed hardware wallets in transit/municipal services; run targeted voucher programs with usage/expiry constraints.
- 18–36 months: scale SME acceptance with settlement and fee perks; pilot invoice-linked B2B disbursements; expand dual-offline device footprint; publish privacy/audit reports.
- 36+ months: normalize rail-under-UI for large shares of retail; embed e-CNY features in enterprise ERPs; align with mBridge corridors in selected trades.

Scorecard (KPIs to watch):

- Share of public disbursements and collections on e-CNY.
- Acceptance density at transit, utilities, healthcare, and public-touchpoint merchants.
- Median settlement latency and effective merchant basis-point cost vs. legacy QR acquiring for SME tickets.
- Count of offline-capable devices (consumer + POS) in the field.
- Volume/share of invoice-linked B2B conditional payments.
- SDK adoption: number of third-party front ends (including Alipay/WeChat) exposing offline/conditional features.
- Security/trust metrics: fraud loss rates, privacy incidents, time-to-reconcile in dual-offline mode.
- mBridge corridor pilot volumes where relevant.

With a scorecard in place, we can look at the potential end-state.

10 Conclusion

The e-CNY is best understood as tokenization with a public purpose. It places a state liability on a programmable rail so that policy, resilience, and settlement live in the infrastructure, while experience and innovation stay at the edge. In the BIS tokenisation blueprint, the winning architecture preserves the singleness of money and the system's elasticity and integrity even as assets and payments go programmable (BIS 2023; BIS 2024). e-CNY addresses those tests at the core.

Success will look unglamorous from the outside. People will keep tapping Alipay and WeChat Pay; behind the glass, a rising share of transactions will settle in central bank money, SMEs will enjoy faster, cheaper settlement, and public-interest flows from disaster relief to tax rebates will run with rail-level conditionality and auditability (People's Bank of China 2021; BIS 2020). Resilience will be measured rather than promised: dual-offline transfers that clear through outages and reconcile quickly without material fraud (People's Bank of China 2022).

Private money will not disappear. Tokenized deposits can power industry workflows and ERP integrations; well-regulated stablecoins may bridge platforms and jurisdictions. The point of a public rail is to give the system a common settlement anchor and policy instrument, not to crowd out edge-layer competition (FSB 2023; BoJ 2024). In corridors where the RMB already matters, wholesale rails like mBridge will quietly make settlement faster and safer without rewriting the capital account (BIS 2024; HKMA 2024a, 2024b).

Failure would be noisy: a high-profile offline security incident; merchant economics that never improve; privacy rules that are ambiguous in practice; or SDKs too immature for developers to care. The antidote is execution: mandate density where it serves the public interest, tangible SME economics, credible privacy governance, and relentless developer support.

The scorecard that matters is practical, not rhetorical: the share of public disbursements and collections on e-CNY; acceptance density in transit and utilities; SME fee and settlement metrics; the installed base of offline-capable devices; uptake of invoice-linked B2B flows; SDK adoption by third-party front-ends; and, where relevant, mBridge corridor volumes. Watch those, and you will know whether the operating-system idea is taking hold.

China does not need a shinier wallet. It needs money that behaves like infrastructure—predictable, policy-addressable, and available when everything else is not. If e-CNY can disappear into that role while anchoring a broader tokenised ecosystem of public and private monies, it will have done exactly what it set out to do.

References

Bank for International Settlements (BIS) (2020) *Central bank digital currencies: foundational principles and core features.* BIS, Basel. https://www.bis.org/publ/othp33.htm. Accessed 18 Oct 2025. (Bank for International Settlements)

Bank for International Settlements (BIS) (2023) *Annual economic report 2023, Chapter III: Blueprint for the future monetary system.* BIS, Basel. https://www.bis.org/publ/arpdf/ar2023e3.pdf. Accessed 18 Oct 2025. (Bank for International Settlements)

Bank for International Settlements (BIS) (2024) *Project mBridge reaches minimum viable product stage.* BIS, Basel (press release, 5 June 2024). https://www.bis.org/press/p240605.htm. Accessed 18 Oct 2025. (Bank for International Settlements)

Bank for International Settlements Innovation Hub; Hong Kong Monetary Authority; Bank of Thailand; Central Bank of the UAE; People's Bank of China—Digital Currency Institute (2021) *Inthanon-LionRock to mBridge: Building a multi-CBDC platform for international payments.* BISIH Hong Kong Centre. https://www.bis.org/publ/othp40.htm. Accessed 18 Oct 2025. (Bank for International Settlements)

Bank of Japan (BoJ) (2024) *Deposit tokenization: survey of overseas initiatives.* BoJ Review 2024-E-9. https://www.boj.or.jp/en/research/wps_rev/rev_2024/data/rev24e09.pdf. Accessed 18 Oct 2025. (Bank of Japan)

Carnegie Endowment for International Peace (2021) *China's digital yuan: an alternative to the dollar-dominated financial system?* https://carnegieendowment.org/research/2021/08/chinas-digital-yuan-an-alternative-to-the-dollar-dominated-financial-system?lang=en. Accessed 18 Oct 2025. (Carnegie Endowment)

DigiChina (2022) Lexicon: "controllable anonymity" (可控匿名) and China's digital yuan. Stanford University Cyber Policy Center. https://digichina.stanford.edu/work/lexicon-controllable-anonymity-or-managed-anonymity-and-chinas-digital-yuan/. Accessed 18 Oct 2025. (DigiChina)

Financial Stability Board (FSB) (2023) *High-level recommendations for the regulation, supervision and oversight of global stablecoin arrangements.* https://www.fsb.org/2023/07/high-level-recommendations-for-the-regulation-supervision-and-oversight-of-global-stablecoin-arrangements-final-report/. Accessed 18 Oct 2025. (Financial Stability Board)

Hong Kong Monetary Authority (HKMA) (2024a) *Expanding the cross-boundary e-CNY pilot in Hong Kong.* Press release, 17 May 2024. https://www.hkma.gov.hk/eng/news-and-media/press-releases/2024/05/20240517-3/. Accessed 18 Oct 2025. (Hong Kong Monetary Authority)

Hong Kong Monetary Authority (HKMA) (2024b) *Project mBridge reaches MVP stage.* Press release, 5 June 2024. https://www.hkma.gov.hk/eng/news-and-media/press-releases/2024/06/20240605-4/. Accessed 18 Oct 2025. (Hong Kong Monetary Authority)

People's Bank of China (2021) Progress of Research & Development of E-CNY in China (white paper). PBoC, Beijing. https://www.pbc.gov.cn/en/3688110/3688172/4157443/4293696/2021071614584691871.pdf. Accessed 18 Oct 2025. (People's Bank of China)

People's Bank of China (2022) Theories and practice of exploring China's e-CNY. PBoC, Beijing. https://www.pbc.gov.cn/en/3935690/3935759/4749192/2022122913350138868.pdf. Accessed 18 Oct 2025. (People's Bank of China)

Tokenization and the Future Monetary System: DCJPY as Tokenized Deposits in Japan

Hiromi Yamaoka

Abstract The modern monetary system with the two-tiered structure of a central bank and commercial banks, supported by fractional reserve system and banks' credit creation, has many benefits such as market-based financial intermediation and elastic supply of money. Tokenization through new digital technologies has potential to further innovate monetary and financial system. In order to design an ideal monetary system for the coming future, it is critical to preserve the advantages of the modern monetary system while maximizing the benefits of innovative technologies, and tokenized deposits are promising solution for achieving these goals. The Digital Currency Forum, which consists of over 100 leading companies and banks in Japan, designed the platform for tokenized deposits denominated by JPY, which was entitled as DCJPY. The first tokenized deposits based on DCJPY were issued in August 2024.

Keywords Tokenization • Monetary system • Blockchain • Central banking • Digital currency

1 Introduction

Blockchain and distributed ledger technology (DLT) have potential to innovate monetary system and financial services through "tokenizing" various assets and values, synchronizing the records of relevant ledgers and enabling the use of smart contracts. For designing an ideal monetary infrastructure for the coming future, it is important to maintain the benefits and advantages of the current monetary system while making full use of new digital technologies. Then, what are the benefits and the advantages of the modern monetary system?

H. Yamaoka (✉)
Digital Currency Forum, Future Institute of Research, Tokyo, Japan
e-mail: h.yamaoka.7w@future.co.jp

S. Yazıcı et al. (eds.), *Tokenisation of Money*, Contributions to Finance and Accounting, https://doi.org/10.1007/978-3-032-22946-5_26

2 Modern Monetary System with Two-tiered Structure

The invention of money drastically increased the efficiency of processing information and enabled wide-scale, consecutive exchanges of goods and services among human beings.[1] Then, the modern monetary system was formed in the nineteenth century, when modern nation states and central banks were established.[2] This system has a "two-tiered" structure with a central bank monopolizing the power to issue the nation's sovereign currency and commercial banks supplying deposits and making loans.[3] This system has many benefits and advantages.

First, commercial bank money (i.e. deposits) and central bank money (i.e. base money consisting of banknotes and reserves) are always exchangeable at parity and on demand. The safety and soundness of deposits are safeguarded by banking regulation and deposit insurance. Through such "singleness of money", each nation can unify its sovereign currency unit, and people do not have to worry about exchange rates between different currency units within the nation.[4] Accordingly, the singleness of money has greatly enhanced the efficiency of economic transactions.

Second, based on fractional reserve system and credit creation, commercial banks can supply credits through making of loans and investments. Through such financial intermediation, commercial banks can contribute to efficient resource allocation driven by market mechanism. Also, commercial banks can supply sufficient amount of money to satisfy the payment and settlement needs of the economy. Such "elastic supply of money" based on each bank's autonomous judgment can facilitate efficient transactions. In monetary aggregate statistics broader aggregates such as M2 and M3 are much larger than M0 (i.e. base money).

Third, the modern monetary system incentivize innovation led by commercial banks and other private entities. Indeed, many innovations such as ATMs, wire-transfers and debit cards have been created by commercial banks and private entities.

Fourth, payment-related data cannot be monopolized by the central bank. The central bank issues banknotes to general public and supply central bank accounts mainly to banks. Since banknotes are anonymous and convey only the information of value, the central banks cannot access to the information and data on people's daily transactions.

Due to those advantages and benefits, the modern monetary system became a standard model in the twentieth century worldwide. This system is based on a sophisticated balance between the nation and the market, and between centralized

---

[1] Professor Caroline Humphery asserted with evidence that wide-scale, consecutive barter transactions were unlikely to occur without the existence of money. See Humphery (1985).

[2] Although Sveriges Riksbank and the Bank of England were established in the seventeenth century, they were close to commercial banks, and they became to monopolize the power of issuing sovereign currencies in the nineteenth century.

[3] Regarding the division of labor between the central bank and commercial banks within the two-tiered monetary system, see Yamaoka (2019).

[4] For material deeply describing the importance of the "singleness of money", see Garratt and Shin (2023).

and de-centralized structures. In this system, the trust and credibility of money are safeguarded by the nation's institutional framework, while the elastic supply of money, credit allocation and innovation are driven by private entities and market mechanism.

3 Central Bank Digital Currencies (CBDCs)

3.1 *Wholesale (Large-value) CBDCs and Retail (General-purpose) CBDCs*

New digital technologies have enabled various types of digital money, such as central bank digital currencies (CBDCs), stablecoins and tokenized deposits, to emerge. This chapter focuses on the CBDCs.[5]

There are two types of CBDCs, which are wholesale CBDCs (large-value CBDCs) and retail CBDCs (general-purpose CBDCs). Since wholesale CBDCs can be regarded as applying blockchain and DLT to central bank RTGS (real-time gross settlement) systems, they do not cause particularly new issues regarding financial stability and monetary policy. Nonetheless, wholesale CBDCs, as blockchain-compatible RTGS, could work as an anchor of future monetary system. This topic will be touched upon later.

3.2 *Issues on Retail CBDCs*[6]

On the contrary to wholesale CBDCs, retail CBDCs may substantially change the structure of monetary system. If retail CBDCs are widely held and used by firms and individuals, it may change the current two-tiered structure into single-tiered one. If firms and individuals withdraw bank deposits and hold CBDCs, commercial banks' financial intermediation would be negatively affected and the size of the central bank's balance sheet would increase. Since the central bank is not a suitable entity to make loans directly to firms and individuals, retail CBDCs might distort market-driven resource allocation. In addition, in a situation of market stress, retail CBDCs could accelerate "digital bank run" and liquidity crises.[7] Moreover, it would be difficult for the central bank to elastically supply retail CBDCs to satisfy the

[5] For detailed analyses on theoretical issues in CBDCs, see Yamaoka and Yanagawa (2019).

[6] For material describing the difficulty in using retail CBDCs as monetary policy tools, see Yamaoka (2021).

[7] If it were not for retail CBDC, nonetheless, digital bank-run could still occur between commercial banks. In this regard, retail CBDCs will not "trigger" digital bank-run but "accelerate" it.

settlement needs of the economy, since retail CBDCs, which are categorized as base money, lack credit creation mechanism.

Imposing quantitative limits on the holding or usage of retail CBDCs could be an option to avoid their large-scale impacts on banking system. Nonetheless, any quantitative limits on CBDCs may impair their utility, since CBDCs, which are free from credit risks, could be useful especially if they are used for large-value settlements. On the other hand, in small payment businesses private-led innovation and entrepreneurship should be strongly encouraged.[8]

In order to maintain the two-tiered structure of monetary system, some central banks support the idea of "indirect" issuance of retail CBDCs, where commercial banks and will work as the central bank's agent to provide retail CBDCs to firms and individuals. In such indirect issuance scheme, nonetheless, commercial banks will be in a difficult situation since they will have to provide both their own liabilities (i.e. deposits) and the central bank's liabilities (i.e. retail CBDCs) to their customers. It will be difficult for commercial banks to explain the difference between them, since they cannot argue that their deposits are riskier than retail CBDCs. Such explanation, which is against the "singleness" of money, may destabilize financial system.

3.3 CBDCs and Narrow Banking

Those issues on retail CBDCs are similar to those of narrow banking proposals in the twentieth century. Although the value of retail CBDCs is stable since they are central bank liabilities, we need to consider various issues such as market-driven financial intermediation, elastic supply of money and financial stability, which are critical in designing desirable financial infrastructure.

4 Stablecoins

4.1 Two Types of Stablecoins

Stablecoins try to stabilize their value through (i) using algorithms or (ii) having back-up assets. The value of the first type of stablecoins often fluctuates, nonetheless. This fact implies that the mechanisms to stabilize the value of currencies are so complicated that it is still difficult to replace them with a pre-determined algorithm. Recently, the first type of stablecoins have been excluded from the legally defined

[8] For example, in Japan, interbank settlements of less than 100 million JPY are netted out through Zengin system, which is a private-based netting system, while interbank settlements of 100 million JPY or above are settled through BOJ-NET, which is the central bank RTGS system.

stablecoins in several countries including as the United States and Japan. Thus, this chapter will focus on the second type of stablecoins with back-up assets.

4.2 Stablecoins and Singleness of Money

Stablecoins could have problems in satisfying the "singleness of money" in a strict sense. Indeed, the value of stablecoins, even though they have back-up assets, sometimes fluctuates. The issuers of stablecoins could have incentives to increase the seigniorage through reducing the quantity or the quality of their back-up assets. These incentives could destabilize the monetary system, as evidenced by the history of "wildcat banks" in nineteenth century in the United States. We have seen several cases where the value of stablecoins were destabilized, as shown in the case of Terra/Luna in 2022. Moreover, if stablecoins have only "fractional" back-up assets, we need to consider how to maintain regulatory level playing field for the issuers of these stablecoins and commercial banks, which are under regulatory requirements of capital and liquidity.

4.3 Stablecoins and Elastic Supply of Money

In order to stabilize the value of stablecoins, some nations including the United States and Japan now legally require stablecoins to be backed up fully by high-quality liquid assets (HQLAs).[9] Even though the value of these stablecoins, which become closer to "narrow banks", tends to be stable, since they would not be supplied elastically to satisfy the settlements needs of the economy since they lack credit creation mechanism. Accordingly, it would be difficult for stablecoins to be dominant settlement instruments due to the constraints of their supply.[10]

4.4 Stablecoins and Measures Against Illicit Activities

In addition, if stablecoins are issued on open and permissionless blockchain, each stablecoin holder will be able to have its crypto-key to access to his or her stablecoins anonymously. Although such technological characteristics protect the privacy of stablecoin holders, they could have problems in terms of KYC (know-your

---

[9] For understanding the U.S. GENIUS Act of 2025, see https://www.congress.gov/bill/119th-congress/senate-bill/394/text

[10] For a detailed analysis of the constraints on stablecoins concerning their elastic supply to the economy, see Garratt et al. (2022).

customers) and AML/CFT (anti-money laundering/ countering the financing of terrorism).

5 Digital Currency Forum and Tokenized Deposits in Japan

5.1 Digital Currency Forum in Japan

In 2020 the Digital Currency Forum, which I have been working as the Chair, was established in Japan. The purpose of the Forum is to design an ideal monetary infrastructure with applying cutting-edge digital technologies. The Forum, which now consists of over 100 leading banks, companies and institutions, has been doing extensive studies and experiments on digital money. The contents and results of those studies and experiments have been published as the Forum's progress reports.

5.2 DCJPY—Two-layered Platform for Tokenized Deposits

The Forum concluded that it would be desirable for blockchain-based digital currencies to be issued initially by commercial banks. Based on this concept, the digital currency platform entitled as "DCJPY" was created by DeCurret DCP Inc., a Japanese IT firm.

DCJPY is designed to innovate monetary system through applying blockchain and DLT to bank deposits, while maintaining the advantages of the current monetary system. Although the Forum did not use the term of "tokenized deposits" at the initial stage of studies, DCJPY can be regarded as the platform for tokenized deposits, which now gather worldwide attention and are being studied by many financial institutions overseas. Thus, this chapter illustrates DCJPY as the platform for JPY-based tokenized deposits.

Tokenized deposits, which are considered as blockchain-based, innovated from of bank deposits, may have various advantages and benefits. Various initiatives are now being taken on tokenized deposits. The front-runner was "JPM Coin" and "Kinexys" led by J.P. Morgan.[11] The project of "Regulated Liability Network (RLN)", led by U.S. and U.K. financial institutions such as Citi, was initiated in 2022.[12] In Germany, several banks have joined the project of "Commercial Bank Money Token (CBMT)" since 2021.[13]

---

[11] https://www.jpmorgan.com/kinexys/index

[12] For a deeper understanding of the structure of the Regulated Liability Network, see Regulated Liability Network (2022). (https://regulatedliabilitynetwork.org/)

[13] https://die-dk.de/en/topics/article/new-working-paper-on-commercial-bank-money-token/

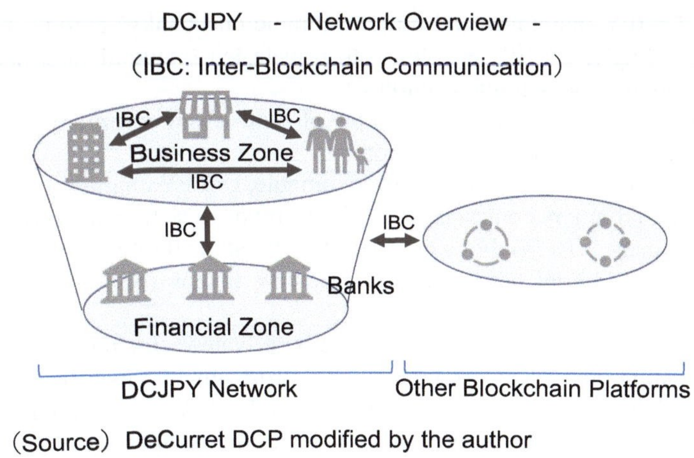

Fig. 1 Two-layered structure of DCJPY (IBC: Inter-Blockchain Communication)

DCJPY has two-layered structure (Fig. 1). The basic layer is entitled as the "Financial Zone", which handles basic transfers of and settlements through tokenized deposits. The upper layer is entitled as the "Business Zone", which is a "programmable" area in which smart contract and other sophisticated functions can be incorporated to satisfy various business needs.[14] Through synchronizing these two zones, the DCJPY can facilitate delivery versus payment (DVP) and straight-through-processing (STP).

5.3 *Possible Benefits of DCJPY*

DCJPY, which is the platform for blockchain-based tokenized deposits, may have various advantages and benefits as an innovative monetary infrastructure.

First, DCJPY satisfies the requirement of the "singleness" of money. Since the tokenized deposits issued on DCJPY can be categorized as bank deposits, they are always exchangeable with base money at parity. DCJPY can make full use of the current institutional frameworks such as banking regulation and deposit insurance to safeguard the trust and confidence to commercial bank liabilities. Accordingly, DCJPY will be able to maintain the sophisticated balance between the state and the market and between centralized and de-centralized structures.

Second, it is unnecessary to impose quantitative limits on the usage of tokenized deposits issued on DCJPY to avoid disintermediation. In addition, commercial banks will be able to provide interests to those tokenized deposits in line with their deposit rates in order to avoid large-scale inflows and outflows of funds.

---

[14] https://www.decurret-dcp.com/en/news/nl-20231012.html

Third, DCJPY maintains and utilizes commercial banks' credit creation functions. Accordingly, DCJPY enables both private led financial intermediation and elastic supply of money to the economy.

Fourth, DCJPY will not cause outflow of funds from commercial banks to the central bank even in a stressed situation.

Fifth, since its Business Zone is programmable, DCJPY enables the use of blockchain, DLT and smart contracts to facilitate innovative transactions such as decentralized finance (DeFi). For example, DCJPY can facilitate efficient transactions of various new digital assets such as security tokens (STs) and non-fungible tokens (NFTs).

Sixth, DCJPY will foster innovation led by private sector initiatives. Firms and financial institutions can incorporate tailored programs into its "Business Zone" to satisfy sophisticated business needs. In addition, DCJPY can be a platform for private entities to utilize information and data regarding payments and settlements.

Seventh, DCJPY can utilize commercial banks' expertise about KYC and AML/CFT. Since commercial banks have been required to perform the duties of KYC and AML/CFT and have accumulated know-hows on this front, it would be better making use of their expertise to prevent illicit activities.

5.4 *Possible Use Cases of DCJPY*

The Digital Currency Forum is conducting various pilot studies, proof of concepts and experiments. For example, in the experiments of regional digital currencies, DCJPY platform was used for circulating the value within a specific region.[15] In this scheme, digitalized local currencies were issued on DCJPY platform to encourage local consumption and to develop regional economy. In addition, DCJPY platform was used by a local government to provide fiscal supports to the residents swiftly.

The Forum also conducted the studies of using DCJPY for cross-border trade finance, in which DCJPY platform synchronized the movements of various trade documents with payments and settlements. The Forum also did an experiment of using DCJPY platform for the transactions of green energy, where environmental value was tokenized into digital assets and traded in exchange for tokenized deposits.

5.5 *Launch of Digital Money on DCJPY for Business Purposes*

The tokenized deposits on DCJPY were issued for business purposes in August 2024 by GMO Aozora Net Bank (https://gmo-aozora.com/), which is an internet-based challenger bank and the subsidiary of Aozora Bank. In this case, the

[15] https://www.decurret-dcp.com/dc-forum/download/.assets/20241217_pr4_en.pdf

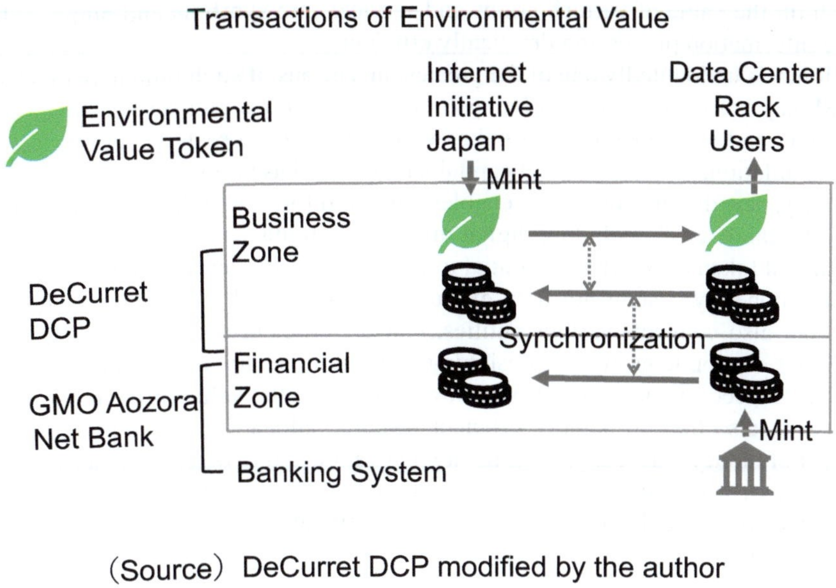

Fig. 2 Use of DCJPY for environmental value transactions

blockchain-based tokenized deposits are used for the transactions of digitalized environmental value created by Internet Initiative Japan (IIJ) (Fig. 2).

There are other on-going projects to issue tokenized deposits based on DCJPY. On September 2, 2025, Japan Post Bank announced that it was planning to issue tokenized deposits based on DCJPY within 2026 fiscal year.[16] On September 16, 2025, SBI Shinsei Bank announced to launch full-scale study on foreign currency transactions using tokenized deposits based on DCJPY.[17]

6 Future Monetary System[18]

6.1 *Digital "Tokenization" and Innovation of Money*

Professor Denise Schmandt-Besserat discovered that human beings created clay "tokens" in ancient Mesopotamia, and that such "tokenization" substantially increased the efficiency of transactions.[19] Human beings' intellectual ability to

---

16 https://www.jp-bank.japanpost.jp/aboutus/press/2025/pdf/pr25090101.pdf

17 https://corp.sbishinseibank.co.jp/en/news/news/20250916a.html

18 For example, in the conference co-hosted by the Center for Advanced Research in Finance of the University of Tokyo and the Payment and Settlement Systems Department of the Bank of Japan, Professor Kazuo Ueda argued for the need to consider an ideal combination of centralized and decentralized structures when designing a future monetary infrastructure. See the University of Tokyo and the Bank of Japan (2016).

19 See Schmandt-Besserat (2019).

transform the value of various goods and services into symbols and numbers have made information processing drastically efficient.

Money is undoubtedly one of the greatest inventions of such human beings' ability. Money has enabled human beings to exchange goods and services over space and time, and to cooperate with unknown others and to create economic society. Prices, inflation, investments and capitalism are also based on money.

Today, new digital technology enables advanced form of "tokenization" and creates "digital tokens", including digital money and digital assets. Such tokenization and digital tokens have great potential to further innovate our monetary system.

The monetary system not only executes payments and settlements of transactions but also connects various entities, realizes efficient resource allocation and facilitates economic growth. In designing an ideal monetary system for the coming future, we need to consider not only how to stabilize the value of payment instruments but also how to achieve efficient resource allocation, to supply sufficient amount of money elastically, to stimulate innovation and to deter illicit activities. In this context, it is fruitful to re-consider the advantages of the current two-tiered monetary system, and why the narrow banking model did not become a solution in a real world.

6.2 *Cost for Creating Trust*

Among them, the cost for creating trust to monetary system is a key issue. Bitcoin, the first crypto-asset, was expected to create their trust through "mining" without relying on the nation. As shown by huge electricity consumption for mining, nonetheless, human beings have not yet found a more efficient system to create the trust than the nation.

In this respect, CBDCs, stablecoins and tokenized deposits are considered to utilize the existing institutional framework to create trust to some extent. We need to consider what is the most efficient way to create trust to future monetary system. The Digital Currency Forum believes that tokenized deposits are most promising in this respect since they can make full use of existing framework with good track records.

6.3 *Resiliency Against Systemic Risks and Regulatory Design Considerations*

In order for monetary systems to operate smoothly and to contribute to the economy, it is important for them to be resilient against cyber-attacks, systemic risks and illicit activities. In other words, monetary systems should have sufficient "integrity" to be relevant in the economy.[20] These issues are critical particularly for retail CBDCs since they are most likely to be targets of cyber attackers and to trigger "flight to safety" in stressed situations. Not only retails CBDCs but also stablecoins and tokenized deposits, nonetheless, may face new challenges regarding cyber-security as long as they adopt blockchain and DLT, which had not been used in traditional monetary infrastructure.

In particular, "permission-less" blockchain where individuals can keep their own private keys may involve risks of creating anonymous or pseudonymous payment tools. On the other hand, tokenized deposits are expected to use "permissioned" blockchain since they use the functions of KYC and AML/CFT performed by banks. In this regard, tokenized deposits based on "permissioned" blockchain accompany less risks than other tools on "permissioned" blockchain in terms of their illicit uses. Besides, since "permissioned" blockchain may still have the "Single Point of Failure (SPF)" as traditional system, the banks functioning as validator nodes are asked to maintain their system resiliency at sufficiently high level.

In the coming future there will be a variety of digital payment instruments including e-money, tokenized deposits and stablecoins. It will be critical to safeguard the stability of the value and the safety of them in order to maintain financial stability. There will be multiple number of schemes for stabilizing their value. For tokenized deposits and CBDCs their stability of the value will be maintained by the soundness of their issuers. For stablecoins and some of e-money their stability of the value will be safeguarded through maintaining the sufficient quantity and quality of collateral. Future regulatory framework should be ready for monitoring both the issuing entities and the collateral of digital currencies. In addition, it will be needed to pay attention to the level-playing field of various digital currencies. For example, since stablecoins without sufficient quantity or quality of collateral will become closer to the liabilities of their issuer, and it could be appropriate to apply banking regulation to it.

6.4 "Unified Ledger"—Nexus of Centralized and De-centralized Infrastructures

The Bank for International Settlements (BIS) expressed the concept of "Unified Ledger", where various infrastructures for digital money and digital assets are inter-linked.[21] In the "Unified Ledger" model, centralized and de-centralized infrastructures are inter-connected through open API (Application Programming Interface), and blockchain-compatible central bank RTGS (real-time gross settlement) systems, which were formerly called "wholesale CBDCs", could work as an anchor of the value of money.

---

[20] See for example, Bank for International Settlements (2025)

[21] See Bank for International Settlements (2025)

DCJPY may have advantages also in this respect. Through connecting its Financial Zone to the central bank RTGS system, DCJPY we could become the integral part of the "Unified Ledger" and automatically synchronize the records on various ledgers across two-tiered structure of the monetary system.

In designing future monetary system, we need to consider a variety of issues including financial intermediation, financial stability, efficient resource allocation and ideal style of financial regulation. We also need to consider the appropriate roles of central bank money in payments and settlements. Issuing a specific kind of digitalized payment instruments is not an ultimate goal, and we should continue seeking for the best possible infrastructure through applying then-available technologies. The Digital Currency Forum will continue making its best effort on this front.

7 Conclusion

Monetary system can be regarded as infrastructure for processing information. Since Tokenization can be regarded as technology for packeting information and incorporating instruction for processing it, tokenization have great potential to innovate monetary system. Indeed, various new tokenized tools and assets such as CBDCs, stablecoins, tokenized deposits, security tokens and non-fungible tokens are invented recently.

In order to design best-possible monetary system for the coming future, it is needed to apply cutting-edge technologies including tokenization to overall monetary system while preserving its benefits and advantages. In this regard, tokenized deposits, which can be regarded as innovated form of bank deposits, may have advantages especially in terms of taking over the benefits of the current two-tiered monetary system including the "singleness of money" and "elastic supply of money" through credit creation.

There will emerge a variety of tokenized financial tools in future monetary system.[22] In order to maximize the benefits of tokenization, we need to seek for the potential of tokenizing not only money but also wide-ranging assets. Tokenized deposits will be able to maximize their capabilities if a variety of securities, assets and central bank reserves are also tokenized so that their movements can be synchronized with those of tokenized deposits. In order to maximize economic welfare through digitalization of finance, we should consider how to apply tokenization technology not only to money but also to overall financial infrastructure in a comprehensive manner.

[22] Although stablecoins may not satisfy the requirement of the "singleness" of money in a strict sense, they can function as safe assets in the portfolio of crypto-asset investments where slight volatility in their value may not be a big problem.

References

Bank for International Settlements (2025) The next-generation monetary and financial system, BIS annual economic report 2025. https://www.bis.org/publ/arpdf/ar2025e3.pdf

Garratt R, Shin HS (2023) Stablecoins versus tokenised deposits: implications for the singleness of money. BIS Bulletin 73

Garratt R, Lee M, Martin A, Torregrossa J (2022) The future of payments is not stablecoins. Liberty Street Economics, Federal Reserve Bank of New York

Humphery C (1985) Barter and economic disintegration. Man 20(1):48–72

Schmandt-Besserat D (2019) The invention of tokens. In: Tokens – culture, connections, communities

The Regulated Liability Network (2022) Digital sovereign currency. Whitepaper

The University of Tokyo and the Bank of Japan (2016) Summary of the conference on "FinTech and the Future of Money" co-hosted by the Center for Advanced Research in Finance (CARF), the University of Tokyo, and the Payment and Settlement Systems Department, the Bank of Japan, on November 18th, 2016

Yamaoka H (2019, September) The future of central banking, accounting, economics, and law: a Convivium.

Yamaoka H (2021) Digital currencies and the future of money. In: The future of financial systems in the digital age. Springer. https://www.researchgate.net/publication/358893101_Digital_Currencies_and_the_Future_of_Money

Yamaoka H, Yanagawa N (2019) Digital innovation, data revolution and Central Bank Digital Currency, Bank of Japan Working Paper 19-E-2. https://www.boj.or.jp/en/research/wps_rev/wps_2019/data/wp19e02.pdf

Blockchain and QR Codes: Revolutionizing Cross-Border Payments and Financial Inclusion in Southeast Asia – A Case Study of Cambodia's Bakong Project

Victor Yaromin

Abstract The financial landscape of Southeast Asia is undergoing a significant transformation, driven by the need for more efficient, inclusive, and interoperable payment systems. Traditional payment infrastructures often face challenges related to high transaction costs, slow processing times, lack of interconnectivity, and limited access for unbanked and underbanked populations. This article examines the innovative use of blockchain technology, specifically Distributed Ledger Technology (DLT), in conjunction with standardized QR (Quick Response) codes to address these challenges and create modern payment solutions. Focusing on Cambodia's groundbreaking "Project Bakong" and its associated "KHQR" standard, this paper explores how these technologies are fostering domestic real-time payments, enabling seamless cross-border transactions, and promoting financial inclusion.

Project Bakong, initiated by the National Bank of Cambodia (NBC), leverages the Hyperledger Iroha blockchain platform to create a unified payment system. This system connects various financial institutions and payment service providers, allowing for real-time, secure, and low-cost peer-to-peer fund transfers and merchant payments. The KHQR standard further enhances this ecosystem by providing a single, interoperable QR code for all participating banks and e-wallets, simplifying the payment experience for both consumers and merchants.

The article analyzes the motivations behind these initiatives, the technological architecture, the implementation strategies, and the observed impacts. It highlights Cambodia's success in establishing direct cross-border QR payment linkages with four key partner countries (Thailand, Vietnam, Malaysia, and Japan), and further extending its international payment capabilities through the integration of major solutions like China's Alipay+, thereby facilitating trade, tourism, and the circula-

See Various LinkedIn posts by Victor Gyugo https://www.linkedin.com/in/viktor-yaromin/ discussing Bakong, KHQR, cross-border payments, and related FinTech developments in Cambodia and Southeast Asia

V. Yaromin (✉)
Morozzi Creative Lab, Phnom Penh, Cambodia
e-mail: viktor@connectingthedotsinfin.tech

S. Yazıcı et al. (eds.), *Tokenisation of Money*, Contributions to Finance and Accounting, https://doi.org/10.1007/978-3-032-22946-5_27

tion of local currencies. Furthermore, the paper discusses the potential benefits, including enhanced efficiency, greater financial inclusion, and support for the digital economy, as well as the challenges and risks, such as cybersecurity, regulatory harmonization, and ensuring widespread adoption. By presenting Cambodia's experience, this article offers valuable insights into the transformative potential of blockchain and QR codes for modernizing payment infrastructures in Southeast Asia and other developing regions.

Keywords Blockchain • Distributed Ledger Technology (DLT) • QR codes • Payment systems • Cross-Border payments • Financial inclusion • Southeast Asia • Cambodia • Bakong • KHQR • Central Bank Digital Currency (CBDC)

1 Introduction

The dawn of the twenty first century has witnessed an unprecedented acceleration in financial technology (FinTech), fundamentally altering how individuals, businesses, and governments conduct transactions. Within this global wave of innovation, Southeast Asia has emerged as a particularly dynamic region, characterized by a burgeoning digital economy, a youthful and tech-savvy population, and a pressing need to overcome legacy challenges in its payment infrastructures. Traditional payment systems in many Southeast Asian nations have often been fragmented, expensive, slow, and lacking in interoperability, thereby hindering economic efficiency and financial inclusion (Ly and Ly 2024).

In response to these challenges, central banks and financial institutions across the region are increasingly exploring and adopting cutting-edge technologies. Among the most promising of these are blockchain, or more broadly, Distributed Ledger Technology (DLT), and standardized Quick Response (QR) code payment systems. Blockchain technology offers the potential for secure, transparent, and decentralized transaction processing, while QR codes provide a simple, low-cost, and accessible interface for digital payments, particularly suitable for mobile-first economies.

This article focuses on the synergistic application of these technologies to create modern, inclusive, and interoperable payment solutions, with a particular emphasis on their role in facilitating cross-border transactions within Southeast Asia. The centerpiece of this analysis is Cambodia's pioneering "Project Bakong," a national payment platform developed by the National Bank of Cambodia (NBC) using Hyperledger Iroha, a permissioned blockchain. Bakong, in conjunction with the national KHQR standard, aims to address issues of interconnectivity, promote the use of the local currency (Khmer Riel—KHR), enhance financial inclusion, and streamline both domestic and international payments.

Cambodia's proactive approach, including the establishment of cross-border QR payment linkages with several ASEAN countries and Japan, provides a compelling case study of how a developing nation can leverage advanced technology to leapfrog traditional developmental stages in its financial system. This paper will delve into the motivations, design, implementation, and impact of Bakong and KHQR, drawing upon official white papers, implementation guidelines, and analyses of its rollout and subsequent regional collaborations. Through this examination, the article seeks to contribute to a deeper understanding of the transformative potential and practical considerations of deploying blockchain and QR code-based payment systems in the unique context of Southeast Asia.

2 The Evolving Landscape of Payment Systems in Southeast Asia

Southeast Asia, a diverse region with varying levels of economic development, presents a complex payments landscape. While some urban centers boast sophisticated digital payment options, a significant portion of the population, particularly in rural areas, remains reliant on cash and faces barriers to accessing formal financial services. The existing payment systems, prior to recent innovations, have been characterized by several key challenges:

1. **Lack of Interconnectivity and Interoperability:** A primary hurdle has been the siloed nature of payment networks. Different banks, e-wallets, and payment service providers often operated on proprietary systems that could not easily communicate with each other. This lack of interoperability meant that transferring funds or making payments between customers of different institutions was often cumbersome, slow, and costly, if possible at all. For merchants, this translated into needing multiple point-of-sale (POS) devices or QR codes to accept payments from various sources.
2. **High Transaction Costs:** Cross-institutional and particularly cross-border payments have traditionally incurred significant fees. These costs are borne by individuals and businesses, acting as a drag on economic activity and discouraging the use of formal payment channels, especially for small-value transactions. The reliance on correspondent banking networks for international transfers often involves multiple intermediaries, each adding to the final cost.
3. **Slow Processing Times:** Settlement finality in traditional systems, especially for interbank and cross-border transactions, could take hours or even days. This delay ties up liquidity and introduces settlement risk, impacting cash flow for businesses and convenience for individuals. Real-time gross settlement (RTGS) systems existed for large-value payments, but retail payment systems often lacked this immediacy.
4. **Limited Financial Inclusion:** According to various reports preceding widespread digital payment adoption, a substantial percentage of the adult population in Southeast Asia was unbanked or underbanked. Barriers to financial inclusion include geographical distance to bank branches, lack of required documentation, low financial literacy, and the perceived high cost of banking services. Cash has remained the dominant mode of transaction for many, limiting their participation

in the digital economy and access to other financial products like credit and insurance.

5. **Dominance of Cash and High Dollarization (in some economies):** In countries like Cambodia, the economy has been highly dollarized, with the US dollar widely used alongside the local currency. While providing some stability, this can limit the central bank's ability to conduct effective monetary policy and seigniorage. Furthermore, the heavy reliance on physical cash for daily transactions is inefficient, costly to manage (printing, distribution, security), and susceptible to risks like counterfeiting and theft.

Recognizing these inefficiencies, governments and central banks in Southeast Asia have been actively promoting the shift towards digital payments. Initiatives have ranged from developing national payment switches and faster payment systems to creating regulatory sandboxes for FinTech innovation. The advent of mobile technology, with high smartphone penetration rates in many ASEAN countries, has provided a fertile ground for mobile-first payment solutions. It is against this backdrop of challenges and opportunities that technologies like blockchain and QR codes have gained prominence, offering pathways to build more integrated, efficient, and inclusive payment ecosystems. Cambodia's Project Bakong and KHQR are prime examples of a concerted effort to address these systemic issues head-on (Fig. 1).

Country	Real-time payments network	Launch date	Operator	QR code standardization
Cambodia	បាគង	October 2020	National Bank of Cambodia	KHQR
Indonesia	BI Fast	December 2021	Bank Indonesia	QRIS QR Code Standar Pembayaran Nasional
Malaysia	PayNet	January 2019	PayNet (Payments Network Malaysia)	DuitNow
Philippines	instaPay PESONet	InstaPay: April 2018 PESONet: November 2017	InstaPay: BancNet PESONet: Philippine Clearing House Corporation	QRPh
Singapore	PAYNOW	July 2017	Banking Computer Services Private Limited a subsidiary of NETS	SGQR
Thailand	PromptPay	January 2017	National ITMX (Interbank Transfer Management and Exchange)	THAI QR PAYMENT
Vietnam	napas 247	June 2021	National Payment Corporation of Vietnam (NAPAS)	VIETQR QR Payment

Fig. 1 QR real-time payments in SE Asia. Source: Thunes

3 Blockchain Technology as a Catalyst for Modern Payment Solutions

The emergence of blockchain technology, and its broader category, Distributed Ledger Technology (DLT), has presented a paradigm shift for various industries, with the financial sector being a primary area of impact (Casino et al. 2019). Originally conceptualized as the underlying technology for cryptocurrencies like Bitcoin, its core principles offer compelling solutions to many of the long-standing challenges in traditional payment systems.

3.1 Fundamentals of Blockchain and DLT

At its core, a blockchain is a continuously growing list of records, called blocks, which are linked and secured using cryptography. Key characteristics relevant to payment systems include:

- **Decentralization/Distribution:** Instead of a central authority maintaining a single ledger, a DLT allows multiple participants (nodes) in a network to hold and synchronize identical copies of the ledger. This enhances resilience against single points of failure and can reduce reliance on intermediaries.
- **Immutability:** Once a transaction is recorded on a block and added to the chain, it is extremely difficult to alter or delete. This is achieved through cryptographic hashing and the linking of blocks, creating a tamper-evident audit trail.
- **Transparency (with Privacy):** While all transactions on a public blockchain can be visible, participants are often represented by pseudonymous addresses. In permissioned (private) blockchains, which are more suitable for financial systems, access to view and validate transactions is restricted to authorized participants, allowing for tailored levels of transparency and privacy.
- **Security:** Cryptographic techniques secure transactions and control access to the ledger. Consensus mechanisms ensure that all participants agree on the validity of transactions before they are added to the ledger, preventing fraudulent activities like double-spending.
- **Consensus Mechanisms:** These are protocols (e.g., Proof-of-Work, Proof-of-Stake, Byzantine Fault Tolerance) by which nodes in a distributed network agree on the state of the ledger and the validity of new transactions. For enterprise and central bank applications, consensus algorithms that are less energy-intensive and offer faster finality, such as those used in permissioned DLTs like Hyperledger Iroha, are preferred.

3.2 *Addressing Payment System Challenges*

Blockchain technology can address the inefficiencies of traditional payment systems in several ways:

- **Enhanced Interoperability:** DLT can serve as a common, neutral platform connecting disparate financial institutions and payment providers, facilitating direct peer-to-peer transactions without needing multiple bilateral integrations.
- **Reduced Costs and Faster Settlement:** By streamlining processes and reducing the number of intermediaries, blockchain can lower transaction fees. Transactions can be settled in near real-time, improving liquidity and reducing settlement risk.
- **Increased Security and Transparency:** The immutability and cryptographic security of DLT can reduce fraud and enhance trust. Regulators can potentially have greater visibility into transaction flows (in permissioned systems) for oversight purposes.
- **Financial Inclusion:** DLT-based payment systems can be accessed via mobile devices, potentially reaching unbanked populations who have mobile phones but lack traditional bank accounts. Simplified Know Your Customer (KYC) processes, as envisioned in some DLT projects, can also lower barriers to entry.

3.3 *Permissioned vs. Permissionless Blockchains*

While public, permissionless blockchains (like Bitcoin) allow anyone to participate, financial institutions and central banks typically favor permissioned (or private/consortium) blockchains. In a permissioned system:

- Participants are known and vetted.
- Access rights and roles are clearly defined.
- Governance structures can be established to manage the network.
- They can be designed for higher transaction throughput and scalability, crucial for national payment systems.

The National Bank of Cambodia's choice of Hyperledger Iroha, a permissioned DLT platform, for Project Bakong aligns with these considerations, aiming to build a secure, efficient, and controlled national payment backbone. This strategic adoption of DLT is a key step in modernizing Cambodia's financial infrastructure and enabling innovative services like QR code payments and cross-border transactions.

4 Project Bakong: A Case Study from Cambodia

Project Bakong, officially launched by the National Bank of Cambodia (NBC) in October 2020 after a pilot phase, represents one of the world's first deployments of a blockchain-based payment system initiated by a central bank (World Economic Forum 2021), often referred to in the context of Central Bank Digital Currency (CBDC) explorations (National Bank of Cambodia 2020). It aims to create a modern, efficient, and inclusive financial backbone for Cambodia.

4.1 Background and Objectives

The NBC embarked on Project Bakong with several key objectives:

1. **Addressing Interconnectivity and Interoperability:** To overcome the fragmentation in the existing payment landscape where different banks and Payment Service Institutions (PSIs) operated in silos. Bakong aims to bring all participants onto a single platform.
2. **Attaining Efficiency:** To reduce transaction costs, increase the speed of payments (aiming for real-time settlement), and enhance the overall security of the payment system.
3. **Promoting Financial Inclusion:** To expand access to financial services for the unbanked and underbanked population, leveraging Cambodia's high mobile phone penetration rate. The Bakong mobile application and simplified KYC procedures are central to this goal.
4. **Easing Khmer Riel (KHR) Cash Payment and Promoting Local Currency Usage:** To encourage the use of the KHR for digital transactions, thereby reducing reliance on physical cash and potentially mitigating the high degree of dollarization in the Cambodian economy.
5. **Modernizing National Payment Infrastructure:** To leapfrog traditional payment system development stages by adopting cutting-edge DLT.

4.2 Technological Foundation: Hyperledger Iroha

Project Bakong is built upon Hyperledger Iroha, an open-source, permissioned blockchain platform hosted by the Linux Foundation. Soramitsu, a Japanese technology company, collaborated with the NBC in developing and implementing the system. Key features of Hyperledger Iroha that make it suitable for Bakong include:

- **Permissioned Network:** Only authorized institutions (banks, PSIs) can join the Bakong network as validating nodes or participants, ensuring a controlled environment.

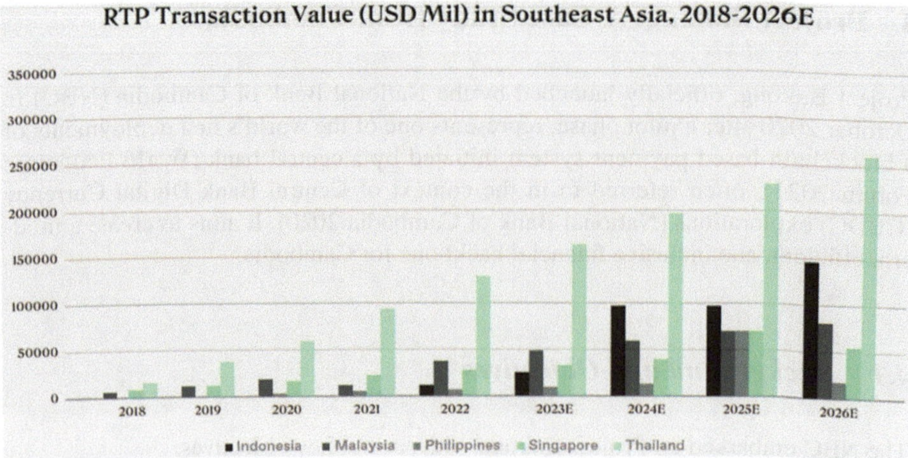

Fig. 2 High volumes of RTP Transaction Value (USD M$) in SE Asia 2018–2026E. Source: Thunes

- **Scalability and Performance:** Designed for enterprise use, Iroha aims to handle a high volume of transactions with low latency, crucial for a national payment system. The Bakong system reportedly processes transactions in less than 5 s with a throughput of 1,000–2,000 transactions per second.
- **Byzantine Fault Tolerant (BFT) Consensus:** Iroha uses a BFT consensus algorithm (Yet Another Consensus—YAC), which ensures system integrity even if some nodes fail or act maliciously.
- **Role-Based Access Control and Multi-Signature Capabilities:** These features allow for the modeling of complex business processes and robust security controls.
- **Account-Based Model:** Users and institutions have accounts on the system, and transactions involve the transfer of digital assets (representing KHR or USD) between these accounts (Fig. 2).

4.3 Key Features of Bakong

- **Real-Time Peer-to-Peer (P2P) Transactions:** Users can send and receive money instantly to anyone else on the Bakong network, regardless of their primary banking institution.
- **Mobile Application:** A user-friendly mobile app for iOS and Android allows users to create Bakong accounts, link them to their existing bank accounts (if any), and perform transactions (send, receive, pay via QR, deposit).
- **QR Code Integration (KHQR):** Bakong is deeply integrated with the KHQR standard, enabling seamless QR code payments at participating merchants.

- **Dual Currency Support:** Transactions can be conducted in both KHR and USD, reflecting Cambodia's dual-currency environment.
- **Interoperability with Existing Systems:** Bakong is designed to interface with existing payment systems like FAST (Fast and Secure Transfer), allowing for a smooth transition and broader connectivity.

4.4 Architecture Overview

- **Bakong Core:** The DLT platform itself, comprising nodes run by the NBC and potentially other participants, maintaining the distributed ledger.
- **Payment Gateway:** Financial institutions connect to the Bakong Core via a payment gateway. Each institution manages its customers (end-users) within its domain on the Bakong system, including KYC/AML responsibilities.
- **End-User Interaction:** End-users access Bakong services through the official Bakong mobile app or potentially through their own bank's mobile app if it integrates with Bakong via APIs.

Project Bakong is not strictly a CBDC in the sense of the central bank issuing digital fiat currency directly to the public as a liability of the central bank. Instead, it is a DLT-based payment system that tokenizes commercial bank money (deposits) for transactions on the platform (The Block Research 2025). However, it shares many characteristics and objectives with CBDC projects and is a significant step in that direction. Its successful implementation and growing adoption, both domestically and for cross-border payments, make it a vital case study for other nations (Fig. 3).

5 The Role of QR Codes in Enhancing Accessibility and Interoperability: The KHQR Standard

While blockchain technology provides a robust and efficient backend infrastructure for modern payment systems like Bakong, the user-facing interface is equally crucial for driving adoption and ensuring ease of use. In this regard, Quick Response (QR) codes have emerged as a highly effective, low-cost, and versatile tool for facilitating digital payments, particularly in mobile-first economies across Southeast Asia. Cambodia has strategically leveraged QR code technology through its national standard, KHQR, to complement and enhance the Bakong ecosystem.

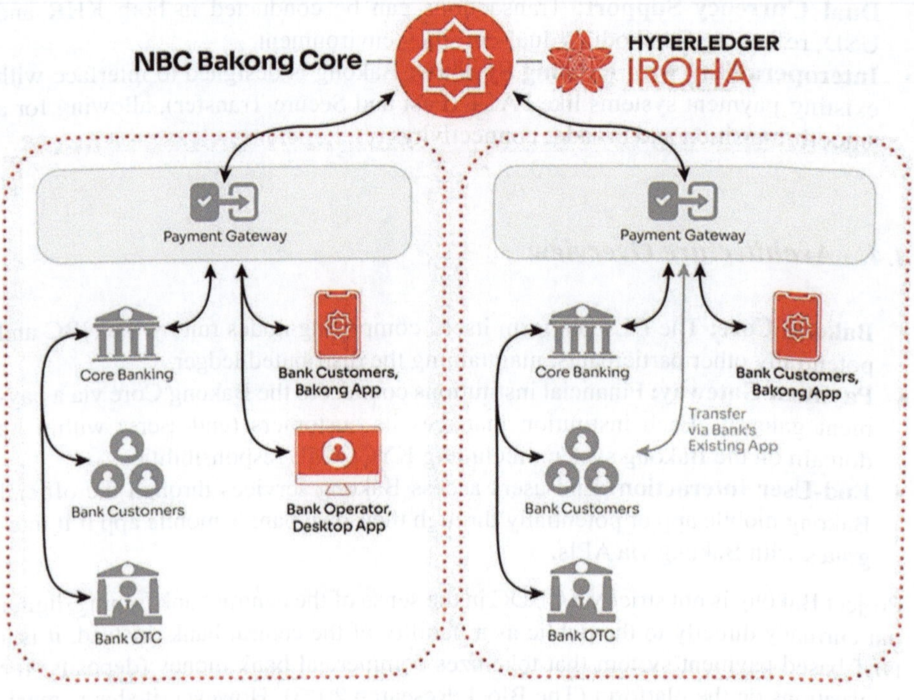

Fig. 3 Interconnection of payment gateways

5.1 Introduction to QR Code Payments

QR codes are two-dimensional barcodes that can store a significant amount of information and can be easily scanned using a smartphone camera. In the context of payments, QR codes can be used in two primary modes:

1. **Merchant-Presented Mode:** The merchant displays a QR code (either static or dynamically generated for each transaction). The customer scans the QR code using their mobile banking or payment app, enters the amount (if not pre-filled), and authorizes the payment.
2. **Customer-Presented Mode:** The customer generates a QR code on their mobile app, which the merchant scans using a POS device or another mobile device to initiate the payment.

QR code payments offer several advantages:

- **Low Cost:** Compared to traditional POS terminals that require hardware investment and maintenance, QR codes can be displayed on a simple printout or a screen, making them highly accessible for small and micro-merchants.
- **Ease of Use:** Scanning a QR code is generally faster and more intuitive than manually entering payment details.
- **Versatility:** QR codes can facilitate P2P transfers, P2M (Person-to-Merchant) payments, and even bill payments.

5.2 *The KHQR Standard*

Recognizing the potential of QR codes but also the risk of fragmentation if multiple proprietary QR systems proliferated, the National Bank of Cambodia, in collaboration with the Association of Banks in Cambodia (ABC), introduced the KHQR standard. KHQR is the standardized QR code specification for retail payments in Cambodia.

5.3 *Key Objectives and Features of KHQR*

- **Interoperability:** The primary goal of KHQR is to enable interoperability across different banks, e-wallets, and payment service providers. A single KHQR code displayed by a merchant can be scanned by customers using any participating mobile banking app or Bakong app (Sereywath 2020). This eliminates the need for merchants to display multiple QR codes from different acquirers.
- **Consistent User Experience:** KHQR aims to provide a uniform and familiar payment experience for both consumers and merchants, regardless of the payment app used.
- **Promotion of Mobile Payments:** By simplifying QR payments, KHQR encourages wider adoption of mobile retail payments throughout Cambodia.
- **Foundation for Cross-Border Payments:** A standardized domestic QR system like KHQR is a crucial building block for enabling cross-border QR payment linkages with other countries that have similar national standards.
- **Integration with Bakong:** KHQR is intrinsically linked with the Bakong payment network, which often acts as the payment switch facilitating transactions initiated via KHQR scans. The QR code itself contains the necessary information (e.g., merchant Bakong account ID, transaction details for dynamic QRs) to route the payment through the Bakong system.

5.4 *How KHQR Works with Bakong*

1. **Generation:** Merchants, whether individuals or corporates, can generate their KHQR codes. This can be done via the Bakong mobile/desktop app, the Bakong website, or through their financial institution if it supports KHQR generation. The KHQR code embeds merchant account information, which is often their Bakong account ID or an account linked through the Bakong network.
2. **Scanning and Payment:** A customer using any participating mobile banking app (or the Bakong app itself) scans the merchant's KHQR code.
3. **Information Processing:** The customer's app reads the information embedded in the KHQR code.

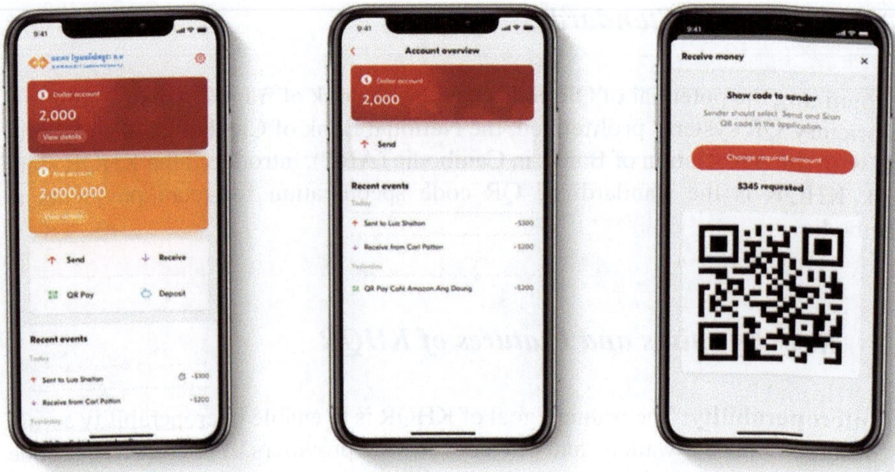

Fig. 4 User flow of KHQR

4. **Transaction Initiation:** The customer confirms the payment amount (if it's a static QR or if prompted) and authorizes the transaction.
5. **Clearing and Settlement:** The payment instruction is routed, often via the Bakong network acting as a switch. Funds are debited from the customer's account (or their linked Bakong account) and credited to the merchant's account in near real-time.
6. **Notification:** Both the customer and the merchant receive a notification confirming the transaction (Fig. 4).

5.5 *Benefits of KHQR*

- **For Consumers:** No more confusion with multiple QR codes. They can use their preferred banking app for payments wherever KHQR is accepted.
- **For Merchants:** Saves counter space (single QR stand). Provides a simple, fast, and secure payment solution. Enables acceptance of payments from customers of any participating bank or e-wallet without needing multiple contracts.

The KHQR standard, by fostering a unified and interoperable QR payment ecosystem built upon the Bakong network, has been instrumental in accelerating the adoption of digital payments in Cambodia and laying the groundwork for seamless cross-border payment initiatives.

6 Enabling Cross-Border Payments in Southeast Asia

The vision of a deeply integrated Southeast Asian economic community hinges significantly on the ability to conduct seamless and efficient cross-border transactions (Boston Consulting Group & ASEAN BAC 2023). Historically, these transactions have been plagued by high costs, slow speeds, and complex processes, often relying on traditional correspondent banking networks. The advent of DLT-based payment systems like Bakong, coupled with standardized national QR codes like KHQR, has opened new avenues for revolutionizing cross-border payments in the region.

6.1 Significance of Cross-Border Payments

Efficient cross-border payments are vital for:

- **Facilitating Regional Trade:** Simplifying payments for goods and services traded between ASEAN nations.
- **Boosting Tourism:** Allowing tourists to use their familiar domestic payment apps in other ASEAN countries, enhancing convenience and potentially increasing spending.
- **Supporting Migrant Workers and Remittances:** Providing cheaper and faster ways for migrant workers to send money home.
- **Promoting Local Currency Usage:** Enabling direct exchange and settlement in local currencies can reduce reliance on intermediary currencies like the USD, potentially lowering costs and exchange rate risks.
- **Strengthening Economic Integration:** Fostering closer financial ties and contributing to the broader goals of the ASEAN Economic Community.

6.2 Bakong and KHQR as Enablers of Cross-Border Linkages

Cambodia, through the National Bank of Cambodia (NBC), has been at the forefront of establishing bilateral cross-border QR payment linkages. The Bakong system and the KHQR standard are foundational to these efforts. The general model involves connecting Cambodia's KHQR system with the national QR standards of partner countries. This allows:

- **Inbound Payments:** Tourists or visitors from a partner country can use their native mobile payment application to scan KHQR codes displayed by Cambodian merchants. The transaction is processed in real-time, with currency conversion handled seamlessly in the background.

- **Outbound Payments:** Cambodian residents and Bakong users can travel to a partner country and use their Bakong app (or participating bank app) to scan the partner country's national QR codes for payments.

6.3 Key Cross-Border Initiatives by NBC (Leveraging Bakong/KHQR)

Based on the provided documents and general knowledge of the region's developments:

1. **Cambodia-Thailand:** This was one of the early and significant linkages, allowing citizens of both countries to make QR payments in the other's territory. It supports tourism and border trade.
2. **Cambodia-Vietnam:** Officially launched in December 2023, this linkage enables seamless and secure QR code payments between the two neighboring countries, aiming to boost trade, tourism, and make it easier for Cambodians in Vietnam to send money home.
3. **Cambodia-Malaysia:** Collaboration has been established to link their national payment systems for cross-border QR payments, further strengthening financial interconnectivity in Southeast Asia.
4. **Cambodia-Japan:** A Memorandum of Cooperation on "Unified QR Code-Based Payment" was signed in December 2023 between the NBC and Japan's Ministry of Economy, Trade and Industry. This aims to drive widespread adoption of cross-border payment systems using QR code technology, enhancing local currency circulation and boosting tourism between the two nations.

6.4 Technical and Operational Aspects

These linkages typically involve:

- **Interoperability between National QR Standards:** Ensuring that the QR codes of one country can be read and processed by the payment apps of the other.
- **Payment Switching Infrastructure:** Often, the respective national payment switches (like Bakong for Cambodia) are connected, or a common switch/hub might be used.
- **FX and Settlement Mechanisms:** Clear mechanisms for foreign exchange conversion and inter-country settlement are established, often aiming for settlement in local currencies to reduce costs.
- **Regulatory Cooperation:** Collaboration between the central banks of the participating countries is essential for establishing rules, standards, and oversight (Fig. 5).

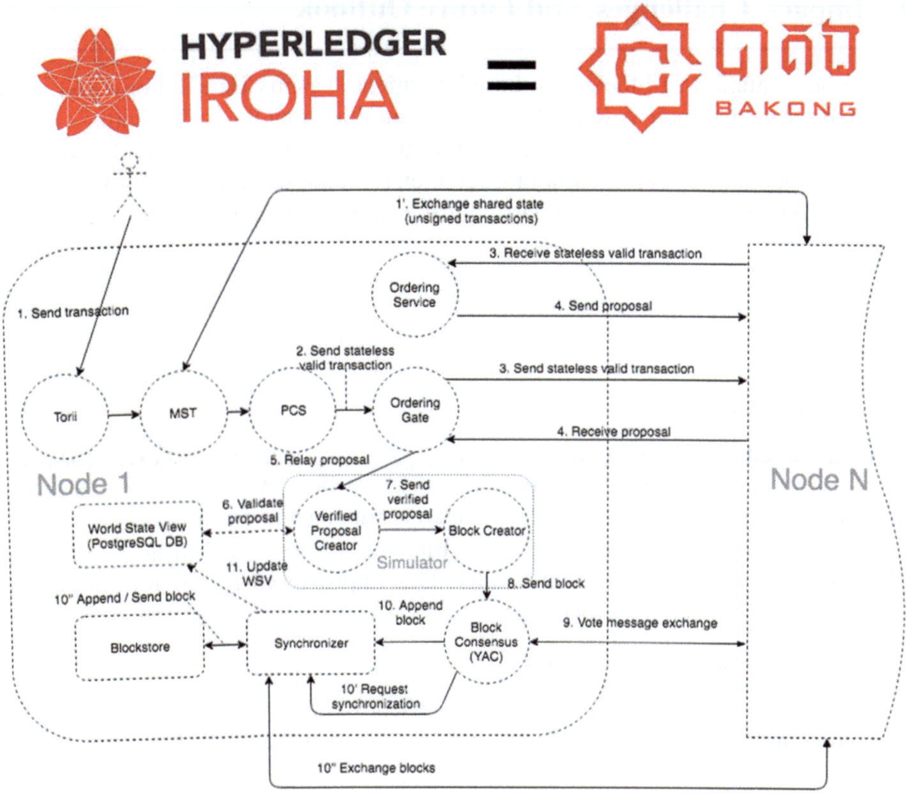

Fig. 5 What is inside Bakong

6.5 *Benefits Realized*

- **Enhanced Convenience:** For travelers and businesses.
- **Reduced Transaction Costs:** Compared to traditional methods like credit cards or money changers.
- **Increased Transaction Speed:** Real-time or near real-time processing.
- **Promotion of Local Currencies:** Transactions are often directly converted between the local currencies involved.
- **Financial Inclusion:** Extends the benefits of digital payments across borders.

While these initiatives are transformative, challenges remain, including ensuring robust security against cross-border fraud, harmonizing technical standards further, navigating different regulatory landscapes, and achieving widespread merchant and consumer adoption across all participating nations. Nevertheless, Cambodia's proactive approach demonstrates the significant potential for modern payment technologies to reshape regional economic interactions.

7 Impact, Challenges, and Future Outlook

The implementation of blockchain-based payment systems like Bakong and standardized QR codes such as KHQR has had a tangible impact on Cambodia's financial ecosystem and offers a glimpse into the future of payments in Southeast Asia. However, this journey is not without its challenges, and the future outlook involves both exciting opportunities and areas requiring careful navigation.

7.1 Impact

1. **Efficiency Gains:**
   - **Reduced Costs:** Bakong aims for zero or very low transaction fees for end-users, making digital payments more accessible. The streamlined process reduces operational costs for participating financial institutions.
   - **Increased Speed:** Transactions on Bakong are processed in near real-time (under 5 s), with settlement finality. This improves cash flow for merchants and convenience for consumers.
2. **Enhanced Financial Inclusion:**
   - The Bakong mobile app, with its user-friendly interface and simplified KYC options, has made it easier for unbanked and underbanked individuals to access formal financial services.
   - The widespread adoption of KHQR by merchants, including small businesses, has expanded the network of digital payment acceptance points.
   - As of recent reports, Bakong has seen significant user growth, indicating progress in bringing more Cambodians into the formal financial system.
3. **Promotion of Local Currency (KHR) Usage:**
   - By facilitating easy and low-cost digital transactions in KHR, Bakong and KHQR encourage its use over physical cash and potentially reduce the dominance of the US dollar in daily transactions. This supports the NBC's broader de-dollarization efforts and strengthens monetary policy transmission.
4. **Modernized Payment Infrastructure and Interoperability:**
   - Bakong has created a unified platform connecting previously fragmented players, significantly improving interoperability within Cambodia's domestic payment system.
   - The successful cross-border QR payment linkages demonstrate its capability to integrate with international payment systems.

5. **Boost to Digital Economy and Innovation:**
    - A robust digital payment infrastructure is a cornerstone of a thriving digital economy, enabling e-commerce, digital services, and FinTech innovation.

7.2 *Challenges*

1. **Cybersecurity Risks:** As with any digital system, Bakong and KHQR are susceptible to cyber threats, including malware, fraud, and hacking attempts. Ensuring the resilience and security of the DLT platform, payment gateways, and end-user applications is an ongoing priority. Cross-border linkages introduce further complexities in managing cybersecurity risks across jurisdictions.
2. **Regulatory Complexities and Harmonization:** While domestic regulation is managed by the NBC, cross-border payment systems require close cooperation and harmonization of regulatory frameworks (e.g., AML/CFT, data privacy, consumer protection) between participating countries. Differing regulations can pose hurdles.
3. **Widespread Adoption and Digital Literacy:** Despite impressive growth, achieving universal adoption requires continuous efforts in promoting digital and financial literacy, especially in rural areas. Building trust in digital payment systems is also crucial.
4. **Competition and Integration with Existing/Global Players:** The entry of large global payment players (e.g., Alipay+) into markets like Cambodia presents both opportunities for collaboration and challenges in terms of competition for local banks and payment providers (Chea 2024). Ensuring a level playing field and managing data security concerns are important.
5. **Scalability and Performance under Stress:** While initial tests show good performance, the system must be able to scale efficiently and maintain performance as transaction volumes grow significantly and during peak load times.
6. **Operational Risks:** The speed and continuous availability of fast payment systems mean that any operational incident (e.g., system downtime) can have an immediate and widespread impact on users. Robust business continuity and disaster recovery plans are essential.

7.3 *Future Outlook*

1. **Expansion of Cross-Border Linkages:** The trend of establishing bilateral and potentially multilateral cross-border QR payment linkages is expected to continue, with Bakong playing a key role for Cambodia in connecting with more countries in ASEAN and beyond.

2. **Evolution towards CBDC:** Project Bakong is a significant step in exploring the functionalities and implications of a CBDC. The NBC may leverage the experience from Bakong for future development of a full-fledged retail or wholesale CBDC.
3. **Integration of Value-Added Services:** The Bakong platform could potentially support a wider range of financial services beyond basic payments, such as digital identity, smart contracts for automated payments, and access to credit or insurance products.
4. **Focus on Data Analytics and Policy Making:** The transaction data generated by the system (while respecting privacy) can provide valuable insights for economic analysis and policy-making by the NBC.
5. **Continued Technological Advancement:** The underlying DLT and QR code technologies will continue to evolve. The Bakong system will need to adapt to incorporate new features, security enhancements, and performance improvements.

The journey of Bakong and KHQR underscores a commitment to leveraging technology for national development. While challenges persist, the proactive approach taken by the National Bank of Cambodia offers a promising model for other nations seeking to modernize their payment systems and foster inclusive economic growth.

8 Conclusion

The transformation of payment systems in Southeast Asia, driven by the imperative for greater efficiency, inclusivity, and interoperability, is being significantly shaped by the adoption of innovative technologies like blockchain and standardized QR codes. Cambodia's Project Bakong, powered by the Hyperledger Iroha DLT and complemented by the national KHQR standard, stands as a compelling testament to this revolution. This initiative by the National Bank of Cambodia has not only modernized the domestic payment landscape but has also positioned the nation as a proactive participant in the burgeoning network of cross-border digital payment linkages within the region and beyond.

This article has demonstrated that Project Bakong was conceived to address fundamental challenges inherent in traditional payment systems, including fragmentation, high costs, slow settlement times, and financial exclusion. By creating a unified, DLT-based platform, Bakong has facilitated real-time, low-cost transactions in both Khmer Riel and US dollars, connecting various financial institutions and making digital payments accessible to a wider segment of the population through a user-friendly mobile application. The KHQR standard has further amplified these benefits by ensuring that a single QR code can be used across all participating payment providers, simplifying the experience for consumers and merchants alike.

The strategic vision of the National Bank of Cambodia extends beyond domestic improvements. The successful establishment of cross-border QR payment arrangements with countries such as Thailand, Vietnam, Malaysia, and Japan underscores the potential of such systems to foster regional economic integration, boost tourism, facilitate trade, and promote the use of local currencies in international transactions. These linkages are crucial steps towards realizing a more interconnected and financially harmonized Southeast Asia.

However, the journey is ongoing and not without its hurdles. Cybersecurity remains a paramount concern, necessitating continuous vigilance and robust defense mechanisms. Regulatory harmonization across borders, ensuring digital and financial literacy for all citizens, and managing the competitive landscape are critical areas that require sustained attention. The scalability and resilience of these new infrastructures must also be continually assessed and enhanced as adoption grows.

In conclusion, the Cambodian experience with Project Bakong and KHQR offers invaluable lessons and a source of inspiration. It showcases how a developing nation can strategically leverage advanced technologies to leapfrog conventional development paths, build a more inclusive financial system, and actively contribute to regional payment modernization. As Southeast Asia continues its march towards a more integrated digital economy, the principles of interoperability, security, efficiency, and financial inclusion, as embodied by initiatives like Bakong, will undoubtedly remain central to shaping the future of payments. The continued evolution of these systems, potentially paving the way for broader CBDC adoption and further FinTech innovation, promises an exciting and dynamic future for the region's financial sector.

References

Boston Consulting Group & ASEAN Business Advisory Council (2023) Interoperable QR code payment ecosystem in ASEAN: what it means for the world. https://www.bcg.com/publications/2023/southeast-asia-qr-code-payment-ecosystem-in-asean. Accessed 23 July 2025

Casino F, Dasaklis TK, Patsakis C (2019) A systematic literature review of blockchain-based applications: current status, classification and open issues. Telematics Inform 36:55–81. https://doi.org/10.1016/j.tele.2018.11.006. Accessed 23 July 2025

Chea S (2024) Remarks – official launching ceremony of cross-border QR code payment between Bakong and Alipay Plus. Bank for International Settlements. https://www.bis.org/review/r251616f.pdf. Accessed 23 July 2025

Ly R, Ly B (2024) Digital payment systems in an emerging economy. Comput Hum Behav Rep 14:100517. https://doi.org/10.1016/j.chbr.2024.100517. Accessed 23 July 2025

National Bank of Cambodia (2020) Project Bakong: next generation payment system (White Paper). Soramitsu. https://soramitsu.co.jp/bakong/whitepaper. Accessed 23 July 2025

Sereywath L (2020) National Bank of Cambodia. Bakong as a payment switch – a single QR Code for receiving payment from any mobile banking apps. https://bakong.nbc.gov.kh/en/download/KHQR/integration/KHQR%20Content%20Guideline%20v.1.3.pdf. Accessed 23 July 2025

The Block Research (2025) Billions to trillions: stablecoin use-cases poised to expand the market. Global Dollar Network. https://www.theblock.co/post/354675/billions-to-trillions-stablecoin-use-cases-poised-to-expand-the-market. Accessed 23 July 2025

World Economic Forum (2021) Cambodia's digital currency can show other central banks the way. https://www.weforum.org/stories/2021/08/cambodias-digital-currency-ishowing-other-central-banks-the-way/. Accessed 23 July 2025

Critical Views on Tokenised Money

Will Tokenised Money Overthrow Existing Financial Infrastructures? TradFi vs DeFi: Who Will Win?

Michael Salmony

Abstract Tokenised money, and stablecoins in particular, represent a paradigm shift in how value can be transferred. By encapsulating monetary value into secure digital tokens and sending them directly over the internet, they enable near-instant, atomic settlement—a "digital bearer instrument" akin to passing cash, but online. This chapter examines whether such tokenised forms of money will upend traditional financial infrastructures or ultimately integrate with them. Key questions are explored around technical advantages, interoperability between privately issued tokens, the role of banks versus non-banks, regulatory and sovereignty implications, and use cases from cross-border remittances to micropayments. We draw parallels to past financial innovations (e.g. Open Banking) to temper expectations, noting that even technically superior solutions can take years to achieve broad uptake. Ultimately, tokenised money's fate lies in resolving open challenges—user experience, standards, regulation, risk—and in navigating scenarios from disruptive upheaval to harmonious integration. The chapter concludes that while tokenised money could become an integral part of the future monetary ecosystem, much work remains to ensure it realises its promise as "fiat made for the internet" in a safe, widely accepted manner.

Keywords Token · Defi · TradFi · Challenges

1 Introduction

The emergence of tokenised money—especially fiat-pegged stablecoins—has prompted intense debate about the future of payments and banking. This promise—explored at length in other chapters—has fuelled extraordinary growth in stablecoin usage over the past few years.

M. Salmony (✉)
Payments Innovation Consulting, Heidelberg, Germany
e-mail: salmony@payments-innovation.com

S. Yazıcı et al. (eds.), *Tokenisation of Money*, Contributions to Finance and Accounting, https://doi.org/10.1007/978-3-032-22946-5_28

Will tokenised money overthrow existing financial infrastructures? The optimist's view is that stablecoins and related tokens could "leapfrog" legacy payment rails that are often slow, costly, and fragmented—especially for cross-currency and cross-border transactions.

However, history urges caution before predicting an imminent overthrow of the status quo. The financial industry is riddled with examples of superior technologies that took far longer than expected to reach scale—or never did. The recent experience of Open Banking in Europe is instructive: despite regulations (PSD2/PSD3/PSR/FIDA) intended to revolutionise data access and traditional payments, years after its introduction adoption has fallen short of expectations, with many banks treating it as a compliance burden rather than an innovation opportunity (Muhn 2025). The lesson is that even when a new way of working is technically and economically superior, entrenched behaviours, legacy infrastructure, existing business models that incumbents feel they need to protect and regulatory complexity can delay or stifle change. For tokenised money, this means overcoming not just technical challenges, but also regulatory hurdles, trust deficits, and integration into everyday commerce.

2 Obstacles on the Road to Mainstream Adoption

For all its promise, tokenised money still remains, to a large extent, a tool of early adopters (tech-savvy users, crypto traders, institutions, fintech firms) rather than the general public or in retail. Significant obstacles must be overcome before stablecoins are ready for mainstream, everyday use. Perhaps the most immediate challenge to mainstream public adoption is the user experience (UX). Handling stablecoins today often requires navigating unfamiliar wallet applications, managing private cryptographic keys or passwords, and dealing with concepts like blockchain incurs gas fees, obscure topics like "slippage tolerance settings" etc.—all of which can be daunting to non-technical users. There are different types of wallets with varying trade-offs, none of which yet provide the seamless simplicity of, say, a contactless card or a mobile banking app for the average person.

On one end, fully open, self-custodial wallets like MetaMask give users control of their keys but demand high technical competence: if you lose your seed phrase, your funds are irretrievably gone. The onboarding might involve installing browser extensions, writing down 24-word recovery phrases, and understanding network settings—steps that cause most newcomers to give up in frustration. On the other end, more user-friendly wallets (like those integrated in fintech apps, exchanges or neo-banks) typically hold custody of the stablecoins on the user's behalf but often restrict transfers to within their own network or partners, losing the global promise.

Another major hurdle is fragmentation and lack of interoperability. The tokenised world is currently a patchwork of different blockchains, proprietary stablecoin issuers, and closed-loop ecosystems. This makes transfer of value between islands (see Fig. 1) very complex. As of 2025, stablecoins exist on dozens of

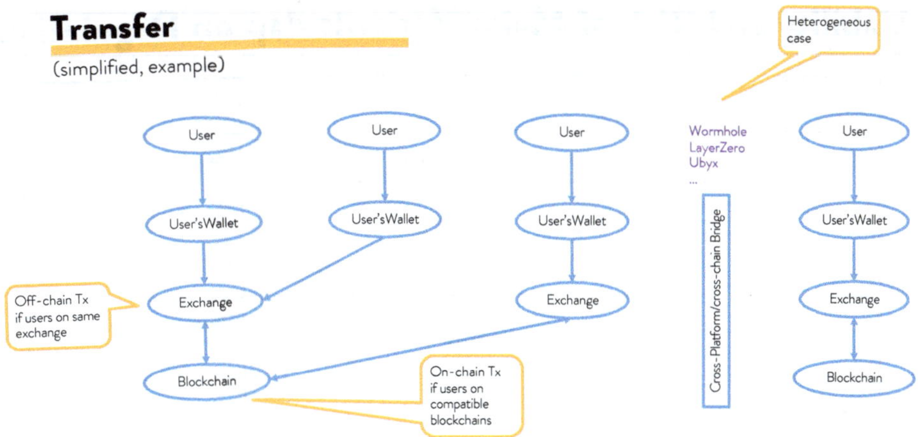

Fig. 1 Depending on whether the sender and receiver are on different wallets, exchanges, blockchains ... transfer of value between them may be different (and difficult). An untenable situation, not suitable for mainstream. (source: Author)

blockchains—USDT alone is on over 10 chains—which are not inherently interoperable. Moving a token from one chain to another often requires using third-party "bridge" services, which can be risky (many hacks have targeted token bridges).

Interoperability challenges extend to issuer fragmentation as well. We may see a proliferation of privately issued tokens: for example, a "Walmart dollar" stablecoin for retail, a "JP Morgan dollar" for corporate settlements, a "PayPal Dollar" and so on. Some efforts are underway to address this: industry groups and standards bodies are exploring common protocols to make stablecoin transfers chain-agnostic and cross-platform.

Acceptance and merchant integration form another piece of the adoption puzzle. Even if consumers hold stablecoins, will they be able to spend them easily for everyday purchases? Today, very few brick-and-mortar merchants natively accept stablecoins or crypto. This chicken-and-egg situation requires building payment acceptance networks and possibly more regulatory clarity (Some bridges to existing infrastructure are emerging: for instance, Visa and Mastercard each have begun to partner with stablecoin companies to offer payment cards that auto-convert stablecoins to fiat at the point of sale.

Regulatory and compliance obstacles loom large as well. Financial services is a heavily regulated domain for good reason—to prevent fraud, protect consumers, and ensure system stability. Stablecoins straddle the worlds of banking, payments, and securities, raising complex questions and need to distance themselves from the World of crypto that is beset by fraud. Certainly the risks, volatility and liabilities of different forms of tokenised money vary significantly (see Fig. 2).

Compliance with KYC/AML rules is thus a key challenge: how to prevent stablecoins from being used for illicit transfers, given they can move freely like cash? In

Liability and Risk of Major Variants dep on Regulation

	Liability on	Risk	Volatility
CBDC	Central bank	v low	None
CBMT/ Tokenised deposits	Commercial bank	low (subject to that bank's health)	None
Regulated Stablecoins (MiCA)	Private issuer	low (backed 1:1, over several banks, ...)	None (dep. on currency)
US Stablecoins	Private issuer	low (- issuer risk, + backed by Treasury bills = state)	None
E-Money (non-DLT)	Private issuer	Low (subject to issuer)	None (regulated, reserve requirements, 1:1 convertability, ...)
Unregulated Stablecoins (also algorithmic)	Private issuer	high	Opaque reserves, risks of depegging, redemption crises, ...
Crypto	none	v high	No underlying assets (except scarcity, hype)

Fig. 2 Liabilities and risks of various tokenised assets. (Source: Author)

any case, until a consistent global regulatory framework is in place, many players will approach global stablecoins cautiously.

Finally, trust and stability are significant adoption factors. The crypto sector's recent history has seen high-profile collapses and scandals—from the death spiral of Terra/Luna's "algorithmic" stablecoin (which was not stable at all) in 2022, to the FTX exchange bankruptcy in 2022, which eroded trust in digital assets. While fully reserved, fiat-backed, regulated stablecoins aim to avoid such failures, users and business may remain wary. Concerns persist about transparency of reserves (e.g. Tether's past opacity leading to fines), the risk of a run if holders rush to redeem, and operational vulnerabilities (cyberattacks, key theft, etc.). If stablecoins are to become part of critical financial infrastructure, they must prove resilient under stress (see Fig. 3). Incidents like temporary de-peggings (e.g. when USDC lost its $1 peg for a short time in March 2023 due to panic over reserve exposure to a failing bank (CNBC 2023) highlight that even well-backed stablecoins can face market confidence crises.

In summary, making stablecoins and tokenised money *truly ready* for mainstream use means solving a complex multi-dimensional equation: Greatly improve ease-of-use and user trust, achieve interoperability and ubiquity of acceptance, comply with or shape regulatory frameworks, and maintain stability and security. These are non-trivial challenges.

3 Future Development Options

In the coming years, we may witness a competition or convergence among the various tokenised money models. It is possible that:

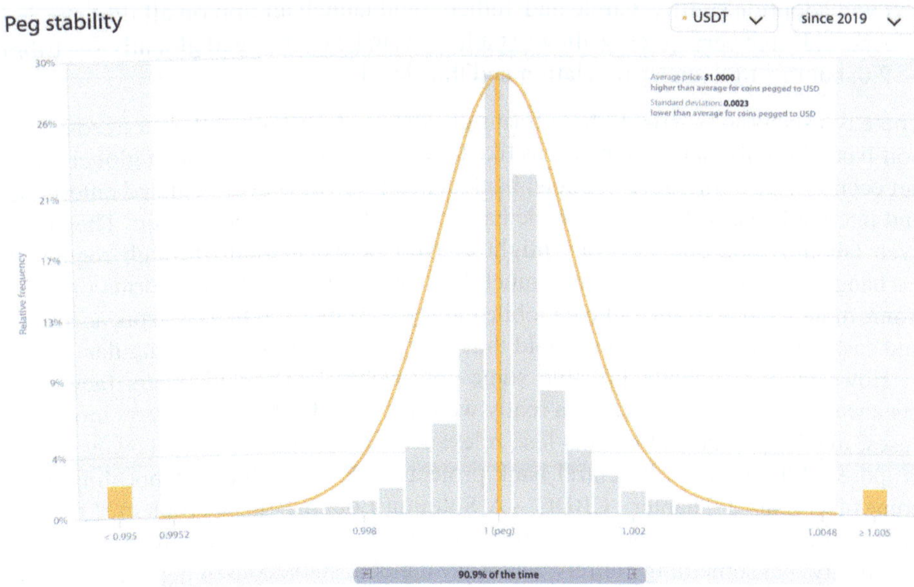

Fig. 3 USDT peg stability: variation of the prices on exchanges (secondary market), where most trading takes place. E.g. in times of crisis, people accept lower returns for quick redemption—as even high-quality "liquid" reserves may not be immediately available. (source: Cambridge Digital Money Dashboard (Cambridge 2025)—"the maintenance of the peg is not always guaranteed and stablecoins can experience significant price deviations from their intended value")

- Some private stablecoins (especially USD-backed) continue to dominate global volume, effectively extending the reach of the U.S. dollar into digital realms (with geopolitical implications).
- Banks respond to the "attack on TradFi" by actively pushing tokenised deposit networks, leveraging their trust and client base to offer similar functionality in a slightly more closed loop—thereby keeping corporate clients from drifting to non-bank stablecoin providers. (As of 2025, major banks' CEOs like Jane Fraser of Citi are explicitly exploring issuing a Citi stablecoin and focusing on tokenised deposits, signalling banks do not intend to miss out.)
- Central banks accelerate CBDC projects to ensure public money has a place in the tokenised future (e.g. for resilience and inclusion) and to counteract any perceived loss of monetary control to private networks. Europe, however, seems to be increasingly alone in this approach.
- Big Tech firms or Fintechs might also enter strongly—recall Facebook's Libra (renamed Diem) attempt in 2019, which was (rightly) thwarted by regulators. But in 2025, Meta (Facebook) is again reportedly exploring payments and possibly stablecoins for its billions of users. PayPal launched its own USD stablecoin. If a tech giant successfully integrates a stablecoin into social media or mobile devices (e.g., an "Apple stablecoin" riding on the hundreds of millions of iPhones now equipped with NFC for contactless payments), that could drive

retail adoption swiftly. Circle and Tether could launch an app on all iPhones and Androids that very quickly allows stablecoins to be exchanged globally—a Libra 2.0, but this time under regulation and thus legal.

There is a scenario where all these forms coexist, each serving different needs: e.g., non-bank digitally-native stablecoins like USDC/USDT serve the open global internet economy and emerging markets; bank deposit tokens serve regulated enterprise and interbank needs; CBDCs provide baseline public utility and backup. They may even (should) interoperate—one might convert between them through regulated exchanges or automatic protocols, much like one converts different forms of electronic money today (think of how mobile money in Kenya connects to bank accounts and cash). The future of money could thus very likely be plural, not singular.

However, it is equally possible some approaches "win" and others fade. For instance, if central banks deliver a really well-designed CBDC that covers most use cases, maybe private stablecoins lose relevance (or are restricted by law, as some propose). Alternatively, if central bank projects stall or produce unappealing outcomes [see Part 2 Chapter "CBDC – A Solution Looking for a Problem?" by the author in this book], the private sector solutions might run ahead. There is even a possibility that something entirely new—say a global stablecoin or a global consortium coin—might emerge to become a universal token standard. So far, attempts like Libra have failed, but perhaps a coalition of reputable institutions could launch a fully reserve-backed global token that gains trust as "the digital cash of the internet." Citi has long promoted a concept called the Regulated Liability Network (RLN), envisioning a network where central bank money, commercial bank money, and e-money all interoperate—hinting that a collaborative approach could prevail (Citi 2022).

In any event, we are still in the early days of this evolution. The coming decade will likely see experimentation with all models. Some will thrive, some may turn out to be dead ends. It is worth recalling that technological transitions often see many contenders before consolidation.

4 Banks, TradFi Infrastructure and the Question of Displacement

One of the central questions is whether tokenised money will cause existing financial infrastructures to become obsolete, or whether it will integrate and upgrade them without complete disintermediation. Will we still need the SWIFT network with multi-hop correspondent banking, batch, store-and-forward networks unavailable at weekends for international payments if businesses all start using stablecoins? Will card networks lose volume to direct token transfers? And crucially, what is the role of banks in a world of tokenised, peer-to-peer money?

The original vision of cryptocurrency pioneers was explicitly to bypass banks and traditional intermediaries—to create a parallel financial system where individuals could be their own bank. Stablecoins to some extent carry that ethos forward (at least the public blockchain-based ones): you can hold and transmit dollar value without a bank account, using just a wallet. If widely adopted, this could indeed threaten the traditional deposit-taking model of banks. For instance, if consumers in an economy decided to hold a significant portion of their funds in a private stablecoin wallet instead of a bank deposit, banks would lose a source of cheap funding (deposits) and might face disintermediation in payments. This scenario also worries regulators (Rodrigues 2025) because it could reduce the control over monetary policy and severely impact bank-based credit creation. However, for such a shift to happen at scale, stablecoins would need to be extremely trusted, convenient and connected—a high bar, as discussed.

A more likely near-term scenario is a hybrid model: banks themselves become key players in the tokenised money ecosystem, rather than being displaced by it. There are several reasons to believe banks will adapt rather than become obsolete. Firstly, banks excel at handling compliance (KYC/AML), risk management, and customer connection—all of which remain needed in a tokenised world. Many users will prefer a bank or regulated institution to hold custody of their tokens or provide insured stability, rather than taking on personal responsibility for safekeeping. Already, many stablecoin arrangements rely on banks: the reserves backing stablecoins are often kept in custody banks or invested through banking partners. It is telling that even disruptor Circle's USDC reserves are partly managed by BlackRock and held at banks like BNY Mellon, essentially embedding stablecoins within the traditional financial stack. In parallel, banks are exploring issuing their own forms of tokenised money (deposit tokens), thereby leveraging their huge customer base. JP Morgan's CEO Jamie Dimon, while sceptical in tone, has been clear: "We're going to be involved in [JPMorgan deposit coin] and stablecoins – to understand it, to be good at it". Banks see that if clients want these capabilities (fast 24/7 settlement, on-chain finance integration), they need to offer them or risk losing clients to Fintechs.

However, reducing banks to the role of providing compliance (KYC, AML, etc.), connectivity, trust, branding and a good user experience (by embedding tokenised money in normal banking apps) may just be "helping the opposition" and accelerate the cannibalisation. This may not only impact transaction banking (money being moved not through traditional banking channels) but also, more seriously, impact core banking and revenue pools. Beyond the future potential impact of DeFi lending (BoE 2021), we may also see a more short-term impact as pointed out by (ECB 2025):

> „… some platforms offer interest on stablecoin holdings, although stablecoins as such do not normally offer interest. Income can also be generated by lending stablecoins, providing liquidity, or through "yield farming". All of these generate a return, similar to a savings account … If interest-bearing stablecoins became common and more businesses started using them, they could divert deposits from traditional banks…"

Thus we have already seen a risk of deposit-flight through CBDC, now the core business of banking—lending—may be impacted also with Stablecoins.

In terms of infrastructure like payment networks and messaging systems (SWIFT, ACH, card networks, etc.), these incumbents are not standing still either. SWIFT, for example, is running experiments around tokenised assets, trying to position itself as an interoperability layer for new networks just as it was for old ones. Card companies Visa/Mastercard are actively investing in crypto and stablecoin integration—Visa has developed ways to settle transactions using USDC on Ethereum for certain partners, effectively starting to accept stablecoin payments into its network (Visa 2023). Mastercard launched a programme to help banks offer crypto and is enabling stablecoin wallet providers to issue cards. These moves imply that rather than being overthrown overnight, existing networks may incorporate tokenised money into their pipelines. The result could be a coexistence for quite some time: traditional rails for many retail transactions, tokenised rails for specific use cases and new domains, with bridging between them.

Focussing on cross-border payments—an area where traditional infrastructure is often criticised as slow and costly. There are now multiple parallel initiatives: SWIFT GPI has sped up legacy transfers, new instant payment linkages like the BIS's Nexus project aim to connect national real-time payment systems and meanwhile stablecoins are already serving as de facto rails in crypto markets and some remittances. It is thus likely that cross-border will stay a patchwork for some time.

We should also consider resilience and risk in new vs old infrastructures. Traditional banking and payment systems, for all their flaws, have redundancies and regulatory safeguards. A fully tokenised system might have new points of failure.

In extreme disruptive scenarios, one could envision a near-total bypass of banks: for instance, a future where large corporations keep most liquidity in stablecoins, transact with each other on distributed networks, and even SMEs use decentralised finance (DeFi) protocols for borrowing/lending, thereby sidelining commercial banks. However, any such shift would face regulatory intervention if it threatened financial stability. Governments might then respond with mandatory CBDCs or stricter rules to pull activity back into traditional oversight.

In conclusion, while tokenised money could in theory "bypass the banks", in practice a more likely outcome is a reshaping of banks' roles and an upgrade of financial infrastructure rather than a wholesale replacement. Banks may transform from traditional ledger-keepers to "stablecoin service providers"—issuing their own tokens, providing conversion and guarantee services, and leveraging their trust to bring tokenisation mainstream. Traditional networks like SWIFT or Visa may pivot to become interoperability layers or incorporate token rails, remaining relevant by evolving. As with past technological disruptions, incumbents that embrace change can often survive or even thrive, whereas those that ignore it risk irrelevance. The balance of evidence suggests many incumbents are now embracing tokenisation (if cautiously), indicating a blended future. That said, one cannot rule out a more disruptive scenario if an inflection point is reached where network effects tip overwhelmingly in favour of tokenised rails (much as cell phones rapidly displaced landlines at a certain point). The tipping point for money might be, for example, if a major central bank or a consortium launches a widely accessible token system that is clearly superior—at that moment, old rails could see a rapid sunset. So the question of overthrow versus coexistence remains open, hinging on how quickly the new technology matures and whether incumbents successfully co-opt it.

5 Use Cases and Impact: From Cross-Border to Micropayments and Inclusion

To gauge where tokenised money might take hold first, it is instructive to look at the concrete use cases being pursued and the problems they aim to solve that traditional infrastructure has not.

1. **Cross-Border Payments:** This is often cited as the "killer app" for stablecoins. The pain points of cross-border transfers—high cost (average fees of 6% for remittances), slow speed (days), and opaque status/routing—are well-known. Despite decades of effort (G20 has had an active programme to improve cross-border payments), progress has been modest in many corridors. Tokenised money offers a way to essentially bypass the old chain of correspondent banks with a direct internet-based transfer. In practice, we already see thousands of small businesses using stablecoins to pay suppliers or remote workers internationally, because it is faster than waiting for wire transfers. Remittance companies are also integrating stablecoins on the back-end to move funds between countries before disbursing locally. For example, rather than holding pools of various currencies, a remittance firm might convert customer funds to USDC, send USDC to the destination country, and convert to local currency for payout—reducing reliance on correspondent bank liquidity. On a larger scale, some countries experiencing hyperinflation or currency crises (e.g. in parts of Latin America, Africa) have unofficially dollarised via stablecoins—people hold USDT as a safer store of value than the local currency and even make peer-to-peer trades and payments with it. (Feingold 2025) mentions stablecoins serving underbanked populations. If stablecoin usage continues rising in these contexts, it could push the global remittance costs down and volumes up, contributing to economic welfare (remittances often being a lifeline in developing economies). Cross-border business payments could also become more efficient, aiding global trade. Global stablecoins acting as "bridges" between currencies might finally achieve something like an instant global dollar that anyone can access, which has mixed implications (good for efficiency, but concerning for local monetary sovereignty as discussed).
2. **B2B and Treasury Payments:** Outside of retail, many predict that business-to-business (B2B) payments and corporate treasury operations will be the first major domain of stablecoin adoption (and indeed that is already happening). Corporates demand speed, certainty, and possibly round-the-clock capability for moving large sums—e.g. moving funds between subsidiaries, paying employees around the globe or funding accounts on exchanges to manage risk. Stablecoins offer 24/7 instant settlement, which is very appealing to treasurers who otherwise

have to wait for wire cut-off times or deal with bank holidays. Dara Khosrowshahi, CEO of Uber, noted that for a company moving billions across countries, stablecoins are "super interesting" as a way to streamline global liquidity. If companies like Uber start shifting significant payment flows to stablecoins, banks that are not supporting stablecoin capabilities could see their best clients migrate their business elsewhere. Conversely, banks enabling this (JPM, Citi, etc.) can lock in those clients by catering to their needs. The demand from corporate treasurers is real but many are "stablecoin curious but lost on implementation"—meaning there's a gap in practical know-how and solutions. This presents an opportunity for payment integrators and fintechs to help companies integrate stablecoins into ERPs and cash management systems (some even call it a "strategic imperative" for integrators). If a robust ecosystem of tools emerges (for accounting, compliance, etc.), B2B usage could ramp up quickly, since the value proposition (cost and time saving) is evident. Trade finance and supply chain payments are another B2B angle: projects are exploring tokenised invoices or letters of credit that pay out via stablecoin when conditions are met, which could simplify historically paper-heavy processes. In our electronic times it is worth noting that half of the $58Tr annual global trade is still done on paper (SWIFT 2021/2024). A single cross-border transaction can involve the exchange of 36 documents and 240 copies among up to 30 different stakeholders (WEF 2025). Half of US B2B commerce is still done with cheques. So the potential to improve, digitise and add value is enormous—maybe stablecoins can accelerate parts of this process.

3. **Micropayments and Machine-to-Machine (M2M) transactions:** Traditional finance has largely failed to enable true efficient micropayments (say a few cents or fractions of a cent) and frictionless M2M commerce, despite decades of attempts. Tokenised money finally makes it feasible for machines to transact autonomously in real time because the overhead per transaction can be extremely low (especially on certain purpose-built networks). One can envision IoT devices using stablecoins to pay per usage: an electric vehicle could continuously pay a streaming service for each song/podcast played in the in-car media entertainment, a connected printer could charge per printed page and instead deliver toner cartridges when needed "for free" (a completely new business model), a smart meter could pull electricity from the currently cheapest provider at that minute, a phone could connect to the best GSM network at the current location and in the B2B space totally new pay-per-use models become feasible. AI agents could be allocated budgets in stablecoins to purchase data or services on the fly (and indeed startups are arming AI agents with crypto wallets for this purpose (Andreessen Horowitz 2025)). This could become a significant slice of economic activity if AI-driven processes scale. To put it dramatically, stablecoins (or similar crypto-native rails) may be the only viable path to support real-time, autonomous, and scalable agentic payments because legacy systems may not be able to handle the volume or granularity (Coinbase 2025). Though these use cases are still emerging, companies like PayPal are betting on it: PayPal in 2025 announced a "financial OS for AI agents" leveraging its stablecoin and network

(Forbes 2025). If that bet pans out, stablecoins might quietly become the behind-the-scenes currency of a machine economy, largely invisible to consumers but powering new services (The machines might trade stablecoins with each other as "digital oil" greasing the machine economy).

4. **Retail Payments and E-Commerce:** This is the most visible use case but also one of the toughest to crack due to competition with existing methods which have been highly optimised over decades. Nonetheless, stablecoin advocates have their eyes on retail. The dream scenario: you go to a coffee shop and pay directly from your digital wallet to the merchant's wallet, no banks or card companies taking a cut in between—an "internet of value" equivalent of handing over a banknote. For this to happen, a few things need to align: user-friendly wallet apps (which could be big tech wallets like an updated Apple Pay, bank or fintech apps), merchant acceptance (point-of-sale integration or QR code payments), and some economic incentive (like lower cost or loyalty benefits). There are examples to draw hope from: in Brazil, the Pix instant payment system (not blockchain, but analogous result: direct account-to-account) was adopted at lightning speed and now accounts for nearly 40% of electronic payments just 3 years after launch, with over 42 billion transactions in 2023 (EPC 2024). Similarly, India's UPI system saw 117 billion transactions in 2023, making up 75% of retail digital payments by volume (Shukla 2024). These show that if a payment method is sufficiently convenient, low-cost, and widely supported (with a push from authorities or big players), consumer habits can change quickly—even leapfrogging cards in some cases. Stablecoins could ride on smartphone ubiquity much like Pix and UPI did (those systems require just a phone app and phone number or QR code to pay). If, say, a stablecoin wallet came pre-installed on iPhones and Androids, allowing contactless NFC stablecoin payments at any POS globally, that could be a game-changer. Android and finally Apple did have to open up the NFC to third-party financial apps), which allows non-Apple/Google payment apps. A large stablecoin issuer using this facility or partnering with a tech giant could distribute a ready-to-use retail payment app to hundreds of millions of users, which also works even at POS (via NFC/QR/etc), very rapidly. The memory of Facebook's Libra attempt suggests regulators will scrutinise such moves heavily, but if done within regulatory bounds, it could finally push stablecoins into daily retail usage.

   An intermediate step we see is cards linked to stablecoin balances. For instance, Crypto.com and others offer Visa cards where you preload crypto or Stablecoins into the card, and it converts on swipe. This does not overthrow Visa—it uses it—but it does allow users to indirectly spend stablecoins anywhere. The volume on those is not huge yet, but major exchanges and fintechs are rolling out more such programs, effectively treating stablecoins as another funding source akin to a bank account. The convenience of letting people spend their digital assets without manual conversion will likely increase stablecoin appeal. Meanwhile, e-commerce merchants online could more accept stablecoins (via plugins or payment processors that handle crypto) since this is "just" software integration and may not require expensive moves like new hardware or staff training. Over time, if enough flows stay on token rails, a circular economy could form where stablecoins rarely need conversion.

5. **Financial Inclusion and Emerging Markets:** Perhaps the most socially impactful use case is giving people who lack access to banking an entry into digital finance. Indeed Bill Gates has regularly promoted the advantages of increased financial inclusion as being beneficial on a par with increased healthcare for developing countries. Over a billion people have mobile phones but no bank accounts (World Bank 2021). Stablecoins plus mobile wallets could allow them to store money safely (and to transact or save in a stable value currency). In countries with volatile currencies, having access to a USD/EUR stablecoin is effectively what people often want (although national regulators of course see this critically). This can protect savings from inflation, make people more independent of corrupt local governments and their unstable monetary systems and enable participation in global commerce (e.g., a freelancer in Nigeria can get paid in USDC for work for a US company, whereas getting a USD bank account would be impossible). Both Tether and Circle have reported growth in stablecoin usage in regions like Latin America and Africa, often citing serving the underbanked as part of their mission. There are anecdotes of communities using USDT as an unofficial local currency (e.g. in parts of Venezuela). Of course, this raises sovereignty issues and regulatory dilemmas—no central bank likes to see an unofficial currency take over and potentially lose control of their monetary system. It can also significantly lower remittance costs, directly benefiting low-income households where the earner works abroad.

   However, it is worth tempering the enthusiasm with practical challenges: for a truly inclusive solution, people need an easy way to cash in/out of stablecoins into local currency for daily expenses (unless the economy around them starts accepting stablecoin directly). That means agent networks or exchanges bridging to physical cash—which is being built in some places (see M-Pesa) but is still a bottleneck. Additionally, reliance on the US dollar (through stablecoins) could increase exposure to US monetary policy, tariffs or currency swings in countries that do not control that currency, potentially introducing new systemic risks. Regulators in emerging markets will have to weigh allowing stablecoin use (and perhaps regulating it like foreign currency) versus banning it to protect their own currency (with the risk people just go underground or use crypto anyway). We might see a split: some emerging markets proactively integrate and regulate stablecoins to boost their fintech sectors (e.g. UAE, Singapore positioning as crypto hubs), whereas others ban or strictly limit them.

6. **Other Use Cases (DeFi, Capital Markets, etc):** Another domain, more on the fringe of mainstream but important in innovation terms, is the wider topic of decentralised finance (DeFi). Stablecoins are the lifeblood of DeFi applications (used in lending, trading, derivatives on blockchain). While this mostly serves crypto traders today, some argue the DeFi sector could evolve to provide financial services (loans, yield, insurance) to anyone globally in a disintermediated way. If that were to happen, stablecoins would be the medium through which credit flows outside traditional banking. That could be rather disruptive (imagine

businesses borrowing stablecoins from a DeFi protocol instead of a bank). As we saw, BigTechs and Fintechs are already an increasing provider of funding to many segments, especially those not well served by traditional banking (e.g. SMEs).

It is early for that scenario; nonetheless, traditional finance is eyeing DeFi's innovations like automated market-making and 24/7 markets. In capital markets, tokenisation of securities coupled with tokenised money could streamline trading and settlement (T + 0 settlement with tokenised cash could eliminate counterparty risk in trades). Some stock exchanges and banks are piloting tokenised bonds and equities that settle via digital cash tokens. If those pilots succeed, the plumbing of capital markets in a decade might be token-based, making trades instant and potentially reducing the role of clearinghouses. That may be more of an infrastructure overhaul than a user-facing change, but it underscores that tokenised money's impact could permeate many layers of finance, reducing latency and intermediaries in transactions of all kinds and severely impacting traditional means.

Across these use cases, the overarching pattern is addressing pain points that existing systems have not solved: whether it is speed (cross-border, B2B), cost (remittances, micropayments), access (inclusion, 24/7 availability), or new functionality (M2M, AI integration). Tokenised money is not a solution looking for a problem (as was the case with early Blockchain efforts)—these problems are real. The open question is execution: can Tokenisation deliver in practice at scale, outweighing the drawbacks and convincing users? The evidence so far is mixed but already promising in specific segments. We see real adoption in certain areas (e.g., $7 trillion+ stablecoin transaction volume in a quarter indicates real usage, albeit heavily in trading).

Ultimately, tokenised money could follow a path similar to the internet or mobile adoption: starting with niche/geek uses, then quietly becoming ubiquitous in the background of everyday life. We might reach a point where, for example, a person is using stablecoin rails without knowing it—perhaps their bank app or payment app automatically chooses to route some transfers via a stablecoin network if it is faster/cheaper, just as your phone chooses Wi-Fi or cellular based on best signal without you noticing. At that stage, the overthrow vs coexistence question becomes semantic.

In conclusion of this section, each use case's success will contribute to tokenised money's overall penetration. Cross-border and B2B usage could drive volume and legitimacy first (we are already seeing acceptance for these). As trust builds, and infrastructure matures, retail and inclusion use cases might follow, especially with big tech distribution. Large payment players (banks, card networks, etc) likely begin by using tokenised money for their own global backbones before opening retail use cases. Micropayments and machine use might become a large new market that ensures constant demand for token transactions. The timeline is uncertain—it might be gradual and then sudden, or a steady incremental growth. But it is telling that even cautious observers cannot deny that stablecoins are becoming economically relevant. When there is unmet demand (e.g., for cheap global payments), solutions tend to find a way in.

6 Future Ecosystem: Scalability, Security, and Reduced Intermediation

Peering further into the future, we must ask: what will the architecture of money look like if tokenisation succeeds on a broad scale? The current generation of blockchain networks, while revolutionary, have well-known limitations in scalability, energy efficiency, and even privacy. Energy efficiency has improved with Ethereum's switch to proof-of-stake (99% energy reduction) and will improve further as new consensus methods and new L1/L2 networks optimised for financial transactions are deployed. It is conceivable that by the time tokenised money is mainstream, the technology underlying it might not resemble today's blockchains at all—or it may be a vastly improved version.

One provocative question is whether scalable implementations will entirely "move away from DLT and Blockchain" to other distributed architectures that mitigate current concerns. Research into next-gen consensus (like Byzantine Fault Tolerant algorithms that have been known for decades but are now being adapted to blockchain contexts) promises sub-millisecond latencies and high throughput. It is quite plausible that in a few years, the distinction between a "blockchain" and a regular distributed database will blur—we might have permissioned or hybrid ledgers that deliver the trust guarantees needed but operate much like fast databases. In fact, some argue that a "closed, permissioned, private blockchain" is essentially just a database. That might be the endgame: the technical term blockchain disappears into the background, and we just have highly connected, secure modern databases (ledgers) run by networks of institutions (or even central banks) powering token transactions.

The following timeline diagram shows the historical perspective from the Crypto visionaries who envisaged a system independent of banks and government (as a reaction to the financial crisis), through many turbulences, failures, fraud and corruption to the current increasing legislated system with real stablecoins (not just in name) and by some 202x future, possibly without Blockchain—just tokenised money on scalable, connected, efficient traditional IT (Fig. 4).

This paints a scenario where the experimental, open wild-west phase (where multiple blockchains compete and crypto runs anarchically) eventually gives way to a more mature modern world. In that future, tokenised money would be ubiquitous and instantaneous, but the technology might be almost invisible, described in plain terms like "the global digital payment network" rather than "the blockchain." We can draw an analogy to the internet: in the early 90s people talked about TCP/IP protocols and dial-up modems; today we just say "online banking" or "streaming video" without referencing the protocols (which have also upgraded significantly). Similarly, future token systems might incorporate features like quantum resistance (to future-proof against quantum computing threats to cryptography), built-in privacy layers (so transactions can be confidential but still verifiable), and multi-layer architectures for scalability. Some of these are already in development (e.g.,

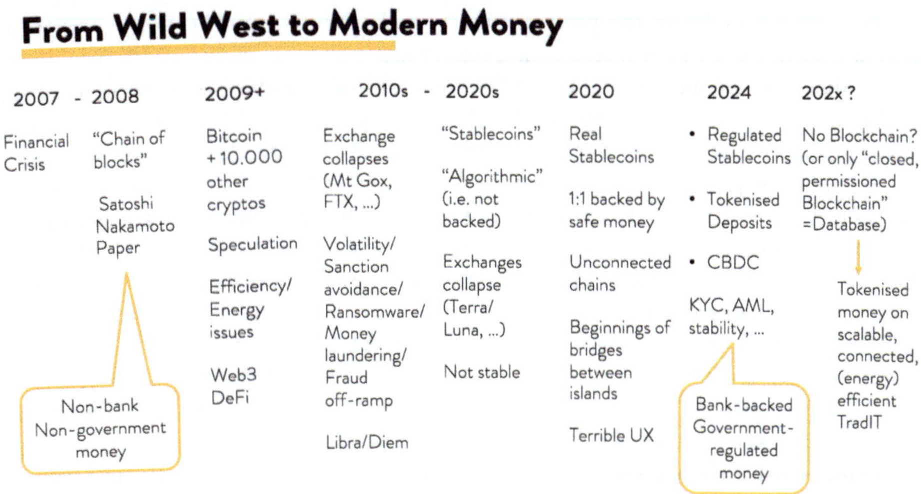

Fig. 4 Historical perspective on evolution from Crypto vision to regulated, safe, scalable modern money (via many catastrophes en route). (source: Author)

zero-knowledge proofs to allow private transactions on public ledgers, or new L1/ L2 architectures to scale throughput).

One of the selling points of tokenised money is the prospect of fewer intermediaries in transactions. If Alice can pay Bob directly, why involve three banks and a clearinghouse? In practice, however, as noted, we may just get different intermediaries: wallet providers, exchanges, payment gateways, custodians, etc. A worry expressed is that we might end up with "just as many intermediaries as before, just with new names". The answer depends on the design choices we make. If the world of tokenised money is dominated by a few big tech or big bank players (each with their own wallet ecosystem), then yes, we have simply relocated intermediation. But if open protocols and interoperability win out, we could achieve more consolidation: a token payment might involve just a sender's wallet software and a receiver's wallet software (with maybe an automated market maker in between if FX conversion is needed).

6.1 *Beyond Technology—Governance, Legal Frameworks, Trust*

Beyond all the technical discussions, the topic of governance in not to be underestimated. "Blockchains are not mythical forces of nature born out of immaculate conception or benevolence of selfless individuals. They are fundamentally just databases and the questions everyone should be asking are: who developed it? who maintains it? why? who is incentivized to run it and how? what happens when it fails, who is liable and who picks up the phone in that case?" (Nordea 2025). Putting trust on technology alone will not lead to good outcomes.

Furthermore we must be clear that "Ownership" of money or real-world assets is not a matter of holding a string of bits. "It is a legal, enforceable right that depends on an ecosystem of verifiable relationships, contracts, custodians, jurisdictions, and most importantly, people and institutions who can be held accountable. Without that accountability, what you are holding is not a real-world asset. You are holding a fragile digital representation of one, with no recourse if things fall apart." Ledgers—however implemented (paper, database, blockchain)—exist because someone operates them, someone maintains them, and someone believes in their relevance. But if the ecosystem around a ledger dissolves—if developers walk away, if economic incentives dry up, if validators leave or community trust collapses the infrastructure can simply vanish. When that happens, the tokens, no matter how many audits or whitepapers once vouched for them, are reduced to orphaned entries in a system that no longer exists. There's no fallback, no legal claim, no escalation path. The "ownership" becomes an entry in a defunct database. The thinking that a Blockchain proves reliable ownership is not a limitation of current technology—"it is a misunderstanding of what ownership actually is." (Hotti 2025). We hope that all those now promoting selling gold, funds, real estate on the blockchain (and their clients) are aware …

Governance arrangements will also have to form a view on topics like resilience. This is a double-edged issue. On one hand, a decentralised token network (if truly distributed) has no single point of failure—thus theoretically more resilient to one node or one data centre going down. On the other hand, a cashless society reliant on digital tokens alone is vulnerable to cyber threats and power/internet outages. Maybe introducing a bit more centralisation (e.g. an intermediary to oversee), may be a wise choice to trade off some decentralisation for security.

Another element is governance of standards. If tokenised money becomes part of a critical infrastructure, it will likely be subject to oversight and common standards (the internet has bodies like IETF). Already, we see BIS and others pushing for global coordination on digital currency standards to ensure interoperability and avoid a fragmented outcome. Possibly, we might end up with international treaties or at least agreements about how different tokenised islands connect, analogous to telecom standards that allow roaming between networks. Ubyx [see Part 3 Chapter "The Case for a Stablecoin Clearing System: Enabling Ubiquity Through Market Structure Evolution" in this book] may play a critical role in interconnecting regulated licensed islands into a global connected settlement infrastructure.

Crucially regulation and legal frameworks will shape the infrastructure at least as much as technology. If regulators mandate certain features (say, all stablecoins must have an "off switch" for illicit use, or every wallet must be linked to an identified entity above a threshold), then those will be built in. If they prioritize privacy, maybe systems will incorporate privacy tech. The design choices will reflect societal values: do we want a fully traceable money for easy law enforcement, or do we demand some cash-like anonymity for civil liberties? These debates are ongoing. The outcome will influence adoption too: if the public perceives tokenised money as a tool of surveillance (as some fear with CBDCs—see, for example, the recent US anti-CBDC "anti-surveillance" bill), they may resist using it—which could keep cash alive or push people to more underground crypto. On the other hand, if done right, tokenised money could improve privacy (some argue it can be better than today since you might send value using privacy preserving means without revealing as much personal info as, say, a credit card transaction which is tied to much personal information).

6.2 *Revolutionary and Evolutionary Future Scenarios*

Finally, we here sketch two extreme future scenarios for the future infrastructure of payments:

- Disruptive collapse scenario: Traditional rails and institutions fail to adapt, a string of bank crises and Fintech innovations lead to a rapid shift where people lose trust in banks or fiat (perhaps triggered by something like hyperinflation or a global financial crisis)—early symptoms of which were seen after the financial crisis—and they flock to alternative digital monies en masse. In this chaotic scenario, tokenised money might rise as a saviour but also cause instability (imagine a run on banks as everyone moves to a stablecoin). Governments might react harshly (outlawing or forcefully converting stablecoins). This is a tumultuous path and unlikely without severe triggers.
- Harmonious integration scenario: All stakeholders—regulators, banks, tech firms, user groups—work together over the next decades to gradually integrate tokenisation into the financial system. Legacy and new technologies are bridged. Users perhaps hardly notice the transition aside from things getting faster and cheaper. Stability is maintained, and we end up with a hybrid system where money is tokenised but overseen by a combination of existing institutions and new frameworks. No sudden upheaval occurs; rather, an evolution to "modern money" happens much like the evolution to electronic payments from paper—incremental but eventually transformative.

  Note that there could be a divergence by region: one region might lean fully into tokenised infrastructure (say, a country that decides to go "all-in" on tokens or mandate a CBDC, deprecating banknotes and maybe even reducing the role of commercial banks in payments), whereas another region might keep using upgraded traditional systems with only limited token use.

At the end of the day, "modernisation of money" is inevitable; the form it takes is up for us to shape. Tokenisation offers a powerful toolkit to modernise, but it must be deployed in a way that preserves the trust and stability that society expects from money. Stablecoins (and by extension tokenised money) are a new "form factor" of fiat i.e. existing money, but made for the internet—meaning we should focus on making them a safe and effective, not a risky novelty. If we succeed, tomorrow's financial infrastructure will be almost unrecognisable in speed and efficiency, yet quietly familiar in reliability and universality of money as a public good.

7 Conclusion

Tokenised money and stablecoins sit at the frontier of financial innovation, posing both an alluring opportunity and a formidable challenge to the status quo. Over the course of this chapter, we have seen that stablecoins can arguably be viewed as "fiat currency made for the internet era"—combining the trust of traditional money with the agility of modern digital networks. They promise to carry value at the speed of information, slashing transaction times and costs, enabling new kinds of economic activity from microtransactions to machine-driven commerce, and extending financial services to those left on the margins of the current system. In essence, tokenisation allows money to finally catch up with the technological advances of the last decades, removing frictions that we have come to take for granted in finance. We overcome the legacy of structures and processes built when computers were slow and communication expensive.

However, it is equally clear that realising this promise will be an evolutionary journey, hopefully not a Big Bang revolution. Many pieces must fall into place: technological maturity (scalable, secure platforms), regulatory clarity (to foster innovation while managing risks), user-centric design (to make usage intuitive and safe), and collaborative standards (to avoid a fractured ecosystem). The incumbents of traditional finance—banks, payment networks, central banks—are not idle passengers in this journey; they are active drivers or brakes depending on their strategies. As of 2025, their engagement has moved from dismissiveness to cautious experimentation and even competition to harness tokenised money for their own purposes.

That said, we have acknowledged that multiple futures remain possible. There are disruptive scenarios—perhaps less probable, but not impossible—where tokenised money dramatically reduces the role of traditional banks or even triggers shifts in global financial power (for instance, widespread adoption of foreign stablecoins raising monetary sovereignty issues). There are also pessimistic scenarios where tokenised money fails to break out of niche use due to regulatory clampdowns, poor user uptake, or a major loss of confidence event (like a systemic stablecoin failure) setting back trust for years.

These outcomes will depend on how well the open questions are addressed. Key among them:

- Can we achieve interoperability and avoid fragmentation? The success of tokenised money largely hinges on making it as universally acceptable as existing money. Efforts toward common standards, such as those discussed for cross-chain and cross-ledger compatibility, will be decisive. If the industry and regulators together ensure that one digital dollar/euro is as good as another, regardless of issuer or network, then users will adopt it without fear. If not, confusion and inconvenience could significantly dampen enthusiasm.
- Will user experience reach a tipping point? At present the average person finds dealing with crypto wallets intimidating. The technology must become invisible and robust for mainstream adoption—just as one does not need to understand

SMTP to send an email. We need only recall that early internet required technical knowledge (dial-up modems, command-line interfaces) but eventually evolved to something anyone can use. Tokenised money needs an analogous UX revolution. Achieving this likely involves both private-sector innovation (fintech UX design) and perhaps public infrastructure (digital identity frameworks, etc., to simplify KYC).

- How will regulation strike the balance? Regulation will undoubtedly shape the trajectory. Encouragingly, major jurisdictions are moving from uncertainty to establishing rules of the road for stablecoins. Thoughtful regulation can mitigate risks (fraud, runs and illicit use) without smothering innovation. The US's proposed laws and the EU's MiCA show it is possible to create regimes where stablecoins can operate safely and at scale. However, over-regulation or inconsistent global rules could either fragment the market or drive activity underground. A harmonised approach, where authorities coordinate (as they do in Basel banking standards, for example), would best support a stable integration of tokenised money. We also saw the geopolitical angle: concerns about currency dominance and control may influence how open different regions are to foreign stablecoins versus developing their own. Navigating these national interests will be key to avoiding a "splinternet" of digital currencies.
- What role for central bank digital currencies? CBDCs could either complement or crowd out privately issued tokenised monies. The design decisions central banks make (retail vs wholesale focus, anonymity features, involvement of intermediaries, etc.) will affect the competitive landscape. In one future, CBDCs provide the core digital cash and private stablecoins play a niche or on-ramp role. In another, CBDCs take a backseat, or available only as a backup and regulators lean on private issuers to provide digital cash under supervision. It is still too early to tell, as major CBDCs (e.g. digital euro, digital dollar, digital pound) are not yet live—and some may never materialise.
- Will stablecoins prove stable and secure over time? Trust is the bedrock of any monetary system. So far, fiat-backed stablecoins have largely held their pegs quite well in normal times (but see Fig. 1). However, we have seen near-misses (e.g. temporary de-pegs during panics) and the outright failures of algorithmic stablecoins. The stability of tokenised money through different economic cycles and stress events remains to be fully tested. Likewise, the resilience against operational threats (hacks, technical bugs) must be proven. Overcoming these will likely involve not just technical measures but also institutional safeguards: audits, insurance, emergency backstops (possibly central bank liquidity lines for systemic stablecoins, akin to how banks have lender-of-last-resort support). If the public comes to see stablecoins as reliably as bank deposits or cash, then mainstream adoption can accelerate. Building that reputation will take time and prudent management.

The tone of this chapter has been optimistic, and rightly so—the potential benefits of tokenised money for efficiency, inclusion, and innovation are immense. Yet we have been careful not to present it as an inevitability or a panacea. Much like the early days of the internet, there is hype and uncertainty, and it will take sustained effort across sectors to fulfil the vision. Even if tokenised money's rise is slower than boosters hope, its influence is already pushing the financial industry toward needed improvements. One could argue that stablecoins simply lit a fire under banks and payment providers to modernise. For instance, seeing the competition, banks and fintechs have sped up development of instant payment solutions and digital asset strategies. In that sense, stablecoins are catalysing change whether or not they themselves capture the whole market.

A historical perspective reminds us that money has continually evolved in form—from shells, to metal coins, to paper notes, to electronic entries [see Part 1 Chapter "The Main Stages in the History of Money" in this book]. Tokenisation is the next step in that evolution, making money more functional for a digital world. But old forms often persist alongside new ones for long periods. Cheques coexist with electronic transfers for decades; cash still coexists with digital payments. We may find that stablecoins and tokenised money will coexist with traditional forms for quite some time, gradually gaining ground in areas where they demonstrate clear superiority, while perhaps not displacing everything. In an optimistic integrated scenario, the end-user might not even distinguish between, say, a "stablecoin payment" and a "bank payment"—they'll simply be making a payment, and the most efficient technology will be used in the background.

In any outcome, we can be optimistic that the end state will be a better one for users worldwide: payments and transfers that are instant, convenient, and low-cost, greater inclusion of those historically excluded, and a platform for innovation in financial services that can drive economic growth. The journey from "fiat to stablecoins" is not a repudiation of fiat money, but rather its renaissance in a form suited for the twenty-first century. As with any renaissance, it comes with challenges and requires bridging old and new wisdom. If we manage that carefully, tokenised money can indeed herald a new era—not of financial anarchy, but of a more efficient, open, and interconnected financial system that works for everyone.

References

Andreessen Horowitz (2025) An AI needs a wallet of one's own to act agentically. https://a16z.com/big-ideas-in-tech-2025/

Bank of England BoE (2021, March 25) A bottleneck for open banking, Carlos Cañón, Irene Ng, University of Warwick, Dataswift. https://wrap.warwick.ac.uk/id/eprint/160540/13/WRAP-Bottleneck-open-banking-Ng-2021.pdf

Cambridge (2025) *Peg stability*. Cambridge Digital Money Dashboard. https://ccaf.io/cdmd/risks-and-protections#peg-stability

Citi Bank (2022) *The Regulated Liability Network*. https://www.citigroup.com/rcs/citigpa/storage/public/icpublic/The-Regulated-Liability-Network-Whitepaper.pdf

CNBC (2023). "Stablecoin USDC breaks dollar peg after firm reveals it has $3.3 billion in SVB exposure", March 11, 2023. Available at https://www.cnbc.com/2023/03/11/stablecoin-usdc-breaks-dollar-peg-after-firm-reveals-it-has-3point3-billion-in-svb-exposure.html

Coinbase (2025, July 2) Why agentic commerce needs crypto to scale. https://www.coinbase.com/en-de/developer-platform/discover/launches/agentic-commerce

European Central Bank ECB (2025, July 28) From hype to hazard: what stablecoins mean for Europe. https://www.ecb.europa.eu/press/blog/date/2025/html/ecb.blog20250728~e6cb3cf8b5.en.html

European Payments Council EPC (2024). "Pix: the latest updates on Brazil's leading instant payment scheme", 30th May 2024. Available at https://www.europeanpaymentscouncil.eu/news-insights/insight/pix-latest-updates-brazils-leading-instant-payment-scheme

Feingold S (2025, March 26) Stablecoin surge: here's why reserve-backed cryptocurrencies are on the rise. *World Economic Forum* (updated July 21, 2025). https://www.weforum.org/stories/2025/03/stablecoins-cryptocurrency-on-rise-financial-systems/

Forbes (2025, May 6) PayPal's big bet on AI agents and payments like stablecoins. https://www.forbes.com/sites/digital-assets/2025/05/06/paypals-big-bet-on-ai-agents-and-payments-like-stablecoins/

Hotti T (2025) LinkedIn post. https://www.linkedin.com/feed/update/urn:li:activity:7356186793886527488/

Muhn J (2025, March 13) Streamly Snapshot: the real reason open banking has floundered in Europe. *Finovate Blog*. https://finovate.com/streamly-snapshot-the-real-reason-open-banking-has-floundered-in-europe/

Nordea (2025) Sointu, Ville. LinkedIn post. https://www.linkedin.com/feed/update/urn:li:activity:7356590938674098176/

Rodrigues F (2025, July 5) Ex-ECB official urges Europe to back Euro stablecoins or risk losing financial power. *CoinDesk*. https://www.coindesk.com/business/2025/07/05/ex-ecb-official-urges-europe-to-back-euro-stablecoins-or-risk-losing-financial-power

Shukla R (2024, June 26) UPI: revolutionising real-time digital payments in India, interview, European Payments Council. https://www.europeanpaymentscouncil.eu/news-insights/insight/upi-revolutionising-real-time-digital-payments-india

SWIFT (2021/2024) Digitising trade: the time is now (August 2021) and related reports including "Swift outlines its mission to digitise global trade", December 13, 2024. https://www.swift.com/swift-resource/251221/download and https://ctmfile.com/story/swift-outlines-its-mission-to-digitise-global-trade-industry-roundup-13-december

Visa (2023) *Visa on digital currencies and stability*—press releases and blog posts on integrating USDC for settlement (e.g. March 29, 2021).

World Bank (2021) *The global findex database 2021: financial inclusion, digital payments, and resilience in the age of COVID-19*. World Bank, Washington, DC

World Economic Forum WEF (2025, June 13) This initiative could cut the cost of global trade by 25%, Trade & Investment. https://www.weforum.org/stories/2025/06/twin-foundation-global-trade/

Stablecoins, CBDCs, and the New Geopolitics of Money: From Global Competition to Risks

Feride Hilal İmal

Abstract The current landscape, marked by weaponized hegemony and economic interdependencies, shows that financial sovereignty now outweighs military power. Geopolitically, stablecoins and CBDCs are prompting states to rebuild economic sovereignty both at home and abroad. These new digital currencies represent emerging instruments of geopolitical strategy, intertwined with novel tools such as digital diplomacy, data governance, and platform sovereignty. However, while they have the power to reshape payment systems and global dynamics, they also carry risks that require caution. This chapter analyzes the geopolitical impact of stablecoins and CBDCs, the competition among leading economic blocs, and the related risks to financial stability, monetary sovereignty, and data privacy.

Keywords Digital money • Stablecoin • CBDC • Geoeconomics • Digital dollarization • Geopolitical impacts • International competition • mCBDC

1 Introduction

In today's world, financial instruments hold significant strategic importance for states in achieving their political objectives. States use their currencies not only for economic power but as strategic levers. Operating with intricate networks of mutual interdependence, they pursue geopolitical objectives through monetary policies that serve as instruments of pressure, reward, or sanction, tailored to economic and political sensitivities. Thus, the geopolitical power of financial instruments provides an effective means of influence in international relations without direct intervention.

F. H. İmal (✉)
İstanbul Bar Association, İstanbul, Türkiye
e-mail: feride.imal@universalhukuk.com

S. Yazıcı et al. (eds.), *Tokenisation of Money*, Contributions to Finance and Accounting, https://doi.org/10.1007/978-3-032-22946-5_29

In traditional finance, the U.S. dollar dominates international trade and financial transactions. Its role as a reserve currency provides significant advantages to the United States, which has also leveraged the dollar's sanctioning power as a geopolitical tool.

While new digital currencies based on Distributed Ledger Technology (DLT) represent a remarkable financial innovation, they also function as geopolitical instruments with the potential to reshape international power relations. Stablecoins and CBDCs sit at the very center of these power relations, directly influencing the future influence and positioning of states both regionally and globally. The potential of cross-border use of digital money transforms the structural elements of the international financial system, producing geopolitical consequences that extend well beyond the realm of monetary policy.

Nevertheless, alongside the benefits that digital forms of money may offer as instruments of payment, regulators, businesses, and consumers still possess legitimate grounds for exercising caution toward stablecoins and CBDCs. While the advantages of digital currencies in facilitating payments may prove highly functional, risks relating to reserve management, volatility, financial stability, and monetary sovereignty—as well as ongoing regulatory uncertainty—remain significant obstacles to widespread adoption.

This chapter explores the significance of new forms of digital currency as geopolitical instruments that challenge and reshape existing power dynamics, while examining the international competition among the world's three major economies. It also analyzes the profound risks these instruments may pose to the financial system, notwithstanding their promises to address various structural issues in today's global financial landscape.

2 Geopolitical Implications and International Competition

Since the establishment of the Bretton Woods system in 1944, the United States Dollar (USD) has remained the dominant global currency and continues to serve, unequivocally as the cornerstone of the international monetary system.[1] The USD maintains an overwhelming advantage over all other currencies in fulfilling the three essential functions of an international currency—serving as a medium of exchange for cross-border payments, a unit of account, and a reserve asset.[2] Although its share of global foreign exchange reserves has gradually declined from

[1] Bogaardt, Paul Christopher, 2024, From Analog to Digital: The Geopolitical and Socioeconomic Calculus of Central Bank Digital Currencies. CGU Theses & Dissertations, 912, https://scholarship.claremont.edu/cgu_etd/912, Last Accessed: 20.10.2025.

[2] Aliyeva, Gulnare, Geopolitical Implications of Digital Currencies: National Security and Global Power Shifts, 2025, Azerbaijan State University of Economics International Master's and Doctoral Center, https://doi.org/10.58225/tim.2025-2-323-329, Last Accessed: 20.10.2025.

71% in 1999,[3] the USD still represents approximately 59% of total reserves worldwide.[4] The dollar's dominance, reinforced by the U.S. financial markets' capacity to provide global liquidity and stability—confers upon the United States immense financial power and hegemony.[5]

The United States' dominance, and its use of the dollar as a geopolitical instrument to advance foreign policy objectives, have given rise to growing international tensions. The sharp increase in the number of financial sanctions[6] imposed by the U.S. since 2000—such as the freezing of dollar-denominated assets belonging to countries including Russia, Venezuela, Iran, and Libya under U.S. jurisdiction, as well as restrictions on access to the SWIFT network—has underscored the geopolitical leverage derived from dollar hegemony. The intensifying U.S.-China economic rivalry[7] in 2025 has further accelerated efforts by states to reduce their dependence on the USD, prompting central banks to diversify their reserves and leading many countries, most notably Russia and China, to seek alternative payment infrastructures.[8]

The digitization of the financial system is not merely an innovation; when intertwined with geopolitical dynamics, it possesses the power to exert a profound influence on national financial sovereignty. Although Bitcoin did not ultimately realize the challenge Satoshi envisaged, subsequently developed instruments that exhibit the core attributes of sovereign money, chiefly a stable store of value and a unit of account, have become the newest, and perhaps the most favored, tools that states intend to wield in the contest for geopolitical pre-eminence and financial sovereignty. Stablecoins and CBDCs directly influence the future of states' regional and global influence, heralding the emergence of a multipolar digital financial order poised to challenge the existing unipolar monetary structure.[9] Within this framework, the following sections will examine the geopolitical strategies of the European

[3] This decline reflects not so much the rising share of major competitors such as the Euro or the Chinese Renminbi (RMB), but rather the growing prominence of smaller currencies such as the Australian Dollar and the Canadian Dollar. See: Bilotta, Nicola/ Botti, Fabrizio, The (Near) Future of Central Bank Digital Currencies, Risks and Opportunities for the Global Economy and Society, 2021, Lausanne, Switzerland: Peter Lang Verlag, https://www.peterlang.com/document/1068992, Last Accessed: 20.10.2025.

[4] Aliyeva (2025).

[5] Bilotta and Botti (2021).

[6] The Hidden Impact of SWIFT Sanctions on Global Banking, 2025, https://www.lawyer-monthly.com/2025/03/the-hidden-impact-of-swift-sanctions-on-global-banking/ Last Accessed: 20.10.2025.

[7] Gunnella, Vanessa/ Stamato, Giovanni/ Kobayashi, 2025, Alicja The implications of US-China trade tensions for the euro area—lessons from the tariffs imposed by the first Trump Administration, Economic Bulletin Issue 3, https://www.ecb.europa.eu/press/economic-bulletin/html/eb202503.en.html, Last Accessed: 20.09.20205.

[8] Bilotta, Nicola, 2024, The Geoeconomics of Money in the Digital Age, 1st Edition Routledge, London, https://doi.org/10.4324/9781003500957, Last Accessed: 20.10.2025.

[9] Marple (2024).

Union and China in response to the United States' efforts to preserve and extend its monetary hegemony into the digital realm.

2.1 The Dominance of USD Stablecoins

USD stablecoins constitute the predominant currency within the stablecoin ecosystem. As of September 2025, 99% of circulating stablecoins are denominated in USD.[10] Although euro-denominated stablecoins—the second largest segment of the market—have experienced some growth under the European Union's regulatory framework, their market capitalization of merely USD 0.54 billion accounts for only 0.2% of the total market share.[11]

This prevailing dominance within the stablecoin ecosystem simultaneously reinforces the global role and hegemony of the USD. Indeed, USD stablecoins bolster the primacy of the dollar in the digital transformation, effectively granting the United States a de facto advantage over contemporary digital flows.[12]

The United States has adopted a regulatory approach aimed at promoting the development and growth of legally recognized, USD-backed stablecoins worldwide.[13] Through the Guiding and Establishing National Innovation of Stablecoins (GENIUS) Act, enacted on 18 July 2025, the United States actively supports a legal strategy to "dollarize the internet." Under the GENIUS Act, the U.S. intends to regulate the holding of USD stablecoin reserves in U.S. Treasury securities, thereby deepening demand for Treasury bonds and extending the dollar's leading role into programmable finance. For instance, as of September 2025, the two largest stablecoins—Tether (USDT) and USD Coin (USDC)—which together dominate approximately 83% of the total stablecoin market with a market capitalization exceeding

[10] Coindesk Stablecoins & CBDCs Report- September 2025, https://data.coindesk.com/reports/stablecoins-cbdcs-report-september-2025, Last Accessed: 20.10.2025.

[11] Gilles Chemla and others, 2025, Mind the Gap: How Stablecoins Can Secure the UK's Financial Future, Imperial College, Centre for Financial Technology and Centre for Cryptocurrency Research and Engineering, https://imperialcollegelondon.app.box.com/s/ggqi8y0jyr3969w863bfiz-pz8g9wj549/file/1986432747899, Last Accessed: 20.10.2025.

[12] Raffelini, Alessandro, 2025, The Global Stablecoin Race And A New Globalization: Digital Rails, Trade Policy, And Geopolitical Realignment Via China's Yuan Stablecoin And Emerging Digital Economic Areas, World Wide Journal of Multidisciplinary Research and Development, https://www.researchgate.net/publication/395899005_The_Global_Stablecoin_Race_and_a_New_Globalization_Digital_Rails_Trade_Policy_and_Geopolitical_Realignment_via_China's_Yuan_Stablecoin_and_Emerging_Digital_Economic_Areas, Last Accessed: 20.09.2025.

[13] The White House, Strengthening American Leadership in Digital Financial Technology, 23 January 2025, https://www.whitehouse.gov/presidential-actions/2025/01/strengthening-american-leadership-in-digital-financial-technology/, Last Accessed: 20.09.2025.

USD 280 billion, hold roughly USD 123 billion in U.S. Treasury bonds.[14] This positions their issuers among the largest corporate holders of such securities.[15]

This regulatory framework simultaneously brings USD stablecoins—now commanding 99% of the market—under a formal legal structure, thereby extending the United States' national jurisdiction on a global scale (long-arm jurisdiction).[16] Such global reach and expansion exert a profound influence on the sovereignty of nations as well as on the broader international political and economic landscape.[17]

2.2 *Global Responses to Dominance*

The overwhelming dominance of USD stablecoins in the market not only strengthens the United States' financial system and global influence through its Treasury markets but also consolidates the dollar's supremacy in the digital domain. In response, over 130 countries—representing 98% of global GDP—are actively researching or implementing CBDCs. Increasingly, these nations are integrating their CBDCs through regional collaborations, creating shared payment infrastructures. For example, organizations such as ASEAN, the African Union, and the Gulf Cooperation Council are working on joint digital payment infrastructures through regional cooperation, seeking to establish a multipolar monetary order as an alternative to the traditional Bretton Woods system.[18] This trend, referred to as "monetary disarmament," argues that CBDCs may generate asymmetric digital power dynamics among nation-states.[19] Other major powers, including the European Union and China, are developing strategic regulatory and infrastructural solutions—such as MiCA/Digital Euro initiatives and RMB-backed stablecoin/e-CNY systems—to counter this "digital dollarization," preserve monetary sovereignty, and advance the international role of their respective currencies.

---

[14] Raffelini (2025).

[15] Gilles (2025).

[16] Raffelini (2025).

[17] Jin, Sheng, 2025, The Potential Risks and Global Governance of Stablecoins: a Dual Perspective Based on Economics and Politics, Law and Financial Markets Review, DOI: 10.1080/17521440.2025.2569313, Last Accessed: 20.10.2025.

[18] The Role of Stablecoins in Financial Sovereignty, Digital Euro Association. Digital Euro Association Working Group, The Role of Stablecoins in Financial Sovereignty, 2025, https://digital-euro-association.de/hubfs/DEA%20-%20The%20Role%20of%20Stablecoins%20in%20Financial%20Sovereignty.pdf?hsLang=en, Last Accessed: 20.09.2025.

[19] Marple (2024).

2.2.1 European Union

The euro continues to lag significantly behind the U.S. dollar in terms of global foreign exchange reserves and international transactions.[20] While the European Union remains heavily dependent on the USD for global trade and energy imports, it lacks a pan-European payment system and widespread domestic mobile payment applications, in contrast to China.[21] Having failed to establish its own card scheme, the EU remains reliant on U.S.-based private actors such as Mastercard and Visa for international payments;[22] indeed, thirteen European countries are entirely dependent on non-European card providers.[23] Consequently, the EU faces geopolitical risks including exposure to external policy leverage, compromised control over critical data, and diminished economic resilience. This situation poses a substantial threat to the EU's strategic autonomy.[24] Against this backdrop, the EU harbors deep concerns over the overwhelming rise of USD stablecoins and the digitalization of the global financial system.[25]

The European Union expresses concern over the risks to monetary policy and monetary sovereignty that could arise should USD stablecoins attain dominance within the eurozone. Of particular apprehension is the potential realization of a digital dollarization scenario, which could undermine the central bank's control over price stability in the real economy.[26]

Like China and other major powers, the European Union is pursuing strategies aimed at de-dollarization and enhancing the international role of its currency through CBDCs. Although reducing reliance on the U.S. dollar remains a formidable challenge, the European Central Bank and other European central banks have initiated collaborative efforts with institutions such as the Bank for International Settlements and the Bank of Japan to develop alternative infrastructures for cross-border payments through multi-CBDC (mCBDC) arrangements. In addition, in response to the strong network effects and liquidity of USD stablecoins, the EU seeks to cultivate a competitive euro-stablecoin ecosystem.[27]

To this end, the European Union has structured its strategy around two main pillars: the MiCA regulation targeting stablecoins and the Digital Euro project. As the first regulatory actor in this domain, the EU, through the MiCA Regulation, has placed stablecoins used as a means of payment under a regional regulatory

---

[20] Digital Euro Association Working Group, The Role of Stablecoins in Financial Sovereignty 2025.

[21] Bilotta (2024).

[22] Bilotta and Botti (2021).

[23] Bezemer, Dirk/ Sanders, Mark/ Kramer, Brenda/ Simić, Aleksandar, 2025, Stablecoins and Digital Euro: Friends or Foes of European Monetary Policy?, European Parliament, Monetary Dialogue Papers, https://www.europarl.europa.eu/RegData/etudes/IDAN/2025/764387/ECTI_IDA(2025)764387_EN.pdf, Last Accessed: 20.09.2025

[24] Bilotta (2024).

[25] Bezemer et al. (2025).

[26] Digital Euro Association Working Group, The Role of Stablecoins in Financial Sovereignty, 2025.

[27] Digital Euro Association Working Group, The Role of Stablecoins in Financial Sovereignty, 2025.

framework,[28] while the European Central Bank's Digital Euro initiative complements this approach. Together, they form an integral part of Europe's strategy to promote monetary competition and assert digital sovereignty.[29] Moreover, the EU aims both to eliminate dependence on payment rails for cross-border transactions controlled by U.S. companies under the current system and to mitigate the risk of erosion of sovereign payment infrastructure posed by the increasing role of U.S.-based stablecoins in intra-European payments. In this context, the Digital Euro project and the MiCA Regulation represent not merely financial innovation but a comprehensive strategy devised by the European Central Bank (ECB) as a direct response to concerns regarding financial stability and monetary sovereignty.[30]

Through the MiCA Regulation, the European Union seeks to prevent stablecoins pegged to foreign currencies from attaining systemic dominance as a means of payment within Europe.[31] Under this framework, the use of a non-EU stablecoin in payments is capped at either 1 million transactions per day or €200 million.[32] Furthermore, the MiCA Regulation prohibits the payment of interest to stablecoin holders, aiming to counter incentives for their use as a store of value and to discourage disintermediation of the banking system.[33]

Although the European Union, through MiCA, has established the world's first and most mature regulatory framework for stablecoins, market dynamics indicate that users overwhelmingly continue to prefer USD stablecoins.[34]

The European Central Bank views the Digital Euro as a potential instrument to strengthen the international role of the euro and reduce dependence on foreign payment infrastructures. According to the ECB, U.S.-based companies, which currently hold strong dominance within payment systems, could further consolidate their market power by issuing their own stablecoins, thereby creating a risk to monetary sovereignty in the euro area. In this context, the Digital Euro is regarded as a critical tool for maintaining the euro's domestic market dominance.[35]

The ECB emphasizes that, unlike private payment service providers, the participation of a non-commercial central bank in the Digital Euro will enhance privacy and strengthen the transmission mechanism of monetary policy to the real economy.[36]

---

[28] Digital Euro Association Working Group, The Role of Stablecoins in Financial Sovereignty, 2025.

[29] European Central Bank (ECB), 2023, Progress on the Investigation Phase of a Digital Euro—Third Report, https://www.ecb.europa.eu/euro/digital_euro/timeline/profuse/shared/pdf/ecb.degov230424_progress.en.pdf, Last Accessed: 20.09.2025.

[30] Bezemer/Sanders/Kramer/Simić (2025).

[31] Digital Euro Association Working Group, The Role of Stablecoins in Financial Sovereignty, 2025.

[32] Gilles (2025).

[33] Digital Euro Association Working Group, The Role of Stablecoins in Financial Sovereignty, 2025.

[34] Raffelini (2025).

[35] Bezemer et al. (2025).

[36] Passacantando, Franco, 2023, The Digital Euro: Challenges and Opportunities, Digitalization And Geopolitics: Catalytic Forces In The (Future) International Monetary System (Eds Bilotta Nicola, Botti Fabrizio) Edizioni Nuova Cultura, https://www.iai.it/sites/default/files/iairs_10.pdf, Last Accessed: 20.10.2025.

In addition to safeguarding monetary sovereignty, the ECB plans to impose low holding limits on the Digital Euro to mitigate the risk of disintermediation of commercial banks.[37] However, these restrictions pose a significant obstacle to the Digital Euro's ability to compete with USD stablecoins or bank deposits as a store of value. While such limits protect commercial banks, they conflict with the ECB's strategic objective of competing effectively with foreign stablecoins. Indeed, the restricted issuance of a digital version of cash—which, in principle, can be held in unlimited quantities—has been criticized on this very basis.[38]

2.2.2 China and the Internationalization of the RMB

Despite its economic size and role in the global economy, China remains heavily reliant on foreign networks, the U.S. dollar and U.S. Treasury securities for international transactions. This dependence renders China highly vulnerable to fluctuations in the dollar.[39] While the United States was preoccupied with election cycles and policy shifts, and Europe moved slowly to develop and implement robust regulatory frameworks such as the MiCA Regulation, China acted proactively by supporting yuan (RMB)-backed stablecoins and internationalizing e-CNY operations. This enabled the early launch of the e-CNY as far back as 2014, positioning China as a leader in the CBDC issuance race.[40] China's CBDC initiative represents a significant geopolitical maneuver with the potential to reshape the global financial architecture and diminish U.S. financial leverage. Moreover, the e-CNY project is directly linked to China's broader objective of internationalizing the RMB.[41]

Similarly, China is pursuing a strategy of establishing Digital Economic Areas (DEAs) in collaboration with other countries to mitigate exposure to U.S. sanctions. China regards these objectives as a strategic necessity, driven by concerns over financial penalties and commercial disputes arising from dependence on the USD and Western-centric payment systems.[42]

China is pursuing a two-tiered strategy, comprising a domestic layer with the e-CNY and an external layer supported by RMB-pegged stablecoins under Hong Kong's licensing regime. The entire framework is built upon existing infrastructures, including the "Cross-Border Interbank Payment System (CIPS)," established in 2015 to facilitate RMB payments abroad without routing through U.S.

---

[37] Bezemer et al. (2025).

[38] Bezemer et al. (2025).

[39] Bilotta (2024).

[40] Knoerich, Jan, 2023, China's New Digital Currency: Implications for Renminbi Internationalization and the US Dollar, Digitalization And Geopolitics: Catalytic Forces in the (Future) International Monetary System (Eds Bilotta Nicola, Botti Fabrizio) Edizioni Nuova Cultura, https://www.iai.it/sites/default/files/iairs_10.pdf, Last Accessed: 20.10.2025.

[41] Raffelini (2025).

[42] Raffelini (2025).

correspondent banks or foreign clearinghouses, and mBridge, the Bank for International Settlements' multi-CBDC project for international payments.[43]

Moreover, China aims to enhance the international influence of the RMB by integrating the e-CNY with the Belt and Road Initiative (BRI), an RMB-based trade and payments network launched in 2013 that, as of 2025, connects 150 countries and has achieved a transaction volume of USD 1.17 trillion.[44] China seeks to strengthen the role of the RMB both as a means of payment and as a tool of geopolitical influence by combining its long-standing objective of providing a stable trade infrastructure—less vulnerable to U.S. sanctions and SWIFT transit points—with the development of China-centered Digital Economic Areas (DEAs) through CBDCs and stablecoins.[45] China's CBDC initiative is not merely a financial innovation but a strategic instrument aimed at reshaping global economic hegemony. The rise of CBDCs is viewed as part of a broader restructuring of the international monetary system toward a multipolar, institutionalized cooperation system.[46]

Nevertheless, China faces several challenges in achieving this objective. Despite its efforts, the RMB remains a minority player against decades of entrenched U.S. dominance, which is reinforced by strong network effects, institutional depth, and trust. Moreover, although collaboration has been established with regional countries and states subject to U.S. sanctions, such as Russia and Iran, Western nations—positioned amid the U.S.-China economic rivalry—are likely to hesitate in aligning against the United States.[47] Additionally, the strict control of data under the e-CNY, coupled with incompatibilities with data protection laws governing cross-border data transfers, presents a significant obstacle to the global promotion and adoption of the e-CNY.[48]

3 Risks and Challenges

Although new digital currencies offer promising opportunities for the financial system and carry significant geopolitical relevance, their adoption is accompanied by several risks and challenges arising from both their technology and their potential scale. Developments in the stablecoin ecosystem, in particular, have shown regulators how quickly theoretical risks can turn into real and immediate concerns. Before these instruments, whose full risk-benefit impact is still difficult to predict, are adopted; it is essential to establish regulatory standards that preserve the expected advantages of the ecosystem while addressing the risks analyzed in this chapter.

43 Raffelini (2025).
44 Raffelini (2025).
45 Boros and Horváth (2022).
46 Aliyeva (2025).
47 Boros and Horváth (2022).
48 Bilotta and Botti (2021).

3.1 Risks Specific to Stablecoins

As a form of private money, stablecoins carry a range of risks, foremost among them threats to financial stability and monetary sovereignty. Trust is the cornerstone of any instrument used in the financial system. Trust is the cornerstone of any instrument used in the financial system.

The emphasis on "stability," embedded in both the name and definitions of stablecoins, creates a perception that they are backed by an unconditional asset class. This perception fosters confidence that stablecoins can be redeemed at par, both under normal conditions and during times of market stress. However, this does not guarantee that these instruments are stable.[49] The stability of a stablecoin is not an intrinsic or privileged attribute; rather, it is a characteristic that can only be achieved through a well-designed and effective risk management approach.[50] Consequently, this trust may be undermined if high-risk reserves are held, if reserves are inadequately safeguarded, redemption rights are uncertain, or operational risks materialize. For instance, in October 2018, concerns regarding whether Tether—the largest stablecoin—was fully backed by U.S. dollars, contrary to the issuer's claims, triggered a sharp de-pegging of Tether. Subsequently, in April 2019, an investigation into Tether's relationship with Bitfinex sparked another episode of peg volatility.[51] Such a loss of confidence may extend beyond a single issuer, adversely affecting trust in other stablecoins and the broader stablecoin ecosystem. Such a loss of confidence may extend beyond a single issuer, adversely affecting trust in other stablecoins and the broader stablecoin ecosystem.[52]

Moreover, if global stablecoins (GSC),[53] which have the potential for adoption and accessibility across multiple jurisdictions and the capacity to achieve significant volume, were to be employed as a common store of value, even minor fluctuations

[49] D'avernas, Adrien/ Maurin, Vincent/ Vandeweyer, 2022, Quentin, Can Stablecoins Be Stable?, University of Chicago, Becker Friedman Institute for Economics Working Paper No. 2022–131, Proceedings of the EUROFIDAI-ESSEC Paris December Finance Meeting 2022, https://ssrn.com/abstract=4226027, Last Accessed: 20.09.2025; Ferreira, Agata, 2021, The Curious Case of Stablecoins – Balancing Risks and Rewards?, Journal of International Economic Law, 24, 755–778, https://doi.org/10.1093/jiel/jgab036, Last Accessed: 20.09.2025.

[50] ECB Crypto Assets Task Force (CATF), 2020, Stablecoins: Implications for Monetary Policy, Financial Stability, Market Infrastructure and Payments, and Banking Supervision in the Euro Area, ECB Occasional Paper Series, No 247, https://www.ecb.europa.eu/pub/pdf/scpops/ecb.op247~fe3df92991.en.pdf, Last Accessed: 20.09.2025.

[51] Ahmed Rashad/Aldasoro, Iñaki/Duley, 2024, Chanelle, Public Information and Stablecoin Runs, BIS Working Papers No 1164, https://www.bis.org/publ/work1164.pdf, Last Accessed: 20.09.2025.

[52] FSB, Addressing the Regulatory, Supervisory and Oversight Challenges Raised By "Global Stablecoin" Arrangements Consultative Document, 14 April 2020, https://www.fsb.org/wp-content/uploads/P140420-1.pdf, Last Accessed: 20.09.2025, (FSB Global Stablecoin Consultative Document 14 April 2020).

[53] FSB Global Stablecoin Consultative Document 14 April 2020.

may lead to significant variations in users' wealth. Such volatility may be substantial enough to influence spending behavior and economic decision-making.[54]

Another risk posed by GSC relates to monetary sovereignty.[55] A private sector-issued means of payment may, particularly in jurisdictions where trust in the national currency has eroded due to hyperinflation or similar factors, be perceived as more valuable than the national currency itself.[56] In certain developing countries experiencing hyperinflation, where access to cash is limited or physically carrying cash is perilous, digital payment instruments can become more advantageous than legal tender. In such contexts, payment tools like stablecoins may gain widespread acceptance and, in effect, function as de facto legal tender, signaling a loss shift in the traditional monetary function of national currencies.

A 2024 report by the FSB identified higher levels of interest and activity in stablecoins within emerging market and developing economies (EMDEs) compared to advanced economies.[57] The report identifies several reasons for the interest in stablecoins in countries such as Türkiye, Thailand, Brazil, Indonesia, Russia, and Ukraine. Among these are the use of stablecoins—particularly those pegged to the U.S. dollar—as a store of value against devaluation or capital flow management measures (CFMs); the liquidity advantages they offer for taking speculative positions in various crypto assets, as opposed to other trading pairs; and, in certain cases, their facilitation of cross-border payments and remittances. However, the widespread adoption of foreign-currency-pegged global stablecoins (GSCs) in EMDEs, in the absence of a comprehensive regulatory framework, renders these economies more vulnerable to financial risks compared to advanced economies.[58]

As of 2025, approximately 90% of the stablecoin market capitalization is accounted for by just two issuers.[59] In such instances of market concentration, the issuer of a stablecoin that has achieved large-scale adoption—even in advanced economies—may become a key player within the financial ecosystem. This, in turn, may impact the national monetary policy. Likewise, the GENIUS Act in the United States, which requires stablecoin reserves to be held in Treasury securities, suggests that by 2030, large-scale stablecoin issuers could become among the largest holders

---

54 Arner, Douglas/Auer, Raphael/Frost, 2020, Jon, BIS Working Papers No 905 Stablecoins: Risks, Potential and Regulation, https://www.bis.org/publ/work905.pdf, Last Accessed: 20.09.2025.

55 FSB Global Stablecoin Consultative Document 14 April 2020.

56 FSB, Review of the FSB High-Level Recommendations of the Regulation, Supervision and Oversight of "Global Stablecoin" Arrangements Consultative Report, 11 October 2022, https://www.fsb.org/wp-content/uploads/P111022-4.pdf, Last Accessed: 20.09.2025.

57 FSB, Cross-border Regulatory and Supervisory Issues of Global Stablecoin Arrangements in EMDEs, 23 July 2024, https://www.fsb.org/wp-content/uploads/P230724.pdf, Last Accessed: 20.09.2025.

58 FSB, Cross-border Regulatory and Supervisory Issues of Global Stablecoin Arrangements in EMDEs, 2024.

59 These two stablecoins are USDT and USDC. See: CoinDesk Data, Stablecoins & CBDCs Report, September 2025; For related analyses, see also: Aldasoro, Iñaki/ Aquilina, Matteo/Lewrick Ulf /Lim, 2025, Sang Hyuk, Stablecoin Growth—Policy Challenges and Approaches, BIS Bulletin No 108, https://www.bis.org/publ/bisbull108.pdf, Last Accessed: 20.09.2025.

of U.S. Treasury bonds.[60] This scenario would not only elevate demand for Treasury securities but could also render government debt markets increasingly dependent on stablecoin issuance.

Indeed, while central banks pursue public objectives such as the sustainability of financial stability through their monetary policies, stablecoin issuers—as commercial entities—bear no public mandate and thus cannot be expected to assume responsibility for safeguarding the public interest.[61]

Moreover, the migration of liquidity towards stablecoins may give rise to destabilizing capital flows and shadow banking activities. In such a scenario, the local banking system may face liquidity shortages, potentially destabilizing foreign exchange rates, financing, and intermediation services, which may harm the financial system.[62] Similarly, in 2007, money market funds—a shadow banking instrument—evolved into entities that extended more credit than traditional banks, thereby triggering the financial crises of Northern Rock and Lehman Brothers and producing a destructive impact whose costs were borne by the global financial system.

Furthermore, stablecoin issuers will possess a vast influx of data linked to money -an intersection of payment instruments and technology that is largely absent in the current system. The competitive dynamic between states and large technology companies, already considered potential threats to the financial system due to their data-driven power, could assume a different dimension when this data is directly associated with monetary instruments. Given these companies' existing track records regarding data protection, it remains doubtful whether they can fully fulfil their obligations with respect to data linked to money.

3.2 *Risks Specific to CBDCs*

CBDCs signal a profound transformation in the mechanisms through which central banks create and transmit money.[63] However, this transformation carries risks that must be carefully considered, particularly with respect to financial stability, the effectiveness of monetary policy, and international power dynamics.

---

60 Bankers Association for Finance and Trade (BAFT), 2025, BAFT Whitepaper on the Impact of Stablecoins on Payments, https://www.baft.org/document/baft-white-paper-on-the-impact-of-stablecoins-on-payments/, Last Accessed: 20.09.2025.

61 Hsu, Michael J., 2022, Thoughts on the Architecture of Stablecoins, Remarks Before the Institute of International Economic Law at Georgetown University Law Center, https://www.occ.gov/news-issuances/speeches/2022/pub-speech-2022-37.pdf, Last Accessed: 20.09.2025.

62 Arner et al. (2020).

63 Auer, Raphael/Böhme, Rainer, 2020, The Technology of Retail Central Bank Digital Currency, BIS Quarterly Review, 85–100, https://www.bis.org/publ/qtrpdf/r_qt2003j.pdf, Last Accessed: 20.09.2025.

In the current system, a two-tiered monetary structure exists between commercial banks and central banks, which CBDCs have the potential to disrupt, thereby weakening the fundamental functions of the banking sector. By eliminating the intermediary role of banks, CBDCs, issued directly by central banks, could trigger deposit withdrawals from commercial banks. This resulting deposit disintermediation may reduce banks' lending capacity and create liquidity constraints.[64] It could also diminish banks' ability to attract deposits, exerting upward pressure on interest rates. Designing CBDCs to bear interest could transform central banks beyond their traditional boundaries, positioning them as direct market participants and potentially disrupting the balance between monetary policy implementation and financial intermediation functions.[65] Moreover, the traditional role of the central bank as the "lender of last resort", a key pillar of financial security in the existing system, could be altered, with central banks assuming the position of primary lender. These potential risks pose systemic effects that should not be underestimated, impacting financial stability, competitive balance, and potentially the independence of central bank policy.[66]

Likewise, a 2025 report by the European Parliament highlighted that a poorly designed digital euro could weaken the private banking sector and excessively centralize the economic intermediation functions of central banks.[67] In such a scenario, the emergence of a new form of "public monopoly" within the financial system becomes a distinct possibility.

The trust generated by CBDCs, as liabilities of the central bank, could prompt rapid conversions of deposits and funds to CBDCs during periods of financial crisis, potentially triggering bank runs. Given that such runs would occur digitally (in the form of digital bank runs), they could unfold much more quickly and extensively than traditional bank panics.[68] For this reason, CBDCs must be carefully designed and introduced in a controlled manner. To mitigate these risks, central banks are exploring measures related to CBDC design, including whether they should bear interest, the imposition of holding limits, and layered access models that channel usage through banks.[69]

By affecting reserve levels, CBDCs could weaken central banks' ability to control interest rates for price stability, manage reserves, and implement monetary policy aimed at interbank market liquidity.

---

64 Abad, Jorge/Nuño Galo/Thomas, Carlos, 2024, CBDC and the Operational Framework of Monetary Policy, BIS Working Papers No 1126, https://www.bis.org/publ/work1126.pdf, Last Accessed: 20.09.2025.

65 Bank for International Settlements (BIS), 2021, CBDCs: Financial Stability Implications, https://www.bis.org/publ/othp42_fin_stab.pdf, Last Accessed: 20.09.2025.

66 Abad et al. (2024).

67 Bezemer et al. (2025).

68 Bank for International Settlements (BIS), CBDCs: Financial Stability Implications, September 2021.

69 Ulrich, Bindseil, 2020, Tiered CBDC and the Financial System, January, https://ssrn.com/abstract=3513422, Last Accessed: 20.09.2025.

Moreover, CBDCs enable transactions to be monitored directly by central banks, a capability that carries significant implications for financial privacy. While governmental oversight can offer advantages in combating issues such as tax evasion, money laundering, and the financing of terrorism, it also presents the potential for use as a tool of societal control and punitive measures, particularly under non-democratic regimes.[70] The expansion of state surveillance and the consequent erosion of individual privacy pose serious risks to fundamental rights and freedoms, including economic freedom of expression, giving rise to legal, ethical, and human rights considerations that demand careful scrutiny.[71]

CBDCs also entail technical and cybersecurity risks that could profoundly impact the financial system. These systems require highly advanced technical infrastructure and robust cybersecurity measures. Any cyberattack or technical disruption could propagate throughout the entire payment ecosystem. Moreover, such incidents have the potential not only to cause technical failures but also to trigger macroeconomic and political crises.[72]

On the other hand, many countries rely on private technology firms to develop the technical infrastructure of their CBDC systems or use externally dependent systems. Central banks generally assume a policymaking and regulatory role rather than an operational one. Consequently, their technological capabilities are limited, and they lack an established structure for operating these systems. This situation raises issues of technological sovereignty, both in relation to the technology providers and to other countries supplying the technical infrastructure.[73]

4 Conclusion

The current geoeconomic order is characterized by heightened strategic competition among major powers and challenges to the Western-led financial system, resulting in a more contested global economy. The global circulation of U.S.-based stablecoins is giving rise to a new form of dollarization—"digital dollarization"—while financial geopolitics is increasingly shaped by the private sector, with stablecoin issuers anticipated to become among the largest holders of U.S. Treasury securities.

[70] The Digital Dollar Project, 2025, Modernizing the U.S. Dollar for the Future of Digital Networks, https://digitaldollarproject.org/wp-content/uploads/2025/03/Modernizing-the-US-Dollar-for-the-Future-of-Digital-Networks-1.pdf, Last Accessed: 20.09.2025.

[71] Skinner, Christina P., 2024, Central Bank Digital Currency as New Public Money, 172 University of Pennsylvania Law Review,151, https://doi.org/10.58112/uplr.172-1.3, Last Accessed: 20.09.2025.

[72] Citi Global Perspectives & Solutions, 2025, Digital Dollars: Banks and Public Sector Drive Blockchain Adoption, https://www.citigroup.com/rcs/citigpa/storage/public/GPS_Report_Blockchain_Digital_Dollar.pdf, Last Accessed: 20.09.2025.

[73] Ulrich (2020).

The continuity of the global dollar system is thus linked not only to central banks but also to the sustainability of private issuers and platform economies.

At the same time, the world is undergoing a structural shift from U.S. dollar hegemony—intensified by the use of economic sanctions as a weapon and amplified by digitalization—toward a multipolar, fragmented system. Historically, it has been observed that currency dominance can fluctuate in tandem with shifts in global power dynamics.

The rise of digital currencies may give impetus to the formation of new financial alliances and blocs. Regional partnerships can influence the adoption of digital currencies, and regional digital currencies may evolve into alternative or complementary multipolar cooperation systems, facilitating trade outside the dollar and beyond the reach of Western sanctions. While this could represent a strategic victory against U.S. hegemony, it may simultaneously accelerate the fragmentation of the international monetary system, favoring closed economic blocs and parallel systems over open and free trade, thereby impeding global economic integration.

Stablecoins and CBDCs, which lie at the heart of the digital transformation of the financial system, have become emblematic of strategic competition over the future of the financial architecture. While both instruments offer significant benefits within the payments ecosystem, they simultaneously possess the potential to reshape geopolitical power balances—a potential that is inextricably intertwined with substantial risks to monetary sovereignty, financial stability, and privacy.

Stablecoins, in particular, represent a striking example of how an innovation led by the private sector can evolve into a systemic force. Likewise, the expansion of a monetary structure based on private issuers may transform a fragile market participant into a shadow banking instrument, posing risks to financial stability. Conversely, CBDCs—introduced by public authorities as tools to safeguard monetary sovereignty—bring forth new areas of concern, including digital surveillance, data privacy, technological dependency, and the potential contraction of individual freedoms.

Integrating these new forms of digital money into the financial system necessitates the re-establishment of the historical balance between efficiency and sovereignty, innovation and stability, as well as privacy and oversight, in conjunction with geopolitical objectives. Future policy design must regard these instruments not as alternatives but as complementary components, aligning public oversight and private sector innovation within a coherent and harmonious framework.

The future of digital finance will be shaped not merely by the digitalization of currencies, but also by global regulatory coordination, cyber resilience, interoperability standards, and principles of international governance. An effective and diversified digital monetary ecosystem can only be achieved through the establishment of a multilateral financial order founded upon the principle of mutual interdependence.

References

Abad J, Nuño G, Thomas C (2024) CBDC and the Operational Framework of Monetary Policy, BIS Working Papers No 1126. https://www.bis.org/publ/work1126.pdf. Accessed 20 Sept 2025

Ahmed R, Aldasoro I, Duley C (2024) Public information and stablecoin runs, BIS Working Papers No 1164. https://www.bis.org/publ/work1164.pdf Accessed 20 Sept 2025

Aldasoro I, Aquilina M, Lewrick U, Lim SH (2025) Stablecoin growth—policy challenges and approaches, BIS Bulletin No 108. https://www.bis.org/publ/bisbull108.pdf. Accessed 20 Sept 2025

Aliyeva G (2025) Geopolitical implications of digital currencies: national security and global power shifts. Azerbaijan State University of Economics International Master's and Doctoral Center. https://doi.org/10.58225/tim.2025-2-323-329. Accessed 20 Oct 2025

Arner D, Auer R, Frost J (2020) BIS Working Papers No 905 Stablecoins: risks, potential and regulation. https://www.bis.org/publ/work905.pdf. Accessed 20 Sept 2025

Auer R., Böhme R (2020) The technology of retail central bank digital currency, BIS Quarterly Review, March, 85–100, https://www.bis.org/publ/qtrpdf/r_qt2003j.pdf. Accessed 20 Sept 2025

Bank for International Settlements (BIS) (2021, September) CBDCs: financial stability implications. https://www.bis.org/publ/othp42_fin_stab.pdf. Accessed 20Sept 2025

Bankers Association for Finance and Trade (BAFT) (2025) BAFT Whitepaper on the impact of stablecoins on payments. https://www.baft.org/document/baft-white-paper-on-the-impact-of-stablecoins-on-payments/. Accessed 20 Sept 2025

Bezemer D, Sanders M, Kramer B, Simić, A (2025) Stablecoins and Digital Euro: friends or foes of European monetary policy?, European Parliament, Monetary Dialogue Papers. https://www.europarl.europa.eu/RegData/etudes/IDAN/2025/764387/ECTI_IDA(2025)764387_EN.pdf. Accessed 20 Sept 2025

Bilotta N (2024) The geoeconomics of money in the digital age, 1st edn. Routledge, London. https://doi.org/10.4324/9781003500957. Accessed 20 Oct 2025

Bilotta N, Botti F (2021) The (near) future of central bank digital currencies, risks and opportunities for the global economy and society. Peter Lang Verlag, Lausanne. https://www.peterlang.com/document/1068992. Accessed 20 Oct 2025

Bogaardt PC (2024) From analog to digital: the geopolitical and socioeconomic calculus of central bank digital currencies. CGU Theses & Dissertations, 912. https://scholarship.claremont.edu/cgu_etd/912. Accessed 20 Oct 2025

Boros E, Horváth M (2022) Central bank digital currency: the next money revolution? Central bank digital currencies in the dimension of geopolitics, Public Financ Q, 67(4), 506–521 https://doi.org/10.35551/PFQ_2022_4_2. Accessed 20 Oct 2025

Citi Global Perspectives & Solutions (2025) Digital dollars: banks and public sector drive blockchain adoption. https://www.citigroup.com/rcs/citigpa/storage/public/GPS_Report_Blockchain_Digital_Dollar.pdf. Accessed 20 Sept 2025

Coindesk Stablecoins & CBDCs Report (2025, September). https://data.coindesk.com/reports/stablecoins-cbdcs-report-september-2025. Accessed 20 Oct 2025

D'avernas A, Maurin V, Vandeweyer Q (2022) Can stablecoins be stable? 2022, University of Chicago, Becker Friedman Institute for Economics Working Paper No. 2022–131, Proceedings of the EUROFIDAI-ESSEC Paris December Finance Meeting 2022. https://ssrn.com/abstract=4226027. Accessed 20 Sept 2025

Digital Euro Association Working Group (2025) The role of stablecoins in financial sovereignty. https://digital-euro-association.de/hubfs/DEA%20-%20The%20Role%20of%20Stablecoins%20in%20Financial%20Sovereignty.pdf?hsLang=en. Accessed 20 Sept 2025

ECB Crypto Assets Task Force (CATF) (2020) Stablecoins: implications for monetary policy, financial stability, market infrastructure and payments, and banking supervision in the euro area. ECB Occasional Paper Series, No 247. https://www.ecb.europa.eu/pub/pdf/scpops/ecb.op247~fe3df92991.en.pdf. Accessed 20 Sept 2025

European Central Bank (ECB) (2023) Progress on the investigation phase of a Digital Euro—third report. https://www.ecb.europa.eu/euro/digital_euro/timeline/profuse/shared/pdf/ecb.degov230424_progress.en.pdf. Accessed 20 Sept 2025

Ferreira A (2021) The curious case of stablecoins – balancing risks and rewards? J Int Econ Law 24:755–778. https://doi.org/10.1093/jiel/jgab036. Accessed 20 Sept 2025

FSB (2020) Addressing the regulatory, supervisory and oversight challenges raised by "global stablecoin" arrangements consultative document. https://www.fsb.org/wp-content/uploads/P140420-1.pdf. Accessed 20 Sept 2025, (FSB Global Stablecoin Consultative Document 14 April 2020)

FSB (2022, October 11) Review of the FSB high-level recommendations of the regulation, supervision and oversight of "global stablecoin" arrangements consultative report. https://www.fsb.org/wp-content/uploads/P111022-4.pdf. Accessed 20 Sept 2025

FSB (2024) Cross-border regulatory and supervisory issues of global stablecoin arrangements in EMDEs. https://www.fsb.org/wp-content/uploads/P230724.pdf. Accessed 20 Sept 2025

Gilles C, et al (2025, September) Mind the gap: how stablecoins can secure the UK's financial future, Imperial College, Centre for Financial Technology and Centre for Cryptocurrency Research and Engineering. https://imperialcollegelondon.app.box.com/s/ggqi8y0jyr3969w863bfiz-pz8g9wj549/file/1986432747899. Accessed 20 Oct 2025

Gunnella V, Stamato G, Kobayashi A (2025) The implications of US-China trade tensions for the euro area—lessons from the tariffs imposed by the first Trump Administration, Economic Bulletin 3. https://www.ecb.europa.eu/press/economic-bulletin/html/eb202503.en.html. Accessed 20 Sept 20205

Hsu MJ (2022) Thoughts on the architecture of stablecoins, remarks before the Institute of International Economic Law at Georgetown University Law Center. https://www.occ.gov/news-issuances/speeches/2022/pub-speech-2022-37.pdf. Accessed 20 Sept 2025

Jin S (2025) The potential risks and global governance of stablecoins: a dual perspective based on economics and politics. Law Financial Mark Rev 18(4):205–225. https://doi.org/10.1080/17521440.2025.2569313. Accessed 20 Oct 2025

Knoerich J (2023) China's new digital currency: implications for renminbi internationalization and the US Dollar. In: Bilotta N, Botti F (eds) Digitalization and geopolitics: catalytic forces in the (future) international monetary system. Edizioni Nuova Cultura. https://www.iai.it/sites/default/files/iairs_10.pdf. Accessed 20 Oct 2025

Marple T (2024) The Geoeconomics of Traditional and Digital Government Money: Strategic Interaction in Central Bank Digital Currencies, in Vinod K. Aggarwal, and Tai Ming Cheung (eds), The Oxford Handbook of Geoeconomics and Economic Statecraft, Oxford Handbooks. https://doi.org/10.1093/oxfordhb/9780197673546.013.13. Accessed 20 Sept 2025

Passacantando F (2023) The Digital Euro: challenges and opportunities. In: Bilotta N, Botti F (eds) Digitalization and geopolitics: catalytic forces in the (future) international monetary system. Edizioni Nuova Cultura. https://www.iai.it/sites/default/files/iairs_10.pdf. Accessed 20 Oct 2025

Raffelini A (2025) The global stablecoin race and a new globalization: digital rails, trade policy, and geopolitical realignment via China's Yuan stablecoin and emerging digital economic areas. World Wide J Multidiscip Res Dev. https://www.researchgate.net/publication/395899005_The_Global_Stablecoin_Race_and_a_New_Globalization_Digital_Rails_Trade_Policy_and_Geopolitical_Realignment_via_China's_Yuan_Stablecoin_and_Emerging_Digital_Economic_Areas. Accessed 20 Sept 2025

Skinner CP (2024) Central bank digital currency as new public money. Univ Pa L Rev 172:151. https://doi.org/10.58112/uplr.172-1.3. Accessed 20 Sept 2025

The Digital Dollar Project (2025) Modernizing the U.S. Dollar for the future of digital networks. https://digitaldollarproject.org/wp-content/uploads/2025/03/Modernizing-the-US-Dollar-for-the-Future-of-Digital-Networks-1.pdf. Accessed 20 Sept 2025

The Hidden Impact of SWIFT Sanctions on Global Banking (2025). https://www.lawyer-monthly.com/2025/03/the-hidden-impact-of-swift-sanctions-on-global-banking/. Accessed 20 Oct 2025

The White House (2025) Strengthening American leadership in digital financial technology. https://www.whitehouse.gov/presidential-actions/2025/01/strengthening-american-leadership-in-digital-financial-technology/. Accessed 20 Sept 2025

Ulrich B (2020, January) Tiered CBDC and the financial system. https://ssrn.com/abstract=3513422. Accessed 20 Sept 2025

The Stablecoin Paradox: From Decentralized Ideals to Re-Intermediation and Financial Engineering

C. Coşkun Küçüközmen

Abstract Stablecoins have emerged as the dominant transactional infrastructure of the digital asset economy, filling the functional void left by the volatility of native cryptocurrencies. Originally conceived as instruments to stabilize decentralized finance, fiat-backed stablecoins have instead produced a paradoxical outcome: rather than disintermediating the financial system, they have reinforced new forms of centralization and deepened linkages to sovereign debt markets, regulatory authority, and traditional financial intermediaries. This chapter examines the stablecoin phenomenon through four analytical lenses. First, it analyzes the geopolitical implications of dollar-denominated stablecoins, arguing that they function as instruments of digital dollarization that extend U.S. monetary power. Second, it contrasts the U.S. embrace of private stablecoins with the European Union's defensive regulatory posture under MiCA, emphasizing institutional stickiness and payment efficiency. Third, it explores the corporate adoption barrier created by International Financial Reporting Standards, highlighting tensions between accounting form and economic substance. Finally, the chapter surveys emerging financial engineering approaches that seek to design endogenous stability through risk tranching and internal restructuring. By synthesizing political economy, regulation, accounting, and financial design perspectives, the chapter assesses whether stablecoins represent a digitization of existing monetary hierarchies or a still-incomplete step toward a new monetary paradigm.

Keywords Stablecoins · Digital dollarization · Monetary sovereignty · Re-intermediation · Treasury markets · Financial stability · IFRS · Cash equivalents · Crypto-dollarization · Endogenous stability · Tranching

The author thanks his research assistant Doğu Çeteci who is currently pursuing an MSc in Economics at the University of St Andrews (UK), for his valuable technical support in structuring, formatting, and integrating revisions during the final stages of this chapter.

C. C. Küçüközmen (✉)
Faculty of Business, İzmir University of Economics, İzmir, Türkiye
e-mail: coskun.kucukozmen@ieu.edu.tr

S. Yazıcı et al. (eds.), *Tokenisation of Money*, Contributions to Finance and Accounting, https://doi.org/10.1007/978-3-032-22946-5_30

1 Introduction

The cryptocurrency movement originated with a radical critique of centralized finance. The publication of the Bitcoin whitepaper in 2008 articulated a vision of money that would operate without trusted intermediaries, replacing institutional discretion with cryptographic proof and algorithmic consensus. The slogan "Don't Trust, Verify" captured this ambition: a financial system in which trust would be embedded in code rather than vested in banks or central authorities.

More than a decade later, the outcomes of this experiment are mixed. While Bitcoin and other crypto-assets have succeeded as speculative stores of value and as vehicles for censorship-resistant transactions, they have largely failed to perform the classical monetary functions of unit of account and medium of exchange. Extreme price volatility has rendered them impractical for everyday payments, wage contracts, and financial reporting. In response, the ecosystem has converged on stablecoins as a pragmatic solution.

Stablecoins, particularly those backed by fiat currencies, have become an increasingly important component of digital asset markets. Their use has expanded rapidly in trading, cross-border payments, and as settlement instruments across both decentralized and centralized platforms. Although they still account for only a fraction of global financial activity, their growing prominence within crypto ecosystems is striking. Yet this expansion has come at the cost of reintroducing intermediaries and concentrated power structures that the crypto movement initially sought to escape. This tension lies at the heart of what this chapter terms the 'Stablecoin Paradox.'

2 The Geopolitics of Digital Money: Dollar Hegemony vs. European Sovereignty

Although stablecoins circulate on borderless blockchain networks, their economic significance is deeply embedded in geopolitical realities. Currency dominance, regulatory authority, and sovereign debt markets shape both their design and their implications. A comparison between the United States and the European Union reveals sharply divergent approaches to the rise of private digital money.

2.1 *The "Crypto-Dollar" and the Centralization Paradox*

The rise of dollar-denominated stablecoins represents a paradoxical outcome for decentralized finance. In order to achieve price stability, the market has gravitated toward fiat-backed tokens issued by private entities and supported by custodial banks and sovereign debt instruments. Users must therefore trust issuers, auditors, and regulators rather than purely algorithmic mechanisms.

This re-centralization has served U.S. geopolitical interests. By allowing private actors to issue digital representations of the dollar, the United States has effectively outsourced the digitization of its currency. Following the passage of the GENIUS Act, U.S. policymakers have explicitly framed regulated dollar stablecoins as tools to reinforce dollar dominance in a digital world. As Smart (2026) notes, widespread adoption of dollar-denominated stablecoins could increase global demand for U.S. Treasury securities, enhance the effectiveness of financial sanctions, and cement U.S. influence over emerging financial standards.

Early cryptocurrency narratives emphasized the ambition of reducing reliance on traditional financial intermediaries rather than eliminating intermediation altogether. As Prasad (2025) astutely observes, the subsequent evolution of the stablecoin market has produced what he terms a "paradox of centralization." In practice, the extreme volatility of native crypto-assets such as Bitcoin limited their suitability for everyday transactions, prompting the ecosystem to gravitate toward fiat-backed stablecoins. While these instruments introduced new efficiencies, they also reaffirmed the functional necessity of intermediaries, whether for issuance, custody, payment acceptance, fraud mitigation, or system interoperability, often reconstituting established financial roles in new institutional forms.

This shift fundamentally altered the trust model of the ecosystem. Users no longer rely solely on algorithmic consensus but must place trust in the private issuers (such as Tether or Circle) and the commercial banks holding the underlying reserves. Consequently, power has not been decentralized; it has merely been shifted from regulated traditional banks to less-regulated "shadow" issuers who retain the power to freeze assets and censor transactions.

Crucially, this centralization has served the geopolitical interests of the United States, creating a mechanism often described colloquially as a "GENIUS Act" of monetary policy. By allowing private entities to issue digital tokens pegged to the dollar, the US has effectively outsourced the digitization of its currency.

- **Reserve Demand:** Issuers of major stablecoins (USDT, USDC) are required to hold reserves, predominantly composed of US Treasury bills. This creates a structural, non-inflationary demand for US government debt.
- **Eurodollar 2.0:** Just as the Eurodollar markets of the twentieth century extended the dollar's reach offshore, dollar-backed stablecoins allow the USD to penetrate emerging markets and blockchain ecosystems where local banking infrastructure is weak or capital controls are strict.

Thus, rather than threatening fiat, stablecoins have arguably become its most potent vectors in the digital space.

2.2 The European Fortress: Institutional Stickiness and Monetary Defense

In contrast to the tacit encouragement seen in the US dollar sphere, the European perspective is characterized by caution and a defense of monetary sovereignty. Bezemer et al. (2023) provide a comprehensive assessment of whether stablecoins pose a threat to the European Central Bank's (ECB) monetary policy. Their conclusion is markedly less alarmist than the prevailing narrative in the US, attributing the resilience of the Eurozone to structural and institutional "stickiness."

They also argue that the threat of stablecoins undermining the ECB's transmission mechanisms, specifically the interest rate and bank lending channels is overstated in the short to medium term. Their analysis rests on three pillars:

1. **The Interest Rate Channel:** Monetary policy operates in part through the central bank's ability to influence economic conditions by adjusting interest rates. Most euro-denominated stablecoins currently do not remunerate holdings, which reduces their attractiveness as stores of value during periods of monetary tightening. While some stablecoin-based arrangements, particularly in the US, have begun to introduce interest-bearing or yield-linked mechanisms, these features remain limited, unevenly accessible, and institutionally distinct from traditional bank deposits, thereby constraining the effectiveness of stablecoins as substitutes for regulated deposit instruments in the euro area.
2. **Institutional Barriers and Efficiency:** Unlike the US, where domestic payment settlement can be relatively slow and costly, the euro area benefits from the Single Euro Payments Area (SEPA), including SEPA Instant Credit Transfer, which enables near-instant, low-cost fiat settlement for most domestic and intra-EU transactions. This institutional infrastructure significantly weakens the efficiency-based case for stablecoins as a domestic payment solution within the EU. However, stablecoins may retain a more limited value proposition in facilitating cross-border transactions between the euro area and non-EU jurisdictions, where payment frictions, currency conversion costs, and settlement delays remain more pronounced.
3. **Currency Mismatch Risks:** The authors note that "dollarization" (or cryptoization) typically occurs in economies with high inflation and low institutional trust. The Eurozone, despite recent inflationary pressures, does not fit this profile. Contracts, taxes, and wages are rigidly denominated in Euros, creating a high barrier to entry for foreign-denominated stablecoins.

2.3 Regulatory Divergence: Innovation vs. Stability

Differences in economic structure and financial architecture have given rise to divergent regulatory approaches. The European Union has moved pre-emptively with the Markets in Crypto-Assets (MiCA) regulation, which imposes strict governance and reserve requirements and, crucially, volume caps on non-euro-denominated stablecoins used as a medium of exchange. These measures are designed to limit the scale of foreign stablecoins and thereby reduce potential systemic risks to the euro area. In contrast to US-dollar stablecoins, which are typically backed by short-dated US Treasury securities and central-government liabilities, euro-denominated stablecoins tend to rely more heavily on commercial bank deposits and bank-issued instruments. This difference in backing structures implies a higher exposure to banking-sector fragility in the European case, reinforcing the EU's preference for precautionary regulation.

A residual vulnerability nonetheless remains in this defensive strategy. While the regulatory perimeter is robust, the EU's offensive alternative, the digital euro, faces internal design trade-offs. If the digital euro is engineered too conservatively, for example through tight holding limits or limited functionality in order to safeguard commercial bank funding, it risks failing to match the flexibility and usability of private stablecoins. Existing analyses emphasize that this tension may constrain the digital euro's ability to serve as a credible private-sector substitute without undermining financial stability.

In summary, whereas the United States has allowed private stablecoins, largely underpinned by sovereign debt markets, to expand as a complementary instrument reinforcing dollar dominance, Europe has relied more heavily on regulatory barriers and the efficiency of its existing banking and payment infrastructure to protect monetary sovereignty. As the analysis now turns from macro-level monetary considerations to the micro-level of corporate balance sheets, a further challenge emerges: how these instruments should be classified in a manner consistent with their underlying economic substance.

3 The Corporate Dilemma: Accounting Form Versus Economic Substance

Beyond geopolitics, the adoption of stablecoins by corporations and institutional investors hinges on their treatment within financial reporting frameworks. For treasurers and auditors, efficiency gains, particularly in cross-border payments and crypto on- and off-ramps, are relevant considerations. Ultimately, however, the decisive issue is not technological efficiency alone, but how stablecoins should be classified on the balance sheet.

Under current International Financial Reporting Standards, most crypto-assets, including stablecoins, are classified as intangible assets under IAS 38. This classification obscures their liquidity and undermines their usefulness for cash management. Hampl and Gyönyörová (2022) argue that this treatment misrepresents economic reality, particularly for high-quality fiat-backed stablecoins used primarily for payments.

Applying the criteria of IAS 7, the authors show that while stablecoins cannot qualify as 'cash' due to the absence of legal tender status, some may plausibly meet the definition of 'cash equivalents.' However, redemption rights, minimum thresholds, and issuer opacity, especially in the case of USDT, remain critical obstacles. Until accounting standards evolve, institutional adoption is likely to remain constrained.

3.1 *The IFRS Classification Gridlock*

Current International Financial Reporting Standards (IFRS) present a conundrum for corporate treasurers. As Hampl and Gyönyörová (2022) articulate in their technical analysis, the default classification of crypto-assets, including stablecoins, often falls under "Intangible Assets" (IAS 38). This classification is problematic for liquidity management; intangible assets are typically viewed as illiquid and do not contribute to key financial metrics like the "Current Ratio." If a company holds millions in USD Coin (USDC) for payments, but must report it alongside software licenses or patents rather than cash, the firm's financial health may appear artificially distorted to creditors and investors.

The pressing research question posed by Hampl and Gyönyörová (2022) is whether fiat-backed stablecoins can qualify as "Cash" or "Cash Equivalents" under IAS 7, thereby allowing them to sit in the most liquid tier of the balance sheet.

3.2 *Failed Tests and New Definitions*

The authors' rigorous application of IAS 7 reveals a binary outcome. First, stablecoins definitively fail the test for "Cash." They lack the status of legal tender and remain negligible as a unit of account in pricing goods and services globally. However, the nuance lies in the category of "Cash Equivalents."

According to IAS 7, a cash equivalent must satisfy four criteria: it must be short-term, highly liquid, convertible to a known amount of cash, and subject to an insignificant risk of changes in value. Hampl and Gyönyörová's empirical analysis of the 11 largest fiat-backed stablecoins challenges the skepticism often found in regulatory circles:

- **Volatility and Risk:** Through comparative analysis with traditional money market funds and short-term government bonds, the authors demonstrate that leading stablecoins exhibit volatility profiles low enough to satisfy the "insignificant risk" criterion.
- **Liquidity:** The depth of secondary markets (crypto exchanges) ensures that these assets can be converted to fiat almost instantly, often faster than redeeming shares in a traditional money market fund.

3.3 The Redemption Risk: The Case of Tether

Despite favorable liquidity data, the legal structure of redemption rights remains a critical barrier. The study highlights a bifurcation in the market between transparent, regulated issuers and opaque incumbents. Specifically, the authors point to Tether (USDT) as a cautionary example. While USDT maintains a peg in secondary markets, the primary redemption mechanism is often restricted by high minimum thresholds (e.g., $100,000) and significant fees.

From an accounting perspective, if a holder cannot legally force the issuer to convert the token back to fiat at par (1:1) without significant friction, the asset fails the strict definition of a cash equivalent. This finding suggests that accounting standards may inadvertently act as a quality filter, incentivizing the market to shift toward fully regulated, transparent issuers like Circle (USDC) or Paxos, whose contractual terms align more closely with cash-like instruments.

3.4 Substance Over Form

The ultimate argument put forth by Hampl and Gyönyörová (2022) is one of "Substance over Form." They argue that excluding high-quality fiat-backed stablecoins from cash equivalents effectively misinforms the users of financial statements. If a digital asset behaves like money, is stored like money, and is used to settle debts like money, reporting it as an intangible asset violates the core accounting principle of representing economic reality.

This friction suggests that the next phase of stablecoin evolution will not just be technological, but administrative. Until standard-setting bodies like the IASB update their interpretations to accommodate these "digital cash equivalents," institutional adoption will face an invisible but formidable glass ceiling.

4 Stablecoins, Financial Stability, and Treasury Markets

Stablecoins have become deeply intertwined with global sovereign debt markets. Issuers of major dollar-pegged stablecoins hold substantial volumes of short-term U.S. Treasury securities, making them significant participants in money markets. Financial Times reporting (Martin 2025) indicates that these holdings rival those of some foreign official investors.

This integration has ambiguous implications for financial stability. On the one hand, inflows into stablecoins increase demand for Treasuries and may compress yields. On the other hand, large-scale redemptions could force rapid asset sales, transmitting volatility into core funding markets. In effect, stablecoin issuers perform liquidity transformation similar to shadow banks, but without access to central bank backstops.

Attempts to design stability without explicit reserve backing have further illustrated the fragility of purely algorithmic approaches. The collapse of the Terra/Luna ecosystem demonstrated how reflexive price dynamics and loss of confidence can overwhelm rule-based stabilization mechanisms in the absence of credible collateral or institutional backstops. Rather than resolving the Stablecoin Paradox, such designs expose its limits: efforts to eliminate centralized trust entirely often reintroduce instability at scale, reinforcing the trade-off between decentralization and monetary robustness.

While the geopolitical and accounting debates focus on how to integrate stablecoins into the existing world, a parallel stream of research asks a more fundamental question: Is the design of the asset itself flawed? The vulnerability of current stablecoins lies in their reliance on *exogenous* stability. Fiat-backed coins rely on the honesty of off-chain custodians, while algorithmic models rely on fickle market sentiment. Both have historically failed, either through opacity (Tether) or "death spirals" (Terra/Luna).

4.1 The Flaw of "One Token Fits All"

Cao et al. (2025) argue that the core fragility of the crypto ecosystem stems from a failure to segregate risk. In traditional finance, risk is stratified; a Treasury bond buyer does not hold the same instrument as a hedge fund speculator. In crypto, however, protocols often conflate the store-of-value function with speculative incentives. To solve this, the authors propose a return to first principles using financial engineering, specifically the concept of "risk tranching" borrowed from the structured finance world (e.g., CDOs, Collateralized Debt Obligations).

4.2 Tranching: The CDO Model Applied to Crypto

The proposed design abandons the idea of a single token in favor of a dual-class structure backed by a pool of volatile crypto-assets (like ETH):

1. **Class A (The Stablecoin):** This acts as the "Senior Tranche." It is designed to be risk-free (or near risk-free), similar to a senior bond. It holds the first claim on the underlying collateral. Its goal is strictly capital preservation and stability.
2. **Class B (The Risk Absorber):** This acts as the "Equity Tranche." It is a leveraged, high-risk instrument that absorbs all the volatility of the underlying collateral. In exchange for protecting Class A, Class B holders receive outsized returns (leveraged gains) during bull markets.

This separation aligns incentives: "Safe" users (Class A) get stability without needing to trust a bank, while "risk-seeking" users (Class B) get leverage without needing a centralized exchange.

4.3 *The Reset Mechanism: Solving the Liquidation Spiral*

The most significant contribution of the Cao et al.(2025) model is the elimination of the "fire sale" risk. In current over-collateralized systems (like MakerDAO), if the price of collateral drops, the protocol must sell ETH on the open market to repay debt. In a crash, this selling pressure drives prices down further, causing more liquidations—a feedback loop known as a **liquidation spiral**.

They introduce a **"Reset Mechanism"** to replace external liquidation with internal restructuring.

- **Downward Reset:** If the collateral value drops significantly, the protocol does not sell assets. Instead, it mathematically restructures the claims. Class B holders are partially or fully wiped out (their equity is used to cover the loss), and the system resets with new parameters.
- **Upward Reset:** Conversely, if collateral skyrockets, gains are realized and distributed to Class B, resetting the leverage ratio to keeping the system balanced.

By using an **endogenous** accounting adjustment rather than an **exogenous** market trade, the system becomes immune to liquidity dry-ups in the external market.

4.4 *A Return to "Don't Trust, Verify"*

This engineering-heavy approach offers a philosophical counter-argument to the centralization trends discussed by Prasad (2025). By embedding option-pricing logic and automated risk constraints directly into smart contracts, the model shifts monetary credibility away from discretionary governance toward formalized, transparent rules. In doing so, it removes the need for a "GENIUS Act," a central-bank backstop, or reliance on regulated deposit-taking institutions. Stability is not guaranteed by institutional authority, but by ex-ante mathematical design and continuous collateral rebalancing. This perspective suggests that the future of stablecoins may not lie in digitizing existing sovereign currencies (as in USDT or USDC), but in constructing crypto-native synthetic assets that function as money precisely because they minimize institutional dependence.

Seen through this lens, stablecoins are increasingly positioned not merely as crypto-native instruments but as a competing layer of financial infrastructure, as explicitly noted by Asgari (2026). While proponents emphasize their efficiency, programmability, and suitability for a digital economy, incumbent banks and regulators perceive a deeper challenge: that these arrangements replicate core banking functions, payments, maturity transformation, and yield-like returns without relying on the traditional prudential perimeter. The resulting regulatory and political tension reflects not only concerns over stability, but a broader contest between institution-based trust and rule-based, algorithmic monetary design.

5 Discussion: The Asymmetric Reality in the Global South

Recent empirical evidence supports this bottom-up pattern of crypto-dollarization in emerging markets. Drawing on firm-level reporting, Stafford (2025) documents that in regions such as sub-Saharan Africa, Southeast Asia, and Latin America, stablecoins—particularly USD-pegged tokens such as USDT—are increasingly used for wages, trade settlement, and fundraising within specific cross-border payment networks and digital-native firms. While stablecoins still account for a negligible share of aggregate money and payment volumes globally, they can represent a substantial share of transactional activity within certain corridors, platforms, and user communities operating across borders. Their appeal lies not in technological novelty but in access to a reliable proxy for the US dollar in environments characterized by high inflation, capital controls, and fragile banking systems. From a systemic perspective, this usage pattern nonetheless reinforces demand for US Treasury bills, as stablecoin issuers back outstanding tokens with short-term sovereign debt, effectively channeling savings from the Global South into US public finance (Stafford 2025).

This dynamic should not be interpreted as politically uncontested or irreversible. In practice, episodes of crypto-dollarization have already triggered regulatory push-back, ranging from tighter controls on exchanges and on-ramps to explicit restrictions on stablecoin usage and foreign-currency substitution. For regulators in countries such as Turkey, Argentina, and Nigeria, the expansion of stablecoins poses a direct challenge to monetary sovereignty, making policy responses, whether through enforcement, taxation, capital controls, or the promotion of state-backed digital alternatives both likely and inevitable. The resulting tension underscores that crypto-dollarization is not a stable end state, but a contested and evolving equilibrium between private monetary instruments and state authority.

This trend validates Prasad's (2025) "GENIUS Act" hypothesis, albeit with a darker twist for developing nations. Demand for stablecoins in the Global South contributes at the margin to US public debt financing through increased demand for Treasury-backed reserves, while simultaneously weakening the monetary autonomy of local central banks. Unlike the euro area, which possesses the institutional capacity to limit stablecoin penetration, many developing economies lack credible domestic alternatives. As a result, stablecoins in these contexts function not as a niche speculative asset, but as an emergent parallel financial infrastructure, shadow banking in its most literal sense.

This asymmetry exposes a gap in the literature: Western-centric regulatory models may fail to capture the dynamics of stablecoin adoption in regions where the state struggles to provide stable money. In this setting, the engineering-based approaches proposed by Cao et al. (2025) take on added relevance. If stablecoins can be designed to achieve robustness without dependence on US banking rails, they may offer a neutral monetary instrument rather than a vector of digital dollar dominance.

6 Conclusion

Stablecoins represent one of the most consequential developments in contemporary finance. Born from a desire to disintermediate the banking system, they have paradoxically become vehicles for re-intermediation, binding crypto markets to sovereign debt, regulatory authority, and centralized trust. Geopolitically, they extend U.S. dollar power while challenging other monetary regimes. Institutionally, they expose gaps in accounting standards and financial supervision. The Stablecoin Paradox is not a problem to be solved, but a structural condition of a financial system attempting to reconcile decentralized technological ideals with the enduring realities of monetary power, regulation, and trust.

References

Asgari N (2026) The stablecoin war: wall street vs crypto over the future of money. Financial Times, February 2

Bezemer D, Sanders M, Kramer B, Simić A (2023) Stablecoins and digital euro: friends or foes of European monetary policy? Sustainable Finance Lab

Cao Y, Dai M, Kou S, Li L, Yang C (2025) Designing stablecoins. Math Financ 35(1):263–294

Hampl F, Gyönyörová L (2022) Can fiat-backed stablecoins be considered cash or cash equivalents under international financial reporting standards rules?

Martin K (2025) Why we should worry about the rise of stablecoins. Financial Times, June 6

Prasad ES (2025, December) The stablecoin paradox. Finance & Development. International Monetary Fund

Smart C (2026) Trump's crypto gamble: how a stablecoin could preserve dollar dominance—or shatter it. Foreign Affairs, January 19

Stafford P (2025) How stablecoins are entering the financial system. Financial Times June 12

Concluding Synthesis: Probabilistic Scenarios for the Future of Money

Selim Yazıcı, C. Coşkun Küçüközmen, and Michael Salmony

Abstract This concluding chapter synthesises the book's exploration of tokenised money, encompassing central bank digital currencies (CBDCs), commercial bank money tokens, and stablecoins, through a structured, forward-looking framework of probabilistic scenarios. Rather than offering deterministic predictions, the authors draw on long-standing expertise in payments, regulation, and financial infrastructure to map plausible trajectories across regions and technological dimensions over the coming decade. The analysis proceeds in four stages. First, an idealised, perfectly tokenised scenario of seamless global interoperability is examined and assessed as highly unlikely in the medium term, given entrenched regulatory divergence, fragmented infrastructure, and geopolitical constraints. Second, regional scenarios are developed for the United States, Europe, Asia, and beyond: US dollar-denominated stablecoins are expected to consolidate their dominance in global settlement corridors; Europe is projected to progress cautiously, led by regulation rather than market adoption; Asia's wallet-based ecosystems are seen as continuing to expand while accommodating multiple monetary form factors; and emerging economies, particularly those in inflation-prone or geopolitically motivated contexts, may increasingly turn to dollar stablecoins or regionally anchored alternatives. Third, transversal scenarios are offered on infrastructure evolution, corporate and B2B adoption, the risk of confidence shocks, and the atomisation of money into distinct Digital Currency Areas. A gradual token adoption scenario is considered the most plausible infrastructure trajectory, with B2B use cases expected to lead

S. Yazıcı (✉)
Department of Business Administration, Faculty of Political Sciences, Istanbul University, Istanbul, Türkiye
e-mail: selim@istanbul.edu.tr

C.C. Küçüközmen
Faculty of Business, Izmir University of Economics, Izmir, Türkiye
e-mail: coskun.kucukozmen@ieu.edu.tr

M. Salmony
Payments Innovation Consulting, Heidelberg, Germany
e-mail: salmony@payments-innovation.com

S. Yazıcı et al. (eds.), *Tokenisation of Money*, Contributions to Finance and Accounting, https://doi.org/10.1007/978-3-032-22946-5_31

consumer adoption across most markets. Finally, a high-level evolution timeline is proposed, spanning regulatory experimentation in 2026–2027 through to final broad consumer integration, even in retail, beyond 2040. The chapter concludes that tokenised money constitutes a genuine structural force in the evolution of the payments and banking landscape, yet one whose transformative potential will be realised unevenly and subject to the complex interplay of trust, governance, sovereignty, and institutional inertia that has always attended monetary innovation.

Keywords Tokenised money · Stablecoins · CBDC - Digital currency - Payments infrastructure · Distributed ledger technology · Fintech regulation · Monetary sovereignty · Scenario analysis

In this book, we have explored the *why, what, how, where, and when* of tokenised money, drawing on the perspectives of practitioners, policymakers, technologists, and researchers directly engaged in shaping these developments. Rather than repeating prior arguments, this concluding chapter synthesises our analysis through a structured forward-looking lens. We do not offer prediction in the deterministic sense. No one has a crystal ball, so what follows is necessarily speculative. That said, drawing on long experience in payments and fintech, we offer a best-effort view of plausible developments over the coming decade.

To address the question, "How will the many variants of tokenised money (CBDC, commercial bank money tokens, stablecoins, and others) develop across regions (US, China, Europe, and beyond) over the medium term?", we propose the analytical framework below.

Analytical Framework

We use a "multi-scenario approach" since we do not expect a single global trajectory. Instead, we anticipate differentiated outcomes across geographies and across diverse forms of tokenised money. The framework combines *regional scenarios* with *transversal thematic axes* to analyse the evolution of tokenised money over the next 5–10 years. This dual structure allows comparison between local/regional developments and broader technological or institutional trends.

The "probabilities" assigned reflect our judgments informed by experience across payments, regulation, and financial infrastructure (we acknowledge that quantitative probabilities at this stage are particularly speculative and open to debate). They are intentionally approximate and overlapping. They do not sum to 100%, as several developments may occur simultaneously across different layers (e.g., infrastructure evolution, regional divergence, and B2B adoption). This framework therefore serves not as prophecy, but as structured synthesis: a map of plausible monetary futures.

Caveat

The following is an honest, best-effort prediction on the evolution of tokenised money by the independent editors, with no bias for or against any particular solution or region. This bold evaluation goes against some predictions by interested parties and may thus be seen by some as controversial.

Structure

1. Idealised future scenario
2. Likely future scenarios by region (US, Europe, Asia, and others)
3. Likely future transversal scenarios in the medium term
4. Summary: Likely High-level Evolution Timeline

1 Idealised Future Scenario

- Fiat money, stablecoins, CBDCs, commercial bank money tokens (CMBT), and other forms interoperate seamlessly on a global basis.
- Strong integration into B2B workflows and a harmonised user experiences drive broad adoption by businesses and consumers.

Probability: <1% in the medium term

This scenario is often presented as "the end state" by some advocates of "new rails": everything connected, frictionless, and globally interoperable. Some indeed present this as the current evolution. We, however, consider it highly unlikely over the medium term (5–10 years). Even more modest, regional evolutions in payments have regularly been shown to take more than 10 years - so such a transformational, global revolution towards unified tokenisation will likely not happen in the medium timeframe considered here.

Key blockers include diverging legal and regulatory regimes; fragmented infrastructure; inconsistent governance and liability models; differences in compliance (KYC/AML) and privacy expectations; lack of widely adopted standards; geopolitical constraints; and the need to contain bad actors before mass adoption becomes feasible; and more. All these need to be solved/harmonised for tokenisation to scale globally and become harmonised.

However it is important to highlight that this—in our opinion likely but more futuristic scenario - commercial banks may no longer be at the centre of payments, savings, and lending… A seismic shift whose implications are sometimes underestimated and for which incumbents are well advised to prepare now.

Over the longer term (10+ years), aspects of this idealised scenario will become more and more plausible if harmonisation of legislation, standards, and market practices increase and if a dominant economic and technical models emerge and converge.

2 Likely Future Scenarios by Region

2.1 Likely Scenario for the US in Medium Term

- US fiat (the dollar) remains the dominant global reserve currency and medium of exchange.
- Dollar-denominated stablecoins expand their role in global tokenised payments and settlement, reinforcing US influence in many corridors (with notable exceptions where anti-US politics or capital controls intervene).
- Adoption is likely to be fastest in (i) emerging economies, (ii) countries with unstable domestic currencies, and (iii) regions with heavy trade or financial links to the US.

Probability: ~80%

2.2 Likely Scenario for Europe in Medium Term

- The euro remains strong as a local currency, despite recurring economic and political headwinds.
- A digital euro, if launched, may see limited day-to-day usage in the medium term despite substantial investment and policy effort.
- Based on the time of writing, many consider that Europe will fall further behind in digital race after massive distraction, delays and costs of CBDC. However the "offline" Digital Euro shows a valuable perspective of a new modern form of cash.
- European tokenised money (including euro stablecoins, deposit tokens, and bank-led models) continues to be explored through pilots and niche deployments, but achieving critical mass, even within Europe, remains uncertain.
- In particular Euro-denominated Stablecoins and European Stablecoin providers make little significant inroads against globally increasingly dominant US players.
- US dollar stablecoins may not gain broad traction for *domestic* European retail payments (where instant payments, low fees, consumer protections, and a stable currency already reduce the problem to be solved).
- However, the use of dollar stablecoins for cross-border, B2B settlement and certain consumer corridors (such as global remittance) may become increasingly significant.

Probability: ~80%

2.3 *Likely Scenario for Asia in Medium Term*

- Wallet-based ecosystems continue to expand across many parts of the region (for example, China and Southeast Asia; with Japan following a distinct path).
- Stablecoins and other new monetary form factors become increasingly integrated into wallets where they offer clear advantages (for example, in cross-border use cases or where local frictions remain).
- China's e-CNY remains relatively constrained in domestic usage in the medium term, but continued policy commitment, infrastructure investment, targeted partnerships and selected international corridors may support gradual expansion. If India continues to connect further (politically, economically) with China, common initiatives leveraging UPI, also for more global context (see BRICS) are to be expected.
- Japan continues to evaluate options (including bank-led, technology-led and infrastructure-led approaches) and may progress incrementally as social and regulatory consensus develops.

Probability: ~80%

2.4 *Likely Scenario for Other Regions in Medium Term*

- Middle East initiatives (including policy-led digital currency experiments like Digital Dirham and tokenisation of real-world assets) remain important to watch.
- In parts of Africa, Latin America, Türkiye and other inflation-prone, fragmented or high-friction markets, dollar stablecoins may increasingly serve as an alternative store of value and settlement medium, likely prompting local policy responses to protect monetary sovereignty.
- Bloc dynamics (like BRICS) may matter: Some countries may seek alternatives to US-dominated stablecoin rails for strategic reasons, potentially leading to regionally anchored tokenised money arrangements.
- Geopolitical fragmentation and a shift toward economic security and local sovereignty may reinforce fragmentation rather than convergence.

Summary of Likely Scenarios by Region (Medium Term)

- Europe: Regulation-led and stability-focused; experimentation continues, but mass adoption may be slower. Goal: Prevent excesses by industry, banks, bad actors through regulation.
- US: Market-led; private stablecoins play an outsized role in global settlement and innovation. Goal: Make the most money.
- Asia: Innovation- and wallet-led; multiple monetary form factors co-exist within dominant consumer platforms. Goal: Develop that which helps people/solves a problem.

- Middle East: Policy-led; region-specific models and strategic hub ambitions shape experimentation. Goal: Establish Middle East as a new and different global hub for tech-driven finance versus US/China.
- Switzerland: Bank-grade, infrastructure-driven tokenisation; international pilots often remain pilots. Goal: Technology
- Africa: Highly heterogeneous; tokenised money may increase interoperability in some corridors, but outcomes will vary markedly by country. US Stablecoins (connection to stable currency) and China eYuan (aligned with China's investments in region) may experience heavy adoption. South Africa remains special case (more like Western world). Goal: Get out of the current fragmentation, increase efficiency, access, inclusion.

We summarise the above directional expectations: in the medium term, (i) a strong global role for US dollar stablecoins, (ii) the emergence of regionally focused alternatives (like BRICS) in selected blocs and corridors, and (iii) a comparatively smaller role for tokenised money in European domestic retail payments, even if Europe remains influential (maybe even a role model) in regulation and standards.

Special Attention on BRICS and Other Corridors
One dimension sometimes underweighted in Western debates is the potential role of BRICS in shaping tokenised money. Several countries—including some within BRICS and parts of the Islamic world—have strategic incentives to reduce reliance on US-dominated payment and settlement rails. Thus, from our perspective on the future of money, there is politically a high motivation to create alternatives to US-denominated tokens, and US providers like Circle and Tether, etc. to ensure sovereignty.

This does not guarantee a single "BRICS token" or a single "Sharia token" (serving the Islamic world). However, it increases the plausibility of regionally anchored tokenised money initiatives and corridor-specific arrangements, especially where sovereignty concerns, sanctions risk, or local values drive design and policy choices.

Overall, we therefore expect the tokenised money landscape to remain diversified and pluralistic, rather than converging quickly on one global model.

3 Likely Future Transversal Scenarios in the Medium Term

So far, we have considered the geographic/political/regulatory plurality, but there are also other dimensions, for example the technology dimension which we also believe will continue to diversify with little convergence initially. It is to be hoped that we will see the emergence of a reduced number of networks/platforms/technologies/standards in the medium term. The dimensions of this will be examined in this section.

3.1 *Infrastructure/Technology*

We briefly sketch three infrastructure scenarios on the adoption, within our considered 5–10 year timeframe, of the underlying technology (such as distributed ledger technology (DLT) and related architectures): (1) an "all-in" scenario, where most money and payments migrate on-chain; (2) a "status quo" scenario, where blockchains remain marginal; and (3) a gradual adoption scenario - of DLT and other supporting technologies - which we consider most likely.

(1) "All-in" DLT scenario

- Large parts of the industry (merchants, banks, payments) move on-chain and rely primarily on blockchain-based settlement (see, for example, DK 2022).

Probability: <10%

(2) Status quo scenario

- Tokenised rails remain peripheral; traditional infrastructures (for example, instant-payment systems and SWIFT) continue to improve incrementally.

Probability: ~30%

(3) Gradual adoption scenario

- Interoperability between regulated forms of money improves (fiat, regulated stablecoins, bank-issued tokens, and selected CBDC forms).
- Consumer-facing platforms increasingly integrate tokenised money in the back end (their "rails") for cost, speed, or product reasons, improving usability, connectivity cost and speed without requiring consumers to "think crypto".
- Fiat remains dominant for everyday domestic retail payments in almost all markets.
- Wholesale experimentation, especially in cross-border, continues; some DLT-based wholesale initiatives may be scaled back where the new technology (e.g. DLT-based wCBDC) does not deliver clear advantages over upgraded conventional infrastructure.
- Cross-border stablecoin propositions increase competitive pressure on correspondent banking; traditional rails remain widely used but face growing substitution, especially in specific corridors.
- The downsides of DLT/Blockchain (costs of consensus, issues on privacy, scalability, etc) and their need/suitability in an environment where regulated/KYCed participants know and trust eachother may lead to a move back to high-performance distributed databases as the carriers of tokens (Oracle 2026). In any case it is to be wished and expected that the discussion around tokenisation moves away from technology to focus more on use cases/business models, especially in mature markets.

Probability: >70%

3.2 *Corporate, B2B, and Treasury*

Finally, we look beyond the geographic scenarios and the technology/infrastructure scenarios sketched above, since we also envisage a diversity of other transversal developments. Initially we look at the B2B use case.

- Adoption of tokenised money increases in corporate use cases where it saves cost, reduces settlement time, or improves liquidity management (for example, cross-border settlement, trade finance workflows, and international payroll).
- Tokenised money becomes more integrated into supply chains and treasury operations.
- ERP and payments service providers increasingly offer simplified access for merchants, B2B, and even SMEs.
- Banks continue to fall behind FinTechs in token services for B2B, especially to SMEs. As money becomes increasingly tokenised, banks' core services (e.g. lending) become increasingly challenged by new actors.
- B2B use cases are likely to lead, ahead of consumer adoption, except in specific high-friction corridors such as remittances.

Probability: ~90%

3.3 *Additional Controversial Future Scenarios*

3.3.1 Atomisation of Tokenised Money: Digital Currency Areas (DCA) and Global Splintering

- Different regulations (Divergence across regulatory regimes n.d.), capital controls, policy priorities and market practices lead to siloed digital currency areas becoming more entrenched.
- Bilateral or corridor-based arrangements between DCAs will emerge for economically important routes, but global interoperability remains limited and complex.
- Competing regional developments persist (for example, wallet-dominated Asian ecosystems, dollar stablecoin ecosystems, bank-led token models, and policy-led regional initiatives).
- Asian Wallets, US Stablecoins, EU Fiat, Middle Eastern Digital Dinar, Singapore, Switzerland, … remain competing global segments.

Probability: ~70%

3.3.2 A Confidence Shock: Collapse of Tokenised Money—It Was All a Bubble!

- High-profile failures, frauds, hacks, or repeated consumer harm reduce political and public appetite for tokenised money initiatives.
- The lack of standardisation, scalability, performance, privacy concerns of blockchain technology, continued UX failure, fragmentation of disconnected silos prevent mass adoption (see past tech and market initiatives n.d.).
- Industry attention shifts toward other priorities (for example, AI-enabled financial infrastructure), while tokenisation continues but at a slower and more uneven pace.

Probability: ~20%

4 Summary: A Plausible High-Level Evolution Timeline

Summarising all our speculations above, we would like to offer the following timeline along which tokenised money may evolve:

- 2026–2027: Increasing regulatory clarity, pilots, and consortium building; tokenised money remains primarily experimental outside a few scaling niches.
- 2028–2030: Integration and scaling in specific corridors and use cases; token backend rails begin to substitute legacy layers in targeted niches.
- 2030–2035: Gradual convergence in standards and interfaces; fiat remains dominant, while tokenised money becomes increasingly common in the back end.
- 2035 onwards: Broader corporate and SME adoption in wholesale and cross-border contexts; consumer adoption grows where it is integrated into mainstream wallets and payment experiences.
- 2040 onwards: Tokenised money becomes a standard feature in many consumer wallets; fiat (whether tokenised or not) remains the primary unit of account in all jurisdictions.

Top-level Summary

The current stablecoin expansion represents a fundamental shift from previous cryptocurrency cycles, now embedding itself within mainstream financial infrastructure. With the stablecoin market reaching hundreds of billions and major payment platforms investing heavily in stablecoin infrastructure through acquisitions and partnerships, this technology has moved beyond speculative novelty into practical utility (Morgan Stanley, 2025; Stripe's Bridge n.d.). However, expectations must remain measured: the vision of frictionless, globally interoperable digital payments remains distant, constrained by fragmented regulatory frameworks, competing technical standards, and divergent geopolitical interests.

Nevertheless, tokenisation constitutes a genuine structural force poised to reshape segments of the payments and banking landscape (IMF, 2026) The global proliferation of dollar-based stablecoins, combined with emerging regional alternatives tailored to specific economic blocs and payment corridors, suggests that while the path forward will be uneven and fragmented, the transformative potential of tokenisation is increasingly difficult to dismiss.

Final Remarks: Future of Money

At its core, the tokenisation of money represents more than a mere technological upgrade to existing payment rails. It embodies a fundamental reimagining of how value is represented, transferred, and settled in a digital-first economy. Whether manifested as central bank digital currencies, commercial bank money tokens, or private stablecoins, tokenised money promises efficiency, composability, and global near-instantaneous settlement. A new form-factor of money made for the internet. These are the attributes that could unlock entirely new categories of financial products and services. Yet this promise must be tempered by recognition that money is not simply a technology but a social institution, deeply embedded in legal frameworks, cultural practices, and power structures. The successful integration of tokenised forms will therefore depend not merely on technical elegance but on navigating complex questions of trust, governance, privacy, and sovereignty that have always attended monetary innovation.

This book arrives at a pivotal moment in the evolution of digital finance. Published as regulators worldwide grapple with how to accommodate tokenised money within existing frameworks, as central banks deliberate the merits and risks of issuing their own digital currencies, and as private stablecoin issuers scale to systemic significance, the timing could not be more relevant. The contributions assembled here offer readers a rare vantage point, grounded perspectives from practitioners, policymakers, and researchers who are actively shaping these developments, rather than speculating from the sidelines. As such, this volume serves not merely as a chronicle of current initiatives but as an essential reference for understanding the critical junctures and decision points that will determine whether tokenised money fulfils its transformative potential or fragments into a patchwork of incompatible systems.

Looking further ahead, the monetary landscape of 2050 may bear little resemblance to what we know today. Perhaps by then, the distinction between "traditional" and "tokenised" money will have dissolved, with digital bearer instruments seamlessly integrated into every facet of economic life; from automated supply chain settlements that trigger upon verified delivery, to personalised micro-insurance contracts that adjust premiums in real-time based on behavioural data, to cross-border remittances that clear in seconds rather than days. Alternatively, we may witness the crystallisation of distinct digital currency zones, each optimised for different priorities: privacy-preserving retail payments in some jurisdictions, fully transparent wholesale settlement in others, with carefully managed gateways between them. What seems certain is that the next quarter-century will reshape fundamental assumptions about money itself, who issues it, who controls it, how it moves, and what purposes it serves. Whether this transformation leads to greater financial inclusion, enhanced efficiency, and democratised access, or instead reinforces existing power asymmetries and creates new forms of exclusion, will depend on choices made today and in the years immediately ahead. This book, we hope, provides the analytical foundation for making those choices wisely.

References

Adrian, Tobias. 2026. "Tokenized Finance". IMF Note 2026/001, International Monetary Fund, Washington, DC. https://www.imf.org/-/media/files/publications/imf-notes/2026/english/insea2026001.pdf

Divergence across regulatory regimes (for example, EU MiCA, the US GENIUS Act, and debates on privacy, holding limits, interest-bearing stablecoins, backing policy, and the role of CBDCs) suggests limited global policy convergence in the medium term (n.d.)

German Banking Association, "New working paper on Commercial Bank Money Token", 5 Dec 2022, https://die-dk.de/en/topics/article/new-working-paper-on-commercial-bank-money-token/

Gourav Sarkar, Oracle Digital Assets & Blockchain Platform, CB-DC Conference, Kuala Lumpur, May 2026, "How Oracle Solutions Address Real-world Challenges"

For example, Morgan Stanley noted stablecoin market capitalisation reaching $300bn in September 2025. https://www.morganstanley.com/im/en-pt/institutional-investor/insights/articles/modernizing-financial-infrastructure.html

Past tech and market initiatives that struggled to reach sustainable scale and are now consigned to the cemetery of industry failures include (among others) WAP, the metaverse hype cycle, and Libra/Diem (n.d.)

Stripe's Bridge acquisition was widely reported at approximately $1.1bn (n.d.). https://fintech-magazine.com/articles/stripe-completes-us-1-1bn-bridge-acquisition

MIX
Papier aus verantwortungsvollen Quellen
Paper from responsible sources
FSC® C105338

If you have any concerns about our products,
you can contact us on
ProductSafety@springernature.com

In case Publisher is established outside the EU,
the EU authorized representative is:
Springer Nature Customer Service Center GmbH
Europaplatz 3, 69115 Heidelberg, Germany

Printed by Libri Plureos GmbH
in Hamburg, Germany